A History of Ancient Philosophy

Giovanni Reale

A History of Ancient Philosophy

IV. The Schools of the Imperial Age

EDITED AND TRANSLATED FROM THE FIFTH ITALIAN EDITION

John R. Catan

State University of New York Press

Published by
State University of New York Press

©1990 State University of New York

For information, address State University of New York
Press, State University Plaza, Albany, N.Y., 12246

Library of Congress Cataloging-in-Publication Data

Reale, Giovanni.

      A History of Ancient Philosophy

      Translation of : Storia della filosofia antica.
      Includes bibliography.
      Contents: — 3. The systems of the Hellenistic
Age — 4. The schools of the imperial age / edited and
translated from the fifth Italian edition [by] John R.
Catan.
      1. Philosophy, Ancient—History. I. Catan, John R.
I. Title.
B171.R4213 1990   180   84-16310
ISBN 0-7914-0128-6 (v. 4)
ISBN 0-7914-0129-4 (pbk. : v. 4)

10 9 8 7 6 5 4 3 2 1

This volume is dedicated to the memory of Aunt Sue Oliva

Table of Contents

First Part

THE FINAL DEVELOPMENTS AND THE DISSOLUTION OF THE PERIPATETIC SCHOOL AND THE GREAT HELLENISTIC SCHOOLS

First Section

THE REDISCOVERY OF THE ESOTERIC WORKS OF ARISTOTLE, NEO-ARISTOTELIANISM, AND THE LIMITS OF ITS HISTORICAL-PHILOSOPHICAL IMPORTANCE.

Second Section

THE FOUNDATION AND STRUCTURE OF THE SYSTEM OF PLOTINUS

Third Section

THE DEVELOPMENTS OF NEOPLATONISM AND THE
END OF ANCIENT GREEK-PAGAN PHILOSOPHY

Foreword

The fourth volume of the *History of Philosophy* contains the treatment of the Schools of philosophy and the movements of philosophic and religious thought covering the period of time which encompasses, with some exceptions, the end of the Pagan Era to the beginning of the sixth century of the Christian Era. Just as the preceding period, beginning from the death of Alexander the Great to the end of the Pagan Era (which is the Hellenistic period), has been somewhat obscured and not been fully appreciated or basically esteemed, even if for very different reasons, so also has this part the history of Greek-pagan philosophy suffered a similar fate.

Many historians have seen in these centuries little more than the monotnous repetition of old ideas, that is, the inexorable decline of the Hellenic genius, which in the course of a slow depletion was finally extinguished. They have preferred to turn their attention to the parallel birth of Christian thought because of its more stimulating aspects.

In point of fact, the complex picture of the Schools of this age, seen from the outside, would seem to present nothing more than a series of attempts to propose and interpret again older positions, which they rarely seem to truly advance. We witness, in the course of these centuries, the rediscovery of Aristotelianism, the final resurgence of Epicureanism, the rebirth of Pyrrhonism, the revival of Cynicism, the rebirth of Pythagoreanism, and, especially, a renewal of Platonism, which in successive stages becomes a kind of philosophical ecumenism (from which Christianity itself drew much in order to elaborate and critically support its conceptions). Therefore, it would appear that the uniqueness which can be found in this picture is limited to the qualifier "neo," which distinguishes the various currents of thought: neo-Aristotelian, neo-Stoic, neo-Skeptic, neo-Cynic, neo-Pythagorean, neo-Platonic (we ought not speak of neo-Epicurean, since the teachings of the School remained unchanged and embalmed, as the ancients said, always "in deep peace"). "Neo" would seem to be a qualifier which in this case has changed, although perhaps in a limited way, the substance which it modified.

Taking everything into account, a real originality can be recognized almost solely in "neo-Platonism," that is, in the Neoplatonism of Plotinus. In regard to this author, the consensus is almost unanimous. In fact, it is recognized that some pages of the *Enneads* reach heights comparable only to those reached by some Platonic dialogues or some of the treatises of Aristotle. Also, the great influence that Plotinus had throughout the whole course of the history of Western philosophy from late antiquity to the medieval period, from humanism and the renaissance to the romantic age, as well as in the various forms of contemporary spirituality cannot be gainsaid.

But this is the point to which we wish to call the attention of the reader, who perhaps will be rightly concerned with Plotinus and reserve all or almost all of his attention for him. Plotinus can be encompassed only within the historical period in which he is placed and according to the currents of thought which preceded him and opened the path for him. The *Enneads* presupposed many things which were not demonstrated, but were simply stated as already acquired. This happened because by the third century CE these doctrines were actually considered to be accepted by the general consensus of philosophers. The *Enneads*, furthermore, are characterized by a climate of distinct religiousness and by a spiritual atmosphere impregnated with a strong mystical sense. But even this climate and atmosphere had already been prepared and was widely spread in large measure as a result of other currents of thought.

The unique contribution of the present volume is the attempt to reconstruct the history of these spiritual components which took Greek speculation to its final brilliant fulfillment in order to uncover all that is "unstated" which accompanies, in a subterranean way, that which in the *Enneads* was instead explicitly stated. This had been accomplished up till now only, or chiefly, within the confines of highly specialized and basically philologically-oriented studies whose emphasis has not been historical and philosophical. And the reader who has the patience to follow us will become aware, we believe, that never, as in this case, is the statement more true that the key to understanding the "major" thinkers is precisely to be found in the "minor" thinkers.

Nevertheless, stated in these terms, our task would seem to be reductive. In fact, many "minor" thinkers who are treated in this volume are not simply preparations for Plotinus, but also have significance in their own right, as we will fully demonstrate, even though we firmly believe in a certain hierarchy and in differences in their levels of importance, which is today stubbornly flattened out by everyone with the result that all antiquity (and especially this part of antiquity) has the relevance of a museum piece or a repository for antiquities.

Seen from within all the Schools, the authors treated in this volume have presented to us their specific message, which we have tried to emphasize throughout. We are therefore convinced that the history of philosophy is not solely constituted of novel ideas, but should also be concerned with how old ideas are handed down by the tradition and how they are constricted and disappear or are expanded and strengthened, increasing in this way through the absorption of other ideas and generating something original..

This volume follows step-by-step the final revival of the ancient Schools and their dissolution, paralleling the rebirth, the affirmations, and the sensational victory of Platonism with the complex ebb and flow of the various currents in the measure in which, overall, they made that result possible.

The basic thesis which guides the reconstruction is the following: The great Schools which began in the Hellenistic Age immediately after the death of Alexander the Great (as we have shown in the third volume) were characterized by the neglect of the significance and the loss of the results of the "second voyage," and consequently attempted to reconstruct a materialistic and immanentistic vision of reality. In addition, the philosophies of early Hellenism were great secular faiths in man and in the possibility of his achieving, by himself, the supreme goal which for the Greeks was essentially the goal of "eudaimonia," or, as we would say today, using a term which is not wholly adequate, happiness. On the contrary, in the Imperial Age these convictions were slowly sloughed off and out of the eclectic volcanic magma produced from the explosive mixture of the ideas of the various Schools (which, as we will show, were only relatively, not absolutely, opposed) there re-emerged slowly but surely those conceptions bound to the "second voyage" which penetrated in various ways into almost all the Schools and became, finally, the minimum common denominator among them all. Thus they reintroduced the concepts of the incorporeal and the transcendent; but nature (immanently and corporeally conceived) ceased to be the basis for the elucidation of moral law. However, God (transcendent and incorporeal) began to be called the "measure," and the rule of life was pointed out as the "imitation of God," the "following of God," or more precisely, the "assimilation to God" and, at its extreme, the notion of "ecstatic union" with him., in conclusion, the renewal, the continuation, and the completion of the "second voyage" is what is offered by the Greek thought of these final centuries.

This idea is dominant, it seems to us, and it is indeed a thread of Ariadne to help us through the labyrinth of the Schools, the movements, and the currents of thought which characterized late Greco-pagan antiquity. It has also enabled us to properly locate a series of developments which are not usually acknowledged nor adequately defined.

It will be seen, for example, that in the majority of cases the currents of thought which differ from the Platonic in these centuries become differentiated from the original stock (even if not exclusively) in the measure in which they accept the Platonic positions. The neo-Aristotelianism of the last Peripatetics and of Alexander of Aphrodisias, on the basis of the more recent discoveries of specialized studies, reveals the following "novelty," which is the acceptance of Platonic doctrines, even mystical ones. Something of an analogy has been recognized by some scholars even with respect to the neo-Stoics, in which, indeed, among many aporias, some Platonic positions became determinative, and the "imitation of God" became an explicitly thematicized moral concept. Philo reread and interpreted the *Bible* in function of some Greek categories, among the most important of which were Platonic ones (he expressly maintained the notion that the theory of Ideas of Plato is a Mosaic truth). Neo-Pythagoreanism reproposed a synthesis between the doctrine of numbers and the Platonic categories which had already occurred in the first

Academy (although in a different manner). And again, Platonism, together with Pythagoreanism, dominated the philosophical, mystical, and religious literature so typical of this era, such as the *Corpus Hermeticum* and the *Chaldean Oracles.*.

From the middle of the first century BCE and ending with Plotinus, Platonism developed with characteristics that are "intermediate" between those of the old and those of neo-Platonism; therefore, it is called "Middle Platonism," now correctly applied. And it is this "Middle" Platonism which reaches the early Fathers of the Church and which is used for the rational exploration of the Gospel message.

The reconstruction of the thought of Plotinus, which constitutes the largest part of this volume, is focused through a reinterpretation of the concept of "emanation" which is totally different from Eastern doctrines of emanationism, or the various forms of monism and pantheism, which the West has recognized, and which again is further revealed as a *unicum* (a *singularity*) in the history of ideas. Through this reconstruction (which it is impossible to anticipate here because of the limits of space, but which the reader can see taken up again in the concluding chapter on Plotinus) we used numerous contributions which have been recently published on Plotinus and which produced relevant advances in research.

Also, in the reconstruction of Neoplatonism after Plotinus we have made use of more recent studies, those which literally overturn the traditional account which is traceable to Zeller, and now have also overturned current scholarly judgments.

But before we conclude, let us turn to some necessary cautions.

This period of late ancient philosophy is one which has been least adequately dealt with historically, and it is hence understandable that it has also been marked by divergent treatments and by being subject to remarkable disagreement in different histories of philosophy. (The *clichés* adopted from the writers of textbooks are, for the most part, wholly inadequate for understanding the complexities of the period.) Instead, advanced scientific research and the resultant new contributions end in a consistently precise and detailed understanding which defines the peculiar traits of this phase of the thought of the ancients, and thus a new historiographic systematization of the material is imposed upon us.

The contributions of various scholars (which we will note in the appropriate places), beyond leading for a time to analytic research on this period in order to understand Plotinus, have permitted us to redesign some sections and chapters in a unique way. The reader will find, for example, expositions of Middle Platonism and neo-Pythagoreanism made with new criteria. We have attempted a reconstruction of Middle Platonism which seeks to bring to the fore the homogeneity of its problems beyond the variety of its solutions and currents. We have proposed a rereading of neo-Pythagoreanism which distinguishes two phases: one of the Hellenistic Age, which we can call Middle Pythagoreanism; one of the Imperial Age, that is, the properly Neoplatonic one, which seems to offer the possibility of a better understanding of the specific character of the movement. The reader will find, in addition, a very ample presentation of Hermeticism accompanied by an exposition of the doctrines of the *Chaldean Oracles* with just as much detail. This was necessary because specialized studies have demonstrated that such documents in which philosophy seems to have only an ancillary function in reality reflected in a clear manner the sentiments, the anxieties, and the mystico-religious aspirations of the epoch, qualities on which the philosophy of that time tends more and more to be founded and confounded. Furthermore, as we will see, the *Chaldean Oracles*, both in the turbid magico-theurgic aspect which marks them and in their theoretical formulation, constitute a source of inspiration for late Neoplatonism as a kind of "pagan Bible," and are even the landmark which permits the settling of the basic difference between the Neoplatonism of Plotinus and his School and that of the succeeding Neoplatonists.

Also, the notion that the treatises of Philo nourished a "Jewish philosophy" is justified in this new vision. Philo, in recent research, is no longer the eclectic mixer of the ideas of the past. But, on the one hand he is the founder of "religious philosophy" (thus, a kind of precursor of Christian philosophy), and, on the other hand, he is a thinker who, through the impact of biblical theology, has carried into the Greek area, and in particular into the scope of the Alexandrians, new ideas destined to give clear advances also in the sphere of the succeeding Greco-pagan philosophy and which will result in benefits for numerous thinkers, including even Plotinus himself.

The philosophy of Plato constituted, therefore, the true source of the speculations of this era. Invariably, as in the case of the thinkers of these five centuries, it will be true to say with Emerson that "Plato is philosophy," or, if you prefer, what is said with exquisite irony by Montaigne: "Shake and agitate Plato as you will, everyone is proud of appropriating him, and in so doing put him where they like."

We remind the reader, especially after the publication of the first edition of the present volume, that we have focused the researches of our students concerning the themes treated herein by asking for their assistance and by welcoming important contributions of colleagues on the same issues in the collection under our direction in order to throw further light on this period so obscured by scholars in the past.

Putting aside minor contributions, we wish to point out the following ones:

Nine treatises on Philo of Alexandria were published in three volumes by Rusconi (in 1978, 1981, and 1984 respectively). In addition, R. Radice has edited an imposing and basic annotated Philonian bibliography with the title: *Filone di Alessandria, Bibliografia generale* (Naples: Bibliopolis, 1983).

Concerning Middle Platonism, C. Mazzarelli prepared the first general annotated bibliography (published in the *Rivista di Filosofia neo-scolastico* in1980 and 1982) and he is presently preparing an edition of the fragments of some Middle Platonists.

Again in the collection published by Rusconi, we introduced a new translation with critical apparatus of the *Dialogues of Seneca* edited by A. Marastoni (1979), a new translation with critical apparatus for the whole of Epictetus which we edited together with C. Cassanmagnago (1982), and the translation of the *De mysteriis* attributed to Iamblichus, edited by A.R. Sodano with a full and exhaustive commentary.

Finally, other translations of the works of Philo and Proclus never available before in Italian are already in advanced stages of completion.

Giovanni Reale
Milan, Italy

Preface to the American Edition

The translation of this fourth volume of my *History of Ancient Philosophy* which Professor John Catan has now completed is based on the fifth edition, published in Italian in 1987 within ten years after the first edition, which was published in 1978.

One might ask: would the interest of readers and the success of this volume have been an easy matter to predict?

The reply to this question, after the fact, would seem to be evident enough. The period which this volume considered embraced five centuries, the first five centuries of the Christian era, which are, in a certain sense, among the most complex and intricate and in which the final revival and the final flicker of ancient-pagan thought paralleling the birth and diffusion of Christian thought is presented. For a series of easily understandable reasons, the scholars of ancient-pagan thought chose to concentrate themselves on the classical period, or even (but fewer) on the Hellenistic age, and for the most part neglected this period of the Imperial age. Instead, the scholars with specialized scholarly interests in this period concentrated chiefly on nascent Christian thought, with an exception made in favor of Plotinus.

As a matter of fact, works presenting an overall view of this period are very scarce or, if produced, deal with it from a narrow perspective. In the first half of this century, K. Praechter published his *Die Philosophie des Altertums* (in the famous series *Grundriss der Geschichte der Philosophie* commenced by Ueberweg), which was very accurate with respect to our period, but is now obsolete and is in the course of a complete re-editing. The great work edited by A.H. Armstrong, *A History of Later Greek and Medieval Philosophy* (1970), contains some excellent pages, but is profoundly selective and neglects throughout numerous important positions.

Instead, detailed and specialized works are, again, widespread on aspects of this period which for a long time were relatively unknown, but which now impose themselves as necessary for any attempt at an overview of the period.e have separated the two worlds, that is, ancient pagan thought from early Christian thought, leaving the latter alone (we will eventually be concerned with it in some future work) because it brings to a head preceding thought and opens perspectives through which the succeeding centuries can be understood, and so we concentrated on pagan thought in this volume. Only in this way was it possible to focus basically on those specific categories which have dominated Greek-pagan thought and moreover to understand the presuppositions and the consequences which they implied. For these reasons, we have given considerable space, for example, even to religious-philosophical phenomena such as those connected with the *Corpus Hermeticum* and the *Chaldean Oracles*, which are truly indispensable for the understanding of the spiritual climate of this period of ancient thought and from which, hence, it is not possible to prescind. (Surprisingly, even an historian of ancient thought of the caliber of E. Zeller, in the previous century, believed that he could lightly treat the *Chaldean Oracles* which, on the contrary, are an essential support for the whole of Neoplatonism from Iamblichus onwards.)

Certainly Plotinus is at the highest apex of the whole of this period of ancient philosophy. But if we neglect the background and all the streams of vital nutriment with which the thought of Plotinus is fed, we will not understand him, or we will understand him only in part. Consequently, we have dedicated a large part of this volume to Plotinus, concentrating on what we call his "creative contemplation" or "contemplative creation." We have shown its precise foundation and metaphysical consequences. In particular, we hope to liberate the reader from old errors which still continue to victimize many scholars. Plotinus was not an 'emanationist,' this is the thesis which we demonstrate in detail, and hence we were able to provide an interpretation which involves a very complex and fecund perspective, as the reader will discover in the pages concerned with its demonstration and documentation.

Finally, the reader should keep in mind that we did not consider many aspects of the thought of these five centuries simply for extrinsic reasons, but precisely because of that perspective which is today called by the German word "Wirkungsgeschichte," that is, the history of the influences and the effects produced by doctrines. And anyone who follows us and takes a stand within this perspective will be able to comprehend very well, we believe, how in these five centuries all the results of Greek thought are measured in terms of the impact of Plato and by Platonism, which stand out clearly as the most fruitful and vital stream of the whole of ancient thought.

Dr. Catan has labored hard in the translation of this volume, because some positions which we treated and some Greek texts we translated could not be compared to any models at his disposal in English. I wish him, hence, a full measure of success and extend my thanks for the laborious task which he tackled in order to bring this complex work to a successful conclusion.

Giovanni Reale
Milan, Italy

Translator's Preface

I would like to thank my colleague Dr. Joseph Gilbert, who read through the manuscript in its first incarnation and saved me from many infelicitous and murky passages, as well as my friend and former student Mr. Peter MacLellan for his help in preparing the text for the camera and proofing the final text. I also have an even heavier burden of gratitude to render to Melody Brinkman, who read all of the revisions and who brings to the editing of the manuscript an excellent command of English grammar, as well as her attention to detail and the complete formatting of the text for camera-ready copy.

To the publishers who have given their permission for the use of their translations of works of the many figures encountered in the Imperial Age, I am grateful. Many translations were compared and were of use in producing my own translations, among them the indispensable Loeb Classical Library Series and their recently published *Plotinus*, translated by A. H. Armstrong, [volumes I-VII 1966-1989]. I also wish to thank Oxford University Press for permission to use a few extracts from E. R. Dodd's translation of *Proclus: The Elements of Theology*, as well as Selene Books of El Paso, Texas and their reprints of the old translations by Thomas Taylor of Proclus, Numenius, and Porphyry, and Shambhala Press of Boston for the *Hermetica*. In many cases the Italian translations which I used in making my translations were amazingly close to the English translations of the Loeb Classical Library Series although not in every detail.

In the matter of the names of ancient figures, I have responded to some intemperate criticism by consulting the *Oxford Classical Dictionary* and using its spellings of proper names. Spelling in some cases seems to be an inexact science, even among the experts. If any past misspellings have caused readers any inconvenience in their researches, I beg their pardon.

I have found the Italian translations of classical sources quite competent and in some cases superior in their grasp of the sense to some of their English counterparts. Some readers have complained about my use of the term "Movent" for the more traditional "Mover" in those contexts which are concerned with the Aristotelian final cause(s). I opted for "Movent(s), because the English "Mover" too easily connotes "moving, or efficient causality," which is foreign to Aristotle's understanding of the kind of causality exercised by the unmoved Movent(s) of the *Metaphysics* Book Lambda. This was the practice of my teacher, Father Joseph Owens, C.Ss.R., in his masterpiece *The Doctrine of Being in the Aristotelian Metaphysics,* and I am convinced by his argument and I follow his example. I also continued the practice of capitalizing "god" [God] to avoid Christian connotations foreign to Greek-pagan philosophy and used BCE for BC and CE for AD to use a religously neutral nomenclature.

I am also grateful to the publisher, State University of New York Press, to its Director Mr. William Eastman, to Ms. Elizabeth Moore, and to Ms. Dana Foote for persevering in what has become a very long project. I would also like to thank the anonymous technical support people at WordPerfect Corporation as well as Peter J. Winz of SoftCraft, Inc. for their assistance in getting the text ready for the camera. The copy was entirely formatted using Xerox® Ventura Publisher: Professional Extension, the text was processed using WordPerfect® (5.0), the screen and print fonts were provided by BitStream® Fonts™ (Dutch) through SoftCraft© LaserFonts software package, which also provided the classical Greek font in various pitches. I am also indebted to the women of the *Documentation Preparation Center* (S. U. C. at Brockport), to the Director Vicki Willis, as well as to Terry Collins and Loretta Lonnen, for rekeying from my hard copy when I inadvertently erased my files and, finally, to the administrators of State University College at Brockport (President John E. Van de Wetering, Vice-President Robert D. Marcus, Dean Robert J. Gemmett and Dean Thomas Bonner) for the fine support services for research and scholarship which they have made available to the college.

I have dedicated this volume to the memory of my dear Aunt Sue, who passed away during the long preparation of the volume. She was a second mother to me and is sorely missed.

J. R. Catan
Adams Basin, New York

The Schools of the Imperial Age

«φεύγωμεν δὴ φίλην ἐς πατρίδα,
ἀληθέστερον ἄν τις παρακελεύοιτο
...πατρὶς δὴ ἡμῖν, ὅθεν παρήλθ-
ομεν, καὶ πατὴρ ἐκεῖ.»

"This would be truer advice, 'Let us
fly to our dear country,' ...Our country from which we came is there, our
Father is there."

Plotinus, *Enneads* 1.6.8

First Part

THE FINAL DEVELOPMENTS AND THE DISSOLUTION OF THE PERIPATETIC SCHOOL AND THE GREAT HELLENISTIC SCHOOLS

«οἷς μέλει τοῦ ἔχειν τι θεῖον ἐν αὐτοῖς, τούτοις προνοητέον τοῦ δύνασθαι νοεῖν τι καὶ τοιοῦτον.»

"Those who care to have something of the divine in themselves ought to be concerned with being capable of thinking something like it."

Alexander of Aphrodisias,
De anima 91.5ff.

«ἔκκοψον τὸ τεθνηκὸς τῆς ψυχῆς καὶ γνώσῃ τὸν θεόν.»

"Cut out that which is death in your soul and you will know God."

Musonius Rufus, Frag. 53

THE REDISCOVERY OF THE ESOTERIC WORKS OF ARISTOTLE, NEO-ARISTOTELIANISM, AND THE LIMITS OF ITS HISTORICAL-PHILOSOPHICAL IMPORTANCE

«ὃν [*sc.* νοῦν ποιητικόν] ὁ νοῶν νοῦς, ὅταν
αὐτὸν νοῇ, ἐκεῖνός πως γίνεται, εἴ γε τὸ
νοεῖν ἐν τῷ λαβεῖν τὸ εἶδος τὸ νοού-
μενον καὶ ὁμοιωθῆναι αὐτῷ.»

"The [human] mind which knows the
productive [divine] mind becomes, in a
certain sense, this, since knowing consists in the reception of the intelligible
form and in becoming similar to it."

> Alexander of Aphrodisias,
> *De anima* 89.21ff.

«δοκεῖ θεῖόν τι εἶναι ἡ ἀρετὴ καὶ
ὁμοίωσίς τις τῷ θεῷ τὸ γὰρ θεῖον
οὐ κατὰ τὸ εὖ πάσχειν ἀλλὰ κατὰ
τὸ εὖ ποιεῖν νοεῖται.»

"Virtue seems to be something
Divine and a kind of assimilation to
God: in fact it is characteristic of the
Divine not to receive good but to do
good."

> Aspasius, *In Arist. Eth. Nic.* 99.4ff.

I. The Two-Century Eclipse of the Peripatos in the Hellenistic Age

1. Lycon

From about 270 BCE up to the middle of the first century BCE, the life of the Peripatos went on in a climate of mediocrity and oppressive gloominess. The School continued to reap some success as an institution of an educational nature, but it was practically absent from the ongoing debate of ideas. The men who led it turned out to have an unremarkable philosophical capacity, and were capable of doing nothing other than making a fainthearted attempt of an eclectic nature to deal with some of the leading issues of the period.

Around 270 BCE, Lycon became the scholarch of the School, succeeding Strato, and he continued to be dominant in the School for almost a half century.[1] He wrote works which were recognized for their fine style, but not for their profound content, as Cicero tells us:

> Lycon has a verbose style, and his thoughts are somewhat barren.[2]

His philosophical interests were limited to ethics. He defined the highest good as "spiritual joy," or the "joy of the soul."[3]

Lycon was obviously influenced by the Stoa, since he tried to reduce as much as was possible the great distress which comes from the things which are foreign to the soul, as, for example, the afflictions which come from the body and fate. Cicero writes:

> In order to diminish anguish he [Lycon] says that it is prompted by inconsequential circumstances, pains of fortune and of body, not by evils of the soul.[4]

The principal interests of Lycon, then, were not philosophical, but were rather educational and pedagogic in nature. This evaluation can be derived from the explicit testimonies of the ancients.[5]

2. Hieronymus of Rhodes

A contemporary of Lycon, Hieronymus of Rhodes,[6] on the contrary, maintained doctrines clearly impregnated by Epicureanism. For this reason, Lycon, who was instead inspired by the rigorousness of the Stoa, was very unsympathetic to him. Hieronymus held that the highest good is the *absence of pain*, thereby understanding pain as the greatest evil. Here are some of the numerous testimonies of Cicero which are very crucial for the understanding of Hieronymus:

> "Remember, then," I said, "the definition that Hieronymus of Rhodes gives of the highest good, the standard to which all other things should be referred?"
> "Yes," said he, "that he considers the goal to be the absence of pain."
> "And again, what does he think about pleasure?"

"He says that it is not desirable for itself alone.

"Therefore he maintains that it is one thing to feel joy, and another to feel pain."[7]

"Nor is it necessary to listen to Hieronymus, for him the highest good is identified with what is the same as is occasionally, or rather only too frequently, upheld by you, the absence of pain. Since if pain is an evil, to be without this evil is not sufficient to constitute the good life."[8]

It is clear that by maintaining this conception of the highest good Hieronymus went far beyond Peripatetic philosophy, as Cicero himself clearly pointed out:

I passed over many writers, including the learned and entertaining Hieronymus. *Indeed I know no reason for calling the latter a Peripatetic at all*; since he proposed the highest good as the absence of pain; and one who differs about the highest good has a different philosophical system altogether.[9]

3. Ariston of Ceos (Keos)

The writings of Ariston of Ceos (Keos), like those of his teacher, Lycon,[10] whom he succeeded, must be singled out for their elegant style, but not for their speculative depth. This can be confirmed from the testimony of Cicero:

Lycon's pupil, Ariston, was polished and graceful, but did not have the depth that we expect to find in a great thinker; his writings are certainly very urbane, but his style was somehow lacking in authority.[11]

In point of fact, his ethical reflections, judging from the few fragments which have come down to us, must be said to be superficial and not indicative of a first rate philosophical mind. As a result, we may say that Ariston continues that phenomenological tendency begun by Theophrastus with his work *Characters*, that is, a philosophical tendency which is theoretically disengaged and mainly descriptive in nature.[12]

4. Critolaus of Phaselis

The next scholarch of the Peripatos (perhaps immediately after Ariston) was Critolaus of Phaselis.[13] Although he expressed the intention of remaining faithful to the doctrines of the founders of the school, he showed himself to be sensitive to the influence of the Stoa. In fact, if on the one hand he defended the Aristotelian notion of the eternity of the world and of the human race,[14] on the other hand he abandoned the Stagirite and maintained positions quite close to those of the Porch, advocating the materiality of the soul and identifying *psyché*) with the "quinta essentia," which is explicitly referred to as *aither* =the fifth element).[15] In addition, contrary to Aristotle, Critolaus maintained the thesis that pleasure is an evil:

Critolaus the Peripatetic maintained that pleasure is an evil and the many other evils are produced from it.[16]

In his doctrine of the good, then, a typical attempt at an eclectic accommodation between the Peripatos and the Stoa is apparent. Critolaus repeated the

Peripatetic doctrine that there are three classes of goods, but maintained that the exterior goods and the goods of the body (although they are indeed goods and not merely "indifferents") are incommensurably inferior to virtue, that is, to the goods *of the soul and the goods of the spirit.* Cicero writes:

> And here I ask for the significance of the famous balance of Critolaus. Critolaus claims that if on one side of a scale the goods that belong to the soul were put, and on the other the goods that belong to the body which are exterior goods, the first side will sink so far down that not the earth nor the sea could, with their weight, restore the balance.[17]

But this was a solution which was necessarily doomed to failure, insofar as it forced a union of the Peripatos with the Stoa, because the Stoa defined the notion of "good" as virtue thus excluding everything else from the definition.

5.   Diodorus of Tyre

Diodorus of Tyre was a pupil of Critolaus and his successor as scholarch.[18] Diodorus maintained, as his teacher did, that the soul and the intellect were constituted of *aither* and hence that they were material.[19]

Instead, in ethics, he attempted a peculiar compromise which simultaneously tried to satisfy the Peripatetic, the Stoic, and the Epicurean positions on the problem. Diodorus attempted to satisfy the Peripatetics by identifying the highest good with virtue, and the Stoics by positing virtue as clearly superior to all other goods, and, finally, the Epicureans by affirming (as Hieronymus had done previously) that happiness consisted in the absence of pain.[20]

Diodorus of Tyre is the last of the Peripatetics of this epoch of whom we can be sure that he filled the office of scholarch.

It is possible that the successor of Diodorus was Erinneus, of whom we know very little. Some people who were to have a certain importance in the political fortunes of Athens were linked to this Peripatetic, as for example Athenion, who became a tyrant, and especially Apellicon of Teos, who rescued the esoteric works of Aristotle and published them.[21] However, we want to speak more fully about this issue because we find it not only basic to a fundamental understanding of the history of the Peripatos, but also, in a certain sense, basic to the understanding of all Western thought, which was conditioned in a substantial way by the esoteric works of Aristotle.

II. The Rediscovery of the Esoteric Writings of Aristotle, the Great Edition of Andronicus of Rhodes, and the Slow Rebirth of Aristotelian Philosophy in the First Century before the Common Era

1. The misadventures of the esoteric writings of Aristotle and their publication

We have sufficiently informed the reader about the misadventures of the Aristotelian writings through what we have written in the preceding volume. Aristotle published works only for a large readership (the so-called exoteric works), for the most part in a dialogue format, composed almost wholly in the years in which he was a member of the Academy of Plato. These works (today we only know about them from indirect fragments) were widely diffused and were, with a few exceptions, the only ones accessible to everyone in the Hellenistic Age, that is, in the years which elapsed from the death of Theophrastus to the beginning of the first century BCE.

The so-called "works derived from schoolroom activity" (that is to say, the writings [λóγοι] which Aristotle prepared for his lectures and which were composed beginning from the period in which the Stagirite founded his first School at Assos), because of their highly specialized and technical content, not only were not published, but in all likelihood were never polished and arranged from a literary standpoint. They remained in an unfinished state, which would make them suitable only for use within the School (and that is why they are called esoteric or acroamatic works). Certainly some copies of these works were made, at least of some of them, or of some of their parts. But these copies would have been quite limited in number, since they were works which were not intended for publication and further they were written in a style incomprehensible to anyone not belonging to the School. In their totality, these works were the patrimony of the library of the Peripatos only up to the death of Theophrastus, who established in a will before he died that the library would be exclusively inherited by Neleus, whereas the buildings and the garden of the School would instead be the inheritance of the whole community. Here is an extract of the will of Theophrastus which has been handed down to us by Diogenes Laertius:

> The whole of my library I give to Neleus. The garden and the walk and the houses adjoining the garden, all and sundry, I give and bequeath to such of my friends hereinafter named as may wish to study literature and philosophy there in common, since it is not possible for all men to be always in residence, on condition that no one alienates these goods or applies them to his private use, but so that they hold it like a temple in joint possession and live, as is right and proper, on terms of familiarity and friendship. Let the community

consist of Hipparchus, Neleus, Strato, Callinus, Demotimus, Demaratus, Callisthenes, Melantes, Pancreon, Nicippus...[2]

We do not know why Theophrastus decided to do something which was fraught with such serious consequences, that is, to make private and hence transferable a treasure of such importance as the library, and to maintain on the contrary the real estate of the School as common and inalienable, since the School would have had a greater need of the library than of the real estate. It may be that he tried in this way to guarantee to Neleus the succession to the scholarchate of the School, which we know subsequently went to Strato.[3]

It is quite true that to an old follower of the Peripatos like Neleus the new doctrinal direction impressed on the School by Strato turned out to be not only unpalatable but even intolerable. Perhaps an acrimonious disagreement broke out between Neleus and Strato, and the very grave decision of taking away the library from the Peripatos and Athens was a consequence of that falling out. And thus the library of the Peripatos, which also contained the books collected by Aristotle and Theophrastus in addition to the original manuscripts of their own works, went from Athens to Scepsis, a town of Troas. Neleus perhaps sold many works to the library of Alexandria, but jealously held onto the invaluable manuscripts of Aristotle and Theophrastus for himself. The heirs of Neleus, lacking any interest in philosophy and culture, were concerned solely to safeguard those manuscripts from the greed of the Attilide kings of Pergamum (who were searching out works for their library at Pergamum which they hoped would rival that of Alexandria). The heirs could think of no other solution, in this situation, except to conceal the manuscripts in a cellar (this must have occurred in the first half of the second century BCE). Between the end of the second century and the beginning of the first century BCE, Apellicon of Teos, of whom we have previously spoken, succeeded in acquiring them (at considerable expense). He brought them to Athens, where he tried to repair the damage (produced by mold and insects), but in a quite arbitrary and maladroit manner, as was explicitly reported. Then he published the precious texts (which were edited, as a result, for the first time). Unfortunately, they were full of errors and hence not very intelligible.[4]

But the mishaps that befell the Aristotelian writings do not end here. A little after their publication by Apellicon, Athens was conquered and sacked by Sulla, in 86 BCE, and the Lyceum also (as well as the Academy) sustained very great damage.[5] Some scholars think that this led to the destruction and closing of the Peripatos.[6] It is clear that our better witnesses no longer mention any scholarchs after Diodorus of Tyre, and the more recent sources which speak again of scholarchs of the Peripatos leave a gap in this period.[7] Be that as it may, Sulla then seized the precious manuscripts of Aristotle recovered by Apellicon and took them to Rome.[8]

At Rome, the grammarian Tyrannion succeeded in gaining the confidence and hence the cooperation of the librarian who had care of the books of Sulla and so he was allowed to transcribe them. We also know that some books were transcribed haphazardly by inexperienced copyists and these copies once again were circulated, although full of errors. We know almost nothing concerning the substance and the results of the work of Tyrannion. But we do know that Andronicus of Rhodes obtained from Tyrannion the invaluable material which he made use of in his monumental edition of the works of Aristotle (and of Theophrastus) which was destined to become epochal because it changed the destiny, as we have said, not only of the Peripatos, but of Western philosophy as well, insofar as this edition guaranteed the preservation and the diffusion of the works of Aristotle which we are still using to this very day.[9]

This information was given to us by testimonies worthy of credibility, that is, both by the geographer Strabo, who was educated in the Peripatetic school and hence had at his disposal the information firsthand, and also by Plutarch. Some confirmation has also come to us through Posidonius. Before continuing, we wish to quote in their entirety the passages of these authors, because they are documents of exceptional importance. Speaking of the city of Scepsis, Strabo writes:

> From Scepsis came the Socratics Erastus, Coriscus, and Neleus, son of Coriscus, a man who was a follower of both Aristotle and Theophrastus, and he inherited the library of Theophrastus as well as that of Aristotle. In fact, Aristotle left his library to Theophrastus as well as deeding the school; he was the first of whom we know that they collected books and who were taught by the king of Egypt how to systematize a library. Theophrastus left the library to Neleus, who took it to Scepsis and left it to his heirs who were uncultured people and they kept the books locked up and not adequately cared for. But when he discovered the eagerness with which the Attilide kings under whose rule the city was, were searching out books for the establishment of their library at Pergamum, he concealed the books underground in a cave. After some time when the books were already damaged by mold and insects, the descendants of Neleus sold them to Apellicon of Teos for a lot of money, the books of Aristotle as well as those of Theophrastus. But Apellicon was more a bibliophile than a philosopher; and so he tried to reconstruct the damaged parts in order to make new copies, he thus altered the text, completing it in incorrect ways, and published the books full of errors. It happened that the ancient Peripatetics after Theophrastus no longer had the books except a few and of these mostly the exoteric works, such that they were no longer in a position to philosophize in their own way but were reduced to making only bombastic statements. Instead the succeeding Peripatetics, from the time these books came out, were in a better condition to philosophize and to profess Aristotelian philosophy, but they were subsequently forced to affirm many things only on the level of probability, because of the great number of errors in the text. Even Rome contributed much to this situation. In fact, immediately after the death of Apellicon, Sulla conquered Athens seizing and taking back to Rome the

library of Apellicon. There the grammarian Tyrannion who was an admirer of Aristotle, succeeded in getting his hands on them by romancing the librarian. He also made some books by using poor copyists without controlling their copies with the originals, a thing which also happened in other cases when books were copied for commercial reasons both here and at Alexandria.[10]

Plutarch repeated some of this very important information and completed it as follows:

[Sulla] having put to sea with all his ships from Ephesus, on the third day he came to anchor in Piraeus. He was now initiated into the mysteries, and seized for himself the library of Apellicon the Teian, in which were almost all of the treatises of Aristotle and Theophrastus, at the time not yet well known to the general public. But it is said that after the library was carried to Rome, Tyrannion the grammarian arranged most of the works in it, and that Andronicus the Rhodian was furnished by him with copies of them, and published them, and drew up the catalogues now current. The older Peripatetics were evidently of themselves accomplished and learned men, but they seem to have had neither a large nor an exact acquaintance with the writings of Aristotle and Theophrastus, because, the estate of Neleus of Scepsis, to whom Theophrastus bequeathed his books, came into the hands of careless and illiterate people.[11]

Finally, important information about Apellicon comes directly from Posidonius: he confirms that Apellicon actually was a member of a circle of Aristotelians and that he acquired the library of Aristotle because "he was quite wealthy."[12]

In conclusion, all the misadventures of the Aristotelian esoterica can be summarized in the following way: (*a*) Neleus (designated by Theophrastus to inherit the library of the Peripatos) carried the Aristotelian writings to his native city of Scepsis, where they were neither organized nor utilized. (*b*) Some of these writings (at least parts of them) were certainly copied (in addition to those in Athens, copies of the esoteric writings found their way into the library of Alexandria[13] and probably also to Rhodes, in the native land of Eudemus)[14] but they must have been dead works, since they basically were not read or studied and assimilated by any of the philosophers of the Hellenistic Age. (*c*) The rediscovery of the Aristotelian esoterica was the work of Apellicon of Teos, who likewise arranged for their publication, but in very inaccurate copies: as a result, the works remained almost incomprehensible. (*d*) The invaluable manuscripts of Aristotle were then confiscated by Sulla and carried to Rome, where the grammarian Tyrannion set to work systematically and reorganized them (a task which he did not completely carry out). (*e*) Some copies of the esoterica were put in circulation at Rome by some booksellers, but they were again copies which were very inaccurate and made only for a quick profit by poorly controlled copyists. (*f*) The systematic edition of the writings of Aristotle was the work of Andronicus of Rhodes, who also compiled an organized catalog, completing in this way a work which necessarily constituted the indispensable premise and foundation of the rebirth of Aristotelianism.

2. The criteria followed by Andronicus of Rhodes in his edition of the *Corpus Aristotelicum*

How did Andronicus of Rhodes go about the task of editing Aristotle's writings? He did not simply limit himself to producing an intelligible reading of the texts, because he was also concerned with regrouping those writings which treated the same material and rearranging them on the basis of their content. A testimony of Porphyry in this regard is very invaluable. Porphyry writes, explaining the criteria that he used in the publication of the writings of Plotinus:

> He himself [Plotinus] entrusted me with the arrangement and editing of his books—and I promised him in his lifetime and gave undertakings to our other friends—that I would carry out this task. So first of all I did not think it right to leave the books in confusion in order of time as they were issued. *I followed instead the example* of Apollodorus of Athens, who collected the works of Epimarchus the comedian into ten volumes, and *Andronicus the Peripatetic, who classified the works of Aristotle and Theophrastus according to subject, bringing together the discussions of related topics*. So I, as I had fifty-four treatises of Plotinus, divided them into six sets of nine (enneads) it gave me pleasure to find the perfection of the number six along with the nines. I put related treatises together in each ennead, giving the first place to the less difficult questions.[15]

It is clear that only the general principle which guided Andronicus can be determined from the text just read. But modern scholars, by examining the ancient catalogs (those which are prior in origin to the edition of Andronicus),[16] have been able to furnish some important determinations. Andronicus reunited some short treatises that were more or less autonomous (and which also had their own titles) to treatises of greater length concerned with the same content. Sometimes he gave new titles to the works thus assembled.[17] It is probable, for example, that he undertook the organization of all the logical works in a single *corpus* as well as giving the title, the *Organon*, to it.[18] As a matter of fact, he thought that the systematic study of philosophy ought to begin from Aristotelian logic.[19] He proceeded in an analogous way to organize the various separate *logoi* concerning physics, metaphysics, ethics, politics, aesthetics, and rhetoric. The general and particular arrangement which Andronicus gave to the *Corpus Aristotelicum* became definitive. It conditioned all of the succeeding tradition and hence also all modern editions.

In conclusion, the edition of Andronicus truly was epoch making in the complete sense of that term.[20]

3. The exponents and tendencies of Peripatetic philosophy in the first century before the Common Era

If we put aside Apellicon and Tyrannion, who were not philosophers (the former, we are told by Strabo himself, was more a bibliophile than a philosopher, the latter was a grammarian),[21] the exponents of Peripatetic thought in the first century BCE who are known to us are the following: Staseas of Naples, Ariston of Alexandria, Cratippus of Pergamum, Andronicus of Rhodes, Boethus of Sidon, Xenarchus of Seleucia, and Nicolaus of Damascus. The chronological information placing many of these individuals within the first century BCE is uncertain, and the opinions of scholars are in disagreement about the issue. It would be important to have reliable knowledge about the dates of the birth and death of Andronicus and thus the dates of his edition of the *Corpus Aristotelicum* because, as we have said, it is linked to the rebirth of Aristotelianism, and the change of quality in its content and method, since the Peripatetic philosophy of this period depended on this new edition. We have already seen how only a later dating of Andronicus and his edition of the works of Aristotle is plausible, if what our sources tell us is accepted, and if we take into account the grave position in which Athens found itself after the conquest of Sulla, and the heavy damage which the Peripatos sustained, as well as the taking to Rome of the Aristotelian manuscripts. Consequently, a careful consideration of the activity of the philosopher cited above confirms what we have already stated, namely that a series of elements arise in favor of the later dating of the edition of Andronicus, which in all likelihood must have occurred in the course of the two decades succeeding the death of Cicero.[22]

A subsequent and particularly significant circumstance must also be kept in mind, Cicero not only did not know Andronicus, but he did not even know any of the philosophers mentioned above who could have benefited from his edition of Aristotle's works, as the extant evidence attests. Cicero, on the contrary, knew Staseas, Ariston, and Cratippus who all worked in the first half or in the first years of the second half of the century.[23] And the thought of these Peripatetics does not reveal any knowledge of the esoterica through Andronicus. In addition, Cicero speaks of Cratippus (to whom he entrusted the education of his son) as though he were the only Peripatetic of importance at the time, as if he were teaching privately and not as a scholarch of the Peripatos.[24] It is, however, true that the name of one of these three philosophers, Ariston, is mentioned by Simplicius in the list of the ancient commentators on the *Categories*,[25] but it is not certain that he is the one in question, since we know of another Ariston who was active in the Age of Augustus.[26] Nevertheless, if Ariston were also our commentator nothing would be changed, since he came from Alexandria, whose library possessed a good many copies of the *Categories*, and since Apellicon also, as we know, had published the Aristotelian esoteric writings at the beginning of the century in Athens, although in a badly corrupted edition.

On the other hand, keep in mind that Andronicus and the Peripatetics of the first century BCE who were probably influenced by him, developed only the premises to the method and the technique of commentary on the esoterica, which will instead become the typical treatise of the Aristotelianism of the succeeding centuries. Andronicus seems to have written paraphrases rather than commentaries. Boethus of Sidon, his follower, was concerned with various problems and various works of the Stagirite, but his activity of commenting is attested to with certainty only for the *Categories*. Xenarchus seems to have been the author of monographs and not of specific commentaries, while Nicolaus of Damascus is the author of an exposition which was a doxographical compendium.[27]

A brief characterization of the activity and thought of each them will confirm what we stated and permit us to draw well established conclusions. Staseas of Naples, who was born in the last decades of the second century BC,[28] was a rhetorician in addition to being a philosopher. The themes which he treated tell us about the climate of the discussions which again we know about as peculiar to the Peripatos of the third and second centuries BCE. He held for the sake of argument, probably as a criticism of the rigidity of the Stoa, that in order to guarantee the achievement of happiness, external goods are very important (in particular good fortune) as well as corporeal goods. Cicero judged the treatise of Staseas on happiness as clearly inferior to that of Antiochus.[29]

Ariston of Alexandria was first a follower of Antiochus,[30] and Lucullus knew him in the years 86/87 BCE at Alexandria as a member of the circle of the Academicians.[31] It is probable, but not certain, that he is the commentator on the *Categories* of whom Simplicius speaks, as we have previously stated.[32] (The ancients report some observations on the category of relation made by Ariston.)[33] He was concerned, in addition, with the syllogism and added three modes to the first figure of the syllogism and two to the second.[34] What forced Ariston to leave Antiochus is unknown to us; the rediscovery of the works of Aristotle and the edition of Apellicon (not necessarily that of Andronicus) would provide a plausible reason. Cratippus of Pergamum was initially a follower of Antiochus. He was engaged in teaching at Mytilene and from 47/46 BCE at Athens, where he had as a student a son of Cicero.[35] He must have acquired considerable prestige, since Cicero himself considered him as the highest authority and the best of the Peripatetics of that period.[36] No one, however, says that he was scholarch.[37] He must have been chiefly concerned with ethics (moral duty). The only information which we have about him, however, is about the art of divination, from which it is clear that he utilized a Platonic-Aristotelian psychology which he found in the exoteric works of Aristotle. The art of divination of Cratippus is not the one of the *Parva Naturalia* of Aristotle and his doctrine of the *psyché* is not that of the *De Anima*. Hence Cratippus did not know the esoteric works of the Stagirite and thus did not make use of them.[38]

We have already mentioned Andronicus and his editorial activity.[39] Neoplatonic sources tell us that he was the eleventh scholarch of the Peripatos, but they leave a gap (of at least two names) between Diodorus and Andronicus.[40] Consequently, if the following facts are taken into account which belong to the period corresponding to this gap: the siege of Athens by Sulla, the damaging of the Lyceum, the confiscation and transportation to Rome of the esoteric works of Aristotle, and the forced interruption of the activity of the School, then it would be reasonable to conjecture that Andronicus himself was able to reconstruct the Peripatos.[41] The philosophical activity of Andronicus, it should be noted, cannot be reduced to simple exegesis or to a mere commentary on the Aristotelian text. Today we can still get an idea of the freedom with which Andronicus developed the Aristotelian problematic chiefly from what has come down to us relative to his interpretation of the *Categories*.[42] It seems that in psychology as well Andronicus was not close to Aristotle's doctrines, since he conceived the soul as a numerical relation which binds the elements of the body and hence as a number, more precisely as a self-moving number, as did Xenocrates. Moreover, it has also been handed down that Andronicus vacillated between this conception and that which made of the soul not the cause, but the effect of the composition of the elements of the body.[43]

The follower and successor to Andronicus was Boethus of Sidon[44] who, to judge from the testimony which has survived, seems to have interpreted Aristotle in some key positions in a naturalistic mode. In fact, while Andronicus proposed to begin the study of philosophy by starting from logic (which is like an instrument and hence must be known first), Boethus proposed to begin with physics, because this study puts us in contact with the things which are most familiar and known to us, and philosophical inquiry should, in point of fact, proceed from what is more familiar and known to us and then go on to what is less familiar and less known to us.[45] The naturalistic tendency of Boethus is evident also from what he wrote in his *Commentary on the Categories*, especially in his interpretation of the first category, that is, of the substance which for him is matter and the composite and not the form. Indeed, it seems that according to Boethus the form falls outside of the category of substance and enters into the scope of other categories. It is understood, consequently, as he would maintain, that the individual would be not only the primary reality *for us* but also *for nature* as well.[46] Finally, he tried to draw from the texts of Aristotle the doctrine of *oikeiosis* which the Stoa had placed as the foundation of their own ethics (but which perhaps was anticipated previously by Theophrastus), that is, the original goal (the πρῶτον οἰκεῖον) towards which we tend is ourselves in relation to ourselves. In agreement with that view, he says that we do not love anyone in preference to ourselves and finally that we only love others in reference to ourselves.[47]

Xenarchus of Seleucia[48] disagreed with Aristotle on almost every issue. This is evident especially with respect to two points: he denied the existence of the *aither* to the point of composing an entire treatise entitled *Against the Fifth Element*,[49] and he also rejected the existence of the supersensible (and thus the immobile Movent). Here are his words:

> [We must] not have recourse to the intelligible, which has no independent existence by itself, and is only a bare supposition.[50]

Xenarchus, in addition, undoubtedly under the influence of Stoic doctrine together with Boethus of Sidon, maintained that we ourselves are the first object of our desire.[51]

Worthy of mention, finally, is Nicolaus of Damascus who was the advisor to King Herod the Great and had excellent relations with Caesar Augustus.[52] His work *On the Philosophy of Aristotle* is made up of many books; it was to be a rather faithful exposition of the thought of the Stagirite, or more accurately, of the following parts of the thought of Aristotle: physics, metaphysics, cosmology, the doctrine of the elements, meteorology, zoology, psychology, and botany. (From Nicolaus we also have a small treatise *On Plants* which in the medieval period was translated into Latin from Arabic and believed to be the work of Aristotle. What cannot be gainsaid is that it constituted a part of the general work *On the Philosophy of Aristotle*.)[53]

On the basis of what we have said and noted, it is necessary to draw the following conclusions. In the first century BCE there were still some Peripatetics who did not benefit from the rediscovery of the esoteric Aristotle and who continued to discuss problems analogous to those discussed by the Peripatetics of the two preceding centuries and with a essentially identical method. Instead, the Peripatetics who benefited from the rediscovery of the esoterica seem to depend almost totally on the edition of Andronicus. Nevertheless, almost all of these philosophers had a tendency to interpret Aristotle, in some key positions of his system, in a tendentiously naturalistic mode (if not completely, as in the case of Xenarchus, who did so in a more accentuated naturalistic manner), with some concessions to Stoicism. This direction, however, will not be followed by the Peripatos; Aristotle's esoteric writings will be the cornerstone and the interpretation of the esoterica will become canonic, but it will change, in a somewhat palpable way, the theoretic climate, as we will immediately see.

III. The New Course of Aristotelianism in the First Two Centuries of the Common Era

1. The consolidation and diffusion of the commentary genre concerning the esoteric works

Not much has come down to us concerning the Peripatetics who lived in the first two centuries CE and at the beginning of the third, except for Alexander of Aphrodisias, who is an exceptional figure and with whom, as a matter of fact, the history of the Peripatos ended. In addition, the extant documents and testimonies have not been adequately interpreted and analyzed and only in very recent times have they attracted the attention of some scholars. The results achieved so far are somewhat surprising; in any case, they are of such a nature as to shatter the schemas that the historians of the previous century and of the first decade of the present century had imposed on the interpretation of the Peripatetic philosophy of this period and which consequently became canonic.[1]

What are the characteristics of the Peripatetic philosophy of this epoch?

In the first place, to philosophize, for the Peripatetics of this epoch, is almost entirely to interpret and comment on the texts of Aristotle. This task is the common theme uniting the philosophers we are going to consider. The exegesis and commentary on the esoteric works begun by Andronicus and his followers would become, in a certain sense, a method of philosophizing and a special literary form wherever followers of the Stagirite can be recognized. Even after the arrival and nearly absolute predominance of Neoplatonism, it was the only way in which Aristotle continued to be read and understood, namely, by means of the commentary and paraphrase of the esoteric works.[2] Thus it would be impossible to neglect or exaggerate the importance of this activity.

In point of fact, almost all of the Peripatetics of this epoch are remembered as authors of exegetical works and commentaries. Alexander (who was a teacher of Nero) came from an Aeolian town called Aigai. He probably wrote a commentary (or an exegesis) on the *Categories* and perhaps also on the treatise *De Caelo*.[3]

Aspasius, who lived in the first half of the second century CE, is remembered as a commentator on the *Categories*, on the *De Interpretatione*, on the *De Caelo*, on the *Physics*, and on the *Metaphysics*. He also wrote a commentary on the *Nicomachean Ethics*, of which there is still a good part extant (and which, as we will see, contrary to what is often maintained, is a document of great importance).[4]

Adrastus of Aphrodisias was a respected author of commentaries on the *Categories* and the *Physics*. This philosopher also cultivated mathematics and astronomy as well as being especially interested in the *Timaeus*, probably producing a commentary to it (or part of it). Thinkers like Theon of Smyrna, Proclus, and Chalcidius are indebted it would seem to his commentary.[5]

Herminus flourished toward the first half of the second century CE. He wrote commentaries on the *Categories*, on the *De Interpretatione*, on the *Prior Analytics*, and on the *Topics*, as well as devoting himself to a critical treatment of the problems concerning the *Physics*, as we will see.[6]

Aristocles of Messana, instead, wrote a vast work, *On Philosophy*, which offered a wide panorama of the whole history of philosophy in an historical and theoretical vein.[7]

Great numbers of commentaries, finally, were written by Alexander.[8] But we will take him up separately because he clearly stood out among all the other Peripatetics.[9]

This broad consolidation of the method of the commentary to the esoterica and its surprising diffusion (a number of commentaries to the same work seems to even further stimulate the writing of new ones) shows that by now the interests of the followers of Aristotle were concentrated on the works of the School and that in comparison with these published works the exoterica had lost almost all their ancient fascination. Gradually the exoterica were neglected and scarcely utilized and so almost slipped into oblivion. It is clear then, why the exoterica were lost, and only the school works transmitted to us. Paradoxically, after having enjoyed such admiration and esteem the exoteric works were condemned to oblivion, while the esoteric works, after remaining for a long time almost wholly unacknowledged, were destined by history to be perpetually rediscovered.

Ettore Bignone has correctly explained the reasons (about which we will speak at length in the remaining parts of this work) which contributed to producing the revolution we have just mentioned. The men of the first centuries of Hellenism, he notes, loved simplicity and clarity. The writings of the School of the Stagirite in no way fulfill these notions. Therefore, those few scholars who had at their disposal some of the esoteric writings of Aristotle were not at all attracted by them, since they possessed characteristics of style which were so contrary to those required by the taste of that age. "But," Bignone continued, "times change, and with them their spirit. What is a defect in one period becomes an advantage in another. The lucidity which the preceding age prized was the asset of the exoteric works of Aristotle; in the centuries of the Roman Empire they appeared popular. Then men become passionate about the recondite and the mysterious. Effort is the law of style; ideas more than words are valued as are sentences which carry a hidden meaning. The fascination about the Hermetic doctrines of the East had penetrated the Roman spirit. Obscurity does not frighten, rather it fascinates. If the new religions have mysteries for initiates, why not the religion of truth, philosophy? Also, the God of philosophical thinking does not appear to all but only reveals himself to those who merit it, beyond the internal part, in the innermost recesses of the temple. As Pythagoreanism, which is in fashion, so every philosophy must have secret doctrines and sacred 'orgies' of the mind to which only the initiated are admitted. Where they do not exist they are assumed. Clement of Alexandria...discovers them also in the school of Epicurus, all the more so therefore in Aristotle. Lucian, in his *Philosophers for Sale*...when selling Aristotle, proclaims through the auctioneer, in order to increase the price, that he who buys will find two Aristotles in one, the ordinary and the extraordinary. Such a love for the arcane brought gradually to the esoteric works of Aristotle the attention of the later centuries of the declining Classical Age. Conquering the first difficulties they go on to grasp the profundity and beauty of the esoterica. It is finally understood that here is the most profound and fully developed thought of the Stagirite. But in order to achieve this, a long journey through the centuries was necessary and furthermore an increasing longing for infinity as well as an habituation to metaphysical subtlety was required."[10]

2. The Platonic and Middle Platonic influences on the Aristotelianism of the Common Era

What was the theoretical uniqueness of the Aristotelianism of this epoch?

We have seen that the post-Aristotelian Peripatos, beginning first with Theophrastus (and especially with Strato) as well as after the recovery of the esoteric writings during the last century of the pre-Common Era (and perhaps also partly during the first century CE), had embraced a naturalistic and even a materialistic position because some of its exponents had been influenced by the Stoa.[11] On the contrary, the Aristotelianism of the epoch with which we are concerned and, in a particular way, the Aristotelianism of the second century CE reveals the distinct influences of Platonism, and especially of that form of Platonism which arose between the end of the pre-Common Era and the first two centuries CE. As we will see, it reached its acme in the second century CE and almost all the historians of ancient philosophy to the present agree in calling it Middle Platonism.[12]

The sympathies of Aristocles of Messana toward Platonism have been recognized at times. Actually, the judgment of Aristocles on Plato and on his philosophy is, in this respect, so clearly favorable that it cannot but come to our attention. Aristocles writes:

Plato, above all the others, philosophizes in an authentic and perfect way.[13]

Not only is the positive judgment on Plato transparently clear from the fragments of Aristocles, but also his substantial agreement with him. Plato had, in fact, the greatness of having understood that although there is only one science of human and divine things, it must nevertheless be distinguished into three parts, namely, a first concerned with the nature of the Whole, a second about human affairs, and a third concerned with reasoning. He understood as well that the first is the foundation and condition of the second. Plato, in other words, had the merit of having grasped that it was not possible to know human realities without first knowing divine realities.[14]

This unconditioned approval of Platonic philosophy (at least understood in this form which is echoed again in its Middle Platonic elaboration) arose from the conviction of Aristocles that Platonism is fully reconcilable with Aristotelianism, and it seems to be reflected in the fact that Aristocles even calls the Academy "the Peripatos of Plato."[15]

But the situation of Aristocles is not an isolated one. All of the Peripatetic philosophers of the second century mentioned above attest to a definite relationship with Plato. Adrastus of Aphrodisias, as we have previously stated, was deeply concerned with the *Timaeus*,[16] which, as we will see, was almost the "Bible" of Middle Platonism. Herminus took the Platonic concept of the soul as self-moving principle and tried to explain celestial motions with it.[17] But the most important document is the commentary on the *Nicomachean Ethics* of Aspasius, which was judged for some time to be of little value and which, in the light of more recent research, may now be viewed instead as having inestimable historical importance.[18]

Let us see some of the more significant Platonic and Middle Platonic elements present in the commentary of Aspasius. In emphasizing the excellence of the contemplative life and contemplation, Aspasius depended on a dualistic conception of man which judges as nonnatural the union of soul and body and which has precise parallels in texts of Plutarch and other Middle Platonic authors. Our author, in fact, writes:

> If...we were freed from the body, no other task would touch our nature except contemplation; now instead the body, insofar as it is chained to physical pleasures and pains, necessarily is constrained to practice temperance and continence and many other virtues of that kind, of which it is not likely that divinity participates because of the fact that it does not share in corporeal pleasures and pains. It is therefore clearly through a necessity imposed by the body that we are concerned with morality.[19]

We will see in addition that Middle Platonism locates the supreme end of man, in man becoming like God. Consequently, Aspasius agrees completely with this typical Middle Platonic conception and clearly preserves it, obviously going beyond the text of Aristotle on which he is commenting. In order to explain the Aristotelian principle "the good is correctly defined as that to which all things tend," Aspasius writes:

> If [Aristotle] intended the good in the sense of the primary cause and in the most proper sense [that is in the sense of God], the proposition is correct, because all things tend to him and to make themselves similar to him. It is necessary to interpret the tendency in the sense which any being has been

disposed by nature to become similar, insofar as it is possible, to the first and most perfect cause: each, in fact, is forced urgently by its own nature toward its proper perfection; and is forced to this through its inclination to that being which is above all most perfect.[20]

Aspasius still more clearly derives the Middle Platonic doctrine from the Aristotelian affirmation that it is typical of the virtuous man to do good rather than to receive it:

Thereby virtue seems to be something Divine or *like a kind of assimilation to God*; the notion of the Divine implies, in fact, not the reception of the good but doing good.[21]

In addition, in order to indicate God, Aspasius undoubtedly uses the expression "the first God,"[22] which derives from a new hypostatic and hierarchical conception of the divine which belongs to Middle Platonism. He enlarges, then, the Aristotelian conception of divinity in function of the categories of the good and the beautiful, attributing to God a knowledge and a concern for the things of the world which the Stagirite does not admit, at least not on the explicitly thematic level:

For nature the divine is beautiful and good and always actually exercising the most beautiful activities and [the Gods] *know the entities as they are and act to preserve the world in its present state.*[23]

These and other contacts between the doctrines of Aspasius and Middle Platonism involve the conclusion that "in the work of Aspasius there is... preserved, if not a Middle Platonic interpretation of the ethics of Aristotle, yet surely an interpretation which was strongly influenced by Middle Platonism."[24]

In the light of these particular elements which indicate a broad tendency on the part of the Aristotelianism of the second century CE to take up and to appropriate the theses and typical conceptions which parallel the Middle Platonic movement, the conclusions which have been forthcoming in the new reinterpretation of Alexander do not surprise us. They seem to put definitively in jeopardy the cliches in which our philosopher was imprisoned for a long time. They reveal a hidden dimension which is not only unacknowledged, but is even unsuspected by previous scholars. Let us consider the reconstruction and interpretation of the cornerstones of the theoretical thought of Alexander in a detailed manner.[25]

IV. The Neo-Aristotelianism of Alexander of Aphrodisias

1.   The cornerstones of the metaphysics of Alexander and their significance

Alexander of Aphrodisias,[1] as we have already stated, was by far the greatest of the commentators of Aristotle. He was even called "the second Aristotle" because of the accuracy and acuity of his commentaries. He was and is considered the "commentator" par excellence for good reasons.

Alexander was not limited, however, to simply commenting; he also wrote works of a theoretical nature. They are in great part extant and have a certain significance and, when correctly understood, an undoubted originality. It is true that he did not present himself strictly as a philosopher as he wished simply to be a faithful interpreter of the thought of the Stagirite, but it is likewise true that in reality he goes beyond the Stagirite and his innovations had notable echoes in Medieval as well as Renaissance thought.[2]

What is the originality of Alexander and what is its significance?

Not long ago it was maintained that his reinterpretation of Aristotelianism was conducted in a "naturalistic" and even in a "nominalistic" mode. It was also maintained that this reinterpretation, in some way, was similar to that achieved in a previous time by Straton of Lampsacus, third scholarch of the Peripatos. But lately a wholly new and in many respects surprising understanding of our philosopher has been discovered. It is even said that Alexander was anti-naturalistic, mystical, and Platonic, and in some respects pre-Neoplatonic.

The metaphysical cornerstones on which the traditional interpretation of Alexander was supported and which instead are now interpreted according to an opposed view are the following.

(*a*) Aristotle affirmed that the concrete individual has the greatest reality, while the universal has the greatest truth, and that while the individual is primary for us (viz., primary in sensation and sensory experience), the universal is prior in nature (the individual is primary subjectively, the universal is primary objectively). On the contrary, Alexander stated that the individual is primary in all senses, not only for us, but also in nature. Simplicius writes:

> Alexander claimed that individual substances [τὰς ἀτόμους οὐσίας] are prior in nature to the universals; in fact, unless there were individuals, there could not be anything else.[3]

(*b*) Aristotle affirmed that the intelligible forms (those which inform the sensibles) do not exist "separately" except in the mind and in mental activity, but he clearly attributed to these forms metaphysical status. Alexander was persuaded, instead, that the being of the intelligibles consists only in their "being thought," and that hence the intelligibles (the intelligible forms of sensible realities) cease to be as soon as they cease to be thought).[4]

(c) The denial of the autonomy of the form and the affirmation that it can only exist in matter (or in thought as an "abstraction") moved Alexander to affirm, contrary to Aristotle, the impossibility for that particular form which is the soul to exist independently from the body and hence to affirm its corruptibility and its mortality.[5]

Consequently, this is how these cornerstones which appeared for such a long period as unequivocal expressions of empiricism, nominalism, and naturalism are today reinterpreted as expressions of a metaphysics with an exactly opposite meaning.

(a) Firstly, Alexander did not entirely attribute reality and truth only to the empirical individual. For individual (indivisible) substance, in fact, he understood both the physical substances constituted of matter and form as well as the meta-empirical realities which are pure forms, pure intelligibles (indeed, pure intelligibles coincide with pure Intelligence, as we will see), as the ancient sources say in an unambiguous way:

> Alexander says that the intelligible and transcendent form [χωριστὸν εἶδος] is also an individual substance.[6]

Alexander interpreted individual substance by trying to locate the prime Movent in its ambit.[7]

We are hence far removed from the position of Straton, as far as the results of the "second voyage" are concerned, and, as we will see, he is preserved from sinking into materialism, as some of the Peripatetics did about whom we have written above,[8] Alexander rejected materialism. As for Plato and for Aristotle, so also for Alexander, not only does the immaterial and immobile exist, but it and it alone can be the cause and explanation of material and mobile beings.

(b) Also, the so-called "nominalism" of Alexander is reoriented. Our philosopher, with the affirmations which we have stated above, did not intend to deny the existence of the self-existent forms, that is, the existence of the purely intelligible forms and hence the transcendent, but he only wanted to preserve the metaphysical inseparability of the forms of sensible things from matter and the non-substantiality of universals. He radicalized (in a somewhat onesided way) certain affirmations of Aristotle, but he did not overturn the Aristotelian positions. Moreover, as recent studies have brought to light, when the Stagirite says that the universal is primary in nature he does not mean by it abstract universals, the universal in the logical sense, but the universal principles, the principles which explain all things; and when Alexander denies that the universal is primary in nature he does not refer to the universal principles, but to the abstract universals, and on this issue Aristotle himself fully agrees.[9]

(c) In the third place, it is true that Alexander denied the immortality of the human soul which for him can live and act only when united to the body and hence must be born and die with it. Nevertheless, if this is true, it is likewise true that he introduces a wholly unusual form of immortality which remains unique in the history of ancient philosophy and which only recently has been fully understood.[10] But of this we will speak further on.

(*d*) In addition, keep in mind that Alexander went on to a physical interpretation of the soul and the human mind. But at the same time he also attributes expressly to the human mind the transcendent capacity of grasping the divine Mind and "becoming it," that is, "of being assimilated to it." Hence he admits a form of mystical union which is more Platonic than Aristotelian and even pre-Neoplatonic.[11]

(*e*) Finally, do not forget that even in the interpretation of the relations between the primary intelligible form (which, as we will see, is the agent Mind, that is, God) and the forms of sensible things, Alexander goes back to Plato, adducing a kind of explanation which once more is a prelude to Neoplatonism.[12]

The things which we have said will be clearer from an examination of the principle positions of our philosopher's noetic.

2. The doctrine of Nous and its novelty

Alexander distinguishes three Minds:[13]

(*a*) The physical or material Mind is the Mind which is a pure possibility or potency to know all things (both sensibles and intelligibles);

(*b*) the acquired Mind or Mind *in habitu* is the Mind which by means of the realization of its potentialities possesses its perfection. It is a *habitus* [ἕξις] of knowing (one can also say that the Mind *in habitu* is the mind which has acquired the settled disposition to grasp the form in matter);

(*c*) the agent or productive Mind [νοῦς ποιητικός] is the cause which makes it possible for the material mind to separate the form and hence to become the Mind *in habitu*.

Hence the material Mind is a pure potentiality for abstracting; the mind in habitu is the acquired capacity to abstract; the agent or productive mind is the cause of this capacity.

Consequently, Alexander's doctrine is quite different from the doctrine of the Stagirite, since he does not admit that the agent Intellect is "in our soul";[14] rather he makes it a single entity for all men and even identifies it with the first principle, that is, with the immobile Movent, which is a Thinking on Thinking. (And from this he derives the necessity of the distinction which is not present in Aristotle between the material mind and the mind *in habitu*.) Here is the most explicit passage:

> The agent Mind is separate [χωριστός] and it is impassible and unmixed with otherness and all these characteristics belong to it because it exists separate from matter. It is therefore separate and existent in itself and for itself. In fact none of the forms which are in matter are separate, or they are

only so in thought, and the separation from matter results in their corruption. And it is also impassible because in all things that which suffers is matter and substrate. And being impassible and unmixed with any matter it is also incorruptible, being act and form separated from potentiality and matter. Now Aristotle shows that indeed the first cause has such characteristics and it is also par excellence the Mind. In fact the form without matter is par excellence a Mind. Therefore this Mind is more valuable than the mind in us which is material because the agent is always superior to the patient and that which is separate from matter is superior to that which is joined to matter.[15]

The text above thus engenders the problem of how the agent Mind, which is God, can make the material mind become a mind *in habitu*, that is, how does the material mind acquire the abstracting capacity. What does Alexander say about this? He furnishes two different replies to the problem, both of which not only are not in contrast, but are consistent with each other.

We have already seen that the agent Mind is in its nature both the *supreme intelligible and the supreme mind* and, in addition to this, that it is the cause of the abstractive capacity of the material Mind, both as supreme intelligible, and as supreme Mind as well.

As *supreme intelligible* the productive mind is the cause or condition of the abstracting capacity of our mind. Insofar as the intelligible par excellence is the cause of the intelligibility of all other things, it is the supreme form and giver of forms to all other things. Our mind knows things only in the measure in which they are intelligible and have form, and the *abstractive hexis* is nothing other than the capacity of grasping the intelligible form. Here is the most explicit passage on this point. After having said that the productive mind is the cause of the *hexis* of the material mind, Alexander writes:

This is, in fact, the intelligible form par excellence and in the highest grade, and such is the form separate from matter [τό κυρίως τε καὶ μάλιστα νοητόν εἶδος, τοιοῦτον δὲ τό χωρὶς ὕλης]. In every case, in fact, the being which has a certain property par excellence and in the highest grade is the cause through which other things also have such a property. For example, that which is visible in the highest degree, that is the light, is the cause of being visible for all other visible things; and so also the primary and supreme good is the cause which makes such all the other goods as such; in fact the other goods are judged indeed on the basis of what they contribute in relation to it. Whatever is in the highest degree and through its nature intelligible is clearly the cause of the knowledge of the other intelligibles. And such being will indeed be the productive mind. In fact unless there were an intelligible by nature, there would not even be any other intelligible thing, as was said before. In fact in every case in which a being exists which has a characteristic in the highest degree and another being has that characteristic in a lesser degree this latter derives its characteristic from the former.[16]

Here it is evident that Alexander exploited the Aristotelian positions and expanded them, chiefly in a Platonic sense (remember the doctrine of the *Republic*) and, as has been noted, he anticipates in some way the Plotinian notion of causality for which *propter quod alia, id maximum tale [that which has such (a property) in the highest degree is the cause of others (having that property)].*[17]

But the productive Mind is a cause of the *abstractive hexis* of our intelligence, or rather as the supreme Intelligible which by its own nature is also supreme Mind or Intellect. It is, in short, the direct and immediate action of the productive Mind on the material mind which is postulated by Alexander as necessary in addition to the indirect and mediate action examined above. Here is the most explicit text:

> There is a third Mind besides the two we have mentioned, the productive Mind whose task is to bring the material Mind up to being the Mind *in habitu* [scil., in possession of the noetic hexis], and this productive Mind, as Aristotle says, is analogous to light. In fact as light is the cause for the colors which are visible in potency to become visible in act, so also this third Mind makes the potential and material Minds become actual, by producing in them the noetic hexis [scil., the actualized capacity to think].[18]

Because the productive mind can operate in this way, it is necessary that it enters into our soul and that hence it is present in us. But due to the identification by Alexander of the productive Mind and the primary cause, that is, God, *it is a presence which comes from the outside and which is not a constitutive part of our soul.* The famous "mind which comes from the outside" [νοῦς θύραθεν, *nous thurathen*][19] becomes in Alexander almost the intelligible impression (the transcendent intelligible impression) in our mind which is formed when we think the productive Mind, that is, the presence of an Intelligible which is also the supreme Intelligence (precisely because the supreme Intelligible is the supreme Intelligence) and it is precisely this identification which makes the potential Mind *in habitu*. Alexander writes:

> This [Mind which comes from the outside], which is through its own nature intelligible, becoming present in anyone who thinks by being thought by this, becomes present as mind in anyone who thinks and comes to be thought from the outside.[20]

The presence in us of the Mind which comes from the outside and which is at the same time the intelligible and Mind gives us the capacity of separating the intelligible forms of things and recognizing them as intelligibles *by positing itself as the goal of the reference:*

> This [productive Mind] is through its nature Intelligible and Mind in act, being the cause which to the material mind by means of the reference to a form which is precisely [the productive Mind], permits to separate, imitate and think any of the immanent forms in matter and render them intelligible and the productive Mind is called the Mind which comes from the outside.[21]

In conclusion, the form and intelligibility of things depends on the productive Mind as well as our mind's capacity for intelligence, that is, our capacity of grasping the intelligible. We are here closer to the theory of being and the notion of causality found in the *Republic* of Plato than to that found in the *De anima* or Book Lambda of the Aristotelian *Metaphysics*.[22]

3. The presence of a mystical component in the metaphysics of Alexander

The traditional interpretation is focused chiefly on the fact that Alexander denied that the *Nous poietikós* was a function or part of our soul; in order to affirm that, so the argument goes, our philosopher had to break the "mystical unity" of our mind with that of the divine. Thus the traditional interpretation is able to qualify Alexander's noetic and metaphysics as "naturalistic."

In point of fact, as more recent and better documented studies have shown, not only is this notion unfounded, but the doctrine of Alexander which states that our minds can act only through contact with the divine Mind justifies the opposite characterization.

To see how this can be defended, consider the following. The human mind is the capacity to abstract the forms of sensible things, that is, the intelligible immanent in matter, but not through its own power, but only through a kind of participation in the divine Mind which, as we have seen, is what makes our Mind move from being a material mind to a Mind *in habitu*. The immediate participation with the divine Mind, which is what Alexander calls "the Mind which comes from the outside," is therefore the necessary condition, the *sine qua non* of human knowledge. It is moreover clear that while knowledge of material forms is of a mediate (abstractive) character the contact with the divine Mind can only be *immediate* and hence of an *intuitive character*. Alexander speaks even of the "assimilation of our minds to the divine Mind," of "our minds becoming equal to the divine Mind,"[23] using a language which is refulgent with the terminology of the Middle Platonists.

This observation should be contrasted with the fact that Alexander speaks of the *mortality of the soul*. Because our soul is a form bound to matter, it cannot exist apart and hence cannot survive the death of the body.[24]

But if this is true, it is also true that Alexander does not in this way simply set aside the problem. For while he preserves the mortality of *our soul*, and in particular of the material or potential mind and of the Mind *in habitu* (which is simply the actuation and perfection of the former), he also speaks of the *immortality of the "Mind which comes from the outside."* In this way he maintains a conception that, as we have already said, has not been encountered either in the preceding history of Greek thought or in what followed. When we intuitively grasp the *Nous poietikós*, that is, the divine Mind, our mind *becomes* this Mind and *is assimilated* to it and hence becomes in a certain sense immortal. But because we know that the grasp of the divine Mind on the part of our mind is what Alexander calls "the Mind which comes from the outside," it follows that immortality is proper to (and only for) this Mind, while *our individual Mind* is mortal. Alexander thought, perhaps, that there was a kind of *impersonal immortality*. It is certain that he had arrived at this conception due to the admission of a "mystical union," that is, of an assimilation and an intimate joining of the human with the divine Mine. Here is the most important text:

> The Mind, therefore, which thinks the Intelligible [= divine Mind] *is immortal;* it is not the Mind which is a substrate, i.e., the material Mind (this in fact corrupts when the soul corrupts, of which it is a capacity, and when it is corrupted even its hexis is corrupted with it, i.e., its capacity, its perfection), but it is a question of the mind which becomes like the divine Mind when it thinks (because in fact the divine Mind becomes like each of the things thought, because it thinks them, and whatever be the thing thought the mind, because it thinks it becomes similar to it), and this mind is the Mind which comes into us from the outside and is incorruptible. In fact other things thought [= the other intelligibles which are abstracted from sensible things] also come from the outside, but they are not mind and become mind only because they are thought. That, instead, comes from the outside properly as mind. That alone, in fact, among all the things that are thought, is Mind in itself independent of being thought. And it is incorruptible because such is precisely its nature.[25]

Therefore, not only is the divine Mind incorruptible, but so also is the Mind which enters into us "from the outside," or, if you wish, that which of the divine Mind, by thinking, we receive within ourselves.

Thus, in order to fully satisfy these new mystical exigencies, Aristotelianism must make its own some doctrines of Platonism and lose its own identity. It is understandable, therefore, that after Alexander Aristotelianism could only survive as a propaedeutic or complementary aspect of Platonism.

THE FINAL TESTIMONY OF THE FOLLOWERS OF THE PHILOSOPHY OF THE GARDEN AND THE WORDS OF EPICURUS INCISED IN STONE

" 'Epicurus,' inquis, dixit: 'Quid tibi cum alieno?' Quod verum est, meum est. Perseverabo Epicurum tibi ingerere, ut isti, qui in verba iurant, nec quid dicatur aestimant, sed a quo, sciant, quae optima sunt, esse communia."

" 'Epicurus,' you reply, 'uttered these words; what are you doing with another's property?' Any truth, I maintain, is my own property. And I shall continue to heap quotations from Epicurus upon you, so that all persons who swear by the words of another, and put a value upon the speaker and not upon the thing spoken, may understand that the best ideas are common property."

Seneca, *Epistle* 12, 11

I. The Revival of Epicureanism in the First Two Centuries of the Common Era

1. Testimony concerning the vitality and diffusion of the philosophy of the Garden in the Imperial Age

We have already examined, in the preceding volume,[1] the developments of Epicureanism during the Hellenistic Age and the important position which the philosophy of the Garden held in Italy within the circle of Philodemus, especially as a result of the great poem of Lucretius in the first half of the last century BCE. But Lucretius died in the 50s BCE and Philodemus in the 40s BCE, while from a letter of Cicero in 51 BCE we know, as we have already noted, that the house of Epicurus and the related grounds had been sold and there was a proposal to construct new buildings in that area. It would be better to read the letter of Cicero (which, although quite important, is little known) in which he, on behalf of the Epicurean philosopher Patro, Phaedrus, and Pomponius Atticus himself, earnestly entreated C. Memmius, who had acquired the land, to preserve the house of Epicurus and the place in which the greatest of men had lived and walked:

> With Patro the Epicurean I am in complete accord, except that I emphatically disagree with him in philosophy. But not only in the early days at Rome, while he showed deference to you too and all your friends, did he cultivate my acquaintance in a special degree, but lately also, when he realized all his wishes in the way of privileges and rewards, he regarded me as practically the leading man among his defenders and friends: and now again he has been introduced and recommended to me by Phaedrus, of whom, when I was a boy, before I knew Philo, I entertained a high opinion as a philosopher, but afterwards as an honest, amiable, and obliging man.
>
> This Patro, then, sent me a letter when I was at Rome, asking me to make his peace with you, and beg of you to yield possession to him of some tumbledown house or other (you know which one), which once belonged to Epicurus (*nescio quid illud Epicuri parietinarum sibi concederes*); but I wrote nothing to you for the simple reason that I did not want your scheme of building [*aedificationis tuae consilium*] to be interfered with by any recommendation of mine. But when he also asked me, on my arrival at Athens to write to you to the same effect, he had his request granted to him for no other reason than because your friends were unanimously agreed that you had thrown to the winds all that building scheme of yours. If that is so, and is now of absolutely no importance to you, I should like you, if your feelings have been ever so slightly hurt by the wrongheadedness of certain persons (I know that coterie), to allow yourself to incline towards leniency, whether because your own exceptional kindliness, or even as a compliment to me. For my part, if you ask me what my own opinion is, I fail

to see either why he is so obstinately set upon it, or why you are so stoutly opposing him, except, of course, that one could far less easily allow you than him to be so needlessly troubled. And yet I am well aware that you know all about Patro's petition and the merits of his case. He avers that he must keep intact his own honor and responsibility, the sanctity of testamentary dispositions, the authority of Epicurus, the solemn injunction of Phaedrus, the residence, the domicile, the very footprints of the most illustrious men [*honorem, officium, testamentorum ius, Epicuri auctoritatem, Phaedri obstentationem, sedem, domicilium, vestigia summorum hominum sibi tuenda esse dicit*]. If we are inclined to find fault with the object of his present efforts, we may as well make mock of the poor fellow's whole life and the principles he follows in philosophy. But, on my oath, since I bear no particular grudge against the great man and those others who are fascinated by such doctrines. I think perhaps that we ought to forgive Patro, if he is much troubled; even if he is mistaken in being so, it is a mistake due to lack of sense more than lack of morality.

But to waste no more words (I must say it sooner or later), I love Pomponius Atticus as a second brother. He is to me the dearest and the most delightful man in the world. Now Atticus not that he is one of that lot [scil., an Epicurean] being a man of most refined erudition in every branch of liberal learning, but he has a great esteem for Patro, and had a great affection for Phaedrus Atticus, I say, the least self-seeking of men, and the least importunate in making requests, entreats me to do this with as much earnestness as he has ever evinced; and he has no doubt that I could get you to grant him this favor by a single nod, even if it were still your intention to build. Now, however, if he hears that you have abandoned that intention, and that even so I have failed to get from you what I want, he will not suspect you of shabbiness to me, but me of lack of consideration for him. And that is why I beg of you to write to your friends, saying that with your full consent that decree of the Areopagites, which they themselves call a *memoire*, may be rescinded.

But I return to what I said at first. Before persuading yourself to do this at all, I would have you persuade yourself to do it readily, as a kindness to me. Anyhow, let me tell you this if you do what I ask, it will give me the greatest pleasure.[2]

Now it would seem to be possible to draw from this letter with some certitude the conclusion that the Garden had been closed and that the members of the School were dispersed. Patro acted and spoke as if he were an ex-scholarch who was trying at all cost to save from total destruction at least the place in which the school was located. The fact that immediately after 51 BCE there is not much information about the scholarchs of the Garden confirms this conjecture.

The crisis of the Epicurean school at Athens probably lasted for a long time, perhaps continuing into the greater part of the first century CE.[3]

We are able to conclude that the Garden in the second century CE existed as a viable institution from the testimonies of the Neo-Pythagorean Numenius and the Aristotelian Aristocles, and that therefore it must have been re-established.[4] In any case, this may be ascertained without any doubt from some extant inscriptions which reveal that the "diadochoi" of the Epicurean school in Athens in the second century CE[5] were being regularly chosen.

It is easy to understand, therefore, how Diogenes Laertius, who lived in the first half of the third century CE, could, among the various proofs attesting to the probity of Epicurus and of Epicurean philosophy (for which he had a great sympathy) also draws forth the following:

> *The school itself which, while nearly all the others have died out, continues forever without interruption* through numberless reigns of one scholarch after another.[6]

But the most interesting document is perhaps an important letter of Plotina,[7] widow of Trajan who belonged to the Epicurean school of Athens, which was addressed to the Emperor Hadrian and in which she asked for certain concessions for the School and especially the freedom to choose the successor in its direction even in the case in which he did not have Roman citizenship. This proves that the preceding Emperors had placed severe restrictions on the freedom of the School, and that therefore the School itself must have been very lively to have attracted so much attention.

Let us remember, finally, that the Emperor Marcus Aurelius financed with public monies a center for Epicurean philosophy.[8]

The vitality of the Epicureans outside of Athens is also attested to by numerous sources. In fact, Epicureanism probably did not experience any difficulty outside Athens. In the first century CE, Seneca and Pliny the Elder speak of Epicureanism as a movement flourishing in Italy.[9] Lucian of Samosata, in the second century CE, said that the Epicureans were numerous and very active in the Pontus.[10] In the same century Galen wrote numerous works to explain and combat Epicurean philosophy.[11]

But the evidence of greatest interest in the second century CE is the magnificent portico that a wealthy citizen of Oenoanda (in Asia Minor) named Diogenes had constructed with long walls on which were inscribed the teachings of Epicurus. But about this magnificent work, the only one of its kind, we will speak further below;[12] first we want to determine the characteristics of the Epicureanism of this period.

2. The permanent stability of the teachings of Epicureanism and the accentuation of its characteristics as a secular religion

The stability of the teaching, the rigorous orthodoxy and fidelity was almost total, if the teachings of the founder of the school are compared with the characteristic traits not only of the Epicureanism of the Hellenistic Age,[13] but likewise with that of the Imperial Age. It is this peculiarity of the Epicurean philosophy which surprises not only the modern reader but which aroused wonder and admiration even among the ancients, accustomed as they were to witnessing the vivid differences and rivalries which were to be found in other Schools. Numenius of Apamea writes in his book *On the Infidelity of the Academy to Plato* as follows:

> No one has even seen the Epicureans argue against Epicurus about any doctrine in any way: they are convinced of sharing the tenets of a wise man and they themselves have the advantage of bearing his name and rightly indeed. It is also a fact that many times the later Epicureans did not speak against each other nor against Epicurus in anything which was important enough to be recorded. In fact, this is for them an illicit act, even an impious one, and so any innovations were prohibited. Because of this attitude no one dare to do such a thing and thus their teachings always remained self-consistent. The school of Epicurus is like an authentic society which does not allow sedition and possesses a single spirit and a single will: which permitted them to be in the past, present, and likewise in the future faithful followers.[14]

Numenius lived in the second century CE and his remarks reflected (as clearly emerges from the tenor of his words) not only the situation in the past, but also in the present. In fact, so much was he convinced of the doctrinal solidarity of the Epicurean community that he confidently predicted its continuing future.

This doctrinal unity (this "enjoyment of the teachings in great peace," as Numenius said) is undoubtedly a characteristic of religion (it is simply a secular version of religion) in which all the founders of the great schools of the Hellenistic Age tried to cloak their doctrine,[15] but which Epicurus more, or better, than others succeeded effectively in guaranteeing both on the theoretical level as well as on the practical level with the special type and style of life which he himself realized and also with the detailed prescriptions he was able to impart.

While he lived, Epicurus established his birthday so that it was solemnly celebrated and in his will he left provisions that this holiday would be perpetuated (the tenth day of Gamelion [January-February]) every year and that on the twentieth day of each month a reunion was to be held of all the companions in philosophy devoted to his memory and that of Metrodorus (and this came to be called the feast of the *Twentieth*.[16]

We know from Pliny the Elder that in the first century of the CE the Epicureans still celebrated these two occasions, exactly as Epicurus had established them:

> They offer sacrifices on his birthday, and keep his festival, which they call the *eikas* [εἰκας] on the 20th day of every month these of all people, whose desire it is not to be known even when alive![17]

Moreover, Epicurus had expressly prescribed:

Act always as if Epicurus sees you.[18]

And with this precept, although with the attenuation of the "as if," he certainly had transposed and applied to himself the prerogatives of divinity. It is a divinity which sees all the actions of men, and is consciously presented as the supreme authority who supports and guards the norms of the good life and consequently judges them.

The fact is not, therefore, surprising that in complete harmony with the tendencies of these testimonies, as we have seen, Lucretius called Epicurus "a God," nor the fact that in the second century CE Lucian of Samosata called Epicurus "divine priest of truth" and "liberator of those who follow his teachings."[19]

The emphasis on the truly religious character of this philosophy during the first three centuries CE in mutual rapport with the spirit of the new age clearly emerges in the testimonies mentioned even if there is a basic difference. The spirit of the new age was turned toward the transcendent, while Epicureanism was and always remained a religion of the immanent.

3. The prestige achieved by Epicurus and the Epicureans in the Imperial Age

The Epicureans during the Hellenistic Age did not take an active role in the profound philosophical discussions and in the lively debates which occurred among the followers of the various Schools. They were only, at least for the most part, opposed and scorned. All the forms of eclecticism of which we are aware tried to respond to the positions taken by the various Schools, but not the Garden. Cases like that of the Peripatetic Hieronymos, as we have seen,[20] are isolated and scarcely relevant. The Epicureans, in short, condemned themselves to an almost total spiritual isolation.

The situation which existed in the Imperial Age was different. Seneca, who welcomed the basic ideas of the Stoa, that is, of the School which had been the supreme antagonist of the Garden, held an open and favorable attitude toward the teachings of the Epicureans. For him many of the ideas of Epicurus were valuable not only for the followers of the philosophy of the Garden, but generally for all men, in the measure in which they touched on the truth. Here are some of his important comments:

> It is likely that you will ask me why I quote so many of Epicurus' noble words instead of words taken from our own school. But is there any reason why you should regard them as sayings of Epicurus and not common property?[21]

> "Epicurus," you reply, "uttered these words; what are you doing with another's property?" *Any truth, I maintain, is my own property.* And I shall continue to heap quotations from Epicurus upon you, so that all persons who swear by the words of another and put value upon the speaker and not upon the thing spoken may understand that the best ideas are common property.[22]

But what can seem audacious or, at least, unusual about this attitude of Seneca really reflects a change of opinion about Epicurus and the Epicureans, which was widely diffused. Seneca himself reveals it in this passage:

> And how many have been ruined, not rescued by their reputation? *There is Epicurus, for example, mark how greatly he is admired, not only by the more cultured, but also by this ignorant rabble.* This man, however, was unknown to Athens itself, near which he had hidden himself away. And so, when he had already survived by many years his friend Metrodorus, he added in a letter these last words, proclaiming with thankful appreciation the friendship that had existed between them: "So greatly blest were Metrodorus and I that it has been no harm to us to be unknown, and almost unheard of, in the well-known land of Greece." Is it not true, therefore, that men did not discover him until after he had ceased to be? Has not his renown shone forth, for all that? Metrodorus also admits this fact in one of his letters: that Epicurus and he were not well known to the public: but declares that after the lifetime of Epicurus and himself any man who might wish to follow in their footsteps would win great and ready-made renown. Virtue is never lost to view; and yet to have been lost to view is no loss. There will come a day which will reveal her, though hidden away or suppressed by the spite of her contemporaries. That man is born merely for a few, who thinks only of the people of his own generation. Many thousands of years and many thousands of peoples will come after you; it is to these that you should have regard.[23]

Even Marcus Aurelius, in the next century, confidently cites Epicurus and the Epicureans with approval and urges others, when calamity strikes, to "imitate Epicurus."[24]

Again, in the second century CE, Lucian of Samosata tells us of the life of Alexander of Aboniteichos, an adventurer who exploited the superstitions of the people and who presented himself as a prophet of Asclepius the Healer and who thus became immoderately wealthy; Lucian spoke of the firm and critical attitude that the Epicureans allied with the Christians in this had taken in this confrontation, denouncing Alexander's bad faith and lies. Epicureans and Christians hence were united in combating pagan superstition and its exploiters, an alliance wholly contingent and isolated but nonetheless important. Here is an interesting testimony of Lucian:

> Again he [scil., Alexander] established some mysteries with torchlight processions, and other ceremonies which lasted three days. In the first he announced the day, as in Athens, with these words: if an atheist, a Christian, an Epicurean come to spy on the mysteries, be gone: the believers in our God will celebrate them under good auspices. After this he began the procession. He went in front and said: Away with the Christians! And the assembled people replied: Away with the Epicureans![25]

This self-styled prophet, then, encouraged by the furor against the Epicureans, publicly burned the *Maxims* of Epicurus in the public square and threw the ashes into the sea. And as a commentary on this incident here is what Lucian writes:

> The wicked did not know what benefits have accrued through this book for those who read it: what peace, constancy, and liberty dwells in the soul; how free from fears, from vain illusions, from bizarre foolishness, from vain expectations, from excessive desires: and it places in you truth and judgment; and with the purification of the mind not by the torchlight and herbs and with other trifles but with reason, truth, and free speech.[26]

And now we come to the most important testimony concerning the Epicureanism of the Imperial Age, that is, to the inscriptions incised in marble of Diogenes of Oenoanda.

II. Diogenes of Oenoanda

1. The portico constructed by Diogenes of Oenoanda and its purpose

The diffusion of philosophical ideas has usually been entrusted to face-to-face conversation or to books. But in the small city of Oenoanda in Lycia (Asia Minor) a rich convert to the philosophy of the Garden named Diogenes,[1] filled with enthusiasm for the words of Epicurus, decided to propagate them in a totally new way. He acquired a large tract of land on a height and constructed a piazza surrounded by a portico in a rectangular shape furnished with statues. In one of the smaller sides he placed a portal; on the opposite side he perhaps constructed his mausoleum; on the two larger sides, he cut into the stone a rather full and detailed summary of the whole of Epicurus's philosophy, with maxims and aphorisms taken from the works of Epicurus. The inscriptions were probably placed at eye-level and were like a book written in stone.

The excavation carried out on the hill at Oenoanda toward the end of the previous century has brought to light large fragments of this wall-book;[2] some of them hold a particular interest.[3]

Why did Diogenes decide to carry out such an imposing undertaking?

He himself had found in Epicurus a teaching which brought peace and tranquility of soul. For the love of all those men "endowed with good faith" he wanted to place at their disposal the message of salvation so that they would not be lost in vain searching and would not be overcome by vain fears. Here are his words:

> As I was almost at the decline of life through old age, when it is nearly the moment to take leave of life with a beautiful paean to the satiety of all pleasurable things, I wanted to help immediately those endowed with good sense before being forestalled by death. If hence there is only one, two, three, or four, or five, or six (or however more you wish, they be O man, in number of persons of good sense, but in no way many) who would be in a bad disposition of soul, I would call them to me also one by one and would do everything in my power to bring them to the best deliberation. But whereas, as you said above, the greater part of men have a common illness, as in one pestilential epidemic, that is their own false opinions of things, and these patients become always more numeroussince they infect one another like sheep through their spirit of imitation, because it is correct that what I know now come to help also those who will come after us (insofar as they are ours, even if they are as yet unborn), and finally it is due humanity to take care of strangers which we find among ourselves, since therefore the remedies procured by this writing concerns many persons, I wish to place therefore the remedies of salvation by means of this porch. Of all the forms as they come I can speak briefly. We have in fact dissolved the fears which

are without reason our masters; then of the useless pains which we have cut-off at the bottom and the natural ones we have reduced a little with a remedy, their greatness having thus become quite small ...[4]

Diogenes did not want to restrict this message to his fellow citizens. He wanted to extend it also to strangers and even to foreigners, in sum, to all men without distinction whether Greek or barbarian because all men are citizens of a single country which is this world:

And undoubtedly he did all this for so-called strangers, who in reality are not such: because, according to every single subdivision of the earth, everyone has his native land, but in relation to the entire world, the only single land of us all is the whole earth, and the world is thus a single residence.[5]

This thought arose and was nourished especially in the Stoa (in addition to the Cynics), but now the Epicureans as well had taken it up because it agreed with their basic principles.

Hence the portico with its inscriptions was to be a book for everyone, for present generations and those of the future, a book which Diogenes had inscribed upon stone to make it eradicable. Diogenes only asked of visitors to the place the following; first, do not approach the writings distractedly, and second, in case it turns out indifferently for you or even that they generate in you a feeling of aversion, avoid making a fuss and go on your way. Diogenes asked, in short, a complete spiritual openness.[6]

2.   The exposition of the physical doctrines

From the extant fragments it does not seem that Diogenes was concerned expressly with the *Canonic*, but in the course of the exposition of the *Physics* he preserved the fundamental principles of the Epicurean logic and especially the principle of the unconditioned validity of sensation and the firm conviction about the possibility of achieving the truth. He argued against those whose teachings questioned the validity of these principles; against Democritus, who denied the validity of sensations; against the Skeptics, who denied the possibility of achieving the truth and abstained from judgment; and against Aristotle himself[7] (evidently against the exoteric Aristotle), who Platonistically denied the knowability of physical things. The Aristotle against whom Epicurus argued, as the reader will recall, was chiefly the Aristotle of the earlier or youthful writings.[8] (The rediscovery of the esoteric Aristotle would not in any way have interested the Epicureans of the Imperial Age.)

The polemics in which numerous philosophers were involved, from the Presocratics to the Stoics, were evidently maintained as essential by Diogenes with the purpose of avoiding the danger of falling into those errors into which some famous philosophers had previously fallen and therefore in order to guarantee truth, as he expressly said:

Now therefore we accuse the previously mentioned philosophers not in a contentious spirit but with the desire to preserve the truth.[9]

In what concerns the properly physical teachings, at least in the extant fragments, we find again the typical Epicurean doctrines, from the theory of the atoms to that of the infinity of the world, from the doctrine of the soul to that of the simulacra, from the demonstration of the conclusion that death is not dreadful (because the soul, and hence feeling, perishes with the body) to the re-affirmation of the position of the naturalness of language.[10] In addition, Diogenes preserved the tenet that natural phenomena are explained by multiple causes and there is no need to take a position in favor of only one of the possible solutions.[11]

The defense of Diogenes concerned with the accusations against Epicureans of impiety and atheism then is worth mentioning. He expressly refers to the names of some really impious men and true atheists (the accusers of Socrates, and Anaxagoras, Diagorus, and Protagoras),[12] and he vigorously affirmed:

It is not us who strike at the Gods, but it is the others.[13]

3. The exposition of the ethics

The goal of life (the achievement of which is happiness), in the exposition of the ethics of Diogenes, is found in pleasure:

Let us affirm now and always proclaiming to all, Greeks and barbarians, that pleasure offers the highest goal of a better way of living.[14]

In addition he argued vividly against those who place such an end in virtue, which for him is only a means, not an end.[15]

Naturally, as means of achieving *ataraxy*, he reproposed the four-fold remedy.[16]

Moreover, an incisive polemic was waged against various doctrines on the immortality of the soul, as is proved by many explicit references to the doctrine of metempsychosis and to the hybrid thesis of the Stoics, which maintained the survival of the soul for a limited time.[17]

His arguments against the notion of Fate were forceful, as were those against the connected doctrine of divination as well as his defense of the free movement of the atoms and hence of human liberty.[18]

Diogenes defended old age, showing that this age also brings its advantages, and he opposed, finally, those who reproached the aged as "crippled." The extant fragments on this theme are few and badly preserved, but they help us to grasp, in any case, the tenor of the defense by Diogenes.[19] He taught in a faithful Epicurean manner that life can be enjoyed always, right to the end, if we realize that it is a good which, as long as we possess it, cannot be taken away by any evil. For the Epicurean life is always, *insofar as and as long as it lasts*, without exception, the unconditioned good. It is enough to live life as we ought to, that is, making use of the "remedies of salvation" to be happy always.

III. The Dissolution of Epicureanism

The outdoor wall inscriptions of Diogenes of Oenoanda are probably the last significant manifestation of Epicureanism.

Perhaps the Epicurean Diogenianus also belongs to this century. There are some of his extant fragments, although of minor importance, in which he argues against Fate and against diviners.[1]

At the beginning of the third century CE, Diogenes Laertius, if not agreeing with the teaching of the Garden, certainly exhibits an appreciation of it more than of any of the other Schools. The whole of the tenth book of the *Lives and Opinions of Eminent Philosophers*, which is the concluding book of his entire work is devoted to Epicurus and the Garden. It is through this book that those works of Epicurus have been preserved which we can still read in their entirety. Diogenes Laertius, in fact, in the course of his book, in order to explain Epicurean thought in an adequate way, quoted in their entirety the *Letter to Herodotus*, the *Letter to Pythacles*, the *Letter to Menoeceus*, and the famous *Maxims*, which are a summary of the whole philosophy of the Garden.[2]

That Epicureanism was, moreover, still alive in the third century CE is demonstrated by the polemics of Bishop Dionysius of Alexandria[3] and by traces in Lactantius.[4]

Concerning the Garden at Athens, if it had survived into the third century CE then it could not have survived beyond 267 CE, the year in which the invasion of the Herulians destroyed the area in which it is thought that the school building had been situated.[5]

It is nevertheless certain that in the fourth century CE Epicureanism had already disappeared and that, as the Emperor Julian attested, the books of Epicurus had been destroyed and so most of them had disappeared from circulation.[6]

The doctrines of Neoplatonism and Christianity by this time had practically conquered the spirit of the age.

Third Section

THE REBIRTH OF THE PHILOSOPHY OF THE
PORCH AT ROME AND NEO-STOICISM

"Subsilire in coelum ex angulo licet exurge:
modo et te quoque dignum finge deo."

"One may leap to heaven from the very
slums. Only rise: and mold yourself to kinship with your God."

Seneca, *Epistle* 31, 11

I. Final Phase of the Stoa

1. The vitality and diffusion of Stoicism in the Imperial Age

The Stoa was one of the great Schools born in the Hellenistic Age which in the succeeding Imperial Age demonstrated the greatest vitality and the greatest spiritual hold over the hearts of men.

In the properly philosophical field there emerged thinkers like Seneca, Epictetus, and Marcus Aurelius and, although on an inferior level, it is also correct to place along with them Musonius Rufus, chiefly for his noble moral ideals and the lofty character of his educational teaching. (There remains a conspicuous literary inheritance from all these philosophers which in part compensates for the loss of the works of the ancient Stoics. There are many letters, treatises on morality and scientific topics, and tragedies of Seneca extant; we possess the *Memoirs* or *Meditations* of Marcus Aurelius; a goodly number of the lectures of Epictetus transcribed by the historian Arrian have been preserved; and a certain number of discourses belonging to Musonius transcribed by a certain Lucius have also come down to us.) The figure of Hierocles is more modest (we know his *Elements of Ethics*, which is extant on papyrus, and large fragments of his *Philosophoumena*, which were preserved by Stobaeus): he simply reproduced Stoic morality in a didactic and popularizing style.[1]

In the areas of the interpretation of myths and of religion in the first century BCE, Lucius Anneus Cornutus was distinguished for his application of the Stoic method of allegorizing[2] (he composed a textbook which was used to teach children how to interpret names, attributes, and myths relative to the Gods in the sense of the natural theology of the Stoa), as was the grammarian Heraclitus (who interpreted Homer in terms of the Stoic theory of allegorizing) and the learned Alexandrian Chaeremon of Egyptian origin (who applied the allegorical method of interpretation of Egyptian theology).[3]

In the area of science, the astronomers Manilius[4] and especially Cleomedes were notable; the latter composed an introductory textbook to the theory of celestial phenomena in which he violently attacked Epicurus.[5]

The influence of the Stoa was felt in poetry, as can be seen in Persius and Lucan, both followers of Cornutus (Lucan was the nephew of Seneca), and in general in the whole spiritual life of the time, especially in the Roman world.[6]

In conclusion, in the first two centuries CE there was at all levels a rebirth of the Stoa which led to a series of achievements of considerable interest which we will now analyze in detail.

2. The characteristics of Neo-Stoicism
    In order to fully understand the peculiarities of Neo-Stoicism it is neces-

sary by way of introduction to consider the fact that it started and flourished at Rome.[7] The thinkers of the Middle Stoa (Panaetius and Posidonius) had already benefited, at least in a certain respect, from the influence of the Roman spirit;[8] but the new Stoa was nourished almost entirely by the Roman spirit.

It was not an accident that Roman Stoicism was the philosophy which always had the greatest number of adherents and admirers, both in the Republican Period and in the Imperial Age. Indeed, the disappearance of the Republic with the consequent loss of liberty for its citizens and hence with a decrease in all public affairs and activities connected with them notably confirmed in the most sensitive spirits an interest in intellectual pursuits in general and in Stoic philosophy in particular.[9]

Consequently, it is the general characteristics of the Roman spirit which experienced as truly essential only practical problems and not those of a purely theoretical nature which when joined to the particular characteristics of the historical moment of which we are speaking that permit us to explain fully the particular configuration which determined the problematic of the final stage of the Stoa.

(*a*) In the first place, the interest in ethics which had already been brought into the foreground by the Middle Stoa became predominant in the Roman Stoa of the Imperial Age. For some thinkers, it constituted their almost exclusive interest.

(*b*) The interest in the problems of logic and physics diminished considerably, and theology itself, which was part of physics, assumed a coloration which would almost necessarily qualify it as spiritual in orientation.

(*c*) Individuals notably relaxing their ties with the state and society sought their own perfection in the interiority of their own conscience by creating an interior a-political atmosphere which never before then had been encountered in this period of philosophy, at least to this degree.

(*d*) The Roman Stoa consequently developed a sense of an intimate union between God and man which then reached its crowning moment in Neo-Platonism.

(*e*) Platonism, which previously had exercised a certain influence on Posidonius, inspired not a few pages of Roman Stoicism with its own new characteristics derived from "Middle Platonism." In particular, the fact is worth noting that the notion of philosophy and the moral life as an *assimilation to God* and as the *imitation of God*, which as we will see constitutes a signature characteristic of Middle Platonism, exercised an unequivocal influence. Seneca alludes many times to the above-mentioned conception.[10] Musonius spoke of man as the "image of God," and he expressly said that to philosophize is "to follow Zeus."[11] An analogous thought is expressed by Marcus Aurelius.[12]

But here as evidence is a passage of Epictetus which is perhaps the most pointed one in this respect:

Something like this is our picture of the work of the philosopher. The next thing after this is that we seek the means of achieving it. We see, then, that the carpenter becomes a carpenter by first learning something, the helmsman becomes a helmsman by first learning something. May it not be, then, that in our case also it is not sufficient to wish to become noble and good, but that we are under the necessity of learning something first? We seek, then, what this is. Now the philosophers say that the first thing we must learn is this: that there is a God, and he provides for the universe, and that it is impossible for a man to conceal from him, not merely his actions, but even his purposes and his thoughts. Next we must learn what the Gods are like; for whatever their character is discovered to be, the man who is going to please and obey them *must endeavor as best he can to resemble them*. If deity is faithful, he must also be faithful; if free, he must also be free; if beneficent, he must also be beneficent; if high-minded, and so forth; there-fore, *in everything he says and does, he must act as an imitator of God.*[13]

Neo-Stoic anthropology itself was influenced in a certain respect by Middle Platonism, especially Seneca's notion of the dualistic relations existing between the soul and the body, as well as the notion of the clear supremacy of *nous* over *psyché* of Marcus Aurelius, about which we will speak later. And again, the interpretation of *nous* in the daimonological sense, as we will see, was derived from Middle Platonism.

(*f*) Finally, a strong religious sense erupts and transforms in a rather accentuated way the spiritual climate of the old Stoa. In fact, in the writings of the new Stoa we even find a series of precepts which we may call parallels to the Gospel precepts; for example, the common parentage of all men by God, the universal brotherhood of man, the necessity of pardon, love of neighbor, and finally, love for those who do evil, as we will fully document.

(*g*) A significant fact which neatly closes the history of the Stoa deserves to be emphasized. From the very beginning, the philosophers of the Porch had stated that philosophy could be present in a slave or in his master; Seneca stated that a good and great soul could be found in a slave or in a Roman knight. The history of the Stoa ends with the truly beautiful and perfect illustration of this profound conviction in the succession of its final great proponents. Epictetus was a slave, and, what is more, quite disabled; while Marcus Aurelius, who was a great admirer of the slave philosopher, was an Emperor.

II. Seneca

1. The characteristics of the thought of Seneca

The Stoa, which with Panaetius and Posidonius had already opened the door to truth and to the teachings of the other schools, was again more sensitive with Seneca to eclectic positions.[1] The Roman philosopher energetically expressed his spiritual freedom from the teachings of the School in the necessity he felt to listen to all voices and accept them if sound, even when they were in conflict with the views of the founders, Zeno and Chrysippus. He felt compelled to keep searching beyond, beyond the truths already uncovered as well as seeing the importance of appropriating them fully and bringing them to life by examining them. Here are some apt testimonies:

> But when I say "ours," I do not bind myself to some particular one of the Stoic masters; I, too, have the right to form an opinion. Accordingly, I shall follow so-and-so, I shall request so-and-so to divide the question; perhaps, too, when called upon after all the rest, I shall impugn none of my predecessors' opinions, and shall say: "I simply have this much to add."[2]

I shall show, too, that the Stoics also accept this doctrine, not because I have made it my rule to set up nothing contrary to the teaching of Zeno or Chrysippus, but because the matter itself suffers me to adopt their opinion; for if a man always follows the opinion of one person, his place is not in the senate, but in a faction.[3] We may argue with Socrates, we may doubt with Carneades, find peace with Epicurus, overcome human nature with the Stoics, and exceed it with the Cynics. Since Nature allows us to enter into fellowship with every age, why should we not turn from this paltry and fleeting span of time and surrender ourselves with all our soul to the past, which is boundless, which is eternal, which we share with our better.[4] Even certain norms of wisdom preached by Epicurus, despised for a long time by the Stoa, and especially the basic sense of the message of the philosophy of the Garden are refurbished by Seneca because of his attitude of total openness:

> Personally I hold the opinion–I shall express it though the members of our school may protest–that the teachings of Epicurus are upright and holy and, if you consider them closely, austere; for his famous doctrine of pleasure is reduced to small and narrow proportions, and the rule that we Stoics lay down for virtue, this same rule he lays down for pleasure–he bids that it obey Nature. But it takes a very little luxury to satisfy Nature.[5]

It is true, nonetheless, that Seneca is not simply an eclectic. His openness and his freedom in receiving views of the various schools are, therefore, rooted in an authentically Stoic sense that almost always organically assimilates what it takes up. In addition, if it is true that Seneca always starts from Stoicism but does not always remain faithful to it nevertheless it is likewise true that the new conclusions at which he arrives are grasped chiefly at the purely intuitive level without any knowledge on his part of how to elaborate them in adequate theoretical categories which would be different from those elaborated by the Stoics.

But even Plato, who Seneca knew chiefly through Middle Platonism which was then widely diffused, had a strong attraction for him, not only the anthropology and the moral doctrine but even the metaphysics, although the latter was apparently quite removed from the concept that Seneca had of philosophy as the *ars vivendi* [*the art of living*]. Here is the most important text on this issue:

> That is my habit, Lucilius: I try to extract and render useful some element from every field of thought, no matter how far removed it may be from philosophy. Now what could be less likely to reform character than the subjects which we have been discussing? And how can I be made the better men [sic] by the "ideas" of Plato? What can I draw from them that will put a check on my appetites? Perhaps the very thought that all these things which minister to our senses, which arouse and excite us, are by Plato denied a place among things that really exist. Such things are therefore imaginary, and though they for the moment present a certain external appearance, yet they are in no case permanent or substantial; nonetheless, we crave them as if they were always to exist, or as if we were always to possess them. We are weak, watery beings standing in the midst of unrealities; therefore let us turn our minds to the things that are everlasting. Let us look up to the ideal outlines of all things that flit about on high, and to the God who moves among them and plans how he may defend from death that which he could not make imperishable because its substance forbade, and so by reason may overcome the defects of the body. For all things abide, not because they are everlasting, but because they are protected by the care of him who governs all things; but that which was imperishable would need no guardian. The Master Builder keeps them safe, overcoming the weakness of their fabric by his own power. Let us despise everything that is so little an object of value that it makes us doubt whether it exists at all. Let us at the same time reflect, seeing that Providence rescues from its peril the world itself, which is no less mortal than we ourselves, that to some extent our petty bodies can be made to tarry longer upon earth by our own providence, if only we acquire the ability to control and check those pleasures whereby the greater portion of mankind perishes.[6]

2. God and the Divine

Seneca is certainly one of the exponents of the Stoa in whom a certain vacillation in thinking about the divine is quite clear. A tendency to start out from pantheism and the spiritual attitudes we have mentioned above, accompanied by an accentuated religious spirit, is clearly evident.

In many passage, in point of fact, Seneca seems quite consistent with the pantheism of the school. God is *Providence*, he is the *immanent Mind* which forms matter, he is *Nature*, he is *Fate*. In his *De beneficiis*, after having exemplified many aspects of the providence of God, Seneca writes:

> "It is nature," you say, "who supplies me with these things." But do you not understand that, when you say this, you merely give another name to God? *For what else is Nature but God and the Divine Reason that pervades the whole universe and all its parts?* You may, as often as you like, address this being who is the author of this world of ours by different names: it will be right for you to call him Jupiter Best and Greatest, and the Thunderer and the Stayer, a title derived, not from the fact that, as the historians have related, the Roman battle-line stayed its flight in answer to prayer, but from the fact that *all things are stayed by his benefits, that he is their Stayer and Stabilizer.* If likewise you should call him *fate*, it would be no falsehood; for since *fate is nothing but a connected chain of causes*, he is the *first of all causes on which the others depend.* Any name that you choose will be properly applied to him if it *connotes some force that operates in the domain of heaven*–his titles may be as countless as are his benefits.[7]

God and the world are identical: God is *all that we see*; and even *the wholeness of what we can see* and of what we cannot see in the sense that he is the totality of phenomena and their reason. On the other hand, Seneca tends to accentuate the privileged role of God, self-caused and the cause of all, most powerful begetter and ruler, and goes as far as to oppose to him matter as soul is opposed to body;[8] in this way he follows the positions opposed to those which are immanentistic and materialistic. Seneca does not succeed, however, in giving a voice to these positions and does not even succeed in determining them and expressing them thematically because he does not possess the tools or sufficient speculative ability. Therefore, it is true that, as the historians of philosophy have noted that, in the ultimate analysis he did not escape from pantheistic Stoicism.

Nevertheless, where the speculation of Seneca is most original, that is, in its psychological analysis, in echoing the innermost voice of the human spirit, in the grasp and interpretation of the interior feeling for the divine, it is to be recognized that, in this sphere, his God takes on spiritual traits and even personal ones, which undoubtedly arise from outside the framework of Stoic metaphysics. Here are some of the graceful pages which illustrate this point. In the Forty-First *Letter*, Seneca writes:

> You are doing an excellent thing, one which will be wholesome for if as you write me you are persisting in your effort to attain sound understanding; it is foolish to pray for this when you can acquire it from yourself. We do not need to uplift our hands towards heaven, or to beg the keeper of the temple to let us approach his idol's ear as if in this way our prayer were more likely to be heard. *God is near you, he is with you, he is within you.* This is what I mean, Lucilius: *a holy spirit indwells within us, one who marks our good and bad deeds*, and is our guardian. As we treat this spirit, so are we treated by

it. Indeed, *no man can be good without the help of God. Can one rise superior to fortune unless God helps him rise? He it is that gives noble and upright counsel. In each good man a God does dwell,* but what God we know not.

If ever you have come upon a grove that is full of ancient trees which have grown to an unusual height, shutting out a view of the sky by a veil of bleached and intertwining branches, then the loftiness of the forest, the seclusion of the spot, and you marvel at the thick unbroken shade in the midst of the open spaces, will prove to you the presence of the deity. Or if a cave, made by the deep crumbling of the rocks, holds up a mountain on its arch, a place not built with hands but hollowed out into such a spaciousness by natural causes, *your soul will be deeply moved by a certain intimation of the existence of God.* We worship the sources of mighty rivers; we erect altars at places where great streams burst suddenly from hidden sources; we adore springs of hot water as divine, and consecrate certain pools because of their dark waters or their immeasurable depth. *If you see a man who is unterrified in the midst of dangers, untouched by desires, happy in adversity, peaceful amid the storm, who looks down upon men from a higher plane, and views the Gods on a footing of equality, will not a feeling of reverence for him steal over you?* Will you not say: "This quality is too great and too lofty to be regarded as resembling this petty body in which it dwells? *A divine power has descended upon that man.*" When a soul rises superior to other souls, when it is under control, when it passes through every experience as if it were of small account, when it smiles at our fears and at our prayers, *it is stirred by a force from heaven. A thing like this cannot stand upright unless it is propped up by the divine. Therefore, a greater part of it abides in that place from whence it came down to earth.* Just as the rays of the sun do indeed touch the earth, but still abide at the source from which they are sent; even so the great and hallowed soul, which has come down in order that we may have a nearer knowledge of divinity, *does indeed associate with us, but still cleaves to its origin; on that source it depends, thither it turns its gaze and strives to go, and it concerns itself with our doings only as a being superior to ourselves.*[9]

God listens, sees, and loves man and in particular he is a friend of the good man. Here are the traits then of a providence which is almost personal and which stands out clearly in this passage illustrating the relation of God with good men and clarifying the providential sense of adversity which befalls the good man:

I shall reconcile you with the Gods, who are best to those who are best. For Nature never permits good to be injured by good; between good men and the Gods there exists a friendship brought about by virtue. Friendship, do I say? Nay, rather there is a tie of relationship and a likeness, since, in truth, a good man differs from God in the element of time only; he is God's pupil, his imitator, and true offspring, whom his all-glorious parent, being no mild task-master of virtues, rears, as strict fathers do, with much severity. And so, when you see that men who are good and acceptable to the Gods labor and sweat and have a difficult road to climb, that the wicked, on the other hand, make merry and abound in pleasures, reflect that our children please us by their modesty, but slave-boys by their forwardness; that we hold in check the former by sterner discipline, while we encourage the latter to be bold. Be assured that the same is true of God. *He does not make a spoiled pet of a good man; he tests him, hardens him, and fits him for his own service.*[10]

Clearly God, in this passage and in other parallel passages, is represented as having little in common with the characteristics of the pneuma-God or the fiery-breath God.

3. The conception of man

An analogous phenomena in relation to theology is also encountered in psychology. Seneca accepted the Platonic tripartition of the soul but he subsumed it into the ruling part; or better described, he considered the three parts of the soul as three powers of the "ruling part" of the *psyché*, as Posidonius had previously held.

But Seneca emphasized the duality between body and soul much more than the Middle Stoa had done, with an emphasis redolent with the imagery of the Platonic *Phaedo*. The body is heavy, a bond, a chain, a prison for the soul; the soul is the true man, which tends to free itself from the body in order to achieve its true nature. Our philosopher says in one of his most famous moral treatises:

> Those things that men's untutored hearts revere, sunk in the bondage of their bodies–jewels, gold, silver, and polished tables, huge and round–all these are *earthly dross*, for which the untainted spirit, *conscious of its own nature, can have no love, since it is itself light and unencumbered, waiting only to be released from the body before it soars to highest heaven.* Meanwhile, *hampered by mortal limbs* and encompassed by the *heavy burden of the flesh*, it surveys, as best it can, the things of heaven in swift and winged thought. And so the mind can never suffer exile, *since it is free, kindred to the Gods, and at home in every world and every age; for its thought ranges over all heaven and projects itself into all past and future time.* This *poor body, the prison and fetter of the soul* is tossed hither and thither; upon it punishments, upon it robberies, upon it diseases work their will. *But the soul itself is sacred and eternal, and upon it no hand can be laid.*[11]

In *Letter* 65, we read:

> For all these questions [of philosophy], ... elevate and lighten the soul, which is weighed down by a *heavy burden* and desires to be freed and to return to the elements of which it was once a part. *For this body of ours is a weight upon the soul and its penance; as the load presses down the soul is crushed and is in bondage,* unless philosophy has come to its assistance and has bid it take fresh courage by contemplating the universe, and has turned it from things earthy to things divine. There it has its liberty, there it can roam abroad; meantime it escapes *the custody in which it is bound,* and renews its life in heaven.[12]

In Letter 92:

> But He in whose body virtue dwells, and spirit e'er present, is *equal to the Gods; mindful of his origin, he strives to return thither.* No man does wrong in attempting to *regain the heights from which he once came down.* And why should you not believe that something of divinity exists in one who is part of God.[13]

In *Letter* 102 Seneca even asserts that the day which we greatly fear as the last of our life is instead "the day of our birth into immortality," the day in which, putting aside the shell of our body, the mysteries of nature will be unveiled for us and a clear light "will close in upon us."[14] It is evident that these conceptions are inconsistent with the Stoic affirmations that the soul is a body,[15] that is, a pneumatic substance and a subtle breath,[16] statements which Seneca nevertheless affirms. The truth of the matter is that, on the intuitive level, Seneca went beyond Stoic materialism; but then, because he lacked speculative categories to ground and develop such intuitions, he left them unsupported, in mid-air, as we have already said. In fact, Seneca reveals an unusually intensive acquaintance with the writings of some Platonists, but at the same time, it is patent that what he derived from them is only a series of corollaries, although very important ones, but not their ontological grounds.

4. Conscience

Seneca discovers *conscience* as a spiritual force which is fundamental to human morality once more on the basis of the psychological analysis in which he excelled, and he places it in the foreground in such a way as none among Greek or Roman philosophers had done previously.

Pohlenz indicates that the source of Seneca's inspiration about the "voice of conscience," familiar to popular Roman ethics as well as to Cicero himself, was precisely the influence of Sextius, who inspired by the Pythagoreans, also recommended a daily examination of conscience.[17]

Actually, the *De ira* contains a very clear testimony in this respect:

> All our senses ought to be trained to endurance. They are naturally long-suffering, if only the mind desists from weakening them. *This should be summoned to give an account of itself every day.* Sextius had this habit, and when the day was over and he had retired to his nightly rest, he would put these questions to his soul: "What bad habit have you cured today? What fault have you resisted? In what respect are you better?" Anger will cease and become more controllable if it finds that *it must appear before a judge every day.* Can anything be more excellent than this practice of *thoroughly sifting the whole day*? And how delightful the sleep that follows this self-examination—how tranquil it is, how deep and untroubled, when the soul has either praised or admonished itself, and when this secret examiner and critic of self has given report of its own character! I avail myself of this privilege, and *every day I plead my cause before the bar of self.* When the light has been

removed from sight, and my wife, long aware of my habit, has become silent, *I scan the whole of my day and retrace all my deeds and words*. I conceal nothing from myself, I omit nothing. For why should I shrink from any of my mistakes, when I may commune thus with myself? "See that you never do that again; I will pardon you this time. In that dispute, you spoke offensively; after this don't have encounters with ignorant people; those who have never learned do not want to learn. You reproved that man more frankly than you ought, and consequently you have not so much mended him as offended him. In the future, consider not only the truth of what you say, but also whether the man to whom you are speaking can endure the truth. A good man accepts reproof gladly; the worse a man is the more bitterly he resents it."[18]

In addition to God, our own conscience is the real, infallible, and inexorable judge of our moral life. Therefore, Seneca writes:

Nothing shall I ever do for the sake of opinion, *everything for the sake of my conscience*. Whatever I shall do when I alone am witness I shall count as done beneath the gaze of the Roman people.[19]

The awareness of good and evil in man, hence, is original and uneliminable.

The structural awareness of good and evil is conscience. No one can reject it, because man cannot reject himself. The evil-doer may flee from the punishment of the law, but not from conscience, which inexorably goads him and which is a most implacable judge. In *Letter* 97 we read:

The evil-doer has often another tribunal which is never kind: his conscience. Because the first and worst penalty for sin is to have committed sin and crime, though fortune deck it out with her favors, though she protect and take it in her charge, can never go unpunished; since the punishment of crime lies in the crime itself. But nonetheless do these second penalties press close upon the heels of the first—constant fear, constant terror, and distrust of one's own security....Let us disagree with Epicurus on the one point, when he declares that there is no natural justice; and that crime should be avoided because one cannot escape the fear which results therefrom; let us agree with him on the other—that *bad deeds are lashed by the whip of conscience*, and that conscience is tortured to the greatest degree because unending anxiety drives and whips it on, and it cannot rely upon the guarantors of its own peace of mind. For this, Epicurus, is the very proof that we are by nature reluctant to commit crime, because even under circumstances of safety there is no one who does not feel fear. Good luck frees many men from punishment, but no man from fear. And why should this be if it were not that we have ingrained in us a loathing for that which Nature has condemned? Hence *even men who hide their sins can never count upon remaining hidden; for their conscience convicts them and reveals them to themselves. But it is the property of guilt to be in fear.*[20]

This conception of the voice of conscience is only partially in agreement with Stoic principles. In the measure in which the Stoa makes of our reason an emanation or a moment of the cosmic reason, it can handily explain conscience as the imprint of the laws of the eternal logos on the human logos; but, as long as it pretends to reduce this logos to fire, to a fiery breath, or to a body, then it would take away any possibility whatever of comprehending the notion of conscience: a fire or a conscious breath as interior judge of good and evil does not make consistent sense. As can be seen, the *spiritual* conception of conscience expressed by Seneca would be more in harmony with anti-materialistic and hence anti-Stoic presuppositions.

5. Will

As we have seen above, the Stoa insisted on the fact that the disposition of the soul determined the morality of an action; but this disposition of the soul was derived and resolved in conformity with the fundamental intellectualistic tendency of the whole of Greek ethics into knowledge, into *episteme* (*science*) which belongs to wisdom. *Seneca goes beyond this and speaks expressly of will*, and in fact, for the first time in classical thought, *he speaks of the will as a distinct power apart from knowledge.* In this discovery, Seneca was assisted in a specific manner by linguistic considerations of the Latin language, because the Greek language has, in point of fact, no term corresponding completely to the Latin word *voluntas*.

Latin expresses by the word *voluntas* an ethical experience which Greek expresses in a different way. Because it is a novelty of great importance, we wish to explain it by quoting from Pohlenz, who has understood the issue better than any other scholar. "For Seneca the decisive factor in self-education is will. *It is a trait which is non-Greek but Roman which was introduced by Seneca into the Stoa.* In Cicero it was still contained within the general Greek theoretical position...and to this latter were bound all those thinkers, like Musonius, who preserved the Greek language in the teaching of philosophy. Seneca writes and thinks in Latin. When he composed the *De beneficiis* for *dianoia*...he substituted almost involuntarily *voluntas*, and once it found a formulation, Roman thinking extended it to other fields of ethics. The instinct of conservation of the Stoics became in Seneca an instinctive *will-to-live*. But will reveals its specific power especially in moral education: '*Quid tibi opus est, ut bonus sis? Velle!*' (*Letter* 80.4). Seneca does not insert will into a psychological system, nor does he do it with conscience. 'No one can say what is the origin of the will' (*Letter* 37.5). In any case, it is not a fact of the intellect, *velle non discitur*. The will for the good bursts out of the depths of the soul and must involve a persevering work because it came through a clear vision of the goal and is changed into good intention. Neither is the will sufficient by itself; only with the knowledge of the good does it become possible, in its most pure and elevated form. In practice, however, the will acquires even more importance than knowledge, and moral exhortation becomes an appeal to the power of the will: 'Better to lack knowledge for a fool than will!' The ancient Stoa divided men into the wise and the foolish; Seneca adds another distinction, between the good and evil will. Seneca once made with satisfaction the following observation with regard to himself: 'A great part of progress consists in the will to progress. I am steady about this: I will, I will, with all my heart.' Hence wisdom to which man must tend consists for him in this, that 'man wills or does not will always the same things.'...By giving such a strong emphasis to will Seneca opens a breach in the intellectualism of the ancient Stoa."[21]

6. The sense of sin

Another trait which distinguishes Seneca from the Stoa, as well as from the whole of Greek philosophers, is the *accentuated sense of sin and the faults by which all men are stained.* Man is necessarily a sinner, says our philosopher. And this is an affirmation which is in clear opposition to the alleged perfection that the ancient Stoa dogmatically attributed to its wise man. But—on the contrary, Seneca thinks—if anyone were never to sin, he would not be a man; the wise man himself, insofar as he stays a human being, cannot not sin. Here is a splendid passage from the *De ira*:

> If we are willing in all matters to play the just judge, let us convince ourselves first of this–that no one of us is free from fault. For most of our indignation arises from our saying, "I am not to blame," "I have done nothing wrong." Say, rather, you admit nothing wrong! We chafe against the censure of some reprimand or chastisement although at the very time we are at fault because we are adding to wrong-doing arrogance and obstinacy. What man is there who can claim that in the eyes of every law he is innocent? But assuming that this may be, how limited the innocence whose standard of virtue is the law! How much more comprehensive is the principle of duty than that of law! How many are the demands laid upon us by the sense of duty, humanity, generosity, justice, integrity–all of which lie outside the statute books! But even under that other exceedingly narrow definition of innocence we cannot vouch for our claim. Some sins we have committed some we have contemplated, some we have desired, some we have encouraged; in the case of some we are innocent only because we did not succeed.[22]

If a great city were to allow only persons to live who were absolvable by a severe judge, notes Seneca again, such a city would immediately fall into the greatest desolation, because everyone, even if in different ways, is a sinner. And not only for some period in the past or in the present but forever.[23]

It is clear then, with such a vision of man, that Seneca could only attribute to the Stoic notion of the "wise man" nothing but an ideal significance: the wise man only has the value of a model, that is, a deontological value. In reality, that wise man does not exist; only human beings exist who can gradually remove themselves from sin, but without being able to totally eliminate it.[24]

It is evident that these conceptions are connected to the discovery of the notion of *voluntas*. In fact, if morality were to depend on knowledge and only on it, and if sin were to be reduced to an error in judgment, then it is clear that it is logically impossible to grasp and affirm that man is and remains a sinner up to his death, because once he achieves knowledge, *by that very fact* he ceases to err and hence to sin. If, on the contrary, evil and sin depend on *voluntas*, then the argument is wholly different. Sin is no longer a simple logical error but becomes something much more complex, and the fact that one can sin while knowing the good indeed becomes explainable, because the *will responds to solicitations which are not simply those derived from knowledge.* It is hence the will which makes us good or wicked, and liberty is situated in it. Unfortunately, Seneca had developed these truths only on the descriptive and intuitive level, because he did not know how to ground them ontologically. Yet even within these limits what he said in this regard, due to the intellectual premises of the school from which he began and to which he constantly continued to appeal,[25] is noteworthy and important.

7. The equality of all human beings and mutual love

Seneca, within the Stoa, was the thinker who most strongly opposed the institution of slavery and social distinctions. His view was that true value and nobility are imparted only by virtue, and virtue is at the command of everyone indiscriminately. It requires only *natural man* Seneca writes in the Forty-Fourth *Letter*:

> If there is any good in philosophy it is this–that it never looks into pedigrees: all men, if traced back to their original source, spring from the gods. You are a Roman knight, and your persistent work promoted you to this class: yet surely there are many to whom the fourteen rows are barred; the senate chamber is not open to all: the army too, is scrupulous in choosing those whom it admits to toil and danger. But a *noble mind is free to all men*; according to this text, we may all gain distinction. Philosophy neither rejects nor selects anyone; its light shines for all.[26]

Nobility and social slavery depend on fortune and caprice. Everyone numbers among their most distant ancestors both slaves and nobles, so in terms of origin all men were equal. The only nobility which has true meaning is that which man constructs within the dimension of spirit:

> A hall full of smoke-begrimed busts does not make the nobleman. No past life has been lived to lend us glory, and that which has existed before us is not ours; *the soul alone renders us noble, and it may rise superior to Fortune out of any earlier condition, no matter what that condition has been.* Suppose, then, that you were not a Roman knight, but freedman, you might nevertheless by your own effort come to be the only free man amid a throng of gentlemen. "How?" you ask. Simply by distinguishing between good and bad things without patterning your opinion from the populace.[27]

Speaking, then, of the highest value, of the value which transcends time, in the Thirty-First *Letter*, Seneca writes:

What is this value? It is the soul, but the soul that is upright, good, and great. What else could you call such a soul than *a God dwelling as a guest in a human body*? A soul like this may *descend into a Roman knight just as well as into a freedman's son or a slave's*. For what is a Roman knight, or a freedman's son, or a slave? They are mere titles, born of ambition or of wrong. *One may leap to heaven from the very slums. Only rise and mold yourself to kinship with your God.*[28]

In *Letter* Forty-Seven, explicitly concerned with how to treat slaves, Seneca writes:

They are slaves, hence men. They are slaves, hence comrades. They are slaves, hence unpretentious friends.[29]

Here is the norm which Seneca proposes to regulate the way in which the master should behave himself with a slave or a superior to an inferior:

Treat your inferiors as you would be treated by your betters.[30]

This is a maxim which is very close to the spirit of the Gospels.[31]

In what concerns the relation between men, in general, Seneca posits as its basis brotherhood and love:

How to deal with men? What is our purpose? What precepts do we offer? Should we bid them refrain from bloodshed? *What a little thing it is not to harm one whom you ought to help*! It is indeed worthy of great praise, when man treats man with kindness! Shall we advise stretching forth the hand to the shipwrecked sailor, or pointing out the way to the wanderer, or sharing a crust with the starving? Yes, if I can only tell you first everything which ought to be afforded or withheld; meantime, I can lay down for mankind a rule, in short compass, for our duties in human relationships: all that you behold, that which comprises both God and man, is one—we are the parts of one great body. *Nature produced us related to one another, since she created us from the same source and to the same end.* She engendered in us mutual affection, and made us prone to friendships. She established fairness and justice; according to her ruling, it is more wretched to commit than to suffer injury. *Through her orders let our hands be ready for all that needs to be helped.* Let this verse be in your heart and on your lips: "I am a man; and nothing human do I consider foreign to me." *Let us possess things in common; for birth is ours in common. Our relations with one another are like a stone arch, which would collapse if the stones did not mutually support each other, and which is upheld in this very way.*[32]

By reaching beyond Greek ethics, Seneca achieved an understanding not only that we ought to render good for the good which has been done and not to return evil for the evil which has been done, but even that we ought to *render good to the one who has done evil.*[33]

8. The purported relationship between Seneca and St. Paul

The elevated concept of God, the spirituality of man, the notion of human weakness, the brotherhood of man, and the proclamation of good-will and love, which in Seneca has the kind of significance which we have seen, have given rise to the well-known legend of some actual relationship between our philosopher and St. Paul and even to an apocryphal Epistle from the philosopher to the Apostle and vice versa.[34]

In reality, the thought of Seneca and the religion of St. Paul move on two parallel lines which do not intersect and the points of contact between them are more apparent than real. Concetto Marchesi, who has been one of the most serious scholars of Seneca, has clearly noted the heterogeneity of the two doctrines and has felicitously expressed it in the quotation which follows: "Between the doctrine of Seneca and the religion of St. Paul is an abyss: for Seneca man redeems himself by the use of reason, for St. Paul redemption is left to God in the plunge into faith; in Christianity God is the savior of man, in the teaching of Seneca man saves himself; for Paul the miracle descends from heaven towards humanity, for Seneca the human soul rises towards the heights. Seneca believed in human virtue; for Paul human virtue is vain. "My preaching," said Paul to the Corinthians[35]—"does not consist in the persuasive discourse of human wisdom, but in a demonstration of the spirit and power, because our faith is grounded not on the wisdom of men but on the power of God'; and further on he adds[36]:"If anyone among you imagines that he is saved by the wisdom of this world, become a fool in order to be saved."[37] But the wisdom of Seneca was only a wisdom of this age, that is, of this world.

III. Musonius Rufus

1. The accentuation of the practical aspect of philosophy

An eclectic attitude is clearly recognizable also in Musonius[1] due to the presence of some doctrines of Socraticism (understood in an Hellenistic manner) and Cynicism (Diogenes and Socrates are the two philosophers most often cited by Musonius).

The position of Cynicism can be noticed first in the strong reduction of the theoretical aspect of philosophy to the practical one. Musonius says:

> He who demands everywhere demonstrations even where things are clear or wants many demonstrations there where a few are enough is undoubtedly obtuse and stupid.[2]

We are hence far removed from the Stoicism of Chrysippus, who gave logic very great importance. Musonius did not condemn logic, in fact, he maintained it was necessary and was quite severe with his followers who committed logical errors. Epictetus, who was of the school of Musonius, reports that one day he replied to his teacher, who had censured him for an omission committed in a syllogism, that after all it was not as though he had set fire to the Capitolium; Musonius himself replied that in this precise case, in the sphere of logic, the omission corresponded exactly to burning down the Capitolium.[3]

Musonius maintained nevertheless that logic ought to be reduced to an indispensable minimum and that philosophy would be truly useful only in the measure in which it knew how to come down to the practical. Here are his words in this regard:

> I say that the teacher, when he is truly a philosopher, ought not to bring a bag of words or demonstrations to his pupils, but he ought to touch each point insofar as it is appropriate, striking the mind of the listener, presenting persuasive arguments, avoiding those that are difficult, and especially attracting the listener by helping him see that he is by speaking of the most useful things and is acting according to what he maintains: the student, for his part, ought to stretch out towards that which is said and be careful not inadvertently to accept error, and not try, by Zeus, to hear many demonstrations about what is true, but clear ones, and to follow in his life those precepts which are persuasive and true. Only in this way will he benefit from philosophy, if he acts in accord with the reasoning which he has accepted, insofar as it is veracious.[4]

Consequently, it is clear that Musonius maintained that the *practical* was more effective than *theory* and judged as authentic philosophers those who know not only how to *reason well*, but those who know how to *live well*. Here is an important passage:

> How could it be more important to know the theory of anything than to

have the ability to do it and make things according to the indications of the theory? And actually the practical guides us to making, while knowledge of the theory of a thing enables us to speak about it. Theory certainly contributes to action, as it teaches how we ought to act, and it is in that order prior to the practical, since it is impossible for one who is not habituated to the theory to be practical in making something beautiful; but with respect to power the practical surpasses theory because it is more effective than theory as a guide for human actions.[5]

2. Practice as the actuation of virtue and goodness

Strictly connected to this conviction (and even a coherent consequence of it) is the affirmation of the *necessity of practice*. Virtue, which constitutes the true goal of every human being, male or female, is impossible without practice.[6] In other words, virtue is like the art of medicine or music; it is not only theory but requires practice, and one who wishes to be virtuous ought not to be content with *apprehending* these teachings which lead to virtue but he must diligently *practice living* according to these teachings. This practice, which is proper to philosophers and which leads to virtue, is the most complex and the most difficult which exists. First, since man is constituted of soul and body and the body serves as an instrument, there will be a two-fold order of practices; one which looks to the body and soul together and one which looks to the soul alone. To habituate the body to hunger, to thirst, to renouncing pleasures, to enduring fatigue is a practice which strengthens the body and soul at the same time. The proper exercise of the soul consists in the demonstration of the nature of true goods and true evils and *to know how to follow* the former and *to avoid* the latter.[7]

This elevation of practice was already one of the components of Socraticism, but it was brought to the fore only by Cynicism. It constituted, indeed, a corrective for Socratic intellectualism, but it was not a conscious one. Practice supposes, in fact, a *will*; but neither the Cynics nor Musonius were able to point out that this is, indeed, the foundation of practice.

The things "which appear as goods" but which in reality are not so, for Musonius, as previously for the ancient Stoa, are pleasures, riches, life itself, and in general anything which does not share in virtue, while things "which appear to be evils" but which in reality are not so are fatigue, poverty, exile, old age, and death itself.

Musonius came, in fact, to raise to the highest moral level struggle (toil, labor, or effort) which is strictly connected to practice; and he affirmed that those who do not wish to struggle "declared themselves unworthy of any benefits."[8]

Concerning exile, Musonius pointed out on the basis of concepts which were dear both to the Cynics and the Stoics that in reality a human being cannot be deprived of his fatherland except by understanding this in the most restricted sense, since the whole cosmos is the authentic fatherland of man:

> Is not the world the common fatherland of all men, as Socrates thought? Therefore it is not consistent with truth to maintain that you are exiled from your native land if you are far from the place of your birth and upbringing, for you are only deprived of a city, much more so if you claim to be yourself a real person. Such a man does not condemn nor value a place as if it were the cause of happiness or unhappiness. He puts everything on himself and upholds citizenship in the city of Zeus, which is made up of men and Gods. Euripides expressed it in the same sense also where he says: *Every region of heaven is open to the eagle, every land is native to the noble man.*[9]

The conviction expressed by Musonius, that the appropriate means for a philosopher to earn himself a living through farming, is worthy of attention. It obliges him to a kind of natural life, and it favors in all senses the commitment to toil and struggle, about which we spoke above, and permits him not to need others to satisfy his own necessities.[10]

Contrary to both the Cynics and to many Stoics, Musonius had a strong social sense, taken from the Roman *ethos*, which led him to elevate the institution of matrimony "as a great thing and worthy of the highest respect," since it is the very basis of society.[11]

3. New starting points

As in the other representatives of Neo-Stoicism so also in Musonius, as we have pointed out, the precepts appealed to have precise analogs in the *Gospels*, even if they are justified with different reasons, in particular the precept of love and forgiveness. Questioned about whether the philosopher must bring an action in law in the case of being abused, Musonius replied by denying that it could be done licitly. He justified his assertion not only by having recourse to the Cynic disapproval which the philosopher must have for blows and censure, but also by extending positively and fruitfully forgiveness towards those who offend. Here is the interesting passage:

> To accept the offenses without hatred and not to be implacable against those who act evilly, to be on the contrary for these motives of good hope, is proper to placid and cordial natures. How much better that the philosopher show such dispositions to maintain as worthy of forgiveness he who has offended him rather than believe in defending by appealing to the causes and to lawsuits and, in reality, to detract from himself with conduct which is not consistent with his words! Because he who thinks that he is a good man is never offended by evil men.[12]

Even the Middle Platonist influence on Musonius (to which scholars have scarcely attended until now) is operative on the Neo-Stoics as well and not in a purely implicit manner. Here is, for example, how the concept of man as the image of God, quite traditional in its general lines, is amplified in the Middle Platonic sense:

In general, man alone among terrestrial beings is an image of God (μίμημα θεοῦ), he has virtues similar to him, because not even among the Gods can we suppose anything superior to prudence, to justice, and even to courage and temperance. And as God, by the presence of these virtues, is victorious over pleasure and victorious over immoderation, he is superior to the passions and to envy and jealousy, magnanimous, loving towards man (because it is of such a nature that we imagine God to be); in this way we think that man, who is the image of him, when living according to nature is in the same condition as God, and in this way he is enviable: being enviable, he will himself also be happy, because we only envy the happy.[13]

In addition, in responding to the question "do we need to obey parents in all things," Musonius, in order to justify his assertion that obedience is not needed by a father when forbidding something good (or when commanding something not good), for example, when he forbids doing philosophy, writes:

Your father forbids you to philosophize, but the father of all, men and Gods, Zeus, commands you and imposes it on you. His order, his law is that man be just, noble, beneficent, sober, magnanimous, above fatigue, above pleasures, free of all envy and all deception: to speak briefly the law of Zeus commands all men to be good human beings. But being good is itself what it is to be a philosopher! *Now if by obeying a father you place yourself behind a man, and by philosophizing behind Zeus, it is clear that it is better to philosophize than not to philosophize.* But, by Zeus, your father, who will reprove you, will close in your face the door of the house in order that you do not philosophize. Perhaps he will do it: but he will not be able to force you far away from philosophy unless you wish it, because we do not philosophize with our hands or with our feet or with another part of the body but with our soul and precisely with a small part of our soul which we call reason. And reason God has placed in the best place so that it be invisible and unassailable and beyond every restriction free and independent.[14]

Beyond the notion of philosophizing as "the going among Zeus's retinue" (τῷ Διΐ ἕπεσθαι), he also mentions here the notions of interiority and liberty, which in Seneca, and perhaps again more emphatically in Epictetus and in Marcus Aurelius, come to be proclaimed and supported. In fact, Musonius seems to have even anticipated the great principle which is the basis of the system of Epictetus and which represents the most rigorous consequences of the moral principles of the Stoa in its most intimate and spiritual meaning:

Of existing things, God has put some in our power, others not. In our power he has placed the most beautiful and important thing, *through which he himself is happy, that is, the use of the representations.* When this use is correctly exercised there is liberty, serenity, tranquility, and security: there is also justice, law, mastery of oneself and every virtue. All the other things he has not placed in our power. Hence *it is necessary that we also agree with God* and divide the objects according to his views, and that we try to obtain in any way those which are in our power; the others which are not, we leave to the universe and we willingly hand over to him whatever he has chosen to ask us: our sons, our fatherland, our body or similar things.[15]

The whole philosophy of Epictetus is nothing except the systematic grounding and an explication of this principle, as we shall see.

IV. Epictetus, the Slave Philosopher

1. The characteristics of the Stoicism of Epictetus

The Stoa, in the person of Epictetus, concretely showed that a slave can be a philosopher and can be free, not in the ordinary sense of "free," but rather in the sense of "free in spirit." Epictetus was forcibly taken to Rome from Hierapolis (in Phrygia) and was the property of a freedman of Nero's named Epaphroditus, who released him from slavery.[1] But true liberty did not come to Epictetus by the act of manumission, but rather it was grasped through Musonius Rufus,[2] who taught him the doctrines of the Stoa. He also learned true freedom through Socrates and through Antisthenes, who taught him liberty of spirit. And so there vibrated in the heart of Epictetus more than in any of the other Stoics, a constant enduring love of freedom,[3] a strong desire to achieve it in his life, and the unswerving conviction that it can only be found in philosophy.

As Socrates did not write anything and assigned to the living word and to dialogue with his followers all of his thought, so Epictetus did likewise.

The characteristics of the philosophy of Epictetus are for the most part the same ones found in Seneca, Musonius, and Marcus Aurelius; a deep and almost exclusive interest in ethics, a marked sense of interiority, a strong sense of the bond between God and man, and a notable religious sensibility. Epictetus is to be distinguished from the aforementioned by a deeply felt tendency to return to the *origins of the Stoa*, especially to Chrysippus, whom he admired more than any other adherent of the school. Therefore, eclectic tendencies in him are mitigated by this explicit tendency to return to the ancient Stoa and by his desire to bring to life the original teachings.[4] (This phenomenon of returning to origins is also found in exponents of other Schools.) To point this out is, however, far from making the thought of Epictetus a mere repetition of the thought of the ancient Stoa; although it does preserve him from the doctrinal infiltration of the other schools, it did not prevent him from utilizing the Socratic method or from accepting the teaching of Diogenes the Cynic even though adapting it to his own needs. This tendency does not even prevent the acceptance of some new doctrines of his epoch, both those of a philosophical character (in particular those of Middle Platonism) as well as those of a religious and mystico-ascetic nature. Epictetus often pushes to the limits his religiousness and his sensibility about divinity as well as his conception of the relationship between God and man in a way which formally seems to touch on Christianity. Nevertheless, through the above-mentioned connection to the origins of Stoicism, he remained in his spirit essentially a Stoic, which is clearly quite removed from Christianity. Epictetus remained absolutely ignorant of the existence of the supernatural and grace, because he was in a dimension of thought in which God, soul, and salvation are theoretically grounded in the domain of Stoic *physis.*[5]

2. The fundamental principle of the ethics of Epictetus

The great principle of Stoic ethics consists in the clear distinction between things which are *good, evil,* and *indifferent*; goods are only those of a moral nature, evils are their contraries, indifferent things are all those other things which concern the body and external things. Epictetus reformulated the principle, keeping its spirit but giving it a more effective blend. Things are distinguished into two classes: (*a*) those which are *in our power* and (*b*) those which *are not in our power*; good and evil are found exclusively in the class of things which are in our power because they depend on our will, and not in the latter class because things which are not in our power are not dependent on our will. Here is how he enunciated this principle in his famous *Manual*:

> Some things are under our control, while others are not under our control. Under our control are conception, choice, desire, aversion, and, in a word, everything that is our own doing; not under our control are our body, our property, reputation, office, and, in a word, everything that is not our doing. Furthermore, the things under our control are by nature free, unhindered, and unimpeded; while the things not under our control are weak, servile, subject to hindrance, and not our own.[6]

All the difficulties of life and the errors we commit depend on *not taking this fundamental distinction into account*. In fact, if we consider as free and within our power things which are not in fact free and which are totally independent of our will, we will be totally deluded, we will lament our fate and curse men and things. If, instead, we identify things which are not in our power and consequently act and consider as ours only those things which actually belong to us, then we will not find any impediments and delusions, because no one can take them away or injure them insofar as they cannot be reached from outside of ourselves. The passage quoted above continues:

> Remember, therefore, that if what is naturally slavish you think to be free, and what is not your own to be your own, you will be hampered, will grieve, will be in a turmoil, and will blame both Gods and men; while if you think only what is your own to be your own, and what is not your own to be, as it really is, not your own, then no one will ever be able to exert compulsion upon you, no one will hinder you, you will blame no one, will find fault with no one, will do nothing against your will, you will have no personal enemy, no one will harm you, for neither is there any harm that can touch you.[7]

In this distinction there is no place for compromises through the "indifferents" and through the "intermediate things"; the choice hence is very radical, peremptory, and ultimate. The two classes of things cannot be followed simultaneously, because the one implies the loss of the other and vice versa. Epictetus, in addressing a follower, says, for example:

> You must be one person, either good or bad; you must labor to improve either your own governing principle or externals; you must work hard either on the inner man or on things outside; that is, play either the role of a philosopher or else of an ordinary man.[8]

And again:

> You cannot be continually giving attention to both externals and your own governing principle. But if you want the former, let the latter go; otherwise you will have neither the latter nor the former, being drawn in both directions. If you want the latter, you must let the former go.[9]

One who chooses the second class of things, physical life, the body and its pleasures, material well-being both of things and the men who dispense them not only embraces delusions and misfortunes which we have already spoken about, but *he even loses his liberty* and becomes more a slave than the ordinary slave, because he will have as masters whom he must obey, soothe, and please all those things and those men who establish or dispense these goods and these material advantages.[10]

One who instead rejects as a whole those things which do not depend on him becomes truly free, lives life as he wishes, and consequently achieves spiritual peace and contentment of soul.[11]

Epictetus did not dare affirm that he is totally free; he confessed that he tried to get closer to this freedom in spite of the fact that he had not succeeded in standing up to all his "slave-masters," but he pointed out an exemplary model of liberty in Diogenes the Cynic. And actually, the great ethical principle of Epictetus is a reformulation of the Stoic principle rooted precisely in the ground of the Cynic experience. Here is the liberty of Diogenes, which for Epictetus is liberty in its highest form:

> Diogenes was free. How did that come about? It was not because he was born of free parents, for he was not, but because he himself was free, because he had cast off all the handles of slavery, and there was no way in which a person could get close and lay hold of him to enslave him. Everything he had was easily loosened, everything was merely tied on. If you had laid hold of his property, he would have let it go rather than followed you for its sake; if you had laid hold of his leg, he would let his leg go, if of his whole paltry body, his whole paltry body; and so also of his kindred, friends, and country. *He knew the source from which he had received them, and from whom, and upon what conditions.* His true ancestors, indeed, the Gods, and his real country he would never have abandoned, nor would he have suffered another to yield them more obedience and submission, nor could any other man have died more cheerfully for his country. For it was never his wont to seek to appear to do anything in behalf of the universe, but he bore in mind that everything which has come into being has its source there, and is done on behalf of that country, and is entrusted to us by him who

governs it. Therefore, see what he himself says and writes: "For this reason," he says "you are permitted, O Diogenes, to converse as you please with the king of the Persians and with Archidamus, the king of the Lacedaemonians." Was it, indeed, because he was born of free parents? No doubt it was because they were all the children of slaves that the Athenians and Lacedaemonians and Corinthians were unable to converse with these monarchs as they pleased, but were afraid of them and paid court to them! Why, then, someone asks, are you permitted? "Because I do not regard my paltry body as my own; because I need nothing; because the law, and nothing else, is everything to me." This it is which allowed him to be a free man.[12]

It is scarcely necessary to emphasize that the law of which he speaks here is the universal law, the law of reality, the law of God, God himself.

In such ways "slave-masters" are unmasked and rejected, the body we have on loan and hence it does not belong to us; it can be taken from us at any time and we ought not be preoccupied with it, because how long it lasts does not depend on us, just as what happens to it does not totally depend on us. The same can be said of everything intrinsically linked to the body. And the same can be said of everything which happens and which we cannot in any way change and which hence we must accept, or better still we must consciously will [that is, make a virtue of our necessity]:

Do not seek to have everything that happens happen as you wish, but wish for everything to happen as it actually does happen, and your life will be serene.[13]

This and only this is true liberty both for the ancient as well as for the new Stoicism.

Therefore, the new Stoicism teaches that we ought to attend to the things which are in our power; for these alone are free and these alone are goods, they are inalienable goods, they are sufficient, they are what guarantee the tranquility of the soul. Everything which concerns the body and the things connected to it does not depend on us and hence ought not to pre-occupy us, because it is not of concern to us and hence is not evil.

3.   An ethically relevant tripartition of philosophy

As is well known, the Stoa and in general all the Hellenistic schools distinguished philosophy into logic, physics, and ethics. Epictetus did not repudiate this division, but (what was certainly a consequence of the failing interest in the first two) he formulated another division of philosophy, which has clear roots and an ethical motivation, and which offers, in a certain sense, an outline of its procedure.

There are three fields of study in which the man who is going to be good and excellent must first have been trained.

(1) The first has to do with *desire and aversion*, that he may never fail to get what he desires, nor fall into what he avoids;

(2) the second with cases *of choice and of refusal*, and, in general, with duty, that he may act in an orderly fashion, upon good reasons, and not carelessly;

(3) the third in the *avoidance of error* [= the positive action of avoiding error] and in rashness in judgment and, in general, about cases of assent.[14]

As can be seen, the distinctions do not have a theoretical significance, that is, they are not an attempt to fix the boundaries of knowledge, but they are intended to specify the applications which must successively be acquired by anyone who wishes to achieve freedom and moral excellence, and hence it has a pedagogical and moral significance.

(1) The first area to conquer is that of the passions, and it is "the most important and in the highest degree urgent"[15] Epictetus says:

> The passions do not arise except a desire fails to attain its object, or an aversion falls into what it would avoid. This is the field of study which introduces to us confusions, tumults, misfortunes, and calamities; and sorrow, lamentations, envies; and makes us envious and jealouspassions which make it impossible for us to listen to reason.[16]

Consequently, according to Epictetus, the ruling and overcoming of the passions is attained on the grounds of the great principle enunciated above, that is, it depends on the fact that the things which truly concern us are those of the soul and that these alone depend on our will, while all other things which do not depend on our will are to be entirely disregarded and ought therefore not touch or even cause an itch in us in any way. In this sense, Epictetus expressed firmly the necessity of renouncing desires and suppressing strong emotions.

(2) The second domain to rule with reason is impulse (or aversion), which moves us to act (or not at act). Insofar as we have a body, we are in a relationship with things and with others and we must hence direct our impulses and actions which are derived from impulses in a correct manner. Epictetus says:

> For I ought not to be unfeeling like a statue, but should maintain relations, both natural and acquired, as a religious man, as a son, a brother, a father, a citizen.[17]

This is the sphere of the *kathekonta (duties)*, to use the language of the Stoic school. And duties are nothing other than those actions which we ought to accomplish in relation to our body, to parents, and to other men, *respecting the dictates of reason*. Here is how he formulates the golden rule which regulates duties:

> Our duties are in general measured by our social relationships. He is father. One is called upon to take care of him, to give way to him in all things, to submit when he reviles or strokes you. "But he is a bad father." Did nature, then, bring you into relationship with a good father? No, but simply with a father. "My brother does me wrong." Very well, then, maintain the relation

that you have toward him; and do not consider what he is doing, but what you will have to do, if your moral purpose is to be in harmony with nature. For no one will harm you without your consent; you will have been harmed only when you think you are harmed. In this way, therefore, you will discover what duty to expect of your neighbor, your fellow citizen, your commanding officer, if you acquire the habit of looking at your social relations with them.[18]

In addition, again, this sense of duty towards others is compounded in Epictetus, unlike in the ancient Stoa, of deep humanity and love. Man, in fact, he says, is "an animal who loves and wishes to be loved."[19]

(3) Here is the way that Epictetus characterized the third domain:

The third belongs only to those who are already making progress; it has to do with the element of certainty in the matters which have just been mentioned, so that even in dreams, or drunkenness, or a state of melancholy-madness, a man may not be taken unaware by the appearance of an untested sense-impression.[20]

Now, it is interesting to notice that although this is a problem of logic and as such it should have preceded any other consideration it is the last one for Epictetus. In this way, what we have noticed many times in the previous volume is made explicit. These systems (doctrines aimed at solving the problem of living) do not deduce their solutions from a logic nor from an ontology, but from a sense of a life-lived, from a premise perceived by intuition or acknowledged because of a form of faith. The premise is one that they then explicate in a rational manner and try to ground rationally. This position is made quite explicit in Epictetus.

4. Prohaíresis or basic moral choice

Instead of an abstract criterion of truth as the foundation of morality, Epictetus posits prohaíresis; and this confirms further what we have said in the conclusion of the previous section.

The ancient Stoics do not speak of prohaíresis, nor does Epictetus refer to the Aristotelian notion of prohaíresis, which, as we know, signifies the choice of the immediate means for the realization of goals (goals, let us remember, for Aristotle are not objects of choice, but of will).[21] The prohaíresis of Epictetus indicates rather a condition of pre-choice, or pre-decision, which determines in general what is good and what is not good.[22] The succeeding choices of individual objects and of individual actions depend, hence, on this general "pre-choice." In conclusion, prohaíresis is the basic decision and choice which man makes once for all and through which he is determined, hence, the distinctiveness of his moral being and on which will wholly depend what he will do and how he will do it.

It is clear that an authentic prohaíresis, for Epictetus, coincides substantially with the acceptance of his great principle which distinguishes the things which are in *our power* from those that *are not in our power* and establishes that good things are exclusively the former, while the others are not and do not concern us. And it is also clear that from this basic choice, once it is operative, the particular choices, the individual actions, issue forth from it as a consequence.[23]

Prohaíresis determines, therefore, the structure of our moral being. Consequently Epictetus can correctly affirm:

> Because you are not flesh, nor hair, but moral purpose; if you get that beautiful, then you will be beautiful.
>
> *Moral choice [prohaíresis]* is only good when it is correctly disposed and *moral choice* is only evil when it is not correctly disposed. Tell me, therefore, what are the indifferent things: tell me the consequences which follow from it.
>
> What *not depend on my moral choice [aprohaíreta]* is nothing to me.
>
> –Tell me then what things remain goods?
>
> –The right use of representations and a right *moral choice [prohaíresis]*.[24]

Virtue and vice, happiness and unhappiness, in sum, depend on *prohaíresis*. It is the finest thing in man.[25] Here is a passage in which Epictetus expresses throughly his thought on this issue:

> Man, be neither ungrateful for these gifts, nor yet forgetful of the better things, but for sight and hearing, yes and, by Zeus, for life itself and for what is conducive to it, for dry fruits, for wine, for olive oil, give thanks unto God; *and at the same time remember that He has given you something better than all these things–the faculty which can make use of them, pass judgment upon them, estimate the value of each.* For what is that which, in the case of each of these faculties, shows what it is worth? Is it each faculty itself? Did you ever hear the faculty of sight say anything about itself? Or the faculty of vision? No, but they have been appointed as servants and slaves to minister to the faculty which makes use of external impressions. And if you ask, what each thing is worth, of whom do you ask? Who is to answer you? How, then, can any other faculty be superior to this which both uses the rest as its servants, and itself passes judgment upon each several thing and pronounces upon it? For which one of them knows what it is and what it is worth? Which one of them knows when one ought to use it, and when not? What is the faculty that opens and closes the eyes, and turns them away from the things from which it should turn them, but directs them toward other things? The faculty of sight? No, but the faculty of *moral choice* [προαιρετικὴ δύναμις]. What is the faculty that closes and opens the ears? What is that faculty by virtue of which men are curious and inquisitive, or again, unmoved by what is said? The faculty of hearing? No, it is none other than the faculty of *moral choice*. When, then, this faculty sees that all the other faculties which surround it are blind and deaf, and unable to see anything but the very acts for which they have been appointed to serve and minister unto it, while it alone sees clearly and surveys, not only all the rest, determining what each is worth, but itself also, is it likely to pronounce that

anything else is supreme but itself? And what else can the open eye do but see? But whether it ought to see someone's wife and how, what faculty tells it? That of *moral choice*. And what faculty tells a man whether he ought to believe what he has been told, or disbelieve, and, if he believes, whether he ought to be provoked by it or not? Is it not that of *moral choice*? And this faculty of speech and of the adornment of language, if it really is a separate faculty, what else does it do, when discourse arises about some topic, but ornament and compose the words, as hairdressers do the hair? But whether it is better to speak than to keep silence, and to do so in this way, or in that, and whether this is appropriate or not appropriate, and the proper occasion and utility of each action–what else tells us all this but the faculty of moral purpose? Would you, then, have it come forward and condemn itself? "What then," says an objector, "if the matter stands like this, and it is possible for that which serves to be superior to what it serves—the horse to the rider, or the dog to the hunter, or his instrument to the harper, or his servants to the king?" Well, what faculty is it that uses the services of the rest in this way? *moral choice* [προαίρεσις]. What is it that destroys the whole man, sometimes by hunger, sometimes by a noose, sometimes by hurling him over a cliff? *Moral choice*. Is there, then, anything stronger than this among men? Yet how can the things that are subject to hindrance be stronger than that which is unhindered? What are by their very nature capable of hindering the faculty of vision? Both moral purpose and things that lie outside its sphere. The same hinder vision; and so it is also with speech. But what is by its very nature capable of hindering *moral purpose? Nothing that lies outside its sphere, but only itself when perverted. For this reason moral purpose becomes the only vice, or the only virtue.*[26]

Prohaíresis to the modern reader could seem to be an act of will (*voluntas*). If this were so, the ethics of Epictetus would be a voluntaristic ethics. But such is not the case; *prohaíresis* is an act of reason, it is a cognitive judgment. Epictetus says:

"But," says someone, "if a person subjects me to the fear of death, he compels me." "No, it is not what you are subjected to that impels you, but the fact that *you decide it is better for you to do* something of the sort than to die. Once more, then, it is the judgment [δόγμα] of your own will which compelled you, that is, *prohaíresis* compelled *prohaíresis*."[27]

In this passage *prohaíresis* and *dogma* or judgment are clearly identified. And again:

...only the act which proceeds from correct *judgments* is well done, and that which proceeds from bad *judgments* is badly done. Yet until you learn the judgment from which a man performs each separate act, neither praise his action, nor blame it.[28]

In this regard Pohlenz made many sound observations, "*Prohaíresis* is the general and basic judgment concerned with the value of things. It is undoubted that it necessarily translates into appetites, practical impulses, and that it implies the choice of a determined way of life. Nevertheless it always remains an act of the intellect, and the 'willing' is determined only in a second phase by the representation of the particular goal which is shown to us by the decisions of the intellect. It is hence certainly erroneous to translate *prohaíresis* as '*voluntas*'[*will*]; it is likewise different from the *voluntas* of Seneca. The ethics of Epictetus is not voluntaristic; it continues and develops the fundamental Socratic conception."[29]

As for Socrates, so also for Epictetus, each wants the good and useful and what any choices are is what is *judged* good and useful; virtue is correct choice, vice is an erroneous choice due to ignorance of the truly good and useful:

> –Cannot a man, then, think that something is profitable to him, and yet not choose it?
>
> –He cannot.
>
> –How of her [Medea] who says, "Now, now, I learn what horrors I intend. But passion overcomes sober thoughts"?
>
> –It is because the very gratification of her passion and the taking of vengeance on her husband she regards as *more profitable than the saving of her children.*
>
> –Yes, but she is deceived.
>
> –Show her clearly that she is deceived and she will not do it; but so long as you do not show it, what else has she to follow but that which appears to her to be true?[30]

Greek thought never liberated itself entirely from Socratic intellectualism, for it assigned almost the whole meaning and greatness of man to his logos. The intuitional voluntarism of Seneca, for reasons indicated above, could not be fruitful.

5. The new rational attitude toward the divine

Epictetus does not reject the immanentistic conception which belongs to the Stoa, but admits into it a very strong spiritual and religious content. But nonetheless he cannot abandon pantheism and Stoic materialism, because he lacked the theoretic conception of the supersensible and the transcendent. And thus the religious ferment which he accepts does not allow him to overcome pantheistic materialism, but it does bring him to a position which is almost a break, in many respects, with the doctrine of the ancient Stoa: God is intelligence, is science, is right reason, is good. God is providence, who cares not only about things in general but about each of us in particular. To obey the logos and to do good means therefore to be obedient to God, serve God, it means to give praise to God. Liberty coincides with submission to the divine will.[31]

In addition, for Epictetus, we come from God and we are fragments of divinity, and we return to God at death.

Here is a passage which gives a better sense of the new attitude towards God, his providence, his all-embracing vision, and the new conception of the bond between God and man:

> Yet nonetheless [Zeus] has stationed by each man's side as guardian his
> particular genius,–and has committed the man to his care,–and that too a
> guardian who never sleeps and is not to be beguiled. For to what other
> guardian, better or more careful, could He have committed each one of us?
> Wherefore, *when you close your doors and make darkness within, remember*
> *never to say that you are alone, for you are not alone; nay, God is within, and*
> *your own daimon is within.* And what need have they of light in order to see
> what you are doing? Yes, and to this God you also ought to swear allegiance,
> as the soldiers do to Caesar. They are but hirelings, yet they swear that they
> will put the safety of Caesar above everything; you, on the other hand, *must*
> *put yourselves above all things.*[32]

And the break with notion of a *physis-God* is again quite evident in the passage
which follows:

> As for me, I would prefer that death overtook me occupied with nothing
> but my own *moral choice* trying to make it *tranquil,* unhampered, uncon-
> strained, free. This is what I wish to be engaged in when death finds me, so
> that I may be able to say to God, "Have I in any respect transgressed Your
> commands? Have I in any respect misused the resources which You gave
> me, or used my senses to no purpose, or my preconceptions? Have I ever
> found any fault with You? Have I blamed Your governance at all? I fell
> sick, when it was Your will; so did other men, but I willingly. I became poor,
> it being Your will, but with joy. I have held no office, because You did not
> will it, and I never set my heart upon office. Have You even seen me for
> that reason greatly dejected? Have I not ever come before You with a
> radiant countenance, ready for any injunctions or orders You might give?
> And now it is Your will that I leave this festival; I go, I am full of gratitude
> to You that You have deemed me worthy to take part in this festival with
> You, and to see Your works, and to understand Your governance." Be this
> my thought, this my writing, this my reading, when death comes upon me."[33]

6.   The kinship of man with God and the brotherhood of man

The theme of the relationship of human beings with God, which is already
present in the ancient Stoa also assumes a strongly spiritual and, one might say,
almost a Christian inflection. Here is a passage on this issue which is especially
informative:

> But you are a being of primary importance; *you are a fragment of God; you*
> *within you a part of Him.* Why, then, are you ignorant of your own kinship?
> Why do you not know the source from which you have sprung? Will you not
> bear in mind, whenever you eat, who you are that eat, and whom you are
> nourishing? Whenever you indulge in intercourse with women, who you are
> that do this? Whenever you mix in society, whenever you take physical
> exercise, whenever you converse, do you not know that *you are nourishing*
> *God, exercising God?* *You are bearing God about with you, you poor wretch,*

and know it not! Do you suppose I am speaking of some external God, made of silver and gold? It is within yourself that you bear Him, and do not perceive that you are defiling yourself that you bear Him, and do not perceive that you are defiling Him with impure thoughts and filthy actions. Yet in the presence of even an image of God you would not dare to do anything of the things you are now doing. But when God Himself is present within you, seeing and hearing everything, are you not ashamed to be thinking and doing such things as these, O insensible of your own nature, and object of God's wrath![34]

And again:

If a man could only subscribe heart and soul, as he ought, to this doctrine, that *we are all primarily begotten of God, and that God is the father of all men as well as of Gods*, I think that he will entertain no ignoble or mean thought about himself. Yet, if Caesar adopts you no one will be able to endure your conceit, but if you know that you are a son of Zeus, will you not be elated? As it is, however, we are not, but inasmuch as these two elements were co-mingles in our begetting, on the other hand the body, which we have in common with the brutes, and, on the other, reason and intelligence, which we have in common with the Gods, some of us incline toward the former relationship, which is unblessed by fortune and is mortal, and only few toward that which is divine and blessed. Since, then, it is inevitable that every man, whoever he be, should deal with each thing according to the opinion which he forms about it, these few, who think that by their birth they are called to fidelity, to self-respect, and to unerring judgments in the use of eternal impressions, cherish no mean or ignoble thoughts about themselves, whereas the multitude do quite the opposite. "For what am I? A miserable, paltry man!" say they, and, "Lo, my wretched, paltry flesh!" Wretched indeed, but you have also something better than your paltry flesh. Why then abandon that and cleave to this? It is because of this kinship with flesh that those of us who incline toward it become like wolves faithless and treacherous and hurtful, and others like lions, wild and savage and untamed: but most of us become foxes, that is to say, rascals of the animal kingdom. For what else is a slanderous and malicious man but a fox, or something even more rascally and degraded? Take heed, therefore, and beware that you become not one of these rascally creatures.[35]

From here Epictetus derives the most convincing demonstration of the Stoic idea that man and God form a single society, the true universal society, beyond and above the native earth of our origin where the body was born:

If what is said by the philosophers regarding the kinship of God and men be true, what other course remains for men but that which Socrates took when asked to what country he belonged, never to say "I am an Athenian," or "I am a Corinthian," but "I am a citizen of the universe"? For why do you say that you are an Athenian, instead of mentioning merely that corner into which your paltry body was cast at birth? Or is it clear you take the place which has a higher degree of authority and comprehends not merely that corner of yours, but also your family and, in a word, the source from which your race has come, your ancestors down to yourself, "Athenian" or "Corinthian"? Well, then, anyone who has attentively studied the administration of the universe and has learned that "the greatest and most authoritative and most comprehensive of all governments is this one, which is composed of men and God, and that from Him have descended the seeds of being, not merely to my father or to my grandfather, but to all things that are begotten and that grow upon earth, and chiefly to rational beings, seeing that by nature it is theirs alone to have communion in the society of God, being intertwined with him through the reason,"–why should not such a man call himself a citizen of the universe? Why should he not call himself a son of God? And why shall he fear anything that happens among men? What! Shall kinship with Caesar or any other of them that have great power at Rome be sufficient to enable men to live securely, proof against contempt, and in fear of nothing whatsoever, but to have God as our maker, and father, and guardian,–shall this not suffice to deliver us from griefs and fears?[36]

And from this point the necessary consequence is derived, namely, the meaning of the brotherhood of all human beings in the common bond with God; the distinction between master and slave no longer has any meaning:

Now when someone asked him how it is possible to eat acceptably to the Gods, he said, "If it is done justly and graciously and fairly and restrainedly and decently, is it not also done acceptably to the Gods? And when you have asked for warm water and the slave does not heed you; or if he does heed you but brings in tepid water; or if he is not even to be found in the house, then to refrain from anger and not explode, is not this acceptable to the Gods?"

–How, then, can a man bear with such persons?

–Slave, will you not bear with *your own brother, who has Zeus as his progenitor and is, as it were, a son born of the same seed as yourself and of the same sowing from above*, but if you have been stationed in a like position above others, will you forthwith set yourself up as a tyrant? Do you not remember what you are, and over whom you rule? They are kinsmen. *They are brothers by nature*. They are the offspring of Zeus.

–But I have a deed of sale for them, and they have none for me.

–Do you see whither you bend your gaze, that it is to the earth, that it is to the pit, that it is to these wretched laws of ours, the laws of the dead, and that it is not to the laws of the Gods that you look?[37]

7. The praise to God

We have also seen then how in the ambit of the ancient Stoa Cleanthes would religiously color Stoic ontology and would even introduce prayer as a song of praise in his *Hymn to Zeus*. Epictetus takes to extreme limits this attitude. To sing praises to God is even the chief task which he assigns to himself, it is the part which he maintains is assigned to him. And by rereading the hymn of Cleanthes and this hymn of Epictetus, which is much more unassuming and unpretentious, but likewise so much more touching, it will be important to take notice of the significant shift that has now directly affected the notion of God. In Cleanthes, God is impersonal law, impersonal Providence, *physis*, destiny which merits a hymn, God, however, does not listen to it; while in Epictetus there is an irresistible tendency to assume, although in a purely implicit way, the spiritual traits of a personal God who knows and can listen to the hymn which is sung to him:

> Are these the only works of Providence in us? Now, what language is adequate to praise them all or bring them home to our minds as they deserve? Why, if we had sense, ought we to do anything else, publicly and privately, than hymning and praising the Deity, and rehearsing his benefits? Ought we not, as we dig and plough and eat, to sing the hymn of praise to God? "Great is God, that He has furnished us these instruments wherewith we shall till the earth. Great is God, that he has given us hands, and power to swallow, and a belly, and power to grow unconsciously, and to breathe while asleep." This is what we ought to sing on every occasion, and above all to sing the greatest and divinest hymn, that God has given us the faculty to comprehend these things and to follow the path of reason. What then? Since most of you have become blind, ought there not to be someone to fulfill this office for you, and in behalf of all sing the hymn of praise to God? Why, what else can I, a lame old man, do but sing hymns to God? If indeed I were a nightingale, I should be singing as a nightingale; if a swan, as a swan. But as it is, I am a rational being, therefore I must be singing hymns of praise to God. This is my task; I do it, and will not desert this post, as long as it may be given to me to fill it; and I exhort you to join me in this same song.[38]

Unfortunately, as we have previously seen confirmed in Seneca as well as in Epictetus, none of them knows how to place this new doctrine on an adequate metaphysical foundation. In fact, here, more than in any other place, does Stoic materialism reveal its basic inadequacy. Much that Epictetus says about human beings would be quite correct theoretically within the parameters of a dualistic metaphysics of a Platonic type, but not in the monistic materialism of the Stoa. Much of what he says about God would even require more mature metaphysical reasoning than that achieved by Plato or Aristotle.

V. Marcus Aurelius, the Emperor Philosopher

1. The characteristics of the Stoicism of Marcus Aurelius

The Emperor Marcus Aurelius[1] was a fervent admirer of the slave Epictetus. With him Stoicism ascended to the throne of the greatest Empire, and with him also it ended. Marcus Aurelius is the final figure of importance which the spiritual movement of the Stoa included.

There are eclectic tendencies quite visible also in Marcus Aurelius. He did not hesitate, following Seneca's lead, to accept statements about wisdom which he took even from Epicurus in addition to the now predominant Middle Platonic positions. Likewise he proceeded to exploit the tenet of the Heracliteans that "all things are flowing," which was unknown to the Stoa and was thus borrowed most probably from the Skeptic Aenesidemus, who, as we shall see, considered Skepticism as the way which leads to Heracliteanism.[2]

He is the one who greatly limits philosophy to the moral sphere among the exponents of the new Stoa, coloring it, no less than Seneca and Epictetus, with strong religious tints. The Stoa for half a millennium had helped men to live by its moral doctrines more than by its logic or physics. Its logic and physics had gradually become worn out, diminished, and even sclerotic, while, on the contrary, its morality had been revived and flourished again because it continued to respond to the actual needs of men, unchanged even in changing times. With Marcus Aurelius we are at the end of a parabolic arc: the *Meditations* are the final affirmation of that faith, which, five hundred years before, Zeno of Athens had proclaimed to the world. After him even this faith will no longer satisfy, man will yearn now for a higher faith.

2. The cosmic flux and the transiency of all things

One of the characteristics of the thought of Marcus Aurelius which greatly impresses the reader of his *Meditations* is the persistence with which he explains and expresses the transient nature of things, their inexorable passing, their monotony, their insignificance, and their emptiness.

Here are some eloquent reflections about the turbulent character of change which, according to Marcus Aurelius, clings to and devours everything:

> How quickly all things disappear, in the universe the bodies themselves, but in time the remembrance of them; what is the nature of sensible things, and particularly those which attract with the bait of pleasure or terrify by pain, or are noised abroad by vapory fame; how worthless, and contemptible, and sordid, and perishable, and dead they are![3]

> Of the life of man the duration is but a point, its substance streaming and the perception dull, and the composition of the while body subject to putrefaction, and the soul a whirl, and fortune hard to divine, and fame a

thing devoid of judgment. And to say in a word, everything which belongs to the body is a stream, and what belongs to the soul is a dream and vapor, and life is a warfare and a stranger's sojourn, and after-fame is oblivion.[4]

Everything is only for a day, both that which remembers and that which is remembered.[5]

As a river consisting of all things that come into being, yes, a rushing torrent, is Time. No sooner is a thing sighted than it is carried past, and lo, another is passing, and it too will be carried away.[6]

Think often on the swiftness with which the things that exist and that are coming into existence are swept past us and carried out of sight. For all substance is a river in ceaseless flow, its activities ever changing and its causes subject to countless variations, and scarcely anything stable; and ever beside us is this infinity of the past and yawning abyss of the future, wherein all things are disappearing.[7]

Some things are hastening to be, others to be no more, while of those that hasten into being some part is already extinct. Fluxes and changes perpetually renew the world, just as the unbroken march of time makes ever new the infinity of ages. In this river of change, which of the things which swirl past him, whereon no firm foothold is possible, should a man prize so highly? As well fall in love with a sparrow that flits past and in a moment is gone from our eyes. In fact a man's life itself is but as an exhalation from blood and an inhalation from air. For just as it is to draw in the air once into our lungs and give it back again, as we do every moment, so it is to give back thither, whence you did draw it first, your faculty of breathing which you did receive at your birth yesterday or the day before.[8]

Asia, Europe, corners of the Universe: the whole Ocean a drop in the Universe: Athos but a little clod therein: all the present a point in Eternity:– everything on a tiny scale, so easily changed, so quickly vanished.[9]

Change is the universal experience. You are yourself undergoing a perpetual transformation and, in some sort, decay: yes, and the whole Universe as well.[10]

The substance of the Universe is a torrent, it sweeps everything along.[11]

All that your eyes behold will soon perish and they who live to see it perish will in their turn perish no less quickly; and he who outlives all his contemporaries and he who dies before his time will be as one in the grave.[12]

And here are some thoughts on the monotony of all things:

Even if your life is to last three thousand years or for the matter of that thirty thousand, yet bear in mind that no one ever parts with any other life than the one he is now living, nor lives any other than that which he now parts with. The longest life, then, and the shortest amount to the same. For the present time is of equal duration for all, while that which we lose is not ours; and consequently what is parted with is obviously a mere moment. No man can part with either the past or the future. For how can a man be deprived of what he does not possess? These two things, then, must needs be remembered: the one, that all things from time everlasting have been cast in the same mold and repeated cycle after cycle, and so it makes no difference whether a man sees the same things recur through a hundred years or two hundred, or through eternity: the other, that the longest liver and he whose time to die comes soonest part with no more the one than the other. For it is but the present that a man can be deprived of, if, as is the fact, it is this alone that he has, and what he has not a man cannot part with.[13]

He, who sees what now is, has seen all that ever has been from times everlasting, and that shall be to eternity; for all things are of one lineage and one likeness.[14]

Look up, look down, everywhere you will find the same things, whereof histories ancient, medieval, and modern are full; and full of them at this day are cities and houses. There is nothing new. Everything is familiar, everything fleeting.[15]

And in this "there is nothing new" (οὐδὲν καινόν) it is impossible not to hear an echo of the *nihil sub sole novi* [*nothing new under the sun*] of *Ecclesiastes*.[16]

But even the theme of the *vanity of all things*[17] (which probably, as we mentioned previously, is derived—at least in part—from Aenesidemus[18]) is closely connected with those views set out above, which then in Marcus Aurelius became a salient feature:

Expressions once in use are now obsolete. So also the names of those much be-sung heroes of old are in some sense obsolete, Camillus, Caeso, Volesus, Dentatus, and a little later Scipio and Cato, then also Augustus, and then Hadrian and Antoninus. For all things quickly fade away and become legendary, and soon absolute oblivion encairns them. And here I speak of those who made an extraordinary blaze in the world. For the rest, as soon as the breath is out of their bodies, it is, out of sight, out of mind. But what, when all is said, is even everlasting remembrance? Wholly vanity.[19]

In a word, fail not to note how short-lived are all mortal things, and how paltry–yesterday a little mucus, tomorrow a mummy or burnt ash.[20]

Seeds of decay in the underlying material of everything–water, dust, bones, reek! Again, marble but nodules of earth, and gold and silver but dross, garments merely hair-tufts, and purple only blood. And so with everything else. The soul [understood as pneuma], too, another like thing and liable to change from this to that.[21]

This sense of things[22] is by now decidedly removed from the Greek sense, not only of the Classical Age, but likewise of early Hellenism. The ancient world was dissolving and Christianity was inexorably conquering men's souls. It is at this time that the greatest spiritual revolution was in progress, emptying everything of its ancient meaning. And it is this revolution, indeed, which gave to human beings the sense of the emptiness of everything.[23]

But Marcus Aurelius is profoundly convinced that the ancient Stoic teachings are again in a condition to show that things and life, beyond their apparent emptiness, have a meaning. On the ontological and cosmological plane there is the vision of a pantheistic One-Totality, rising and embracing everything, which redeems the individual's existence from meaninglessness and emptiness. On the anthropological and ethical plane it is a moral duty which gives meaning to life. And on this plane Marcus Aurelius ends in more than one position which almost subsumes Christian principles or, in any case, with the refining of some conceptions of Stoic ethics to the point of taking them quite close to conceptions from the Gospels. Naturally, the point of contact remains very extrinsic, because the foundations of the two positions remain antithetical; but the ancient Stoic materialism is shaken even more, as we will see, than in Seneca and Epictetus.

3.   The reaffirmation of Stoic pantheistic monism

The first consideration on the basis of which the pessimistic attitude toward things and life is overcome, as we said above, is of an ontological character. That flux which drags all things down *does not carry them into eternal nothingness*; similarly it *does not bring them forward out of nothingness*, but they come from *being eternal and return to being eternal*. There is one matter out of which things are made and one soul which enlivens all things and similarly one mind which rules all things. And thus the totality of things is established in a single great living thing, which Marcus Aurelius says is ordered and harmonious.

> That which comes after always has a close relationship to what has gone before. For it is not like some enumeration of items separately taken and following a mere hard and fast sequence, but there is a rational connection; and just as existing things have been combined in a harmonious order, so also events do not only demonstrate a pure and simple sequence, but a wondrous relationship among them.[24]

> For, in fine, there is one harmony of all things, and just as from all bodies the Universe is made up into such a body as it is, so from all causes is Destiny made up into such a cause.[25]

> Meditate often on the intimate union and mutual interdependence of all things in the Universe. For in a manner all things are mutually intertwined, and thus all things have a liking for one another. For these things are consequent one on another by reason of their contracting and expanding motion, the sympathy that breathes through them, and the unity of all substance.[26]

> All things are mutually intertwined, and the tie is sacred, and scarcely anything is alien the one to the other. For all things have been ranged side by side and together help to order one ordered Universe. For there is both one Universe made up of all things and one God immanent in all things, and one Substance, and one Law, one Reason common to all intelligent creatures, and one Truth: if indeed there is also one perfecting of living creatures that have the same origin and share the same reason.[27]

But there is more. In this completely peaceful and harmonious universe man occupies a privileged position, the meaning of his life does not spring forth only from being a piece of a marvelous mosaic. Man possesses something which raises him above everything and places him in proximity to the Gods. And on this point Marcus Aurelius does not hesitate to shatter orthodox Stoicism in order to guarantee this radical distinction between man and other things and the point of contact of man with the Gods. We will see exactly in what way this occurs.

4. A new anthropology: man as body, soul, and mind

The Stoa, as we know, had distinguished in man body and soul and had given a clear superiority to soul. Nevertheless—and this too we have noted many times—the distinction could never be a radical one because soul is always a material entity, a hot breath, i.e., a pneuma, and hence is of the same ontological nature as the body. Marcus Aurelius fractured this division by assuming three principles as constitutive of man, (a) the *body* (σῶμα) which is flesh; (b) the *soul* (ψυχή) which is breath or pneuma, and (c) superior to the soul itself is *mind* (νοῦς). And while the Stoa identified the *hegemonic* or ruling principle of man with the highest part of the soul, Marcus Aurelius placed it outside of the soul and identified it with *nous*, with the mind. Here are the passages in which this innovation can be found:

> This that I am, whatever it be, is mere *flesh* and a little *breath* [= pneuma or breath] and the *ruling reason* [= the hegemonic]. Away with your books! Be no longer drawn aside by them, it is not allowed. But as one already dying disdains the flesh, it is naught but gore and bones and a network compact of nerves and veins and arteries. Look at the breath too, what sort of thing is it; air, and not even that always the same, but every minute belched forth and again gulped down. Then, thirdly, *there is the ruling reason*. Put your thought thus.[28]

> Body, soul, and intelligence, for the body sensations, for the soul desires, for the intelligence axioms. To receive impressions by way of the senses is not denied to cattle; to be as puppets pulled by the strings of desire is common to wild beasts and to pathics and to a Phalaris and a Nero. Yet to have the intelligence a guide to what they judge their duty is an attribute of those also who do not believe in Gods and those who fail their country in its need and those who do their deeds behind closed doors. If then all else is the common property of the classes mentioned, there is left as the characteristic of the good man to delight in and to welcome what befalls and what is being spun for him by destiny; and not to sully the divine *genius* [δαίμων] that is enthroned in his chest, nor yet to perplex it with a multitude of impressions, but to maintain it to the end in a gracious serenity, in orderly obedience to God [ἑπόμενος θεῷ], uttering no word that is not true and doing no deed that is not just.[29]

> You are formed of three things in combination—*body, vital breath, intelligence*. Of these the first two are indeed yours, insofar as you must have them in your keeping, but the *third alone is in any true sense yours*. Wherefore, if you cut off from yourself, that is from your mind, all that others do or say and all that you have done or said, and all that harasses you

in the future, or whatever you are involved in independently of your will by the body which envelops you and the breath that is twined with it, and whatever the circumambient rotation outside of you sweeps along, so that your intellective faculty, delivered from the contingencies of destiny, may live pure and undetached by itself, doing what is just, desiring what befalls it, speaking the truth–if, I say, you strip from this ruling reason all that clings to it from the bodily influences and the things that lie beyond in time and the things that are past, if you fashion yourself like the Empedoclean–*Sphere to its circle true in its poise well-rounded rejoicing*–and school yourself to life that life only which is yours, namely the present, so shall you be able to pass through the remnant of your days calmly, kindly, and at peace with your own *genius* [δαίμων].[30]

Many problems arise because of this radical innovation. Chiefly, (*a*) from whence did Marcus Aurelius get the doctrine? (*b*) In addition, what is this *nous*, this mind from the ontological viewpoint? (*c*) From whence is it derived? (*d*) What is its function? (*e*) What is its destiny?

Marcus Aurelius has only partial and somewhat vague and ambiguous answers to these questions.

(*a*) First, it could not have been derived from Plato or Aristotle, as some have thought, since they do not oppose soul and mind (*nous*) in this way. It was undoubtedly inspired by a leaning or tendency toward the spiritual or immaterial which became stronger and which could not accept the reduction of what was most elevated in man to a mere material pneuma. In our view, it is almost certain that the doctrine is derived from Middle Platonism, which presents on a thematic level the tenet of the superiority of *nous* over *psyché*, as we will see further on. It is nevertheless evident that Marcus Aurelius was preoccupied with exactly this, *to show that man is not reduced, as are all other things, to a purely physical component and not even to something vital.* Mind (νοῦς) arises decisively beyond the vital and the physical, and because of this superiority the destiny and happiness of human beings is decided only through and with *nous*. In fact, Marcus Aurelius, as the Middle Platonists, undoubtedly identified our *nous* with our *daimon* and also proposed as their fundamental principle "to follow God."[31]

(*b*) But as clear as this specific function of *nous* is in the context of the *Meditations*, its ontological nature is at the same time obscure. And it could not be otherwise: in fact, and the reader will by now easily have grasped this fact, in order to give the mind an ontological status which is above the pneumatic and material nature of the physical world, once more the categories of the supersensible and immaterial are indispensable. In other words, it was indispensable to leave behind the Stoic ontological sphere which can only contain the material and corporeal. But Marcus Aurelius was far from being able not only to critically recover these categories, but also simply to realize the basic implications which the admission of a *nous* above *psyché* involved.

And when our philosopher says that *nous* is a *daimon* (δαίμων), which is a fragment of the divine substance itself, evidently he did not solve the problem, but merely shifted it, because once again, beyond the implicit negation that God is pneuma or fire, we are not given any positive determination of the nature of God. From Middle Platonism then Marcus Aurelius, as the other Neo-Stoics, only took some corollaries and not their foundation.

(*c*) We thus have a reply to the further problem of the derivation of *nous*. Marcus Aurelius writes:

> If the intellectual capacity is common to us all, common too is the reason, which makes us rational creatures. If so, that reason also is common which tells us to do or not to do. If so, law also is common. If so, we are citizens. If so, we are fellow-members of an organized community. If so, the Universe is as it were a state—for of what other single polity can the whole race of mankind be said to be fellow-members?–and from it, this common State, we get the intellectual, the rational, and the legal instinct, or whence do we get them? For just as the earthy part has been portioned off for me from some earth, and the watery from another element, and aerial from some source, and the hot and fiery from some source of its own–for nothing comes from the one-existent, any more than it disappears into nothingness–so also the intellect has undoubtedly come from somewhere.[32]

> Among irrational creatures one life is distributed, and among the rational one intellectual soul has been parceled out. Just as also there is one earth for all the things that are of the earth; and one is the light whereby we see, and one the air we all breathe that have sight and life.[33]

> There is one light of the sun, even thought its continuity be broken by walls, mountains, and countless other things. There is one common substance, even though it be broken up into countless bodies individually characterized. There is one soul, though it be broken up among countless natures and with individual limitations. There is one intelligent soul, though it seem to be divided. Of the things mentioned, however, all the other parts, such as breath, are the material substratum of things, devoid of sensation and the ties of mutual affinity–yet even they are knit together by the faculty of intelligence and the gravitation which draws them together. But the mind is peculiarly impelled towards what is akin to it, and coalesces with it, and there is no break in the feeling of social fellowship.[34]

As is evident, Marcus Aurelius admitted a *universal intellectual soul* beyond a *universal matter* and beyond a *universal pneumatic soul* of which individual souls are but fragments or moments. This universal mind or intellect is God, a pantheistic conception of God, which contains and absorbs all into itself. But, for the same reasons indicated above, the relations of this God with universal pneumatic soul and with universal matter are not clear, nor does it seem that Marcus Aurelius was acutely aware of any of the aporematic implications that these relations structurally involve.

(*d*) If man emerges as transcending all things through his rational soul, then it is clear that the meaning of life could only be decided in it and through it. And the nature itself of the mind (*nous*) indicates a way of life to be followed. It is a general law of nature that like is joined to like.[35] And like for the mind (*nous*) moves in two directions, in a horizontal one, so to speak, that is, in the direction of other men and in a vertical one, in the direction of the divine mind (*nous*). And thus the moral task for man will be explained in a social dimension by loving and assisting human beings, and in a religious dimension by living with the Gods. Marcus Aurelius expressly writes:

> To live with the Gods. To live precisely with the Gods who accept their happiness in the destiny assigned them and to obey the commands, which come from the genius [δαίμων] which Jupiter has given to each one of us as our ruling part, our guide, and which is like a fragment of him [ἀπόσπασμα ἑαυτοῦ]. And this genius is wholly our intelligence and reason.[36]

(*e*) Contrary to what one would expect, Marcus Aurelius does not affirm the immortality of the human *nous*. In some passages he repeats the Socratic dilemma that death is either a *dissolution* or *a step into another life.*[37] But his though on this issue ought to be typical of a Stoic, that is, that the souls of human beings are preserved after death, but only for a limited duration of time, as is clear in the following passage:

> If souls outlive their bodies, how does the air contain them from times beyond ken? How does the earth contain the bodies of those who have been buried in it for such endless ages? For just as on earth the change of these bodies, after continuance for a certain indefinite time, followed by dissolution, makes room for other dead bodies, so souls, when transferred into the air, after lasting for a certain time, suffer change and are diffused and become fire, being taken again into the Seminal Reason of the Whole, and so allow room for those that subsequently take up their abode there.[38]

It is true that Marcus Aurelius seems to speak of the pneumatic soul as primary; but it is likewise true that the mention of the re-absorption into the Creative Principle of the universe, that is, into the *Logos Spermatikós* [*Seminal Reason*] leads us to believe that the fate of the intellective soul is identical. In any case, immortality is a conception which remains outside the scope of our philosopher's views.[39] On this point Marcus Aurelius remains strictly a Stoic, the fate of the soul after death *does not enter into the decision about the meaning of life*; moral duty is imposed of itself, absolutely, and has in itself its own *telos* [*goal*] for the reasons seen.

5. The refuge in interiority

On the basis of what was said above it is not difficult to understand that for Marcus Aurelius the intellective soul (νοῦς) constitutes our true self, the secure refuge into which we retire in order to defend ourselves against any danger and in order to find the necessary energy with which to live a life worthy of being human.

> When forced, as it seems, by your environment to be utterly disquieted, return with all speed into your self, staying in discord no longer than you must. By constant recurrence to the harmony, you will gain more command over it.[40]

> Never forget that the ruling Reason shows itself unconquerable when, concentrated in itself, it is content with itself, so it does nothing that it does not will, even if it refuse from mere opposition and not from reason–much more, then, if it judge of a thing on reasonable grounds and advisedly. Therefore the Mind, unmastered by passions, is a very citadel, for a man has no fortress more impregnable wherein to find refuge and be untaken for ever. He indeed who has not seen this is ignorant, but he that has seen it and takes not refuge therein is luckless.[41]

But here is a passage which puts together perfectly this conception of the refuge in interiority and which also illustrates the essential principles which, according to Marcus Aurelius, are to be uncovered in the interiority of man:

> Men seek retreats for themselves, houses in the country, sea-shores, and mountains; and you too are apt to desire such things very much. But this is altogether a mark of the most common sort of men, for it is in your power whenever most you choose to retire into yourself. For nowhere either with more quiet or more freedom from trouble does a man retire than into his own soul, particularly when he has within him such thoughts that by looking into them he is immediately in perfect tranquility; and I affirm that tranquility is nothing else than the good ordering of the mind. Constantly then give to yourself this retreat, and renew yourself; and let your principles be brief and fundamental, which, as soon as you shall recur to them, will be sufficient to cleanse, the soul completely, and to send you back free from all discontent with the things to which you return.

> For with what are you discontented? With the badness of men? Recall to your mind this conclusion, that rational animals exist for one another, and that to endure is a part of justice, and that men do wrong involuntarily; and consider how many already, after mutual enmity, suspicion, hatred, and fighting, have been stretched dead, reduced to ashes; and be quiet at last.

> But perhaps you are dissatisfied with that which is assigned to you out of the universe?

> Recall to your recollection this alternative; either there is providence or atoms; or remember the arguments by which is has been proved that the world is a kind of political community.

> But perhaps corporeal things will still fasten upon you.

> Consider then further that the mind mingles not with the breath, or the moving gently or violently, when it has once drawn itself apart and discovered its own power, and think also of all that you have heard and assented to about pain and pleasure.

> But perhaps the desire of the thing called fame will torment you.

> See how soon everything is forgotten, and look at the chaos of infinite time

on each side of the present, and the emptiness of applause, and the chan-
geableness and wont of judgment and those who pretend to give praise, and
the narrowness of the space with which it is circumscribed. For the whole
earth is a point, and how small a nook in it is this your dwelling, and how few
are there in it, and what kind of people are they who will praise you. This
then remains, remember to retire into this little territory of your own, and
above all do not distract or strain yourself, but be free, and look at things as
a man, as a human being, as a citizen, as a mortal. But among the things
closest to hand to which you should turn, let there be these which are two.
One is that things do not touch the soul, for they are external and remain
removable, but our perturbations come only from the opinion which is
within. The other is that all these things, which you see, change immediately
and will no longer be; and constantly bear in mind how many of these
changes you have already witnessed.

The universe is transformation, life, opinion.[42]

The ruling principle, that is, the intellective soul which is our *daimon*, is
invincible, if we want it to be. Nothing can impede it, nothing can subdue it,
nothing can touch it, neither fire nor iron, nor the violence of any kind, if we
do not wish it. Only judgment which comes forth from it concerning things
can influence it; but then it is not the things which afflict it, but the false
opinions which it produced.[43] When kept rightly and uncorrupted, *nous* is the
refuge which gives man absolute peace.

6. The new spirit

Previously the ancient Stoa had emphasized the general bond which
embraced all men, but only the Roman Neo-Stoicism elevated this bond to
the precept of love. Marcus Aurelius went without restraints in this direction.
Here are some illuminating remarks:

And again it is of a rational soul to love a neighbor, that is truth and
humility....[44]

This inclination in human nature to love other men is based on the fact
that in all human beings *nous*, or mind is present, and it is wholly derived from
God and is a particle of divinity:

And you forget how strong is the kinship between man and mankind, for it
is a community not of corpuscles, of seed or blood, but of intelligence. And
you forget this too, that each man's intelligence is God and has emanated
from Him; and this, that nothing is a man's very own, but that his babe, his
body, his very soul came forth from Him; and this, that everything is but
opinion; and this; that it is only the present moment that a man lives and the
present moment only that he loses.[45]

Here is another notion found in Marcus Aurelius which is close to the Gospel
precept of doing good for goodness sake without looking for or waiting for public
recognition or reward:

One man, when he has done another a kindness, is ready also to reckon on a return. A second is not ready to do this, but yet in his heart of hearts ranks the other as a debtor, and he is conscious of what he has done. But a third is in a manner not conscious of it, but is like the vine that has borne a cluster of grapes, and when it has once borne its due fruit looks for no reward beyond, as it is with a steed when it has run its course, a hound when it has singled out the trail, a bee when she has made her comb. And so a man when he has done one thing well, does not cry it abroad, but takes himself to a second, as a vine to bear afresh her clusters in due season. A man then must be of those who act thus as it were unconsciously.[46]

The Emperor even goes as far as to say the following:

It is a man's special privilege to love even those who stumble. And this love follows as soon as you reflect that they are of kin to you and that they do wrong involuntarily and through ignorance, and that within a little while both they and you will be dead; and this, above all, that the man has done you no hurt; for he has not made your ruling Reason worse than it was before.[47]

The religious sentiment in Marcus Aurelius was also much further developed than in that of the ancient Stoa.[48]

"To give thanks to the God from the depths of the heart,"[49] "to always have God in mind,"[50] "to pray to the Gods,"[51] "to live with the Gods"[52] are meaningful expressions which occur again and again in the *Meditations* but now charged with a new meaning. But more fully indicative in this regard is the following thought:

Either the Gods have no power or they have power. If they have no power, why pray to them? But if they have power, why not rather pray that they should give you freedom from fear of any of these things and from lust for any of these things and from grief at any of these things [rather] than that they should grant this or refuse that. For obviously if they can assist men at all, they can assist them in this. But perhaps thou wilt say, The Gods have put this in my power. Then is it not better to use what is in thy power like a free man than to concern yourself with what is not in your power like a slave and an abject? And who told you that the Gods do not co-operate with us even in the things that are in our power? Begin at any rate with prayers for such things and you will see.[53]

For a Stoic, so proud of the things which are in his power, appealing to divine help, even in such things as are within his power, is not a little indicative of the profound need for God that Marcus Aurelius, as also many other men of his epoch, felt.

Unfortunately, Marcus Aurelius judged the attitude of Christians who faced death in order to witness to their faith to be theatrical in character.[54] In point of fact he appropriated that attitude, and in some way made it his own, although for his own purposes:

You have but a short time left to live. Live as on a mountain; for whether it be here or there, matters not provided that, wherever a man live, he live as a citizen of the World-City. Let men look upon you, cite you, as a man in very deed that lives according to nature. *If they cannot bear with you, let them slay you.* For it were better so than to live their life.[55]

But it is perhaps less likely that men do not tolerate but slay those who live *according to nature*; rather they do not easily tolerate those who live according to principles which transcend nature.

VI. The Dissolution of the Philosophy of the Stoa

Stoicism undoubtedly celebrated its greatest triumph with Marcus Aurelius insofar as, as has been correctly noted, "an emperor, the sovereign of the whole known world, professed Stoicism and lived as a Stoic."[1] But immediately after Marcus Aurelius, Stoicism began its inevitable decline, and in the next few generations, in the third century CE, it disappeared as an autonomous philosophical current.

A passage of a work of Longinus, reported by Porphyry in his *Life of Plotinus*, contains a precious document about the last Stoics, reduced now to wearily repeating the dogmas of the ancient Stoa, and, together with it, about the testimony of their end.[2]

The reasons which provoked the crisis of the most vigorous spiritual movement of the Hellenistic Age are of two different orders and have already been discussed so frequently in what we said above that it will be sufficient here to briefly recall them.

The greatest obstacle which impeded the survival of Stoicism was its *basic materialism* which the spiritual currents of Platonic inspiration could not surmount. We have seen in the ancient Stoa how materialism became, at least in part, a Procrustean bed, and how, especially in the Roman Stoa, the contradictions between the spiritual positions and the materialistic foundations became an explosive mixture, provoking a whole series of fractures and, in particular, involving the impossibility of a sound theoretical justification of the most important innovations, which were achieved almost solely on an intuitive level. A whole series of theological and anthropological corollaries, as we have seen, in Seneca, Musonius, in Epictetus, and Marcus Aurelius could be justified only on the basis of a spiritual, that is, non-materialistic metaphysics. It is not difficult to understand, therefore, how the massive attacks conducted against the materialistic foundations of the Stoic system by the Middle Platonists, Neo-Pythagoreans, and Plotinus himself, struck their objective fully, because the very foundations had already been weakened by the last of the Stoics themselves. Finally, Platonism and the non-materialistic attitude at first penetrated into the Stoa as some "corollary" positions, so to speak, then the power of these positions increased more and more until finally the foundations disintegrated. After the coming of Neoplatonism and after its uncontested triumph, only those propositions and teachings of Stoicism which were not necessarily bound up with materialism or which could be freed from it survived.

The other great force which contributed in a specific way to the demise of Stoicism was the Christian religion. We have seen previously that the ancient Stoics were the upholders of some moral ideas which anticipate some traits of the Christian ethic and that numerous maxims of the Roman

Stoics could be compared in detail with some evangelical maxims. But once again we are faced with intuitions which in various measures go beyond the theoretical framework proper to Stoicism and which, if adequately developed, would have shattered this framework. Actually, beyond a series of corollary points of contact there is a fundamental and radical opposition at the basis of Stoicism and Christianity which Max Pohlenz has correctly pointed out in the following way, "Jesus did not turn man to himself, but exhorted him to have faith in God, and notwithstanding the many coincidences in particulars, we cannot avoid seeing the abyss which separates his purely religious sentiment from that of the humane ethic of the Stoic. How deep this abyss is depends chiefly upon this consideration. In Greek thought the concept of nature is the point of departure as well as the point of arrival. Nature is the force which rules the great complex of cosmic events by its eternal laws, but it is simply that which determines the essence of man and constitutes the norm of his action; morality is nothing but the full development of the rational nature of man. The language in which Jesus expressed himself does not have a word which corresponds to the Greek concept of *physis*; for him the world was the work of God, who—and this notion was as inconceivable for the Stoics as it was for the Epicureans—had created it from nothing and rules the course of its changes. Not his own reason, but God prescribed to man those things that ought to be done or avoided, what is good and what is evil, what is moral. Here, immoral action does not represent simply a violation of the laws of nature, but it is an act of disobedience to God, sin; the goal for man is not to lead a life according to nature in harmony with the *logos*, but only a life in God according to the will of God. The *eudaimonia* of man consists on earth in peace, which is superior to all reason, and it is completed in the beatitude in Heaven. If the Stoa believed in the power of man to realize his own destiny through correct knowledge and action, Jesus, although claiming that man must involve himself in the work of his own salvation, promised to the weak the grace of a merciful God and pardon for sins. We can ascertain that the need for establishing a relationship with God in the Stoics of the Imperial Age increases; God, however, always remains the universal reason, one being in its essence, with the human spirit, completely different from the Father Who is in heaven, with Whom Jesus is found in direct communion and to Whom he wishes to guide other men."[3]

In conclusion, on a philosophical plane Stoicism was conquered by speculative currents which recovered the results of the Platonic "second voyage," strengthening the claim at all levels of the tenets of the immaterial; whereas on a religious plane, it was conquered by a new faith which opened up into the domain of the supernatural.

Fourth Section

THE REBIRTH OF PYRRHONISM AND NEO-SKEPTICISM

«ὁ σκεπτικὸς διὰ τὸ φιλάνθρωπος εἶναι
τὴν τῶν δογματικῶν οἴησίν τε καὶ
προπέτειαν κατὰ δύναμιν ἰᾶσθαι λόγῳ
βούλεται.»

"The Skeptic, being a lover of humankind,
desires to cure by speech, as best he can,
the self-conceit and rashness of the dogmatist."

Sextus Empiricus, *Outlines of Pyrrhonism* 3.280

I. Aenesidemus and the Reinterpretation of Pyrrhonism

1. The reasons for the rebirth of Pyrrhonism and its characteristics

The conviction gradually developed in the Academy (as we saw in the preceding volume), after the scholarchate of Carneades and his student Clitomachus, that it was necessary to return to dogmatism. The conviction also grew of the necessity to borrow in an eclectic way and chiefly from the Stoa many of those doctrines which in the past had been the object of the most violent criticism.[1] Probably it was because of the return of the Academy to a kind of Stoic-like dogmatism which must have pushed some of its exponents, still convinced of the validity of the skeptical positions welcomed by Arcesilaus and Carneades, to break away from the school, as they could not share in any way the new course set by Philo and Antiochus.

Evidently, they were not even able to present themselves as continuators or restorers of the Skeptic tradition of the Academy, which at the time had evidently fallen into disrepute and which, in fact, the Academicians not only tried to limit but even to deny. There seems to be no other option for them except the alternative of a direct resumption of the original skepticism, that is, of the views of Pyrrho and his school.

This must have been precisely the task which was proposed by Aenesidemus and his followers, that is, to clearly burn the bridges to the Academy and take the school to Alexandria.

The chronological placement of Aenesidemus is discussed a good deal but, because of most of the data which are extant, we are forced (and in a rather definitive manner) to place him in the age of Cicero, that is, after Antiochus of Ascalon had transformed Academic philosophy in a dogmatic, eclectic, and Stoicizing direction. The title of the major work of Aenesidemus, *An Introductory Outline to the Philosophy of Pyrrho*, as well as being dedicated to Lucius Aelius Tubero, a well-known Roman ambassador to the circle of the Academicians, seems to be comprised of a well-thought-out, challenging, and innovative program. The fact, then, that Cicero ignored Aenesidemus and considered Skepticism as something defunct at that time can offer a useful later element in the chronological placement of the rebirth of Pyrrhonism. The work of Aenesidemus was probably written in the years immediately following the death of Cicero which is about 43 BCE.[2] Now let us read the principle thematic points of this work which have been preserved by Photius with great fidelity and which reproduced almost to the letter the text of Aenesidemus. Photius writes:

> The general aim of the work of [Aenesidemus] is that of establishing that nothing can be understood in a stable way either by means of sensations or by reasoning and it is because of this that neither the Pyrrhonians nor the

other philosophers know the truth of things, but the adherents of the philosophers of the other sects do not know even that they are getting tired and consumed in vain in continuing torments, and do not know in addition this also, that is, that nothing which they believed they understand is truly comprehended. On the contrary, he who philosophizes like Pyrrho is happy chiefly because he is a wise man, because of the fact that above all he knows that nothing is comprehended by him stably; and concerning those things which can be known he is such as to give his own assent no more to the affirmation than to its negation. In the first book, introducing a distinction between the Pyrrhonians and the Academicians, Aenesidemus states these words: philosophers are dogmatics and posit certain things without uncertainty and reject others without hesitation; on the contrary, the adherents of Pyrrho profess doubt and are free of all dogma: no one of them absolutely had affirmed that all things are incomprehensible nor are they comprehensible, but that they are no more so this (οὐδὲ μᾶλλον) than in any other way, either sometimes they are comprehensible and sometimes are not comprehensible, or for one are incomprehensible and for another are not comprehensible at all. Neither have they said that all things together or some of them are understandable, but that they are understandable no more (οὐδὲν μᾶλλον) than they are not understandable, or that they are sometimes understandable and at other times are not more understandable, or that they are understandable for the one and for the other are not understandable. And, actually, there is neither truth nor falsity, neither probably nor improbable, neither being nor non-being, but the same thing, that is to say, is no more (οὐ μᾶλλον) true than false, nor more probable than improbable, nor more being than non-being neither sometimes this and at other times that other, neither for one in such a way and for another in such other. In general, in fact, the Pyrrhonists define nothing, and they do not define either this, that nothing can be defined, but they say to speak without knowing how to express what is the object of their thought. The philosophers of the Academy they uphold,especially those contemporaries, sometimes go back to Stoic opinions, and if there is a need to say the truth, they seem to be Stoics who argue with other Stoics. In the second place [the Academics] make [dogmatic assertions] on many topics. They introduce virtue and stupidity, positing as principles good and evil, truth and falsity, probability and improbability, being and non-being, and they define many things stably. They say their doubts only concern cataleptic impressions. Therefore the followers of Pyrrho in not defining anything remain absolutely faultless; on the contrary, the philosophers of the Academy, Aenesidemus says, lay themselves open to the same reproaches they make to other philosophers, but the graver fact is that, while they doubt about all questions which are the objects of discussion, they maintain their unity and they do not contradict, and those who contradict, do not realize it. In fact, to posit something and eliminate it without any doubt, and at the same time to affirm that things exist which can generally be perceived, implies an evident contradiction; since how is it possible that one who knows that this given thing is true and this other false is still in a position of doubt and of indecision and not chose clearly the one and not avoid the other? In fact, it is not known that this is good or evil, or that this is true and this other false and that this is being and this other is non-being, then there is need certainly to admit that each of these things is not comprehensible; if, on the contrary, each of these things can be perceived with sensation or with reason, then there is need to say that each of these things is comprehensible. These and others similar to these are the arguments that Aenesidemus presents at the beginning of his work in order to demonstrate the difference between the Pyrrhonians and the Academics.[3]

The radical disagreements between the positions held by the Academics of the first century BCE and the Skeptics who intended to remain faithful to the Pyrrhonian spirit could not be better expressed. In a summary way, we may characterize the divergences on the basis of what Photius said in the passage just quoted, as follows:

[1] The Academics had appropriated the doctrine of the Stoa.

[2] The Academics had fallen into clearly dogmatic affirmations and their profession of doubt had been emptied of meaning.

[3] The Academics had limited their doubt only to comprehensive or cataleptic representations.

[4] The Academics, in addition, by admitting the distinction between good and evil, true and false, probable and improbable, had ended with admitting again what they seemed to have firmly rejected, that is to say, the comprehensibility of things (hence, the possibility of comprehensive representations).

[5] The Academics, finally, in their negations had manifested a dogmatic attitude; in fact, the true Skeptic not only must not affirm, but he also must not deny anything with certainty. On the contrary, the authentic skeptical and anti-dogmatic attitude in the Pyrrhonian sense is *that of total suspension both of affirmation and non-affirmation.* Here it is in a concise way:

[1] The Pyrrhonian does not say (*a*) either that all things are not comprehensible by means of sensation or that they are comprehensible, but he does say that *they are no more comprehensible than they are not comprehensible*; (*b*) either that they are *at times* comprehensible and *at times* not comprehensible, but that *they are not any more comprehensible at times than they are not comprehensible at times*; (*c*) either that they are comprehensible *for a given man* and not comprehensible *for another man*, but that *they are not more comprehensible for a given man than they are not comprehensible for another man.*

[2] The Pyrrhonian does not say (*a*) that things or some things are comprehensible by means of reasoning, but he does say that *they are not more comprehensible than not comprehensible by reasoning*; (*b*) either that *at times* they are comprehensible by means of reasoning and *at times* not, but that *they are not at times more comprehensible by means of reasoning than at times not*

comprehensible; (c) either that for a given man they are comprehensible by reasoning and *for another man* not comprehensible, but that *they are not comprehensible or not comprehensible to a given man by means of reasoning more than they are such to another man.*

[3] A thing is neither true nor false for the Pyrrhonian, neither probable nor not probable, neither being nor non-being but rather *it is no more true than false, no more probable than improbable, no more existent than not existent* (it is not more true than false, it is not more probable than not probable, it is not more existent than it is not existent).

In this way a radically new proposal was made by sweeping away not only the eclectic and Stoicizing Academy but even some of the concessions of Arcesilaus and especially of Carneades, insofar as Aenesidemus truly and expressly rejected the distinction between the probable and the not-probable.[4] Nevertheless, Aenesidemus was also able to exploit certain contributions of the skeptic Academy of Arcesilaus and Carneades. It can be claimed, in fact, that the Neo-Pyrrhonism or Neo-Skepticism of Aenesidemus unified some Pyrrhonian positions with some Academic-Skeptical ones by reinterpreting and amplifying some of the Pyrrhonian reasons on the basis of a clever use of Academic dialectic, appropriately purified and more rigorously applied, in the way which we will immediately consider.

2. The ten tropes, or the list of the highest categories of doubt

The statement that no thing is *more this than that* (οὐ μᾶλλον), as we have previously seen in Pyrrho,[5] implies the denial of the validity of the principles of identity, of contradiction, and the excluded middle. Furthermore it implies the denial of substance and the stability of the being of things, and, hence it implies their total indetermination or, as Aenesidemus also said, their *disorder* (ἀνωμαλία) and their *confusion* (ταραχή). This is precisely the condition of things which in a programmatic way Aenesidemus tried to show in the first place, that is, how it is always possible to counterpose considerations having equal credibility to the apparently persuasive power of things, considerations which would annul (or at the least counter-balance in the opposite direction) that seemingly persuasive force. He composed for this purpose what we today would call a table or list of the highest categories of doubt. The ancients called them *tropes* which develop into the suspension of judgment, that is, the modes or the formal reasons by which we achieve or better by which we *must* achieve the recognition of the indeterminate character of things. Hence it is that the *tropes* involve the suspension of judgment, that is *epoché* (a term which Aenesidemus took over from the Academic tradition but which, as we already have seen, expressed, enriched, and determined in a conceptually more precise way the spiritual attitude which was previously Pyrrhonian).

The *tropes* are conceived, therefore, as the way which necessarily leads in a convergent manner to the suspension of judgment. Certainly much of the material gathered by Aenesidemus in his list of *tropes* was taken from ancient Skepticism (some of the examples even seem to echo the experience of Pyrrho in his travels to the East following Alexander, for example, in the explicit recalling of the fact that Demophon, who was Alexander's factotum, "got warm in the shade, and shivered in the sun"). One part of the material could perhaps have been taken from Academic skepticism itself; but the arrangement of all the material (and its completion) from which the list of the ten *tropes* arises surely belongs to Aenesidemus.

Here is how Diogenes Laertius summarized the notions previously explained which inspired the list of the *tropes*:

> Thus the Pyrrhonian principle, Aenesidemus says in the *Introduction to his Pyrrhonics*, is but a report on phenomena or on any kind of judgment, *a report in which all things are brought to bear on one another, and in the comparison are found to present much anomaly and confusion*. As to the contradictions in their doubts, *they would first show the ways in which things gain credence, and then by the same methods they would destroy belief in them*; for they say those things gain credence which either the senses are agreed upon or which never or at least rarely change, as well as things which become habitual or are determined by law and those which please or excite wonder. *They showed, then, on the basis of that which is contrary to what induces belief, that the probabilities on both sides are equal.* Perplexities arise from the agreements between appearances or judgments [= that which has been thought], and these perplexities they distinguished under ten different modes (κατὰ δέκα τρόπους) in which the subjects in question appeared to vary.[6]

But let us go on now to analytically examine each of the ten modes, *tropes*, taking as our main evidence is the text of Diogenes Laertius and strengthening it by the parallel testimony of Sextus Empiricus but used only as a complement, since the latter, in part, reinterpreted and recast the list in function of a personal rethinking of skepticism which we will discuss fully further on. The testimony of Philo of Alexandria, who lived a little after Aenesidemus and who refers in great part to these modes, or *tropes* in a detailed way, is also of great historical importance.[7]

[1] The first mode, or *trope*, reveals the numberless differences which can be found among various living beings at all levels. They especially mark the differences in the constitution of the senses, which obviously involve sensations that are not only diverse but contrasting. It cannot be said that man enjoys, with respect to other animals, a privileged position; in fact, for some senses the opposite is precisely the case. This contrast existing between the different sensations of different living beings, therefore, demands suspension of judgment. Philo writes:

> In fact all the differences which are recognized in the animals, not just in one respect but in all respects, are almost innumerable with regard to their

birth and constitution, to nutrition, and to their lifestyle, with respect to their likes and to their dislikes, to their sentient activity and their movements, with respect to particulars, infinite affections of the body and of the soul.[8]

Diogenes Laertius writes:

The first [*trope*] relates to the differences between living creatures in respect of those things which give them pleasure or pain, or are useful or harmful to them. By this it is inferred that they do not receive the same impressions from the same things, with the result that such a conflict necessarily leads to suspension of judgment. For some creatures multiply without intercourse, for example, creatures that live in fire, the Arabian phoenix and worms; others by union, such as man and the rest. Some are distinguished in one way, some in another, and for this reason they differ in their senses also, hawks for instance being most keen-sighted, and dogs having a most acute sense of smell. It is natural that if the senses, e.g., eyes, of animals differ, so also will the impressions produced upon them.[9]

Finally, Sextus writes:

I have drawn this comparison...having already sufficient proved, as I think, that we cannot prefer our own sense-impressions to those of the irrational animals.[10]

[2] The second mode, or *trope* moves from the consideration of living beings in general to men in particular and to the innumerable differences which can be verified in fact among men. Given also (but not conceded) that the perceptions and the feelings of men would be superior to those of animals, the situation would not change. In fact, men differ among themselves notably in what they call body and soul and these differences are such as to involve in different men different perceptions, different thoughts, different feelings, as well as different practical attitudes (different to the point of there even being contradiction between them). Therefore, suspension of judgment is required from these considerations.

Let us read, in order, the testimonies of Sextus Empiricus, Diogenes Laertius, and Philo of Alexandria:

The second mode, or *trope*...is based on the differences in men; for even if we grant for the sake of argument that men are more worthy of credence than irrational animals, we shall find that even our own differences of themselves lead to suspension of judgment. For man, you know, is said to be compounded of two things, soul and body, and in both these we differ one from another. [There follow numerous illustrative examples of these differences.] Necessarily, therefore, the differences in men afford a further reason for bringing in suspension of judgment.[11]

The second mode, or *trope*, has reference to the natures and idiosyncrasies of men [= the particular temperaments]; for instance, Demophon, Alexander's butler, used to get warm in the shade and shiver in the sun. Andron of Argos is reported by Aristotle to have traveled across the waterless deserts of Libya without drinking. Moreover, one man fancies the profession of medicine, another farming, and another commerce; and the same ways of life are injurious to one man but beneficial to another; from which it follows that judgment must be suspended.[12]

There are the diversities on all subjects which, to pass from animals in general, we find also in men in particular. Not only do their judgments on the same objects vary at different times, but different persons receive different impressions of pleasure or its reverse from the same things. For what is disliked by some is enjoyed by others, and contrariwise what some receive with open arms as acceptable and agreeable to their nature is utterly scouted by others as alien and repugnant.[13]

[3] But also by restricting our consideration to only the individual, hence, without opposing one individual to another, and without acting on the differences which distinguish one with respect to the other, we are led to the same conclusions and the necessity of suspending judgment imposes itself. In fact, the structure of the various senses is different and the related sensations are hence diverse. Sextus adduces numerous examples (the eye sees a distinctive feature in a picture, which through the sense of touch is perceived instead as smooth; honey pleases the palate and displeases the eyes, etc.), and he proceeds to a series of rather complicated considerations. Diogenes Laertius reports the *trope* in a concise manner as follows:

> The third mode, or *trope*, depends on the differences between the sense-channels in different cases, for an apple gives the impression of being pale yellow in color to the sight, sweet to the taste and fragrant to smell. An object of the same shape is made to appear different by differences in the mirrors reflecting it. Thus it follows that what appears is no more such and such a thing (μὴ μᾶλλον) than something different.[14]

[4] In addition, in the same individual not only are the structures of the senses different but so are the dispositions, conditions, states of mind different and changeable, all of which consequently condition the representations. It all verifies the conclusion that our representations differ according to whether we are healthy or ill, young or old, in our right mind or out of it, happy or unhappy and thus as a consequence, for this reason as well, we must suspend judgment.

The fuller exposition of this *trope* is perhaps that of Diogenes Laertius:

> The fourth mode is that due to differences of condition and to changes in general; for instance, health, illness, sleep, waking, joy, sorrow, youth, old age, courage, fear, want, fullness, hate, love, heat, cold, to say nothing of breathing freely and having the passages obstructed. The impressions received thus appear to vary according to the nature of the conditions. Nay, even the state of madmen is not contrary to nature; for why should their state be so more than ours? Even to our view the sun has the appearance of standing still. And Theon of Tithorea used to go to bed and walk in his sleep, while Pericles' slave did the same on the housetop.[15]

The fifth mode, or *trope*, notes the differences and the contradictory character of the opinions of men about moral values (good and evil, beautiful and ugly, true and false), about the Gods, and about the generation and corruption of the world according to their different educations and different laws or according to whether they belong to different ethnic groups and places or also to different philosophical sects.

The most effective and concise presentation of this *trope* is perhaps that of Philo:

> And are we not warned against giving over-ready credence to uncertainties by other considerations? I allude to certain facts, the evidence for which is found practically over the whole world as known to us facts which entail on Greek and barbarian alike the universal tendency to error which positive judgment brings. By these I mean of course ways of life from boyhood upwards, traditional usages, ancient awls, not a single one of which is regarded in the same light universally, but every country, nation and city, or rather every village and house, indeed every man, woman and infant child takes a totally different view of it. As a proof of this we see that what is base with us is noble with others, what is seemly and just with us is unseemly or unjust with them, our holy is their unholy, our lawful their unlawful, our laudable their blameworthy, our meritorious their criminal, and in all other matters their judgment is the opposite of ours. ...Since then the divers customs of divers persons are not distinguished merely by some slight difference, but exhibit an absolute contrast, amounting to bitter antagonism, it is inevitable that the impressions made upon the mind should differ and that the judgments formed should be at war with each other.[16]

Diogenes Laertius adds:

> Different peoples believe in different Gods; some in providence, other not. In burying their dead, the Egyptians embalm them; the Romans burn them; the Paeonians throw them into lakes. As to what is true, then, let suspensions of judgment be our practice.[17]

[6] The sixth mode, or *trope*, points out that nothing appears in itself and through itself as it is, but only and always in various ways mixed with others, and that our representation as a result is always conditioned, so that it is necessary also in this regard to suspend judgment. Here is how Philo referred to this *trope*:

> Nor is this strange. For anyone who penetrates deeper into things and views them in a purer light, will recognize that no single thing presents itself to us in its own absolute nature but all contain interlacings and intermixtures of the most complicated kind. For instance, how do we apprehend colors? Surely by means of the externals, air and light, and the internal moisture in the eye itself. How do we discriminate between sweet and bitter? Can we do so without the juices in the mouth, both those which are in accord with nature and those which are not? Surely not. Again, do the odors produced by burning incense present to us the natures of the substances in a pure and

simple form, or in a combination, in which themselves and air, or sometimes also the fire which dissolves the material, are joined with the faculty possessed by the nostrils? From this we deduce that we do not apprehend colors, but only the combination produced by the light and the material substances to which the colors belong, nor smells, but only the mixture of the emanation from the substances with the all-admitting air; nor flavors, but only the something produced by the application of what we taste to the moisture in our mouths.[18]

[7] The seventh mode, or *trope*, emphasizes that distances, different positions, and places condition our impressions of things to the point that once again the suspension of judgment becomes necessary. Diogenes Laertius writes:

> In this mode, or *trope*, things which are thought to be large appear small, square things round; flat things appear to have projections, straight things to be bent, and colorless colored. So the sun, on account of its distance, appears small, mountains when far away appear misty and smooth, but when near at hand rugged. Furthermore, the sun at it rising has a certain appearance, but has a dissimilar appearance when in mid-heaven, and the same body one appearance in a wood and another in open country. The image again varies according to the position of the object, and a dove's neck according to the way it is turned. Since, then, it is not possible to observe these things apart from places and positions, their real nature is unknowable.[19]

[8] The eighth mode, or *trope*, points out that quantity and quantitative relations condition our impressions in a radical way. For example, silver filings appear black when considered as individual grains while considered in a mass appear white. And grains of sand individually appear rough, in a mass give the appearance of softness. Analogously, the effects which things produce vary according to their quantity. In a special way, then, the effect of composites varies with the variety of quantitative relations of the components. Therefore Sextus Empiricus concludes:

> For there the exact blending of the simple drugs makes the compound wholesome, but when the slightest oversight is made in the measuring, as sometimes happens, the compound is not only unwholesome but frequently even most harmful and deleterious. Thus the argument from quantities and compositions causes confusion as to the real nature of the external substances. Probably, therefore, this mode, or *[trope]*, also will bring us around to suspension of judgment . . .[20]

[9] The ninth mode, or *trope*, indicates that we know things more or less by putting them *in relationship* with other things and that outside of such relations individual things are *in themselves* unknowable. This *trope*, which is called on *relativity*, is well-stated by Philo as follows:

Again, everyone knows that practically nothing at all which exists is intelligible by itself and in itself, but everything is appreciated only by comparison with its opposite; as small by comparison with great, dry with wet, hot with cold, light with heavy, black with white, weak with strong, few with many. The same rule holds with all that concerns virtue and vice. We only know the profitable through the hurtful, the noble by contrast with the base, the just and good in general by comparison with the unjust and evil. And indeed if we consider we shall see that everything else in the world is judged on the same pattern. For in itself each thing is beyond our apprehension, and it is only by bringing it into relation with something else that it seems to be known. Now that which is incapable of attesting itself and needs to be vouched for by something else, gives no sure ground for belief. And it follows that on this principle we can estimate at their true value lightly-made affirmations and negations on any subject whatever.[21]

[10] The final mode, or *trope*, notes that the continuity, the frequency, and the rarity with which phenomena appear necessarily conditions our judgment. Here are some well-stated examples from Sextus Empiricus:

The sun is, of course, much more amazing than a comet; yet because we see the sun constantly but the comet rarely we are so amazed by the comet that we even regard it as a divine potent, while the sun causes no amazement at all. If, however, we were to conceive of the sun as appearing but rarely and setting rarely, and illuminating everything all at once and throwing everything into shadow suddenly, then we should experience much amazement at the sight. An earthquake also does not cause the same alarm in those who experience it for the first time and those who have grown accustomed to such things.[22]

Therefore, because the same things according to whether we see them rarely or frequently appear precious and marvelous or not so, for this reason the suspension of judgment is also necessary.[23]

3. The negation of truth, of the principle of causality, and of the possibility of meta-empirical inference

The list of the *tropes* allows us again to see the complete outline of the difficulties which impede the attribution of soundness to our representations and especially to our sense representations. But the compilation of this list only represents a first contribution to the relaunching of Pyrrhonism on the part of Aenesidemus. Our philosopher, in fact, tried to reconstruct in outline the difficulties which impede the establishment of science and attempted to destroy in a systematic way the conditions and the foundations which science postulates. In order to do this, he had to give weight to some of the arguments which had previously been made by Academic skepticism.

One of the most penetrating scholars of skepticism wrote in this regard, "it is probably under the influence of the new Academy, to which we have reason to believe that he had originally belonged, and in order to respond to the new demands of the philosophy of his time, that Aenesidemus was moved to overcome by a subtle and profound criticism the ideas essential to science. After a philosophy like that of Carneades which had proclaimed the impossibility of science and brought to the foreground the insufficiency of sensible knowledge, a skepticism, if it wished to maintain its own rank among the competing systems, could not be content any more to simply enumerate opinions or contradictory appearances and take pleasure in the easy play of oppositions that we find in the ten *tropes*. It needed to proceed further and show not only that no science had been constructed, but even that it could never be produced. And this is precisely what Aenesidemus tried to do."[24]

Consequently, the possibility of science supposes in general three conditions: (*a*) the existence of *truths*, (*b*) the existence of *causes* (of principles or causal reasons), and (*c*) the possibility of *meta-empirical inferences*, that is, the possibility of understanding things which are seen as "signs"(*effects*) of things which are not seen (and which can be postulated precisely as necessary causes for the explanation of the things which are seen).

Aenesidemus tried to systematically destroy all three of these cornerstones of science. Let us see, in detail, the arguments by which he accomplished this task.

(*a*) Concerning truth, our philosopher, as Sextus Empiricus tells us, must have argued in this way:

> If...anything true exists, it is either sensible or intelligible or both intelligible and sensible. But it is neither sensible nor intelligible nor both together...therefore there does not exist anything true.[25]

Aenesidemus argued that the truth cannot be something *sensible* by noting that sensations are "a-rational" and that it is not possible for knowledge to be derived in an "a-rational" manner (and this is the revolutionary viewpoint of Epicurus's argument which, as we have seen, saw in the a-rationality of sensation the guarantor of truth).[26] Our philosopher argued that the truth cannot be something *intelligible* because the intelligible is not thought commonly by all, and if, on the other hand, it is thought only by some, then it is subject to controversy (this argument is evidently aimed against all rationalists). Finally, Aenesidemus argued that the truth cannot be something *both-sensible-and-intelligible* by noting that in this case the preceding difficulties noted are combined because in addition to the contrast existing between sensible things and that existing between intelligible things (the objects of thought) the mutual contrast is added which exists between sensible things and intelligible things (this argument is directed against those maintaining that the achievement of truth depends on both the senses and reason).[27]

(*b*) The reasoning of Aenesidemus is still more radical with respect to *causes*, since he tried to show the inconceivability of the existence of a causal relation, that is, of a connection of cause and effect. Now to be sure the cosmology and the theory of being of the Greeks was surely directed toward discovering causes. Aristotle, indeed, had even demonstrated that *science* and all *arts* in general are differentiated from mere experience precisely in the measure in which they seek the why, that is, the cause.[28] Therefore, the denial of the existence of a cause or of the causal nexus necessarily involves the destruction of the possibility of cosmology, a theory of being, and in general any science and art which is scientifically grounded.

Aenesidemus reasoned as follows. The causal nexus cannot have a place either between bodies or between non-bodies, or further, between the bodily and the non-bodily or vice versa. In order to grasp the context surrounding the reasons our philosopher used to sustain these views, it is necessary to take into account that the predominant mentality of his epoch was materialistic and that he did not succeed in any way in freeing himself from that mentality (in the second half of the first century BCE the rebirth of Platonism had not definitively commenced), so it is true that the concepts of "corporeal" and "incorporeal" to which he made reference were in content essentially the same as those of the Garden and the Stoa.[29]

Actually, the notion of a causal nexus and causation were understood by Aenesidemus either as a material transfer of the nature of the agent into that of the patient (an influx which involves an almost total mixture of agent and patient), or as an absurd and inconceivable physical multiplication of entities, or as a derivation of the effect from the cause conditioned by something which is pre-contained in the nature of the cause and which hence cannot exist except by having the same nature (and which, in the end, leaves the effect indistinguishable from the cause).[30]

Here is an example of an argument according to which a body cannot be the cause of another body:

> For it acts on another thing either while continuing by itself or after uniting with the other. But while it remains by itself it would not be able to effect anything more than itself and its own nature; and when united with another it would not be able to produce a third thing which was not previously in existence. For neither is the one thing able to become two, nor do the two produce a third thing. For if one is able to become two, each of the units which have so become, being one, will produce two, and each of the four, being one, will make two, and similarly each unit of the eight, and so on ad infinitum; but it is wholly absurd to say that an infinite number proceeds from one; therefore it is also absurd to say that anything more is generated from the one.[31]

The presence of the materialistic assumption is revealed in a still stronger fashion in the subsequent reasoning by which Aenesidemus intended to show the impossibility of the "incorporeal" as the cause of the incorporeal. In fact, our philosopher also adds the following to the argument previously touched on: the incorporeal is "an intangible nature," and hence can neither be active nor passive; consequently it cannot be a cause of another incorporeal nor be caused by it.[32]

Naturally Aenesidemus also rejects the possibility that the incorporeal can be the cause of the corporeal or vice versa, that the corporeal can be the cause of the incorporeal, because the nature of the incorporeal "does not contain in itself" the nature of the corporeal and vice versa. For example (and in this example the materialistic mentality that we spoke about is very much in evidence) the horse cannot be caused by a plane-tree, because in it "there is not contained" the nature of a plane-tree.[33] Finally Aenesidemus notes what follows:

> Yet if the one does exist in the other [the immaterial in the material or vice versa], even so the one will not spring from the other. For if either of them is existent, it does not come into existence from the other, but it is already in existence and being already in existence it does not become, since becoming is the process toward existence.[34]

But in order to strike down the etiological mentality of the Greeks at its ultimate source, Aenesidemus wanted to complete these arguments with a new list of modes, or *tropes*, that is, with a new list of paradigmatic modes according to which those who posit causes would inevitably fall into error. Hence the new *tropes* would be the built-in errors into which every attempt to construct an etiology would necessarily fall. Here are these *tropes*, which Aenesidemus held were eight in number:

[1] The first *trope* consists in the invalid assumption of reaching something invisible and not evident (precisely, the cause) without the warrant of anything which is visible and evident.

[2] The second consists in the pretense of explaining the causes of whatever is the object of inquiry limiting the explanation to but one cause, while multiple causes may possibly exist.

[3] The third consists in the claim of being able to infer causes which do not have order so as to explain, on the contrary, what manifests order (as the Epicureans do, for example, who pretend to infer from the disorder of the atoms the explanation of the world which is, on the contrary, ordered).

[4] The fourth consists in the claim that things which are not visible behave as visible things do, whereas their behavior could very well involve quite different and singular ways.

[5] The fifth consists in the claim of philosophers to establish the causes on the basis of their own hypothesis concerning the primary elements (hypotheses which differ according to the various philosophical sects) and not on the basis of methods and notions commonly agreed upon.

[6] The sixth consists in the claim to accept as a cause only what agrees with their own hypothesis and of rejecting what, on the contrary, is not in accord with it, even if it has equally persuasive force.

[7] The seventh consists in the acceptance of causes in conflict with the phenomena or else in conflict with the hypothesis of the philosophers.

[8] The eighth consists in the claim of explaining things which appear in a doubtful way with causes which are equally doubtful.[35]

This list undoubtedly flowed from an acute and critical mind; it would not be difficult to show that many causal explanations of the "dogmatists," especially those of the Epicureans and Stoics, fall into one or more of these errors (as we have pointed out in relation to the third *trope*). But we must not forget that Aenesidemus, in the construction of these criteria and in the compilation of this list, was permeated by that etiological mentality (which was in fact typically Greek) that he wanted to destroy. He, in fact, went on to a detailed and accurate *determination of the causes* without which it would be impossible *to inquire into the causes* (he would, in short, *discover the causes for which it is impossible to discover any further causes*). This is one of the most compelling and elegant examples which shows that some truths reaffirm themselves in the very act of trying to deny them.

(*c*) We proceed now, after our listing of the modes, or *tropes* which denounce the errors into which the etiological mentality falls and the pretense of finding the causes of phenomena, to the *problem of inference* or, to use ancient terminology, to the problem of "signs," to which Aenesidemus devoted a detailed analysis, perhaps the first which was produced in the ancient period.[36]

The very significant principle "that what appears is a glimpse of the invisible" (ὄψις ἀδήλων τὰ φαινόμενα) is involved in all Greek philosophy and science.[37] According to this principle it is possible, by starting from what is apparent to the senses, to ascend to what does not fall under the scope of the senses, that is, "to infer," by starting from phenomena, meta-phenomenal causes. The phenomenon becomes thus a *sign* which is *the indicator of something else* (i.e., what does not fall under the senses), the non-phenomenal cause. It is this principle which Aenesidemus intended to contest. Photius writes:

> In the fourth book [of the *Pyrrhonian Discourses*] he says that visible things which we call signs of things invisible are not precisely that and that those who believe this are stupid and deceived by a useless sentiment.[38]

Sextus states further:

> Aenesidemus, in the fourth book of his Pyrrhonian Discourses, propounds an argument on the same subject and to much the same effect in the following form: "If apparent things appear alike to all those in a similar condition, and signs are apparent things, signs appear alike to all those in a similar condition. But signs do not appear alike to all those in a similar condition; and apparent things appear alike to those in a similar condition; therefore signs are not apparent things."[39]

In order to clarify the reasoning of Aenesidemus, Sextus observes that the same pathological phenomena which are manifested in an illness, for example, can appear to three doctors who are consulted, and who are hence in similar condition, as signs of three different causes.[40] What it means precisely is that the signs are not as a matter of fact "phenomena," "things which appear." Or better yet, it means that the things which appear can be understood as "signs" only arbitrarily, and thus without any restraint. To put it in other words, at the very moment in which a phenomenon is to be interpreted as a "sign," it is placed by us on a meta-phenomenal level, insofar as that phenomenon is understood as the *effect* (which appears) of a *cause* (which does not appear), that is, it unwarrantedly assumes the existence of an ontological/metaphysical nexus, cause-effect and its universal validity.

Later Skepticism (perhaps beginning from Menodotus) introduced the important distinction between "recalled signs" and "referential signs." The *recalled sign* is one which is constantly united to a determined thing in a preceding observation; when this thing does not appear in an evident way it can lead us to recall it to mind, as for example the smoke which is coming from a chimney enables us to recall the fire which is not visible. The *referential sign*, on the contrary, is one which, although it is not observed together with the thing of which it is a sign, nevertheless "through its nature and constitution" indicates this thing, as for example, when we say that the movements of the body are signs of the soul. Empirical Skepticism will accept the *recalled sign* and reject the *inferential sign*. But it is only this latter notion of sign which Aenesidemus attacked, because it is the one which permits us to understand *what appears as a glimpse into the invisible.*[41]

4. The relations between the skepticism of Aenesidemus and Heracliteanism

Sextus Empiricus writes that Aenesidemus was linked by his skepticism to Heracliteanism and in the *Outlines of Pyrrhonism* he writes:

> Aenesidemus says that the skeptical road is a way which leads to the Heraclitean philosophy.[42]

Sextus contests the thesis of Aenesidemus by noting that Heracliteanism falls into dogmatism, since it infers that the contraries *exist* in the same object because the contraries appear in the same object; whereas Skepticism precisely does not say anything about the *being* of the object (not even in the negative form of Heracliteanism) but is strictly limited to the *appearance* of phenomena.[43]

This remark of Sextus depends naturally on his "empirical" skepticism, which is based on a clear distinction between the *external object* and the *representations* which are produced in us by it, or, in modern terminology, between "things in themselves" and the "phenomena" (things as they appear). But this distinction does not belong either to ancient Pyrrhonism or to the Neo-Pyrrhonism of Aenesidemus. Both Pyrrho and Aenesidemus reduce being to the appearance, the *in itself* into the *for us*, the substance into the accidents.[44] This very conception of things, in the measure in which it destroys the stable basis of being and substance, leads directly to Heracliteanism, or better to that form of Heracliteanism, which putting aside the metaphysics of the *logos* and the harmony of contraries, previously begun by Cratylus, had put the emphasis on the universal mobility and instability of all things.[45]

Some scholars have correctly attended to the fact that in the *Theaetetus* of Plato there is expressed a position or thought of Heraclitean origin which is close to the position of Aenesidemus (obviously Aenesidemus, insofar as he was an Academic, must have been well acquainted with this dialogue).[46]

Now in the *Theaetetus* Plato notes that discussing and reasoning with the supporters of these "Heraclitean" doctrines is quite difficult and he says:

> But if you ask one of them a question, he pulls out puzzling little phrases, like arrows from a quiver, and shoots them off; and if you try to get hold of an explanation of what he has said, you will be struck with another phrase of novel and distorted wording, and you never make any progress whatsoever with any of them, nor do they themselves with one another, for that matter, but they take good care *to allow nothing to be settled either in an argument or in their minds*, thinking, I suppose, that this is being stationary; *but they wage bitter war against the stationary, and, so far as they can, they banish it altogether.*[47]

These thinkers who affirm that "all is in motion," Plato remarks further on, must understand "movement" or "change" in two senses, that is, in the sense of *alteration* (change of quality) and in the sense of *local-motion* (change of place) and they must admit that all things are moved in these two senses. But if this is so, the qualities sensed (for example, the colors) do not remain ever equal and thus not even the sentient subject remains identically himself, and hence the following "skeptical" consequences, which Plato draws coherently in this passage:

> Socrates: *Then we must not speak of seeing more than not-seeing,* or *of any other perception more than of non-perception*, if all things are in all kinds of motion.
> Theodorus: No, we must not.
> Socrates: And yet perception is knowledge, as Theaetetus and I said.
> Theodorus: Yes, you did say that.
> Socrates: Then when we were asked "what is knowledge?" we answered *no more what knowledge is than what non-knowledge is.*
> Theodorus: So it seems.
> Socrates: This would be a fine result of the correction of our answer, when we were so eager to show that all things were in motion, just for the purpose of making that answer prove to be correct. But his I think did prove to be true, that if all things are in motion, every answer to any question whatever is equally correct, and we may say it is thus or not thus or, if you prefer, "becomes thus," *to avoid giving them fixity by using the word 'is'.*

Theodorus: You are right.

Socrates: Except, Theodorus, that I said "thus" and "not thus," *but we ought not even to say "thus"; for "thus" would no longer be in motion; nor, again, "not thus." For there is no motion in "thus" either; but some other expression must be supplied for those who maintain this doctrine, since now they have, according to their own hypothesis, no words, unless it be perhaps the word "no how." That might be most fitting for them, since it is indefinite.*[48]

Now, notice that the epistemological position that Plato infers from Heracliteanism is expressed completely by the formula "no more this than that"(οὐ μᾶλλον) which Pyrrho,[49] and then Aenesidemus posited at the core of their rethinking of skepticism.[50]

But there is more. Sextus Empiricus refers to the fact that Aenesidemus and his followers reduced the various forms of movements distinguished by Aristotle to only two, that is, to *alteration* and *local-motion*, precisely to those two types of motion about which we read in the passage of the Platonic *Theaetetus*.[51]

Hippolytus confirms it in what he says about Pyrrho:

All reality is *fluid and changing and never remains in the same place.*[52]

Hence, Plato has deduced the fundamental assertion of Skepticism and vice versa *ante litteram* [*before the text*] from Heracliteanism by a dialectical reasoning process. From his basic skeptical assertion *Aenesidemus has returned to Heracliteanism and has affirmed, as we have previously seen, that skepticism is the way which precisely leads to Heracliteanism.* The accounts are in complete agreement, thence, provided that, as we have previously mentioned, the pure phenomenalism of Aenesidemus is not confused with the dualistic phenomenalism of Sextus. The issue has been best clarified by a French scholar on skepticism in a fine passage, which is worth reading in its entirety, "In the text of Photius...it is said that 'the Pyrrhonians determine nothing and not even this, that nothing is determined.' The universality of the 'not more...than' as of the 'not to determine anything,' hence, does not imply any doubt. It follows that the notion itself of an indeterminate being (of a reality inaccessible in itself, not able to be decided, of which nothing can be said, etc.) is not entirely excluded from the field of the application of these formulas. Consequently, the phenomenon is no more simply a 'phenomenon' than a reality in itself. Aenesidemus say so expressly, there is neither being nor non-being and the same thing is not more a being than a non-being (Photius 170a7-9). We can see all the determinations concerning being destroy themselves; the phenomenon destroys its determination of a simple phenomenon, being is no more 'being' than 'non-being,' etc. The argument of Aenesidemus is thus to be understood: Skepticism introduces us to the philosophy of Heracliteans because the contrariety in the *appearances* is *likewise* the contrariety in the *being* itself of things. The passage from appearances to being is impossible when the fixed opposition between being and phenomena is maintained. But such a dogmatic opposition is precisely abolished. The being concealed behind the phenomenon (*adelon*) can no more be being than non-being. But no-more-being-this-than-that is precisely what is said of things in their appearing. Therefore the differences of the two aspects of things vanishes. Nothing impedes this, on condition that there remains no fixity to the dogmatic opposition between being and its appearance. To say, 'being contains in itself the opposition to itself' signifies a departure from the beings of our general awareness and from dogmatism in order to dissolve them. In fact, being which is opposed to itself can never be the being of the general and dogmatic awareness, that is, it is no longer truly being, if it is authentically being (and that is what Aristotle wanted to say) then it is devoid of contradiction. It is hence evident that the proof of contrariety and the inconsistency of the appearances leads to an Heraclitean vision (or a neo-Heraclitean one) of total inconsistency, since appearance in the Pyrrhonian sense and Aenesidemus's is nothing other than being, which signifies that there is precisely neither 'being,' nor 'essence,' nor a 'basis' of things, but only surface without depth, an absolute surface."[53]

5. Moral ideas

That Aenesidemus must have been basically concerned with moral ideas especially in the last three books of the *Pyrrhonian Discourses*, which chiefly aimed at destroying the positions of his adversaries in this area, can be derived from the meager summary which Photius has left us.[54]

He denies that the concepts of *good*, of *evil*, and of the *indifferents* (preferables and the non-preferables) would enter into the domain of human understanding and knowledge. He criticizes, in addition, the validity of the conceptions proposed by the dogmatists relative to virtue. Finally, he systematically contests the possibility of understanding as the goal of man, happiness, pleasure, wisdom, or anything like it, opposing all philosophical schools. He upholds without any possibility of mediation the non-existence of a *telos* [goal].[55]

Actually, in a universe constituted by mobile and unstable appearances and in a vision of reality in which the *logos* is reduced to the *memory* of phenomena and what is in some way the object of thought according to which all things are revealed as anomalous and confused, there is no place in any way for a *telos*, since a goal would imply the opposite, that is, stability, harmony, and order.

The only goal for the preceding Skeptics as well[56] would be the *suspension of judgment* with the state of the soul called *imperturbability*, which is its consequence.[57]

Aristocles even says that according to Aenesidemus *aphasia* (the suspension of judgment) was followed by "pleasure."[58] If Aristocles is not incorrect,

Aenesidemus, as sometimes scholars have pointed out, understood the term 'pleasure' in a wide sense and essentially as a synonym of ataraxy.

In any case, that attitude of total separation from things, which involves the wise man in *ne sentire quidem* [*not to feel anything*] and which we have seen to be the distinguishing mark of the ethics of Pyrrho,[59] remains foreign to Aenesidemus; but probably it is an existential attitude acquired by the founder of Skepticism through his Eastern experiences and, as such, incapable of separation from those experiences.

II. Agrippa and The Developments
of Neo-Skepticism

1. The Skeptics after Aenesidemus

We have hardly any information about the history of Skepticism after Aenesidemus. We know a fair amount about Sextus Empiricus (through his principal works), who lived about two centuries after Aenesidemus.[1] Strangely, Sextus Empiricus, a real mine of information about almost all the thinkers of Greece prior to him as scholars have at times noted, is, on the contrary, stingy about information relative to the history of his sect after Aenesidemus, especially about the names of the scholarchs and its more important exponents.

Fortunately, Diogenes Laertius fills in part of this lacuna, furnishing us the list of the scholarchs (or at least a list of names of a series of persons linked by the relationship of master and student), although he is in no position to tell us very much about many of them. Aenesidemus taught Zeuxippus, a fellow-citizen of Cnossus; he in turn instructed Zeuxis "γώνιοπους" (crooked-foot), and there was a disciple of Zeuxis named Antiochus of Ascalon. The latter taught an empirical physician named Menodotus of Nicomedia and Theiodus of Laodicea. Menodotus was the teacher of Herodotus of Tarsus, of whom Sextus Empiricus was a pupil. The official list of the leading Skeptics ends with Saturninus, called Cythenas, a student of Sextus.[2] Beyond these names Diogenes records the name of Agrippa (and Apelles, who wrote a book dedicated to Agrippa),[3] who as we shall see, was the author of a new list of *tropes* of great value. Licinius Sura (about whom Pliny the Younger speaks)[4] is remembered among those who had a great sympathy for skeptical thought, as well as Favorinus (of whom Aulus Gellius was a student), who was more a polymath than a philosopher.[5]

We are able to deduce from the information given by Diogenes Laertius that the basic positions of Aenesidemus (the resolution of all reality into appearances or 'phenomena' and the establishment of the simple phenomenon as the criterion) were maintained without important variations up to the time of Antiochus of Laodicea. Let us read a passage of Diogenes Laertius which will be helpful in this respect:

> Aenesidemus too in the first book of his *Outlines of Pyrrhonism* says that Pyrrho determines nothing dogmatically, because of the possibility of contradiction, but guides himself by apparent facts. Aenesidemus says the same in his works *Against Wisdom* and *On Inquiry*. Furthermore Zeuxis, the friend of Aenesidemus in his work *On Two-sided Arguments*, Antiochus of Laodicea, and Apelles in his *Agrippa* all hold to phenomena alone. Therefore *the apparent is the Skeptic's criterion, as indeed Aenesidemus says*....Against this criterion of appearances the dogmatic philosophers urge that, when the same appearan-

ces produce in us different impressions, e.g., a round or square tower, the Skeptic, unless he gives the preference to one or the other, will be unable to take any course; if on the other hand, say they, he follows either view, he is then no longer allowing equal value to all apparent facts. The Skeptics reply that, when different impressions are produced, they must both be said to appear; *for things which are apparent are so called because they appear.*[6]

The connection of the Skeptics with the empirical tendency of medicine from Menodotus on down is always underlined by Diogenes Laertius.[7] This connection had probably been pointed out at a much earlier time. In fact as many scholars have indicated, some names of the persons belonging to the group of skeptical philosophers are likewise found in the list of representatives of the empirical trend in medicine, and it is probably not simply an accidental similarity in their names.[8] Moreover, it is beyond doubt that only with Menodotus did the alliance between Skepticism and empirical medicine become truly significant to the point of creating a new development in the history of Neo-Pyrrhonism. Agrippa, who as it would seem was the most important person in the span of time which goes from Aenesidemus to Sextus Empiricus, maintained, on the contrary, the same positions as Aenesidemus and carried to their extreme consequences some of the doctrines that he had made important, as we will see.

2. The new list of the *tropes* of Agrippa

Agrippa[9] was not satisfied with the list of the ten *tropes*, or grounds of doubt, put together by Aenesidemus. He took the opportunity to formulate a new group of them, not so much with the purpose of substituting them for those of Aenesidemus, but in order to give a greater variety of arguments with which to refute the arrogance of the Dogmatists. In reality, as we will immediately see, the new list more than enriches its predecessor; it subsumes it and clearly surpasses it. Here are five modes, or *tropes*, from the new list:[10]

[1] The first mode, or *trope*, concerns differences of opinions and shows how on any question both those raised by philosophers and those raised through ordinary living are so in contrast and confused as to impose suspension of judgment.

[2] The second mode, or *trope*, notes that if we want to resolve a question it is necessary to bring forth a proof; now no one proves something exhaustively: every proof requires further things proved and this itself requires further proof and so becomes a regress to infinity. Here is how Sextus Empiricus describes this mode, or *trope*:

> The mode based upon regress ad infinitum is that whereby we assert that the thing adduced as a proof of the matter proposed needs a further proof, and this again another, and so on *ad infinitum,* so that the consequence is suspension as we possess no starting-point for our argument.[11]

[3] This third mode, or *trope*, concerns relations and points out that each thing cannot be considered through itself, but only in relation both to the subject who judges (the judging subject) and to other things which are perceived together with it.

[4] The fourth mode, or *trope*, notes that the Dogmatists, in order to avoid the regress to infinity, assume their first principles without demonstrating them assuming thus that they are immediately creditable and this assumption is purely gratuitous. Sextus Empiricus writes:

> We have the mode based on hypothesis when the Dogmatists, being forced to recede ad infinitum, take as their starting-point something which they do not establish by argument but claim to assume as granted simply and without demonstration.[12]

Diogenes Laertius explains it further:

> The inconsistency of such premises is revealed by the fact that others will adopt the contrary hypothesis.[13]

[5] The fifth mode, or *trope*, concerns the so-called "circular reasoning" [*petitio principii* "*begging the question*"] which is verified when, in order to give a reason for something which is sought, the very reason is assumed that is adduced to explain it, or better, when the thing which is assumed as explaining [the explanans] and the thing which is to be explained [the explanandum] reciprocally require each other. Sextus writes:

> The mode of circular reasoning is the form used when the proof itself which ought to establish the matter of inquiry requires confirmation derived from that matter; in this case, being unable to assume either in order to establish the other, we suspend judgment about both.[14]

3. The meaning of the new list of the *tropes*

Notice that the first and the third modes, or *tropes*, summarize, as a matter of fact, the ten *tropes* of Aenesidemus (the third, in particular, on relations or better on relativity is the minimum common denominator of all the *tropes* of Aenesidemus, as we have previously noted above). The other three *tropes* carry us forward and are such that if appropriately utilized they make suspect not only the validity of impressions, but also the validity of every kind of reasoning and inquiry about both sensible and intelligible things.

Here, for example, is how Sextus explains the way in which all reasoning about the intelligible encounters the five grounds of doubt or *tropes*:

> For if it should be said that it is a matter of unsettled controversy [scil. into which those who admit the intelligible fall], the necessity of our suspending judgment will be granted. And if, on the other hand, the controversy admits of decision, then if the decision rests on an intelligible object we shall be driven to the regress *ad infinitum,* and to circular reasoning if it rests on a sensible; for since the sensible again is controverted and cannot be decided by means of itself because of the regress ad infinitum, it will require the

intelligible object, just as also the intelligible will require the sensible. For these reasons, again, he who assumes anything by hypothesis will be acting illogically. Moreover, objects of thought, or intelligibles, are relative; for they are so named on account of their relation to the person thinking, and if they had really possessed the nature they are said to possess, there would have been no controversy about them. Thus the intelligible also is referred to the five modes, so that in all cases we are compelled to suspend judgment concerning the object presented.[15]

In conclusion, the *tropes* of Agrippa take aim not only at impressions, but the very possibility of reasoning itself, imprisoning them, so to say, in a kind of deadly triangle. He who claims to explain something through reasoning (*a*) either is lost in a regress to infinity or (*b*) falls into a vicious circle (*c*) assumes merely hypothetical points of departure (that is, the indemonstrables).

The view of Brochard on the significance and value of these *tropes* is the best commentary: "The five *tropes* can be considered as the most radical and most precise formulas which have ever been given to skepticism. In a certain sense, even today they are irresistible. Whoever accepts the discussion about principles, whoever does not declare them superior to reasoning and known through an immediate intuition of the spirit, which is admitted only through an act of primitive faith, of which he is unable to give an account, and which has no need of justification, would not be in condition to escape this subtle dialectic. Again, the force by means of which the Dogmatism of every period loosens the grip of Skepticism has been foreseen by Agrippa: it is what he calls the hypothesis, the act of faith by means of which the principles are posited as true. He was only wrong in calling it arbitrary. He did not have to qualify it as arbitrary but rather as free. It is undoubtedly true that we are free to refuse adherence to primitive truth; this is what Agrippa saw clearly. But the correct adherence to them is also free. Now between those who reject this adherence and those who concede it the balance is not equal, as the Skeptic believes. Nature inclines us on the one side, the side of truth, and the fact that we can make no use of freedom or that we can abuse it proves nothing against the legitimate use which can be made of it. but if the use is made of one's freedom (and this is what dogmatism always does, what it must do) in this way it needs to be acknowledged that in a certain sense the Dogmatist gives reasons to the Skeptic. It is appropriate to say that reason cannot justify everything, that reduced to its own power it is impotent to produce all its warrants, at this point we have to search for the principle of truth and science."[16]

III. Sextus Empiricus and the Final Developments of Ancient Skepticism

1. A brief characterization of the tendencies of Greek medicine with particular regard to the empirical tendency

We have already pointed out above that the history of ancient skepticism in its final phase is characterized by a close alliance with empirical medicine. It is therefore necessary to determine the essential traits of this tendency of Greek medicine, and indeed, in order to grasp its distinctive characteristics, it is also necessary to indicate its other tendencies.[1]

The most ancient tendency of Greek medicine, and from a certain viewpoint perhaps the most important, is that of the "doctrinal" or "reasoning" physicians (λογικοί), which dates back even to the great Hippocrates of Cos. The common held conviction of doctrinal physicians was that it was possible *to discover the hidden causes* of the different pathological phenomena encountered in experience as well as the conviction that the essentials of the medical art (both in its cognitive aspects and its practical-therapeutic aspects) would consist precisely in the discovery of these causes. Hippocrates thought that the causes of an illness depended on some alteration of the constituents of the temperament of each man which, as is known, was determined, according to his theory, by a particular mixture (κρᾶσις) of the four fundamental humors (sanguine, phlegmatic, irascible, and melancholic). Other physicians held that the causes of illness should rather be sought for in the quality of the blood, or in certain movements of the blood. Still others (the so-called pneumatic physicians) pointed out, instead, that the causes of illness were in the poor circulation of a subtle fluid called *pneuma* which passed through the whole body.

A second tendency, constituted by the so-called "methodic" physicians, was founded by Themison of Laodicea (second half of the first century BCE) and continued by Thessalus of Tralles, a town of Lydia (end of first century CE), and by Soranus of Ephesus (second century CE). The thrust of the methodic physicians precisely modified the methodological position of the doctrinal physicians by challenging their etiological mentality. The methodic physicians maintained, in fact, that *it was not possible either to affirm or deny* anything whatever about the *hidden causes* of illnesses without, however, presuming to be able to establish that the said causes would be certainly inconceivable. They clung, therefore, to the phenomena and tried to draw from them what was of benefit to the sick person, following the judgment about the mere necessity of the affections. Sextus Empiricus, who had a great sympathy for this tendency (at least in his *Outlines of Pyrrhonism*) writes in this respect:

So then, just as the Skeptic, in virtue of the compulsion of the affections, is guided by thirst to drink and by hunger to food, and in like manner to other such objects, in the same way the methodical physician is guided by the pathological affections to the corresponding remedies—by contraction to dilation, as when one seeks refuge in heat from the contraction due to the application of cold, or by fluxion to the stoppage of it, as when persons in a hot bath, dripping with perspiration and in a relaxed condition, seek to put a stop to it and for this reason rush off into the cool air. It is plain, too, that conditions which are alien compel us to take measures for their removal, seeing that even the dog when it is pricked by a thorn proceeds to remove it.[2]

Sextus notes in addition that the methodic physicians, like the Skeptics, do not have "dogmas" and use words with "indifference," that is, without dogmatic presumptions. In this way, for example, they use the word "indication" (indicative sign) not in a dogmatic sense but in the sense of "guides" derived from the apparent affections according to or contrary to nature, as we have seen above.

The third tendency is that of the "empirical" physicians, who had some precursors in the third century BCE. Philinus of Cos, a pupil of Herophilus, is alleged to have been its founder, but Serapion of Alexandria is the actual founder. In the first century BCE Heraclides of Tarentum acquired a considerable reputation, chiefly through his book *On the Empirical Sect*. But the empirical tendency was very widespread in the Common Era between the first and second century, especially with Menodotus of Nicomedia, of whom we will immediately speak below.

This tendency agreed with the methodic physicians in their rejection of the etiological mentality, but went further to affirm even that the "causes" of illnesses are *inconceivable*. They also agreed with the methodic tendency in granting primary status in every thing to the phenomena and to experience; in fact, on this point they meant to be more radical; the empirical physicians must also take into account experiences about the circumstances and the individuality of the subject (the *idiosyncrasies*) without sacrificing in any way the particular to the general. As previously with Serapion and Apollonius Mys, who was a little later, the empirical physicians, as seems to be recoverable from the titles of their works (which are, respectively, *With Three Means* and *The Tripod*), developed their method in the following three stages:

(*a*) The physician, starting from the pathological case with which he is struggling, must proceed in the first place to *personal and direct observation* of the phenomena relative to it, both the antecedent, concomitant, and consequent phenomena (this was the so-called *autopsia* phase).

(*b*) The personal and direct observation (the *autopsia*) was followed by the *history*, that is, the discovery, collection, and critical analysis of the observations made *by other physicians*, especially in the past, and preserved in their writings. It is hardly necessary to point out that one of the tasks of critical analysis of these documents, and in fact the principal task, was that of discerning both the results of actual experience, and the results of reasoning as well as any improper reasoning.

(c) The third phase was constituted by the so-called "passage from like to like." It was a "passage" which was wholly diverse in nature from a causal inference because it was rigidly limited to the phenomena (it was in a fact a purely empirical process from one affection to another affection, from one part of an organism to another, from one treatment to another treatment). In order to distinguish this phase in the clearest possible way from the method of analogical reasoning used by the Dogmatics to reach the causes, the empirical physicians called it *epilogismus* (ἐπιλογισμός), in order to emphasize that it was a matter of reasoning or rational calculation which indeed went from the phenomenon to the phenomenon without in any way going beyond them. It was, therefore, the most discussed point of the method, insofar as it is true that extreme polemical statements were advanced against it. We know, in fact, that the Pyrrhonian Cassius maintained that this process of like to like was foreign to the empirical method and Menodotus not only did not consider it as a constitutive phase of the method itself, but did not even make use of it; on the contrary, Theoda of Laodicea (who, as we know, was a co-follower of Menodotus) considered this process indispensable unless one wished to debase medicine to a mere empirical knack.[3]

We have already pointed out the hypothesis advanced by scholars that the existence of relations between empirical medicine and Skepticism could be proven even prior to Menodotus by the fact that some names of empirical physicians correspond to the names of Skeptic philosophers or persons who were linked to them: Heraclides of Tarentum, for example, one of the most famous empirical physicians, could be that same Heraclides who, according to Diogenes Laertius, was the teacher of Aenesidemus; the physician Zeuxis could be Zeuxis (the follower of a follower of Aenesidemus) of whom, again, Diogenes speaks. It is generally certain, and we have stated this above, that only with Menodotus was there an attempt to systematically fuse empirical medicine with Skepticism and that with him alone, consequently, is a real development verified in the history of Skepticism.[4]

2. Menodotus between empirical medicine and Skepticism

Up to what point the attempt of Menodotus of Nicomedia was pushed is impossible to establish, given the sparseness of the testimony which is primarily about his philosophical thought. Probably medical interests and mentality prevailed in him and within the limits of medicine he would achieve, more than in that of philosophical speculation, his most significant contributions. The fact is worthy of note that the great Galen (who judged Menodotus very severely from a moral viewpoint) argued against him and mentioned him by name a few times.[5] Menodotus fought against the opponents of empirical medicine not only with firmness but even with animosity and acrimony. In order to demonstrate the vanity of the pretensions of the inquiry into the causes, he pushed beyond the proclamation of the necessity for the suspension of judgment (*epoché*), even on positions of negative dogmatism, by stating that the positions of his opponents were certainly false.[6]

We know that Menodotus did not maintain that Academic skepticism was reconcilable with Pyrrhonism and that hence it could re-enter into its history. The original Pyrrhonism was already dead with Timon and would rise up again only with Ptolemy of Cyrene (who was the teacher of the empirical physician Heraclides of Tarentum, of whom we have already spoken above), that is, in the first century BCE. Consequently, he rejected the notion that Plato could be considered a Skeptic, a notion that was maintained, to the contrary, by some Academics. In fact, Menodotus argues, if Plato accepted the Ideas, Providence, and Virtue, he was a Dogmatic; whether he granted them as probable and prefers them as such, again he is far from being a Skeptic, but does participate in the dogmatic attitude; and such conclusions do not change even if Plato expressed himself, on some issues, in a skeptical way.[7]

It is possible that from Menodotus there arose, as we have already seen, the distinction between *indicative signs* and *recalling signs* (and the following clarifications of the legitimacy of this latter), which was not yet present in Aenesidemus and his followers and which certainly presupposes the achievement of the empirical perspective (Sextus Empiricus, as we will see, considered it as a distinction already acquired). The recalled sign is, in fact, to speak in modern terms, a mere mnemonic association between two or more phenomena acquired through experience (that is, by having many times encountered in experience these phenomena as connected) which permits us, when presented with one of these phenomena (for example, the smoke), to "infer" the other, viz., the other phenomena (for example, the fire, its light, and heat).[8]

It is evident, nevertheless, that generally next to the negative moment belonging to Pyrrhonian Skepticism Menodotus placed the positive movement consisting of the need for experience and the use of the empirical method. It is precisely this positive connection to experience which characterized the novelty of the final phase of the Skepticism begun by Menodotus, but it came to maturity and full consciousness only with Sextus Empiricus.[9]

3.   The new plane on which Sextus Empiricus reformulated Skepticism
We have tried to show above that the original phenomenalism of Pyrrho (and in large measure also that of Aenesidemus) was a pure phenomenalism, viz., a form of phenomenalism which was not based on the dualistic presup-

position of the existence of a "thing-in-itself" but which entirely reduced the being and substance of things to phenomena. The reality of things, in short, was resolved into its appearances without remainder.[10]

On the contrary, the phenomenalism of Sextus is formulated in terms which are clearly *dualistic*; the *phenomenon* becomes the *impression* or the *sensible affection of the subject* and as such is *opposed to the object*, to the "external thing," to the thing which is other than the subject and which it presupposes as the cause of the sensible affection of the subject itself. It can thus be stated that, while the phenomenalism of Pyrrho and Aenesidemus, insofar as it resolved reality into its appearance, was a form of absolute phenomenalism and hence *metaphysical*, whereas the phenomenalism of Sextus Empiricus was a form of phenomenalism which was clearly empirical and *anti-metaphysical* (remember, that the phenomenalism of Pyrrho led expressly to the admission of a "nature of the divine and the good" which lives eternally and from which "derives to man the most equal and just life" and that the phenomenalism of Aenesidemus led likewise expressly to a Heraclitean vision of reality).[11] The phenomena as mere affections of the subject did not resolve into themselves all reality but left outside of themselves the "external object," which was declared if not unknowable in principle (an affirmation which would be a form of negative dogmatism), at the least, unknowable in fact.

But let us see some informative examples provided by the definition of Skepticism that Sextus provides in his *Outlines of Pyrrhonism*:

> Skepticism is an ability, or mental attitude, which opposes *appearances* to *judgments* in any way whatsoever, with the result that owing to the equipollence of the objects and reasons thus opposed we are brought firstly to a state of mental suspense and next to a state of "unperturbedness" or quietude.[12]

Sextus, then, analyses the terms immediately:

> By the word "phenomena" [τὰ φαινόμενα] we mean, now, the "objects of the senses" [τὰ αἰσθητά] and whence we contrast them with the "objects of thought" [τὰ νοητά, τὰ νοούμενα].[13]

In order to explain the numerous presuppositions which are involved in these affirmations and thus to comprehend the new position of Sextus, many clarifications must be made.

In the first place, our philosopher expressly formulated the equation existing between the *phenomenon* and the *sensory datum*. (We will see further, immediately below, in what way phenomenon and sensory datum, as we have previously noted, are reduced to nothing more than an *affection* of the subject.)

In the second place the "noumenon" of which he speaks here is not the "object external" to perception, the "thing-in-itself" of which we have spoken above, but it is the simple intellectual impression, considered as purely phenomenal. In fact, the "external object," as we will see better below, is opposed both to sensory perception and to intellectual cognition, which are considered by Sextus as being equally *subjective*.

In the third place, Sextus—in the play of the opposition of phenomena to phenomena, of intellectual perceptions to intellectual perceptions, and of these to those and vice-versa for the purpose of showing their equality of credibility and non-credibility and hence for the purpose of reaching "suspension of judgment"—does not at all treat the phenomena by the same standard as he does the "noumena" or intellectual perceptions. Moreover, he confers on the former a primarily positive value and on the latter a chiefly negative value, so also the other formulation of the principle of Skepticism, which is proposed a few lines from the first one, yields much more significant results:

> The main basic principle of the Skeptic system is that of opposing to every proposition [λòγos] an equal proposition; for we believe that as a consequence of this we end by ceasing to dogmatize.[14]

Actually, for Sextus a reasoning process can keep in check another reasoning process and a sensory datum (a phenomenon) can challenge a reasoning process, but not vice versa.

In the fourth place, as a consequence of the above-mentioned distinctions, Sextus admits that it is all right for the Skeptic *to assent to some things, to the impressions linked to sensory impressions*; it is a purely empirical assent and as such not dogmatic. Here are the words of our philosopher:

> When we say that the Skeptic refrains from dogmatizing we do not use the term "dogma," as some do, in the broader sense of "approval of a thing" *(for the Skeptic gives assent to the feelings which are the necessary results of sense-impressions*, and he would not, for example, say when feeling hot or cold "I believe that I am not hot or cold"); but we say that "he does not dogmatize" using "dogma" in the sense, which some give it, of "assent to one of the non-evident objects of scientific inquiry"; for the Pyrrhonian philosopher assents to nothing that is non-evident.[15]

And again:

> Those who say that "the Skeptics abolish appearances," or phenomena, seem to me to be unacquainted with the statements of our School. For, as we said above, *we do not overthrow the affective sense-impressions which induce our assent voluntarily; and these impressions are "the appearances"*.[16]

Moreover, Sextus expressly mentions that the skeptical formulas are employed for obscure things and not for phenomena.[17]

In the fifth place (and with this remark we return to the fundamental question from which we began our discussion), Sextus succeeds in attributing to "phenomenon" the new connotation *only to the detriment of the rigorousness and consistency of the skeptical argument*. In order to distinguish this new connotation he is forced to have recourse to a series of pre-suppositions which, without taking cognizance of the fact, he infers from the "dogmatic" mentality which is the point under contention and thus he "begs the question." Our philosopher writes:

> For as apparent things merely establish the fact that they appear, and are not capable also of showing that they really subsist.[18]

Now observe that this distinction between the *phenomenon* (τὸ φαινόμενον) and the existing object (τὸ ὑποκείμενον cannot be meaningful unless it presupposes the dogmatic distinction between *to appear* and *to be* which gives a precise meaning to the concept of an *object existing beyond the phenomenon* but which the Skeptic could not in any way construct, since he lacks all the conceptual tools necessary for task.

But Sextus also goes beyond this. In showing how one is the "impressed object" and the other the "object which is real," he writes:

> Furthermore, the presentation is an effect of the object presented, and the object presented is the *cause* of the presentation and is capable of impressing the sensitive faculty, and the *effect is different from the cause which produces it*. Hence, since the mind apprehends the presentations, it will be receiving the effects of the presented objects but not the external objects themselves. And should anyone argue from the feelings and affections it experiences that it apprehends the external object [τὰ ἐκτὸς], we shall adduce the difficulties previously stated.[19]

As is evident, he even presupposes the concept of *cause*, as well as the concept of causal inference, which Skeptics believe they have placed wholly outside of consideration.

In conclusion, we can say that the new plane on which Sextus Empiricus proceeds in reformulating Skepticism is precisely given by the new concept of the phenomenon understood as an *affection of a subject* in opposition to an *external object*, that is, in opposition to an object existing outside of the subject (beyond the phenomenon).

All the formulas and all the canonic principles of Skepticism come to be proposed again in this dualistic manner, now by playing on the subjective "impression," now on the "external object," now on both. In this way all the Skeptic principles are represented by Sextus not as "true in an absolute sense," but precisely only as *expressions of what the Skeptic feels*. Our philosopher writes:

> Besides this we must also remember that we [Skeptics] do not employ them [scil., the skeptical principles] universally about all things, but about those which are non-evident and are objects of dogmatic inquiry; and that we state *what appears to us* and do not make any positive declarations *as to the real nature of external objects*.[20]

Here again is what Sextus writes with respect to aphasia:

> *Non-assertion* (ἀφασία), then, is avoidance of assertion (φάσις) in the general sense in which it is said to include both affirmation and negation, so

that non-assertion is a mental condition of ours because of which we refuse either to affirm or to deny anything. Hence it is plain that we adopt non-assertion also not as though things are in reality of such a kind as wholly to induce non-assertion, but as indicating that we now, at the time of uttering it, are in this condition regarding the problems now before us. It must also be born in mind that what, as we say, we neither posit nor deny, is some one of the dogmatic statements made about what is non-apparent; for we yield to those things which move us emotionally and drive us compulsorily to assent.[21]

Analogously, the reinterpretation of the grounds of doubt, the modes, or *tropes*, of Aenesidemus is conducted according to this new vision, and the suspension of judgment becomes not the suspension of judgment in general, but the suspension of judgment *about the nature of external objects* (περὶ τῆς φύσεως τῶν ἐκτὸς ὑποκειμένων). And thus, stated in general, the problem for Sextus becomes this, whether the (subjective) *appearance* of the object corresponds to its (objective) *being*:

No one, perhaps, disputes that the underlying object has this or that appearance; the point in dispute is whether the object is in reality such as it appears to be.[22]

4. Life without dogma, or life without philosophy, according to Sextus

The fusion of the doctrines of Skepticism with empiricism involved also, within the domain of ethics, a notable departure from the original position of Pyrrhonism. Sextus, in fact, constructs a kind of *ethics of common sense*, very elementary and purposefully primitive. He writes:

Hence, not only do we not fight against living experience, but we even lend it our support by assenting undogmatically to what it relies on, while opposing the private inventions of the Dogmatists.[23]

And again:

For it is, I think, sufficient to conduct one's life empirically and undogmatically in accordance with the rules and beliefs that are commonly accepted, suspending judgment regarding the statements derived from dogmatic subtlety and furthest removed from the usage of life.[24]

To live according to common experience and according to custom (συνήθεια) is possible, according to Sextus, by conforming to these four elementary rules: (*a*) follow the dictates of nature, which through the senses and reason tell us what is useful; (*b*) follow the impulses of our impressions which push us, for example, to eat when we are hungry or to drink when we are thirsty; (*c*) respect the laws and customs of your own country and hence accept, from the practical viewpoint, the relative evaluation of piety as good and impiety as evil; (*d*) do not remain inactive, but exercise an art. Here is the most significant text:

Adhering, then, to appearances we live in accordance with the normal rules of life, undogmatically, seeing that we cannot remain wholly inactive. And it would seem that this regulation of life is fourfold, and that one part of it lies in the guidance of Nature, another in the constraint of the passions, another in the tradition of laws and customs, another in the instruction of the arts. Nature's guidance is that by which we are naturally capable of sensation and thought; constraint of the passions is that whereby hunger drives us to food and thirst to drink; tradition of customs and laws, that whereby we regard piety in the conduct of life as good, but impiety as evil; instruction of the arts, that whereby we are not inactive in such arts as we adopt. But we make all these statements undogmatically.[25]

Note, something that at first glance can be disconcerting, concerning the third point that Sextus, while he is pre-occupied with analyzing and refuting the demonstration of the existence of God offered by the Dogmatics, states that the Skeptics are not atheists:

Following the ordinary view, we affirm undogmatically that Gods exist and reverence Gods and ascribe to them foreknowledge.[26]

This re-evaluation of the *ordinary view* involves the abandonment of the ideal of absolute indifference and of imperturbability pursued by Pyrrho. The empirical Skeptic preaches not *apatheia* (ἀπάθεια) but *metriopatheia* (μετριοπαθεία), the moderation of the necessary affections. Also the Skeptics suffered hunger, cold, and other similar affections, but rejected the judgment of them as *objective evils*, evil by nature, and thus they limited the turbulence that derived from such affections. That the Skeptics can *ne sentire quidem* [*to be indifferent*, i.e. not to prefer either this or that] is an idea that, on the basis of his re-evaluation of experience, Sextus can no longer take into consideration.[27]

In addition, the evaluation of ordinary life involves as well a precise evaluation of the *useful*. The goal for which the arts are cultivated (to cultivate the arts, remember, is the fourth rule of the empirical ethic of Sextus) is stated in the notion "of use for living."[28]

Finally, the fact is worth noting that the achievement of imperturbability, that is, of *quietude* (ἀταραξία), presented by Sextus is almost like a casual consequence of the renunciation by the Skeptic of judging the truth, that is, it is a casual and unexpected consequence of the *suspension of judgment*. What befalls the Skeptic is something like what happened to the painter Apelles, who wanted to depict the foam on the mouth of a horse and, failing to do that, gave up and literally "threw in the sponge," viz., he threw a sponge with which he cleaned brushes against the painting and the sponge, struck the mouth of the house by chance, and left an imprint which looked like foam:

The man who determines nothing as to what is naturally good or bad neither shuns nor pursues anything eagerly; and, in consequence, he is unperturbed. The Skeptic, in fact, had the same experience which is said to have befallen the painter Apelles. Once, they say, when he was painting a horse and wished to represent in the painting the horse's foam, he was so unsuccessful that he gave up the attempt and flung at the picture the sponge on which he used to wipe the paints off his brush, and the mark of the sponge produced the effect of a horse's foam. So, too, the Skeptics were in hopes of gaining quietude by means of a decision regarding the disparity of the objects of sense and of thought, *and being unable to effect this they suspended judgment; and they found that quietude, as if by chance, followed upon their suspense, even as a shadow follows its substance.*[29]

5. The systematic critique by Sextus of all the sciences and philosophy

The most conspicuous part of the output of Sextus (at least of what is extant) is of a critical character. Concerning the *Outlines of Pyrrhonism*, only the first book has a "systematic" character while the other two develop an organic critique of dogmatic philosophy divided into three sections consolidated and codified in the Hellenistic Age. All eleven books which constitute the work commonly cited by the title *Adversus mathematicos*[30] are of a purely critical character: in the first six books he refutes the arts and sciences (grammar, rhetoric, geometry and arithmetic, astronomy, and music), while in the other five he refutes the logic, physics, and ethics of the Dogmatists.

It would be impossible to give an account of the critiques by Sextus in an exhaustive way, not only in a work of synthesis as is ours, but even in a monograph-length treatment, given that he, as has been correctly noted, succeeded in putting together a "skeptical encyclopedia of the philosophical sciences."[31] Nor can its complex arguments be reduced to a few principles, since the negative dialectic prevails which was in fashion among the Academics. It has recourse, frequently enough, to the facile trick of using the very weapons of the adversary against him and to a series of interminable *ad hominem* arguments. It gives, in addition, the impression that Sextus does not entirely intend to present us only with his personal contributions, for he proceeds to catalog all the contributions of his predecessors among which he placed his personal ones. Hence it unfolds with a content which can be considered the common patrimony of the Skeptic's sect.

Concerning the criticism of the arts (grammar, rhetoric, geometry, arithmetic, astronomy, and music), Sextus, as we have previously pointed out, wholly rejects the doctrinaire apparatus which constitutes them and the etiological mentality which is at their base. What the moral art properly understood must aim at is being of assistance in the conduct of life. The basis of the arts is not established by abstract reason, but by experience and by the systematic observation of phenomena. Consequently, of the traditional arts Sextus preserved them only as much as they are useful to accomplish the goal indicated and as much of them as can be justified on the basis of the empirical method.[32]

The refutation of the philosophers, rather more vigorous and penetrating, follows a detailed order in the division into three parts and likewise into a subdivision of these parts. It is an order taken from the dogmatic mentality itself. On the other hand, this is inevitable, since the skeptical refutation (ἀντίρρησις) is nothing except a hand-to-hand struggle against such a mentality, against what has resulted from it, and against the way in which it was produced. In essence, Sextus wanted to produce a series of reasons against the reasons produced by the Dogmatists on all the essential problems of philosophy. He did not do this simply in order to conclude that the Dogmatists are certainly wrong (since this would be nothing more than a reverse dogmatism which would propose again with the very same certainty what the Dogmatists had felt in being correct), but ultimately it was rather in giving "equal weight to arguments" which, in regard to the various philosophical questions, exclude each other, and hence which does not terminate in a negative judgment but in the *suspension of judgment*. It is to be understood that Sextus located in this "refutation of the Dogmatists" his greatest task.

A rough outline of the approach followed by our philosopher follows.

In the sphere of logic to the corresponding reasons of the Dogmatists, he opposes arguments intended to demonstrate with equal force what follows: (*a*) there exists no criterion for truth; (*b*) even granted that it existed, it would be ineffective because truth does not exist; (*c*) not only is it not possible to affirm anything about things which (to the Dogmatists) appear evident lacking a *criterion*, but it is not even possible, for stronger reasons, to go from evident things to those not evident, that is, from phenomena to their presumed source and to the presumed cause, and hence (*a*) referential signs do not exist, that may bring to light hidden causes, (but only recalled signs) and (*b*) demonstrations do not exist, that is, the discovery by reasoning of non-manifest conclusions. Sextus criticizes consequently the deductive syllogism, as well as inductive reasoning and the definition itself.

In the domain of physics, Sextus particularly subjects to his *antirrhesis* the reasoning of the Dogmatists concerning deity, the causes and the principles, whole and part, body and non-body, the various forms of change, place, time, and number.

In the area of ethics, finally, Sextus concentrated on three points: he criticizes the dogmatic conception of good and evil, he criticizes the claim that there exists an art of living, and he criticizes the claim that such an art, if it existed, could be taught.

In this tournament of reasons against reasons Sextus showed himself rather scrupulous and often accurately presented the doctrines of his adversaries which he then refuted, and thus he showed himself to be well-informed on large sectors of the vast sweep of ancient thought prior to him (from this viewpoint his work remains a real mine of information for the reconstruction of the thought of those authors whose works are no longer extant). The shape of the problems and the angle from which they are seen, as we said above, are those which are proper to the Hellenistic Age, in particular to the Stoics (it is significant, for example, that in the two books directed against the logicians Sextus shows an ignorance of the logic of Aristotle and in particular the syllogistic of the *Analytics*, and argued chiefly against Stoic logic; but there are many examples of this kind which could be shown also in the books against the Physicists and the Ethicians; Sextus does not seem to have benefited from the rebirth of Platonism or Aristotelianism which in his century, as we saw, had already begun to flourish).[33]

In the field of dialectic in which he constructed his arguments in opposition to those of the Dogmatics, the reasoning process is of the same nature as the way current among Academics, and that hence it reveals its Stoic origins. The arguments are in general pregnant, relevant, and also of diverse effectiveness, some capricious and sophistic, when they are not simply boring. But Sextus is in part aware of it because he states at the end of his *Outlines of Pyrrhonism* that the weight and character of his arguments are proportioned to the arrogance of the discourse of the Dogmatists he intends to refute.[34]

Finally, Sextus sometimes appealed positively to experience and to the evidence of the facts against the claims of theory, but not in any systematic way. And thus certain anticipations of ideas which were much later developed by Locke, Hume, and J. S. Mill and which scholars have at times pointed out remain in Sextus little more than isolated intuitions.[35]

Sextus, contrary to what has been maintained by many French scholars,[36]

does not anticipate modern positivism (just as empirical medicine does not anticipate the inductive method which belongs to modern science), *because he did not in any way come up with a new logic*.[37] And he did not construct a new logic for two necessary reasons. He was too distrustful of the constructive aspect of thought, which is indispensable for the uncovering of laws and the bonds which link phenomena, and he had too little trust in the possibility of the experience of things allowing for truth. For Sextus reason serves almost entirely as a weapon against dogmatic arguments and is used almost solely as a tactic for survival, that is, for a practical aim.[38]

The position of Sextus can best be summarized in this paragraph from a modern scholar of Skepticism who shares the position of Skepticism himself: "Life only is worth pursuing, and philosophy primarily consists in ridding oneself of dogmatic philosophies which speculate about uncertainties; and which describes as the Democriteans would, measures as the Platonists would, or imagines as the Stoics would, the so-called truths about the invisible."[39]

IV. The Exhaustion of Skepticism

The ancients preserved only one name of a Skeptic philosopher after Sextus, that₁of Saturninus, a student of Sextus himself, who also was an "empirical." We know nothing more of him and hence it can be argued that he did not depart from the positions of his teacher. Otherwise with Sextus Empiricus Skepticism achieved its unsurpassable Column of Heracles and, in fact, celebrated together both its own victory as well as its own destruction. Sextus himself shows some glimmer of recognition of this fact. In regard to the canonic formula of Skepticism, he writes in the *Outlines of Pyrrhonism*:

> For, in regard to all the Skeptic expressions, we must grasp first the fact that we make no positive assertion respecting their absolute truth, since we say that *they may possibly be confuted by themselves*, seeing that they themselves are included in the things to which their doubt applies, just as purgative drugs do not merely eliminate the humors from the body, but also expel themselves along with the humors.[2]

And in the greater work, in regard to the objection that the Skeptic demonstration intended to demonstrate the non-existence of demonstration also destroys itself, Sextus writes:

> So also when we say that no proof exists we imply in our statement the exception of the argument which proves that proof does not exist; for this alone is proof. And even if it does banish itself, the existence of proof is not thereby confirmed. For there are many things which produce the same effect on themselves as they produce on other things. Just as, for example, fire after consuming the fuel destroys also itself, and like purgatives after driving the fluids out of the bodies expel themselves as well, so too the argument against proof, after abolishing every proof, can cancel itself also![3]

These examples are marvelous, and in our view express as well as it is possible to express one of the historical functions which ancient Skepticism fulfilled, in fact perhaps even its principal one, that is, a cathartic or liberating function. Ancient Skepticism actually did not destroy ancient philosophy, which survived and lived again a stretch of glorious history after it, but it did destroy a *certain philosophy* or better a *certain dogmatic mentality* bound to this philosophy. *It destroyed that dogmatic mentality which was created by the great Hellenistic systems, especially by the Stoic system.* And the fact that Skepticism in its various forms was born, developed, and died in synchrony with the birth, development, and death of the great Hellenistic systems is very instructive. It is also indicative that the above mentioned mentality did not survive Sextus. After Sextus, philosophy embarked on a journey toward other shores.

Sextus, naturally, could not foresee any of this. An Italian scholar has recently commented, "Sextus is far from suspecting that almost contemporaneously with him and in the same city of Alexandria frequented by him there was outlined that teaching of Ammonius Saccas, which was destined to move ancient thought toward a different goal from that of Skepticism. He does not foresee that a new dogmatic construct began to be constructed on the base of those same Doric columns which had been shaken by him, although they did not tumble down. And if the authentic historian, by using all the developments and the perspectives of the past, is in a certain sense also able to foresee this, we must unfortunately admit that Sextus did not succeed in foreseeing anything, because from the past he had not taken anything other than the wreck of all of philosophical civilization. His historical-critical analysis, in fact, is carried out in such a way as to come close to the absurd and almost exhausted polemic of *Philosophies for Sale* without protracting it to infinity with damage to all contenders. According to Sextus, the history of Greek philosophy, examined with the rigor of a well-ordered logic, must end in a peaceful and resigned recognition of all the errors of the Dogmatics. And to this end, although he furnished it with an abundance of vigorous argument, he did not intend to reserve for himself the last word, since he did not produce any better sequel because he had already rejected every possible sequel out of hand whether good or bad."[4]

If this is true, it is likewise true that Sextus *could foresee nothing* for the reasons given above, that is, because (as his Skeptic predecessors) *he did not go beyond that mentality created by Hellenism, and supported as he was by the dialectical method, he could destroy that mentality only by destroying himself with the same stroke.*

Moreover, an eloquent confirmation of what we have said is to be found in the fact that the new philosophical currents of which we will speak have a strong religious inspiration with points of authentic mysticism, and they not only do not fear Skepticism, insofar as they appeal to forms and modes of knowledge different from those which Skepticism had criticized, but in certain cases they confidently accept some results of Skepticism precisely in order to open new perspectives.[5]

Fifth Section

THE REBIRTH OF CYNICISM

« ... ἀνθρώπου μὲν εἶναι τὸ ἁμαρτάνειν,
θεοῦ δὲ ἢ ἀνδρὸς ἰσοθέου τὰ πταισθέντα
ἐπανορθοῦν. »

"... It is human, he thought, to err, but
divine (whether in God or man) to put the
error to right."

Demonax, quoted by Lucian,
Life of Demonax 7

I. The Revival of Cynicism in the Imperial Age and its Characteristics

We have said, in the preceding volume,[1] that Cynicism had already reached its apex at the beginning of the Hellenistic Age and that it had used up, so to speak, all its possibilities and resources. In fact, immediately after Diogenes and Crates Cynicism lost most of its original strength, showing a tendency to compromise and hence manifesting a decline which in some of its exponents terminates in almost a total loss of awareness of its own identity, so much so that towards the end of the Pagan Era almost nothing further is stated about the Cynics.[2] The vitality of Cynicism is not, however, totally exhausted. In fact, it re-awakens in the Imperial Age (the first Cynic who is known by name, Demetrius, probably lived towards the middle of the first century CE) and it continued to live or survive up to the end of the sixth century CE, that is, for about half a millennium.

A question spontaneously arises in relation to this surprising phenomenon: did this revival of Cynicism in the Imperial Age examine the ideas of ancient Cynicism and achieve new perspectives or was it only a restatement, more or less sterile and dry, of what had previously been acquired and thus a mere "repetition"?

In order to respond to such a question it is necessary to refer to the three components which distinguish this very special philosophy and which also indicate three precise directions according to which it acts in the spiritual life of the ancient world. These components are (*a*) "the Cynic life," (*b*) "the Cynic doctrine," (*c*) "the mode of expression," or "the literary form," belonging to the works of the Cynics.

Let us take up the last point above (*c*) first. In this respect Cynicism had given its best in the first centuries of the Hellenistic Age.[3] In particular, the "diatribe" had become an authentic "literary genre," widely diffused and almost irreplaceable. Deprived at the time of the sarcasm and the caustic pungency belonging to the original Cynicism, the "diatribe" was adopted by many philosophers of the Imperial Age, not only by the Stoics, who in certain respects were close to Cynicism (remember the *Diatribe* of Epictetus), but even by thinkers with no connection to Cynicism, for example, Philo of Alexandria and even Plotinus (certain passages of the Philonian works as well as some chapters of the *Enneads* undoubtedly have the form of a diatribe). Consequently, this "literary genre" created by Cynicism became autonomous and hence was no longer an exclusive vehicle for Cynic teaching.

The second point (*b*) concerns the authentic "Cynic doctrine," namely that the revived Cynicism could not achieve significant novelty for structural reasons already noted in our previous volume.[4] In fact previously with

Diogenes the Cynic the doctrine achieved the extreme limits of its radicalization, that is, its unsurpassable "Columns of Heracles." Therefore there are only two remaining possibilities: (1) either a re-proposal of Cynicism, which takes up the demands of a contemporary doctrine (in particular, Stoicism, which in the Imperial Age, as we have seen, on account of its tendencies already gravitated more than in the preceding age to the Cynic position, especially in some adherents) and in some way shows itself susceptible to the religious and mystical demands belonging to the new age, (2) or the possibility of re-proposing, although with some limitations, the radicalism of original Cynicism by giving value in various ways especially to the libertarian position. In effect, the Cynics of the Imperial Age who are known to us clearly have followed either one of these two ways, but without knowing how to reach results of significant import, as we will see.

Finally (*a*), the "Cynic life" in the Imperial Age for a long time was a real and very strong attraction and stimuli. (*a*) *It was, hence, the practical aspect of Cynicism which had real impact in the epoch under consideration.* It explains, hence, rather well the fact that Antisthenes, founder of Cynicism, little by little was put in the shade and finally eclipsed by Diogenes and Crates; in fact, Antisthenes did not live, except partially, a full "Cynic life," which instead was created and lived in an exemplary way by Diogenes and Crates. The *Letters*, a *pseudepigrapha* falsely attributed to the ancient Cynics, and which are forgeries (produced at the beginning of the first century of the Common Era) have the purpose of raising once again and defending Cynic teaching and attracting adherents to it. The Letters are almost wholly attributed to Diogenes and Crates (fifty-one are attributed to Diogenes and thirty-six to Crates) while only one among those extant is jointly attributed to Antisthenes and to Menippus. But in this regard if the re-proposal of the paradigm of the "Cynic life" found some chosen followers who agreed with its sincere intent, it found likewise numerous dilettantes who misrepresented its significance and who contributed progressively to discrediting it and hence frustrating it, as we will see.

II. The Stoicizing and Religious Currents of Cynicism in the Imperial Age

1. Demetrius

Demetrius, who as we have already mentioned is the first name of a Cynic of the Imperial Age of whom we have additional information, was a contemporary of Seneca[1] and was admired and greatly revered by him. Here are some eloquent passages taken from the *De beneficiis*, the *Letters*, and the *De providentia*:

> Demetrius the Cynic [is] a philosopher of great importance, to my mind, even compared to the greatest.[2]

> But a little while ago I reminded you of Demetrius,...a man of consummate wisdom, though he himself disclaimed it, of steadfast firmness in all his purposes, of an eloquence fitted to deal with the mightiest subjects, not given to graces, nor finical about words, but proceeding to its theme with great spirit, as impulse inspired it. I doubt not that this man was endowed by divine providence with such a life, with such power of speech in order that our age might not lack either a model or a reproach.[3]

> Demetrius, for instance, the best of men, I take about with me, and leaving the wearers of purple and fine linen, I talk with him, half-naked as he is, and hold him in high esteem. Why should I not hold him in high esteem? I have found that he lacks nothing. It is in the power of any man to despise all things, but of no man to possess all things. The shortest cut to riches is to despise riches. Our friend Demetrius, however, lives not merely as if he has learned to despise all things, but as if he has handed them over for others to possess.[4]

Demetrius maintained the necessity of reducing philosophy to an awareness of a few precepts and to their rigorous application. There are, he said, many interesting knowledges and the acquisition of them is very agreeable, but only a few are essential and these few are easy to grasp, since nature has providently brought everyone to them. And here is what these essential rules are:

> The soul that can scorn all the accidents of fortune, that can rise superior to fears, that does not freely covet boundless wealth, but has learned to seek its riches from itself; the soul that can cast out all dread of men and gods, and knows that it has not much to fear from man and nothing from God; that despising all those things which, while they enrich, harass life, can rise to the height of seeing that death is not the source of any evil, but the end of many; the soul that can dedicate itself to virtue, and think that every path to which she calls is smooth; that, social creature that it is and born for the common good, views the world as the universal home of mankind, that can bare its conscience to the gods, and respecting itself more than all others, always live as if in the sight of men—such a soul, remote from storms, stands on the solid ground beneath a blue sky,

and has attained to perfect knowledge of what is useful and essential. All other matters are but the diversions of a leisure hour; for when the soul has once found this safe retreat, it may also make excursions into things that bring polish, not strength, to its powers.[5]

In this context, *ponos* (πόνος), or labor, and *askesis* (ἄσκησις), or discipline, regain all their ancient meaning, viz., the tempering of the soul which makes it capable of confronting all the adversities of life. An existence which never has the conflicts of destiny and is never provoked by adversities for Demetrius is a "dead sea,"[6] hence human beings who have never been struck by adversity, far from being happy, as the many believe, are in reality unhappy. Seneca writes this aphorism:

No one seem to me more unhappy than a human being to whom no adversities have occurred.[7]

Finally, the Cynicism of Demetrius is colored by a considerable religious sentiment close to what had inspired the Stoic Cleanthes. It is again Seneca who reports the most important testimony in this respect:

Here is another spirited utterance which, I remember, I heard that most valiant man, Demetrius, make: "Immortal gods," he said, "I have this one complaint to make against you, that you did not earlier make known your will to me; for I should have reached the sooner that condition in which, after being summoned, I now am. Do you wish to take my children?—it was for you that I fathered them. Do you wish to take some member of my body?—take it; no great thing am I offering you; very soon I shall leave the whole. Do you wish to take my life?—why not? I shall make no protest against your taking back what once you gave. With my free consent you shall have whatever you may ask of me. What, then, is my trouble? I should have preferred to offer than relinquish. What was the need to take by force? You might have had it as a free gift. Yet even now you will not take it by force, because nothing can be wrenched away from a man unless he withholds it.[8]

This is a conception which expresses a particular attitude toward life which also reappears in Roman Neo-Stoicism, that is, in Seneca himself and especially in Epictetus, as we have seen above.

2.   Dio Cocceianus (Chrysostomos)

It is the tenet of Demetrius that only adversity reveals the true moral character of a human being and that one is to be considered unhappy who is not tried by and steeped in misfortune. This doctrine has an outstanding confirmation in the vicissitudes of the life of Dio Chrysostomos.

Born of a wealthy family of high social standing in the city of Prusa in Bithynia,[9] Dio was trained at first in literary studies and started out as a rhetorician in Rome (as a "sophist," to use the terminology current in that epoch), and he even wrote a work against philosophers in general and one against Musonius in particular. In Rome he was on familiar terms with men of high rank and, by reason of the close bond of friendship which he had with

Titus Flavius Sabinus (for a short time co-consul with Domitian), Dio was condemned to exile, because he was one of those suspected of plotting against the Emperor Domitian.

Banished from Bithynia and from Italy, forced to wander in inhospitable countries and to earn a living with the lowliest of work, although deprived of all that he had acquired, he passed his life cheerfully; he was able to discover his ultimate vocation because of the demands of these adverse circumstances and thus he became a "philosopher." He discovered anew in this way the soundness of Cynic philosophy, which claimed that in being deprived of everything and in leading the life of "primitives," contrary to common opinion, lay the most authentic good.[10]

Here is how Dio himself, in a highly informative passage, describes his own conversion to Cynic philosophy:

> And the men whom I met [scil., in my wanderings from place to place] on catching sight of me, would sometimes call me a tramp and sometimes a beggar, though some did call me a philosopher. From this it came about gradually and without any planning or any self-conceit on my part that I acquired this name. Now the great majority of those styled philosophers proclaim themselves such, just as the Olympian heralds proclaim the victors; but in my case, when the other folk applied this name to me, I was not able always and in all instances to have the matter out with them. And very likely, as it turned out, I did profit somewhat by the general report about me. For many would approach me and ask what was my opinion about good and evil. As a result, I was forced to think about these matters that I might be able to answer my questioners. Furthermore, they would invite me to come before the public and speak. Consequently it became necessary for me to speak also about the duties of man and about the things that were likely, in my opinion to profit him. And the opinion I had was that pretty well all men are fools, and that no one does any of the things he should do, or considers how to rid himself of the evils that beset him and of his great ignorance and confusion of mind, so as to live a more virtuous and a better life; but that they all are being thrown into confusion and are swept round and round in the same place and about practically the same objects, to wit, money and reputation and certain pleasures of the body, while no one is able to rid himself of these and set his own soul free; just as, I fancy, things that get into a whirlpool are tossed and rolled without being able to free themselves from it.[11]

The writings of Dio dating back to this period of exile repeat the chief cornerstones of Cynic doctrine without much originality, if not without politeness and vigor, and the figure of Diogenes predominates uncontestedly in them. These writings exalt in a particular way the liberating power of the teaching of Diogenes. They state the soundness of the Cynic list of values by redefining certain aspects of Cynic shamelessness (ἀναίδεια) and markedly emphasize the importance of the struggle against pleasure.[12]

Here is an important passage of the *Discourse on Virtue*:

> And when a certain man asked whether he too came to see the contest, he
> said, "No, but to take part." Then when the man laughed and asked him
> who his competitors were, he said with that customary glance of his: "The
> toughest there are and the hardest to beat, men whom no Greek can look
> straight in the eye; not competitors, however, who sprint or wrestle or jump,
> not those that box, throw the spear, and hurl the discus, but those that
> chasten a man." "Who are they, pray?" asked the other. "Hardships," he
> replied, "very severe and insuperable for gluttonous and folly-stricken men
> who feast the livelong day and snore at night, but which yield to thin, spare
> men, whose waists are more pinched in than those of wasps. Or do you think
> those potbellies are good for anything?—creatures whom sensible people
> ought to lead around, subject to the ceremony of purification, and then
> thrust beyond the borders, or, rather, kill, quarter, and use as food, just as
> people do with the flesh of large fish, don't you know, boiling it in brine and
> melting out the fat, the way our people at home in Pontus do with the lard
> of pigs when they want to anoint themselves. For I think these men have
> less soul than hogs. But the noble man holds his hardships to be his greatest
> antagonists, and with them he is even wont to battle day and night, not to
> obtain a stalk of celery, like goats, nor an olive or pine-needle circlet [the
> victors of the Olympian and Isthmian Games were crowned with them], but
> to win happiness and virtue throughout all the days of his life... [13]

These adversaries, Dio tells us, must be attacked with extreme decisive-
ness, that is, as must be done in dealing with fire which if attacked without
hesitation can be extinguished; if not it will get a secure upperhand. [14]

But a much worse adversary for Dio as well as for the ancient Cynics is
pleasure, which does not use force but is sly and seduces us with ruinous
attractions, as did the enchantress Circe, of whom Homer speaks, who attracted in this way the companions of Ulysses and then transformed them into
pigs and savage animals. Pleasure threatens in every possible way, even during
sleep, by means of insidious dreams. In order to defend against pleasure it is
necessary to be as distant as possible from it and to have dealings with it only
out of strict necessity. Therefore Dio concludes:

> And herein the strongest man is indeed strongest, one might almost say,
> who can keep the farthest away from pleasures; for it is impossible to dwell
> with pleasure or even to dally with her for any length of time without being
> completely enslaved. Hence when she gets the mastery and overpowers the
> soul by her charms, the rest of Circe's sorcery at once follows. [15]

At the death of Domitian, Dio returned to Rome, and with the end of his
exile his "Cynic life" was also terminated; his philosophical vision itself
widened, taking up Stoic concepts and even some Platonic suggestions for
living.

The speech which has the title *Euboic* shows strong Cynic influences, in it
the story is told of a family of hunters who, far from the city, live close to nature,

serenely, satisfying only the most elementary and essential needs, without desiring superfluities and without vain ambitions; they achieved unknowingly, in this way, the ideal life. Dio had no doubt that to live in poverty and not in the midst of riches represents "life in conformity with nature (κατὰ φύσιν)."[16]

On the basis of this conception of a clearly moral character he proposed the solution of the social problem of the poverty of the lower classes which in the great cities had become more and more serious. It would be necessary for those he defines as the "respectable poor," that is, the poor who live an honest life, to leave the cities and live in the countryside, and there they would be taught to gain their livelihood in a more natural way.[17] It is clear that Dio intended to present this program not only with a theoretic aim but as his concrete solution to the grave social problems of the historical times in which he lived.

Another group of his writings of a political character composed in a period after his exile again reflect Cynic ideas, but they are contained in the widest Stoic perspective of the universal kingdom of which Zeus is the king.[18] The ideal governor is, for Dio, the monarch, and the ideal king is the best of men, that is, a virtuous man. Let us read the *Fourth Oration*, where the protagonists are Diogenes (the spokesman for Dio) and Alexander (who probably represents, in some way, the Emperor Trajan, around whom the discourse revolves):

> Hereupon he [Alexander] put the following question to Diogenes.
>
> –'How," said he, "could one be the best king?"
>
> –At this the other, eyeing him sternly, answered, "But no one can be a bad king any more than he can be a bad good man; *for the king is the best one among men, since he is most brave and righteous and humane, and cannot be overcome by any toil or by any appetite*".[19]

The king must be a "shepherd of the people," according to the famous saying of Homer,[20] and he must be the imitator of the most great of all kings, of the king who governs the whole universe, Zeus. Let us read, for example, in the *First Oration*:

> So too among kings, since they, I see, derive their powers and their stewardship from Zeus, the one who, keeping his eyes upon Zeus, orders and governs his people with justice and equity in accordance with the laws and ordinances of Zeus, enjoys a happy lot and a fortunate end.[21]

And a little further on, Dio says:

> It was my purpose, after finishing the description of the good king, to discuss next that supreme king and ruler whom mortals and those who administer the affairs of mortals must always imitate in discharging their responsibilities, directing and conforming (ἀφομοιοῦντας) their ways as far as possible to his pattern.[22]

Other works, on the contrary, bend decisively towards the teaching of the Stoa, for example, the *Thirty-Sixth Oration*, which contains a truly Stoic cosmology, and the *Twelfth Oration* (called the *Olympic*), which shows that the idea of God is inborn in all existing human beings, both Greeks and barbarians.

Also in Dio, as in concurrent Neo-Stoicism, the idea of kinship (συγγένεια) and of the natural bonds which unite men to the Gods, and hence the idea of the brotherhood of all men, is present.[23] And as in the parallel movement of Middle Platonism, so in Dio, there is not only the idea previously mentioned above, which is that men must imitate the Gods and become like them,[24] but even the teaching that the daimon of man is his Nous, or his Mind (note: not the simple ψυχή, but νοῦς!):

> Showing that the good and the bad spirits that bring happiness and misery are not outside the man, and that each one's intelligence (ὁ δὲ ἴδιος ἑκάστου νοῦς)—this and nothing more—is the guiding spirit of its owner, that the wise and good man's spirit is good, the evil man's evil, and likewise the free man's is free, the slave's slavish, the kingly and high-minded man's kingly, the abject and base man's abject.[25]

III. The Current of Cynicism of the Imperial Age Inspired by Contentious Ancient Radicalism

1. Oenomaus of Gadara

The radical and contentious component of ancient Cynicism (which found its most typical expression in *shamelessness* (ἀναίδεια) and in the notion of untrammeled *freedom of speech*, (παρρησία) as we have seen) returned in Oenomaus.[1] In his writings he probably treated the entire span of the Cynic thematic, but there has come down to us detailed information and ample extracts of only one work, that has the title of *The Charlatans Exposed* [Γοήτων φώρα = Κατὰ χρηστηρίων].[2] In this work, Oenomaus mounts a full-scale attack against oracles and against the possibility of prophecy and divination. He examines in an analytic way the most well-known prophecies of the Oracle at Delphi, shows their inconsistency and capriciousness, and adduces some philosophical reasons against the possibility of the prophecies themselves.

The philosophical analyses (the only ones, in this respect, which are of interest to us) were not based on a general rejection of the existence of divinity and demons. In fact, Oenomaus, as in general the Cynics, was not an atheist. He maintained, nevertheless, that God is not concerned with human affairs and that hence there would be nothing daimoniacal or divine in the so-called prophecies but only examples of human cheating. The analysis, in a word, appealed to the contradictions existing between affirmations of the existence of Fate or of Necessity which governs everything, on the one hand, and the admission of human liberty, on the other. Divination shows its absurdity in the measure in which it appeals at the same time to both these presuppositions which are mutually exclusive. Our philosopher writes:

> It is wholly ridiculous to be able at the same time to say that something depends on a human being and that nevertheless it is dominated by Destiny.[3]

This contradiction renders absurd the credibility of oracles (and divination in general) in every sense of the term. In the first place, it makes absurd the supposed liberty of the prophet Apollo, because if everything were necessary, Apollo at Delphi could not remain silent, not even if he wished it, and in every moment he, far from being able to do his own will, must be doing what Necessity has ordered.[4] In the second place, supposing also that oracles were possible, they would have no meaning, in the measure in which they commanded anything, since by admitting Necessity, nothing would remain within the power of human beings.

In this vivid argument it can be surmised that Oenomaus must be chiefly attacking the Stoics, who with their teaching on Fate have precisely claimed to give a philosophical basis for divination.[5]

The Stoics, according to Oenomaus, were not consistent; in fact, they affirm that man can be virtuous. In addition they are securely persuaded at the same time that human beings can be such *not by contravening their will*, but only through *spontaneous deliberation*. Consequently, if this is so, there is no one, "God or Sophist that he may be," that can dare affirm that this spontaneous deliberation depends on Necessity, by reason of the evident contradiction; and if this is so, their fatalism cannot be sustained. And with a rattling of the Cynic sword of untrammeled *freedom of speech*, (παρρησία) Oenomaus concludes:

> And if he dares to affirm it [scil., that what is deliberately chosen also depends on Necessity]. We will not formulate more arguments against him, but we will take a very hard scourge akin to that which teachers use to reproach unruly pupils and will break their legs.[6]

2. Demonax of Cyprus

Demonax[7] was also an exponent of the radical current of Cynicism, and he was a contemporary of Oenomaus. His teachers were Epictetus, Timocrates of Heraclea, Agathobulus, and Demetrius. Actually, Demonax ameliorated in some points certain excesses of Cynicism: "he did not misrepresent his habits and his manner in order to be admired," Lucian says,[8] that is, in order to attract, by being ostentatious, the attention of the people, and especially he did not indulge in the extreme gestures typical of Cynic *shamelessness* (ἀναίδεια). On the other hand, he expressly confessed that he not only admired Diogenes, but respected Socrates and loved Aristippus.[9] He also studied the thought of other philosophers, and not superficially, which was not common among the Cynics.[10] From Cynicism comes, in the first place, his great love of liberty and speaking freely (παρρησία) and the notion that happiness consists in liberty.

Here are some important testimonies from Lucian:

> Demonax...despised all human goods, he did not wish anything other than to be free and to speak freely...[11]
> Asked for a definition of happiness, he said that only the free were happy.
> –'Well," said the questioner, "there is no lack of free men."
> –'I count no one free who is subject to hopes and fears."
> –"Your ask impossibilities; of these two we are all very much the slaves."
> –"Once you grasp the nature of human affairs," said Demonax, "you will find that they justify neither hope nor fear, since both pain and pleasure are to have an end."[12]

Also, his attitudes toward popular religion, the Mysteries, the beliefs about the soul and its fate in the hereafter, were in full agreement with Cynic radicalism, and because of this he was accused and indicted on the basis of a formal accusation that he had never been seen sacrificing to the Gods and had never been initiated into the Eleusian mysteries. (He defended himself brilliantly against the accusation by maintaining in the first place that the Gods had no need of the sacrifices made by humans, and with respect to the mysteries he maintained that he could not in any way respect them and not speak of them to the non-initiates; thus, if they were evil, he would have revealed it in order to dissuade the non-initiates from evil things, and if they were good things, he would have to speak to everyone about them because of his love for all humanity.)[13]

Concerning his opinions about the immortality of the soul and its fate, here is what Lucian says:

> He was once asked if the soul is immortal. He replied that, 'It was immortal like everything else.'[14]

> Some one asked him what he took the next world to be like. "Wait a bit, and I will send you the information."[15]

Also, the cult of discipline and work was important for him and he praised *self-sufficiency* (αὐτάρχεια).[16]

Demonax upheld, in addition, the philanthropic component of Cynicism, which Crates especially had been known to esteem. Lucian wrote in this regard:

> He was never known to shout or be over vehement or angry, even when he had to correct; he touched offenses, but pardoned offenders, saying that the doctors' was the right model, who treat sickness but are not angry with the sick. It is human, he thought, to err, but divine (whether in God or man) to put the error right.[17]

And again:

> He was fond of playing peace-maker between brothers at variance, or presiding over the restoration of marital harmony. He could say a word in season, too, before an agitated political assembly, which would turn the scale in favor of patriotic duty. Such was the temper that philosophy produced in him, kindly, mild, and cheerful. Nothing ever grieved him except the illness or death of a friend, friendship being the one among blessings that he put highest; and indeed he was every man's friend, counting among his kindred whatever had human shape.[18]

And finally:

> He lived to be nearly a hundred, free from disease and pain, burdening no man, asking no man's favor, serving his friends, and having no enemies. Not Athens only, but all Greece was so in love with him that as he passed the great would give him place and there would be a general hush. Towards the end of his long life he would go uninvited into the first house that offered, and there get his dinner and his bed, the household regarding it as the visit of some heavenly being which brought them a blessing. When they saw him go by, the baker-wives would contend for the honor of supplying him, and a happy woman was the actual donor. Children too used to call him father, and bring him offerings of fruit.[19]

3. Peregrinus Proteus

We are informed fully about Peregrinus (called Proteus because he wished it so)[20] just as about Demonax, only by Lucian, but in a totally different mode.[21] Lucian writes almost a panegyric about Demonax with the conscious intention of pointing him out as an exemplar, while against Peregrinus he writes a libel, with the conscious intention of exposing him to public scorn. How much Lucian succeeds in idealizing the former and in vilifying the latter is difficult to say. It is certain that what little Aulus Gellius has to say about Peregrinus (he heard him speak at Athens) seems to be of a different quality.[22]

Peregrinus presents the most inconceivable fusion of religiosity or better of mysticism and typically Cynic anarchic radicalism, united to a good deal of the spirit of adventure.

He was suspected of parricide, and therefore he left his native city of Parium in Mysia and settled in the Holy Land. (Lucian says that Peregrinus strangled his father, "not wishing him to live beyond sixty years of age," and that his lengthy stay away from his native land was a self-condemnation to exile.) In the Holy Land he was involved with Christians, whose doctrines he seemed to have shared, and in fact, he wrote "many books" on these doctrines.[23] For being one of the people often seen with Christians (or generally considered such) he was thrown in jail, which brought him great fame and authority among the Christians. Lucian did not believe at all that Peregrinus was in good faith in his adherence to the Christian religion and writes:

> So it was then in the case of Peregrinus; much money came to him from them by reason of his imprisonment, and he procured not a little revenue from it. The poor wretches [scil., the Christians] have convinced themselves, first and foremost, that they are going to be immortal and live for all time, in consequence of which they despise death and even willingly give themselves into custody, most of them. Furthermore, their first lawgiver persuaded them that they are all brothers of one another after they have transgressed once for all by denying the Greek gods and by worshipping that crucified sophist himself and living under his laws. Therefore they despise all things indiscriminately and consider them common property, receiving such doctrines traditionally without any definite evidence. So if any charlatan and trickster, able to profit by occasions, comes among them, he quickly acquires sudden wealth by imposing upon simple folk.[24]

Liberated by the Proconsul, Peregrinus returned to his native land, where again, says Lucian, in order to avoid a trial due to the persisting scorn for the death of his father which was blamed on him, he left to the people his remaining possessions. And when he presented himself to the assembly with the typical Cynic garb (long hair, torn cloak, knap-sack on his shoulders, and a stick in his hand), the people saluted him as a true philosopher and follower of Diogenes and Crates.[25]

He then turned to wandering, receiving again the support of the Christians, who yet, after some time, abandoned him (Lucian wants us to believe that the cause of the break had been the eating of "some forbidden food," but from the way in which he says it, he shows that he did not believe it himself).[26]

After having searched in vain to recover the possessions left to the people, Peregrinus went to Egypt to study with the Cynic Agathobulus, in order to graduate, says Lucian with unabashed irony, in the doctrine which taught that public masturbation is an "indifferent thing" (this reference is to a typical example of Cynic *shamelessness* [ἀναίδεια]).[27]

He was hence in Italy, from whence he was expelled, says Lucian, because he worked hard at speaking evil of everyone, profiting shrewdly from the indulgence of the Emperor; his followers said, instead, that he was expelled for his *frank and bold speech* (παρρησία) typical of Cynics.[28]

He returned to Greece, Lucian says, and continued to exercise his bad-mouthing until he because a figure of contempt to all, and decided to commit suicide in flames on the occasion of the Olympic games, desiring to be spoken of at all costs and to achieve fame with posterity. Peregrinus and his followers would allege, naturally, the best motivation; the fiery death was to serve the good of all men, that is, in order to teach them to scorn death and to suffer torments.[29]

Actually, we know that the model Peregrinus intended to imitate, besides that of Heracles, was that of the Indian sages. In the past, the Cynic Onesicritus of Astypalaea (who had participated in the expedition of Alexander to the East) recognized in the way of living and of thinking of the Indian sages close parallels with the Cynics.[30]

Again, Lucian, who would not have minded helping Peregrinus to the pyre, says that these were the exact words of Peregrinus:

> He said that to a life of gold he wished to place a crown of gold: having lived as Heracles he wished to die as Heracles, and "to vanish into the air." "I wish," he said, "to do a great service to mankind, by showing them how to scorn death..."[31]

In conclusion, Peregrinus Proteus was certainly more than an adventurer, which is the way that Lucian depicts him. The numerous followers that he had, both among Christians and among Pagans when he embraced Cynicism, and the testimony of Aulus Gellius, confirms it in an undeniable way.[32]

Aulus Gellius expressly says that he knew and saw Peregrinus personally when he stayed at Athens: he was a "*virum gravem et constantem* [*serious and steady fellow*]," Gellius found him "*in quodam tugurio extra urbem* [*in a kind of hut outside the city*]," and speaks of having made many visits and listened to him speak about many things "*utiliter et honester* [*worthily and usefully*]."[33]

Unfortunately, Gellius mentions only one point of the teaching of Proteus, but it is worth considering, namely, that the wise man must not sin, not even if his sin were to remain unknown to everyone, both to Gods and to men, since he does not need to abstain from committing sins for fear of punishment of or of having a bad reputation, but for the love of the good as such.[34]

Peregrinus Proteus represents, as we have indicated previously, a fleeting moment in the meeting of Cynicism (in addition to its Eastern component) with a mysticism which becomes more and more widespread not only among Christians but also among pagans and which constitutes one of the distinguishing characteristics of the Imperial Age.

IV. The Cynicism of the Imperial Age as a Phenomena of the Masses and its Internal Contradictions

The important Cynic figures after the second century CE are unknown to us. We know some names of Cynics belonging to the fourth century CE through the writings of the Emperor Julian, but, for us, they are faceless names.[1]

We know a little more about the Cynic Maximus, who lived in the fourth century CE and combined Cynicism and Christianity.[2] Finally, we have information about the Cynic Sallustius, who lived at the beginning of the sixth century CE, but who seems to have returned to the asceticism of the ancient Cynics as well as acting again, in that respect, as Dio Chrysostomos did.[3]

But the success of the Cynicism of the Imperial Age was not due, as we have previously stated above, either to original doctrinal reëlaborations made by outstanding thinkers or to literary innovations about the *kynikós tropos*, but it was due to the enormous attraction of the Cynic life, of the *kynikós bios* [the Cynic life]. And the embracing of the Cynic life in the Imperial Age became an authentic mass phenomenon which mostly interested the poorest classes of society, who believed that they had found a means in the *kynikós bios* to avoid their unhappy condition, as a means of liberation. It can safely be said that no philosophy of antiquity had a diffusion on the popular level even distantly comparable to that of the Cynics and, in this sense, the definition of Cynicism as "a philosophy of the Greek proletariat"[4] has its own justification. It is nevertheless certain that this popularity arose and was especially created from an ambiguous understanding of Cynic doctrines. It is evident in fact, from our sources, that many (even most of the adepts) mistook the spirit of the Cynic life for its exterior manifestations and maintained that is sufficient to put on Cynic attire (cloak, knap-sack, and walking stick) and go wandering around the countryside like real indigents, imitating the rough manners and repeating the hackneyed formulas of Diogenes, in order to be authentic Cynics. It was inevitable that because of this mindless inanity a great deal of discredit fell on Cynicism.

The most effective description of the phenomenon of popular Cynicism is given by Lucian in the *Fugitives* in which Philosophy is presented in the act of lamenting with Zeus for the sad fate befalling it because of the work of these self-styled Cynic philosophers. Here is an important passage:

> Zeus: You have not yet told me what wrongs have been done you, Philosophy; you merely vent your indignation.
>
> Philosophy: But do listen, Zeus, and hear how great they are. There is an abominable class of men, for the most part slaves and hirelings, who had nothing to do with me in childhood for lack of leisure, since they were performing the work of slaves or hirelings or leaning such trades as you

would expect their like to learn—cobbling, building, busying themselves with fuller's tubs, or carding wool to make it easy for the women to work, easy to wind, and easy to draw off when they twist a yarn or spin a thread. Well, while they were following such occupations in youth, they did not even know my name. But when they began to be reckoned as adults and noticed how much respect my companions have from the multitude and how men tolerate their plain-speaking, delight in their ministrations, hearken to their advice, and cower under their censure, they consider all this to be a suzerainty of no mean order.

Now to learn all that is requisite for such a calling would have been a long task, say rather an impossible one. Their trades, however, were petty, laborious, and barely able to supply them with just enough. To some, moreover, servitude seemed grievous and (as indeed it is) intolerable. It seemed best to them, therefore, as they reflected upon the matter, to let go their last anchor, which men that sail the seas call the "sacred" one; so, resorting to good old Desperation, inviting the support, too, of Hardihood, Stupidity, and Shamelessness, who are their principal partisans, and committing to memory novel terms of abuse, in order to have them at hand and at their tongue's end, with these as their only countersigns (you perceive what a rare equipment it is for philosophy), they very plausibly transform themselves in looks and apparel to counterfeit my very self, doing, I vow, the same sort of thing that Aesop says the jackass in Cyme did, who put on a lion skin and began to bray harshly, claiming to be a lion himself; and no doubt there were actually some who believed him!

What characterizes us is very easily attainable, as you know, and open to imitation—I mean what meets the eye. It does not require much ceremony to don a short cloak, sling on a wallet, carry a staff in one's hand, and shout—say rather, bray, or howl, and slang everyone. Assurance of not suffering for it was bound to be afforded them by the usual respect for the cloth. Freedom is in prospect, against the will of their master, who, even if he should care to assert possession by force, would get beaten with the staff. Bread, too, is no longer scanty or, as before, limited to bannocks of barley; and what goes with it is not salt fish or thyme but meat of all sorts and wine of the sweetest, and money from whomsoever they will; for they collect tribute, going from house to house, or, as they themselves express it, they "shear the sheep"; and they expect many to give, either out of respect of their cloth or for fear of their abusive language.

Moreover, they discerned, I assume, the further advantage that they would be on an equal footing with true philosophers, and that there would be nobody who could pass judgment and draw distinctions in such matters, if only the externals were similar. For, to begin with, they do not even tolerate investigation if you question them ever so temperately and concisely; at once they begin shouting and take refuge in their peculiar citadel, abusiveness and a ready staff. Also, if you ask about their works, their words are copious, and if you wish to judge them by their words, they want you to consider their lives.

Consequently, every city is filled with such upstarts, particularly with those who enter the names of Diogenes, Antisthenes, and Crates as their patrons and enlist in the army of the dog. Those fellows have not in any way imitated the good that there is in the nature of dogs, as, for instance, guarding property, keeping at home, loving their masters, or remembering kindnesses, but their barking, gluttony, thievishness, excessive interest in females, truckling, fawning upon people who give them things, and hanging about tables—all this they have copied with painful accuracy.

You shall see what will happen presently. All the men in the workshops will spring to their feet and leave their trades deserted when they see that by toiling and moiling from morning till night, doubled over their tasks, they merely eke out a bare existence from such wage-earning, while idle frauds live in unlimited plenty, asking for things in a lordly way, getting them without effort, acting indignant if they do not, and bestowing no praise even if they do. It seems to them that this is "life in the age of Kronos," and really that sheer honey is distilling into their mouths from the sky!

They think would not be so dreadful if they offended against us only by being what they are. But although outwardly and in public they appear very reverend and stern, if they get a handsome boy or a pretty woman in their clutches or hope to, it is best to veil their conduct in silence. Some even carry off the wives of their hosts, to seduce them after the pattern of that young Trojan, pretending that the women are going to become philosophers; then they tender them, as common property, to all their associates and think they are carrying out a tenet of Plato's, when they do not know on what terms that holy man thought it right for women to be so regarded. What they do at drinking-parties, how intoxicated they become, would make a long story. And while they do all this, you cannot imagine how they berate drunkenness and adultery and lewdness and covetousness. Indeed you could not find any two things so opposed to each other as their words and their deeds. For instance, they claim to hate toadying, when as far as that goes they are able to outdo Gnathonides or Sruthias; and although they exhort everyone else to tell the truth, they cannot so much as move their tongues except in a lie. To all of them pleasure is nominally an odious thing and Epicurus a foeman; but in practice they do everything for the sake of it. In irascibility, pettishness, and proneness to anger they are beyond young children; indeed, they give no little amusement to onlookers when their blood boils up in them for some trivial reason, so that they look livid in color, with a reckless, insane stare, and foam (or rather, venom) fills their mouths.

And "may you never chance to be there when that vile filth of theirs is exuded! *As to gold or silver, Heracles! I do not want even to own it. An obol is enough, so that I can buy lupines, for a spring or a stream will supply me with drink.*" Then after a little they demand, not obols for a few drachmas, but whole fortunes. What shipman could make as much from his cargoes as philosophy contributes to these fellows in the way of gain? And then, when they have levied tribute and stocked themselves up to their heart's content, throwing off that ill-conditioned philosopher's cloak, they buy farms every now and then, and luxurious clothing, and long-haired pages, and whole apartment-houses, bidding a long farewell to the wallet of Crates, the mantle of Antisthenes, and the jar of Diogenes.

The unschooled, seeing all this, now spit scornfully at philosophy, thinking that all of us are like this and blaming me for my teachings, so that for a long time now it has been impossible for me to win over a single one of them. I am in the same fix as Penelope, for truly all that I weave is instantly unravelled again; and Stupidity and Wrongdoing laugh in my face to see that I cannot bring my work to completion and my toil to an end.[5]

Lucian knows very well, notwithstanding his constant polemic, that authentic Cynicism is quite different than this quite degenerate imitation. His praise of the Cynic Demonax, who he singled out, as we have had occasion to remark above, as a true model to imitate, is the most eloquent proof of what we have said.[6]

However before Lucian, Seneca,[7] Musonius,[8] and especially Epictetus[9] had drastically distinguished authentic Cynicism from its degenerate forms. In fact, Epictetus, in the same moment in which he rebelled against the parodies of the Cynic life, *kynikós bios*, to which he was witness, went on to an authentic idealization of the traits of that which, for him, must be "true" Cynicism by making more strident, in this way again, the contradictions into which the Cynicism of the epoch floundered.

Here is what Epictetus prescribed for those who aspired to be true Cynics:

First, in all that pertains to yourself directly you must change completely from your present practices, and must cease to blame God or man; you must utterly wipe out desire, and must turn your aversion toward the things which lie within the province of the moral purpose, and these only; you must feel no anger, no rage, nor envy, no pity.[10]

Even more important is this other passage in which Epictetus opposes the "true" Cynic (who for him was the Cynic of past times, the true follower of Diogenes) to the Cynics of his period:

And how is it possible for a man who has nothing, who is naked, without home or hearth, in squalor, without a slave, without a city, to live serenely? Behold, God has sent you the man who will show in practice that it is possible. "Look at me," he says, "I am without a home, without a city, without property, without a slave; I sleep on the ground; I have neither wife nor children, no miserable governor's mansion, but only earth, and sky, and one rough cloak. Yet what do I lack? Am I not free from pain and fear, am I not free? When has anyone among you seen me failing to get what I desire, or falling into what I would avoid? When have I ever found fault with either God or man? When have I ever blamed anyone? Has anyone among you seen me with a gloomy face? And how do I face those persons before whom you stand in fear and awe? Do I not face them as slaves? Who, when he lays eyes upon me, does not feel that he is seeing his king and his master?"

Lo, these are words that befit a Cynic, this is his character, and his plan of life. *But no, you say what makes a Cynic is a contemptible wallet, a staff, and* big jaws; to devour everything you give him, or stow it away, or to revile tactlessly the people he meets, or to show off his fine shoulder. Do you see the spirit in which you are intending to set your hand to so great an enterprise? First take a mirror, look at your shoulders, find out what kind of loins and thighs you have. Man, it's an Olympic contest in which you are intending to enter your name, not some cheap and miserable contest or other. In the Olympic games it is not possible for you merely to be beaten and then leave; but, in the first place you needs must disgrace yourself in the sight of the whole civilized world, not merely before the men of Athens, Lacedaemon, or Nicopolis; and, in the second place, the man who carelessly gets up and leaves must needs be flogged, and before he is flogged he has to suffer thirst, and scorching heat, and swallow quantities of wrestler's sand.

Think the matter over more carefully, know yourself, ask the Deity, do not attempt the task without God. For if God so advises you, be assured that He wishes you either to become great, or to receive many stripes. For this too is a very pleasant strand woven into the Cynic's pattern of life; he must needs be flogged like an ass, and while he is being flogged he must love the men who flog him, as though he were the father or brother of them all.[11]

The situation could not have been much different in the fourth century CE. In the writings of the Emperor Julian, we find again, in fact, that same interweaving of opposed sentiments toward ancient Cynicism, on the one side, and toward the self-styled contemporary Cynics, on the other, which we have pointed out in Epictetus.[12]

For Julian, the Cynic philosophy of the founders (that is, that of Diogenes and Crates), is the "most natural and universal"[13] philosophy, because it does not require study nor special knowledge and it is based on two very elementary principles: (*a*) "know thyself," and (*b*) "reject vain opinions and follow the truth."[14] In the Cynics who were his contemporaries Julian did not see the incarnation of these principles, but he encountered rather the humiliation of philosophy and the presumptions that divided Cynics, ignorance, audacity, and impudence, or, as he also says, the heaping of insults on the Gods and the braying at men are "the very short way" for the achievement of virtue.[15]

Julian even tried to compare the Cynics of his time to the Christians who renounce the world.[16] The comparison in the mind of Julian expresses the maximum contempt (for him, an apostate, the Christians are "Galilean sacrileges"). Instead, he expresses a profound truth (just as in modern times the definition of the Cynics as the "Capuchins of antiquity" has had a varied success). Actually, what many of the Cynics of the Imperial Age undoubtedly attempted in the Cynic life, *kynikós bios*, was what the anchorites in the East and then the monks in the West tried to achieve within the confines of Christianity.

And, indeed, the future was to belong to them.

Second Part

The Rediscovery of the Incorporeal and the Transcendent

PHILO OF ALEXANDRIA, THE REVIVAL OF PLATONISM AND PYTHAGOREANISM, THE HERMETIC WRITINGS, AND THE CHALDEAN ORACLES

«Τί δή ἐστι τὸ ὄν;
«Αὐτος δὲ οὐκέτι σχηματισθήσομαι
οὐδ᾽ ἀγνοεῖν φήσω τὸ ὄνομα τοῦ
ἀσωμάτου· καὶ γὰρ κινδυνεύει νῦν ἤδη
ἥδιον εἶναι εἰπεῖν μᾶλλον ἢ μὴ εἰπεῖν.
Καὶ δῆτα λέγω τὸ ὄνομα αὐτῷ εἶναι
τοῦτο τὸ πάλαι ζητούμενον.»

"What is being?"
"I no longer pretend and I will not say for ignorance the name of the incorporeal: at
this point, in fact, it is easier to name it
rather than to be silent. And I say immediately
that what its name is, has been searched out
already many times."

Numenius, Frags. 3 and 6 (des Places)

First Section

PHILO OF ALEXANDRIA AND MOSAIC PHILOSOPHY

« ὁ δ᾽ ἀπογνοὺς ἑαυτὸν γινώσκει τὸν ὄντα.»

"The man who has despaired of himself is beginning to know Him that is."

       Philo of Alexandria, *De Somniis* 1.60

« μόνον οὖν ἀψευδὲς καὶ βέβαιον ἀγαθὸν ἡ πρὸς θεὸν πίστις.»

"Faith in God, then, is the one sure and infallible good."

       Philo of Alexandria, *On Abraham* 268

I. The Origin, the Components, and the Basic Problems of the Philosophy of Philo of Alexandria

1. The origin of Philonian thought and its role in the history of ancient philosophy

Philo undoubtedly is a person who in the language of today we would speak of as being at a "critical juncture."[1]

He is a man of two epochs, of two cultures; he was not exempt from a series of contradictions (although unduly emphasized by many scholars) which arise from the fact that he expresses new ideas with old terminology and by the fact that the new ideas which he wants to express are derived from a tradition and a mentality which is very different (and in certain cases antithetical) to the Hellenic culture from which he received his vocabulary and his conceptual tools. Nevertheless, beyond these contradictions the "critical juncture" of which we spoke is evident on almost every page of his remarkable work. Philo shook to the roots the landmark doctrines which for three centuries had supported the thought of the great Hellenistic schools. In fact, he produced a break in the dominant materialism by the recovery of the incorporeal, which he proclaimed and defended in a very energetic way; to the immanentistic vision he opposed a transcendent conception even more advanced than anything the Greeks had known up to that time; in addition, he drastically limited the unconditioned faith in the self-sufficiency (αὐτάρχει) (a) of human beings by showing the necessity for transcending reason and joining it to God and to divine revelation in order to truly resolve ultimate problems; finally, he made an opening in the closed vision of the world and the merely immanentistic and naturalistic life proper to Hellenism with a vibrant religious consciousness and intense mysticism fated to change the climate of philosophical thinking in a radical manner.

This remarkable change happened in Alexandria. It was the work of a man who was not a Greek, but a Jew educated by Greek culture who was also educated by and imbued with Jewish belief and firmly convinced of the divine inspiration of the Scriptures.

All these circumstances are essential not only for the understanding of Philo, but also for all remaining Greek thought about which we are to speak.

The city of Alexandria was exposed more than any other to the influence of the Orient, both for geographical reasons as well as because of its openness to spiritual, cultural, and social currents, an openness which was especially encouraged by the ethnic diversity which molded the mental attitudes of its populace. At Alexandria the most important attempts at a synthesis occurred- between the typically Hellenic rationalistic spirit, and the Eastern which was, on the contrary, religious and radical in nature.[2]

So among the various currents of Greek philosophy there were two particularly suited to guarantee the mediation between Hellenic rationalism and Eastern religiousness and mysticism; the Pythagorean and especially Platonism. And from these two philosophies, at Alexandria, a few decades before Philo, a movement began to develop to get away from that sclerotic eclectic Stoicism (which was formed at the beginning of the second century BCE), as we will see.[3]

This particular ambiance would not simply by itself be sufficient to produce that splendid attempt at the fusion of biblical theology and Hellenic philosophy unless there had been present, as we have previously pointed out, a man like Philo, nourished by both cultures. Philo was profoundly convinced both of the excellence of the former and of the non-substitutable and the non-renounceable nature of the latter. Further, he was a Jew in every sense of the word as well as being a fervent admirer of the Greeks. No Greek, in fact, would have felt at that time the necessity of attempting this kind of mediation between these two conceptions of reality. And no Greek especially would have had the possibility of embarking on the apprenticeship necessary to grasp the categories of Jewish thought and particularly to understand the entire system of Jewish belief down to its fundamentals, in addition to all the categories of Greek thought.

The attempt to unite Jewish religion and Greek philosophy produced by Philo, with its uncertainties and its numerous aporias, constitutes an event of exceptional importance not only within the confines of the intellectual history of Greece but also of Judaism as well. *Because Philo began that alliance of biblical faith and Hellenic philosophical reason which was destined to have such a great success through the diffusion of the Christian message and from which arose the categories of thought of the succeeding centuries and from which its importance extended to all mankind.*[4]

With Philo, as has been correctly noted, the history of "Christian" philosophy (i.e., religious philosophy) and hence "European" philosophy begins.

Also within the limits of the development of the succeeding history of Greek philosophy, which rejects the Christian message and remains bound to a pagan mentality, and which will occupy us in a specific way, Philo had an important role to play. A whole series of concepts (at the head of which was the reëmergence of the immaterial) which were put into circulation, again by Philo, reappear in the school at Alexandria, founded by Ammonius, from which Neoplatonism developed and from which Plotinus came forth. In addition, Numenius, of whom we will speak further on,[5]

read, admired, and assimilated some basic doctrines from Philo, as many extant and incontrovertible fragments attest, and Numenius was one of the philosophers who exerted a special influence on the thought of Plotinus.

2. The Hellenic component

How and to which of the Greek schools did Philo go to master their categories in order to produce his synthesis of biblical religion and philosophy? Already from what we have said above the reply should be apparent: the Pythagorean and the Platonic components are his source of continual inspiration, but in a special way it is Platonism which is the privileged source. Actually, the ancient Fathers of the Church considered Philo a Pythagorean, and especially a Platonist.[6]

Some modern scholars have instead noted the influence of the Stoa.[7]

These are undoubtedly significant, but Philo systematically emptied all Stoic concepts of their materialistic and immanentistic content and restructured them in a transcendent, non-material sense. Nevertheless, there is an ineradicable and clear influence of Cynicism, especially in the doctrine of pleasure as evil and hence as a source of sin. Skepticism itself, although limited in its consequences within Plato's perspective, is nevertheless accepted and wisely developed in certain of its positions; especially, as we have said above, where Philo accepts the *tropes* (τρόποι), or the grounds of doubt of Aenesidemus. He concludes, therefore, that reason cannot overcome the impasse created by the "grounds of doubt" if it does not ally itself to faith and together with faith attempt to approach the Absolute.[8]

Recently there has been an emphasis also on the influence of the exoteric works of Aristotle which, as we know, were rather near to Platonic thought. There has also been noted, finally, certain points of contact with the *Treatise on the Cosmos*, a work attributed to Aristotle which, in any case, contains extensive references to the teachings of the Aristotelian exoterica.[9]

In order to complete this overview on origins, it is necessary to point out that Philo was acquainted with almost the whole span of the problematic of the history of Greek philosophy from the Presocratics (among whom he admired especially Parmenides and Empedocles, as "divine men") to the great exponents of the Hellenistic schools. And it is also necessary to recognize that he was in some way indebted to all of them in the formation of his philosophical consciousness, even to those philosophers with whom he disagreed, like the Sophists and the Epicureans.[10]

We will conclude this excursus, then, by asking a question: was the philosophy which Philo used for the interpretation of the *Bible* an eclecticism, that is, an eclecticism dominant at his period, as some scholars maintain? In our judgment, the answer to this question is a decisive negative. Above all those convictions which had by then become the common patrimony of almost all the schools and which constituted a truly philosophical *koiné*, just as above each particular doctrine taken from each school in Philo, very often the spirit of Platonism predominates as we have already pointed out. The numerous Stoic concepts which he used, as we have previously pointed out, are systematically released from their materialistic and immanentistic bonds and are advanced again within the context of an immaterialistically inspired metaphysics (involving the transcendent and the immaterial). Pythagoreanism itself was utilized only to a certain degree, especially in the development of the symbolic interpretation of numbers and in the allegorical exegesis of certain passages of the *Bible* [*T ᵉnak*]. In particular, Philo did not agree, which is significant enough, with the identification of the Ideas with numbers and maintained the eidetic-paradigmatic aspect of the Platonic doctrine of Ideas in all its purity. He even used Aristotelian doctrines which were in accord or easily reconciled with Platonism. atonism.

But what type of Platonism is being proposed by our philosopher? It is a new form of Platonism which is *recast in some essential points*. For example, Philo completely reinstated the notion of the incorporeal, and thus he is linked to the true spirit of Platonism beyond the misconceptions of the eclectic Academy; but he also restored the concept of God, placing it above the Ideas, as well as reconstituting the notion of the Ideas by making them the constructs or thoughts of God. He further transformed, in the creationist sense, the demiurgic activity of the divinity, as well as renewing the concept of moral law by making its precepts the "commandments" of the Almighty. Finally, he renovated the concept of man by introducing revolutionary novelties into the conception of the soul, which shattered not only the schemas of Platonic psychology, but also those of all Greek philosophy.

We will see that some of these transformations, which also belong to other Platonists and in point of fact constitute the distinctive traits of Middle Platonism, as we have said, arose at Alexandria a little before Philo and achieved their maximum development in the second century of the Common Era.[11]

Here we will be simply limited to mentioning these reforms, reserving a detailed discussion of them for later. First, in fact, it is necessary to say something about the properly Jewish component in Philonian thought.

3. The Jewish Component

The texts which constitute the "be all and end all" for Philo are not those of the philosophers but those of the Scriptures. Thus it is in these texts that we must search for the truly inspired nucleus and hence for the unifying principle of his thought.[12]

The text of the *Bible* to which Philo referred is not the original Hebrew, but the so-called Greek *Septuagint* translation. It was begun at Alexandria during the reign of Ptolemy Philadelphus (285-246 BCE) in order to respond to the needs of the Greek-speaking Jewish community formed at Alexandria. Some scholars, in fact, maintain that Philo himself did not know Hebrew or at least did not know it expertly.[13]

The translation of the Septuagint evidently facilitated Philo's task because it constituted a first mediation between Judaism and Hellenism. The Greek terms and expressions into which the corresponding Hebrew terms and expressions were translated inevitably reflected the peculiar cultural character of the Greek matrix from which they were derived. Any translation, in particular if made in a non-superficial way, is in some sense an interpretation, that is, a mediation. But Philo was convinced, just as of the original Hebrew text, that the Greek translation of the *Bible* was also inspired by God, and, because of this, it had equal value. God, Philo says, has "inspired" the translators in the choice of Greek words with which they translated the originals so that, properly speaking, they were not translators but "hierophants and prophets."[14]

Philo knew and meditated on almost the whole *Bible*, since he cites passages from almost eighteen of the books of which it is constituted. But he treated in an absolutely special way the first five books, viz., the *Pentateuch*, that is, the *Law* (*Torah*, in Hebrew; *Nomos*, in Greek). He considered Moses, its author, the greatest prophet and maintained that the Mosaic message, insofar as it is inspired by God, is the highest one issuing from the mouth of a human being. The message of Moses was for him, as a logical consequence, the truth which must be the measure, and the doctrines of all the philosophers must be gauged by it. Moreover, he maintained that some of the fundamental doctrines of the Greek philosophers had some precise antecedents in Moses.[15]

The notion of "Mosaic philosophy" with the clarifications made above appears then to be a better way to characterize Philonian thought.[16]

Accordingly, the works of Philo are, with the exception of a few chiefly for extrinsic purposes, commentaries, especially allegorical commentaries on the *Pentateuch* (the other passages of other books of the *Bible* to which he refers are always used in the context of the interpretation of the *Pentateuch*). In Philo's judgment, it contains the whole truth on God, the universe, man, and his destiny.

4. Philonian allegories and their Greek and Jewish antecedents

We have spoken of the commentaries in general as well as of the "allegorical commentaries" which Philo made of the *Pentateuch*, and it is opportune now to point out that not only the latter prevailed, in terms of quantity and quality, but that *the allegories are the real spiritual key to understanding our author*. The method of Philonian philosophizing is identical with allegory, which consists, in particular, in the tracing and explanation of the significance which is placed on the persons, acts, and events narrated in the *Pentateuch*.[17]

What are the origin, nature, and characteristics of Philonian allegorizing?

First, the method of allegorical interpretation in the time of Philo was widespread both in the pagan ambiance as well as in the Jewish milieu.

In the sphere of Hellenic culture the Alexandrian grammarians interpreted Homer and Hesiod in an allegorical way, and previously in the precincts of the ancient Stoa pagan mythology had been interpreted as a symbol of physical-theological truth. Nevertheless, for the Stoics the allegorical interpretation was a complementary method, that is, an ancillary, and not in any way essential to their properly philosophical method.[18]

Scholars note, not without reason, the idea that truth is hidden under symbols. Consequently, the emergence into the foreground of a procedure aimed at uncovering the truth under the symbol must have had its origin in the mileau of the *Mysteries*. In particular, in the Orphic mysteries, especially in their more developed stage, the initiation into them no longer simply consisted in a knowledge of the myths and in the participation in their ceremonial presentation, but in the penetration and comprehension of their inner hidden meaning. Towards the end of the second century CE the grammarian Dionysius Thrax significantly placed in opposition to the Delphic Oracle which communicated in clear language and literal expressions, Orpheus who used symbols and thus Dionysius emphasized the superiority of "speaking by means of symbols."[19]

A document in which the allegorical interpretation is predominant is the so-called *List of Cebes* (*Cebetis Tabula*), a neo-Pythagorean *pseudepigraphon* (about which more later). In this work the figures supposedly painted by "a disciple of Pythagoras and Parmenides" (on a salver offered as a gift to Kronos) are interpreted as symbols of the ethical life, various moral states of the soul, of good and evil, and what is neither good or evil. In addition, the interpretation of the tray is presented as a sort of initiation, or at least as the revelation of an esoteric wisdom which the author of the work maintained he had received from the maker himself of the salver.[20]

It is probably in this pagan document, that the allegorical method which is quite close to the Philonian procedure was applied, developed, and is to be found.

Furthermore, it is Philo himself who likens the allegorical interpretation of the Scriptures to the *initiation into the Mysteries*. But if certain modern interpreters have too often insisted on the influence of the Hellenistic mysteries, pushing it to truly exaggerated extremes, it is still undeniably true that the expressions of our author echo with the terminology of the Mysteries.[21]

The sources of Jewish inspiration must also be of no less importance.

For a long time scholars have inferred some parallels between Philo and the extant fragments under the name of Aristobulus[22] as well as between Philo and the authors, respectively, of the *Letter of Aristea*[23] and the *Wisdom of Solomon*.[24]

But it is Philo himself who informs us about the existence of the allegorical exegesis of the *Bible* in the Jewish milieu, although not with the precise and circumstantial evidence that we moderns would like. He tells us of the "inspired men" to whom he listened and who interpreted many of the things contained in the *Bible* as "visible symbols of invisible things," "expressible symbols of an inexpressible reality."[25]

Philo also attributed to the Jewish community of the Essenes, who lived in the Holy Land, the practice of meditation on most of the passages of the *Bible*, precisely by means of symbols.[26] Also of the Jewish community of the Therapeuti who settled in Egypt, Philo says that they systematically practiced allegorical interpretation and they likened the literal sense to the body of a living thing, the allegorical method to its soul.[27]

All of these components would have had a role to play, although in different ways, in the development of the allegorical method of Philo. It is certain, nevertheless, that no one had applied the allegorical method with such breadth and profundity as Philo did. Christian thought will be in Philo's debt; less than a century later it will take up the allegorical reading of the *Bible* again, redirecting it with new and fruitful results.

Before going on, it is again important to note two points for the correct understanding of the Philonian allegorical method: (*a*) Philo maintained that the words of the *Bible* indeed had a literal sense; in fact, he rejects, as a norm, the assimilation of the biblical account simply to a myth. The literal sense is placed, in his judgment, at an unequivocally inferior position and it stays outside of Mosaic teaching, while the allegorical interpretation is set in a decidedly superior position, reaching the very soul of this teaching. Both meanings are considered to be divinely revealed.[28]

(*b*) Philo himself, as an allegorical interpreter, maintains that he shares in divine inspiration.[29]

II. Philo and the Prelude to a Great Development in Western Thought

1. The first formulation of the problem of the relations between divine revelation and philosophy, that is, between faith and reason

We have pointed out above the firm faith of Philo in revelation, that is, in the divine inspiration of Scripture and especially his confidence in the divine assistance for himself in the allegorical interpretation of the books of Moses.

It is evident that we are here faced with an important development in Western thought, insofar as philosophical thought not only faced new problems, but problems of such a nature and character that, in order to be resolved, *they would put in a state of crisis the classical concept of philosophy and they would involve the achievement of heretofore unforeseen perspectives.* It was establishing the relations between divine revelation and philosophy, that is, between *faith*, which alone can believe in a superior divine revelation, and *philosophical reason*, which involves for the human *logos* [reason] the explanation and justification of all things. And it was a matter, consequently, of ascertaining from whom and by what the agreements would be controlled between the teachings contained in the revealed texts on the one hand and in the writings, the fruit of autonomous Greek philosophical thought, on the other, and to establish which should have the supremacy—whether faith in revelation, or the autonomous inquiry of human reason.

The great turning point of western thought will be visible in a very clear manner (especially in its multiple implications and consequences) chiefly in the birth and development of Christian Patristics and then in medieval scholasticism (also with the parallel development of Muslim and Jewish medieval philosophy). But it would be a grave mistake to think that pagan philosophy, in its survival beyond five centuries after the birth of Christianity, did not resent this development, or that it resented it only in a casual manner, as we will see.

In order to comprehend the novelty of this problem and its relevance it is well to remember that the Greek thought of the Classical Age as well as that of the Hellenistic Age had never found itself in the position of coming to terms with a "divine revelation" or with a doctrine considered as revealed, like that of the *Bible*, which Philo was the first to face, or the *Gospels* on which the Fathers of the Church were engaged, or the *Qu'ran* against which Muslim thinkers measured themselves. The Hellenic religions did not have unchanging teachings comparable to those of other religions, nor did it have a priestly caste whose chief task was to guard it; and what is more important, pagan beliefs were not exactly considered "teachings revealed by God" in the Biblical sense, as we have pointed out in the first volume.[1]

The philosophers who accepted certain parts of the message of the Orphic mysteries, especially Plato, would appeal, as a mode of seeing, to the dimension of a divine inspiration (assimilable in a very rough way to revelation). But for Plato it is clear that "divine inspiration" and "divine revelation" only played the role of a stimulus or impetus which was immediately transformed into reasoned discourse, or, it had the role of an inducement repeatedly taken up into the *logos*, as an enrichment of the *logos* itself.[2]

Besides, the case of Plato is especially significant because he made reference many times to *divine inspiration* and to the *divine mania* (that divine *mania* which is the source of great art, of oracles, of divination, and the erotic), and because the thinkers of the Imperial Age, beginning from Philo himself are in possession of the language with which Plato had described these states, but which is now to be located in a totally new spiritual dimension.[3]

First it is important to say that Plato, in the notion of "divine inspiration," even though with different nuances of meaning, implicitly saw it as a chiefly negative notion consisting in the fact that it brings man "outside sense," "outside of reason." Thus for him, the properly philosophical moment, which implies awareness and the full possession of reason, will necessarily be superior. Dialectic is, and always will be, the culminating moment for Plato, and dialectic is, and always will be, the path to true wisdom.[4]

Nevertheless, for Plato as well as for all the ancient Greeks, the notion of a "divine revelation" such as an "historical event," that is, as a message which could be presented to human beings as the solution to the basic problems concerning God, man, and his life, and which would qualify as the "word of God," as we have said, could not be involved in any experience whatsoever. It would have only been a human desire, a poignant yearning which was clearly articulated in that page of the *Phaedo* we chose as an epigraph for this work:

> I think, Socrates, as perhaps you do yourself, that it is either impossible or very difficult to acquire clear knowledge about these matters [on the destiny of man and on his ultimate fate in this life]. And yet he is a weakling who does not test in every way what is said about them and persevere until he is worn out by studying them on every side. For he must do one of two things; either he must learn or discover the truth about these matters, or if that is impossible, he must take whatever human doctrine is best and hardest to disprove and, embarking upon it as upon a raft, sail upon it through life in the midst of dangers, *unless he can sail upon some stronger vessel, some divine revelation, and make his voyage more safely and more securely.*[5]

This means that a "divine revelation," "the word of a God" which tells us what man's destiny is, would have to be supreme, because, just as a ship is a shelter against storms, it would be a safe means for crossing the sea of life, and it would conduct us to the safe harbor which we all aspire to reach. Otherwise, we are confined to human reasoning (philosophy): which is like a raft, which can save us, but with all the attendant risks that can easily be avoided by those who travel by ship.

So what is for Plato a mere hope is for Philo a reality. Philo has at his disposal the use of the Platonic image, both the "ship" and the "raft," that is, both "a divine revelation" and "philosophical thought," both the message transmitted through Moses that God made known to men and the word of human wisdom which arose from many centuries of the intellectual labor of the Greeks. In what way can there be relations between the two "messages"? To which of the two should priority be given by one who wishes to philosophize?

Philo does not only reply to this question in a clear and unequivocal way, but he also gives a solution destined to become a model and to define an epoch. Philo himself is the thinker who first gave an interpretation of the relation between philosophy (reason, the human word) and revelation (the divine word) in terms of an "ancillary subordination" of the former to the latter. He formulated a doctrine which through the Fathers of the Church will pass on to the Scholastics and to Western thought and which will remain canonic for centuries.[6]

Hellenistic philosophy had already presented the sciences and the particular arts as "ancillaries" to philosophy and this idea had been accepted by Philo, who elaborated it further. Just as the arts and the special sciences on which the general culture are based are in service to philosophy, so also, analogously, philosophy is in service to "wisdom" (σοφία). For by "wisdom," as we will see further on, Philo understands especially the Mosaic-Biblical revelation.

Here is a very important text in this regard:

> And indeed just as the sciences on which the general culture [τὰ ἐγύκλια] contribute to the acquisition of philosophy [φιλοσοφία], so does philosophy to the getting of wisdom [σοφία]. For philosophy is the practice or study of wisdom, and wisdom is the knowledge of things divine and human and their causes. And therefore just as the general culture is the bond-servant [δούλη] of philosophy, so must philosophy be the servant of wisdom [φιλοσοφία δούλη σοφίας].[7]

The foundation of the wisdom of which Philo speaks is faith, understood as a firm and unshakable confidence which is opposed to the uncertainty of human reasoning. In the *Allegorical Interpretation* Philo writes, for example:

> So then it is best to trust God and not our dim reasonings and insecure conjectures: "Abraham believed God and was held to be righteous" (*Gen.* 15: 6); and the precedence which Moses takes is testified to by the words he is "faithful in all My house" (*Num.* 12: 7). But if we repose our trust in our own reasonings, we shall construct and build up the city of Mind that corrupts the truth.[8]

And in *On Abraham* our philosopher affirms unequivocally:

III. Metaphysics, Theology, and the Theory of Being of Philo

1. The overcoming of the materialistic and immanentistic presuppositions of the Hellenistic systems and the reaffirmation of the incorporeal and the transcendent

The changes in the Hellenistic framework of philosophical knowledge, as we have said, must depend directly on the erosion of the foundations on which it was erected. It is clear, in fact, that Philo removes theology from the sphere of cosmology and locates it within ethics *because he rejects the materialistic and immanentistic conception of God and the divine maintained by all the Hellenistic schools especially the Stoa* and he even radically realigns the meaning and nature of cosmology itself.

Actually, from the beginning to the end of the writings of our philosopher he affirmed the *reality of the incorporeal* in that connotation and in that ontological and metaphysical significance which had been intensely and consistently denied by the adherents not only of the Garden, the Stoa, and the Skeptics, but also by the very heterodox followers of the Academy and the Peripatos. Now in the incorporeal Philo pointed to the true cause of the corporeal and consequently, by overturning the common perspective of all the Hellenistic schools, he refuses to concede any ontological autonomy to the corporeal, that is, he denies that the corporeal contains its own justification. In this way, the metaphysical achievement of Plato is further enriched and developed in function of some essential elements derived from the Scriptures.

God is an incorporeal being and the *Logos*, the *Powers*, the Ideas, and the world of Ideas (which we will see Philo completely reinterprets by changing their status in a major way) as well as souls are incorporeal entities. Now, both God and the *Logos*, the *Powers*, the intelligible cosmos, and souls have, at different levels and in different respects, a well-defined roles as causes and foundations of the sensible. Therefore, it can be correctly said that the corporeal exists only because the incorporeal exists, since the incorporeal produces it, sustains it, and maintains it.[1]

Since Philo overturned a reigning paradigm which had dominated the philosophical culture for roughly three centuries almost uncontested, it is an opportune time to read some of his statements in this regard. Here is how the attribute of the "incorporeal" expressly used of God by Philo[2] is analyzed, for example, in the *Allegorical Interpretations*:

> "And the Lord God said, It is not good that the man should be alone, let us make for him a helper corresponding to him" (*Gen.* 2: 18). Why, O prophet, is it not good that the man should be alone? Because, he says, it is good that the Alone should be alone: but God, being One, is alone and unique, and like God there is nothing. Hence, since it is good that He Who is should be

alone—for indeed with regard to Him alone can the statement "it is good" be made—it follows that it would not be good that the mans hould be alone. There is another way in which we may understand the statement that God is alone. It may mean that neither before creation was there anything with God, nor, when the universe had come into being, does anything take its place with Him; for there is absolutely nothing which He needs. A yet better interpretation is the following. God is alone, a Unity, *in the sense that His nature is simple [φύσις ἁπλῆ], not composite, whereas each one of us and of all other created beings is made up of many things*. I, for example, am many things in one. I am soul and body. To soul belong rational and irrational parts, and to body, again, different properties, warm and cold, heavy and light, dry and moist. *But God is not a composite being, consisting of many parts, nor is he mixed with aught else*. For whatever is added to God, is either superior or inferior or equal to Him. But there is nothing equal or superior to God. And no lesser thing is resolved into Him. If He do so assimilate any lesser thing, He also will be lessened. And if He can be made less, He will also be capable of corruption; and even to imagine this were blasphemous.[3]

The incorporeality of God is identical, therefore, with his *absolute simplicity* (the absolute absence of composition and parts, the presence of which are instead the peculiarcharacteristic of the corporeal) and *absolute incorruptibility*.

As the concept of incorporeality completely regained its meaning, it was paralleled in this respect by the concept of *transcendence* as well. It became superior even to the notion of Plato and Aristotle in clarity and detail, for reasons which we will specify further on. Here are some penetrating affirmations:

For not even the whole world would be a place fit for God to make His abode, since God is His own place, and He is filled by Himself, and sufficient for Himself, filling and containing all other things in their destitution and barrenness and emptiness, but Himself contained by nothing else, seeing that He is Himself One and the Whole.[4]

Philo is strongly convinced that the doctrine of the necessary existence of the "incorporeal Ideas," that is, of the incorporeal paradigms or prototypes which function as the exemplary cause of corporeal realities, is to be maintained as the capstone of the Mosaic revelation.[5]

Here is how Philo argues against those who reject the existence of the "incorporeal Ideas" in *The Special Laws*:

For the heads under which the impious and unholy can be characterized are not one, but many and different. Some aver that the *Incorporeal Ideas* or Forms are an empty name devoid of any real substance of fact, and thus they abolish in things the most essential element of their being, namely the archetypal patterns of all qualities in what exists, and on which the form and dimensions of each separate thing was modeled. These the holy table of the law speak of as "crushed," for just as anything crushed has lost its quality and form and may be literally said to be nothing more than shapeless matter, so the creed which abolishes the Forms confuses everything and reduces it to the pre-elemental state of existence, that state devoid of shape and quality. Could anything be more preposterous than this? For when out of that confused matter God produced all things, He did not do so with His own handiwork, since His nature, happy and blessed as it was, forbade that He should touch the limitless chaotic matter. Instead He made full use of the incorporeal potencies well denoted by their name of Forms to enable each kind to take its appropriate shape. But this other creed brings in its train no little disorder and confusion. For by abolishing the agencies which created the qualities, it abolishes the qualities also.[6]

Finally, in what concerns the soul, as we will see, Philo not only tends to distinguish *psyché* from *nous* in a marked way so as to emphasize the privileged status of the latter, but he also introduces remarkable novelties which carry his position beyond that of Plato himself.[7]

2. The new conception of God

The center of the Philonian system is established by a rational attitude and a conception of God radically new with respect to the preceding Greek tradition, as we will immediately see.

First, he distinguishes in an extremely clear way especially on the theoretical level with more detail than was done by his predecessors, two different problems: (*a*) that of the *demonstration of the existence of God* and (*b*) that of the *determination of his nature and essence*. The first problem, he says, is not difficult; the second, instead, not only is difficult, but is even insoluble. In other words, according to our philosopher, the existence of God is *understandable*, his essence, on the contrary, is *incomprehensible* to man.[8]

Although the fact that the existence of God is understandable, notes Philo, not all men achieve this understanding, or not all achieve it in an adequate manner. The *atheists* do not succeed in understanding it, they absolutely deny the existence of God. Not even those who we today call *agnostics*, that is, those who maintain that they cannot decide whether or not God exists begin to understand it. On the other hand, the *superstitious* understand the existence of God poorly; rather than based on a sound use of reason, they rely indiscriminately (that is, acritically) on traditions. In addition, those who pretend to explain everything with physical science and end in identifying God with the world poorly understand it, that is, those who are *pantheists*. Again, they poorly understand who, inasmuch as they posit the world as uncreated end in this way by admiring the creature more than the Creator and by supposing the existence of an inactive God. Finally, the *polytheists* poorly understand the existence of God since they introduce a multiplicity of deities, male and female, young and old, and hence they do not comprehend the idea of a unique being which alone truly exists.[9]

Against all these types of ignorance of God Philo pronounces a severe judgment. He especially singles out the atheists as those who win the first prize in the impiety sweepstakes and he calls them impotents, since they are deprived of the essential notion of the Creator of all things and consequently have become incapable of generating wisdom.[10]

In addition, he defines the polytheists with a caustic image as "sons of prostitutes" like the sons of prostitutes they do not know who their true fathers are and must consider all men such who frequent their mothers, so also, they do not recognize the existence of the one true God and are forced to invent the existence of a great number of Gods.[11]

The proofs which Philo adduces in favor of the existence of God are of a physical-teleological character, or, if you prefer, they are of a cosmological-teleological nature wholly derived from the Greek philosophical tradition and in particular from Socrates, Plato, and Aristotle.[12] Here are two of the more important ones:

We see then that any piece of work always involves the knowledge of a workman. Who can look upon statues or painting without thinking at once of a sculptor or painter? Who can see clothes or ships or houses without getting the idea of a weaver and a shipwright and a housebuilder? And when one enters a well-ordered city in which the arrangements for civil life are very admirably managed, what else will he suppose but that this city is directed by good rulers? So then he who comes to the truly Great City, this world, and beholds hills and plains teeming with animals and plants, the rivers, spring-fed or winter torrents, streaming along, the seas with expanses, the air with its happily tempered phases, the yearly seasons passing into each other, and then the sun and moon ruling the day and night, and the other heavenly bodies fixed or planetary and the whole firmament revolving in rhythmic order, must he not naturally or rather necessarily gain the conception of the Maker and Father and Ruler also? For none of the works of human art is self-made, and the highest art and knowledge is shewn in this universe, so that surely it has been wrought by one of excellent knowledge and absolute perfection. In this way we have gained the conception of the existence of God.[13]

For it cannot be that while in yourself there is a mind appointed as your ruler which all the community of the body obeys and each of the senses follows, the world, the fairest, and greatest and most perfect work of all, of which everything else is a part, is without a king who holds it together and directs it with justice. That the king is invisible need not cause you to wonder, for neither is the mind in yourself visible. Anyone who reflects on these things and learns from no distant source, but from one near at hand, namely himself, and what makes him what he is, will know for certain the world is not the primal God but a work of the primal God and Father of all Who, though invisible, yet brings all things to light, revealing the natures of great and small. For He did not deem it right to be apprehended by the eyes of the body, perhaps because it was contrary to holiness that the mortal should touch the eternal, perhaps too because of weakness of our sight. For our sight could not have borne the rays that pour from Him that is, since it is not even able to look upon the beams of the sun.[14]

This *a posteriori* procedure or, as Philo says, "from low to high" (κάτωθεν ἄνω)[15] which consists in an inference beginning from things and judging them incapable of justifying themselves, rises to that cause which alone can explain them; the *a posteriori* procedure consists in a complex work of mediation. But Philo affirms that there is another way of arriving at the knowledge of the existence of God. It is a type of knowledge which does not move from low to high, but which comes directly and immediately from the high. Such a knowledge is reversed, however, for the elect, for those who are "true servants and lovers of God."[16] It is a knowledge which God gives on his own initiative as a gift to those who pray for it and it makes them worthy, as happened in a prototypical way to Moses.

Here is a very important passage:

> There is a mind more perfect and more thoroughly cleansed, which has undergone initiation into the great mysteries, a mind which gains its knowledge of the First Cause *not from created things, as one may learn the substance from the shadow, but lifting its eyes above and beyond creation obtains a clear vision of the uncreated One*, so as from Him to apprehend both Himself, and His shadow. To apprehend that was, we saw, to apprehend both the Word and this world. The mind of which I speak is Moses who says, 'Manifest Yourself to me, let me see You that I may know You'(*Exod.* 33: 13); 'for I would not that You should be manifested to me by means of heaven or earth or water or air or any created thing at all, nor would I find the reflection of Your being in aught else than in You Who are God, for the reflections in created things are dissolved, but those in the Uncreated will continue abiding and sure and eternal.' This is why God has expressly called Moses and why He spoke to Him.[17]

Here is how Philo further explains this type of immediate knowledge:

> How this access has been obtained may be well seen through an illustration. Do we behold the sun which sense perceives by any other thing than the sun, or the stars by any others than the stars, and in general is not light seen by light? In the same way God too is His own brightness and is discerned through Himself alone, without anything co-operating or being able to co-operate in giving a perfect apprehension of His existence. They then do but make a happy guess, who are at pains to discern the Uncreated, and Creator of all from His creation, and are on the same footing as those who try to trace the nature of the monad from the dyad, whereas observation of the dyad should begin with the monad which is the starting point. The seekers for truth are those who envisage God through God, light through light.[18]

In this privileged knowledge of the existence of God it is not so much the man who sees God, but it is "God who let himself be seen by man." In sum, it is a divine initiative which comes to man and offers him, as we said, the vision of himself gratuitously. We are, then, in the presence of an idea completely unknown to Greek philosophical thought, *that of a gratuitous gift which God makes to men for love of them.*

The immediate knowledge God can give to man, "giving himself to be seen," concerns only his *existence* and not his *nature or essence*, which as we have previously mentioned remains incomprehensible to all men, since it transcends them infinitely. God replies to the prayer of Moses calling on Him to manifest His nature:

> He replies, "Your zeal I approve as praiseworthy, but the request cannot fitly be granted to any that are brought into being by creation. I freely bestow what is in accordance with the recipient; for not all that I can give with ease is within man's power to take, and therefore to him that is worthy of My grace I extend all the boons which he is capable of receiving. *But the apprehension of Me is something more than human nature, yes even the whole heaven and universe will be able to contain.*[19]

It is clear from this text that the nature of God cannot be understood by man by reason of His *absolute transcendence*. God transcends not only human nature but likewise the nature of the heavens and the whole universe. God is totally other with respect to everything which is known to us, or, saying it in Philonian terminology, "there is nothing which is like to God."[20]

In fact, Philo even says that God is above the One and the Monad itself, that He is above all life and virtue, beyond science, beyond the Good itself.[21]

The repeated assertions of our philosopher that God is "without qualities" *(apoios)* means precisely this, that He is beyond all possible qualitative determinations (i.e., God is beyond any form or quality).[22]

God transcends not only being and the sensible world, but also the intelligible world and its entities, because, as we shall see, He is the creator of both. Therefore God is the font of all reality. He is nowhere and at the same time He is everywhere, the whole of reality is full of Him and He contains all.[23]

The transcendence of God also necessarily involves his epistemological transcendence, which renders him unknowable to man, and consequently it renders him likewise ineffable, that is inexpressible and not denominable by names.[24]

This doctrine, of which there are traces in preceding thought, but without adequate justification and development, can be considered a novelty introduced by Philo, at least in the formulation which he gave to it (the absolute transcendence depends, in the ultimate analysis, on the notion of creation, which was missing in preceding speculation) and is the foundation of that which much later, in the sphere of Christian speculation, would be called "negative theology." Nevertheless, it does not lack influence in the sphere of pagan philosophy: we find it, in fact, in the *Didaskalikos* of Albinus and especially in the *Enneads* of Plotinus.[25]

It is nevertheless interesting that Philo recommends constant pursuit in the inquiry into the essence of God; in fact, even if this continues to be formally incomprehensible, nonetheless, hesays, man can achieve a grasp of some properties which can be referred to the essence of God, just as happens to the eyes, although incapable of seeing the sun directly, we try to grasp its reflection and the final extension of the splendor of its rays on earth.[26]

Actually, the different properties of God to which Philo refers in his writings either express in various ways the radical differences between Him and all other things or they express some aspects of His activity. It is in this way that God is said to be incorporeal, one, simple, self-sufficient, perfect, immobile, immutable, eternal, omnipresent, omniscient, omnipotent (and hence infinite), creator and father of all things, provident, revealer of laws and so on.[27]

There is nevertheless a name which, according to Philo, denominates God in a special way, in the sense that it does not simply express one of his activities or one of his *Powers*, but in a way that is close to arising from his very activities and *Powers*. This name is *Being*, or *Entity*, or *Existent*. The famous passage of *Exodus* in which God replies to Moses, who wishes to know his name, is in the *Septuagint* translation: "I AM HE WHO IS" (ἐγώ εἰμι ὁ ὤν), "I am Being." Philo did not fully develop the metaphysical connotations of this expression; but not only did he use this name in a systematic way, but here and there seems to maintain that God is self-defined as Being par excellence, insofar as He is that Being which is and will always be and in addition is that Being which through its very nature also makes other beings exist, the Being which is fully being and is the source of all other beings.

> God replied [to Moses]: "First tell them that I AM HE WHO IS [ὁ ὤν], that they may learn the difference between what IS and whatis not, and also the further lesson that no name at all can properly be used of Me, *to Whom alone being belongs*.[28]

> Thus in another place, when he had inquired whether He that IS has any name, he came to know full well that He has no proper name (*Exod*. 6: 3), and that whatever name anyone may use of Him he will use by license of language; *for it is not the nature of Him that IS to be spoken of, but simply to be*. Testimony to this is afforded also by the divine response made to Moses' question whether He has a name, even "I AM HE THAT IS" (*Exod*. 3:14). It was given in order that, since there are not in God things which man can comprehend, man may recognize His subsistence.[29]

> So Moses "taking his tent sets it up outside the camp" (*Exod*. 33:7), and places its abode far from the bodily encampment, expecting that only thus might he become a perfect suppliant and worshipper of God. Of this tent he says that it has received the title of "Tent of Testimony," using his words

quite advisedly, to show that the Tent of the Existent One really IS, and does not merely have the title. For, among the virtues, that of God really IS, actually existing, inasmuch as *God alone has true being* (θεὸς μόνος ἐν τῷ εἶναι ὑφέστηκεν). This is why Moses will say of Him as best he may in human speech, "I AM HE THAT IS" (*Exod.* 3:14), implying that others lesser than He have not being, as being indeed is, but exist in semblance only, and are conventionally said to exist.[30]

3. The first philosophical formulation of the doctrine of Creation

Philo is the first thinker to introduce into philosophy the doctrine of creation by borrowing it from the *Bible* and trying to mediate it through the Platonic doctrine of the *Timaeus*. Succeeding pagan thought will allow this achievement, which will be the foundation of Christian thought, to be utterly neglected.

Actually many scholars maintain that Philo gave more weight to the narration of the *Timaeus* than to that of the *Bible*, and that in a certain way he considered matter eternal (at least implicitly) and had hence reduced in the ultimate analysis the creative activity of God to a demiurgic activity, that is, to an organizing activity of a pre-existent material. In point of fact such is not the case. Philo pushed well beyond the *Timaeus*, even if he did not achieve and did not ground the theory of creation with all the clarity that we might desire (having been the beneficiaries of successive elaborations by Christian thought).

By going back to the above-mentioned discussion about the properties of God, we can say that the most important is that of acting, doing, and producing:

> *For it belongs to God to act,* and this we may not ascribe to any created being. What belongs to the created is *to suffer*.[31]

> *For God never leaves off making,* but even as it is the property of fire to burn and of snow to chill, so it is the property of God to make: nay more so by far, *inasmuch as He is to all besides the source of action*.[32]

What kind of activity is this "making" (ποιεῖν) of God?

Some scholars, as we have pointed out above, basing themselves on some texts in which Philo speaks the language of Greek philosophy, have maintained that it is *demiurgic activity*.

Here are some of these texts:

> There are some people who, having the world in admiration rather than the Maker of the world, pronounce it to be without beginning and everlasting, while with impious falsehood they postulate in God a vast inactivity; whereas we ought on the contrary to be astonished at His powers as Maker and Father, and not to assign to the world a disproportionate majesty. Moses, both because he had attained the very summit of philosophy, and because he had been divinely instructed in the greater and most essential part of Nature's lore, could not fail to recognize that the universal must consist of

two parts, one part *active cause* and the other *passive cause*; and that the active Cause is the perfectly pure and unsullied Mind of the universe, transcending virtue, transcending knowledge, transcending the good itself and the beautiful itself; *while the passive part is in itself incapable of life and motion, but, when set in motion and shaped and quickened by Mind, changes into the most perfect masterpiece, namely this world.* Those who assert that this world is unoriginate unconsciously eliminate that which of all incentives to piety is the most beneficial and the most indispensable, namely providence.[33]

Now just such a power [of the supreme Being] is that by which the universe was made, one that has as its source nothing less than true goodness. For should one conceive a wish to search for the cause, for the sake of which this whole was created, it seems to me that he would not be wrong in saying, what indeed one of the ancient philosophers [scil. Plato] did say, that the Father and Maker of all is good; and because of this He grudged not a share in his own excellent nature *to an existent which has of itself nothing fair and lovely, while it is capable of becoming all things.* For of itself it was without order, without quality, without soul, (without likeness); it was full of inconsistency, ill-adjustment, disharmony: but it was capable of turning and undergoing a complete change to the best, the very contrary of all these, to order, quality, life, correspondence, identity, likeness, perfect adjustment, to harmony, to all that is characteristic of the more excellent model.[34]

They judge that the master art of God by which He wrought all things is one that admits of no heightening or lowering of intensity but always remains the same and that through its transcendent excellence it has wrought in perfection each thing that is, every number and every form that tends to perfectness being used to the full by the Maker. For He judged equally about the little and the great, to use Moses's words (*Deut.* 1: 17), when He generated and shaped each thing, nor was He led by the insignificance of the material to diminish, or by its splendor to increase, the art which He applied. For all craftsmen of repute, whatever materials they use, whether they be costly or of the cheapest, wish so to use them, that their work shall be worthy of praise. In fact people have been known to produce a higher class of work with the cheaper than with the most costly substances; their feeling for beauty was enhanced and by additional science they wished to compensate for inferiority of material. But with God no kind of material is held in honor, and therefore He bestowed upon them all the same art, and in equal measure. And so in the holy Scriptures we read, "God saw all things which he had made and behold, they were very good"(*Gen.* 1: 31), and things which receive the same praise must be of equal honor in the eyes of the praiser. Now God praised not the material which He had used for His work, material soul-less, discordant and dissoluble, and indeed in itself perishable, irregular, unequal, but He praised the works of His own art, which were consummated through a single exercise of power equal and uniform, and through knowledge ever one and the same. And thus by the rules of proportion everything was accounted similar and equal to everything else, according to the principle which His art and His knowledge followed.[35]

Nevertheless, these and similar passages may lead the reader astray because they inevitably carry us back to the Platonic notions, concealing all the novel conceptions which Philo introduces. First, he does not quite say that matter is co-eternal with God and that it pre-exists the creation of the world. In addition, from some passages of *On Providence* it would seem to be permissible to infer the creation of matter itself.[36]

An analogous conclusion can also be drawn by interpreting *On Creation of the World* without restricting it to the Platonic framework.[37] In addition, and this is clearly noted by the interpreters, the Ideas which function as paradigms and exemplary causes in Plato are ungenerated and eternal; on the contrary, for Philo, they are conceived as produced by divine thought and hence as *created by God*. But we will speak further on about this argument.

On the other hand, Philo himself places in evidence two very important points:(*a*) the activity of God produces things which did not exist, it produces all things from *not being*;(*b*) God is not hence only a "demiurge," but is a"creator."

Here are some texts:

> For God has produced the world, his most perfect work, out of non-being into being [ἐκ τοῦ μὴ ὄντος εἰς τό εἶναι].[38]

> God has brought the totality of things out of non-being.[39]

> So God when He gave birth to all things, not only brought them into sight, but also made things which before were not [ἃ πρότερον οὐκ ἦν, ἐποίησεν] not just handling material *as a demiurge, but being Himself its Creator* [οὐ δημιουργός μόνον ἀλλὰ καὶ κτίστης αὐτός ὤν].[40]

Finally, Philo upholds and emphasizes a further point, that *everything is a grace and gift of God*: nothing belongs to itself, but all in all belongs to him; everything is gratuitous and a free gift of his goodness. This is a way of thinking and feeling possible only within a creationist context.

Here are some important texts:

> The righteous man exploring the nature of existence makes a surprising find, in this one discovery, that all things are a grace of God [χάριν ὄντα τοῦ θεοῦ τὰ σύμπαντα], and that creation has no gift of grace to bestow, for neither has it any possession, since all things are God's possession, and for this reason grace to belongs to Him alone as a thing that is His very own. Thus to those who ask what the origin of creation is the right answer would be, that it is the *goodness and grace of God* [ἀγαθότης καὶ χάρις τοῦ θεοῦ], after which He bestowed on the race that stands next after Him. For *all things in the world and the world itself is a free gift and act of kindness and grace on God's part.*[41] All things are the grace or gift of God: earth, water, air, fire, sun, stars, heaven, all plants and animals. But God has bestowed no gift of grace on Himself, for He does not need it, but He has given the

world to the world, and its parts to themselves and to each other, yes and to the All.[42]

From these notions of a Creator-God and of creation as a gratuitous gift depends as we will see, a series of essential changes which Philo developed on different levels.

4. The doctrine of the *Logos*

A series of novelties are involved in the notion of creation, in the first place, on the ontological-metaphysical level, beginning with the theory of the *Logos*, which takes on truly unexpected connotations. Unfortunately Philo speaks frequently of the *Logos*, but chiefly through allusions. What is more, he speaks in different contexts and from different perspectives, so that it is easy to understand how scholars have proposed different and sometimes opposed interpretations. In this way, we are dependent on hints because of the complexity of the matter and the problematic character of the texts.

God, Philo explains, wanted to create the sensible world in an appropriate way, so he produced the *intelligible world* first, which has the function of being an *incorporeal model* according to which the corporeal world is to be realized the way an architect "creates" who wants to construct a great city. First of all he creates the project mentally and only afterward is it translated into reality. So the divine *Logos* is the activity or power of God which creates the intelligible reality which functions as a model or ideal paradigm. Here is the famous passage from *On the Creation of the World* which expounds this doctrine:

> Just such must be our thoughts [it is understood that the reference is to the example of an architect who wishes to construct a city] about God. We must suppose that, when He was minded to found the one great city [scil. the universe], He conceived *beforehand* the models of its parts, and that out of these He constituted and brought to completion a world discernible only by the mind, and *then*, with that for a pattern, the world which our senses can perceive. As, then, the city which was fashioned beforehand within the mind of the architect held no place in the outer world, but had been engraved in the soul of the artificer as by a seal; even so the universe that consisted of ideas would have no other location than the Divine Reason, which was the Author of this ordered frame. For what other place could there be for His powers sufficient to receive and contain, I say not all but, any one of them whatever uncompounded and untempered?[43]

And a little further on in the same work, we read:

> Should a man desire to use words in a more simple and direct way, he would say that *the world discerned only by the intellect is nothing else than the Word of God when He was already engaged in the act of creation*. For (to revert to our illustration) the city discernible by the intellect alone is nothing else than the reasoning faculty of the architect in the act of planning to found the city.[44]

In these passages the divine *Logos* would seem to be the same as the *activity of divine thinking*, that is, with divine reasoning, or better, with the divine *Nous*, with that which is not distinct from God himself.[45]

But Philo immediately distinguishes the *Logos* from God and makes it almost an hypostasis, even calling it "first born of the uncreated father," "second God," "image of God." In some passages he also speaks of it as an instrumental and efficient cause. In other passages he speaks of it, instead, as the Archangel, as the mediator between Creator and creatures (insofaras it is not uncreated like God, but not created like a creature of this world), the Herald of the peace of God, the preserver of the peace of God in the world. The *Logos* of Philo expresses, in addition (and this is very important), the fundamental connotations of the biblical notion of "wisdom" as well as of the biblical "word of God," which is a creative and productive word. Finally, the *Logos* also expresses the ethical significance of the message by which God guides men to the good, the significance of a saving word.[46]

In all these meanings the *Logos* signifies an incorporeal reality which is beyond the sensible, a transcendent. But because the sensible world is construed according to an intelligible model, that is, according to the *Logos*, and, in fact, by means of the instrumentality of the *Logos*, there is in this way, a *Logos* immanent to the sensible world, or better, an immanent aspect of the *Logos*, which is simply the actions, and hence, the various effects of the incorporeal *Logos* in the corporeal world. In this immanent sense, the *Logos* is the bond which holds the world together, the principle which conserves it, the rule which governs it, and so on.[47]

It is impossible not to notice in this doctrine of the *Logos* as archetype of all reality, that is, as a thought which contains within itself the whole intelligible cosmos, an anticipation of the second hypostasis of Plotinus (*Nous*)[48] without reckoning, evidently, the connotations of this conception with that of the *Prologue of Saint John's Gospel* and the germs which it contains of certain doctrines which will mature in the sphere of Christian thought.[49]

5. The doctrine of Powers

The same difficulties as those in regard to the *Logos* reappear also for the doctrine of the *Powers* (δυνάμεις) and for the same reasons.

We have seen that God is an unceasing activity; now, the *Powers* are precisely the multiple manifestations of this activity. It is evident that in this context *Powers* does not mean potentiality in the Aristotelian sense, but rather force, action, or activities. We also have seen that the *Logos* is reduced to one of these activities, or *Powers*, thinking (which we will see is a privileged *Power* reuniting all other *Powers*).

So the three levels recognized in the *Logos* are also distinguishable in the *Powers*. They, if considered in God, are indeed the divine properties themselves. But Philo does not speak explicitly about this aspect of the *Powers*.

Considered in themselves, they are in a certain sense incorporeal intermediary entities between God and the world. Finally, if considered as immanent to the world, they are the interface between the physical universe and the incorporeal.[50]

Because God is not finite, there are innumerable manifestations of his activity, that is, his *Powers* are innumerable. Philo mentions nevertheless only a limited number of them and, as a rule, speaks only of the two principal ones and to these he subordinates all the rest. The two principal *Powers* are the Creative Power, that is, the Power by which the Creator produces the universe (which is indicated by the term θεός, God, understood in the restricted sense and interpreted as deriving from τίθημι, which means *to do, to create*) and the Ruling *Power* with which the Creator governs what he has created (which is indicated by the term κύριος, which means Lord). These two *Powers* correspond, as scholars have shown, to those two aspects of the divinity which the ancient Hebraic tradition indicated with the names of *Elohim* and *Yahweh* [*Jehovah, Jahveh*]. *Elohim* expresses the power and the force of good and hence of the act of creation, *Yahweh* the legislative and punishing force. (Note that the translation of the *Septuagint* renders *Elohim* by θεός and *Yahweh* with κύριος.) The Creative *Power* is connected, for example, to the beneficent *Power* and the propitiatory *Power*. The Legislative *Power*, for example, is connected to the Ruling *Power*.[51]

It is evident that, God being unique, the *Powers* which are multiple do not reveal anything except the reflections and projections of God. This is true, naturally, for the two principal ones.

Here is one of the most beautiful passages on this subject:

> When, then, as at noon-tide God shines around the soul, and the light of the mind fills it through and through and the shadows are driven from it by the rays which pour all around it, the single object present to it a triple vision, one representing the reality, the other two the shadows reflected from it. Our life in the light which our senses perceive gives us a somewhat similar experience, for objects standing or moving often cast two shadows at once. No one, however, should think that the "shadows" can be properly spoken of as God. To call them so is loose speaking, serving merely to give a clearer view of the fact which we are explaining, since the real truth is otherwise. Rather, (as anyone who has approached nearest to the truth would say), the central place is held by the Father of the Universe, Who in the sacred scriptures is called He that IS as His proper name, while on either side of Him are the senior potencies, the nearest to Him, the creative and the kingly [θεός is in fact derived as we said from τίθημι]. The title of the former is God, since it made and ordered the All; the title of the later is Lord, since it is the fundamental right of the maker to rule and control what he has brought into being. So the central Being with each of His potencies as his squire presents to the mind which has vision the appearance sometimes of one, sometimes, of three: of one, when that mind is highly purified and,

passing beyond not merely the multiplicity of other numbers, but even the dyad which is next to the unit, presses on to the ideal form which is free from mixture and complexity, and being self-contained needs nothing more; of three, when, as yet uninitiated into the highest mysteries, it is still a votary only of the minor rites and unable to apprehend the Existent alone by Itself and apart from all else, but only through Its actions, as either creative or ruling. This is, as they say, a "second bestvoyage"; yet all the same there is in it an element of a way of thinking such as God approves. But the former state of mind has not merely an element. It is in itself the divinely-approved way, or rather it is the truth, higher than a way of thinking, more precious than anything which is merely thought.[52]

The relation between the *Logos* and the two highest *Powers* (and hence, between the *Logos* and all the other *Powers*, which are subordinated to the two principal ones, as we have seen) is expressly thematized by Philo. In some texts[53] he considers the *Logos* as source of the other *Powers*; in others, instead, he attributes to the *Logos* the function of reuniting the other *Powers* (thus as, and we will immediately see, reuniting in itself all the Ideas), as for example, in the important text *On the Cherubim* (where he interprets the Cherubim as symbols of the *Powers* and the sword of fire as symbols of the *Logos*):

> The [divine oracle] says to me that God is truly only one but the first and highest powers are two, that is, goodness and sovereignty and that with his goodness has created all things and with his sovereignty rules creation. A third power, *which reunites the other two, being in the midst of them and it is the Logos: in fact, it is with the Logos that God is both Sovereign and Good.*[54]

6. The doctrine of the Ideas and the Philonian reform

We have previously mentioned the revival on the part of Philo of the doctrine of the Ideas and the essential change which he imposed on them. The Ideas went from being ungenerated to *being created by God in the act of thinking them, and thus were archetypes of the sensible world*. They become, in this way, the thoughts of God, in the sense that God creates them by thinking them, but they are not exhausted in the simple activity of being thought. They become likewise *beings*, that is, realities in the sense that we have seen. The "place of the Ideas" becomes the *Logos* which includes them in their totality as an "intelligible cosmos" (an expression unknown to Plato and—as it seems—coined by Philo).[55]

Scholars have frequently asked who was the first to introduce the doctrine of the Ideas as the thoughts of God,[56] but they almost never have had the courage to yield to the evidence presented and conclude that on the basis of the documents at our disposal; no one before Philo presented this doctrine with such fullness and detail. In our judgment, this is evidence which serves as solid proof and which cannot easily be refuted. The concept of creation is necessary in order to transform the Platonic Ideas into an intelligible cosmos produced by a mind which also contains them. Prior to Philo there had surely been some attempts to place the Ideas in the divine mind, but the foundation is surely absent which could guarantee the success of the attempt. After Philo, on the contrary, the reduction of the Ideas to divine thoughts will become a doctrine which always continues to expand; but in order to find some philosophers who proposed it with adequate metaphysical basis, it is necessary to go directly to the final Middle Platonists (and especially to Albinus), who placed it in their hypostatic vision of the supersensible, and even to Plotinus who, not incidentally, came out of the Alexandrian milieu.

Naturally, insofar as created by God, the Ideas cease to be "the Being which truly is," that is, absolute being (τὸ ὄντως ὄν) and absolute being becomes God, a God who, being in fact the Being par excellence, can bring forth the totality of things from not-being, as we have seen above.[57]

And again, as created, the Ideas also cease to be absolute paradigms and becomes "images" which are in their turn paradigms. The absolute model is God. The *Logos* is already the firstimage, a perfect image which in its turn functions as a model for the beings which follow. And while the *Logos* is a perfect image of God and the model of all things, the Ideas are particular images, and hence particular models of each individual thing.[58]

It scarcely needs to be pointed out that the creation of the Ideas on the part of God is *not* a temporal act (as the generation of the *Logos* and the *Powers* is not one either), because it does not occur in time. Time arises with the world, as Plato has previously explained in the *Timaeus*. God is prior, in a metaphysical sense, to the Ideas which he creates, insofar as he is their source, and hence he is prior also in the hierarchical sense (that is, above them). Analogically, the Ideas are prior to the world in the metaphysical and axiological sense, insofar as they are the model and the paradigmatic principle, while the world is *posterior* to God and to the Ideas *even in the chronological sense,* because the stated dimension of time is born with the world.[59]

Philo, in addition, connected the Ideas with the *Powers* in various ways.[60]

Notwithstanding the fluidity of the language with which he presents them in this regard, it can be said that the Ideas in general differ from the *Powers* for the following reasons: (*a*) they have a *more limited function* (the *Powers* go back to the general aspects of the divine activity, as we have seen, while the Ideas, in the most proper acceptation of the term, are, more specifically, particular moments of the thinking activity of God); (*b*) this function is precisely that of being *models or exemplary causes*. On the other hand, it is necessary to note, in relation to the fact that the *Logos* in which they are found, functions also as instrumental and efficient cause in the creation of the world, as we have previously said, then in this particular respect the Ideas, insofar as they produce things, can be considered and said to be *Powers* or productive activities.[61]

Interestingly, contrary to Plato, Philo admitted that there were Ideas of the mind and of the soul with consequences which we will examine further on.[62]

Finally, just as the *Logos* and the *Powers*, so also the Ideas have an aspect in respect of which they are immanent to the sensibles as *concrete forms* of concrete things. Precisely in this regard let us recall that they had been created by God, that is, in order to be able to produce a completely unified physical world.[63]

7. The souls without bodies and the Angels

There is a further matter to be considered in order to bring to a close the presentation of the Philonian conception of the incorporeal world, that is, the question of the "Angels" of which the *Bible* speaks.

Philo interpreted Angels as corresponding to those things which in pagan thought were called "Daimons."[64]

The Angels are "bodiless souls" who live chiefly in the air, souls totally devoid of the irrational part and functioning as ministers of God. It is not that God, Philo appropriately notes, has need of informants or helpers, but it is necessary for us to have intermediaries and arbitrators in confronting the immense force of his power.[65]

Nevertheless, in the angelology of Philo the Hellenic component plays an important role, but not a determinative one. The notion of "Angel" is an extremely fluid expression which at times is even applied to the *Logos*[66] and at other times to the appearance God can assume in manifesting Himself to souls which are still united to their bodies,[67] and hence are a particular manifestation of the Power of God (Heb. *shekinah*).

Nonetheless, as much as Philo takes from classical daimonology, in the context of his creationist theology, so much does he change its meaning. In fact, the concept of an Angel as "intermediary between God and men" is inserted into the general conception of creation as a "gift," and comes to be itself one of the ways in which this gift is realized. The Angel is sent to us in various ways because we, in various ways, can rise again to God.

IV. The Anthropology and Moral Philosophy of Philo

1. The new conception of the nature of man or the three dimensions of being human

Scholars have frequently lamented the uncertainty and presumed contradictions in the Philonian conception of man, but they are for the most part referring to the categories of Hellenic philosophy. They have noted that it is very difficult, if not impossible in certain cases, to make everything that Philo says about the nature of man consistent with them. Only a few have noted that, on the contrary, we find ourselves confronted with an authentically revolutionary conception (that Philo achieved gradually) which ends by clearly shattering the positions of classical philosophy from which Philo began.

First, in *On the Creation of the World*, although they still play a dominating role, Greek conceptions, in particular those drawn from Plato and the early Aristotle, are for the most part modified by the context of a creationist conception into which they are placed. It is God himself who intervened in the creation of each individual human being, so between God and each soul (the single individual) there is a bond unknown to preceding thought. The biblical narratives of the creation of man, found respectively in *Genesis* 1:26ff. and 2:7 and due, in all probability, to extrinsic reasons, are interpreted by Philo as referring to two stages of creation, that is, respectively, to the moment of the creation of the intelligible cosmos and to the moment of the physical cosmos in accordance with his general metaphysical conception about which we spoke above. At first ("at first," viz., in the ideal, non-chronological sense) God creates *the ideal model of man*, the eternal pattern which, in a certain sense, is identical with the *Logos*; next, he molds the concrete man at the same time in which he creates the physical world and time. Philo calls the ideal model of man "created man" (man in the image and likeness of God) which he calls his empirical realization "molded man."

Here is a passage in which Philo furnishes the interpretation of *Genesis* 1:26ff.

> After all the rest, as I have said, Moses tells that man was created after *the image of God and after His likeness*(*Gen.* 1:26). Right well does he say this, for nothing earth-born is more like God than man. Let no one represent the likeness as one to a bodily form; for neither is God in human form, nor is the human body God-like. No, it is in respect of the *Mind* (νοῦς), the sovereign element of the *soul* (ψυχή), that the word "image" is used; for after the pattern of a single Mind, even the Mind of the Universe as an archetype, the mind in each of those who successively came into being was molded. It is in a fashion a god to him who carries and enshrines it as an object of reverence; for the human mind evidently occupies a position in

men precisely answering to that which the great Ruler occupies in all the world. It is invisible while itself seeing all things, and while comprehending the substances of others, it is as to its own substance unperceived; and while it opens by arts and sciences roads branching in many directions, all of them great highways, it comes through land and sea investigating what either element contains. Again, when soaring wing it has contemplated the atmosphere and all its phases, it is borne yet higher to the aither and the circuit of heaven, and is whirled round with the dances of the planets and fixed stars, in accordance with the laws of perfect music, following that love of wisdom which guides its steps. And so, carrying its gaze beyond the confines of all substance discernible by sense, it comes to a point at which it reaches out after the intelligible world.[1]

Here is the passage in which Philo interpreted *Genesis* 2:7ff.:

After that he says "God formed man by taking clay from the earth, and breathed into his face the breath of life"(*Gen.* 2:7). By this also he shows very clearly that there is a vast difference between *the man thus formed* and *the man that came into existence earlier after the image of God* [scil.: in the narration of *Gen* 1:26ff.] for the man so formed is an object of sense-perception, partaking already of such or such quality, consisting of body and soul, man or woman, by nature mortal; while he that was after the (Divine) image was an idea or type or seal, an object of thought (only), incorporeal, neither male nor female, by nature incorruptible. It says, however, that the formation of the individual man, the object of sense, is a composite one made up of *earthly substance* and of *Divine breath* [πνεύματος θείου]: for it says that the body was made through the Artificer taking clay and molding out of it a human form, *but that the soul was originated from nothing created whatever*, but *from the Father and Ruler of all*: for that which He breathed in was nothing else than a Divine breath [πνεῦμα θεῖον] that migrated hither from that blissful and happy existence for the benefit of our race, to the end that, even if it is mortal in respect of its visible part, it may in respect of the part that is invisible be rendered immortal. Hence it may with propriety be said that man is the borderl and between mortal and immortal nature, partaking of each so far as is needful, and that he was created at once mortal and immortal in respect of the body but in respect of the mind immortal.[2]

Nevertheless, in these texts, notwithstanding the creationist perspective, man is still conceived as composed of *body* and *soul*, wherefore by "soul" is meant mind. The non-rational soul also belongs to animals, while in man the rational soul is added to non-rational soul, that is, the mind (the distinction between "soul" and "mind" which is much more accentuated than in Plato or Aristotle will become a trait typical of Middle Platonism and of succeeding Greek philosophy, as we will see). Human beings, in conclusion, are still conceived in two dimensions, body and intelligence, the one mortal, the other immortal and "divine."

But gradually, Philo develops a more advanced conception by injecting a third dimension into man's nature of such a kind as to radically upset the significance, the value, and the character of the other two. According to this new conception, in which biblical components become predominant, man is constituted by (1) body, (2) soul-mind, and (3) Spirit which comes from God. According to this perspective the human mind is corruptible insofar as it is a "terrestrial" mind, unless God does not provide us with a "potency for true life," which is his Spirit (πνεῦμα).[3]

Let us read two fundamental texts taken from *Allegorical Interpretations*. Here is the first text in which Philo re-interprets *Genesis* 2:7ff.:

> "And God formed the man by taking clay from the earth, and breathed into his face a breath of life, and the man became a living soul" (*Genesis* 2:7). There are two types of men; the one a heavenly man, the other an earthly [= the paradigmatic ideal man and real men]. The heavenly man, being made after the image of God, is altogether without part or lot in corruptible and terrestrial substance [insofar as he is an incorporeal paradigmatic ideal]; but the earthly one was compacted out of the matter scattered here and there, which Moses calls "clay." For this reason he says that the heavenly man was not molded, but was stamped with the image of God; while the earthly is a *molded work* of the Artificer, but *not His offspring*. We must account the man made out of the earth to be mind [νοῦς] mingling with, but not yet blended with, body. *But this earthlike mind is in reality also corruptible* [γεώδης καὶ φθαρτός], *were not God to breathe into it a power of real life*; when He does so, it does not any more undergo molding, but becomes a soul, not an in efficient and imperfectly formed soul, but one endowed with mind and actually alive; for he says, *"man became a living a soul."*[4]

Therefore, mind of itself, that is, without the breath of divine power, is corruptible, as is everything else.

The most explicit and important text is the following:

> "Breathed into," we note, is equivalent to "inspired" or "be-souled," the soulless [= vivifying the things of life]; for God forbid that we should be infected with such monstrous folly as to think that God employs for in breathing organs such as mouth or nostrils; for God is not only not in the form of man, but belongs to no class or kind. Yet the expression clearly brings out something that accords with nature. For it implies of necessity three things, (*a*) that which inbreathes,(*b*) that which receives, (*c*) that which is inbreathed: (*a*) that which inbreathes is God, (*b*)that which receives is the mind [νοῦς], (*c*) that which is inbreathed is the spirit or breath [πνεῦμα]. What, then, do weinfer from these premises? A union of the three comes about, as God projects the power that proceeds from Himself through the mediant breath till it reaches the subject. And for what purpose save that we may obtain a conception of Him? For how could the soul have conceived of God, had He not *breathe* into it and mightily *laid hold* of it? *For the mind*

> *of man would never have ventured to soar so high as to grasp the nature of God, had not God Himself drawn it up to Himself, so far as it was possible that the mind of man should be drawn up, and stamped it with the impress of the powers that are within the scope of its understanding.*[5]

It is clear that the human soul (the human mind) would be an impoverished thing considered in itself if God did not breathe his Spirit [πνεῦμα] into it. The bond of man to the divine is achieved, for Philo no longer as it was for the Greeks, through the soul not even in its highest part, the mind but through the Spirit which comes immediately from God. Consequently, man has a life which moves in three dimensions, as we said above: (1) according to the dimension of the purely physical animal (body), (2) according to the rational dimension (soul-mind), (3) according to the highest, divine transcendent dimension of Spirit. The soul-mind, of itself mortal, becomes immortal because God gifts it with His Spirit, and the soul binds itself to the Spirit and lives according to the Spirit. The supports on which Plato had based the immortality of the soul are thus eliminated. The soul is not of itself immortal, but can become so because it knows how to live according to the Spirit.

All the most remarkable and novel doctrines which Philo introduces into ethics belong to this third dimension, the Spirit of God, which he derives directly from the interpretation of the biblical doctrine of creation. The moral thought of Philo becomes inseparable from faith and religion and it surges into an authentic mystical and ecstatic union with God, as we will see.[6]

2. The overcoming of the ethical intellectualism of Greek philosophy and the proclamation of faith as the highest virtue

All of Greek ethics was based, as we have seen in the course of this work, on two fundamental presuppositions: (*a*) man with only the power of reason can know *physis*, being, the absolute, and consequently can derive through reason alone, the norms of his moral life which themselves are based on the laws of *physis*; (*b*) human virtue or *areté* has its roots in reason and knowledge and in fact it is knowledge in the sense of reason understood as the *necessary and sufficient* condition for moral action.

Philo counterposes to these fundamental convictions of the Greeks, conceptions that are of a clearly opposed nature.

(*a*) Human reason is not sufficient for the achievement of truth and those who obstinately cling to it will fall into a form of atheistic pride of which Cain is the symbol. The wise cling not to human reason but to God, with humility, and this type of man is symbolized by Abel. Let us read in *On the Sacrifices of Abel and Cain*:

> It is a fact that there are two opposite and contending views of life, one which ascribes all things to the mind [= to human reason] as our master, whether we are using our reason or our senses, in motion or at rest, the other which follows God, whose handiwork it believes itself to be. The first of these views

is figured by Cain who is called "Possession," because he thinks he possesses all things, the other by Abel, whose name means "one who refers (all things) to God."[7]

The conception of man which posits in human reason the supreme guide is expressed in the clearest manner in the Protagorean doctrine of "man as the measure of all things," while on the contrary, in the noble conception based on a creator, God is the measure of all things.[8]

Moreover, according to Philo, the lesson to be drawn from Greek skepticism is the demonstration of the failure of reason, that is, of the claim of reason itself to achieve through itself the truth, and hence it is a kind of demonstration of the correctness of the contrary conviction, that is, of the necessity of arriving at truth *by means of faith in God.*[9]

Man does not achieve truth if truth does not come to him. The biblical God has not only created the world and is revealed in its works, but he has also revealed his existence to some directly and to all through these chosen ones (the prophets). Not only has he given the laws of life by establishing the laws of nature, but he has explained these laws once again through the prophets inspired by him.

(*b*) In addition, reason and knowledge are necessary in order to live well, but they are not sufficient conditions. They necessitate *liberty and the will to choose the good and to reject evil.* Man can easily know the better thing and choose the worse, indeed, simply because he has been created with the free choice between good and evil. Here is a passage in which liberty and will (free will, to use a term coined in the context of Christian thought) are clearly affirmed as man's prerogative, and moral good and evil and in general moral responsibility are joined to them:

> For it is mind alone which the Father who begat it judged worthy of freedom, and loosening the fetters of necessity, suffered it to range as it listed, and of the free-will [τὸ ἑκούσιον] which is His most peculiar possession and most worthy of His majesty gave it such portion as it was capable of receiving. For the other living creatures in whose souls the mind, the element set apart for liberty, has no place, have been committed under yoke and bridle to the service of men, as slaves to a master. But man, possessed of a *spontaneous and self-determined will,* whose activities for the most part rest on deliberate choice, is with reason blamed for what he does wrong with intent, *praised when he acts rightly of his own will.* In the others, the plants and animals, no praise is due if they bear well, nor blame if they fare ill; for their movements and changes in either direction come to them from no deliberate choice or volition of their own. *But the soul of man alone has received from God the faculty of voluntary movement* [τὴν ἑκούσιον κίνησιν], *and in this way especially is made like to Him,* and thus being liberated, as far as might be, from that hard and ruthless mistress, necessity, may justly be charged with guilt, in that it does not honor its Liberator. And there it will rightly pay the inexorable penalty which is meted to ungrateful freedmen.[10]

In addition, for the first time the obligatory character of the moral law is justified and grounded. All Greek philosophers had labored to deduce the "ought" of *moral obligation* from *being* (from *physis*); for Philo, instead, this deduction no longer constitutes a problem, because moral laws are *commands* of God, an *obligation which he imposes as Creator* and which he reveals further, both directly as well as indirectly. And for the first time all the necessary elements are assembled which can explain "sin," or moral fault. Sin is not the result of an error of reason, a poor calculation, but a disobedience to a command, that is, an unwillingness to do the will of God.

We are in the presence of a profound overturning of a perspective in comparison with the moral rationalism of the Greeks which depends once again on the conception of a Creator God and Revealer and consequently on a new conception of the relations existing between the Creator and his privileged creatures, human beings.

Finally, the break with Hellenic rationalism involves the introduction of a new virtue, that of faith, which is placed at the very apex of all the virtues. The "theological" virtue of *faith in God* becomes thus the "queen of the virtues," and in fact "wisdom" itself is reduced to it, that "wisdom" which for Aristotle was the supreme "dianoetic" virtue.[11]

The new "wise man" is the man who has faith in God, who places all his trust in Him, giving all to Him, trying in all possible ways "to follow Him" and "to imitate Him."[12]

Along with faith emerges *hope* (ἐλπίς) and *love*. Thus gradually those things which will become the "theological virtues" of Christian thought are delineated.[13]

And Philo defines immortal life itself in terms of the key notion of love:

> The most beautiful definition of immortal life is this: to be possessed by a desire and a love of God not bound by flesh and body.[14]

3. The journey to God, mystical union with God, and ecstasy

The whole philosophy of Philo is, in the ultimate analysis, *a journey to God* and his allegorical interpretations of the persons and events narrated in the *Bible*, as we have said, are indeed a history of which these persons and events are the symbols of the stages of the soul in its journey to God.

There are three fundamental stages in this journey within which there are further distinguishable moments.[15]

(1) The first stage consists in the abandoning of the contemplation and adoration of the cosmos (the Chaldaic mentality, as Philo called it) in order to return to the goal of "knowing oneself." Philo undoubtedly considered the "contemplation of the cosmos," if kept within correct limits, a form of wisdom, and hence considered a life spent in this sense to be higher than a life which is dispersed in making and doing external things; nevertheless, he censures the

dangers and the extreme fragility of such a life. The dangers consist in the fact that man can carry (and in many cases has actually carried) it to the point of forgetfulness of the very Creator for the benefit of the created, that is, we could say, to the practical absolutizing of the cosmos itself. The fragility of the contemplation of the cosmos, even if correctly practiced, consists in the fact that although the cosmos can be used to rise up to God as to its Creator, it does not permit us to achieve the further knowledge of the effective relation of God to man and hence does not permit the realization of a union with God.

We are also here in the presence of a hiatus in the predominant spirit of Greek philosophy, which is for the most part *cosmocentric*. Aristotle writes:

> *There exists other things far more divine in their nature than man,* for instance, to mention the most visible, *the things of which the cosmos is composed.* These considerations show that wisdom is both scientific knowledge and intellect as regard the things of the most exalted nature.[16]

Philo ends by overturning this perspective. The most divine thing by nature among visible, created things is man, who is a true microcosmos and something more, since as we have seen, he is the single creature which God has made like Himself and in which He even infused His Spirit. Therefore it is easy to see that the trueway to God does not pass through the cosmos, but through man:

> Come down therefore from heaven, and, when you have come down, do not begin in turn to pass in review earth and sea and rivers, and plants and animals in their various kinds; *but explore yourselves only and your own nature, and make your abode with yourselves and not elsewhere*: for by observing the conditions prevailing in your own individual household, the element that is master in it, and that which is in subjection, the living and lifeless element, the rational and the irrational, the immortal and the mortal, the better and the worse, you will gain forthwith a sure knowledge of God and of His works.[17]

(2) The second stage for man consists in self-knowledge aimed at ascertaining, says Philo by means of an Homeric citation, "what there is of good and evil in your palace," that is, within yourself.

This second stage implies a knowledge (*a*) of our *body*, (*b*) of our *senses*, and (*c*) of our *language* and the successive detachment from these three which are deceptive. (*a*) The body, in fact, is said to be a sort of "disgraceful prison" which imprisons by pleasures and desires. (*b*) The senses alienate us, so to speak, and attract us toward objects of their own longing, making us renounce what is proper to us for what is exterior and foreign. (*c*) Language deceives by the beautiful appearance of words; the words risk veiling rather than unveiling the truly beautiful, that is, that which presents the appearance instead of the reality, the copy instead of the prototype.[18]

The detachment and separation from these three realities evidently does not mean to cease to use them; this would only be possible with death, but it means to acquire the "mentality of strangers" in their use, that is, to detach oneself from them through judgment and to be able to go beyond them through reason. It means, as Philo likewise explains, to recognize that they are not ours in reality, but of God, and to offer them to Him.[19]

(3) The third stage consists in the fleeing into our soul as well as understanding that our soul itself (the same as our mind) must be surpassed since, if it does not raise its eyes above itself, that is, to the incorporeal realities and to God, it finds itself inevitably in the service of something which is merely human and terrestrial.[20]

Here is a significant passage:

> "Even as you have quitted the others, *quit yourself, depart from yourself.*" And what does this "departing" mean? It means "do not lay up as treasure for yourself, your gifts of thinking, purposing, apprehending, but *bring them and dedicate them to Him Who is the source of accurate thinking and unerring apprehension." This dedication will be enshrined in the holier of the great sanctuaries.*"[21]

This "leaving from self," that is, from the soul itself or mind, which is a "gift" of our thought to Him Who is the Cause, is identical with a mystical and *ecstatic union with God.*"[22]

The meaning of this journey to God is very clear: from consciousness of the cosmos we have to pass to consciousness of ourselves; but the essential moment consists *in the grasping consciously that we are a nothing.* It is exactly in the moment in which we recognize our own nothingness, that is, in the moment in which we comprehend that everything which we have is not ours and we give back to God what God has given to us, that God gives Himself to us. Here are three important passages on this issue:

> And this is nature's law: he who has thoroughly comprehended himself, thoroughly despairs of himself, having as a step to this ascertained the nothingness in all respects of created being. And the man who has despaired of himself is beginning to know Him that IS.[23]
>
> It is just when he knows his own nothingness, that the creature should come into the presence of his Maker.[24]
>
> A great and transcendent soul does such a boast bespeak, to soar above created being, to pass beyond its boundaries, to hold fast to the Uncreated alone, following the sacred admonitions in which we are told to cling to Him (*Deut.* 30:20), and therefore to those who thus cling and serve Him without ceasing he give Himself as portion.[25]

The happy life consists in this transcending of the human in the divine, in "living with all of oneself for God rather than for oneself."[26]

Second Section

MIDDLE PLATONISM AND THE REDISCOVERY OF PLATONIC METAPHYSICS

« ἀκόλουθον οὖν τῇ ἀρχῇ τὸ τέλος
εἴη ἂν τὸ ἐξομοιωθῆναι θεῷ, θεῷ
δηλονότι τῷ ἐπουρανίῳ, μὴ τῷ μὰ Δία
ὑπερουρανίῳ, ὃς οὐκ ἀρετὴν ἔχει,
ἀμείνων δ᾽ ἐστὶ ταύτης.»

"The end which follows upon the principle
is to become like God, to the celestial God,
evidently, and not to the supercelestial Gods,
who have no virtue, but is better than this."

Albinus, *Didaskalikos* 28.3

I. The Development, Characteristics, and Exponents of Middle Platonism

1. The ultimate fate of the Academy and development of Middle Platonism

In the preceding volume we have seen that in the course of the troubled history of the Academy various phases are distinguishable, characterized by fundamental speculative tendencies each somewhat different from the other.[1] Some ancient authors we have previously mentioned had come to distinguish five Academies in the span of time which moves from Plato to Antiochus of Ascalon: (1) that of Plato and his first successors, (2) that of Arcesilaus, (3) that of Carneades and Clitomachus, (4) that of Philo of Larissa and Charmides, (5) that of Antiochus of Ascalon.[2] If we take into account the fact, as we have seen, that Arcesilaus and Carneades, notwithstanding their differences, were essentially Skeptics, and that Philo of Larissa, after having spent many years defending skeptical ideas, ended by espousing an eclectic position with the acceptance of the attitude brought to prominence by his ex-follower Antiochus, then the phases of the history of the Academy can be reduced to three: (1) the *ancient*, (2) the *new or skeptical*, and (3) the *eclectic*.[3] It is, in addition, worth pointing out that the late and cautious concessions of Philo of Larissa to eclecticism were not considered by contemporaries as a clear rejection of the skeptical neo-Academic position, whereas the eclecticism of Antiochus was considered a real dogmatism. It becomes understandable, therefore, why Cicero, who as we know accepted the ideas of Philo of Larissa and tried to develop them in his own way, maintained that he must adopt, in more than one instance, a cautious distance from Antiochus and from his followers, rejecting the acceptance of their Stoic-inspired dogmatism.[4]

It is certain, in any case, that Antiochus signals a break in the Academic skeptical tradition; but it is likewise certain, as we will see immediately, *that with Antiochus the Academy was exhausted and the new form of Platonism which immediately spread cannot be traced back to Antiochus, nor can it be directly linked to him, as not a few scholars have erroneously believed.*[5]

Let us pause now over the final events of the Academy known to us in the first half of the first century BCE. In 88 BCE, Philo of Larissa left Athens and the Academy because of the Mithridatic War and took refuge at Rome whereas it seems he remained until his death.[6] In 86 BCE, Sulla conquered Athens and (as we have previously noted in studying the Peripatos) during the siege of the city "he cut down the sacred trees and groves of the Academy, the most green of the city suburbs as well as those of the Lyceum."[7] Not only were the Academy and the suburbs seriously damaged, but a large part of the city as well (as our sources expressly tell us); the Athenians were slaughtered in great numbers, and many, in the general panic which spread, committed suicide, fearing total destruction of the city itself.[8] It is clear that the damage inflicted by Sulla to Athens must have been of such gravity as to make a rapid repair of the destruction produced by the war impossible, and hence also the reconstruction and re-opening of the Academy were impossible.[9] This is probably the reason why Philo of Larissa (who found in Rome appreciation and followers) must have thought it useless to return to Athens, where there could not have been any real possibility of establishing the school again.

How did Antiochus behave? We know that after having gone to Alexandria between 87 and 84 BCE he returned to Athens, where he taught as an Academic but not in the Academy, for the reasons given above, since it could not in this short time have been reconstructed. Actually, Cicero, who in 79/78 BCE was his auditor at Athens, refers to the fact that *Antiochus taught in a gymnasium called Ptolemy, and that the Academy was a place which was by now almost abandoned.* Here is a passage of Cicero which is instructive in this regard:

> My Dear BrutusOnce I had been attending a lecture of Antiochus, as I was in the habit of doing, with Marcus Piso, in the building called the School of Ptolemy; and with us were my brother Quintus, Titus Pomponius, and Lucius Cicero, whom I loved as a brother but who was really my first cousin. We arranged to take our afternoon stroll in the Academy, chiefly because the place would be quiet and deserted at that hour of the day. Accordingly at the time appointed we met at our rendezvous, Piso's lodgings, and starting out beguiled with conversation on various subjects the three-quarters of a mile from the Dipylon Gate. When we reached the walks of the Academy, which are so deservedly famous, we had them entirely to ourselves, as we had hoped. Thereupon Piso remarked: "Whether it is a natural instinct or a mere illusion, I can't say; but one's emotions are more strongly aroused by seeing the places that tradition records to have been the favorite resort of men of note in former days, than by hearing about their deeds or reading their writings. My own feelings at the present moment are a case in point. I am reminded of Plato, the first philosopher, so we are told, that made a practice of holding discussions in this place; and indeed the garden close at hand yonder not only recalls his memory but seems to bring the actual man before my eyes. This was the haunt of Speusippus, of Xenocrates, and of Xenocrates' pupil Polemo, who used to sit on the very seat we see over there.[10]

Therefore, in 79/78 BCE the Academy was by now a destination in a spiritual journey in which, so to speak, the ghosts of the past were invoked. The fact that our sources say that Antiochus was a disciple of Philo of Larissa and thus an Academic but they do not say that he was a "scholarch" of the Academy is thus understandable. In fact, he could not have been a scholarch, as his predecessors had been, because the Academy as a school, as an institution in the traditional sense, did not exist any longer, and he, hence, could not have been anything except the *inheritor and spiritual head of the thought born and developed there. Antiochus (who as we have previously said, died in Syria* around 60 BCE (*e*) left the patrimony of his school to his brother Ariston.[11] It is probable that it is with Ariston that this Athenian spiritual survival of the Academy finally fades away. In fact, in this period we have no further express mention of the scholarchs of the Academy, and in the succeeding centuries we even have a direct testimony from Seneca which refers to that fact textually:

The Academics both old and new have ceased to have a head.[12]

This is the point at which we wish to arrive. While the Academy ceased to exist in Athens, outside Athens, precisely at Alexandria, *Platonism revived and gained ground with characteristics in large part different from the eclectic-Stoicizing dogmatism of Antiochus.* Eudorus of Alexandria who probably lived in the second half of the first century BCE is the first exponent of whom we have knowledge who belonged to this new tendency of Platonism (but it is not improbable that others, however, again before Eudorus, would have tried to move in this direction).[13] It is certain, in any case, that beginning from the second half of the first century BCE Platonism gently but progressively and constantly continued to differ and to increase in its own consistency and acuity until it culminated in the great Plotinian synthesis which developed in the third century CE and which opened a new path for both Pagan and Christian thought.

Consequently, the great Plotinian synthesis (and the currents of thought that it generated) is correctly called "neo"-Platonism." What, then, will that part of the history of Platonism be called which proceeds from the middle half of the first century CE through the whole of the second century CE? Simply to call it "Platonism," as was done until the previous century, is not correct, since it is not simply a repetition of Plato, or of the doctrine of the ancient Academy. In fact, the attempts to reinterpret in an original way Platonic doctrines in the Platonists of this period are quite visible. They are attempts, in a certain sense, which arrive at results which are preludes to the thought of Plotinus, or they prepare that terrain upon which Neoplatonism will be born by assembling elements that will produce the spiritual climate in which it will be nurtured. It is necessary nevertheless to recognize that it is a thought which is not always unitary, frequently uncertain, and at times even contradictory. It is a thought in which old and new are variously interwoven without ever reaching an exhaustive synthesis. In conclusion, the Platonism of this period has characteristics, so to speak, in the middle between the ancient Platonism of Plato and his immediate followers and the Neoplatonism of Plotinus and his followers. Therefore, the term "Middle Platonism," which signifies in fact a Platonism which stands in the middle between the old and the new, should be considered as justified and perfectly adequate, as we will immediately see in a detailed way below.[14]

2. General characteristics of Middle Platonism

(a) The most typical trait of Middle Platonism, the trait which constitutes the minimum common denominator of the thought of almost all of its exponents without exception, consists in what we could call, by going back to the well-known Platonic image, the renewal of the "second voyage," viz., with the recovery of its essential results, as well as of the principal consequences arising from them. *Middle Platonism, in conclusion, recovers the supersensible, the immaterial, and the transcendent and clearly breaks the chains of the materialism dominant for a long period.* The foundation of the sensible and of the corporeal are pointed out anew in the supersensible and the immaterial, or better in the incorporeal and the metaphysical-theological component of philosophy (in the proper Platonic-Aristotelian sense) not only begins to re-emerge but it is placed in the foreground. In our judgment, it is precisely these characteristics which not only guarantee a place not lacking in importance in the history of ancient thought to Middle Platonism, but which likewise secures the unity of the various tendencies represented by them, that is, that unity which many scholars either have not specified clearly or have even denied. The texts which we will report further on will demonstrate this assertion clearly. (It is appropriate to point out again, in this regard, that Philo of Alexandria himself took up the notion of the "incorporeal," which is not present in the *Bible*, from the incipient Alexandrine Middle Platonism.)[15]

(b) The logical consequences of this renewal of the "second voyage" was the *reproposing of the theory of Ideas*, which as we know represents its most important results. The Middle Platonists, in fact, not only refurbished this doctrine but (at least some of them) rethought it completely, trying to integrate the position taken from Plato with that of Aristotle. Albinus and his circle, as we will see, *considered the Ideas in their transcendent aspect as the thoughts of God* (the intelligible world becomes identified with the activity and with the content of the supreme intelligence) *and in their immanent aspect as the "forms" of things*. Along with the transformation of the theory of Ideas there is as a logical consequence a parallel transformation of the notion of the whole structure of the incorporeal world, with results that, as we will see, are clearly a prelude to Neoplatonism.[16]

(c) The text which the Middle Platonists consider a cornerstone and from which they derive the reinterpretation of the Platonic doctrine was the *Timaeus*. Actually, in the difficult task of reducing the Platonic philosophy to a system and in the attempt to synthesize it, the *Timaeus* was the dialogue which offered a much more secure footing. It is interesting to point out, in this regard, that the Middle Platonists had followed by preference a method opposed to that of the Peripatetics of this period (from Andronicus to Alexander). In fact, the former will maintain that the best way to understand Plato would be by making a *compendium*; the latter instead maintained that the best method for understanding Aristotle would be by producing a *commentary*. Therefore, while the commentary took hold almost exclusively among the Aristotelians,[17] the compendium, as it seems, prevailed instead among the Middle Platonists, even if not a few, especially in the second century CE, seem to be writing commentaries concerned with individual dialogues. The *Didaskalikos* of Albinus, which is extant and complete, is also from this point of view a model document.[18]

(*d*) The "doctrine of the principles" from the esoteric Plato, that is, the *doctrine of the One (ἕν) and the Dyad (δυάς) was in part taken up again, but it remained clearly in the background*. It gained an enormous importance, as we will see, within the sphere of the parallel Neo-Pythagorean movement. This was inevitable since the theoretical system of the *Timaeus* did not allow for the doctrine of the One and the Dyad. On the other hand, the doctrine of the One and the Dyad and its concomitant theory of the Ideal-numbers, as we have seen in Plato, must explain the derivation of the Ideas and the entire world of the Ideas. But the Middle Platonists, once they had reduced the Ideas to the *thoughts of God*, did not have any further need to deduce them or to justify them in any other way, as we will see better further on.[19]

(*e*) The religious sentiment, which in some achieves an authentic mysticism, *moves the Middle Platonists to give a special importance to the doctrine of the Daimons*, which is an ancient doctrine among the Greeks dear to the Orphics and to the Presocratics, who were inspired by Orphism, and dear as well to Plato and the Stoa itself. The accentuation of the transcendence of God and of the divine in relation to man and to the physical world made it necessary to have some "mediators," and in fact as mediators between God and man the Middle Platonists increased the power of the *daimons*. In addition, *daimons* were made powerful in order to justify pagan beliefs. Finally, the strong religious interest pushed some to *re-evaluate Eastern wisdom* in general and as we encounter in Plutarch's writings, in particular the Egyptian one.[20]

(*f*) Also for the Middle Platonists, as for the philosophers of the preceding ages, ethical problems remain paramount, but they are reinterpreted anew and grounded in a novel way. The principle had been "to follow nature" (*physis*) for all the Hellenistic schools and nature was understood in a materialistic and immanentistic sense. The new byword of the Middle Platonists was instead "follow God," "assimilate to God," "imitate God." The rediscovery of transcendence must logically modify step by step the whole vision of life proposed by the Hellenistic Age. *In fact, the Middle Platonists unanimously recognized in the assimilation to the divine transcendence and incorporeality the authentic distinctiveness of the moral life.*[21]

(*g*) On the basis of what we have said it is impossible to directly link Middle Platonism to Antiochus, contrary to what many scholars believed. Although it is true that Antiochus as well as the Middle Platonists turned to "dogmatism" and both attempted to bring together Platonism, Aristotelianism, and Stoicism, it is likewise true that the results of these attempts were *very diverse*. The attempt of Antiochus is a mechanical dogmatic eclecticism, in fact, in its general orientation it is wholly Stoic.[22] On the contrary, Middle Platonic thought, even if accepting elements from various backgrounds, has a fundamental unity which is precisely Platonic and consists, as we have said, in the rediscovery of the incorporeal. *The recovery of the dimension of the transcendent with all its corollaries at all levels is a clear line of demarcation between the dogmatism of Antiochus and Middle Platonism.* Middle Platonism arose, therefore, not from Antiochus, but, on the contrary, by an overturning of the mentality which inspired the philosophy of Antiochus.

3. The exponents and tendencies of Middle Platonism

The names first associated with Middle Platonism, as we have said many times previously, go back to the second half of the first century BCE; they are Dercyllides[23] and, especially, Eudorus of Alexandria.[24]

It is possible to infer a precise enough conclusion from what we have said above about the extinction of the Academy at Athens and what we have noted above in speaking of Philo of Alexandria. Middle Platonism must have arisen not at Athens but at Alexandria, since in this city, before any place else, there was present a strong religious sense and mystical attitude arising through Eastern influence which brought about the recovery of the dimensions of the incorporeal and transcendent which the great Hellenistic philosophers had lost.[25]

Middle Platonism was quickly spread to the West from Alexandria and flourished especially in the second century CE.

In the first half of the first century CE the activity of Thrasyllus whose name is linked to the division of the dialogues of Plato into tetralogies can be located.[26] Onasander also lived in the first century CE.[27] Plutarch[28] who was a follower of the Egyptian Ammonius, who established a circle of Platonists at Athens lived between the first and second century CE.[29] Plutarch was linked to Calvenus Taurus,[30] teacher of Herodes Atticus[31] and of Aulus Gellius.[32] Gaius,[33] in whose school are placed Albinus,[34] and Apuleius,[35] as well as the anonymous author of a commentary on the *Theaetetus* (which is partially extant and which is of no little interest) lived in the first half of the second century CE.[36] To the second century CE also belong Theon of Smyrna[37] Nigrinus (made famous by Lucian),[38] Nicostratus,[39] Atticus,[40] Arpocraton,[41] Celsus,[42] the rhetorician Maximus of Tyre,[43] and Severus;[44] in this epoch Platonism was by now almost an ecumenical movement.[45]

Only a small part of the works of these authors has come down to us, except for a few.[46] We possess complete works of Plutarch, Theon of Smyrna, Albinus, Apuleius, and Maximus of Tyre.[47] We possess only fragments of the other Middle Platonists. Finally, we just know the names of others. The most significant complete extant document, as we said previously, is the *Didas-kalikos* of Albinus.[48]

Some scholars believe that they can distinguish in Middle Platonism two basic tendencies which differ from each other in the following respects: the first is of a *syncretistic* nature, that is, it has a propensity to use the results of the various schools; and the second is more *orthodox*, that is, it has more of a propensity to reject doctrines of other schools in order to follow those which are more authentically Platonic. The circle of Gaius would be an example of the syncretistic tendency, while the exponents of the so-called orthodoxy would be Plutarch, Calvenus Taurus, Nicostratus, and especially Atticus. It is nevertheless important to see that the so-called orthodoxy of these proponents lies more in their intentions than it does in their results. Plutarch, for example, attributes to Plato numerous doctrines which were clearly non-Platonic, and Atticus, who opposed Plato to Aristotle, although he criticized the latter violently, did not represent any more successfully the original Platonic doctrines. In reality, not only is the syncretistic tendency of the circle of Gaius more fruitful but in certain respects it is even more Platonic.[49]

Another distinction can be formulated perhaps in a less inadequate way between the Middle Platonists who gave to their discussions a more philosophical aura and those, on the contrary, who showed special sensitivity to the religious and mystical mentality like Plutarch, Celsus, and Apuleius himself. In Plutarch, as we have previously mentioned, the Eastern component emerges into the foreground. He, in fact, nurtured a great interest in Egyptian religion and mythology, about which he gave interesting allegorical interpretations.[50]

A presentation of Middle Platonism can be made either through the analytic examination of what we know of each individual thinker or by means of the reconstruction of the above-mentioned tendencies or by trying to grasp in a unitary and detailed way the framework of the basic problems and solutions proposed. We have chosen this third method since the first turns out to be very dispersive and the second leads to uncertainty, and hence somewhat implausible results.[51] Before going on to the analysis of the problems, therefore, we want to make a final determination about the limits and the importance of Middle Platonism.

4. The historical and theoretical importance and the limits of Middle Platonism

We can immediately state what is the importance of Middle Platonism, which was for a long time misunderstood. Neoplatonism without the Middle Platonic movement would be almost unexplainable. Plotinus, in his lectures, fundamentally commented on Middle Platonic texts,[52] and on Peripatetic texts influenced by Middle Platonism;[53] in addition, some of his basic problems as well as their solutions were taken from Middle Platonists. Certain affirmations that Plotinus makes in the *Enneads* without any awareness of the need to demonstrate them and with which the modern reader is struck by their lack of demonstration can thus be explained by the fact that they had become common knowledge with Middle Platonism, and as such) Plotinus accepted them.

Middle Platonism, in addition, is important also for the purpose of understanding the first Christian thinkers, that is, the first of the Fathers, who, prior to the birth of Neoplatonism, took from this intellectual movement the categories of thought with which they tried to ground their faith philosophically.[54]

A curious fact is to be noted in this regard: as Neoplatonism, after Plotinus will be used both by some pagan philosophers who favor paganism and by some Christian thinkers who favor Christianity, so it happens also, although in a smaller way, in Middle Platonism. Celsus writes the first philosophical work against the Christians using Middle Platonic categories while the Christians, as we said, would also take their weapons from Middle Platonism in order to elaborate theoretically their own vision of the world and life.

Middle Platonism represents, hence, one of the necessary links in the history of Western thought.

The limits of this movement are established by the fact that the attempts at reinterpreting and systematizing Platonism oscillated and remained incomplete. None of the Middle Platonists, in fact, were able to achieve a definitive or even an illustrative synthesis. Middle Platonism was not lacking men of genius, but it lacked the creative or re-creative genius, and for this reason it is a transitional philosophy, a half-way stop on the journey which leads from Plato to Plotinus.

II. The Metaphysics of Middle Platonism

1.   Incorporeal being, God and his transcendence

We have previously made allusions many times to the rediscovery of the incorporeal and the transcendent and to the consequences of the new notion of reality derived from it. Now we have to examine the manner in which the recovery of the incorporeal involves a new notion of God and the divine and that such a conception is to be especially contrasted with the conceptions of the Stoics, which were far more artful, more capricious, and hence more dangerous.[1] In Plutarch, this anti-Stoic position is very clear:

> And as for his vagaries and transformations when he sends forth fire that sweeps his own self along with it, as they say, and again when he forces it down here and directs it upon the earth and sea and winds and living creatures, and, besides, the terrible things done both to living creatures and to growing vegetationto such tales it is irreverent even to listen.[2]

> For it is neither probable nor fitting that god is, as some philosophers say, mingled with matter, which is altogether passive, and with things, which are subject to countless necessities, chances, and changes.[3]

God, Plutarch states, is transcendent in the sense that he is immutable and immaterial, always identical with himself:

> But he himself is far removed from the earth, uncontaminated and unpolluted and pure from all matter that is subject to destruction and death.[4]

But the most important text of Plutarch is the end of the treatise *De E apud Delphi*, where our philosopher defines God as Being, true Being, opposed to the being of man and all other beings in the physical world, which in reality is not "being": but rather "becoming," that is, being which changes and hence is almost non-being. God is atemporal Being who is not affected by the events of the "past" and the "future": he is immobile Being in the dimension of the eternal. The "E" of the temple of Delphi according to Plutarch means "EI," which means "You are." Therefore God welcomes in his temple man with the slogan "know yourself" and man responds to God with the phrase "You are," which means "You are Being." Let us read this truly important passage in which it seems that we can even detect the echo of the biblical *"Ego sum qui sum"* (which, as we have seen, was basic in the Philonian treatises) as well as the echo of the Parmenidean and Platonic teaching:

> No, it is an address and salutation to the god, complete in itself, which, by being spoken, brings him who utters it to thoughts of the god's power. For the god addresses each one of us as we approach him here with the words 'Know Yourself,' as a form of welcome, which certainly is in no wise of less import than 'Hail'; and we in turn reply to him 'You are *Ei*,' as rendering

unto him a form of address which is truthful, free from deception, and the only one befitting him only, the assertion of Being.

The fact is that we really have no part nor parcel in Being, but everything of a mortal nature is at some stage between coming into existence and passing away, and presents only a dim and uncertain semblance and appearance of itself; and if you apply the whole force of your Mind in your desire to apprehend it, it is like unto the violent grasping of water, which, by squeezing and compression, loses the handful enclosed, as it spurts through the fingers; even so Reason, pursuing the exceedingly clear appearance of every one of those things that are susceptible to modification and change, is baffled by the one aspect of its coming into being, and by the other of its passing away; and thus it is unable to apprehend a single thing that is abiding or really existent.

'It is impossible to step twice in the same river' are the words of Heraclitus, nor is it possible to lay hold twice of any mortal substance in a permanent state; by the suddenness and swiftness of the change in it there 'comes dispersion and, at another time, a gathering together'; or, rather, not at another time nor later, but at the same instant it both settles into its place and forsakes its place; 'it is coming and going.'

Wherefore that which is born of it never attains unto being because of the unceasing and unstaying process of generation, which, ever bringing change, produces from the seed an embryo, then a babe, then a child, and in due course a boy, a young man, a mature man, an elderly man, an old man, causing the first generations and ages to pass away by those which succeed them. But we have ridiculous fear of one death, we who have already died so many deaths, and still are dying! For not only is it true, as Heraclitus used to say, that the death of heat is birth for steam, and the death of steam is birth for water, but the case is even more clearly to be seen in our own selves: the man in his prime passes away when the old man comes into existence, the young man passes away into the man in his prime, the child into the young man, and the babe into the child. Dead is the man of yesterday, for he is passed into the man of to-day; and the man of to-day is dying as he passes into the man of to-morrow. Nobody remains one person, nor is one person; but we become many persons, even as matter is drawn about some one semblance and common mold with imperceptible movement. Else how is it that, if we remain the same persons, we take delight in some things now, whereas earlier we took delight in different things; that we love or hate opposite things, and so too with our admirations, and our disapprovals, and that we use other words and feel other emotions and have no longer the same personal appearance, the same external form, or the same purposes in Mind? For without change it is not reasonable that a person should have different experiences and emotions; and if he changes, he is not the same person; and if he is not the same person, he has no permanent being, but changes his very nature as one personality in him succeeds to another. Our senses, through ignorance of reality, falsely tell us that what appears to be is.

What, then, really is Being? It is that which is eternal, without beginning and without end, to which no length of time brings change. For time is something that is in motion, appearing in connection with moving matter, ever flowing, retaining nothing, a receptacle, as it were, of birth and decay, whose familiar 'afterwards' and 'before,' 'shall be' and 'has been,' when they are uttered, are of themselves a confession of Not Being. For to speak of that which has not yet occurred in terms of Being, or to say of what has already ceased to be, that it is, is silly and absurd. And as for that on which we most rely to support our conception of time, as we utter the words, 'it is here,' 'it is at hand,' 'now'all this again reason, entering in, demolishes utterly. For 'now' is crowded out into the future and the past, when we would look upon it as a culmination; for of necessity it suffers division. And if Nature, when it is measured is subject to the same processes as is the agent that measures it, then there is nothing in Nature that has permanence or even existence, but all things are in the process of creation or destruction according to their relative distribution with respect to time. Wherefore it is irreverent in the case of that which is to say even that it was or shall be; for these are certain deviations, transitions, and alterations, belonging to that which by nature has no permanence in Being.

But if God is (if there be need to say so), and He exists for no fixed time, but for the everlasting ages which are immovable, timeless, and undeviating, in which there is no earlier nor later, no future nor past, nor older nor younger; but He, being One, has with only one 'Now' completely filled 'For ever'; and only when Being is after His pattern is it in reality Being, not having been nor about to be, nor has it had a beginning nor is it destined to come to an end.[5]

We find an analogous order of concepts in Albinus and in the so-called "circle of Gaius." Albinus expressly argued against the pan-corporeal conception of the Stoa according to which only what is a body can act, and he argues for the exactly opposite principle.

He writes thus:

In addition, the efficient causes cannot be other than incorporeal; in fact bodies are passive and changeable and are not always found in the same or identical condition, nor are they steadfast and immutable, and we quickly discover that they are passive also when it seems that there is some activity in them; hence just as there is something which is purely passive, so is there a need for something absolutely active; and this can be nothing other than the incorporeal.[6]

In regard to the incorporeal nature of God, Albinus provides the following demonstration:

God does not have parts because there is nothing existent prior to him; in fact, a part and that out of which something is made exist before that of which it is a part; in fact, the surfaces exist before the solid and the lines before the surfaces; by not having parts therefore it is immobile both with regard to spatial change and qualitative change. If in fact anything changes, it would be either through itself or through another: if were through another, this other would be stronger than it: if through itself, it would change either for the better or for the worse: both these eventualities are absurd. From everything we conclude that He is without a body. This is likewise shown with the following arguments: if God had a body, it would be constituted by matter and form; every body is in fact composed by matter and form which is present in it; this composite is like the Ideas and it participates in them in a way which is difficult to say; it is absurd, then, that God be constituted by matter and form: He would not be in fact simple and originative. Consequently He is incorporeal. And again: if He is a body, He would be constituted by matter, hence we would be either fire, or water, or earth, or air, or something which is derived from these elements; but none of these has the nature of a principle. In addition, it would be subsequent to mater, if He were made of matter: given the absurdity of these conclusions, it is necessary to conceive of Him as incorporeal; in fact, if it is a body, it is corruptible and generated and changeable: but each of these attributes is absurd in its own regard.[7]

Apuleius states analogous concepts which take up again the Platonic "second voyage."

According to Plato there are two realitieswhat we call essence [= substance]from which all things and the world itself are derived: the first is known only by thought, the second can be grasped through the senses. But the first, which is dependent on the eyes of the Mind, is found always in the same condition, equal and similar to itself, as that which truly is; the second, instead, which, as Plato affirms, is born and dies, is grasped by sensible opinion and the irrational. And as the first is considered as true being, so the second is not true being. The first substance or essence is the first God and Mind and the forms of things and soul, the second substance is everything which receives a form and which is generated and has its origin from the model of a superior substance, which can change and transform itself fleeing and dispersing like water from a stream.[8]

The emphasized characteristic of the transcendence of God must involve, as a consequence, the denial of the possibility that man can understand and grasp the essence of God himself and hence the negation of the possibility of expressing it in a definition. This doctrine of the unknowability and ineffability of God, which we have seen in Philo of Alexandria,[9] is affirmed by some Middle Platonists and especially by Albinus in a clear way:

He is ineffable and graspable only with the intellect, as is said because he is neither a genera nor a species nor a specific difference, nor on the other hand can any determination be applied to him, neither evil (since it is not allowable to say this) nor good (since he would be such by participation in something especially good); nor is he indifferent (because he does not correspond to its notion). Neither is any quality applied to him (since he does not have any need of it and he is perfect not dependent on any quality), nor is he without quality (since he is not lacking any quality which can belong to him). He is not a part of anything, neither as a whole has parts, nor consequently is he equal to anything, nor different; nothing in fact can be said which indicates he can be separated from other things; he neither moves or is moved.[10]

Notwithstanding these statements, the Middle Platonists do not proceed, as on the contrary would be done by some Pythagoreans, to the point of also wanting to place God above Mind. Most of them, in fact, maintained that God is identical with the supreme Mind.[11]

Therefore, Platonic metaphysics is taken up again together with the results arrived at by Aristotle, who, as we have seen, had substituted the absolute understood precisely as supreme Mind for the absolute understood as an intelligible idea.[12] In fact, these results would be further enriched by Middle Platonists with a real attempt at the mediation and the overcoming of the existing antithesis between the Platonic and the Aristotelian position concerning metaphysics, as we shall now see.

2. The Ideas as thoughts of God and the distinction between the first intelligibles or transcendent Ideas and the second intelligibles or the immanent forms of things

The conception of the Ideas as thoughts of God has certainly had historical antecedents, as we have already said in speaking about Philo of Alexandria.[13] Scholars have often pointed out that they can trace the anticipation of this doctrine in Xenocrates,[14] in the Stoa,[15] and in Antiochus of Ascalon.[16] But in Xenocrates it is only implicit, while the Stoics and Antiochus completely lacked the conception of the immaterial, and consequently their problematic was located on an entirely different plane. The intuitions which are found in Varro also do not move the issue much further along (while the statements of Seneca prove nothing, because this philosopher, as can gather from what he says about Platonic doctrine, had already read the Middle Platonists' writings).[17]

Instead this doctrine assumes in Philo of Alexandria, as we have seen, other important features and characteristics. But Philo connects the doctrine of Ideas as divine thoughts *through both the biblical concept of creation* and the concept of *Logos*, which was also linked to the biblical notion of Wisdom and the Creative Word of God *more than to Hellenic doctrines*. Albinus instead formulates the same doctrine by using arguments containing categories taken exclusively from Greek thought and hence in an unexpected manner.

Granted the great importance of these doctrines in the succeeding history of Christian and Greek thought, this is an appropriate time to consider it in a detailed manner. In order to fully understand these doctrines, it is necessary to refer to the positions of Plato and Aristotle, which on this question, as we know, were opposed.[18]

Plato had posited as absolute the World of Ideas, that is, the Intelligible, and had placed it above Mind and Intelligence (the Demiurge, which is Intelligence, referred to the Ideas as to entities which were above him). Aristotle, instead, placed as absolute the Mind understood as thought thinking itself (a thinking on thinking). He has made the Ideas immanent in the sensible, making them into the intrinsic "forms" (εἴδη) of things, and he had maintained that only in this way could the fundamental intuition of Plato be supported.

Actually, most of the aporias of the Platonic metaphysics, as we have seen in the appropriate place, depended more on the reasons inferred by Aristotle than on having placed the Ideas *above the demiurgic Intelligence*. In its turn, a series of aporias of Aristotle's metaphysics depended on having placed the Ideas too far *below the divine Mind*, changing them precisely into the immanent "forms" and locating them in matter. The "place of the forms," consequently, for Aristotle could only be the human mind insofar as it abstracts and thinks them and not the divine Mind which only thinks itself.

The Middle Platonists thought it was possible to bring together into a unity the different views of the two philosophers, correcting one with the other and thus bringing them into mutual agreement. The Aristotelian results could be supported by affirming the primary principle to be Mind, but the Platonic world of Ideas could likewise be maintained at the same time *by making it the content of the divine Mind*. The Aristotelian God is a self-thinking Mind; *but the thoughts of God, who thinks himself, of necessity are eternal and immutable, they are eternal paradigms and rules of all things, which is precisely what Plato called the Ideas*. Albinus writes:

> Since the first Intellect is in the highest respect beautiful, it also requires intelligible Objects be in the highest degree beautiful, but in no way more beautiful than Himself; therefore, he think himself, and the *thoughts of himself and this activity are precisely the Ideas*.[19]

And here is a second passage, in which, on the conception of the Ideas as the *thoughts of God*, there is even constructed a demonstration of the existence of the Ideas themselves:

> That the Ideas exist can be demonstrated with the following arguments: be God an intellect or something which thinks, he has thoughts and these thoughts are eternal and immutable; but if this is so, then the Ideas exist. And if matter is, through its own nature, without measure, it needs to find a measure in some other thing which is better and non-material; but the antecedent is true, therefore also the consequent is true. But if that is so, then the Ideas exist as the measure and are non-material.[20]

It is clear that so conceived the *transcendent Ideas* and the *immanent forms* not only do not exclude each other, but the former are principles and causes, whereas the latter as immanent are their consequences and effects. The immanent forms of singular things are the images or reflections of the Ideas impressed by the Demiurge on matter. Albinus consistently calls the Ideas considered as the divine thoughts "the primary intelligibles," and the immanent forms of things "secondary intelligibles."[21]

The confidence with which Albinus espouses these positions shows that he must have had by now a solid tradition behind him, that is, that such doctrines were teachings in large measure already accepted.[22] The doctrine of the Ideas as divine thoughts and the connected distinctions between the primary transcendent intelligibles and the secondary immanent intelligibles represents probably, one of the most felicitous attempts at a synthesis of Plato and Aristotle produced up to that time and an essential achievement of which Plotinus will be the greatest beneficiary.[23]

3. The hierarchy of the divine: toward the doctrine of hypostasis

A common tendency in many Middle Platonists, expressed in a clear way already by the earlier among them, is that of placing *Nous* (Mind) as superior to *psyché* (soul). This doctrine (which was chiefly anticipated by Aristotle)[24] has an anti-materialistic and anti-Stoic[25] meaning in the Middle Platonists. By clearly differentiating between the Mind and the soul and placing Mind as the superior, the bridge with immanentism was definitively broken. (In this respect it is very interesting that Atticus, wanting at all costs to repudiate Aristotle and hence also this distinction, which is precisely of Aristotelian origin, went back to a quite ambiguous position.)[26]

It is clear that in this way a movement towards a doctrine which is a prelude to the Plotinian hypostases must have begun. In fact, *read from a certain viewpoint, not a few passages of the Middle Platonists would even contain, at least inchoately, all three Plotinian hypostases, which are: the One, Nous, and the Soul.*

Thus, for example, in Plutarch, if next to the soul and Mind (which he distinguishes with great clarity) we place the supreme God, who, for him, is Being, but also the supreme One, we obtain a triad which prefigures, precisely, the One of Plotinus.[27] An analogous triad is drawn from a text of Apuleius, who distinguishes: first God, Mind and Ideas, and Soul.[28] Some have thought that the hypostatic hierarchy could be drawn from Albinus.[29] Nevertheless this hierarchical construction is traceable only by someone who has previously read Plotinus. In fact, judging from the clearest text concerning this matter that has come down to us, which is a passage of the *Didaskalikos* of Albinus, the hierarchy of the divine seems to culminate not in a reality which is beyond the Mind, but in the Mind itself, as is clear from the following scheme:

(1) First God or First Mind
(2) Second Mind, or Mind of the soul of the world;
(3) The Soul of the world

The first Mind says Albinus "calls" the soul of the world and turns it toward itself and by returning to itself, it generates the Mind of the world. The cosmos is ordered not directly by the first Mind, but mediately by the second Mind.

Here is the text of Albinus:

> Since the Mind is better than the soul and the Mind in act which thinks all things at once and always is better than the one that is in potency, and more excellent than that is the cause of that and what can be above these, such is the first God, who is the cause of the eternal activity of the Mind of all the heavens. It makes everything move by remaining immobile, as the sun in relation to that which is seen, when it sees it, and as the object of desire moves the desiring, by remaining immobile; thus indeed also this Mind will move the Mind of the whole heavens. Since the first Mind is in the highest way beautiful, it requires that its object also be in the highest way beautiful, but there is nothing more beautiful than itself: therefore it thinks itself and its own thoughts, and this activity is precisely the Idea. In addition the first God is eternal, ineffable, perfect in itself, that is without any needs, eternally complete, that is, eternally perfect: it is the divine, subsistent, truth, and proportionate good. I say that not intending to separate these things but intending to think by means of them a unity. It is good because it benefits all things insofar as it is possible, being the cause of every good; it is beautiful since it is by its own nature perfectly proportioned; it is truth because it is the principle of all truths, just as the sun is the principle of every light; it is father because it is the cause of all and orders the Mind of the heaven and the soul of the world in relation to itself and to its intellections. According to its will, in fact, filling up all things from itself and having revived the soul of the world and *having turned it to itself, it is the cause of its Mind*. This Mind, ordered by the father, orders all of nature in this way.[30]

As can be easily seen, Albinus speaks in a purely hypothetical manner of a First superior to the Mind, but then makes the first God and the first Mind clearly identical.[31]

The identification of the supreme God with the supreme Mind must be considered as typical of Middle Platonism.[32]

Celsus (Aulus Cornelius), instead, seems to place God above Mind and Being itself.[33] But his discussion (which is guided more by religious and mystical interests which are non-philosophical) does not seem to arise from many other well-known Platonic affirmations about the Idea of the Good.[34]

The predominance of this current of thought which derives from the mediation between the Aristotelian metaphysics of the Mind and the Platonic doctrine of Ideas explains, as we have noted previously, the reason for which the Pythagoreanizing doctrines of the esoteric Plato on the One and the Dyad were kept in the shade. In fact, once we have justified the Ideas as thoughts of the divine Mind, the One and the Dyad, which were introduced by Plato precisely in order to deduce the ideal world, as we have already pointed out, come to lose their original significance and importance. Eudorus, according to some scholars, revived that doctrine. But Eudorus belongs to the second half of the first century BCE and it is not precisely certain that he had a theory of the One and the Dyad.[35] In any case, after him Middle Platonism must have become progressively disinterested in the doctrine in question. Besides, the position of Plutarch is significant enough: he also restated the theory of the One and the Dyad, but confined it within a context which was largely marginal.[36] In Albinus it is even absent (and perhaps in most of the Middle Platonists of the second century CE). This doctrine deriving from the esoteric doctrines of Plato is instead the axis around which Neo-Pythagorean speculation rotates, as we have previously said and as we will see better further on.[37]

4. The cosmology of Middle Platonism: matter and the origin of the cosmos

The sensible cosmos for the Middle Platonists is not a simple emanation or an epiphenomenon of the supersensible. In order to explain it they have recourse to "three principles;" in addition to God and the Ideas, there is a "third principle" which is constituted by matter.[38]

Matter is understood both on the basis of the Platonic *Timaeus* and on the basis of later Aristotelian notions. Consequently, they take up again the famous images and expressions of Plato, for example, "nurse," "matrix," and "space," combining them with the Aristotelian concepts of "substrate" and "potentiality." Once again the philosophers of the "circle of Gaius" provide us with the most interesting texts.

Albinus writes:

> It is therefore called by Plato the impressionable matrix, receptacle, nurse, mother, space, substrate not perceptible through sensation and graspable only by means of an illicit reasoning. It has the property of receiving everything which is born, having the function of a nurse in the carrying and receiving all the shapes, but it is of itself without form, without quality and without shape; being formed and signed by these shapes as an impressionable matrix taking the shape from them, but it does not possess in itself any shape or quality. In fact it would not be able to receive impressions and various forms, except it were lacking quality and deprived of those figures which it must accept; we see, in fact, that even those who anoint themselves with perfumed oils, make use of oil which is less odiferous and those who wish to mold forms with wax and clay, work to make as far as is possible these materials to be lacking any form whatever. Certainly, therefore, it is so also for matter, which receives everything, it must receive from everything the extension of its shapes, not having any nature of its own, but it is without quality or shape, in order precisely that it can accept shapes; being such, it is neither a body nor a non-body, but it is a body in potency, as we say that the bronze is a statue in potency insofar as it will become a statue when it takes on the shape.[39]

Here are some further analyses of Apuleius:

> Plato pointed our that matter was ingenerable and incorruptible, that it is neither fire, nor water, nor any of the other primary elements or principles,

but it is prior to all of these, capable of receiving form and shape and in addition ugly and deprived of any formal qualifications: it is God the Artificer who conforms it in its totality. Plato considered it infinite: in fact what is infinite does not have a determined limit to its magnitude and hence since matter is lacking any limit, it can correctly be considered unlimited. But Plato did not admit that it is either a body or not a body; he does not consider it a body, in fact, because no body can be lacking form; in addition it cannot be said that it is without a body, because nothing which is incorporeal can present a body, while potentially and rationally it seems to be a body, and through this it is not graspable, not by any touch, nor with any rational conjecture alone. In fact bodies are known in virtue of their evidence with a concomitant reasoning while that which is deprived of corporeal matter can be cultivated with reasonings. Therefore the characteristic of this matter is grasped with a spurious and ambiguous conjecture.[40]

The genesis of the cosmos is interpreted according to the plan of the *Timaeus*, that is, as an activity of the Demiurge who imposes order on the disorder of the material on the basis of the paradigm of the Ideas.

Plutarch, for example, writes:

The genesis [of the world] is nothing other than the image of being in matter, that which has become is an imitation of being.[41]

So the particulars of the story of the *Timaeus* are collected and preserved almost to the letter.

But a controversy arose on a fundamental point. When Plato speaks of the "generation of the cosmos"(and hence also of the generation of the cosmic soul), did he want to say that the cosmos truly had a beginning in time or did he describe the genesis of the cosmos aiming to represent, by way of imaginative images, a totally different conception? In short: is the story of the genesis of the cosmos to be taken literally or figuratively?

We know that previously in the old Academy the problem came up and was debated because of the criticism of Aristotle, who from the beginning maintained the eternality of the world, reproving Plato for the absurdity of positing a cosmos which is born and which nevertheless *never perishes*.[42] And we also know that the ancient Academics had cleverly maintained that the Platonic story was a pedagogic device and that Plato wished simply to explain in a concrete way the nature of the ontological structure of the cosmos.

In the ambit of Middle Platonism three different replies were given to the problem, each in contrast to the other.

(a) Perhaps Eudorus had already given an allegorical interpretation.[43] Albinus, for his part, took it to a higher level of clarity. He writes in the *Didaskalikos*:

When Plato says that the world is generated, he does not mean it in the sense that there was a time in which the world did not exist, but that the world is always becoming and manifests a more primary principle of its being. And the soul of the world also, which is eternal, God did not create even this, but orders it; and it is said that he created it in this sense: awakening and moving his Mind and himself as from a lethargy and profound sleep, so that they look toward the intelligibles of God, grasping the Ideas and the forms, aiming at thinking them.[44]

To say that the cosmos is born (γέγονε) means two things: (1) that it is perennially dragged into the process of birth, (2) in addition, that it is not self-sufficient and hence it depends on a superior principle (analogously, to say that the world-soul is born means that it depends on a superior principle which made it exist).

Apuleius, then, going back to an interpretation parallel to this one, states that the world which in reality is ungenerated *can appear to be generated* because the things which make it up are all born: we find this notion, with different shadings, maintained also by Calvenus Taurus and by other Middle Platonists.[45]

(*b*) Plutarch returned instead to the literal interpretation, that is, to the notion of the temporal origin of the cosmos, by maintaining that *matter* is eternal and is the shapeless sensible substance from which the cosmos is derived, but not the cosmos, which has been formed. According to Plutarch, matter insofar as it enjoys perennial and chaotic movement, always has a soul: an evil soul, without Mind (soul and mind, remember, are distinguished by Middle Platonists, as we said above). Thus the informed corporeality always existed, endowed with animation and irrational life; God, therefore, created neither matter nor animated things and life, but generated the cosmos giving *order to the matter*, that is, giving *Mind to the soul*.[46]

Atticus also defends the literal interpretation and adds that Plato maintained the notion that the world had a beginning in time in order to endow Providence with an adequate context in which to work out everything. In fact, according to Atticus, the notion of the eternality of the cosmos excludes Providence, insofar as its essential function is to guarantee incorruptibility to the cosmos, which in itself is corruptible.[47]

(*c*) A third position is that of Severus, who went back to the Platonic myth of the *Statesman*,[48] maintaining that the *world as such* is ungenerated, but that our *actual world* is generated (to which previously others had preceded and others will also follow).[49] Finally, Juncus, who is known only for this opinion, maintained that the world as it has been generated by the Demiurge will thus perish when he wills it to.[50]

In addition, there is a "dualistic" tone of an emphatically religious character (probably of Eastern origin) that cosmology and in general the vision of the world assumed in certain Middle Platonists (in a special way, as is obvious, in those more sensitive to the religious problematic).

We have previously said that Plutarch admits the existence of an "evil soul" inhering in shapeless matter.[51] Plato had previously spoken of "evil soul" in the *Laws* in a context that really seems to have more of a hypothetical-dialectical character than an assertive one.[52] Plutarch goes well beyond the affirmations of this passage to achieve a vision of reality in which the two opposed principles of good and evil eternally face each other. This dualistic vision has its most typical expression in the treatise *On Isis and Osiris*. Here Plutarch tries to demonstrate that Egyptian mythology understood in the allegorical sense represents precisely the conception of two rival principles, a conception which to him so to say expresses the conviction of all peoples and all philosophers.[53]

Atticus also admits the existence of an evil-soul,[54] while Celsus affirms clearly that evil is "inherent in matter"[55] and he considered matter hence as a principle antithetical to God, since God, through his nature, is good.[56]

5. The daimonology of Middle Platonism

The special importance given to the transcendence of the supreme God, as we have previously pointed out, involved the necessity of *intermediate hypostases*, that is, *the necessity of conceiving the divine and the supersensible in a hierarchical manner*. But next to the hierarchical conception of a metaphysical and ontological character examined above there is in the ambit of Middle Platonism, *a second hierarchical conception of the divine which is properly mystical and religious in character* strictly connected to pagan polytheism, which once again has precise links to Plato.

The hierarchy of the divine, from this perspective, is as follows:

(1) Supreme God,

(2) Secondary Gods,

(3) *Daimons*.

The supreme God is the one we have previously spoken about above.

The secondary Gods are both incorporeal Gods and hence invisible and visible Gods as, for example, the stars, and they are all powers subordinated in various ways to the supreme God.

The *Daimons* are inferior to the Gods but superior to men. They have, therefore, a nature which can be termed "intermediate." Plutarch, for example, characterizes them as follows:

> Plato and Pythagoras and Xenocrates and Chrysippus, following the lead of early writers on sacred subjects, allege to have been stronger than men and, in their might, greatly surpassing our nature, yet not possessing the divine quality unmixed and uncontaminated, but with a share also in the nature of the soul and in the perceptive faculties of the body, and with a susceptibility to pleasure and pain and to whatsoever other experience is incident to these mutations, and is the source of much disquiet in some and of less in others. For in demigods, as in men, there are divers degrees of virtue and vice.[57]

The *Daimons*, according to the Middle Platonists, are not all equal. So they are distinguishable into two great classes. There are *Daimons* which do not have any dealings with bodies and which constitute the most elevated kind, and there are *Daimons* which, on the contrary, have dealings with bodies and which are souls which, having finished the period of their enfleshment, have been liberated from their bodies. In addition, the souls themselves, even when they are in bodies, can be called *Daimons.*[58]

The *Daimons*, then, are not all equal in another sense, viz., the mixed element is greater in some than in others. It is because of this mixed element that the *Daimons* are subject to affections and changes and, for Plutarch, to death as well.[59]

The possibility of being admitted to the ranks of the Gods is also true for the *Daimons.*[60]

Daimonology, as we have pointed out, is a response to a religious problematic more than to a philosophical one. God and the Gods are not "mixed with men" nor "do they have dealings" with them by reason of their eminence. Therefore, there is need to introduce entities having the function of mediators both to obey and to carry out the commands of the Gods in order to bind together, as much as possible, men and the Gods (a mediation between the lower and the higher). In addition, for Plutarch the *Daimons* need to be introduced also to explain evil and the negative in the world, while the Gods cannot but be good and the source of good; the *Daimons*, by their mixed constitution, can also be evil and sources of evil.[61]

In Plutarch, then, daimonology acquires an importance wholly unique because he explains by means of it the differences of the names and the forms of the worship of the Gods and, in general, polytheistic mythology. Our philosopher notes, in fact, that there is only one supreme God (and only one Providence), who is assisted by "subordinate powers" whose names (and related cults) vary from people to people. The different mythologies of various peoples, in this way, according to our philosopher, receive adequate explanation and justification. In particular, Plutarch adds that the various nefarious acts which the many pagan myths attributed to the Gods in reality are to be attributed not to the Gods but precisely to the *Daimons*, because the Gods are only good while the *Daimons*, as we know, are also wicked.[62] In addition, since the *Daimons* are subject to death, as we said before, it follows that with their death those effects of which they were the causes can suddenly disappear; thus, for example, the sudden decline and extinction of the oracles of some sanctuaries, that is, with the disappearance of the *Daimon* who inspired it, would be explained.[63]

III. The Anthropology and Ethics of Middle Platonism

1. The supreme end of man and his assimilation to God

The notion, as we have already pointed out, which expresses the foundation and the spiritual climate of the Middle Platonic ethics locates the supreme end of man in assimilation to God and to the Divine. The principle is derived from Plato who, as we have seen, had already formulated it in an explicit way; but in the speculations of the Middle Platonists it was to be examined and enriched with totally new corollaries, as we will see. *The supreme imperative "to follow God" is presented in particular as the programmatic overturning of the principle common to all the great Hellenistic philosophies "to follow nature."* The new principle expresses the break between the materialistic constitution of those ethics and the total recovery of the spiritual dimension.[1]

Almost all Middle Platonists agree on this principle: Eudorus,[2] Plutarch,[3] Gaius,[4] Albinus,[5] Apuleius,[6] Theon of Smyrna,[7] Maximus of Tyre,[8] Juncus,[9] and the anonymous author of the *Commentary on the Theaetetus*.[10] The doxographical sources of Middle Platonic provenance preserve it as well in an unmistakable manner.[11] The following passage of Albinus probably constitutes the most advanced point in the elaboration of this doctrine:

Plato, in consequence of all these things, posited as the goal to be assimilated to God insofar as this is possible; this doctrine is treated in various ways. Sometimes, in fact, he says to assimilate to God means to be wise, just and holy, as in the *Theaetetus*; thus one must try to flee from here towards the heights as quickly as he can; the flight is in fact the assimilation to God insofar as it is possible. To be assimilated means to become just, as in the last book of the *Republic*: in fact, he who desires to be just and, caring for virtue, insofar as it is possible for man, wishes to become like God, will never be ignored by the Gods. In the *Phaedo* then, he says that to assimilate to God is to become at the same time temperate and just, in this way approximately: "Therefore they will be the most happy and fortunate and will go to the best places, those who practice the common and proper virtues of the good citizen, which are called temperance and justice." Sometimes he says that the goal is to assimilate to God, sometimes that it is to follow Him, as when he affirms: "God, according to ancient tradition, the principle and goal etc." Sometimes he says both things, as when he says: "The soul which follows God and assimilates to Him etc." The good is the principle of what is right to do and also this is said to come to God; hence, the goal which results from the principle is to assimilate to God, and obviously to the God who is in the Heavens, not to the one who is beyond the Heavens, as this one has no virtue, but is better than it; therefore it can be said that unhappiness is an evil disposition of the inferior divinity, happiness a good disposition. We will be able to become similar to God if we have a suitable nature, if our customs, education, and life are according to the law, and especially if we use our reason, the study and the tradition of the doctrines, so as to keep away from the majority of human concerns and to be always intent on intelligible things. If we wish to be initiated into the highest knowledge, the preparation and the purification of the daimon which is in us must be accomplished through music, arithmetic, astronomy, and geometry and we must be concerned also with our body in gymnastics, which trains and disposes us for war and for peace.[12]

The anonymous author of the *Commentary on the Theaetetus*, in addition, expressly opposes the imitation of God as the foundation of justice and virtue to the Stoic *oikeiosis*:

Plato did not deduce justice from *oikeiosis*, but from becoming like God.[13]

The reader will note in the passage of Albinus read above the affirmation (which at first reading sounds somewhat strange) that the assimilation to God does not mean assimilation to the first God, who is superior to virtue itself, but assimilation to the God who is in the heaven, that is, the second God. The meaning of this affirmation is generally poorly grasped, as is revealed by the following statements of Albinus:

Proceeding in order, now we ought to speak generally about what Plato said about ethics. He maintained that the most precious and great good would not easily be found and being found, it would not be prudent to offer it to all. Certainly only a few selected disciples were allowed to listen to his lecture *On the Good*. Moreover by carefully examining his works, it can be seen that *Plato posited our good in science and contemplation of the primary Good, which can be called God and first Mind.*[14]

If the supreme good is the contemplation of the supreme God, or the first Mind [*Nous*], it is clear that in this contemplation the second God, or second Mind (the Mind of the heavens), achieves its paradigmatic perfection for the reasons which we have spoken above in treating the Albinonian doctrine of the "hypostases." It is precisely the *virtue of the second Mind* (contemplation of the highest God, or first Mind) which is the object of imitation on the part of man. In other words, the supreme end of man, in the measure in which he is capable of it, is to do what in a perfect way the second Mind or God does, namely, to contemplate the Absolute and make it its supreme rule.

2. The spiritual nature of man and the dualistic conception of soul and body

The conception of the supreme end of man as an "assimilation to God" obviously implies an intellectual refoundation of anthropology and a re-affirmation of the presence in man of an incorporeal aspect. Thus Albinus energetically maintained the incorporeality of the soul and in this way the Socratic maxim "take care of your soul," Platonically understood, is reas-serted.[15]

The soul comes from the first God and because of this it is immaterial and incorporeal and is destined to return to the sphere of the divine from which it came to the extent that it purifies itself through the highest knowledge.[16]

In this regard it is necessary to point out that some Middle Platonists, those whom some scholars call "the orthodox," maintained the necessity of returning to a purely Platonic conception of the soul, judging that the Aristotelian psychology was wrong. Atticus, in particular, accuses Aristotle of compromising the doctrine of the immortality of the soul, which is the foundation of ethics, with his distinction between *psyché* and *nous*. And if Aristotle admits the immortality of mind [*nous*], Atticus emphasizes, he cannot explain its origin or its nature nor the relations which it has with individual beings.[17]

Other Middle Platonists, on the contrary, as we have previously pointed out, exploited instead the Aristotelian distinction in an anti-materialistic sense in order to achieve, in a different way and at a higher level, the same objectives which Atticus proposed. Plutarch, for example, writes:

> Now the part submerged and absorbed in the movements of the body is called the soul, whereas the part left free from corruption is called by the multitude the Mind who take it to be within themselves, as they take the reflections of external objects to be in the mirrors; but those who conceive the matter rightly call it daimon as the one which is external.[18]

Also, according to Albinus, the Mind derives from the first God and also from him is called a Daimon while the other parts of the soul are derived from inferior Gods. In particular, then, the possibility itself of the "assimilation to God" in Albinus is grounded on this metaphysical projection of mind [*nous*]:

> Only the Mind and reason in us can reach likeness to the Good [which is the highest Mind].[19]

A final point should be noted in this regard: the affirmation of the liberty of the soul which, as echoed in the famous Platonic doctrine "do not have a master" which means that in its choices the soul is basically devoid of necessity.[20] The Middle Platonists, consequently, argued against the Stoic doctrine on Fate and, even though accepting some aspects of it, tried to reconcile necessity and liberty much more and much better than Chrysippus could have done.

Here is a very important passage of the *Didaskalikos* on this issue:

> Concerning fate Plato thought these things. He says that all is in fate, but that not everything is predetermined. In fact, fate is like a law and it does not establish for example what a person will do, what another person instead will undergo: this in fact would be infinite, since the number of living things is infinite as well as the number of things that could befall anyone; in addition, what is in our power could not be further so and there would not exist praise and blame and other things of this kind; fate establishes instead that if a soul chooses a life and does certain things, certain other things will follow as a consequence. The soul has hence no external master: it is not

held in bonds, and to do or not to do something is totally up to him (to the soul); the consequences of his actions instead will follow according to destiny. For example: from the fact that Paris seized Helen, who depended on him, it will follow that the Greeks will make war for Helen. Thus, in fact, Apollo predicted to Laius: "*If you have a son, your son will kill you.*" In the divine law is contained Laius and the fact that he generated a son, but only that which follows is predetermined.[21]

3. The list of values and virtues

Middle Platonism (and especially the school of Gaius) again took up that list of values which Plato had determined in his final work, viz., the *Laws*,[22] opposing to it the Stoic reduction of every value to only one and re-interpreted some Stoic teachings in a way consistent with this list.

Apuleius, for example, divides goods into two great divisions: (1) divine goods and (2) human goods. Then he subdivides each of these kinds of goods into two further kinds: (1a) God, (1b) virtues, (2a) the good qualities of our body, (2b) the possession of riches, power, and similars. Those of the second kind are only good in relation to the fact that they are subordinated to the first and are used according to reason.[23]

Albinus presents an even more unified systematization. After having said that the supreme good consists in the contemplation of the first Good, that is, the first God, who is the first Mind, he writes:

> He thought that all the things men called good would have this name by their participation, in a certain way, with the first and most precious good, in the same way as those things which are sweet and hot have their names from their participation in the primary sweet and the primary cold. Only our Mind and our reason can achieve assimilation to the good; hence our good is beautiful, noble, divine, amiable, proportioned, and denominated with the names worthy of the divine. Of those things which most people call goods, for example, health, beauty, power, wealth, and other things like these, no one is in itself a good, except that it is used virtuously; in fact, if separated from virtue, they are only on the level of matter and they become evils for those who use them inconsiderately; Plato also called them mortal goods [= goods by participation].[24]

It is clear, then, that the supreme virtue of human beings is contemplative virtue, on which the "assimilation to God" depends. Yet the Middle Platonists confidently made a place also for the ethical virtues by accepting the Aristotelian results and by considering them as virtues related to the a-rational parts of the soul and as realizations of the "golden mean" between excess and defect and hence as the realization of the "correct measure."[25]

True felicity does not depend on human goods, but on those of the divine. They are only those goods which make the soul worthy of returning to the company of the Gods and, with them, to "contemplation on the plain of truth."[26]

4. The ethics of Middle Platonism and the Stoa

The eclectic character of Middle Platonic ethics has frequently been emphasized, for in addition to Platonic tenets Middle Platonists saw no difficulty in accepting Aristotelian as well as Stoic doctrines. A great deal of evidence could be brought forward as proof of this assertion. Nevertheless, *that the Middle Platonists only rarely accept the results after Plato which are opposed to the Platonic spirit has not been adequately appreciated.* In fact, in the great majority of cases they reinterpret and ground again the new results according to the Platonic spirit.

Thus, for example, Albinus expressly shows that the well-known Stoic teaching according to which "only what is morally good is a good" and the consequent reduction of all the remaining values to being "indifferents" is equivalent to the Platonic doctrine that the supreme good consists "in the knowledge of the primary cause" and that only this is "a divine good" while all the others are only "goods by participation," that is, "human goods," and thus all those things which "are separated from the primary cause" are evils.[27]

Also, the Stoic tenet that "virtue is sufficient to itself" insofar as it contains the reason for happiness is maintained by Albinus as wholly Platonic for the reasons which he summarizes as follows:

> Those who possess knowledge which we have said are the most fortunate and happy, now however for the honors which, being such, they will receive, nor in the rewards, but even if they were to be unknown to all men and they were to come to those who are said to be evil, for example, the loss of all their rights, exile, death. On the contrary, those who, without having this knowledge, possess all those things said to be goods, like riches, royal power, health of body, vigor, beauty, in nothing are they more happy.[28]

With respect to the doctrine of *apatheia*, Plutarch shows clearly first that it is an unattainable ideal and then that it is a deceptive goal because it does not take into account the reality of the human soul which, through its own nature, is not passionless. Consequently, the passions can be moderated but not eradicated. The *metriopatheia* which derives in the ultimate analysis from the Platonic notion of the "due measure" becomes thus the ideal for Plutarch.

Here is the maxim which perfectly recapitulates the thought of our philosopher:

> Morally good actions differ from evil ones through their *due measure* (τῷ μετρίῳ).[29]

Albinus argued also against the Stoic notion of the passions and against their reduction to judgments. Moreover, he affirms against the Stoic paradox which categorically divides men into good and wicked the existence of an intermediate position and the capacity to progress toward virtue as well as the existence of degrees of wickedness.[30]

Finally, the persistence of the intellectualistic component should not be overlooked in Middle Platonic ethics. Albinus states that virtue is voluntary, but not vice:

> Since if something exists dependent on us and without a master such is virtue (he who is morally good in fact ought not to be praised if this quality originated from nature or from some divine destiny), virtue is voluntary and consists in an ardent impulse, noble and enduring: from the fact that virtue is voluntary follows the involuntariety of vice. Who in fact would choose voluntarily to have in the most beautiful and valuable part of himself the worse of evils? If, in fact, some aspire to evil, in the first place, they do it believing that they are aspiring not to evil but to the good; and if someone resorts to evil, such a person is absolutely deceived in his intentions of holding far off a greater evil through a smaller evil, and in this way results an involuntary recourse to evil; it is impossible in fact that anyone aspires to evil, desiring to find evil itself, and not by the hope of a good or through the fear of a greater evil.[31]

To affirm that virtue is "voluntary" and that vice, which is its contrary, is "involuntary" is an evident contradiction. It is clear that the presupposition of Socratic intellectualism played a determining role once again. The works of Philo with their Biblical involvements concerning the entire area of morality did not find in Greek culture a hospitable climate in which they could flourish.[32]

Third Section

THE REVIVAL OF PYTHAGOREAN PHILOSOPHY, ITS SUCCESSIVE STAGES, AND THE FINAL FUSION OF NEO-PYTHAGOREANISM AND MIDDLE PLATONISM

« ... δεῖ τινα ἀπελθόντα πόρρω ἀπὸ τῶν αἰσθητῶν ὁμιλῆσαι τῷ ἀγαθῷ μόνῳ μόνον, ἔνθα μήτε τις ἄνθρωπος μήτε τι ζῷον ἕτερον μηδὲ σῶμα μέγα μηδὲ σμικρόν, ἀλλά τις ἄφατος καὶ ἀδιήγητος ἀτεχνῶς ἐρημία θεσπέσιος, ἔνθα τοῦ ἀγαθοῦ ἤθη....»

"... It is necessary that man, after being among sensible things for a long time, enters into an intimate union with the Good, alone to alone, there where there is no individual human being, nor other living being, nor any body, neither great or small, but there there is a marvelous solitude, unspeakable and indescribable, there where the dwelling of the Good is ..."

Numenius, Frag. 2 (des Places)

I. The Documents, the Exponents, the Currents and the Characteristics of the Pythagoreanism of the Hellenistic and the Imperial Ages

1. The misadventures of the Pythagorean School

The ancient Pythagorean school, as we have seen in the first volume,[1] was active up to the first decades of the fourth century BCE. The role it played is essential not only in the development of Presocratic thought, but likewise in the evolution of the thought of Plato, who was greatly influenced by it. From the *Gorgias* to the *Phaedo*, from the *Republic* to the *Philebus*, the role of Pythagoreanism increased more and more and became determinative in the *Timaeus* and in the "unwritten doctrines."

The tradition states that the first Pythagorean who publicly revealed the teaching (which had from the beginning been closely guarded by the sacred bonds of secrecy) was Philolaus, at the time of Socrates. He had been forced to do so by the economic straits in which he found himself. Plato purchased the Pythagorean books made public by Philolaus for one hundred minas.[2] This tradition, however, is suspicious in its details, although undoubtedly containing a kernel of truth, as the consequent events themselves confirm. In the time of Philolaus, the Pythagorean school certainly must have been the victim of a quite serious crisis, so much so that after Philolaus it did not give many signs of life, which may explain how it could come to the point of destroying the "secret" of its teaching and make them public. On the other hand, the fact that Plato knew intimately the teachings of the Pythagorean school is demonstrable from his writings. (Let us bear in mind that Plato was acquainted personally, on his first voyage to Magna Graecia [lower Italy, including Sicily], with a Pythagorean of exceptional reputation named Archytas and who, perhaps, he saw again in 361 BCE on the occasion of his second voyage to Sicily. Plato even owed his liberation during the third voyage to Sicily to Archytas, when Dionysius II held him prisoner, threatening him with death.)[3]

So if the crisis of the Pythagorean school in Magna Graecia produced a break with that tradition and with that line of thought which came down directly from Pythagoras and from his immediate successors, it does not require, however, the destruction of the spiritual and doctrinal attitudes of Pythagoreanism. In fact, they were refurbished and taken to a new metaphysical plane by Plato with the "second voyage"[4] and led to results of considerable importance in the ambit of the first Academy.[5] In this regard, it is appropriate to remember that Aristotle had explicitly emphasized the impressive consequences of Pythagorean thought on Plato, and he was even moved (evidently in a polemical excess) to affirm that in certain key points of his metaphysics Plato had simply repeated Pythagorean teachings, only changing the wording;[6]

in addition, he had firmly denounced the mathematicizing regression of the first Academics and had argued sharply against such tendencies.[7] But Aristotle himself was also attracted to the Pythagoreans in no small measure, inasmuch as he was concerned with them in two critical treatises.[8]

In conclusion, the "Italic" philosophy of the Pythagoreans enjoyed an authentic Athenian period in the Platonic Academy and hence indirectly had an essential role to play in the determination of a series of fundamental categories of what we may call the classical thought of Greece. How long did this Pythagorean influence endure?

Since it was closely linked especially to Platonic-Academic metaphysics, it was subjected consequently to the same vicissitudes. After the scholarchate of Speusippus and Xenocrates at the end of the fourth century BCE, the Academy, as we have previously seen, was in a state of decline which progressively worsened for half a century and then with Arcesilaus it totally embraced a skeptical position wholly alien to Pythagoreanism. At first, the Pythagorean positions were almost entirely absent from the debates concerning the new problems arising from the great Hellenistic schools. The sensibilities of the new age were not attuned to the metaphysics of numbers, nor to the moral doctrines connected to the conception of the transmigration of the soul and its eschatological destiny. The Pythagorean message thus slipped into oblivion, *at least in the dominant culture*, and stayed there until the philosophical ambience was dominated by an uncontested materialistic and immanentistic vision of the world and life. This was common to all the new schools of the Hellenistic Age, that is, during the third and second centuries BCE, or for about 200 years. Only in those circles of individuals who cultivated the Orphic-Pythagorean mysteries or the forms of worship linked to them did there remain alive some elements of Pythagoreanism, but they were not of a philosophical character.[9]

Then, beginning from the first century BCE, Pythagoreanism, paralleling the spiritual and religious demands of the new age, revived, as is shown by a series of witnesses, both in the East and in a special way at Alexandria and in the West, especially at Rome. This hiatus, expressly pointed out by the ancients, and the differences between ancient Pythagoreanism and that revived at the beginning of the first century BCE has induced the historians of philosophy to call this movement "Neo-Pythagoreanism."[10]

For some time, however, scholars have pointed out that even in those centuries in which Pythagoreanism was believed to be totally moribund some writings which were attributed to the ancient Pythagoreans would seem to have been composed and circulated, the so-called *pseudepigrapha* or *pseudopythagorica*, of which we will immediately speak. In the past they were said to have been composed at the beginning of the first century BCE. So this backward displacement of the date of the composition of the *pseudepigrapha*, would seem to place in doubt (at least in a certain understanding) the conviction about the existence of this aforementioned hiatus between "early" and "late" Pythagoreanism, and hence a shift of the chronological parameters relative to the revival of Pythagorean philosophy.

Given the importance of the problem and that the solutions which we propose would introduce new elements of clarification (simply on the level of a working hypothesis and within the limits of a work of synthesis), it is necessary to proceed to some remarks of a more detailed character concerning the documents and the sources relating to the Pythagoreanism of the Hellenistic Age by beginning from the *pseudepigrapha*, which are the most problematic documents.

2. The forgeries attributed to some ancient Pythagoreans in the Hellenistic and the Imperial Age and their probable significance

Scores of writings were circulated (some of them extant in their entirety) under the name of Pythagoras and under the names of members belonging to his family or to the circle of his disciples and followers, whether famous or little known or completely unknown to us (as a group they number more than fifty), which we know for certain are inauthentic because they cite late teachings of various origins drawn especially from Platonic and Academic as well as Aristotelian and Peripatetics works and sometimes even from the Stoics.[11]

Faced with such a mass of forgeries, historians of ancient thought are confronted with the following problems: (1) why were these writings produced? (2) where and when were they produced? (3) what is their significance and value?

A reply to the first question cannot be a simple one. Nevertheless, if we examine the more ample and conspicuous "pieces" extant, their aim seems to be quite patent.

Let us take, for example, some of the writings attributed to Archytas. One of these, almost complete, treats the categories and takes up material for the most part from the well-known work of Aristotle of the same name. So the purpose of the forger who composed it and circulated it under the name of Archytas would be obvious. He wanted to show that the discovery of the doctrine of the categories came from Pythagoreans and that Aristotle can plausibly be said to have taken it from them.[12] In another treatise, *On the Principles* (of which there is a large fragment), the forger attributes to Archytas the doctrine of the "three principles" analogous to what is found in the Middle Platonists, taken from the *Timaeus* of Plato, and reinterpreted in function of some Aristotelian concepts. The three principles are *matter, form,* and *God considered as a moving cause.*[13] God, then, is said to be not only *Nous,* that is, Mind, but superior to Mind,[14] according to the formula which is found in the exoteric works of Aristotle and which already anticipates a position which will be affirmed later on. Again, in this case the forger evidently wanted to make us believe that these doctrines were of Pythagorean origin. Analogously, in the treatise *On the Mind and Sensation* a doctrine clearly taken from the *Republic* of Plato is presented again under the name of Archytas.[15]

Conclusions of an identical type can be drawn from the treatise *On the Origin of the Universe*, circulated under name of Ocellus of Lucania, which aims to attribute to the Pythagorean school doctrines typical of the physics and cosmology of Aristotle and, in particular, the doctrine of the eternity of the cosmos.[16]

Perhaps the clearest example of this kind of literature is the treatise *On the Nature of the Cosmos*, circulated under the name of Timaeus of Locris, which essentially repeats the *Timaeus* of Plato (with some Aristotelian nuances) and which in fact claims to be the supposed original writing by which Plato himself was inspired in composing his great dialogue.[17]

Analogously, a certain number of these *pseudepigrapha* try to lend credence to the notion that the doctrines in morals and politics drawn from Plato and Aristotle originally belonged to the ancient Pythagoreans.[18] In all these documents there is a lack of any serious attempt to locate the doctrines, which were to be presented as Pythagorean, within the context of the theory of numbers and the theory of the supreme principles.

Vice versa, in other *pseudepigrapha* the doctrines of the two opposed principles of the *One or the Monad* and the *Dyad* appear. The Monad is understood as a "generating and determining principle" and the Dyad as an indeterminate principle which is determined by the Monad.[19] The Monad is made to coincide with the principle of the good, with God, and with *Nous*, and in a couple of testimonies, the One tends *to be wholly above Nous*.[20]

Nevertheless, it is immediately clear that the passages which are doctrinally more sophisticated are not original, that is, they are not direct fragments, but are doxographical reports by later authors and hence are of uncertain value. They are attempted forgeries which reveal more awareness and sophistication than the earlier ones.[21]

We will discuss these doctrines later on. But for the present we want to simply note that the *pseudepigrapha* are documents which are heterogeneous in character and that a certain number of them certainly have different origins than that which is indicated by their alleged provenance.

Some are thus simply attempts to put into writing doctrines prevalently Pythagorean which were passed on orally (and hence do not betray that naive and ambiguous purpose of appropriating others' doctrines), as, for example, the well known *Golden Verses of Pythagoras* (the so-called *Carmen Aurea*) attributed to Pythagoras, which preserve for the most part a genuine Pythagorean tradition.[22] Other *pseudepigrapha*, instead, can also be ordinary forgeries prepared with a venal aim, since we are expressly told that the Lybian

King Juba II, who was filled with enthusiasm for Pythagorean philosophy, collected Pythagorean writings. In this circumstances, apocryphal Pythagorean works were produced with the sole purpose of selling them to the gullible King Juba.[23]

In order to conclude this discussion, we believe that many *pseudepigrapha*, in particular those of some "significance" which have come down to us (and which are also the only ones to have had a certain notoriety), are attempts at "re-establishing" Pythagoreanism. The attempt was conducted in an extremely ingenuous manner, that is, by trying to pass off (whether in good or bad faith is irrelevant) famous and clearly Platonic and Aristotelian doctrines as having been in the possession of the ancient Pythagoreans. It is obvious that we are faced with men who, on the one hand, *could no longer count on* a "school" tradition from which they could derive a precise identity and who, on the other hand, *could not yet* propose and reinterpret the Pythagorean principles in a way capable of sustaining the new demands of their time. For reasons of this nature, these writers concealed themselves behind the names of the ancient Pythagoreans. On the contrary, the "neoteroi," the new Pythagoreans, come to another consciousness and spirit, they come with a newly won identity, as we shall see, and for this very reason present themselves without disguise, that is, with their true names and having characteristics which alone authorize us to call them "Neo-Pythagoreans." The conclusion necessarily follows that *between the ancient Pythagoreans and the new there existed an intermediate stage having the characteristics described above and which in an approximate way should be called "Middle Pythagoreanism."*[24]

Where and when the Middle Pythagorean writings arose (and thus we come to the second question stated above) it is impossible to establish with any certainty. One point, nevertheless, seems secure. Relating everything to an Alexandrine background and assigning all of them to the first century BCE as Zeller wanted to do does not seem possible, as recent scholars have demonstrated in different ways.[25] The thesis of Zeller, in our judgment, needs to be corrected as follows. *Neo-Pythagoreanism* seems actually to have had its origin in Alexandria in the first century BCE; however, prior to the first century, in addition to Alexandria also Southern Italy and in fact perhaps chiefly in this setting,[26] these apocrypha began to circulate which we have called Middle Pythagorean. They must not have been, at least originally, very widespread. Moreover, the "provincial" character, that is, the limited speculative field and the absence of doctrinal inspiration, is recognizable and verifiable in them.

Between the old and the new Pythagoreanism, hence beyond that tenuous link forged by the survival into the Hellenistic Age of a certain Pythagorean spirituality linked to the Mysteries and recognized by Zeller himself, there also existed another connection. Even though from the speculative viewpoint (and this answers the last of the questions mentioned above) it has very little value, it is significant, from the historical viewpoint because it contributed to the preparation of an authentic Pythagorean revival, that is to say, an authentic "Neo-Pythagoreanism."

3. The so-called doxographical reports by anonymous Pythagoreans

In addition to the apocrypha, some reports have come down to us on Pythagorean doctrines of a chiefly expository nature made by authors who do to tell us from what sources they drew their information. For this reason, scholars, in order to designate these sources, speak of them as "anonymous Pythagoreans."

The doctrines of these "Anonymi" are referred to by Alexander Polyhistor,[27] Photius,[28] and Sextus Empiricus[29] (in addition to which there can be added the doctrines to which Ovid and Diodorus[30] refer, even if they are of minor importance).[31]

Alexander Polyhistor lived in the first century BCE and probably drew upon very ancient sources, which is particularly interesting because he attempted an unsuccessful synthesis between Pythagorean and Stoic doctrines but *fell unequivocally into a materialistic position.*

Pythagorean doctrines were interpreted in a monistic sense, that is, the Dyad itself is deduced from the Monad; first, numbers are deduced from these two principles, then entities and geometric solids, finally, material elements and the physical cosmos. Here is an important passage:

> Alexander in his *Successions of Philosophers* says that he found in the *Pythagorean Memoirs* the following doctrines as well. The principle of all things is the Monad or Unit; arising from this Monad is the undefined Dyad or two which serves as the material substrate to the Monad, which is cause; from the Monad and the undefined Dyad spring numbers; from numbers, points; from points, lines; from lines, plane figures; from plane figures, solid figures, sensible bodies, the elements of which are four; fire, water, earth, and air; these elements interchange and turn into one another completely and combine to produce a universe animate, intelligent, spherical, with the earth at its center, the earth itself also being spherical and inhabited round about.[32]

After having touched on the pairs of contraries (light and darkness, hot and cold, dry and moist) and their combinations in the determination of the phenomena of the cosmos, he says:

> The sun, the moon, and the other stars are gods; for, in them, there is preponderance of heat, and heat is the cause of life. The moon is illumined by the sun. Gods and men are akin (συγγένεια), inasmuch as man partakes of heat; therefore God takes thought for man. Fate is the cause of things being thus ordered both as a whole and separately. The sun's ray penetrates through the aither, whether cold or dense—the air they call cold aither, and the sea and moisture dense aither—and this ray descends even to the depths

and for this reason quickens all things. All things live which partake of heat—this is why plants are living things—but all have not *soul, which is a detached part of aither, partly the hot and partly the cold, for it partakes of cold aither too*. Soul is distinct from life; it is immortal, since that from which it is detached is immortal.[33]

These statements touch chiefly on the basis for the affinity between God and men which is the *element of heat* as well as the *reduction of the (immortal) soul to hot and cold aither*. The materialistic hypotheses are quite evident. The Pythagorean author or authors who maintain these doctrines place the rediscovery of the problematic of the *incorporeal* outside their ken. We are generally faced with an author or some apocrypha examined above. In fact, the doctrines that they wish to accept and Pythagoreanize are not only Platonic and Aristotelian, but also Stoic in origin, which must be the philosophical positions that were dominant at the time. In addition, they attempt a certain mediation which fails because it takes up again a predominantly Stoic materialism, producing a considerable mismatch with the doctrine of the Monad, since "hot" and "cold" *aither* have nothing to do with the Monad. Note, however, that in its more evolved phase Neo-Pythagoreanism will even develop a polemic against materialism and that, hence, the documents conditioned by this materialistic and immanentistic mentality cannot be considered expressions of the more matre phase of the Pythagorean renewal.

A greater critical awareness and a greater maturity of the Neo-Pythagorean problematic is presented instead by the anonymous author of the *Life of Pythagoras* which Photius has transmitted in a summary form. This anonymous author presented a system which deduced all reality from the Monad, but distinguished the Monad, which belongs to the sphere of *intelligible reality*, from Unity, which instead is the *principle of numbers*. Hence this Pythagorean *has already gone beyond materialism* insofar as he deduces all realities from the intelligible, including bodies. Here are two of the most significant passages from this metaphysical perspective:

> The followers of Pythagoras say that the Monad and Unity are each different. The Monad in fact was considered by them as belonging to the sphere of the intelligible; Unity instead is in the sphere of numbers. Similarly also the Two belongs to the ambit of numerable things, the Dyad instead, they say, is an indeterminate something insofar as the Monad is understood according to equality and measure while the Dyad is understood according to excess and defect; now, the proportion and the measure cannot be greater or lesser, while excess and defect tend toward infinity, for this reason they say that the Dyad is indeterminate. As they relate all things back to numbers, they make them derive from the Monad and the Dyad, they state that everything is number and that the perfect number is ten; now ten is composed by the four first numbers which we count by proceeding through

the order [10 = 1 + 2 + 3 + 4] and through this they call this number as a whole "tetraktys."[34]

The Pythagoreans say that the Monad is the principle of everything, because they say that the point is the principle of the line, the line is the principle of the surface, and the surface is the principle of the solid in three dimensions, that is, of the body. But the Monad is known before the point, so that the Monad is the principle of bodies; consequently all bodies derive from the Monad.[35]

The anonymous author of whom we speak, in addition, reveals an acquaintance with the disputes concerning whether or not Aristotle admitted the immortality of the soul. This would only place him chronologically after the edition of the esoterica made by Andronicus and hence he must have lived after this period.[36]

A later epoch is reflected also in what he says about the goal of ethics as the "imitation of God" and what he says about the separation of the soul from the body.[37]

Man is considered a "microcosmos" not because he is constituted out of all the material elements, but because "he has in himself all the powers of the cosmos," from the lowest to the highest. The point of contact with the divine sharply differentiates here from the materialism of the anonymous author quoted by Alexander Polyhistor and locates it in the rational faculty and in particular in the Mind.[38]

The connection between ethics and metaphysics is completely determined in the notion of the impossibility of knowing oneself without knowing reality in its totality.

To know oneself signifies nothing other than to know the nature of the whole cosmos.[39]

The Pythagoreans whom Sextus Empiricus draws upon belong to the more mature phase.[40]

The framework in which these Pythagoreans are presented to us in his work *Against the Physicists* is very broad-ranging, because it furnishes us with a panorama of the different positions and arguments. The fulcrum of the arguments of the Pythagoreans, in the variety of their formulations, according to Sextus, is a single one and it consists in the deduction from the *incorporeal* (from incorporeal numbers) the whole of reality. This deduction of the incorporeal, hardly touched on by Photius, is instead impressively developed by Sextus. We will take up further on some of these arguments furnished by Sextus. But for the moment we wish to read only a summary which Sextus himself presents in his *Outlines of Pyrrhonism* which gets to the heart of the matter:

> Thus, for example, the School of Pythagoras declare that numbers are also elements of the Universe. They assert, in fact, that phenomena are con-

structed from something, and that the elements must be simple; therefore the elements are non-evident. But of things non-evident, some are corporeal, like atoms and masses, other incorporeal, like figures and forms and numbers. Of these the corporeal are composite, being constructed from length and breadth and depth and solidity, or even weight (cf. Epicurus, frag. 275 Acinar). The elements, therefore, are not only non-evident but also incorporeal. Moreover, each of the incorporeals involves the perception of number, for it is either one or two or more. Thus it is inferred that the non-evident and incorporeal numbers which are involved in all perception are the elements of existing things. Yet not simply [these numbers], but both the Monad also and the Indefinite Dyad which is generated by the expansion of the Monad, and by participation in which the particular dyads become dyads. For they say that it is from these that the rest of the numbers are generated—those, that is, which are involved in the perception of numerables—and the Universe is arranged. For the point presents the relation, or character, of the Monad, and the line that of the Dyad (it being regarded as lying between two points), and the surface that of the Triad (for they describe it as a flowing of the line breadth-wise up to another point placed transversely), and the [solid] body that of the Tetrad; for Body is formed by an ascension of the surface up to a point placed above. It is in this way that they image forth both the bodies and the whole Universe ...[41]

4. The new Pythagoreans who write under their own name

Publius Nigidius Figulus is the first Neo-Pythagorean who is known by his own name and who belongs to the Roman world. Cicero, who was his contemporary, expressly says that he revived the sect which was practically dead at that time.[42] As a matter of fact, Pythagoreanism had continued to exist in the Roman world, chiefly in its ethical, religious, and mysterio-sophic dimensions, even though outside an authentic organized sect or school. This is proven chiefly from the legend according to which King Numa had known Pythagoras, as a consequence of which there arose at the beginning of the second century BCE forgeries of Pythagorean writings attributed to this same King Numa.[43] But the value of Nigidius Figulus was in his re-establishment of Pythagoreanism as a sect and as a school, even if from the speculative viewpoint he did not achieve particularly important results.[44]

At the beginning of the Christian Era there arose the so-called circle of the Sextii, founded by Quintus Sextius and afterwards probably guided by his son (to which Sotion of Alexandria, Lucius Crassicus of Tarantum, and Fabianus Papirius belonged), which had high visibility and disappeared rapidly.[45] Seneca, on whom Sextus exercised a considerable influence, attests to the affinity of the ethics of this thinker with that of the Stoics.[46] The Sextii were quite distinctive since they maintained the *incorporeality of the soul* (Sotion also accepted the doctrine of metempsychosis).[47] One typical characteristic of the school was the practice of the daily examination of conscience, which is also recommended in the *Golden Verses of Pythagoras*.[48]

Neo-Pythagorean metaphysics was represented by Moderatus of Gades, who lived in the first Century CE,[49] by Nicomachus of Gerasa, who lived in the first half of the second century CE,[50] by Numenius of Apamea, who lived in the second half of the same century,[51] and his follower Cronius.[52]

The mystical approach of Neo-Pythagoreanism is represented by Apollonius of Tiana, who lived in the first century CE,[53] of whom Philostratus, in the third century CE at the request of Julia Domna (wife of Septimus Severus), wrote a biography with the intention of presenting Apollonius as the founder of a new religious cult based on interiority and spirituality.[54]

5. Characteristics of the Pythagoreanism of the Hellenistic and Imperial Ages

It is evidently impossible to consider the various documents and authors mentioned above within a unified treatment on the basis of what we have now stated. Zeller attempted to include all of them in a comprehensive synthesis but he found himself faced with different as well as opposed solutions to the important questions. The different documents and authors tended to eliminate a unified treatment and hence Zeller ended in seeing a substantial lack of unity in his treatment emerge because he followed his own original plan.[55]

On the other hand, the claim of Zeller to consider globally this complex material depended on his conjecture that all this literature belonged to the same epoch and came for the most part from the same background. We know this notion is insupportable today.

We have already said that Zeller was correct in supposing that the authentic Neo-Pythagorean movement began in the first century of the Common Era at Alexandria because the documents in our possession lead to this conclusion.[56] (The *acmé* of the movement hence fell within the Imperial Age, that is, in the first two centuries of the Christian Era, insofar as it is true that only in this epoch—with the sole exception of the circle of Nigidius Figulus at Rome—the Pythagoreans were known by their names and their position.) *Zeller therefore incorrectly denied the existence of a Pythagoreanism prior to the first century BCE, that is, in the Hellenistic Age. In fact, many of the Pythagorean pseudepigrapha*, for precise reasons of an historical and philological nature, can be assigned to the third and second (or even to the fourth) centuries before the Common Era with the result that they actually belong doctrinally within another environment. *It will hence be appropriate to distinguish a Pythagoreanism, properly so-called, of the Hellenistic Age and a Pythagoreanism of the Imperial Age. Hence, as we said, there existed a Pythagoreanism midway between the ancient and the new having characteristics to which we have previously referred which are not unifiable with or at least not identifiable with those of the new.*

Let us summarize what we have previously said in the course of the present section and anticipate what we will say in detail in the next. We want to outline in a synthetic framework the characteristics of the two stages of Pythagoreanism which we distinguished and which will simplify the understanding of many of the problems we have discussed.

The traits peculiar to Middle Pythagoreanism are the following:

(1) The authors of this epoch try to give credence to the notion that discoveries from a later period are ancient Pythagorean doctrines by producing a series of apocryphal writings containing these doctrines and attributing them to ancient Pythagoreans.

(2) They show scarcely any awareness of their individual philosophical identity, and precisely for this reason they feel the need to hide behind a mask of anonymity. A center of gravity is missing in their writings. They are frequently limited to presenting the doctrines of Plato and Aristotle again, sometimes almost verbatim.

(3) The doctrine of the highest principles, of the Monad and the Dyad, either is not present or hardly developed and it is not examined in any ontological depth.

(4) They allow materialistic and immanentistic infiltrations, or when they become aroused by a metaphysical notion it is clear that the authors lack any specific sense of the ontological and metaphysical dimension.

(5) With respect to the *pseudepigrapha*, these attempts also probably belong to the more evolved and knowledgeable stage of Middle Pythagoreanism, so, for example, that of the anonymous author quoted by Alexander Polyhistor in which the doctrine of the Monad and the Dyad and the corollary doctrine of numbers becomes explicitly overturned and at the same time combined with Stoic materialism. The reason why we are moved to assign such documents to this phase of Pythagoreanism depends on the fact that the more recent Pythagoreans, the "neoteroi," are anti-materialistic and are in sharp disagreement with both Epicurean atomism and the corporealism and immanentism of the Stoa, but in complete harmony with the parallel Middle Platonic movement.

What then are the characteristics which alone can properly define "Neo-Pythagoreanism," that is, the Pythagoreanism securely datable between the end of the Pagan Era and the first two centuries of the Christian Era?

(1) The authentic Neo-Pythagoreans tend to throw away the cloak of anonymity and to be known by name and doctrine. But this occurred in the Imperial epoch. Naturally this does not happen all at once or exclusively in this period. Some of the same *pseudepigrapha*, for example, (not, however, the

most famous examples) can be dated back to this epoch, insofar as they present some of the characteristics of the Pythagoreanism of this epoch.

(2) The Neo-Pythagoreans have a clear awareness of their identity, insofar as their doctrine reveals a *common denominator*. We know that parallel to the progressive focus on this commonality there is a diminution of their attempts to compare Plato and Aristotle, as well as the philosophers of the Hellenistic Age. However the most ancient authors of the *pseudepigrapha*, the earliest, in their naiveté attempt to show ancient Pythagorean doctrines as the sources of Plato and Aristotle. The anonymous-Photius had in fact established a "diadochic" rule, that is, a "succession," in which Plato and Aristotle figure as members of the Pythagorean school:

> The ninth successor of Pythagoras...was Plato, who was a student of Archytas the Elder; the tenth successor was Aristotle.[57]

Moderatus of Gades and the more recent Pythagoreans simply overdo it. They even get around to accusing Plato and Aristotle and the Academicians of mystification, that is, of having appropriated the doctrines of Pythagoras with minor modifications without saying so and, in fact, they both cite the philosophy of Pythagoras only in its most superficial and dubious aspects in order to discredit it. Porphyry says, as quoted by Moderatus:

> Plato, Aristotle, Speusippus, Aristoxenus, and Xenocrates are said by Pythagoreans, to have appropriated with inconsequential modifications whatever was good in that philosophy; and reunited the ordinary and poor parts and what was thought out successively from the jealous calumniators for the purpose of demolishing and deriding that school and putting aside as their own exclusively what belongs to the sect.[58]

Numenius, who, as we will see, also tried to join Pythagoreanism and Platonism, maintained that Pythagoras not only was not inferior, but in certain respects wholly superior to Plato, and affirms that Socrates himself was a pupil of Pythagoras.[59]

Whereas the Neo-Pythagoreans were completely conscious of what it was which irremediably divided them from Hellenistic schools. The anonymous-Sextus expressly argued, as we know, against the materialism of Epicurus, while Numenius argued explicitly against that of the Stoa.

(3) Let us thus touch on one of the most characteristic qualities of Neo-Pythagoreanism, *the rediscovery and the reaffirmation of the "incorporeal" and the "immaterial," that is, the recovery of those doctrines which had been lost with the systems of the Hellenistic Age.* This is one of the principal historical values of this current which together with Middle Platonism had prepared the foundation for the great Neoplatonic synthesis.

(4) The incorporeal was not understood by the Neo-Pythagoreans in the same way as the Middle Platonists, that is, on the basis of the doctrines of *Nous* of Aristotelian extraction and of those ideas having their source in Plato, but

rather on the basis of the doctrine of the Monad and the Dyad and numbers. Such a doctrine is only indirectly Pythagorean and it links up to the speculations of the ancient Academy of Speusippus and Xenocrates, who, by beginning from the doctrines of the last period of Plato's life, as we noted many times previously, had given an accentuated mathematical development to metaphysics (Aristotle had already decried the philosophy of his times, which was becoming mathematical). Nevertheless, the doctrine of numbers came to be understood in a manner which, with respect to the Academy, greatly accentuated their symbolic character. Numbers expressed something meta-numerical, that is, the most profound principle which because of its difficulty lent itself poorly to simple representation and which instead, by means of numbers, can be clarified in the sense that we will see better further on.

(5) The doctrine of the Monad and the Dyad was subjected to a careful analysis with a peculiar kind of relevance. It began from an original formulation which saw in the Monad and the Dyad the highest pair of contraries. Then it went on to delineate a position which progressively placed the Monad in a position of absolute prominence by distinguishing a *first* from a *second* Monad and by opposing only this last one to the Dyad and also by trying to deduce all reality from the highest Monad, as well as the Dyad itself (on this point, nevertheless, the vocabulary vacillates, some calling the One the first Monad, others instead calling the second the One).

(6) There developed in relation to the theory of the Ideas (which itself was given hardly any importance and only had a role subordinate to the doctrine of numbers and which in addition, in the way noted above, was understood in a theological manner, that is, theosophically) an authentic *arithmology* or *arithmosophia*.

(7) In regard to the notion of man the Neo-Pythagoreans were quite in fashion, maintaining the doctrine of the spirituality of the soul and its immortality (and, consequently, also the doctrine of metempsychosis, which is taken up again and reaffirmed). The end of man involves distancing himself from the sensible and uniting himself with the divine.

(8) The ethics of the Neo-Pythagoreans takes on a strong tinge of mysticism. Philosophy is understood as a divine revelation and the ideal philosopher is identified with Pythagoras not so much as a perfect man but as a Daimon or God or, more generally, a prophet or a superior human being who is in contact with the Gods.

Before passing on to the explanations of these individual points, we must clarify a final question. It is not very exact to consider Numemius a Middle Platonist, as many do, but neither is it correct to consider him like the other Neo-Pythagoreans. In fact, as we will see, Numenius reflects two currents of thought, and for this reason he is treated apart from both of them, insofar as with this attempt he anticipates, to a certain extent, Neoplatonism.

II. The Doctrinal Bases of Neo-Pythagoreanism

1. The recovery of the incorporeal and the reaffirmation of its metaphysical primacy

The rediscovery of the incorporeal and the transcendent as well as the affirmation that the transcendent incorporeal is cause of the corporeal, as we have seen, marked the line of demarcation between Middle and Neo-Pythagoreanism. The most ancient documents, for example, the treatise of the pseudo-Ocellus, as we have previously said, ignored this conception and the problematic connected to it. The anonymous author cited by Alexander Polyhistor made materialistic affirmations of a clearly Stoic character. Some affirmations as well of some *pseudepigrapha* attributed to Pythagoras, of which there is additional information, were also of a decisively immanentistic and Stoic nature.[1]

However, the Neo-Pythagoreans of whom the Middle Platonist Eudorus speaks in the first half-century BCE deduced matter itself and all the things of the world from an absolutely transcendent One.[2]

The anonymous author or authors quoted by Sextus Empiricus present the thematic of the incorporeal as the very center of their theory of being in a vigorous polemic directed chiefly against Epicurean materialism. This, in addition to the passage read above, is proved by the next passage although it is more specific and extremely precise. After having said that the "followers of Pythagoras" attributed "great power" to numbers including making them "the principles of all things," Sextus writes:

> For they say that those who are genuinely philosophizing are like those who work at language. Now the latter first examine the words (for language is composed of words); and since words are formed from the syllables, they scrutinize the syllables first; and as syllables are resolved into the elements of written speech, they investigate these first; so likewise the true physicists, as the Pythagoreans say, when investigating the Universe, ought in the first place to inquire what are the elements into which the Universe can be resolved.—Now to assert that the principle of all things is apparent is contrary to physical science; for every apparent things must be composed of non-apparents, and what is composed of things is not a principle, but rather the component of that compound [is a principle]. Hence one ought not to say that the apparent things are principles of all things, but the components of the apparent things, and these are no longer apparent.— Thus they assumed the principles of existing things to be non-evident and non-apparent, yet they did not do so with one consent. For those who declared that atoms or homoeomeries or molecules or, in general, intelligible bodies are the principles of all existing things proved partly right, but partly went wrong. For insofar as they consider the principles to be non-evi-

dent, their procedure is correct, but insofar as they assume them to be *corporeal* they go wrong. For just as the intelligible and non-evident bodies precede the sensible bodies, so the *incorporeals* (τὰ ἀσώματα) ought to be the principles of the intelligible bodies. And logically so: for just as the elements of a word are not words, *so also the elements of bodies are not bodies*; but they must be either bodies or incorporeals; *certainly, then, they are incorporeals.*—Moreover, it is not admissable to say that it is a property of atoms to be *eternal*, and that on this account they can be the principles of all things although they are corporeal. For, in the first place, those who assert that homeomeries or molecules or minimals and indivisibles are elements assign to them an eternal existence, so that the atoms are no more elements than they. Next, let it be granted that the atoms are in very truth eternal; yet, just as those who allow that the Universe is ingenerable and eternal seek nonetheless, in theory, for the principles which first composed it, so also we—as those Physical philosophers, the Pythagoreans, say—examine theoretically the problem as to what are the components of these eternal bodies perceptible by the reason. Their components, then, are either bodies or incorporeals. And we will not say that they are bodies, since then we should have to say that the components of these also are bodies, and, as the conception thus proceeds ad infinitum that the Whole is without beginning. It only remains, therefore, to declare that the intelligible bodies are composed of incorporeals; and this, too, Epicurus acknowledged, when he said that 'body is conceived by means of a combination of form and magnitude and resistance and weight.' Well then, it is plain from what has been said that the principles of the bodies perceptible by reason *must be incorporeal.*[4]

The affirmation of the transcendence of the highest principle and the distinction between intelligible and sensible are clearer in Moderatus, as we will see.[5]

Nichomachus of Gades also conceived the foundation of all things as being immutable and permanently identical with itself, asserting that the "immaterial entities" (τὰ ἄυλα) are of just such a nature and each thing assumes its own real determinations by participation in them.[6]

In Numenius, as we have previously mentioned and as we will see better further on, the doctrine of the incorporeal is central and is developed with fullness in an explicit polemic with the Stoa.[7]

Let us remember that even in the circle of the Sextii at Rome involved with the moral ideas of the Stoa the thematic of the immaterial emerges as important, at least in the interpretation of the soul, which is said to be "incorporeal."[8]

2. The methodological, metaphysical, and theological meaning of numbers in Neo-Pythagoreanism

The incorporeal, for the Neo-Pythagoreans, cannot be restricted only to the Ideas (as Plato himself had concluded in his esoteric doctrines). The passage of Sextus Empiricus read above continues to justify such a conviction in this way:

> But if certain incorporeals exist before the bodies, these are not already of necessity elements of existing things and primary principles. For see how the Ideas, which are incorporeal, exist before the bodies, according to Plato, and everything which becomes because of its relation to them; yet they are not principles of existing things since each Idea taken separately is said to be a unit, but *two* or *three* or *four* when taken in conjunction with one or more others, so that there is something which transcends their substance, namely *number*, by participation in which the terms one or two or three or a still higher number than these is predicated of them.[9]

It is clear, then, that for the Neo-Pythagoreans the Ideas themselves are not first principles but secondary principles. The primary principles are numbers. But what is meant by saying that numbers are principles? They certainly do not mean number in the archaic sense of the early Pythagoreans[10] (that is, number in an arithmetical or geometrical sense), but rather number in the Platonic and proto-Academic sense and even in a way which is still more sophisticated.

Number for the Pythagoreans has three meanings: (1) one can be called the methodological meaning, (2) the other the ontological-metaphysical meaning, and (3) the last the theological-theosophistical meaning.

(1) The first meaning, which is quite important, is well described in statements made chiefly by Moderatus of Gades (with whom Sextus had many contacts) in his *Pythagorean Commentary*, which Porphyry mentioned.[11] The Pythagoreans behave, said Moderatus, like the grammarians and the geometricians. The former must explain to the student the meaning and value of the elements (vowels and consonants) of words and language, avail themselves of the letters of the alphabet, and then explain that these are not the elements themselves, but "signs" and "indices" of the elements. Analogously, the geometricians, in order to introduce the student to geometry, must draw the figure of a triangle; but then they explain that the triangle is not that particular drawn figure but the concept of which that drawing is the sensible representation. The Neo-Pythagoreans proceed also with the same method and try to overcome the difficulties of expressing with words the supreme principles by availing themselves of numbers for this task. *Numbers are not therefore the principles themselves, but rather the signs and indicators of the principles.*

Let us read the explanation of Moderatus, which helps a great deal to penetrate the mode of thinking typical of this current of thought so frequently misunderstood and devalued precisely because it is not understood:

> Because, he says, they cannot express the primary ideas and the primary principles clearly in words, since they are difficult to conceive and express, they take refuge in numbers, as more easily expressed, in imitation of the

geometrician and the masters of letters. Because, as these set about teaching the value of the elements and the elements themselves, they have recourse to the characters of the alphabet and they say, in order to give a preliminary notion, that these are the elements, and only later do they then explain that these signs are not the primary elements, but simply indices of the true elements; and the geometricians, cannot express with words spiritual things, are satisfied in drawing figures, and they say that, for example, this (imagine a drawn triangle) is a triangle, not however intending to say that this sign which falls under our eyes is a triangle, but that the triangle has such a form, and thus they represent the concept of the triangle; the same would be true for the primary principles and Ideas. The same would hold for the Pythagoreans, who were incapable of expressing verbally the spiritual forms and the primary principles, and so had recourse to demonstration by way of numbers.[12]

Moderatus used some examples which are quite instructive. The Monad indicated, for example, the concept of unity, identity, and equality as well as expressing the reason for which things are connected and harmonized among themselves, which is the cause of the conservation of the universe. The Dyad indicates the concept of inequality, the principle of divisibility, change, and diversity. To name the Dyad and the Two-fold, for the Pythagoreans, means to say the unequal and the diverse:

And thus they call "one" the concept of unity, identity, and equality, and the cause of the co-spiration, harmony, and sympathy as well as of the conservation of the universe, which again has always the same form and essence; while the "one" which is in the particulars is such, united and a co-spiration to the parts, by participation in the primary cause. And the concept of diversity, inequality, everything divisible, changing, and of variable forms, they call a bi-form concept and Dyad; such also is the nature of the Dyad in the particulars. Neither do these notions belong exclusively to these philosophers and are unknown to others; but we also see from other philosophers who communicate the theory of certain unitive forces and the assembling of the great whole, and also proximate to them we find the concepts of identity, inequality, and diversity. These are hence the concepts that because of a greater declarative facility the Pythagoreans are referring to with the name of Monad and Dyad. And for them it is all the same to call them two-fold, unequal, or diverse.[13]

Analogously, the Pythagoreans with the Triad or three-fold signify what by nature has *principle, end*, and *means*. Again, when they speak of the decade as a perfect number they mean that since the decade contains all numbers, and numbers (in the sense specified) are the cause of everything, the decade contains in itself the cause of all, and hence everything.[14]

(2) It is evident, nevertheless, that numbers for the Neo-Pythagoreans were not conventional symbols, as the letters of the alphabet are, nor are they even abstractions nor purely nominal concepts. Numbers express *the very being*

of things, the metaphysical structure of the universe. Moderatus himself, in the same text in which he explained the concepts presented above, also stated:

> The nature of the great whole is defined by way of species and analogies of numbers, and everything which is born and increases and arrives at the end proceeds according to numerical concepts.[15]

There is illumination on the metaphysical aspect of number chiefly from the *Introduction to the Arithmetic* of Nicomachus[16] which we will now take up.

(3) Finally, a third dimension of number must be emphasized that we have called the theological and theosophical, which undoubtedly represents a most baffling, and in a certain sense, a somewhat deceptive aspect of Neo-Pythagoreanism, but which nevertheless must be explained if we want to correctly understand this current of thought both historically and theoretically.

In his *Introduction to Arithmetic* Nichomachus offered us almost a *summa* of the mathematical knowledge of his time and showed a remarkable grasp of mathematics. In his *Theological Arithmetic* (of which Photius has given us a summary) he superimposed on the arguments of the first work accurately carried out both from the methodological and the ontological viewpoint totally different considerations which move beyond the fantastic and into the merely superstitious. In the *Theological Arithmetic*, in fact, Nichomachus, carried to extreme consequences a way of understanding numbers which was very ancient. He identified the numbers from one to ten with Gods and Deities and hence "he worshipped numbers as Deities."[17] Photius, summarizing the book, said that Nicomachus proceeded with extreme arbitrariness in making these identifications (for him the book is worthwhile only for the valuable mathematical knowledge which it involves). Unfortunately he did not report the original reasons but nevertheless we partially succeeded in reconstructing them on the basis of other documents.

Let us see some examples relative to the Monad which are presented as models. Photius writes:

> (Nicomachus of Gades) says besides the Monad, by mixing what is true of it and other ontological features which are peculiar to it with not few fantastic ones, that it would be mind and besides also Male-Female, God and in a certain sense Matter—by mixing together truly the whole—welcoming everything, Receptacle, Chaos, Confusion, Mixture, Absence of Light, Obscurity.[18]

We will try to explain these descriptive nouns and put aside all the other descriptions which follow. anyone who perseveres in reading Photius will have difficulty avoiding the sense of distaste with which the author read and summarized the work of Nicomachus. If, instead, Photius integrated this summary with the *Theological Arithmetic* attributed to Iamblichus,[19] who has taken a lot from Nicomachus, these epithets become very significant.

First, the Monad is completely understandable, on the basis of the position which makes the supreme Principle identical with the supreme Mind. For the same reason it is also God. The Monad is both masculine and feminine since it is the father and mother of all, functioning as form and matter of everything, thus the Neo-Pythagoreans tended to deduce the Dyad from the Monad, that is, matter in addition to form. (Moreover, the Orphic God was said to be masculine and feminine.) In addition, it is "in a certain sense" matter, because, as we have pointed out previously, it is the generator of matter itself. It is the Receiver of all and the Receptacle in addition to and for the same reason, because it is also the "Receptacle of all the seminal reasons," since all the forms are derived from it. It is called Chaos, because from it everything is derived, as from the Chaos of Hesiod. It is said to be Confusion, Mixture, Absence of Light, Obscurity, because "what is due to differentiation in the Monad is still undifferentiated and indistinct."[20]

What is clear is that what Photius laments as fantastic imagery was allegorical representations in which everything is precisely signified and which expresses, so to speak, the "mysticism" of numbers. Whoever neglects this interpretation will not be able to comprehend a certain aspect of Neo-Pythagoreanism which has had a great influence on successive philosophical thought, in particular on Neoplatonism and in general on pagan mysticism.

3. The doctrine of the highest principles of the Monad and the Dyad and the attempted deduction of all reality from a supreme Unity

The central doctrine of the Neo-Pythagorean theory of metaphysics is that of the supreme principles of the Monad and the Dyad, as we have previously pointed out many times. Everything which is positive is made to correspond to the Monad. It is also called Mind and God while the negative and evil are linked to the Dyad. In addition, the former is represented as the "active principle" and the latter as the "passive principle" (according to Stoic terminology, which became gradually emptied of its immanentistic and materialistic contents).[21] Here are some doxographical texts:

> [Pythagoras] puts among the principles the Monad and the indeterminate Dyad. These principles tend, according to him, the one to the efficient and eternal cause, which is the Mind or God, the other to the passive and material cause which is the visible world.[22]

> Pythagoras believes that, among the principles, the Monad and the good are God, that is, the nature of the One, the Mind itself. He says then that evil is alone the indeterminate Dyad around which is the visible cosmos.[23]

> The supreme principles of all things are the first Monad and the indefinite Dyad.... Of these principles the Monad plays the role of efficient cause and the Dyad that of passive matter, and just as they have constructed the numbers composed of these, so also they have built up the Universe and all things in the Universe.[24]

Nevertheless, the *tendency to deduce all reality from the Monad, understood to include the Dyad itself,* became quickly diffused and dominant. This position, which can undoubtedly be defined as a form of "monism," is evidently opposed to the monism of the Stoa, since it is a form of *non-materialistic monism* (the Monad is incorporeal, as we have seen, and the corporeal is derived from the incorporeal; the Monad is immaterial, and from it matter is generated), contrary to the Stoa, which is instead a materialistic monism.

How is such an attempted radical deduction of all reality from a supreme Unity to be accomplished?

The first attempt of which we know is by the anonymous author quoted by Alexander Polyhistor, who seems to be limited to pointing to the *fact* and not the *how* by only stating that "the Dyad is generated from the Monad."[25]

Eudorus also, in the passage we read above, confirms that for the Pythagoreans the One was the principle "both of matter and of all things derived from it."[26] Sextus gives instead a more specific explanation:

Pythagoras moved by these considerations, declared that the One is the principle of existing things, by participation in which each of the existing things is termed one. This One when conceived in its self-identity is conceived as Unity, but when, conceived in its otherness, it is added to itself, and it is the "Indefinite dyad," (ἐπισυντεθεῖσαν δ᾽ἑαυτῇ καθ᾽ἑτερότητα). It is so-called because it is not itself any one of the numbered and definite dadaist, but they are all conceived as dadaist through their participation in it, even as they try to prove in the case of the monad. There are, then, two principles of existing things, the First One, by participation in which all the numbered ones are conceived ones, and the Infinite Dyad, by participation in which the infinite Dyads are twos.[27]

The most interesting statements are those of Moderatus and Nicomachus. They, in fact, not only tend to deduce the Dyad from a supreme One, but they take to its extreme consequences a tendency which was widespread at the end of the first century BCE. They also distinguished the First Monad, the supreme principle, from the second Monad, which through being opposed to the Dyad generates the number series, and so they call the first Monad the "One." It is all worked out in such a way that they seem to have anticipated somewhat vaguely and inchoately the Plotinian hypostases. Syrianus says:

For the Pythagoreans there is a difference between the One and the Monad, discussed by many of the ancient Pythagoreans, like Archytas [understand pseudo-Archytas], who says that, by co-producing, the One and the Monad differ between them and among the more recent Pythagoreans Moderatus and Nicomachus.[28]

But here is the most important testimony which speaks distinctly of the "One" on three levels:

It would seem that the first ones among the Greeks to have this conception of matter were the Pythagoreans, and after them Plato, as Moderatus attests also. In fact, Moderatus following the Pythagoreans shows the Primary One is above being and all essence; then he says that the second One which is being in the absolute sense and the intelligible [= the world of intelligible beings] is the forms, then the third One which is the soul, participates to the primary One and the forms and that the nature which comes last after this [= after the Third One], that is, the nature of sensible things, does not participate these but receives its order by reflection of these (κατ᾽ ἔμφασιν ἐκείνων), because the matter of sensible things is a shadow of non-being which is found primarily in quantity [= in intelligible matter] and is again inferior to it, being derived from it.[29]

Simplicius, who refers these ideas to Moderatus without doubt, explains them in a Neoplatonic sense, but this cannot be a complete invention. Hence Moderatus distinguished the following hypostases according to Simplicius:

(1) The first One as absolutely transcendent was placed above everything.

(2) The Second One, which is the intelligible world, that is, the world of forms, was located in the second position. The Dyad, which is *intelligible matter*, would be connected to this level. Moderatus, in fact, to whom Simplicius himself refers soon after, conceived intelligible matter as pure "quantity" lacking forms which the Primary One produces from itself "by distinguishing it" from itself after having taken away from it all formal determinations.[30]

(3) In the third place was the One-Soul.

(4) Finally, the sensible was conceived as *a reflection of the intelligible* and the matter of the sensible as *the shadow of pure intelligible quantity* that is, *sensible matter* as *the shadow of intelligible matter*).

So the tendency to place the primary principle as transcending the Mind and essence itself is present in some of the *pseudepigrapha* or at least in the testimonies which seem to draw upon the *pseudepigrapha*. The pseudo-Archytas *places God above Nous*[31] and the pseudo-Brontinus places it *above being and essence*,[32] so that the distinction of the two hypostases is plausible and it seems to be confirmed also by Nicomachus.[33] In regard to the deduction of *matter*, then, if the information of Simplicius is precise, we have even in Moderatus a surprising anticipation of the Plotinian position.

The strongly mathematicizing structure of metaphysics must necessarily carry the Neo-Pythagoreans to obscure or anyhow to confine to an inferior position, the theory of Ideas. The Monad and the Dyad are derived from the One and from these two principles numbers and the Ideas which depend on Numbers. It is clear that in the measure in which everything is derived from the first principle, as we have seen, everything is present in it and hence, *in addition to numbers*, the totality of the Ideas is also present. It is hence logical that some Neo-Pythagorean texts would consider numbers (and Ideas) present "as archetypes" in the divine thought,[34] or, in Stoic vocabulary charged with a new meaning, as "seminal reasons"(λόγοι σπερματικοί) present in the supreme Unity.[35]

The belief in *daimons* is also present in the Neo-Pythagoreans, but without any new features in relation to those already discussed with respect to the Middle Platonists and which really belong to the religious aspect of their doctrine.[36]

4. The mystical ideal of human life

We have previously said that a very different way of organizing the anthropological and moral conceptions occurs in the most ancient texts (Middle Pythagorean) than in the more recent (Neo-Pythagorean) texts. In the former, Platonic, Aristotelian, and Stoic[37] doctrines are presented as if they were Pythagorean[38] while the mention of the typical Pythagorean doctrine of metempsychosis[39] is quite infrequent. In the latter, the notion of the spirituality of the soul is revived and the concomitant belief in its eschatological destiny places the end of man in the care of the divine which is in us and in the imitation of God, ending in a mystical union with the divine.

A special place in the history of Pythagorean ethics is occupied by the famous *Golden Verses of Pythagoras*, which are a *summa* of the moral teachings of Pythagoras, an authentic short guide to the spiritual life, or a list of "do's and don'ts". Unfortunately, their date is very uncertain and the variety of dates proposed by scholars ranges over eight centuries (without counting those scholars who maintain them as authentic because, in that case, the span would then be almost a millennium).[40] The chronological placement which is proposed most often is between the end and the beginning of the Common Era (we favor a more ancient date). Its content, in any case, approximates a cognitive method which is not based on philosophical deduction. Most of the material comes from ancient Pythagoreanism and only in a few points is it colored (but rather weakly) by the new mentality. Given the great notoriety and fame which the poem had in the past, we want to read it in its entirety:

> So know and get use to controlling these passions: first of all honor the Gods as the law requires and respect oaths. Honor hence the glorious heroes and the peoples of the earth, acting in conformity with the laws.

> 5   Be respectful of your parents and as many as are bound to you by kinship. For the others make friends with those who are virtuous. Yield to good counsel and agree with advantageous actions. As long as you are able do not take things from your friend over a small wrong; in fact, Power lives close to necessity.

> 10   So know and get use to controlling these passions: first of all the stomach and sleep, then lust and anger. Never act as a result of base thoughts either with another, or when you are alone: be ashamed especially for yourself.

15   In addition practice justice in action as well as speech, do not become accustomed to acting inconsiderately in any matter, but know that it is the fate of everyone to die. Know that wealth is at one time acquired and at another lost.

Concerning the sufferings of men through the divine will, support with good will those which touch you support them with good will and do not worry.

20   It is good that you mitigate them as much as possible and say to yourself: to god men fate does not portion much of these things.

Of men understand that you will hear many evil and good words; but you should not be surprised by this nor allow yourself to be misled by it. If you have said something shameful, bear it with a good heart.

25   That which you say in everything: let no one induce you either in deed or in word to do or say what for you is not the better. Reflect before acting, so that you do not act foolishly. It is a foolish man in fact who acts and speaks inconsiderately. But understand those things which you need not repent.

30   Do not do anything which you do not understand, but grasp everything which is necessary, and thus you will live a very happy life. Do not neglect the health of your body and be moderate in drinking, eating, and in exercise.

Call the measure that which will not harm you.

35   Accustom yourself to a simple mode of life, immune to luxury, and be careful of doing what will attract the envy of others. Do not spend thoughtlessly as one who does not know the correct thing but do not be parsimonious: moderation is the best course in all things.

Do those things which cannot cause you damage and reflect before you do them.

40   Do not give in to sleep because your eyes are drooping without having first passed in review three times the actions of the day: "How have I failed? What have I done? What have I not done well?

Begin from the first question and examine your actions: then blame yourself for the bad and praise yourself for the good.

45   In obligatory matters use every consideration, these are what you must love. Such actions place you in the path of heavenly virtue. It is so for He who reveals the Tetrad to our soul, the source of eternal nature.

Undertake an action after having prayed to the Gods, because it can take you to the finish. Acting in this way, you will know the essence of the immortal Gods and of mortal men and how all things proceed and how they subsist.

50 You will know, as is right, that in everything there is an equal nature, yes, that nothing you hope for is impossible and there is nothing you can flee from.

55 And you will grasp that men suffer for evils that they themselves have brought on themselves; unhappy are those who, being close to good things, do not see them and do not hate them, and few know how to free themselves from evils. Such a fate weighs heavily on men's mind, and they, like a sphere are driven here and there, suffering infinite evils. A deadly country, in fact, of innate disorder secretly damaging them and once aroused leading them to flight

60 O Father Zeus, certainly you could free everyone from many evils by showing everyone their Daimon

But be of good heart because the root of men is divine to which nature reveals its mysteries and shows everything.

65 And if you will understand these things partly you will follow that which I have prescribed for you, and you will heal and liberate the soul from these struggles

Abstain from the foods I told you about; for purification and liberation of the soul is acting with justice, and consider everything putting at the top reason, the best guide.

70 When the body is left behind you will achieve eternal liberty, you will be an immortal and incorruptible God, no longer a mortal being.[41]

The concept of *following in the divine path* and *becoming God* which is in the background of these *Golden Verses of Pythagoras*, emerges instead directly into the foreground in the *Life of Pythagoras* by the anonymous author quoted by Photius, where it takes on a clearly mystical character. Man achieves his end through three stages: (1) by earning intimacy with the Gods, (2) by doing good acts as the Gods do, (3) by wholly distancing himself from the body and the soul:

...the Pythagoreans say that man can become better in three ways: first by means of a close relation with Gods (in fact, due to the contact with them, for this circumstance, it is necessary that they cut themselves off from every form of wickedness, making themselves like a divinity), secondly, in doing good acts (this in fact is proper to God and the imitation of divinity), thirdly in death: in fact, if the soul is separated from the body for a certain time, still being in life yet, becomes better, and in sleep by means of dreams and in ecstatic states [in Greek it is the term ἔκστασις] of the prophetic seizures, in a grade yet greater it becomes better when it is completely separated from the body.[42]

The ideal of life, in a mystical and religious sense, is even further emphasized in the *Life of Apollonius* written by Philostratus and in the *Life of Pythagoras* written by Porphyry and by Iamblichus, the content of which is clearly of Neo-Pythagorean provenance.

Apollonius, if we do not take into account the partially fictional amplifications of Philostratus, certainly reached a high degree of religious and spiritual fervor.[43]

The life which Apollonius led was considered a true model, and Philostratus presents it that way. Apollonius the philosopher, like Pythagoras knew and learned much from the astrologers of Babylonia, the Brahmins of India, and the Gymnosophists of Egypt. He spoke frequently and had communicated often with the Gods, he was a mediator between the Gods and men, he knew the future, he communicated to men a message of true wisdom and, on the basis of this knowledge, performed wondrous actions. (Philostratus makes it quite clear that his wisdom and these wondrous actions do not have anything to do with what seems to be witchcraft and magic, but they directly depend on a true philosophy.)[44]

But even more interesting is the manner in which Pythagoras was idealized and the paradigm which was constructed from this idealization and which was represented in the various *Lives of Pythagoras*. Here is how Philostratus writes, for example:

> The people who praise Pythagoras of Samos tell us that first he was born in Ionia, he was Euphorbus at Troia: who was deceased and lived again and died like Homer sings.... They add that he had dealings with the Gods and that from them he learned what things men appreciate and which not and which of them inspire disputes by nature, by saying that all things the others left to guide by false conjectures about divine things and fall into contrary opinions, but that to him Apollo himself revealed what doctrines ought to be professed and that with him Pallas and the Muses conversed, never simulating the truth and the other Gods, of whom neither the deeds nor the names of the others were known. All which was learned from Pythagoras his followers regarded as law, venerating him as if he had come down from Zeus...[45]

> Porphyry says precisely that some considered Pythagoras as a son of Apollo, and only putatively a son of Mnesarchus.[46]

> Iamblichus, drawing on these sources, says that Abaris, a well-known priest of Apollo, when he saw Pythagoras was convinced that he was Apollo himself.[47]

Pythagoras, for the Pythagoreans, became what Christ was for Christians, the Son of God in human form, and his philosophy became a divine revelation.

III. Numenius of Apamea and the Fusion of Neo-Pythagoreanism and Middle Platonism

1. The philosophical position of Numenius

Neo-Pythagoreanism, with Numenius,[1] achieved its highest development, but at the same time its end, being absorbed into the parallel Middle Platonic movement.

The historians of ancient philosophy usually vacillate in trying to give Numenius a precise place in history. Some consider him more a Platonist or better a Middle Platonist, while others instead consider him a Neo-Pythagorean; an analogous uncertainty is also recognizable among the ancients, but most of them considered him a Pythagorean.[2]

In terms of the extant testimonies and fragments, Numenius considered himself chiefly a follower of Pythagoras as well as Socrates and Plato since he was convinced that both Socrates and Plato, were dependent essentially on Pythagoras and that Plato, consequently, could not be superior to someone to whom he was indebted for his wisdom. In spite of these convictions Numenius felt the need to defend Plato with the work significantly entitled, The Infidelity of the Academics towards Plato, against the misunderstandings of numerous followers who, beginning from Arcesilaus, betrayed him. The Academicians in no way troubled themselves to maintain intact the teachings of their master. Yet Numenius notes that Plato basically deserved that same fidelity and veneration on the part of his followers, through which Pythagoras was elevated to so high a place since, "although not being better with respect to the great Pythagoras, he probably was not in any way inferior."[3]

The Socrates of Numenius professed "the doctrine of the three Gods" which had been taken from Pythagoras, and so Plato, a disciple of Socrates, is a "Pythagorizing" Plato. The betrayal by the followers of Plato would in large part be due to the fact that Plato wrote in an unusual manner, hiding the things which he said, in a sense, "halfway between clarity and obscurity."

The position taken by our philosopher could not therefore be more explicit. He intended to make reëmerge from skeptical and Stoicizing incomprehension the Platonic tenets and to show that these are identical with Pythagorean doctrines.

The doctrines developed by Numenius in the extant fragments, as we will see, largely confirm these programmatic intentions. He tried, although without entirely succeeding, to reconcile those theological and metaphysical doctrines which the Middle Platonists had extracted from a rereading of the *Timaeus* with the doctrine of the Monad, the Dyad, and numbers, which the Neo-Pythagoreans had restated vigorously.

In addition to the things which we said, a third component is essential in order to understand the position of Numenius, the so-called "Eastern component" about which there has been much discussion.[4]

Actually, our philosopher's expressions and repeated assertions testify to his Syrian origin and the influence of the East. Numenius was acquainted with Biblical wisdom and the allegorical interpretations of the *Books of Moses* and the prophets. He was also acquainted with Christian teachings and we know that he interpreted allegorically at least one episode of the Gospel account of Jesus. He was also acquainted with other Eastern peoples, and he accepted the doctrine which admitted that in man there are two souls (one good, the other evil) of Persian [Iranian] origin. But perhaps even more than in a single doctrine the eastern influence is to be seen in the mystical and religious attitudes which had found expression at first at Alexandria and by this time in the second century CE were dominant.[5]

In this way, with the fusion of the two principal currents of thought which had created the new theoretical climate with the mystical component derived from the Near East, there came together all those conditions which were to bring on the birth of Neoplatonism. Numenius, in fact, anticipated, although in a somewhat imperfect manner, the formulation of some of the foundations of the Plotinian system, as we will see.

2. The proclamation of the absolute preëminence of the incorporeal

The Middle Platonic movement was already distinguishable in its origins on the basis of its rediscovery of the incorporeal. Neo-Pythagoreanism also rapidly (or perhaps at the same time) took up this doctrine. consequently, Numenius not only makes this position secure, but gives it an unexpected importance.

The chief metaphysical question, as we know, for the Greek philosophers is "what is being?" It was precisely in this form that Numenius took it up again.[6]

The answer that he gave to the question presupposed not only a general overcoming of materialism, but even its specific overturning.

Being cannot be identified with the material because this is indeterminate, disordered, irrational, unknowable, whereas being must have characteristics which are exactly opposed to these.

Being can in no way be identified with the four elements (water, air, earth, and fire) or with any one of them, because each is derived, transformed, and changed into the other while being does not change. Being cannot, in general, be identified with a body, since bodies are themselves subject to continuous change and need in any case something which would enable them to perdure. This something cannot also be in its turn a body, because if it were so, once again it itself would be in need of a further principle which would guarantee its stability and permanence. Being, hence, must be incorporeal. Being, then, will be an immutable, eternal, and incorporeal reality. Here are two eloquent passages which state these conclusions:

> Being, hence, is eternal, stable, always equal to itself or identical. Being is subject neither to birth nor to death, nor to increase nor to diminution, never did it become more or less. In addition, being does not involve any spatial or other kind of motion. For it does not lie in its nature to be moved, neither backwards or forwards, up or down, right or left; nor will it turn on its axis but it will stand self-poised and stable ever remaining self-similar and identical.[7]

> I cannot any longer pretend nor try to avoid the word *incorporeal*: to this point, in fact, it is more suitable to name it, rather than be silent about it. And I do acknowledge that his name is that which we have so long sought. And let no one mock me if I affirm that the name of the incorporeal is "Substance" and "Being" is the fact that he is not born, nor will he die, nor does he admit any type of motion whatever, nor any change for the better or worse, for he is always simple and unalterable, fixed in the same identical idea, and does not abandon his own identity, either voluntarily or by constraint by another... . He will therefore agree that the Incorporeal is Being is demonstrated.[8]

It is evident that being, understood as incorporeal, for Numenius is not the whole of reality, but only the being that transcends the sensible, that is to say, the sphere of the intelligible:

> I have said that Being was the Incorporeal, and that this was intelligible.[9]

Our philosopher states in agreement with Plato that the sensible or corporeal is not *being* but *becoming*.

> Plato asked: "What is Being?" and designated it is surely as what cannot become. For he said, becoming could not affect Being because it would then be subject to change; and if it were subject to change, it would not be Being.[10]

We are not in the presence, as might be first thought in reading these texts, of Parmenides' ancient theory of being, reformed through the results of the "second voyage" of Plato. In fact, the Being that really is and never becomes nor perishes, that is, the incorporeal, is also the Biblical *"He Who Is."* Numenius was, in fact, convinced that the teaching of Plato corresponded to the ancient teaching of Moses, which he knew well and which, as we have already said, he interpreted in an allegorical manner, as our sources have mentioned.[11]

In fact, Numenius went further still than Philo in this area. Indeed not only was he convinced that the notion of the incorporeal and being professed by Plato corresponded to that of Moses, but he states that Plato basically was nothing but an "Atticizing Moses," that is, a Moses who speaks in Attic Greek. Here is the most significant testimony:

Numenius writes these things [=that being is purely intelligible that it neither becomes nor perishes etc.], when he interprets and clarifies the doctrines of Plato and those earlier of Moses. For good reasons, therefore, the saying is attributed to him which he then passed on and which goes like this: "What is Plato except a Moses who speaks in Attic?"[12]

3. The structure of incorporeal being and the doctrine of the three Gods

What is the structure of being and the incorporeal? We have seen in many authors, especially of the second century CE, that there is a tendency to conceive immaterial reality *in a hierarchical and hypostatic sense* and even a particular configuration of this hierarchy *in a triadic sense* is clearly recognizable. Numenius took this tendency to the highest degree of clarity of anyone before Plotinus. Proclus says:

> Numenius proclaimed three Gods and calls the first "Father"; the second "Creator"; the third "Creation"; in fact according to him, the cosmos is the Third God. So that the Demiurge for him is two-fold: the First and Second God, the cosmos produced by the Demiurge, is the Third. It is better to express it in this way, rather than as he himself says, with the terminology of tragedy, the "ancestor," "the Son," the "Offspring."[13]

The testimony of Proclus requires a series of explanations which are based on the numerous textual fragments of Numenius himself.

First, the Middle Platonists like Numenius found it necessary to distinguish the First God from the Second God in order to guarantee his absolute transcendence and to eliminate any relationship with the world of becoming. The First God has a relationship exclusively with the pure essences that is with the Ideas; instead, the Second God is concerned with the constitution of the cosmos. Numenius maintains that the Idea of the Good, or the Good Itself of which Plato speaks in the *Republic* and on which the other Ideas depend, is identical with the First God. Instead, the Demiurge which constitutes the cosmos, of which Plato speaks in the *Timaeus*, is said to be a "good," *but not the Good*"; it hence is other than the supreme God, and it is precisely the Second God. The world of the supreme Ideas do not depend on him, but they depend on the First God, whereas the world of becoming depends on the Second God. The Second God, *imitating the First*, thinks the essences produced by the First God and reproduces them in the cosmos. The First God is superior to essence, but not to the Mind; in fact, he coincides with the supreme Mind as the Middle Platonists said previously, while the Second God is the Second Mind. Here is the most significant fragment in this regard:

> If Being (οὐσία), and the Idea, is intelligible and if, as is agreed, Mind (νοῦς) is its cause and superior to it, this alone is the Good. For, if the demiurgic God is the principle of generation, then surely the Good is the principle of Being (= of the Ideas). Now, the relation that exists between the demiurgic God and the Good, of which he is the imitator, is analogous to what exists

between Becoming and Being, the former imitates the latter. But if the demiurge of generation is good, the demiurge of Being must be the Good itself, connatured to Being. but as the Second (Divinity), being twofold, he himself produces the Idea of himself, and the cosmos, insofar as he is a demiurge, although he himself remains intelligible. To conclude our reasoning, here are the four names of the four distinct realities: [1] the First God, who is the good itself; [2] the Demiurge, his imitator, who is good; [3] Being (οὐσία), that of the First God and the other of the Second; [4] whose imitation is the beautiful universe which becomes beautiful through participation in the Being of the First [Beautiful being].[14]

The First God, which is absolutely simple, is stable and immobile, or to say it better, it has an immobility which is a "connatural motion." Aristotle spoke of "activity without motion" and it is essentially this about which Numenius is speaking. The First God acts and produces without changing, and on this immutable action depends, in the final analysis, the order, the stability, and the salvation of all beings:

These are the modes of living, of the First God and the Second God. It is clear that the First God must be stable, and that the Second, on the contrary, is in motion. The First hence is concerned with the Intelligible, while the Second is concerned with both the Intelligible and the sensible. And don't be surprised at my statement, because you will hear of things even more fantastic. In contrast to the movement, which belongs to the Second, I call that characteristic of the First God immobility; or rather, an *innate motion*. From this (First God) is shed abroad into the universe the order of the cosmos, its eternal permanence and conservation.[15]

Numenius said also that the First God is as One who "sows the seed of every life" in all things which participate in him, and that the Second God distributes, plants, and transplants into each being.[16] The Second God, instead, as we have previously stated, is in a certain sense twofold. On the one hand he "contemplates" the intelligibles, and on the other hand he acts on matter, constructing the cosmos and governing it. Numenius said expressly that the order which he impressed on matter derived from the sphere of the Ideas and that the terminus of the contemplation from which the demiurgic capacity of judgment comes, is the First God, while the impulse to action comes to him from desire:

He directs this harmony, governing [matter] according to the Ideas, and he looks...toward God which is above, directing his eyes upon him he derives from the contemplation of the divine capacity to judge and from his desire the capacity to act.[17]

What emerges here, although in a somewhat embryonic state, is the concept of "contemplation"(θεωρία) as the foundation of creative activity which, as we will see, constitutes the center of the Plotinian metaphysics.[18]

In the testimony of Proclus from which we began the Third God was identical with cosmos. It is, nevertheless, probable that Numenius understood by the cosmos only its formal aspect (since, as we will see, mater for him is evil) and that, hence, he identified it with the Second aspect of the Second God, which (to judge from the extant evidence) seems to coincide with the soul of the world, or better, with the *good soul* of the world. But in order to understand this point we ought to first examine other conceptions of our philosopher.

4.   The Neo-Pythagorean doctrine of the Monad and the Dyad in the context of the Numenian theory of being

Numenius differs from the Middle Platonists chiefly by reason of his deduction of the doctrine of the Monad and the Dyad which, as we have seen, is a doctrine typical of Neo-Pythagoreans. Nevertheless, the fusion of this doctrine with his trinitarian theology is achieved in a somewhat doubtful way, at least judging from the extant testimonies. Furthermore, he achieved it only at the price of a total break with the most original and novel "monistic" current of Neo-Pythagoreanism.

According to Numenius, the Monad is God while the indefinite Dyad is *sensible* matter. The indefinite Dyad, or the indeterminate Dyad, is *not* generated and is co-eternal with the Monad, while the determined Dyad was generated when it was determined and ordered by God (by the Monad) when the cosmos was created. Further, to deduce the Dyad from the Monad, according to our philosopher, is an absurdity since the Monad must lose its own nature to produce the Dyad (*i.e.*, by reduplication). Here is a testimony of Chalcidius:

> Numenius who followed the teaching of Pythagoras...with whom he states that Plato is in agreement, says that Pythagoras designated God with the name of Monad, matter with that of the Dyad. This indeterminate Dyad was not generated, because only that which is determined was generated. In other words: before being ordered and receiving form and order it was not born or generated, but once it was adorned and embellished by the demiurge it was generated; and thus because generation is a later occurrence, that principle not yet ordered must be understood as not generated and as co-eternal with God, by whom it is then ordered. But some Pythagoreans did not correctly understand the validity of this doctrine, affirming also that the indeterminate Dyad which lacked a measure was produced by the unique Monad when the Monad itself abandons its own nature in order to assume the configuration of the Dyad. And this is not correct since the Monad which exists must cease to be and, what is more, God would be transformed into matter and the Monad into the Dyad without measure and determination: these conceptions are unacceptable to people of even middling education.[19]

Leaving the polemic of Numenius against the Pythagorean "monists" aside, which would carry us too far afield, let us ask first to which of the hypostases does the Monad correspond. Naturally, it would be expected to correspond to the First God, which we are told in addition to being Good is also "One" by means of the well-known Platonic tenet "the Good is One." But an attentive reading of the fragments does not seem to justify this identification entirely, since the First God remains in himself absolutely simple and indivisible, without any relation to the Dyad or to matter. The God who enters into contact with the Dyad-matter and gives it form is, instead, the Second God, which in fact, because of this relation which matter, becomes two-fold because matter is Dyadic, and as such produces a reduplication, as we already stated above. Here is a rather explicit fragment in this regard:

> The First God, who exists in himself, is simple, because he can never be divisible, being in total communion with himself. The Second and Third God are One; nevertheless, entering into contact with matter, which is Dyad, the (One divinity) unifies it but by matter He suffers division, inasmuch as matter is full of desires, and in a perennial flux. But insofar as He is not only turned toward the Intelligible world (which would be more suitable to its own nature), for the reason that while He looks to matter and takes care of it, he forgets Himself. And He comes thus in contact with the Sensible and busics himself with it; and He elevates it up to His own nature, because He was moved by desires for Matter.[20]

The Third God, which is then the Second in its specifically demiurgic function, that is, in its function ordered to informing matter (Dyad), is evidently that which Numenius himself calls "soul of the world," or more precisely, for the reasons which we will soon see, the "good soul" of the world.[21]

Before leaving the argument which we have been considering, we wish to make two more observations.

Whether or not Numenius distinguished the One from the Monad, as some Pythagoreans did, we do not know, but it is possible. In that case, the doctrine of the principles would agree with his trinitarian theology. The First God or the Good itself would be the One (and such is it actually called). The Monad would be the Second God and would be derived by imitation of the One (the Second God is good, as we know, by imitation of the Good, and hence He could also be Monad by imitation of the One), while the Third God would be born in the way explained above, that is, by the contact of the Monad with the Dyad.[22]

It seems, on the contrary, that Numenius considered the Dyad only as *sensible matter* and as intelligible matter as well. According to the extant fragments, in fact, it seems that our philosopher did not use the Dyad for the deduction of the Ideas and Numbers, but only for the deduction of the cosmos. For him the Dyad is the sensible principle opposed to the intelligible world, a principle evil in itself and the source of every evil.

5. Matter, evil soul, and good soul

Matter as an evil principle is not anything inanimate, but (as we have previously seen in Plutarch) is endowed with its own soul (a principle of movement and life), which is also evil and seeks to oppose the work of the Demiurge and Providence, that is, to restrain the action of God which impresses order and rationality on matter. Consequently, since as we have pointed out the doubling of the Second God gives place to a Third, that is, to the aspect or moment properly demiurgic of the Second, which then has its own function of being the soul of the world, it is understandable how Numenius by interpreting literally a passage of the *Laws* of Plato, of which we have previously made mention when we spoke about Plutarch, said that there were *two souls of the world*. Chalcidius says:

> Numenius praises Plato, for having taught the existence of two world souls: one in the highest way beneficent and the second maleficent, that is, matter. For if nature is in even moderate motion, since it moves from its own interior motion, it is necessary that it be alive and animated by soul, according to the laws of all things whose motions are innate.[23]

> Consequently, if the wicked soul is the principle of the irrational life and of the chaotic movement of matter, the good soul is the principle of rationality and order. The good soul hence can only be Mind as has been explicitly attested.[24]

It is understandable, hence, how Numenius considered this soul as "intermediate" between the sensible and the supersensible and defined it as "number deriving from the indivisible Monad and the divisible Dyad."[25] This expression indicates with Pythagorean terminology nothing other than what with Platonic language Numenius himself has defined as the Mind which turns to matter to order it.

On the basis of these doctrines Numenius constructs his vision of man concerning which, unfortunately, very little testimony has come down to us. Our philosopher also assigned *two souls* to man, an evil one in the measure in which it has matter, and a good or rational one.

In addition, given the conception of the soul as absolutely incorporeal Numenius maintained as a necessary presupposition the existence of an intermediate phase in which the soul, before "it is mired in the mud of bodies," *gradually moves away from its original pure state, passes through the celestial spheres, and thus takes on ethereal substance, which permits it to enter into real bodies.* Numenius, in addition, maintained the doctrine of metempsychosis.[26]

It is evident, therefore, that the basic dominating vision of Numenius must be the accentuated mysticism of the *Phaedo*, although certain aspects are completely exaggerated by the introduction of dualistic elements of Eastern origin.

Consider, for example, the liberation of the soul from the prison of the body through the purification of science; the victory of the Good over the evil which is in us as it is in the universe, which constitutes the moral task of human beings; and finally the supreme goal as the ecstatic union with the absolute in which "they enter in intimate union with the Good, one to One."[27]

6. Numenius at the threshold of Neoplatonism

The points of contact which can be noted between Numenius and Plotinus are numerous: some concern a few corollaries, others concern the very foundations of his system.

First, it needs to be recognized that the three Numenian Gods have a series of recognizable features which make them comparable to the three Plotinian hypostases. Nevertheless, although they are quite important, these points are not the most illuminating correspondences.

One the contrary, certain anticipations are determinative, although somewhat imperfectly formulated and expressed, of some of the principles which constitute the central notions of the Plotinian metaphysics.

First, Numenius anticipates the principle which inspires the "procession" of the Plotinian hypostases in which the divine *gives without impoverishing itself.* Here is a very significant Numenian fragment in this regard:

> All things offered as gifts pass into the possession of the one who receives them, being given by the donor (as for example, slaves, riches, incised and minted money); this is the process with earthly and human gifts. When, however, the divine is communicated and passes over from the one to the other, it does not leave the Giver while being of service to the Receiver; not only does the Giver not lose anything thereby, but he gains this further advantage, the memory of his giving (as generosity)...This can be seen when a candle lit from another candle, which has light, does not destroy the first, but because its matter was kindled by the fire of the other.[28]

We have noted and we will only recall the statement of Numenius that the *contemplation* of the Second God which looks to the First is the base on which the possibility of the creation of the cosmos is constructed.

In addition, our philosopher formulated the principle that in a certain sense, *all is in all,* a principle which, with some re-interpretation, becomes central in Plotinus:

> Come on, therefore, rise up to incorporeal reality in itself, in order to judge on the basis of it, in order, all the doctrines on the soul. There are some who affirm that this reality is totally of a homeomeric nature (= constituted of equal parts) identical to itself and one, so that in all its parts it is present in its wholeness. These arrive at placing in individual soul the intelligible world, the Gods, the daimons, the good and all higher realities and affirm that everything is present in the same way in all things, but in each thing according to its proper essence. Of this opinion is certainly Numenius, Plotinus with some differences....According to this opinion the whole essence of the soul

is not different in any way from the Mind, from the Gods, from the supreme genera.[29]

Finally, an impressive anticipation of the doctrine of the Plotinian *unio mystica* [*mystical union*] with the Good is contained in the splendid fragment of the *Treatise on the Good*:

> It is necessary that man, after being separated from sensible things, enters into an intimate union with the Good, one on One, there where there is no human being, nor other living being, nor any body which is great or small, but there is a marvelous solitude, unspeakable, indescribable, there where there is the abode of the Good, its concerns and its splendor, the Good itself in peace and goodness, He, the tranquil One and the Master who is benevolent and transcends his own essence. And, if some one who grasping onto sensible things imagines that the Good flees to him and living in pleasures believes that he achieves the Good, such a one is completely mistaken.[30]

We have now come with Numenius right to the threshold of Neoplatonism.

Fourth Section

THE HERMETIC WRITERS AND THE CHALDEAN ORACLES

« τοῦτό ἐστι τὸ ἀγαθὸν τέλος τοῖς
γνῶσιν ἐσχηκόσι, θεωθῆναι.»

"The happy end to which they come who possess knowledge: is to become God."

Corpus Hermeticum 1.26

« οὐ γὰρ ὑφ᾽ εἱμαρτὴν ἀγέλην πίπτουσι θεουργοί.»

"Theurgians are not part of the masses subject to Fate."

Chaldean Oracles, Frag. 153

I. The Phenomenon of Hermeticism and its Different Aspects

1. Hermes Trismegistus and the Hermetic literature

According to the religious beliefs of the Egyptians, Thoth the very great was the God who invented many sciences and arts and, in particular, the letters of the alphabet, that is, writing.[1] Therefore, he was considered the scribe of the Gods and hence he was the interpreter, revealer, and teacher of divine wisdom and of the divine *logos*. Consequently, the Greeks, when they became acquainted with Egyptian theology, assimilated Thoth to their God Hermes, since he had a similar function of being "interpreter and messenger" of the Gods. In fact, in order to better identify Hermes with the Egyptian Thoth "the very great," they called him by the name of Trismegistus, which is a superlative form of "great" (τρισμέγιστος, which literally means "three times great," the adjective emphasized by repetition). Under the name of this God, in the Hellenistic Age (perhaps previously in the first half of the third century BCE) and especially in the Imperial Age (in particular in the second and third centuries CE), there arose and developed a rich literature having a variety of characteristics and differing contents, joined nevertheless by the claim to be divinely inspired by Hermes "the very great" and hence as a "revelation" of this deity.

To the Fathers of the Church beginning from Tertullian and Lactantius, Hermes Trismegistus seemed, if not a God, at least a prophet, a sort of pagan prophet of Christ who lived at the time of Moses. What impressed them was the elevated theological and moral conceptions which are encountered in some of the Hermetic writings (which were composed in the first centuries of the Imperial Age). He was considered a pagan prophet of Christ during the medieval period, the age of Humanism, as well as during the Renaissance.[2]

Modern research, however, beginning from the eighteenth century has ascertained that the Hermetic writings are *pseudepigrapha*, composed by different authors who hid themselves under the name of the Egyptian God. In our century, moreover, it has been determined that the most important of these writings are not expressions of authentic "Egyptian" wisdom, but rather conceptions which belong to the late Hellenistic Age. Finally, it has been established that they cannot be traced back to a particular religious sect, since they lack indications of anything which is suggestive of a particular religious group.[3]

The Hermetic literature is made up of writings which can be subdivided into two groups.

(1) The works which Festugière calls "popular Hermeticism" which concern the so-called occult sciences, some of which can be traced back to the third century BCE.[4]

(2) The treatises which the same scholar calls "learned Hermeticism," which treat philosophical and especially theological and mystical-religious subjects, the greater part of which seem to have been composed between the second and third century of the Common Era.

The second group of writings, which is the most interesting, is subdivided as follows.

(*a*) The *Corpus Hermeticum*, which consists of seventeen treatises (the first of these, entitled *Poimandres*, is the most unified and the most famous).

(*b*) The *Asclepius*, which is a Latin translation (in the past attributed erroneously to Apuleius) of the *Complete Discourse* originally composed in Greek and which arose probably at the beginning of the fourth century CE.

(*c*) Numerous citations and extracts (some even consistent) which we find quoted by Stobaeus.

(*d*) Testimonies and fragments which are quoted by numerous Christian authors.[5]

In this remarkable mass of writings composed in such varied times and thus of varying content does there exist precise connections and, if they exist, what are they? This is the first problem which we have to tackle.

2.   The basic characteristics of Hermeticism

Repeating some of the remarks previously made above and completing them, we can say the following:

(*a*) Hermeticism is presented as an esoteric doctrine.

(*b*) Hermeticism claims to be a "divine revelation."

(*c*) The divinity speaking is said to be Hermes.

(*d*) Hermeticism in general does not communicate its message by means of rational discourse and logical deductions, but through a kind of "initiation ritual."

These characteristics are found both in the writings of popular Hermeticism as well as in those of learned Hermeticism and they constitute a minimum common denominator, even though a generic one. Festugière correctly points out in this regard: "A trait is…common simply by the fact of the revelation here and there (scil., in the two groups of writings), by the fact that by then, both in order to comprehend and arrange the phenomena and to know and approach close to God, it no more appeals to the procedures of reason alone or to the power of personal reflection, but rather to a divine oracle, to a revelation which is attended to and obtained from divinity; in a word, by the fact that in regard to both science as well as to a spiritual life it has passed from the plane of reason to that of belief, of faith, *which is a great sign of the profound revolution taking place in minds and hearts of men at the end of the Hellenistic epoch.* And it is chiefly this point which ought to be in the foreground."[6]

In regard to the most specific characteristics of this "revelation" and their significance, as we have previously hinted, it is necessary to carry out two different discussions about two different groups of writings.

(1) The first group of writings, which includes astrology, alchemy, magic and the occult sciences in general, reveal perhaps even more or better than some writings of the second group the great decline of the rationalism which belonged to the preceding age. They, in fact, are in many respects the *negation of the spirit which had characterized the science of the Greeks.*

First, the writings involve the negation of that *theoretical-contemplative* aspect which is uniquely Greek. In fact through astrology they wish to know and predict the future for the purposes of deriving some related advantages; through alchemy they want to find suitable procedures to produce gold and hence wealth; through magic they want to dominate the powers of nature for the purposes of acquiring power over things and eventually over human beings.

In addition, these writings are the negation of that *speculative-rational* aspect of Greek science which attempted to discover the *why*, the *cause*, and hence the *universal* (obviously the universal which is proper to each of the individual sciences). In fact these "occult sciences" are especially interested in the *particular*, the *singular*, the *marvelous*.

Festugière's analysis points out the following: "Aristotelian science obscured the singular for the sake of the general, the individual for the universal. What, on the contrary, attracts the new wisdom is the particular properties of each natural thing and a preference for the singular, the marvelous, the *wonder-provoking* characteristics. Since this new knowledge proposes to act on nature, it especially attempts to know the hidden forces of things, those mysterious powers which make certain beings attract certain others (the magnet and iron) or vice versa what repels them; the kinds of plants or parts of animals possessing therapeutic powers or harmful powers, in short, everything which the authors of the *wonderful* and which Pliny calls the laws of sympathy or of antipathy among beings."[7]

Finally, these writings represent the negation of that adamantine faith that the Greeks had nourished about the capacity of human reason to achieve the truth through its own resources. In fact, the hidden peculiarities and powers of things and the relations of sympathy and antipathy are some of the "secrets" of nature and as such are unreachable on the part of *unaided* human reason and hence without the assistance of the Gods. The "revelation" may be invoked rightly in that specific context in which, in the past, reason had been declared absolute sovereign. Festugière quotes[8] in this regard an affirmation of Xenophon (of undoubted Socratic origin) which is to the point, that it is considered foolishness to ask the oracle what is within the power of human talent, that is, what can be known through study, through calculation, and through measurement.[9] What Socrates marked as folly is instead the attitude which characterized the Hermetic writings.

The consequences from all of this are evident and again Festugière has said it in a flawless way: "The new science will be necessarily a mystery, the transmission of a mystery. Those who have knowledge will be the elect, and there will be an infinite distance between these elect and the common people. In addition, the means to obtain the science will no longer be sought in research, the exercise of reason, but in prayer, the act of worship, or, at an inferior level, magical practices: it passed from the intellectual plane to the plane of religion or magic."[10]

(2) The second group of writings presented through its content remarkable analogies with the parallel philosophical currents of Middle Platonism and Neo-Pythagoreanism, but it accentuated the mystical and a-logical aspects. It exacerbated the God-world dualism, it accentuated the character of the transcendence and hence the character of the unknowability and inexpressibility of God. Although Philo, as we have seen, had entered on an analogous path, the Middle Platonists and the Neo-Pythagoreans had also manifested tendencies of this kind. But in the writings of the *Corpus Hermeticum* an even more radical outcome due to its accentuated dualism is reached. The traditional structure of the theological problem is overturned and a new way of knowing (*gnosis*) God is imposed, based no longer on human reason, but on a revelation of God linked to prayer and worship, on direct illumination and on ecstasy. Only when the senses, reason, and speech become diminished, then in the *divine silence* we know God in an ecstatic union, in an authentic fashion "we become Gods." Here is a text which describes in a clear fashion this ecstatic union:

> The vision of the Good is not a thing of fire, as are the sun's rays; it does not blaze down upon us and force us to close our eyes; it shines forth much or little, according as he who gazes on it is able to receive the inflow of the incorporeal radiance. It is more penetrating than visible light in its descent upon us; but it cannot harm us; it is full of immortal life. Even those who are able to imbibe somewhat more than others of that vision are again and again sunk in blind sleep by the body; but when they have been released from the body, then they attain to full fruition of that most lovely sight....Then only will you see it, when you cannot speak of it; for the knowledge of it is deep silence, and suppression of all the senses. He who has apprehended the beauty of the Good can apprehend nothing else; he who has seen it can see nothing else; he cannot hear speech about aught else; he cannot move his body at all; he forgets all bodily sensations and all bodily movements, and is still. But the beauty of the Good bathes his mind in light, and takes all his soul up to itself, and draws it forth from the body, and changes the whole man into eternal substance. For it cannot be...that a soul should become a God while it abides in a human body.[11]

3.   God, the hierarchy of the divine, the development of the cosmos and the man in the *Corpus Hermeticum*

The *Corpus Hermeticum*, as has been pointed out currently by scholars, does not contain a rigorous nor very consistent doctrine. Nevertheless some scholars exaggerated this point somewhat without any apparent justification, since some contradictions are explained easily on the basis of the different periods of composition of the various treatises, while other vacillations and antinomies are encountered also in the parallel philosophical currents and probably derive, at least in part, from the sources from which the Hermetic authors themselves drew.

In regard to God what follows should be noted. He is conceived in connection with the idea, or better, the image of light, and also in function of the concepts of the incorporeal, transcendent, and infinitude (as we have previously pointed out), expressed with forms and definitions which frequently echo Philo and "Mosaic philosophy," in addition to the Middle Platonists. The Neo-Pythagorean concept of the Monad and the Dyad as "principle and root of all things" is also used to characterize God.[12]

Yet just as in Philo and in some Middle Platonists (and then, as we will see, in Plotinus himself), positive theology and negative theology are conjoined in the *Corpus Hermeticum*. On the one hand, it tended to place God above everything and to conceive him as totally other than anything else which exists, "without form or shape," and hence precisely as "lacking essence" and thus wholly ineffable.[13] On the other hand, it recognized that God is good and the father of all things and hence the cause of everything and insofar as he is such it tends to represent him in function of some of the canons of positive theology. The fifth treatise, for example, presents an interesting interweaving of these two positions by maintaining the thesis that God is invisible and at the same time what is most visible.[14]

In addition, there occurs the decisively prevalent identification typical of Middle Platonists of the supreme God with the highest Mind, even if, for example in the second treatise, they would seem to envisage the thesis that God is above Mind itself and cause of itself:

> God is not...the Mind itself, but He is cause of the being of the Mind, it is not the vital breath but cause of the existence of the vital breath, He is not the light but the cause of the existence of the light.[15]

Moreover, although simply as a hypothesis, analogous statements are also found in Albinus, as we have seen, and in any case there is nothing beyond these references.

There is a very interesting point in regard to the conception of the hierarchy of the divine. The *Poimandres*, which is the most coherent of the treatises, presents a series of intermediaries between the First God and the world, evidently taken from Philo on the one hand and from the Middle

Platonists on the other, which is suggestive of the *typical Gnostic tendency* (both pagan and heterodox Christian) *to multiply intermediaries*.

Here is a synoptic outline taken from this treatise.

(1) At the apex stands the supreme God, supreme Light and Mind, having a masculine-feminine nature and hence capable of self-generation.

(2) Then the *Logos*, which is first born son of the supreme God.

(3) From the supreme God is also derived a demiurgic Mind, which is hence a second-born, but it is expressly said to be "consubstantial" with the *Logos*.

(4) Next the *Anthropos*, that is, incorporeal Man, derived from God and who is in the "image of God."

(5) Finally, the Mind which is given to terrestrial man (strictly distinct from the soul and clearly superior to it), which is as much of the divine as there is in human beings (and, in fact in a certain sense, is God himself in man) and that enjoys an essential role in Hermetic ethics and mysticism.

The highest God is, in addition, conceived as articulated "in an infinite number of powers" and also as "archetypic form" and as "the principle of principles, which has no limit"[16] (once again with evident connection to Philo and to Middle Platonism).

The *Logos* and the demiurgic Mind are creators of the cosmos. They act in diverse ways on the *obscurity* or *darkness*, which originally withdrew and which is dualistically conceived as opposed to the light-God (and a *boulé* or Will as well, which derives again from God in a way not made precise and whose relation with *obscurity* is not determined), and they constructed an orderly world. They produced the seven celestial spheres and put them in motion. From the movement of these spheres living beings lacking reason (which in a first stage are all bisexual) are therefore produced.

The generation of the terrestrial man is more complex. The *Anthropos* or incorporeal Man, third-born of the supreme God, wishes to imitate the demiurgic Mind and create something by itself. Obtaining the consent of the Father, the *Anthropos* goes through the seven celestial spheres up to the moon, receiving by participation the powers of each of them; then he appears from the sphere of the moon and sees the sublunar nature. Quickly the *Anthropos* is enamored of this nature and vice versa the nature is enamored of man. More precisely, man is enamored of his image reflected in nature (in water), he is moved by a desire to unite to it, and thus, by joining himself to it, he falls. Terrestrial man with his two-fold spiritual and corporeal nature is born in this way.

The Hermetic author of the *Poimandres* actually complicates his theory of human generation considerably. In fact, from the coupling of incorporeal man with corporeal nature, general man is not immediately born, but there arise seven men (seven like the spheres of the planets), each one both masculine and feminine. Everything remains in this condition until through the will of the supreme God[17] the two sexes of man (of the animals already born through the effect of the movement of the planets) are divided and they receive the biblical commandment to grow and multiply and preserve themselves:

> Increase and multiply abundantly, all you that have been created and made. And let the man that has mind in him recognize that he is immortal, and that the cause of death is carnal desire [eros] and let him know all that exist.[18]

4. The Mind, knowledge, and salvation

The message of "learned Hermeticism" from which is derived all its fame is fundamentally a *doctrine of salvation*, and its metaphysical, theological, cosmological, and anthropological theories are nothing more than the supports of this soteriology.

At the base of the most significant treatises of the *Corpus Hermeticum*, as we have said previously, there is a very accentuated dualistic conception, and consequently a pessimism which was absent or only inchoately present in classical Greek thought and in early Hellenism.[19]

The birth of the terrestrial man is hence due essentially to the fall of *Anthropos*, who wanted to be joined to material nature.[20] And thus Man, from "life and light which he was," is transformed "into soul and Mind" in the sense that his original life becomes soul and his Light becomes Mind. But the material world into which man has fallen is the "pleroma of every evil,"[21] that is, the totality of evil, radical evil. Hence "salvation" could not be otherwise than *liberation and separation from matter*.

So the means for realizing this according to the doctrine of the *Corpus Hermeticum* is knowledge (*gnosis*), while ignorance keeps men riveted to matter and is hence the worst of evils. Therefore salvation is identical with *gnosis*.[22]

But what exactly is Hermetic *gnosis* and how is it actualized? Chiefly, man must *know himself*, he must be convinced that *his true nature is Mind*, and consequently he must try to separate himself from everything in him which is bound to matter, which is darkness and evil. But *because*, as we know, the *Mind is part of God* (God in us), *to know himself in this way means to know God*. Here is a significant passage from the *Poimandres*:

> But why is it that "he who has recognized himself enters into the Good," as it was said in God's speech?..."Because the Father of all consists of Light and Life, and from him Man has sprung."..."Because made of Life and Light, you learn to know that you are made of them, you will go back into Life and Light."[23]

In this *gnosis* Philonian ideas are identifiable, although somewhat transformed in the new context in which they are located. But also, the connected conception of the Mind, interpreted almost as a *divine gift* which man receives thanks to his moral life or as the result of a basic ethical choice, recalls the

Philonian conception of the divine spirit which is given to man because of divine goodness.

But we need to make some distinctions in this regard.

On the one hand, the *Corpus Hermeticum* conceives the Mind as the divine in man almost as if it is a matter of a capacity structurally present in all human beings, as for example in these passages:

> And the soul of man is vehicled thus. The mind has for its vehicle the soul; the soul has for its vehicle the vital spirit; and the vital spirit, traversing the arteries together with the veins and the blood, places in movement the living being and in a certain way transports it.[24]
>
> *Wherever there is soul, there is also Mind*, so as wherever there is life there is also soul; but in the animals devoid of reason, soul is nothing but pure life without Mind. In fact, the Mind is benefactor only to the souls of men: it molds them, having the good as goal; and while in the case of the irrational animals Mind cooperates with the special form of instinct which belongs to each several kind, in men it works against the natural instincts.[25]

In the other passages, instead, it says that the Mind does not belong to all human beings, but to those who honor God.[26]

The two conceptions actually can be reconciled. Festugière explained, in fact, that all human beings possess Mind, but *in a potential state*; it is up to each of them to place it *in act* and hence to truly appropriate it, or not place it in act and to lose it. In effect, this seems to be the key to reading the complex Hermetic doctrine of the Mind.[27]

If the Mind abandons man, it is only by reason of the evil life that human beings lead, and hence it is through the fault of man himself:

> Oftentimes the mind quits the soul; and at such times, the soul can neither see nor hear, but is like a beast devoid of reason. For a soul without mind "can neither say aught nor do aught"; so great is the power of mind. Nor does mind endure a torpid soul; it abandons the soul which is fastened to the body, and held down in the grip of the body. Such a soul, my son, has no mind in it; and therefore such a one ought not to be deemed a man.[28]
>
> If instead it is present in human beings, then it is by reason of the choice of the good that they enact and are thus made worthy of such a divine gift:
>
> God has imparted to all men mind. But mind he did not impart to all....It was his will, my son, that mind should be placed in the midst as a prize that human souls may win.[29]

5. Ecstasy and the eschatology in Hermeticism

Human beings ought not wait for physical death to achieve their goal (*telos*), that is, in order to "become Gods." In fact we can regenerate ourselves, liberating ourselves both from negative and wicked power and from the "torments of darkness" by means of the divine powers of good until we achieve separation from the body, thus purifying our Mind and, in this way, ecstatically join ourselves to the divine Mind, through divine goodness:

What can I say, my son? This thing cannot be taught; and it is not possible for you to see it with your organs of sight, which are fashioned out of material elements. I can tell you nothing but this; I see that by God's mercy there has come to be in me a form which is not fashioned out of matter, and I have passed forth out of myself, and entered into an immortal body. I am not now the man I was; I have been born again in Mind, and the bodily shape which was mind before has been put away from me. I am no longer an object colored and tangible, a thing of spatial dimensions; I am now alien to all this, and to all that you perceive when you gaze with bodily eyesight. To such eyes as yours, my son, I am not now visible.[30]

With physical death human beings first are stripped of their bodies, which return through dissolution to remix with the elements of the cosmos. The irrational powers of the soul return to nature deprived of reason. Hence the soul, rising through the celestial spheres, stripped slowly of the powers it had received from them, achieves the eighth heaven, which is pure *aither*, and here it is maintained only in its pure power. Next, it is united to the Divine Power and becomes itself the divine Power and finally "enters into the God."[31]

II. The *Chaldean Oracles* and their Historical Importance

1.   The origin of the *Chaldean Oracles*

A document which presents many analogies with the Hermetic writings is the so-called *Chaldean Oracles* (χαλδαικὰ λόγια), a work in hexameters of which there are numerous fragments extant.[1] In fact, both in the first and the second of these works we find the same mixture of philosophical doctrines (taken from Middle Platonism and Neo-Pythagoreanism), replete with mythical and fantastic images analogous to a rococo religiosity of Eastern inspiration which is characteristic of the final stages of paganism, as well as an analogous claim to communicate a "revealed" doctrine. In the *Oracles*, indeed, the irrational predominates even more than in the *Corpus Hermeticum* and the speculative component is confused and reduced to a practical and religious purpose to the point of losing its autonomy. Nevertheless given the great importance that these *Oracles* had, especially in the sphere of post-Plotinian Neoplatonism, we ought not limit ourselves only to some brief references.

What is the origin of this work?

From ancient sources it would seem that we can determine that the author was Julian, nicknamed "the Theurgist," son of Julian, said to be "the Chaldaic," who lived at the time of Marcus Aurelius, that is, in the second century CE. Actually, because these *Oracles* are mentioned already in the third century CE by both Christian authors as well as pagan philosophers, and because, as almost all scholars recognize, their content is an expression of a mentality and of a spiritual climate typical of the age of the Antonines, it is not impossible that the author was actually Julian the Theurgist, as by this time many scholars tend to admit, although with suitable cautions.[2]

These *Oracles*, rather than being products of Egyptian wisdom (to which the Hermetic writings refer), are the work of Babylonian wisdom. Actually, Chaldaic sun-worship (worship of the sun and fire) plays a central role in them. About their actual origin E. R. Dodds writes as follows: "By his own account, Julianus received these *Oracles* from the Gods: they were θεοπαράδοτα. Where he in fact got them we do not know....Julianus may of course have forged them; but their diction is so bizarre and bombastic, their thought so obscure and incoherent, as to suggest rather the trance utterances of modern 'spirit guides' than the deliberate efforts of a forger. It seems indeed not impossible, in view of what we know about later theurgy, that they had their origin in the 'revelations' of some visionary or trance medium, and that Julianus's part consisted, as Psellus (or his source Proclus) asserts, in putting them into verse. This would be in accordance with the established practice of official *Oracles*; and the transposition into hexameters would give an opportunity of introducing some semblance of philosophical meaning and system into the rigmarole."[3]

Probably the revelation of the *Oracles* was derived from the Goddess Hecate who in late antiquity was identified with the Goddess of magic and incantations and who to judge from fragments must have had a role of great importance in the work.

2. The philosophical doctrines of the *Chaldean Oracles*

The philosophical doctrines in the *Oracles* can be isolated easily enough from "Chaldean wisdom," as we have previously mentioned, and are close to those of the *Corpus Hermeticum*. They are clearly proximate to that form of Middle Platonism which had absorbed Neo-Pythagorean doctrines and which has its most typical proponent in Numenius of Apamea. (What is more, the *Oracles* and Numenius have similarities which have led some to maintain that they can only be explained by supposing that the philosopher did nothing but a rationalization of the thought-content of the *Oracles*, or that the *Oracles* had put into verse form the ideas of Numenius).[4]

At the top of the hierarchy of the divine the *Oracles* place the Father, who seems to be identified with the First Mind (or *Nous patrikós*) and they identified the Platonic Ideas with the thoughts of this Mind. Here is a fragment (which is the most ample of those extant) in which this conception is expressed with a curious mixture of thought and imagination:

> The Mind of the Father whined as he thought, with a powerful will, the Ideas of all forms, and from one source they all sprang out; because from the Father both intention and accomplishment did come at the same time. But once they were separated by the intelligible Fire, the Ideas split up into intelligent Ideas; because the Sovereign made an intelligible endless model exist before the manifold world. The latter followed in its disorder the first and appeared with its proper form, shaped by every sort of Ideas. There is only one source, from which other Ideas whining spring out. They are divided, inaccessible and are shattered on cosmic bodies; they are similar to swarms and gather around a terrible breast, shining around from every side and very near, in all ways, as intelligent thought which robed with abundance, from the fatherly source, the flower of fire, in the highest point of restless time. It is the original source of the Father, perfect as such, that let these primordial Ideas spring out.[5]

Some scholars evidently manifest some perplexity about the identification of the *Father* with the *paternal Mind* and they think that they are two different hypostases or, anyhow, that the second is to be conceived as subordinated to the first. In reality, the beginning and the end of the fragment read show that they are the same reality and another fragment clearly says that the paternal Mind is "born from itself" (αὐτογένεθλος).[6] We find ourselves, hence, faced with the positions typical of the Middle Platonists and in a certain sense even more accentuated, as we will see.

Again, as in the Middle Platonists it is not the First Mind, the artificer of the world, which is involved but a Second Mind, which is derived from the first. Here are two explicit fragments on this point:

> It is not with a direct action, but by means of a Mind, that First and transcendent Fire includes his Power in the matter; in fact, it is an Mind, born from the First Mind, the craftsman of the igneous world.[7]

> The Father created all things in conformity with perfection and He entrusted them to the Second Mind, that you call "the First," you all that are offspring of man.[8]

This last fragment recalls almost to the letter a parallel fragment of Numenius. In this way, the characterization of the second Mind as the "Dyad," that is, as having a dyadic character insofar as it is holder of the *two-fold function* of "containing the intelligibles" and "of introducing sensation into the world," has, once again, its equivalent in Numenius.[9]

Third in the hierarchial order is the soul, with which the Goddess Hecate is probably identified:

> After the thoughts of the Father, take place, I, the soul; which with my heat animate all things.[10]

In this system, in addition, there is a place naturally for Gods as well as for Daimons; human souls themselves, considered as of divine origin, are capable of returning when they are completely purified to the supreme God. In their descent through the heavens the souls are re-clothed with something like a subtle material tunic, which is a kind of pneumatic material or "vehicle" (ὄχημα), before falling into material bodies. This is a belief of Eastern origin, that the Neoplatonists also, beginning with Porphyry, found congenial and appropriated.[11]

A fragment is worth a special mention which says:

> he Father is all the things, but intelligibly.[12]

This precise statement, as the analogous one which we have previously mentioned in speaking about Numenius,[13] anticipates a principle that will become one of the chief tenets of Neoplatonism.

The doctrines of the *Oracles* examined above are now well known. But along with these we find others of Neo-Pythagorean extraction making reference to the idea of a "triad" which constituted a novelty bound to have, once it was adequately developed, a remarkable future. Unfortunately, the extant fragments about this matter are rather obscure, especially due to their brevity (the ancient authors who record them and comment on them go much beyond the originals). After having qualified the Father, the supreme God, as being the Good, and further also as being the Monad and as the paternal Monad, and after having qualified the second God as the "Dyad" (in the sense explained above), the author of the *Oracles* explains that the supreme God is a "triadic Monad," that is, that *it is one and triune.*

In fact, having seen you triadic Monad, the world has reverenced you.[14]

It is a Monad, that is, a One, as a reality; it is a Triad, that is, triune, through its *capacity* insofar as it is Father, Power, and Mind.

But then the author seems to extend the schema of the triadic conception also to the second Mind:

> From these first two (scil.: the paternal Monad and the Dyad) derives the link of the first Triad, which actually is not first but in which the intelligibles are measured.[15]

In addition, our author seems to apply the triadic schema also to the sphere of the intelligibles, that is, to the Ideas. In fact, he says on the one hand that the Father gives to the second Mind the intelligibles (that is, the Ideas) produced by him,[16] and on the other hand he expressly affirms:

> In fact, the Mind of the father has said that everything would be divided into three...[17]

Consequently, the triadic organization seems to be reflected in all realities:

> A triad contains every thing and every measure.[18]

> In fact in the whole cosmos shines a Triad, that a Monad commands.[19]

The significance of these doctrines seems to us to be altogether clarified in a summary fashion by Hadot (following Lewy) as follows: "It would truly seem that the *Oracles* have provided the raw material of this triadic organization (scil.: what is proper for the Neoplatonists). Actually, they involve many Neo-Pythagorean elements and in particular they place at the top of things a Monad, a Dyad, and a Triad, each of which themselves involves a further triadic aspect. The first Monad was the Father himself, and this Monad was triadic because he possessed in himself Power and Mind. The Dyad corresponded to a second Mind different from the Mind of the Father: he was dyadic in the measure in which he was turned at one time toward the intelligible and toward the sensible, but he was also triadic in the measure in which he contained in himself the Triad. The Triad itself was then likewise the interior number to the Ideas produced by the (supreme) Mind."[20] It is evident that the knowledge of the Divine thus conceived and especially that of the supreme God, that is, of the triadic Monad, ought to be considered as unattainable through the methods proper to traditional philosophy which aimed *to define the nature and essence of God*. To know God in this way, that is, to de-fine it, means to de-termine it, while God lacks any de-terminations. God, according to the *Oracles* (so also in the *Corpus Hermeticum*), is instead attainable in a sort of super-rational union, which is obtained by making the empty within us, that is to say, by emptying the soul and the Mind of the contents and of the thoughts linked to the sensible and to the finite.

The following fragment is interesting in this regard:

There is a sort of Intelligible [scil.: the highest God], whom you must conceive by means of the *flower of the Mind* (νὸου ἄνθος); *because, if you address your Mind towards him and try to grasp it as if you grasped a determinate object, you will not grasp it at all*; because he is the power of a bright sword, glittering with intellectual thrusts. Thus, this sort of Intelligible is not to be conceived with impetuosity, but *by means of the fine flame of a subtle Mind*, which measures all things but this Intelligible; and it is not to be conceived with intensity, but rather with the pure gaze of your soul, diverted (from the sensible), *you will strain your mind, devoid* (of thoughts) *towards the Intelligible*, in order to learn to know the Intelligible, as it exists out of the apprehensions of (human) Mind.[21]

This "flower of the Mind"(νόου ἄνθος) is, in essence, the super-rational power of the soul capable of joining and assimilating to God, what the later Neoplatonists consider the ecstatic capacity of uniting oneself to the One and, with all the proper adjustments, that which the medieval mystics called the *apex mentis* [*the summit of the mind*].

And the "flower of the Mind" presupposes the emptying of the soul and of the Mind of which we have spoken, that is, the total "silence," because, say the *Oracles*, in Silence "God is nurtured."

But while in the Neoplatonists the conception of this super-rationality is philosophically refined and in the mystical Christian is transported to and supported on the plane of the doctrine on grace, in the *Chaldean Oracles* it remains fundamentally conditioned by a magical mentality, as we will see.

Damascius, who had preserved the fragment read above, in order to illustrate the same point reports also this next fragment:

Strong from head to foot, in a refulgent light, with your Mind and your soul armed with a three-point sword [some others translate: with a triple force], cast in your spirit all the symbols of the triad, and do not haunt fired canals, dissipating yourself, but concentrating yourself.[22]

And here evidently we enter into the sphere of "theurgic wisdom" about which we will now speak.

3. The magical wisdom and the theurgy of the *Chaldean Oracles*

That Julian can probably be considered the author of the *Chaldean Oracles* also means that he is the first to have been called (or who proclaimed himself) a "theurgist." The "theurgist" necessarily differs from a "theologian," since the latter, as has been often noted, is limited *to speaking about the Gods*, the former, instead, *calls on the Gods and interacts with them*.

But what is theurgy exactly?

It is a "wisdom" and an "art" of magic *used for mystical and religious purposes*. These purposes are the characteristic attributes which distinguish theurgy from ordinary magic. As we have previously seen, Julian considered it the result of a divine revelation. E. R. Dodds has explained very well that "whereas vulgar magic used names and formulae of religious origin to profane ends, theurgy used the procedures of vulgar magic primarily to a religious end."[23] And these ends are, as we know, the liberation of the soul from the body and from the destiny connected to it and its union with the divine.

E. R. Dodds also tried to show that the procedures of theurgy could probably be distinguished (analogously to those of common magic) into two types: (*a*) those which depended exclusively on the use of *symbola* (of which we will soon speak) and (*b*) those which involved, to use modern terminology, the employment of a *trance* medium.

(*a*) The procedures of the first type probably constitute what was called *telestiké*, which was the practice concerned "mainly with the consecrating (τελεῖν...) and animating magic statues in order to obtain *Oracles* from them." Magical statues were made with a special procedure, filling up the interior cavity with animals, herbs, rocks, and perfumes (or else gem-stones with inscriptions cut into them) considered to be endowed with special powers, especially if put together and arranged in a special way. Every God, Dodds explains again, "has its 'sympathetic' representative in the animal, vegetable and mineral world which is or contains a *symbol* (σύμβολον) of its divine cause and it is hence in a relationship with it."[24] To this practice of making magical statues there goes along, in addition, also oral incantations, in which names and divine epithets are pronounced (some of which are said in a barbaric language, since it is affirmed that if translated into Greek they would lose their divine efficacy). The art of making *magical images* is widely diffused in late paganism and was even defended by the last Neoplatonists as the art of honoring superior powers.

(*b*) The second method used by the theurgist is again explained by E. R. Dodds in the following way: "While *telestiké* sought to induce the presence of a God in an inanimate 'receptacle' (ὑποδοχή), another branch of theurgy aimed at incarnating him temporarily (εἰσκρίνειν) in a human being (κάτοχος or a more specific technical term, δοχεύς). As the former art rested on the wider notion of a natural and spontaneous *sympatheia* (συμπάθεια) between image and original, so did the latter on the widespread belief that spontaneous alterations of personality were due to possession by a God, *daimon*, or deceased human being." In particular, note that the entrance of a divinity into a person, which occurred in theurgic practices, differed from that of the official *Oracles* by the fact that "the God was thought to enter the medium's body not as a spontaneous act of grace but in response to the appeal, even the compulsion, of the operator (κλήτωρ)."[25]

In the extant fragments of the *Oracles* undoubtedly there must be present both of these branches of theurgy, as many sources and the use of technical terms allow us understand, but we do not know up to what point they were developed.

We are not interested in discussing the various problems connected to these techniques. What is of interest to us instead is to focus on the following very important point. These theurgic practices are presented not only as purifications of the soul and union with the divine, but are likewise located within the philosophical schema about which we have spoken above. There they are presented as *necessary instruments* to be used *together with the highest powers in us*, that is, together with that "flower of the Mind" which, by itself, would not seem to be sufficient for its appointed task. The author of the *Oracles* commands in fact, for the liberation of the soul, to "unite (theurgic) actions to the sacred logos."[26] And Michael Psellus (who knows the *Oracles* very well) explains that the "sacred logos" or "sacred thought" corresponds precisely to the "flower of the Mind" and that *simply of itself it is incapable of carrying us up to grasp the divine* and that, according to the author of the *Oracles*, the practice of the theurgic rites is *indispensable*. Psellus then makes a very interesting comparison between the Christian doctrine of Gregory Nazianzen, the purely philosophical doctrine of Plato, and that of the *Oracles*:

> Our theologian Gregory tries to raise the soul towards the divine by means of reason and contemplation: by means of reason insofar as it is in us what is the intellective and better; by means of contemplation, because of the enlightenment which is above us. Plato, in his turn, accepts by means of reason and intuition the intelligible essence. *Instead the Chaldeans say that we cannot rise toward God except by strengthening the vehicle of the soul by means of material rites*. He maintained, in fact, that the soul is purified by rocks, herbs, and by incantation and thus it is moved easily through its ascension.[27]

The *Chaldean Oracles* can arouse in modern readers a series of difficulties of various kinds about their value; nevertheless they constitute a document of noteworthy historical importance, insofar as, both through the triadic schema that they introduce in the conception of reality and further for the "revealed" theurgic "wisdom" which they attempt to join to philosophical "speculation," they would be an obligatory reference point for the late Neoplatonists. The *Oracles* were judged as important as the Platonic dialogues.

In fact, we can certainly say that if these *Oracles* are neglected, then we would be deprived of one of the essential parameters for characterizing the various schools and currents of Neoplatonism. As we will see, they are distinguished either by their non-acceptance of theurgy, pointing to the typical rational aspect of Greek speculation (Plotinus and his school), or by their acceptance of it, or by trying to find a more unified fusion with the tenets of the Greek thought of the past (Iamblichus and some of his followers, as well as all the exponents of the school of Athens), or by endowing theurgy with a total loss of the rational component (as the school of Pergamum and Julian the Apostate).

Third Part

PLOTINUS AND NEOPLATONISM

« ... ἡ σπουδὴ οὐκ ἔξω ἁμαρτίας εἶναι,
ἀλλὰ θεὸν εἶναι.»

"Our concern, though, is not to be out of
sin, but to be god."

Plotinus, *Enneads* 1.2.6

First Section

THE ORIGIN OF NEOPLATONISM: FROM THE SCHOOL OF AMMONIUS AT ALEXANDRIA TO THE SCHOOL OF PLOTINUS AT ROME

«Καὶ οὗτος θεῶν καὶ ἀνθρώπων θείων καὶ εὐδαιμόνων βίος, ἀπολλαγὴ τῶν ἄλλων τῶν τῇδε, βίος ἄν ἡδονος τῶν τῇδε, φυγὴ μόνου πρὸς μόνον.»

"This is the life of gods and of godlike and blessed men, deliverance from the things of this world, a life which takes no delight in the things of this world, escape in solitude to the solitary."

Plotinus, *Enneads* 6.9.11

I. Ammonius 'Saccas' and his School at Alexandria

1. The enigma of Ammonius 'Saccas'

If with Numenius we come to the threshold of Neoplatonism, with Ammonius 'Saccas', who lived between the second and third centuries CE,[1] we surely pass the threshold. In other words, Ammonius is no longer a precursor, but is the *initiator of Neoplatonism*.

Unfortunately, however, Ammonius, like Socrates, wrote nothing and what our most ancient sources tell us of him, if they rightly permit us to affirm the aforementioned fact, nevertheless do not permit us to verify to what level of development he carried Neoplatonic doctrine.

Let us examine the most important evidence concerning our philosopher.

First, we do not know with certainty why Ammonius was called 'Saccas.' The interpretation "carries a sack," referred to for the first time by Bishop Theodoret (Ammonius had worked at the humble task of a carrier of sacks before becoming a philosopher), is not very certain.[2] But also some modern hypotheses seem to have little plausibility. Some, in fact, maintain that 'Saccas' indicates that Ammonius belonged to Indian stock of the Saker or that our philosopher was a Sakka-Muni, a Buddhist monk.[3]

We know, instead, from Porphyry that Ammonius was born and educated in a Christian family and that when he turned to the practice of philosophy, he embraced pagan religion.[4] Eusebius contested this information, accusing Porphyry of having lied and adducing as proof the work of Ammonius entitled, *On the Agreement between Moses and Jesus*.[5] But Ammonius wrote nothing, and Eusebius was victimized by a substitution of persons due to similar names, and likewise due to the fact that the Christian Origen, who was one of the disciples of Ammonius 'Saccas,' was perhaps also a disciple of the Christian Ammonius. Moreover, even the thought of Plotinus, which, as we will see, is closely linked with that of his teacher, leads us to exclude the notion that Ammonius had been a Christian up to the end of his life. Scholars are hence surely on unsound footing when they give credence to the statement of Eusebius (naturally without taking into account, the completely false view of those who believe that Ammonius is the author of the writings attributed to Pseudo-Dionysius).[6]

Ammonius did not belong to those who were acclaimed as celebrities in their own time. He did not look for honors, fame, or numerous disciples, but wanted to live a retiring life, far away from the clamor of the world. He wished, together with a few disciples profoundly committed to him, to cultivate philosophy, understood not only as an intellectual exercise but also and especially as a way of life and as a spiritual discipline. The following passage of Porphyry taken from the *Life of Plotinus* is particularly revealing:

In his twenty-eighth year he [Plotinus] felt the impulse to study philosophy and was recommended to the teachers in Alexandria who then had the highest reputation; but he came away from their lectures so depressed and full of sadness that he told his trouble to one of his friends. *The friend, understanding the desire of his heart, sent him to Ammonius, whom he had not so far tried. He went and heard him, and said to his friend, "This is the man I was looking for."* From that day he stayed continually with Ammonius and acquired so complete a training in philosophy that *he became eager to make acquaintance with the Persian philosophical discipline and that prevailing among the Indians.*[7]

No less indicative are the eleven years that Plotinus spent at the school of Ammonius.[8]

If a man of the quality of Plotinus who quickly tired of the current philosophical celebrities continued to listen to the words of Ammonius for all those years we may justifiably conclude that Ammonius must have been a man of exceptional stature not only in his spiritual qualities but likewise in his doctrines.

Moreover, Porphyry also confirms that the debt of Plotinus to Ammonius with respect to *method* and *content* was considerable:

But he [Plotinus] did not just speak straight out of these books but took a distinctive personal line in his consideration, *and brought the mind of Ammonius'* to bear on the investigation in hand. ...When Origen [Origen the Pagan, co-disciple of Plotinus at the school of Ammonius] once came to a meeting of the school he was filled with embarrassment and wanted to stop lecturing, and when Origen urged him to continue he said, *'It damps one's enthusiasm for speaking when one sees that one's audience knows already what one is going to say'*; and after talking for a little while he brought the session to an end.[9]

Ammonius, as we have previously stated, did not write anything, reserving the communication of his teaching for the living word and spiritual bonds which arise from the intimate understanding between teacher and student. Consequently, out of respect for the peculiar structure given by the master to his own teaching his three most gifted students, Plotinus, Origen (not to be confused, as we will explain below, with the Christian Origen), and Erennius, agreed not to divulge the doctrines which they had taken from the lectures. But Erennius after some time was the first to break the agreement; Origen fairly quickly followed his example by publishing two works; Plotinus instead continued for a long time to follow the example of Ammonius, even after he had founded his own school at Rome, and only ten years later did he begin to put some arguments in writing.[10] But of Erennius' work we have lost everything; of Origen's work we only know their titles;[11] so there only remains the Plotinian *Enneads* as the direct intellectual product of the school of Ammonius. But from this the original teaching of Ammonius can certainly not be extracted. It would be as if we only had the writings of Plato and from them claimed to be able to reach the original thought of Socrates.

The attempt to take from the Christian Origen valid elements for the reconstruction of the philosophy of Ammonius is even more problematic.[12]

Is the thought of Ammonius then destined to remain only an enigma for us?[13]

2.   The testimonies of Hierocles and Nemesius on the thought of Ammonius

Actually, antiquity has passed down testimonies about the thought of Ammonius which date back to the fifth century CE. They were preserved by the Neoplatonist Hierocles of Alexandria and by Nemesius, Bishop of Emesa.[14] Many scholars are not disposed to accept them as creditable, since they cannot understand how and why these authors were in possession of information which the other Neoplatonists ignored. But it is clear that it cannot be categorically denied that some written notes from auditors of Ammonius, although without being published, could have been handed down to Hierocles and Nemesius.

In any case, leaving unprejudiced the question of the truth of these sources, which on the bases of the studies conducted so far are not resolvable in a clear manner, we believe that it is appropriate to explain the principal doctrines that they have attributed to Ammonius.[15]

Ammonius was presented chiefly as the philosopher who, at first, put himself above the dispute and polemics of opposed schools. He was able to reconcile Plato and Aristotle and to communicate to his disciples, especially to Plotinus and Origen, a philosophy freed from a polemical Mind. Ammonius worked this pacification "through divine inspiration," that is, "because instructed by God" (δεοδίδακτος) and "through divine assistance about what is true in philosophy."[16]

All this can be confirmed in what we know from Porphyry and hence is completely creditable.

The Ammonian metaphysical theses which were extracted from Hierocles are very compelling. According to them our philosopher had pointed out the derivation of all reality from God, interpreting the Platonic doctrine in a creationistic sense. Here is a most significant passage:

> Plato ... made an artificer God pre-exist, who ruled the whole order of the visible and invisible universe, not generated from any pre-existent substrate. In fact, his will is sufficient to produce the existence of things. Conjoining physical nature to incorporeal reality, he produced the most perfect cosmos, twofold [= sensible and supersensible] together as *one*.[17]

In this cosmos there are three distinct levels: (1) that of the supreme realities, namely, a creator-God, "the celestial realities," and "the Gods"; (2) that of the intermediate realities: the ethereal nature (air) and good Daimons, who are interpreter and messengers (angels) to men; (3) that of the lowest realities, that is, human souls and men as well as terrestrial animals. In addition, the arrangement is explained as follows:

> The realities from above govern the realities below, and God rules over the whole earth which he has produced and of which he is the father. And this paternal dominion and power is providence, which establishes what is right for everything. Justice which it follows is called fate.[18]

Likewise interesting are the doctrines that Nemesius attributed to Ammonius, but not so much for the demonstration of the incorporeality of the soul in which our philosopher is associated with Numenius in upholding a doctrine already well-known, but rather for the interpretation of the relations between body and soul, the corporeal and incorporeal, which are, on the contrary, quite novel:

> Ammonius, the teacher of Plotinus, said that intelligible realities have a nature such that it can become one with the things which can receive it, like the things which are subject to corruption, *but that even though united to them, remain pure and incorruptible*, as subsisting through them without losing their own proper nature. In fact, in bodies a union produces the complete transformation of the things which are unified, as a transformation occurs in other bodies: thus the elements are transformed into the composite, the food into the blood, the blood into flesh and into the other parts of the body. Instead, *in the case of intelligible reality, the union takes place without any consequent transformation of it*. In fact, through its nature, the intelligible cannot be changed essentially, but either subsists, or goes into not being; instead the intelligible can neither admit change nor go into nothingness. Likewise the soul, which is life, would not be incorruptible if it changed in mixing with the body, it would be other and would no longer be life. But what could it bring to the body except life? Hence the soul in the body is not changed.[19]

The soul, precisely insofar as it is incorporeal, accepting Nemesius' account, is not *in the body* according to Ammonius but is almost as if it were in a recipient. So it is not in the body as in a place, but it has an ontological relation of a totally different nature from that belonging to bodies. The soul is in the body in the same sense in which it is said that "God is in us," as a principle is in that which is principled, in the sense in which the principle produces and rules the principled. Therefore, it ought not be said that the "soul is here," but rather "the soul *acts* here." The activity of the soul in the body is the activity of the principle which vivifies and rules it.[20]

If these testimonies are creditable, then we are able to establish what follows.

Compared to Middle Platonism the novelty of Ammonius would chiefly consist *in the attempt to unify the different levels of being* (the cosmos is two-fold and at the same time one, every level of the hierarchy of the real is the cause of what follows and the first principle is the cause of everything) and even to eliminate the presupposition of eternal matter. As compared to the Neo-Pythagoreans, his novelty consists *in having understood the process of the derivation of all reality as a creation*, determining in this way the tenet which the Neo-Pythagoreans left vague that all things are derived from the One.

Naturally it is conceivable that Nemesius colored Ammonius with Christian hues. But that Ammonius not only could but *ought* to know the doctrine of creation is beyond doubt, since he was born and educated in a Christian family, and since in Alexandria the doctrine had already been made known by Philo. On the other hand, as has been noted by some, the Ammonius of Nemesius is clearly Greek and pagan insofar as he professed polytheism in an unequivocal way.[21] Hence, the doctrine attributed to Ammonius is wholly plausible in the mouth of a man born and educated as a Christian and who then became a pagan.

In addition, the conception of the relation between the soul and body, that is, between the incorporeal and the corporeal, also reveal the acquisition of some of the principles which we will find at the base of the conception of the *Enneads* and about which we will speak fully.

In general, then, the doctrine of the intimate union (*henosis*) between the incorporeal and the corporeal, between God and the cosmos, would be a solid base for a new conception of man and of his *telos* in the sense that the unification of man with the divine would be nothing other than the ethical-religious moment of the general law which governs the whole of reality. And in this way the profound religious structure of the thought of Ammonius would as a result be wholly supported.

But if this were so, the relations between late pagan philosophy and Jewish-Christian thought would have to be reinterpreted in the following way. The unique support on which the last great philosophical system of the Greeks rests unified in a powerful synthesis the whole of reality and allowed all the hypostases and even the material substrate itself to be derived from the first principle, thus linking the corporeal and the incorporeal through the dynamic concept of "activity" and "action." If this is the case, then it would be sound to believe that this notion appeared first in Ammonius, under the aegis of the biblical concept of creation. In Plotinus it was more solidly supported and systematized according to uniquely Greek categories, all of which lead to the theory of the "procession" but nevertheless it would acquire its full meaning only on condition of acceptance of this view. In any case, the sources about which we have spoken do not attribute to Ammonius either the doctrine of the One or the complex and grand theory of Mind [*Nous*] as a synthesis of Being and Thought, which we will find in Plotinus.

3. The followers of Ammonius

We have previously spoken in passing of the followers of Ammonius.

We know nothing about the thought of Erennius, who was the first to break the pact of keeping the doctrines of Ammonius a secret.

We know that, with regard to the pagan Origen in addition to a book entitled *On Daimons*, he published one with the programmatic title of *The Only Creator is the Supreme God*. In this title it is possible to recognize an echo of the doctrines that Hierocles attributes to Ammonius (with verbal coincidences also): it must be directed against those who distinguished the Supreme God from the Creator God. But the first title also reveals a typical position of the school in perfect harmony with those which the above mentioned sources attributes to Ammonius.[22]

Longinus was also connected to the circle of our philosopher, although it was true that his interests were chiefly literary and he was praised as a philologist both by Plotinus and Porphyry.[23] We know one of his philosophical conceptions, but it is a rather significant one. He did not believe that the Ideas were the thoughts of God, but instead maintained that they existed separately from *Nous*. This conception for a certain period of time was maintained also by Porphyry (and perhaps was also held by Ammonius).[24] The treatise *On the Sublime* was attributed to Longinus. It is interesting for many reasons but most scholars consider it unauthentic and therefore do not use it for the reconstruction of the thought of our author.[25]

The Christian Origen does not belong to the group of the above mentioned philosophers and could not even have met Plotinus at Alexandria. Scholars think that it is possible that he attended Ammonius' lectures (who was about ten years his senior) at about 205/210 CE. In 231 CE, it seems, he left Alexandria.[26]

Plotinus came, on the contrary, to Alexandria in 232 CE. His meeting with Ammonius was decisive not only for him, as we have read in a passage of Porphyry, but for the history of thought in the West almost as much as the meeting at Athens of Plato with Socrates. The powerful spiritual energies which Ammonius was able to arouse in his followers and that would have dissipated in a short period of time, instead, because of Plotinus, "will continue forever."

II. The School of Plotinus at Rome and the Origin of the *Enneads*

1. From Alexandria to Rome

Plotinus was twenty-eight years old when he entered the circle of Ammonius 'Saccas,' and he remained there until he was thirty-eight.[1] At the school of Ammonius, as we already know, Plotinus "became eager to make acquaintance with the Persian philosophical discipline and that prevailing among the Indians."[2] The direct contact with Eastern wisdom, hence, must be maintained as the achievement, or at least as the completion, of what he had learned from Ammonius. Moreover, the Gymnosophists, the Magi of the East, as we know, were considered for a long time as one of the principal sources of wisdom.

The expedition of the Roman Emperor Gordian III in 243 CE would seem to offer them a propitious occasion. But it was a dramatic experience which could yield none of the results hoped for. Gordian was killed in Mesopotamia and Plotinus went to Antioch, succeeding only with some difficulty in saving himself. From there he could not or would not return to Alexandria (probably because Ammonius had died), but decided to go to Rome, where arrived in 244 CE when Philip was Emperor.[3] At this point Plotinus had already reached "the halfway mark of the journey of life;" he had reached forty years of age and hence felt mature enough to open his own school in the capital of the empire.

For the decade (244-253 CE) our philosopher gave lectures, following, as we know, the conversations of Ammonius and his method of leaving a great deal of opportunity for discussion and direct investigation for those who attended, but Plotinus wrote nothing down. In this way he maintained faith with the old pact that he made with Erennius and the pagan Origen, even though they had already broken it.[4]

Only beginning from 254 CE did Plotinus begin to write. When Porphyry arrived at Rome in 263 CE, Plotinus had already composed twenty-one treatises. He composed another twenty-four between 264 and 268 CE and the remaining nine after 268 CE.[5]

The information which Porphyry gives on the way in which Plotinus composed his treatises is of great interest to us. He states that Plotinus wrote quickly (without re-reading what he had written, because he had a defect of vision)[6] in a continuous and very orderly manner, almost as if copying from a book, and he could go on doing this for a long time. As a result, his compositions were like a written record of a verbal conversation. And those who do not bear that fact in mind can only understand the spirit of the *Enneads* with great difficulty.

Porphyry was directly entrusted by Plotinus with the task of editing and arranging the various treatises.[7] Now since the treatises as a whole were composed without a clear systematic order, Porphyry decided to follow the method previously adopted by Andronicus of Rhodes in the publication of the esoteric works of Aristotle. He decided to collect together the books which treated the same subject or had direct doctrinal connections among them. Further, Porphyry was influenced by the Pythagorean attitude on the metaphysical meaning of number and combined the "perfection of the number six" and the "ennead," that is, the number nine, and thus he divided the fifty-four Plotinian treatises into six groups of nine each and grouped the related discussions by arranging them according to their difficulty, from the easiest to the most difficult.[8] In this way the *Enneads* was composed which, together with the *Dialogues* of Plato and the esoteric works of Aristotle, contains the most profound philosophical doctrines of ancient philosophy and is one of the most remarkable philosophical works of all time.

2. Characteristics and purposes of the Plotinian school

The school of Plotinus probably was not like any of its predecessors. The authority and prestige which the philosopher had acquired almost to the point of nobility was such that many influenced by "the thought of immanent death" entrusted him with their sons and daughters as "a sacred and divine trust" to be educated and their possessions to be preserved and administered. Consequently the house in which he lived (which belonged to a certain Gemina, whose guest he was) swarmed with young men, women, and widows. In addition, political men came to Plotinus in order to settle disputes and law-suits and they had the greatest confidence in him as a faultless arbitrator.[9]

The Emperor Publ. Lucinius Gallienus himself and his wife Salonina held him in the highest regard, so much so that they took into serious consideration the Plotinian project of erecting a city of philosophers which would be called Platonopolis, in Campania, to which Plotinus himself could go and in which the inhabitants would have to observe "the laws of Plato." The project, however, failed because of the intrigue and plots at the imperial court.[10]

Nevertheless it would be a mistake to argue from all this that Plotinus was interested in political issues or that he had political goals of some kind. The spirit that animates his project of Platonopolis was very different from the spirit which had inspired Plato in his projects, ideals, and political utopias. In fact Plato, wholly impregnated with the spirit and the *ethos* of the Greek *polis*, really aimed, as we have seen in its place, at affecting political activity and at producing a radical transformation both in the theory and practice of politics: he aimed, that is, at a reform of the City-State at its root, in its totality. Plotinus, instead, did not want to propose a project to completely renew the Roman empire in function of philosophical principles, but *simply to construct an oasis of peace, a city made for philosophers*, that is to say (as is clear on the basis of what we will take up immediately), *made for those who want to live a life in a community which makes possible the achievement of the supreme end, that is, union with the divine.* It is not surprising, then, that he expressly dissuaded his disciples from being involved in political activity.

Those who rushed to hear the words of Plotinus had interests of quite a different type.

Moreover, note that anyone who wanted to could attend the reunions.[11] Therefore, there must have been numerous occasional hearers who were attracted simply to them because of the fame of his person and hence from curiosity. Next, there were and these were rather numerous hearers who came with a certain constancy, and among these there were many Roman senators and nobles of Eastern origin. Finally, there were also the authentic "followers." It should not be missed that a certain number of women, referred to by Porphyry, took part in the reunions "all [of whom] were ardently dedicated to philosophy."[12]

Only a few had access directly to the writings of the master and only after they had shown that they possessed the proper intellectual capabilities and moral prerequisites.[13]

Plato had founded the Academy in order to form men through philosophy who would then renovate the state. Aristotle had founded the Peripatos in order to organize research and knowledge in a systematic way. Pyrrho, Epicurus, and Zeno had founded their movements in order to try to lead men to ataraxy, peace, and tranquility of soul. The school of Plotinus tended toward a new and further goal. *It wanted to teach men to free themselves from an earthly life and to be reunited with the divine and to be able to contemplate it up to the peak of a transcendent ecstatic union.* The goal of the new school was, therefore, strongly religious and mystical. It was the same goal which was involved in the project of Platonopolis.

Here are the words of Porphyry which perfectly incorporate this highest *telos* for which our philosopher strove:

> The oracle says that he was mild and kind, most gentle and attractive, and we knew ourselves that he was like this. It says too that he sleeplessly kept his soul pure and ever strove towards the divine *which he loved with all his soul, and did everything to be delivered* and 'escape from the bitter wave of blood-drinking life here.' So to this god-like man above all, who *often raised himself in thought,* according to the ways Plato teaches in the *Banquet, to the First and Transcendent God,* that God appeared who has neither shape nor any intelligible form, but is throned above intellect and all the intelligible. "To Plotinus 'the goal ever near was shown': *for his end and goal was to be united to, to approach the God who is over all things.* Four times while I was with him he attained that goal, in an unspeakable actuality and not in potency only." "I Porphyry, who am now in my sixty-eighth year declare that once I drew near and was united to him."[14]

The final words of the dying Plotinus to the doctor Eustochius were these:

"I have been waiting a long time." Then he said, "Try to bring back the god in us to the divine in the All."[15]

These words truly reflect his spiritual testament and they are like a validation of all his teaching.

III. The Revival and Conclusion of the "Second Voyage"

1. The relation between Plotinus and preceding philosophers

Plotinus presupposes about eight centuries of preceding philosophical speculation and is comprehensible solely on the basis of the essential acquisitions of ancient thought in this period of time.

The list of what Plotinus is in debt to his predecessors is very considerable. To limit ourselves only to essentials, we mention what follows.

The spirit of Pythagoras, or better, of that which afterwards was considered Pythagorean spirit, as well as the doctrine of the supreme principles of the Monad and the Dyad constituted an important component in the formation of his thought.

Our philosopher especially acknowledges in Parmenides the merit of having discovered the identity between Being and Thought. This was a principle which Plotinus reinterpreted in a new way and the conception of which dominated the *Enneads*.

Plato is acknowledged as the absolute, almost always infallible, authority. But the Plato who interests Plotinus is neither the aporematic and problematic Plato of the Socratic dialogues, bristling with doubt and with ironic maieutic qualities, nor even the Plato who pursues the project of the ideal state and gives voice to the great political passions of the Greeks. The Plato who interests Plotinus is the mystical, metaphysical, and theological Plato. Therefore the dialogues which are valuable to him are the *Phaedo, Phaedrus, Symposium, Timaeus,* the central books of the *Republic*, and, in a lesser way, some aspects of the *Sophist*, the *Parmenides*, the *Philebus*, and the *Second Letter*. Plato is never criticized and most frequently is directly mentioned with the use of third person singular pronouns. Plato, as Aristotle for the Scholastics, is, in sum, a firm and central foundation, he is the philosopher par excellence, the supreme authority (we will see that essentially Plotinus did not claim to be anything more than an interpreter of Plato).

The doctrines of Aristotle are instead often criticized, as for example, the doctrine on God as a thinking on thinking, the doctrine of soul as *entelechy*, the conception of *aither*, the doctrine of the categories. Nevertheless, some of the metaphysical and psychological concepts of Aristotle were determinative in the structure of the thought of Plotinus, as we will confirm.

The doctrine of the Stoa was also avoided because of its fundamental materialism, although it has nonetheless a considerable negative presence in the *Enneads*. Plotinus criticizes the materialistic conception of God and the soul, the doctrine of the categories, and the theory of time, which are Stoic. But he accepts the doctrines of universal *sympatheia* and of the *Logos* as well as the position of a unitary conception of the real, although reformulating it on other bases, as well as a series of moral concepts, again bending them in a mystical and spiritual direction.

In fact, Porphyry noted:

> His writings, however are full of concealed Stoic and Peripatetic doctrines. Aristotle's *Metaphysics*, in particular, is concentrated in them.[1]

Even the neglect of Epicurus and the Skeptics would seem to be indicated in the above listing.

But the philosophy of Plotinus would be simply inconceivable outside of the cultural matrix of Alexandria, as it was formed between the first century BCE and the second century CE, that is, without Philo, without Middle Platonism and Neo-Pythagoreanism, whose positions were represented by the school of Ammonius in a very complete synthesis.

Not withstanding these debts and others which we will mention, the philosophy of Plotinus is neither an eclecticism nor a syncretism because in the Plotinian system there is a new inspiration which gives an unexpected meaning to these old doctrines. Dodds has said: "It is true that if you pull Plotinus' system to bits you can usually find for each bit, if not anything that can strictly be called a 'source', at any rate some more or less closely related model or antecedent or stimulus, whether the stimulus came from within the Platonic School or from outside it. Plotinus built his structure very largely out of used pieces, the materials that Greek philosophical tradition presented to him. But the essence of the Plotinian system lies in the new meaning which the whole imposed on the parts; its true originality is not in the materials but in the design (as indeed, I suspect is the case with every great philosophical system)."[2] But if this is true, it needs likewise to be acknowledged that in tracing the new design with the old materials Plotinus received not a few suggestions from the last philosophers named, that is, from Philo, from the Middle Platonists, and from the Neo-Pythagoreans, as modern studies certainly confirm.

But we have to develop a fuller argument on this issue because these philosophical currents flowed in the first two centuries of the Imperial Age and they constituted a great authentic and appropriate prologue to Neoplatonism. This is a fact scarcely acknowledged by the *communis opinio* [*widely-accepted opinion*] of scholars and, even more often, is simply ignored.

2. Plotinus truly carried to full development the positions of Middle Platonism and Neo-Pythagoreanism

The modern reader of the *Enneads* can frequently gain the impression that many conclusions are not demonstrated or at least are not adequately justified. But anyone who stands by this first impression and judges that Plotinian speculation is unfounded would fall into a grave error of historical perspective and prejudice its comprehension in an irreparable way. In fact, it needs to be kept in mind that in the immediately preceding century Middle Platonism and Neo-Pythagoreanism had reached their *acmé*. They had definitively put in question the materialism of the great Hellenistic systems, they had recovered, as we have amply demonstrated above, the results of the Platonic "second voyage" and they had even attempted to integrate them, reëlaborate them, and re-unify them especially by taking into account the Aristotelian achievements and without obscuring any of the positions considered valuable by the systems of the Hellenistic Era.[3]

Plotinus found, hence, a series of philosophical truths already achieve and justified by his predecessors, and because of this he did not find it necessary to demonstrate them again in a more profound way since he considered them as already acquired. Furthermore, Porphyry's testimony in this respect is decisive. Plotinus often had read aloud in his presentations the thought of the Middle Platonists, as we can now confirm by what Porphyry tells us:

> At the Conferences he used to have treatises by various authors read aloud among the Platonists it might be *Severus* or *Cronius, Numenius, Gaius*, or *Atticus*; and among the Peripatetics *Aspasius, Alexander, Adrastus*, or some such writer, at the call of the moment.[4]

As can be seen, the texts of the Middle Platonists, of the Neo-Pythagoreans, and of the late Peripatetics influenced by Middle Platonism constituted the point of departure from which Plotinus moved in his lectures and hence the fertile ground on which his thought was born and developed.

Besides, if we read and meditated upon as much of these authors as is extant (we have nothing of Gaius, but his disciple Albinus, as we have seen, makes up in large part for this loss), the understanding of the philosophical content and the very spiritual climate of the *Enneads* is made wholly accessible.

Another fact is good to remember because it is particularly important for the aim of evaluating the quality of the conclusions that we are proposing. Already in antiquity there had been notice taken of the similarities between some of the positions of Numenius and parallel tenets of Plotinus; in fact, this similarity was judged to be so strong that at Athens Plotinus was even accused of plagiarism, and a follower of Plotinus himself, Amelius, felt that it was necessary to publicly refute such accusations in a published essay.[5] Consequently, if this accusation is undoubtedly unfounded, it is nevertheless undeniable that there are consistent contacts between the philosophy of Plotinus and that of Numenius, as we have pointed out above.

Plotinus, in essence, took the positions given importance by the Middle Platonists and by the more evolved Neo-Pythagoreans and developed them and carried them to full maturity with a depth, a lucidity, and an audacity without equal, right to the point of putting in the shade and making us forget his immediate predecessors. Nevertheless, never as in this case has the principle remained true that the secret for understanding the "greaters" is in large part in understanding the "lessers" who have preceded them. For this reason we have dedicated so much space to the Middle Platonists and the Neo-Pythagoreans (the knowledge of which unfortunately still remains limited to a few specialists): *they alone have put into position those foundations in accordance with which it was possible to rise to the heights which Plotinus, following in the footsteps of Ammonius, was able to ascend.*

It could be objected, against this argument, that Plotinus did not cite by name even one of these authors. But the objection loses all force since it scarcely takes into consideration these three facts. In the first place, Plotinus cites by name only those philosophers who are distant in time from him.[6] In the second place, the philosophers about whom we are talking here were considered exegetes and interpreters of Plato and not original thinkers, and Plotinus considers himself among the interpreters of Plato.[7] Undoubtedly he must judge those of his predecessors simply as men who tapped the same source in which all truth was already contained. Finally, the most significant fact is that Ammonius himself was not cited even once.[8]

3. The relations between Plotinus, Eastern thought, Philo, Gnosticism, and Christianity

In order to understand the complex framework of the diverse cultural components which converge to form Plotinian thought, we must speak again briefly about the problem of Eastern influence, about the Mosaic philosophy of Philo of Alexandria, about Gnosticism, and about Christianity. In what measure did Plotinus draw upon these sources?

The alleged influence of the East on Plotinus has been heavily reduced by modern scholarship. On the other hand, we know that Plotinus wanted very much to have direct experience of the philosophy which was practiced by the Persians [Iranians] and by the Indians, but that, for the reasons previously stated, he did not come into contact with these sources.[9] In addition, the so-called "theory of emanation" of Plotinus has nothing in common with Eastern theories of emanation. We will see, in fact, that properly speaking the doctrine of Plotinus is *not a form of emanationism.*[10] The Eastern sources of Plotinus are reduced to those largely Hellenized in the Alexandrian ambience. More than specific contents, it is a matter of that religious and mystical spirit which was already the product of a mediation and of a synthesis between Eastern and Western categories. It is a matter, in sum, of that spirit which treated as food all the varieties of thought examined which were flourishing at Alexandria at the beginning of the first century CE.

Instead, not only is it probable but it is nearly certain that Philo of Alexandria influenced Plotinus. The books of Philo in Alexandria, a city in which he had worked, were certainly easily accessible. Moreover, indirectly, that is, through Numenius, Plotinus must have known Philo. In fact, the analogies between Philonian thought and Plotinian thought are remarkable. Zeller himself acknowledges even at his time that among all the precursors of Plotinus Philo is precisely the one who presents the most consistent analogies with the thought of the *Enneads*. The Philonian conception of God presents numerous affinities with the Plotinian conception of the Absolute. The doctrine of the *Logos* and of the Powers correspond to the Plotinian doctrine of the second hypostasis, not only in conceptual content, but even in certain lexical expressions (the expression "intelligible cosmos" coined by Philo has the same connotations as it has in Plotinus). The divine activity, creator of all intelligible reality and of the sensible cosmos itself, understood dynamically as a manifestation of the divine power and as the production of effects, in its turn, prefigures, although purely in a parallel and non-convergent direction, the Plotinian doctrine of the procession. The Philonian metaphysics of interiority and the conception of the ultimate end of man found in the mystical-ecstatic union with God then corresponds fully with the pages of the *Enneads*.[11]

The relations of Plotinus with the Gnostics were that they functioned as a polemical antitheses to his doctrines. Naturally, by dialectically confronting them, Plotinus was forced to construct an explanation of his own position. But keep in mind that the ground on which the Gnostics move and on which Plotinus moves is very different. The positive influences of the former on the latter have undoubtedly been exaggerated by some scholars, so much so that we do not know with certainty the Gnostics to whom Plotinus makes reference. Instead, a recent Italian scholar seems to have gone to the heart of the problem in what he explains as follows: "... the Gnostics and Plotinus move in contrasting worlds of thought: the Plotinian doctrine is a series of attempts to resolve the ancient problem of the One-Whole, that is, to put the supreme Principle in relation to the Universe. If we can use the word emanation, for Plotinus it does not have anything in common with Gnostic emanations, which are one of the few examples in European thought of that curious application of the imagination, insofar as it was quite disordered and irrational, to philosophical and theological problems: which is characteristic of that decadent European transposition of Indian thought, to which we give the name theosophy. There are some traces of this contamination between phantasy and reason in late Neoplatonism, with its indiscriminate acceptance of every fictional entity of Chaldean astrology, although even here the native Hellenic rationalism ingenuously attempted, its systematization. There is no such irrationality in Plotinus, not even in the exalted and ecstatic Plotinus, since his mysticism is also Hellenistically influenced by dialectic. The Gnostic systems, if they can be properly so-called, seem to be inspired in part by the syncretism of the epoch, thus by the desire to find a place in their spiritual world for every kind of being which is necessary in all the soteriological or philosophical religions of which they have any knowledge; and in part from the Eastern passion for personifying abstract ideas, characteristic of an age with scholastic tendencies, to which the barbaric names of the Aeons bear witness....Other traits of Gnosticism differentiating them from Plotinus are that the production of the Aeons ["the worlds," cf. H. Jonas, *The Gnostic Religion*, pp. 51-54, esp. 54, n. 2 and 181ff., Ed.] is not necessary or eternal, but depends on the will of the First Principle; and then the sexuality, the erotic "transference" sublimated within the spiritual worlds, characteristic of Simonian and Valentinian Gnosticism. Among the Simonians, a great part is entrusted to the great Mother, great sinner, terrestrial Helena, oscillating between the ancient *epos* [oracle] and the second Faust ["the favored one," cf. H. Jonas, *The Gnostic Religion*, p. 111, Ed.]; while Valentinianism is a true orgy *pornika* [whores' orgy], of desires and couplings. Plotinus is far removed from any of this."[12] Nonetheless, Plotinus was moved in particular by his anti-Gnostic polemic to the full knowledge of the positive nature of the cosmos, which instead is evil, for the Gnostics. Perhaps from certain positions of Gnostic doctrine he was induced to conceive of a problem, foreign to preceding Greek speculation, which involves the Absolute itself, that is, *the problem of why the principle itself exists and the reason for its existence*. But the reply that he made, as we will see, goes well beyond the confines of Gnostic interests and reaches the greatest heights which Western thought has ever achieved.[13]

Plotinus must have had relations with the Christians. Porphyry speaks frequently of numerous Christians at the Plotinian lectures who "lead many into error" in maintaining that "Plato had not plumbed the depths of the intelligible being," so that Plotinus intervened frequently to refute them. But these Christians were mixed together by Porphyry with the Gnostics or even identified *wholly* with them.[14] It is certain, however, that Plotinus expressly took a position against the fundamental doctrine of the *resurrection of the body*.[15] The chief principle of Christianity, *God who becomes flesh, remaining true God and becoming at the same moment true man*, could not be accepted by Plotinus, *either in its revolutionary significance as an historical fact or in its metaphysical and theological significance*. Nor could he have accepted the doctrine of supernatural Grace. Plotinus wanted rather for *man to become God*. In addition, he remained firmly convinced that the powers of man are sufficient for this task: the mystical union with God, that is, the achievement of the supreme *telos* of man, does not happen, as we will see, through supernatural grace, but *through a natural spiritual energy* which enters into the dialectical cycle of *procession (editus)* and *return (reditus)* to the Absolute.[16]

4. The cornerstones of Plotinian thought, their relations with preceding speculation, and their novelty

The complicated framework which we have traced up to this point, which has the aim of making the reader aware of the necessity of understanding a series of complex cornerstones in order to read and understand the *Enneads*, which is the final masterpiece of Greek culture, will be seen even more clearly from the observations that we will now make. Plotinian thought can be wholly analyzed into six fundamental cornerstones:

(1) The fundamental cornerstone consists in the clear distinction between the sensible world and the intelligible world, between corporeal and incorporeal being.

(2) The second cornerstone consists in the determination of the incorporeal in function of a triadic arrangement, that is, in function of the theory of the three hypostases, which are the *One*, the *Mind (Nous)*, and the *Soul (Psyche)*.

(3) The third cornerstone consists in the precise determination of the relations which link the three hypostases, that is, of the process according to which the second is derived from the first and from this the third. The highest level produces the lowest without diminution, giving without impoverishment. (This doctrine is commonly pointed out by the term *emanation*; now, as we will see, such a term is inadequate, insofar as it is the source of every kind of ambiguity and hence needs to be substituted for by the term "procession".)

(4) Closely connected to the doctrine of "procession" of the hypostases is the doctrine according to which sensible matter does not constitute a principle existing in itself, but it itself proceeds from the last hypostasis: the sensible world, consequently, is "deduced" entirely from the supersensible.

(5) Plotinus, as none of the other Greek metaphysicians, was concerned with grounding the unity of all reality. In a certain sense, as we will see, all is in the One and the One is in all, and each of the inferior grades is in the superior and from it is produced and supported. Not only are the supersensible hypostases thus unified, but the corporeal world itself is strictly supported by the incorporeal, at the point at which, by overturning the traditional mode of expressing himself, Plotinus affirms that it is not the soul which is in the body but rather the body which is *in the soul* and hence not the supersensible in the sensible but vice versa. Certainly Plotinus arrives, by pursuing this tack, to the limits of *acosmicism*, but this is precisely the most characteristic trait of his philosophy.

(6) In this ontological context, all "proceeds from" [*exitus*] the Principle (given that there exists nothing opposing him) and therefore a "return to" [*reditus*] the Principle is possible, a full and total reunification with the Principle, which man can realize also while he is yet alive, in a mystical and ecstatic union. Man can separate himself from the external world and enter into himself, taking possession of his true self, which is his soul, and because the soul derives from Mind and Mind from the One man can return to the One. This principle upsets the traditional ordering of values both classical and Hellenistic and transforms ethics into a spiritual *ascesis* and places happiness the human *telos* in ecstatic union with the divine.

Consequently, those cornerstones, even if they have a role equally essential in the *Enneads*, do not have a foundation and a justification proportionate to their nature. What we have said up to here ought to by now have clarified the reason for this apparently strange fact. In reality, Plotinus does not demonstrate but simply affirms and states these cornerstones which the two centuries of speculation preceding him had achieved. He dwells only in part on those which already have been given a justification; instead he insists on the specific novelty contributed by him. And that is why a knowledge of the thought of the first and second centuries CE is indispensable for understanding the *Enneads*.

Let us illustrate this point. The first cornerstone, already fully acquired, is simply assumed by Plotinus: if the modern reader feels the absence of the demonstration of such a conception, Plotinus not only does not feel it, but for precise historical-cultural reasons could not feel it, because, as we have already seen in successive stages, the Middle Platonists and Neo-Pythagoreans, from whom he starts, had already said what was needed.

About the second cornerstone, Plotinus did not dwell on the demonstration *whether there are hypostases* (that is, the existence of a hierarchy in the sphere of the incorporeal), since this was also a current position, but that *the hypostases are three in number* (especially contrary to the Gnostics who multiplied Aeons; Valentine admitted thirty of them, for example). In fact Plotinus upheld this same position as previously accepted by Plato and glimpsed by Parmenides (as, moreover, Numenius had also subscribed to the trinitarian theology previously maintained by Socrates).[17] Plotinus especially tries to demonstrate that the hypostases are *the following three and no others*: the *One* which is beyond being and essence, the Mind (*Nous*) which is the unity of Being and of Thought, and the *Soul*. The third cornerstone (the Soul) is perhaps that which is most discussed together with Mind (*Nous*). However *the determination of the principle according to which the successive hypostases proceed from the first hypostasis and according to which the sensible cosmos itself proceeds from the last hypostasis as well as the determination of the nature of this process is the new and distinctive trait of Neoplatonism.*

Analogous observations could be made about the three remaining cornerstones. In a particular way it is to be marked that the last principal point is perfectly intelligible only if placed within the spiritual climate of the time, in which religious values are placed at the highest level by common consent. Plotinus only gives an adequate speculative foundation to this feeling.

What we have said is sufficient to make comprehensible that *it is impossible to understand Plotinus outside of the background and historical perspective in which he is located.*

5. The method of Plotinus

What is the method of Plotinian speculation? It is the same one which was proper to Platonic speculation, that is to say, "dialectic," understood in its original metaphysical-ontological sense and not merely in the logical-methodological Aristotelian sense and not even obviously in the Stoic sense. Dialectic was, in Plato, not only the method, but the same type of life which characterized the "second voyage," that is, *that method and that type of life which alone move man from being bound to the sensible world, make him ascend to the intelligible world and, once achieved, the intelligible carries him step by step to the supreme reality, to the unbegotten principle, to the unconditioned condition.*[18]

As in Plato, so also in Plotinus there are two stages of dialectic: the first consists in passing from the sensible to the intelligible, the second consists in ascending, step by step, through the intelligible world up to the point of touching the apex of the intelligible. Here is an eloquent passage:

> But how lies the course? Is it alike for all, or is there a distinct method for each class of temperament? For all there are two stages of the path, as they are making upwards or have already gained the upper sphere. The first degree is the conversion from the lower life; the second-held by those that have already made their way to the sphere of the Intelligibles, have set as it were a footprint there but must still advance within the realm lasts until they reach the extreme hold of the place, the Term attained when the topmost peak of the Intellectual realm is won.[19]

Actually, the text speaks of two stages, but then it distinguishes three, insofar as it points out (and we will see further on for what reason) in the same sphere of the intelligible (*a*) the journey into the world of the Mind and (*b*) the moment in which "the terminus of the journey" is achieved, that is, the conclusion of the voyage (ecstasy).

But we will see, in the meantime, what men are in condition to ascend and hence to become dialecticians. According to Plotinus these men are of three kinds: those who have a *musical* nature, those who have an *erotic* nature, and those who have a *philosophical* nature. Essentially they are *men who aspire to the immaterial* and are capable of leaving behind the sensible or who, like men of a philosophical nature, have already in some way performed the separation.

Consequently, the man that has a musical nature first of all will need to be taught to pass from sensible sounds and from sensible beauty which is expressed in them to the spiritual beauty which is superior to them, insinuating in this way philosophical reasons into him.

Analogously, the man who has a passionate nature will need to learn to go beyond beautiful bodies which agitate him and disturb him and he will need to discover the true fascination of incorporeal things and hence to rise up to the world of Mind. The man who has a philosophical nature has already performed this separation and is already prepared for the final journey, that is, he is ready to become a dialectician quickly.[20]

What then precisely is dialectic? Here is the reply of Plotinus:

> It is the Method, or Discipline, that brings with it the power of pronouncing with final truth upon the nature and relation of things what each is, how it differs from others, what common quality all have, to what Kind each belongs and in what rank each stands in its Kind and whether its Being is Authentic-Being, and how many Beings there are, and how many non-Beings to be distinguished from Beings.

> Dialectic treats also of the Good and the not-Good, and of the particulars that fall under each, and of what is the Eternal and what the not-Eternal and of these, it must be understood, not by seeming-knowledge (opinion) but with authentic science. All this accomplished, it gives up its touring of the realm of sense and settles down in the Intellectual Cosmos and there plies its own peculiar Act: it has abandoned all the realm of deceit and falsity, and pastures the Soul in the "Meadows of Truth": it employs the Platonic division to the discernment of the Ideal-Forms, of the Authentic-Being, and of the First-Kinds (or Categories of Being): it establishes, in the light of Intellection, the affiliations of all that issues from these Firsts, until it has traversed the entire Intellectual Realm: then, by means of analysis, it takes the opposite path and returns once more to the First Principle. Now it rests: caught up in the tranquility of that sphere, it is no longer busy about many things: it has arrived at Unity and it contemplates: it leaves to another science all that coil of premises and conclusions called the art of reasoning, much as it leaves the art of writing: some of the matter of logic, no doubt, it considers necessary to clear the ground but it makes itself the judge, here as in everything else; where it sees use, it uses; anything it finds superfluous, it leaves to whatever department of learning or practice may turn that matter to account.[21]

This science, mark it well, does not depend on the external world and is not moved, hence, by sensation, in the sense that *it does not draw its proper principles from sensible experience but from the Mind (Nous) itself by means of the Soul.* Plato had already clearly said that to look directly at sensible things with the senses "blinds the soul" and maintained the necessity of fleeing "into the *logoi*" and to proceed within this sphere.[22] Plotinus affirms, in a still clearer way, that *the principles are given by the Mind (Nous) itself and are evident, provided that they are accepted precisely with Soul, which, as we will see, depends on the Mind (Nous).* Dialectic draws, then, from these principles all the consequences interweaving and separating them up to the point of grasping all the relations which constitute the whole world of the Mind (*Nous*) in an adequate way and even up to accepting beyond the Mind (*Nous*) itself, the One, the Absolute, as we will see.

Two elements are yet to be brought forward in evidence for the purposes of a correct comprehension of Plotinian dialectic.

First, as we have already pointed out, *dialectic is not purely a research method*, that is, *a pure instrument*. It, in fact, does not consist, as for Aristotle and for the Stoics, in the determination of *merely rational procedures*, of the correct way of proceeding in asking and answering questions, but in a process of thought which, as previously with Plato, grasps immediately being and reality:

> Dialectic does not consist of bare theories and rules; it deals with verities; Existences are, as it were, Matter to it, or at least it proceeds methodically towards Existences, and possesses itself, at the one step, of the notions and of the realities.[23]

Secondly, dialectic is a *moral evaluation* for Plotinus, as previously for Plato (and this also we have pointed out), *it is an ascent, it is con-version* (a turning-around). Dialectic cannot exist without virtue, and, in fact, the *highest virtues coincide or are closely linked with dialectic*, given that these virtues are separations from the body, assimilation and identification with the divine, and dialectic precisely takes into account this aim. Plotinian dialectic, in sum, flowers into mysticism.

And thus, with this final feature, we have returned to that initial moment concerning the most peculiar nature of the culmination of Plotinian dialectic. Previously, the Platonic dialectical process ended in the intuition of the Good, that is, in an immediate grasp of the unconditioned. Consequently, Plotinus emphasizes with extreme vigor the extraordinary nature of this final moment boldly opposing it to science, and he even goes on to describe it as a contact, as an assimilation, as an identification, as an ecstasy.[24]

But in order to comprehend this point it is necessary first to examine the entire Plotinian system, and therefore we can characterize it adequately only at the end of our treatment.

IV. The Possible Methods for Interpreting and Expounding Plotinian Thought

1. The interpretations proposed by historians of philosophy

Scholars have been aware for a long time that there are two components of Plotinian thought: one is *subjective*, that is, as we would say today, *existential*; the other, *objective*, and more properly speculative. From the beginning to the end of the *Enneads*, in fact, there emerges the eagerness for the divine and the fervent desire to be united with it, the religious sentiment, and mystical tension; but likewise, from beginning to end of the *Enneads*, the clear attempt to explain rationally the totality of the real and give an account again on a rational basis of that same tension of man and of all things to the divine is evident.

Consequently, then, the interpreters are divided. Some have given special importance to the first component, offering us a series of interpretations which in a *rough manner* of speaking can be called *religious* while the others have emphasized the second component, offering us a series of more *philosophical* and *metaphysical* interpretations.[1]

It is nevertheless to be noted first that these two components in Plotinus are only separated with difficulty. Bréhier has in fact affirmed, and not without reason, that the characteristic trait of Plotinus is properly "the intimate union of these two problems, a union such that the question of knowing which of the two is subordinated to the other cannot be determined."[2] Further, the French scholar later explains: "Plotinus must be placed among those thinkers who have attempted to overcome the conflict between faith and reason (because in this form it will be conditioned by historical circumstances not yet verified in this epoch), but it is a conflict of a very general nature, the conflict between a religious understanding of the universe, that is, an understanding such that our destiny has a meaning, and a rationalistic understanding which seems to destroy any significance for a reality which is the individual destiny of the soul. Plotinus remains one of the most important teachers in the history of philosophy for having posed this problem."[3]

In addition, in every case we are concerned with Plotinus in the history of philosophy only in virtue of the second component, or better, in the measure in which the second component gives meaning to the first. So the philosophical-metaphysical interpretations are undoubtedly more adequate, much more than the religious ones which do not succeed in giving meaning to the religious phase without referring to the philosophical. Again, the philosophical-metaphysical interpretations do not succeed in explaining the existential moment without referring to the ontological component: in sum, they do not attempt to determine the objective stage in order to explain the subjective.

In their way, then, the philosophical interpretations have pursued different routes.

Some scholars have tried to reconstruct the evolution of Plotinian thought and its chronological development.[4] The chronological order of the *Enneads* given to us by Porphyry is unfortunately not wholly trustworthy. In addition, we know that Plotinus began to write towards his fiftieth year, after that for about a decade he had held his lectures, hence when his thought had already matured. It is understandable why these attempts have had somewhat disappointing results.

Those who have instead proposed to systematically reconstruct the Plotinian thought are beset with other difficulties. Plotinus is in a certain sense a very systematic thinker, but the way in which he exposes his own thought is the most unsystematic way that can be imagined. The *Enneads* throughout presuppose the doctrine of the three hypostases and even the whole system already fixed, but nowhere do we find indications of a precise plan to follow for reconstructing it.

It is understandable, therefore, that in this case the interpreters are also divided into two groups. Some have preferred to follow the way we can call "from low to high," that is, the way which begins from matter and the sensible world in order to reach the intelligible world and from the lower hypostases to the highest.[5] Others instead preferred the way which we can call "from high to low," beginning from the highest principle, that is, from the One, descending step by step to the Mind, the Soul, and then to the sensible world.[6] Which of these ways is more correct and more adequate?

2.   The way followed in the present exposition

Actually, in the *Enneads* we can find both of these ways. They are not really antithetical even if they appear to be so. Moreover, we know that previously in Plato as well as in Plotinus dialectic was both a "going up" and a "going down". Nevertheless, those who choose the upward path, from low to high, seem to be in tune with the Aristotelian method, which moves from what is *prior for us* (the sensible) in order to rise to what is *last for us* (the intelligible), just as it is *primary in itself* (the supersensible). But the Aristotelian method is wholly different from the Plotinian one. In fact for Plotinus the sensible world has neither that ontological solidity nor that autonomy which it has in Aristotle and sensations consequently do not have their own cognitive autonomy. As previously pointed out, the soul (our Mind [Nous]) does not grasp principles from sensible things, but from the Mind itself.

On the other hand, Plotinus uses the upward path from low to high only a few times and only when he wishes to prove something, like to verify that the hypostases are three. But usually he uses the downward path from high to low, and so in function of it alone is it possible to adequately understand the "procession" of the hypostases, that is, the way by which one derives from the other and the relations that bind them together.

Moreover, as we will see, the supreme principle, the One, plays a role which absolutely conditions everything in the Plotinian system so that no part of it is intelligible except in relation to it.

The downward path "from high to low" is hence, the one which is more adequate to and conforms better with Plotinian thought.

3.   The articulation of the system

Scholars are in little agreement about the determination of the articulations of the Plotinian system. This is an inevitable consequence of the diverse points of departure which they assume and the diverse interpretation which they give of the nature of Plotinian philosophy.

It seems to us, nevertheless, that this articulation emerges from the *Enneads* in a clear enough manner.

First, because the base of the Plotinian system is the Platonic distinction between the intelligible and the sensible worlds which are between them in the relation of condition to conditioned, it will be necessary to distinguish the treatment of the supersensible world from the sensible and to begin from that distinction.

Concerning the articulation of the treatment of the supersensible, there could not be any doubt: the hierarchical order of the high to the low, from the One to *Nous* to the Soul, is most logical. One who begins from the lower hypostasis, the Soul, in order to rise up to the highest does not succeed in explaining completely the nature of the Plotinian "procession." Thus anyone who begins from the middle hypostasis works arbitrarily.[7]

The treatment of the intelligible world must be followed by that of the sensible world. This is "physics," or better, a true cosmology.

Finally, man, his goal, and how he ought to live in order to achieve it must be treated. This is ethics.

Now if the treatise of the first *Enneads* dedicated to dialectic is re-read, one can find this plan followed. Philosophy has distinct parts: the most noble part is dialectic (which is the knowledge of the intelligible and the immaterial); the two other parts expressly mentioned and declared dependent on dialectic are physics and ethics.[8]

It is quite clear, therefore, that Plotinus is not wholly interested in the treatment of problems of physics considered from a strictly scientific viewpoint. The physical world interests him only as a moment of the "procession" from the Absolute. Analogously, ethics does not have its own solidity, or autonomy, but rather a relative one. Ethics becomes in Plotinus the way of "returning" to the One and only under this perspective is our philosopher interested in the problems of human beings.

Therefore, the Plotinian system emerges in its true shape only by molding the traditional "parts" of philosophy into the new cyclical configuration of the "procession" of all things from the One and their "return" to the One.

Actually, in the Plotinian system there is presented the most daring metaphysical attempt of antiquity, which shakes all the traditional arrangements and puts them in disarray: the hypostases and the world itself are only different grades of the Divine, on every level and in every respect. The One is in all, even if in a different way, according to the capacity each thing has to contain it, and the all is in the One.

As has been correctly pointed out, the "procession" [*exitus*] of the man from the One is "*a path from God to God*," it is also a way "*in God*", because there are only degrees of divine life, an eternal descent and an eternal ascent of the soul, according to a determined rhythm and an immanent law."[9]

On account of this, the "parts" of philosophy lose their traditional meaning and only in the circle of the "procession" [*exitus*] and the "return" [*reditus*] do they acquire their new and transformed meaning.

It is to this issue that we now turn our attention in our exposition.

Second Section

THE FOUNDATION AND STRUCTURE OF THE SYSTEM OF PLOTINUS

«῎Εστι γάρ τι οἷον κέντρον, ἐπὶ δὲ
τούτῳ κύκλος ἀπ' αὐτοῦ ἐκλάμπων,
ἐπὶ δὲ τούτοις ἄλλος, φῶς ἐκ φωτός.»

"For there is a kind of center, and around
this a circle shining out from it, and
beyond these another, light from light: but
outside these there is no longer another
circle of light but this next circle through
lack of its own light needs illumination
from another source."

Plotinus, *Enneads* 4.3.17

I. The First Hypostasis: the One

1. Preliminary demonstration of the existence of the One and of the three
    hypostases

It is impossible to understand the originality of Plotinus and in particular
his personal contribution to the "second voyage" unless one comprehends the
structural reform which he brought to both Platonic and Aristotelian metaphysics and which led to results which were in more than one respect revolutionary. It is quite clear that in Plato there are Plotinian hints *ante litteram*
[*before the text*].[1] In the succeeding history of Platonism and Neo-
Pythagoreanism, these hints, as we have seen,[2] increase greatly, but Plotinus
goes well beyond them to a *true re-establishing of classical metaphysics*.

The ultimate principle of the real for Aristotle, although at different
levels, is *essence* (οὐσία) and Mind (the Mind of the Aristotelian unmoved
Movent); for Plotinus, instead, *the principle is still more ultimate*, He is the One
which is *beyond being and essence and beyond Mind*, He is the One which
transcends *ousia* and *Mind (Nous)*.

But let us see the reasoning by which Plotinus was moved to this doctrine,
according to which the One is *the absolute foundation and principle*.

Every entity in the ultimate sense *is such only in virtue of unity*. If it lacks
unity, in fact, every entity ceases to exist as a thing itself. The existence of the
thing depends on its unity: if this is destroyed the being itself of the thing is
destroyed. Plotinus writes:

> It is in virtue of unity that beings are beings.
> This is equally true of things whose existence is primary and of all that are
> in any degree to be numbered among beings. What could exist at all except
> as one thing? Deprived of unity, a thing ceases to be what it is called: no
> army unless as a unity: a chorus, a flock, must be one thing. Even house and
> ship demand unity, one house, one ship; unity gone, neither remains: thus
> even continuous magnitudes could not exist without an inherent unity;
> break them apart and their very being is altered in the measure of the breach
> of unity.
> Take plant and animal; the material form stands a unity; fallen from that
> into a litter of fragments, the things have lost their being; what was is no
> loner there; it is replaced by quite other things as many others, precisely, as
> possess unity.
> Health, similarly, is the condition of a body acting as a co-ordinate unity.
> Beauty appears when limbs and features are controlled by this principle,
> unity. Moral excellence is of a soul acting as a concordant total, brought to
> unity.[3]

We ask now, once it is established that the being of the entities depends
on their unity, *from what further source does their unity derive?* Plotinus notes

that all physical entities receive their unity from soul (as we will see further on), which is the molding, formative, and coordinating activity of all sensible things and in this sense is the cause and foundation of their unity. May we say that the soul itself is a unity or will we rather say that *soul gives the unity but is not identical with unity* and hence does it derive its unity from something further? Plotinus's reply is very clear: there are *different grades of unity*; the soul has a grade of unity superior to that of bodies, but it is not unity:

> Anything that can be described as a unity is so in the precise degree in which it holds a characteristic being; the less or more the degree of the being, the less or more the unity. Soul, while distinct from unity's very self, is a thing of the greater unity in proportion as it is of the greater, the authentic, being. Absolute unity is not: it is soul and one soul, the unity in some sense a concomitant; there are two things, soul and soul's unity, as there is body with body's unity. The looser aggregates such as a choir are furthest from unity, the more compact are the nearer; soul is nearer yet but still a participant.

> Is soul to be identified with unity on the ground that unless it were one thing it could not be soul? No; unity is equally necessary to every other thing, yet unity stands distinct from them; body and unity are not identical; body, too, is a participant.

> Besides, the soul, even the individual soul, is a manifold, though not composed of parts: it has diverse powers reasoning, desiring, perceiving all held together by this chain of unity. Itself a unity, soul confers unity, but also accepts it.[4]

Hence, the soul introduces unity into the physical world, but it receives it from what exists above, from *Nous*, and from Being.

At this point the problem previously posited in relation to the soul re-appears: *does the One coincide with Being and with Nous (Νοῦς)?* The reply in this case as well is negative. Being and Mind (Nous), although they have a superior grade of unity in relation to soul, are not the One, *because they imply multiplicity*: the duality of knower and known and the multiplicity of the Ideas, the totality of intelligible reality:

> Above all, unity is The First: but Mind, Ideas, and Being, cannot be so; for any member of the realm of Forms is an aggregation, a compound, and therefore since components must precede their compound is later.

> Other considerations also go to show that the Mind cannot be the first. Mind must be about the Intellectual Act: at least in its higher phase, that not concerned with the outer universe, it must be intent upon its Prior; its introversion is a conversion upon the Principle.

> There is no other way of stating the Mind than as that which, holding itself in the presence of The Good and First and looking towards That, is self-present also, self-knowing and knowing itself as All-Being: thus manifold, it is far from being The Unity.

In sum: The Unity cannot be the total of beings for so its oneness is annulled; it cannot be the Mind, for so it would be that total which the Mind is; nor is it Being, for Being is the total of things.[5]

The root of unity, hence, is something which transcends *Mind* (Nous), something absolutely free of any plurality whatsoever *which is One in itself.* Here is an important passage:

> That which engenders the world of sense cannot itself be a sense-world; it must be the Mind and the Intellectual world; similarly, the prior which engenders the Mind and the sphere of Mind cannot be either, but must be something of less multiplicity. The manifold does not rise from the manifold: the Intellectual multiplicity has its source in what is not manifold; by the mere fact of being manifold, the thing is not the first principle: we must look to something earlier.
>
> *All must be grouped under a unity which, as standing outside of all multiplicity and outside of any ordinary simplicity, is the veritably and essentially simplex.*[6]

In conclusion: in searching for the foundation of things, which is unity, we are constrained to rise up from the physical world to the soul (which is the lowest hypostasis), hence from the soul (which has, but is not unity) to Mind (Nous) (which is the second hypostasis), and from Mind (Nous) (which has a higher unity than the soul, but which is still a multiplicity) *to a further absolutely simple principle: the One, which is the first hypostasis, the unconditioned, the Absolute.*

Let us now see, in a more precise way, how Plotinus understood the One.

2.   The infinitude, absolute transcendence and the ineffability of the One

The fundamental characteristic of the One is *infinitude* and from this it is necessary to begin to comprehend the differences between Plotinian metaphysics and that of Plato and Aristotle, which we have alluded to above. Infinitude was attributed to the principle only by some ancient philosophers of *physis* and only in the physical sphere.[7] In Plato and in Aristotle (and in general in Greek thought) the notion was prevalent that the infinite involved imperfection (that it was synonymous with the indeterminate and the incomplete), while the finite (in the sense of the determinate and the complete) was associated with the perfect. Plato understood the first principle (ἀρχή) as *limit* (πέρας) and conceived the Dyad and matter as the unlimited and the infinite (ἄπειρον).[8] Aristotle said it was impossible for an actual infinite to exist, and had conceived the infinite as *purely potential, circumscribing it in the category of quantity*, and had affirmed in addition that the perfect always implies an end and the end, a limit.[9]

It was necessary then in order to revive the ancient conception of the infinite affirmed by the Naturalists [Presocratics] which after all was a spatio-temporal magnitude, to reëstablish it on a new plane on the plane of the immaterial, as had previously been done, at least in a certain measure, by Philo of Alexandria.[10]

Because this radical transformation to which the concept of infinitude was subjected in being transposed to and re-interpreted within the sphere of the immaterial is poorly understood, many historians of philosophy have given the One the most disparate and inadequate interpretations.

What does the infinite within the sphere of the immaterial mean? Here are some statements of Plotinus which are quite clear and most important in this regard:

> Yet its being is not limited; what is there to set bounds to it? Nor, on the other hand, is it infinite in the sense of magnitude; what place can there be to which it must extend, or why should there be movement where there is no lacking? All its infinitude resides in its power; it does not change and will not fail; and in it all that is unfailing finds duration.
>
> It is infinite also by right of being a pure unity with nothing towards which to direct any partial content. Absolutely One, it has never known measure and stands outside of number, and so is under no limit either in regard to any external thing or within itself; for any such determination would bring something of the dual into it. And having no constituent parts it accepts no pattern, forms no shape.[11]
>
> The Unity was never in any other and never belonged to the partible: nor is its impartibility that of extreme minuteness; on the contrary it is great beyond anything, great not in extension but in power, sizeless by its very greatness as even its immediate sequents are impartible not in mass but in might We must therefore take the Unity as infinite not in measureless extension or numerable quantity but in fathomless depths of power.[12]
>
> Consider the life in any living thing; it does not reach only to some fixed point, unable to permeate the entire being; it is omnipresent. If on this again we are asked, How?, we appeal to the character of this power, not subject to quantity but such that though you divide it mentally for ever you still have the same power, infinite to the core; in it there is no Matter to make it grow less and less according to the measured mass.[13]

The Plotinian infinite hence is not a spatial magnitude, or a quantitative infinite (connected to spatiality), but, as in a certain measure previously in Philo of Alexandria, the infinite is understood as an unlimited, inexhaustible, immaterial, *productive power*. In this context evidently the word *potency* (δύναμις) does not assume the significance it had previously of *potentiality*, because this Aristotelian meaning was formally linked to matter and the corporeal, but of *activity*, as previously in Philo.

Hence the potency is identical here with active power, with activity, with pure act or *energeia,* with the metaphysically first pure act. To understand It as infinite Mind creative energy (the One is creator of itself and of all other things, as we will see).

The revolutionary consequences which the positive concept of the *immaterial infinite* requires within the sphere of the "second voyage" are the following.

First, the One cannot be an Idea, nor the first principle, a form, or *ousia* in the Platonic sense because first principles, form, and essence imply for Plato, as we have already said, *determinateness, peras* (πέρας), that is, *limit*: they are and produce limitation and determination. Nor can the One even be compared to the Aristotelian immobile Movents, eternal and separate, because these *ousia* which are self-thinking Thoughts are equally finite and determined.[14] Consequently, being as it was understood by these philosophers was the being of the *eidos* and of the *ousia* (and of what is referred to *ousia*) and as such was finite being, Plotinus was moved to place the One "above being" by these considerations and also for the same reasons "above thought," and he states this tenet in the course of all the *Enneads* with such insistence that he leaves the reader with almost no way of avoiding it. This is a new conception of the transcendent which, in the sphere of the Greeks, does not have anything but vague precedents but has instead a clear antecedent in Philo of Alexandria.[15] The supreme Principle not only transcends the physical world, but transcends *every form of finitude*; He embraces even that finitude in which Plato and Aristotle had imprisoned the intelligible and the Mind.

It is understandable, therefore, how the One for Plotinus tends to have *chiefly negative* determinations (in fact, insofar as He is infinite, He does not become any of the determinations of the finite, which are subsequent to Him), and Plotinus describes Him as *ineffable*:

> Thus The One is in truth *beyond all statement*: any affirmation is of a thing; but "all-transcending, resting above even the most august divine Mind" this is the only true description, since it does not make it a thing among things, nor name it where *no name could identify it*: we can but try to indicate, in our own feeble way, something concerning it. When in our perplexity we object, "Then it is without self-perception, without self-consciousness, ignorant of itself," we must remember that we have been considering it only in its opposites.[16]

Consequently, when Plotinus refers to the One in a positive characterization, he is not speaking contradictorily, as some scholars have thought, because he uses a clearly analogical language, as Philo had done previously. But let us see what are these positive characterizations of the One.

3.   The positive characterizations of the One

Let us begin with the term itself "the One," with which Plotinus designates His supreme Principle. The One, when referred to the Principle, does not mean a *particular one*, that is, *a determined unity*, but He is a One-in-itself, that is, the cause and reason of being of the unity of all other things. The One means

the absolutely simple which is the reason of being of the complex and multiple.
Here is a very eloquent text:

> Anything existing after The First must necessarily arise from that First, whether immediately or as tracing back to it through intervenients; there must be an order of secondaries and tertiaries, in which any second is to be referred to The First, any third to the second.

> *Standing before all things, there must exist a Simplex,* differing from all its sequel, self-gathered not interblended with the forms that rise from it, and yet able in some mode of its own to be present to those others: *it must be authentically a unity,* not merely something elaborated into unity and so in reality no more than unit's counterfeit; it will debar all telling and knowing except that it may be described as transcending Being for if there were nothing outside all alliance and compromise, nothing authentically one, there would be no Source. Untouched by multiplicity, it will be wholly self-sufficing, an absolute First, whereas any not-first demands its earlier, and any non-simplex needs the simplicities within itself as the very foundations of its composite existence..[17]

But keep in mind that these clarifications are somewhat deceptive, since the simplicity of the One *is not a lack,* but on the contrary, *He is infinite power,* as we have seen, that is, He is *infinite richness:* the One, in fact, is the *power of all things,* in the sense that the All brings them into being (from Himself) and maintains them in being, as we will see.[18]

The other term which Plotinus uses frequently in order to designate the absolute Principle is *Agathon,* that is, the Good.[19] It is not a question, evidently, *of a particular good,* but the *Good Himself* or, if you like, not of something that *has* goodness, but which *is* the Good Himself.[20]

Plotinus explains also that, properly speaking, the first Principle is not good of Himself, in the sense that He could not be good to His own advantage because He does not need anything, but He is good for all other things which have need of Him. In this sense, He is Super-Good.

> The ruling self-sufficing principle will be Unity-Absolute, for only in this unity is there a nature above all need whether within itself or in regard to the rest of things. Unity seeks nothing towards its being or its well-being or its safehold upon existence; cause to all, how can it acquire its character outside itself or know any good outside? The good of its being can be no borrowing: This is The Good. Nor has it station; it needs no standing-ground as if inadequate to its own sustaining; what calls for such underpropping is the soulless, some material mass that must be based or fall. This is base to all, cause of universal existence and of ordered station. All that demands place is in need; a First cannot go in need of its sequents: all need is effort towards a first principle; the First, principle to all, must be utterly without need. If the Unity be seeking, it must inevitably be seeking to be something other than itself; it is seeking its own destroyer. Whatever may be said to be in need is needing a good, a preserver; nothing can be a good to The Unity,

therefore *neither can it have will to anything; it is a Beyond-Good, not even to itself a good but to such beings only as may of quality to have part with it.*[21]

In conclusion, He is the absolutely transcendent Good.

On the basis of what we have said to this point we can now clarify the meaning of the affirmations that the One is *beyond thought,* and also *beyond being* (of *ousia* and essence), *beyond thought,* and also *beyond life.* Plotinus did not obviously wish to say that the first is not-being, not-thought, or anything which is deprived of life. He wanted to say, instead, that He is the infinite principle from which being, thought, and life are derived; *He is something superior to His own products.* Actually, Plotinus uses an οἱον (which means "so to speak") in conjunction with these terms when he refers to the One, in other words, in an analogical sense, as we said above, or he even speaks of Super-Thought,[22] and in a certain sense also of Super-Being,[23] and hence of Super-Life.[24]

The One exists, but not in the mode of being of the Ideas and of essences, because these beings had a beginning and are multiple. Analogously, He does not think by getting split into thinking and thought, since such a separation implies a break in unity, and hence His thinking transcends our possibility of determining Him and grasping Him. Otherwise, even if Plotinus sharply denies that the One thinks Himself or is conscious whereas on the other hand the Mind (*Nous*), as we will see, thinks and is conscious of Himself, nevertheless he also denies that the One is unconscious. Consequently, Plotinus resolutely denies that the One lacks life even if His life is not the life proper to Mind (*Nous*) or to soul:

> [The One]...it is therefore *no unconscious thing*: all its content and accompaniment are its possession; it is self-distinguishing throughout; it is the seat of *life* as of all things; it is itself, that self-intellection which, stemming from an inner consciousness, takes place in eternal repose, that is to say, in a mode other than that of the Mind.[25]

And again:

> But how admit a Principle void of self-knowledge, self-awareness; surely the First must be able to say "I possess being."
>
> But he does not possess being.
>
> Then, at least he must say "I am good"?
>
> No: once more, that would be an affirmation of Being.
>
> But surely he may affirm merely the goodness, adding nothing: the goodness would be taken without the being and all duality avoided?
>
> No: such self-awareness as good must inevitably carry the affirmation "I am the Good"; otherwise there would be merely the unattached conception of goodness with no recognition of identity; any such Intellection would inevitably include the affirmation "I am."
>
> If that Intellection were the Good, then the Intellection would not be self-Intellection but Intellection of the Good; not the Supreme but that

Intellection would be the Good: if on the contrary that Intellection of the Good is distinct from the Good, at once the Good exists before its knowing; all-sufficiently good in itself, it needs none of that knowing of its own nature.[26]

Thus the Plotinian Absolute is a thought which is beyond thought (meta-thought). He is an intuition which is beyond intuition (meta-intuition). He is a life which is beyond life (meta-life). His volition as we will see is also beyond volition (meta-volition).

4. The One as free self-productive activity

The One is the reason for the being of everything which follows on Him and is such through His being what He is. But Plotinus is not content with an explanation on this level. He is not content to say that since the One is, and is what He is, then from the One everything else proceeds. Plotinus asks an even more radical question and in this way touches on the extreme limits of metaphysical possibility: *why is the One what He is?* Such a question asked in other terms is equivalent to the following: why is there an Absolute and why is the Absolute as He is?

Thus (*a*) it is to exclude that He is *by chance* or *by accident*, because only things of the sensible world exist in this way, subject to the vagaries of change. Not even (*b*) can He exist *through free choice of the type which presupposes the existence of contraries through which He must work*, because *He is beyond all of this*. Neither (*c*) can it be said that *He exists necessarily*, because necessity is subsequent to Him, and in fact He is indeed the law and the necessity of other things. Not even (*d*) can He be said in comparison with the Absolute to be a being, or an essence, or a determinate nature and *thus explain His activity in function of His nature* because, as we know, He transcends being and essence and His "activity" itself is such only in an analogical sense.

Operari sequitur esse [activity follows on being], the medievals will say. Plotinus, instead, in order to characterize his Absolute, would say the opposite: *esse sequitur operari [being follows on activity]*; or better still, *being and act in the Absolute coincide: the first principle is self-acting, creates Himself, is self-productive activity*. Here is an noteworthy passage:

Where since we must use such words the essential act is identical with the being and this identity must obtain in The Good since it holds even in Mind there the act is no more determined by the Being than the Being by the Act. Thus "acting according to its nature" does not apply; the Act, the Life, so to speak, cannot be held to issue from the Being; the Being accompanies the Act in an eternal association: from the two (Being and Act) it forms itself into The Good, self-springing and unspringing.[27]

In Him will corresponds to His act and hence to His being. He is the will to be what He is, He is total and Absolute liberty. In addition, Plotinus says He wished to be what He is because He is *the Highest of everything*, He is the supreme value and supreme positive. Here is a passage in which Plotinus describes the Absolute as *causa sui* [*self-caused*]. It is a passage in which Platonic and Aristotelian limits are transcended and in which the ancient metaphysics and, in fact, all metaphysics truly reach their extreme limits. It is without doubt the most powerful passage of reflection which antiquity has left us:

> Our inquiry obliges us to use terms not strictly applicable: we must insist, once more, that not even for the propose of forming the concept of the Supreme may we make it a duality; if now we do, it is merely for the sake of conveying conviction, as some cost of verbal accuracy.

> If, then, we allow Activities in the Supreme and make them depend on will and certainly Act cannot There be will-less and these Activities are to be the very essence, then will and essence in the Supreme must be identical. This admitted, as He will to be so He is; it is no more true to say that He wills and acts as his nature determines than that his essence is as He wills and acts. Thus He is wholly master of Himself and hold his very being at his will.

> Consider also that every being in its pursuit of its good seeks to be that good rather than what it is; it judges itself most truly to be when it partakes of its good: in so far as it thus draws on its good its being is its choice: much more then must the very Principle, The Good, be desirable in itself when any fragment of it is very desirable to the extern and becomes the chosen essence promoting that extern's will and identical with the will that gave the existence.

> If then this Principle is the means of determination to everything else, we see at once that self-possession must belong primarily to it, so that through it others in their turn may be self-belonging: what we must call its essence comports its will to possess such a manner of being; we can form no idea of it without including in it the will towards itself as it is. It must be a consistent self willing its being and being what it wills; its will and itself must be one thing, all the more one from the absence of distinction between a given nature and one which would be preferred. What could The Good have wished to be other than what it is? Suppose it had the choice of being what it preferred, power to alter the nature, it could not prefer to be something else; it could have not fault to find with anything in its nature, as if that nature were imposed by force; The Good is what from always it wished and wishes to be. For the Good is precisely a willing towards itself, towards a good not gained by any wiles or even attracted to it by force of its nature; The Good is what it chose to be and, in fact, there was never anything outside it to which it could be drawn.

> It may be added that nothing contains in its essence the principle of its own satisfaction; there will be inner discord: but this hypostasis of the Good must necessarily have self-option, the will towards the self; if it had not, it could not bring satisfaction to the beings whose contentment demands participation in it or imagination of it.

Once more, we must be patient with language; we are forced for reasons of exposition to apply to the Supreme terms which strictly are ruled out; everywhere we must read "So to speak." The Good, then, exists; it holds its existence through choice and will, conditions of its very being: yet it cannot be a manifold; therefore the will and the essential being must be taken as one identity; the act of the will must be self-determined and the being self-caused; thus reason shows the Supreme to be its own Author. For if the act of will springs from God Himself and is as it were his operation and the same will is identical with his essence, He must be self-established. He is not, therefore, "what He has happened to be" but what He has willed to be.[28]

And a little before this passage Plotinus had expressly noted:

...what He is, He is not [so] because He could not be otherwise, but because [to be] so is best.[29]

From this Plotinus derives the notion that the supreme Principle not only is the loveable, but likewise He is love, the love of self:

Lovable, very love, the Supreme is also self-love in that He is lovely no otherwise than from Himself and in Himself. Self-presence can hold only in the identity of associated with associating; since in the Supreme, associated and associating are one, seeker and sought one the sought serving as Hypostasis and substrate of the seeker once more God's being and his seeking are identical.[30]

Holding the supreme place or rather no holder but Himself the Supreme all lies subject to Him; He has "happened" to them, but they, all, to Him or rather they stand there before Him looking upon Him, not He upon them. He is borne, so to speak, to the inmost of Himself in love of that pure radiance which He is, He Himself being that which He loves.[31]

Therefore, the One is self-productive activity, Absolute creative liberty, cause of Himself, He is what exists in and for Himself; He is "the transcendent Himself."[32]

5. The procession of all things from the One

Why and how are other things derived from the One? Why did the One, satisfied with Himself, not stay within Himself? It is after all, as we have had on many occasions noted, to ask a very difficult metaphysical question. Plotinus gives a very lucid response:

The mind demands the existence of these Being, but it is still in trouble over the problem endlessly debated by the most ancient philosophers: from such a unity as we have declared The One to be, how does anything at all come into substantial existence, any multiplicity, dyad, or number? Why has the Primary not remained self-gathered so that there be none of this profusion of the manifold which we observe in existence and yet are compelled to trace to that absolute unity?[33]

The Plotinian response to this question represents one of the high points of the metaphysics of antiquity. His response, as we will see, is most original and even constitutes a *singular* moment in the history of ideas in the West.

In responding to the question Plotinus makes use of, several times, the splendid images which have justly become famous. But precisely insofar as they are images they remain ambiguous unless they become conceptually articulated. Unfortunately, some interpreters let themselves draw more from the images than from conceptual articulations with grave prejudice to the comprehension of the thought of our philosopher. It is nevertheless necessary to start from the most famous of these images in order to better determine the theoretic conception of which they are a preliminary representation.

The most well-known one is certainly that of light. The derivation of things from the One is represented as the radiation of a light from a luminous source in the form of a succession of circles gradually decreasing in luminosity, while the source of light itself remains without diminution in its expansion wholly about. The first circle of light after the source of light is *Mind* (Nous), that is, the second hypostasis; the next circle is the Soul, that is, the third hypostasis. The circle which follows afterwards signifies the moment of the extinguishing of light and symbolizes matter, which needs an external source of illumination, being at this point in darkness:

> There is, we may put it, something that is center; about it, a circle of light shed from it; round center and first circle alike, another circle, light from light; outside that again, not another circle of light but one which, lacking light of its own, must borrow.

> The last we may figure to ourselves as an outer ring, or rather sphere, of a nature to receive light from that third realm, its next higher, in proportion to the light which that itself receives. Thus all begins with the great light, shining self-centered; in accordance with the reigning plan (that of emanation) this gives forth its brilliance; the later (divine) existents (souls) add their radiation some of them remaining above while there are some that are drawn further downward, attracted by the splendor of the object they illuminate.[34]

And here in this other passage Plotinus represents the image of light mixed in with others which became no less famous: the fire which gives off heat, the odoriferous substance which gives off perfume, the living thing which, come to maturity, generates:

> Given this immobility in the Supreme, it can neither have yielded assent nor uttered decree nor stirred in any way towards the existence of a secondary.

> What happened, then? What are we to conceive as rising in the neighborhood of that immobility?

> It must be a circumradiation produced from the Supreme but from the Supreme unaltering and may be compared to the brilliant light encircling the sun and ceaselessly generated from that unchanging substance.

All existences, as long they retain their character, produce about themselves, from their essence, in virtue of the power which must be in them some necessary, outward-facing hypostasis continuously attached to them and representing in image the engendering archetypes: thus fire gives out its heat; snow is cold not merely to itself; fragrant substances are a notable instance; for, as long as they last, something is diffused from them and perceived wherever they are present.

Again, all that is fully achieved engenders: therefore the eternally achieved engenders eternally an eternal being. At the same time, the offspring is always minor: what then are we to think of that All-Perfect but that it can produce nothing less than the very greatest that is later than itself? This greatest, later than the divine unity, must be the Divine Mind, and it must be the second of all existence, for it is that which sees The One on which alone it leans while the First has no need whatever of it. the offspring of the prior to the Divine Mind can be no other than that Mind itself and thus is the loftiest being in the universe, all else following upon it the Soul, for example, being an utterance and act of the Mind as that is an utterance and act of The One.[35]

The other two famous images are that of the inexhaustible spring which generates rivers and that of the tree:

And what will such a Principle essentially be?

The potentiality of the Universe: the potentiality whose non-existence would mean the non-existence of all the Universe and even of the Mind which is the primary Life and all Life.

This Principle on the thither side of Life is the cause of Life for that Manifestation of Life which is the Universe of things is not the First Activity; it is itself poured forth, so to speak, like water from a spring.

Imagine a spring that has no source outside itself; it gives itself to all the rivers, yet is never exhausted by what they take, but remains always integrally as it was; the tides that proceed from it are at one within it before they run their several ways, yet all, in some sense, know beforehand down what channels they will pour their streams.

Or: think of the Life coursing throughout some mighty tree while yet it is the stationary Principle of the whole, in no sense scattered over all that extent but, as it were, vested in the root: it is the giver of the entire and manifold life of the tree, but remains unmoved itself, not manifold but the Principle of that manifold life.[36]

Finally, less acclaimed but no less interesting is the image of concentric circles: the One is at the center, the second hypostasis is an unmoving circle, while the soul is a moving circle:

The total scheme may be summarized in the illustration of The Good as a center, the Mind as an unmoving circle, the Soul as a circle in motion, its moving being its aspiration: the Mind possesses and has ever embraced that which is beyond being; the Soul must seek it still: the sphere of the universe by its possession of the Soul thus aspirant, is moved to the aspiration which falls within its own nature; this is no more than such power as body may have, the mode of pursuit possible where the object pursued is debarred from entrance; it is the motion of coiling about, with ceaseless return upon the same path in other words, it is circuit.[37]

But note that the circles are necessarily generated from the center, as Plotinus explains in the following passage, illustrating especially the relation between the center and the first circle and then turning again to the image of light:

> A circle related in its path to a center must be admitted to owe its scope to that center; it has something of the nature of that center in that the radial lines converging on that one central point assimilate their impinging ends to the point of convergence and of departure, the dominant radii and terminals: the terminals are of one nature with the center, feeble reproductions of it, since the center is, in a certain sense, the source of terminals and radii impinging at every point upon it; these lines reveal the center; they are the development of that undeveloped.
>
> In the same way we are to take Mind and being. This combined power springs from the supreme, an outflow and as it were development from That and remaining dependent upon that Intellective nature, showing forth that, so to speak, Mind-in-Unity which is not the Mind since it is no duality. No more than in the circle are the lines or circumferences to be identified with that center which is the source of both: radii and circle are images given forth by indwelling power and, as products of a certain vigor in it, not cut off from it.
>
> Thus the Intellective power circles around the Supreme which stands to it as archetype to image; the archetype is Mind-in-Unity; the image in its manifold movement round about its prior has produced the multiplicity by which it is constituted Mind that prior has no movement; it generates Mind by its sheer wealth.
>
> Such a power, author of Mind author of being how does it lend itself to chance, to hazard, to any "so it happened"?
>
> What is present in Mind is present, though in a far transcendent mode, in the One: so in a light diffused afar from one light shining within itself, the diffused is vestige, the source is the true light; but the Mind the diffused and image light, is not different in kind from its prior; and it is not a thing of chance but at every point is reason and cause.
>
> The Supreme is cause of the cause.[38]

These are the images: but, as we mentioned above, they have been taken literally and some interpreters are even fixated on them with the resulting misunderstanding or total incomprehension of the concepts which ought to have been clarified. It is on their basis that what is spoken of as "emanationism" and even "pantheism" and "monism" has been defended. Actually, the matter is much more complex than these expressions would lead one to believe and only after giving a final exposition and interpretation of *the whole Plotinian system* will it be possible to understand *in toto* (completely) the multiple ramifications of what is truly meant by the Plotinian "procession from the One." For the moment, nevertheless, we can clarify an essential doctrine through which the procession appears in an unexpected light.

First, this conclusion can be drawn from all the images: the Principle *remains* (μένει) and by remaining He generates in the sense that *His generative acts do not impoverish Him*, nor lessen, nor condition Him. What is generated is inferior to the generator and *does not serve the generator*; the generated has need of the generator, not vice versa.[39] We must look further into this issue. Given His infinite perfection and His transcendent power does the generator perhaps necessarily create? Can the source of light not send light, the spring of water not gush water, the perfumed body not "send forth" perfume? It is precisely on this point that the images tend to be deceptive by revealing only *one aspect of Plotinian thought and veiling the other*, its most original aspect.

Plotinus distinguishes, in fact, two different types of *activity* of the One (and of the other hypostases as well): (*a*) the activity *of* the being and (*b*) the activity which derives *from* the being: the former is immanent *to* the being, so to speak, while the latter is *from* the being and directed *to* the outside. In other words, the activity of the being coincides with the individual being, while the activity which derives from the being is directed to another. Consequently, applying this distinction to the One, it must be said (*a*) there is an activity *of* the One, (*b*) there is an activity which derives *from* the One: (*a*) the activity *of* the One is that which makes it to be and preserves it and makes it "perdure"; (*b*) instead, the activity which derives *from* the One is that which makes, so that from the One derives or better "proceeds" another reality. It is clear that the activity *from* the One depends formally on the activity *of* the One itself.[40] But before drawing the consequences which arise from such a principle, let us read the passage which is fundamental but not very well-known by many in which such a principle is explained in clear terms.

> But how from amid perfect rest can an Act arise?
>
> There is in everything the Act of the Essence and the Act going out from the Essence: the first Act if the thing itself in its realized identity, the second Act is an inevitably following outgo from the first, an emanation distinct from the thing itself.
>
> Thus even in fire there is warmth comported by its essential nature and there is the warmth going instantaneously outward from that characterizing heat by the fact that fire, remaining unchangeably fire, utters the Act native to its essential reality.
>
> So it is in the divine also: or rather we have there the earlier form of the double act: the divine remains in its own unchanging being, but from its perfection and from the Act included in its nature there emanates the secondary or issuing Act which as the output of a mighty power, the mightiest there is attains to Real Being as second to that which stands above

all Being. That transcendent was the potentiality of the All; this secondary is the All made actual.[41]

So by applying this doctrine to the problem about which we have spoken above, we can extract a solution opposed to that which has frequently been presented by not taking the passage into account. It is true that things proceed from the One because the One is what He is, that is, overflowing with infinite power; but we have also seen above that the activity *of* the One *consists precisely in willing to be that which He is*, that is, *in the liberty of being what He is*, to that the activity which proceeds *from* the One and which necessarily follows upon the activity *of* the One (*i.e.*, the so-called "emanation") *constitutes a willed necessity in a certain sense, that is a necessity posited by a free act, or better, the consequences of a free act.* Therefore it has been recently and correctly remarked that from all of this it must be concluded that "the will of the One to be his own nature is the direct cause of the emanation *from* his nature" and that therefore, *in a certain sense*, "creation is free no more and no less than the One itself is free."[42] We prefer to say that the creation (the procession) is a necessity which follows on a free act of the will of the One.

This is of itself sufficient to show the great novelty of the Plotinian procession. But only the examination of the other hypostases could furnish all the elements necessary to grasp it fully.[43]

II. The Second Hypostasis: the Mind (*Nous*)

1. The two-fold relation which binds the One and the Mind (Nous)

The generation of the hypostases implies beyond the two illustrated above, a further activity which is no less essential to these, since without it the hypostases could not exist. It involves *the activity of "turning around" to the principle from which any hypostasis derives in order "to look at it" and in order "to contemplate it."* This "contemplative activity" is not in any way expressed in the famous images examined above. Consequently, it has been wholly misunderstood (and sometimes ignored) even by famous interpreters, while in reality it represents one of the centers around which the Plotinian metaphysics moves.

In particular, with regard to the second hypostasis which we are now engaged in discussing, the Power or activity of the First does not immediately generate Mind (Nous), but something "indeterminate" or "unformed." This determines and becomes a world of forms by *turning* to the One, *looking* at and *contemplating* the One and fecundated and filled by Him by means of such a "contemplation" (and in addition, as we will see, by contemplating Himself fecundated by the contemplation of the One).

This *indeterminate and unformed product* of the One (before turning to contemplate the One) is said by Plotinus to be intelligible "otherness," "intelligible matter," and also "first motion," intelligible motion. Here is a very important text in this regard:

> For that differentiation within the Cognizable which produces Matter has always existed and it is the cleavage which produces the Matter there: it is the first movement; and movement and differentiation are convertible terms since the two things arose as one: *this motion, this cleavage, away from The First is indetermination (= Matter) needing The First to its determination which achieves by its Return*, remaining, until then, an Alienism, still lacking good; unlit by the Supernatural. It is from The First that light comes, and, until this be absorbed, no light in any recipient of light can be authentic; the recipient is itself without light since light is from elsewhere.[1]

The esoteric language ought not to throw us off track: this *matter* and this *intelligible motion* is nothing other than *indefinite thought* (or as we can also say, indefinite being), *which is determined precisely by turning toward the One.*

In order to express his conception, Plotinus uses also the famous "Pythagorean" and "Platonic" principles of the One and the Dyad. The product of the One is the "indefinite Dyad," which, coming together with the One, generates the Ideas. This signifies: (*a*) what the One produces is not another One but a Dyad, because thought presupposes the object of thought and hence, implies a duality; (*b*) further, this indeterminate duality is determined through its turning to the One, thus generating the world of Ideas and hence becoming Mind, as we will see.[2]

But Plotinus is certainly happier when he sticks to the new concepts of his own invention leaving aside ideas of both Platonic-Aristotelian and Neo-Pythagorean extraction. Consequently, we spoke above of the Mind (Nous) which is not entirely and simply the power which "proceeds" from the One, but that this power, in order to be Mind, must "turn around" to the One and contemplate it. But—and this is a most important point—also such a "turning around" to the One *is not yet the Mind (Nous) but the cause and the condition which makes it be so.* Plotinus, in fact, distinguishes two stages: (*a*) the "turning around" of the power to the One, which fecundates, fills up totally the power itself, and (*b*) the "reflecting" of this power on itself previously fecundated. The two stages (which are obviously only logically and not chronologically distinguishable) explain the two aspects of the Nous (Mind), or Principle (*a*) In the first moment, substance, essence, being (the content of thought) is born; (*b*) in the second moment, thought is born. This two-fold character of the moments likewise explains *the birth of multiplicity*, not only the duality of knower and known, but also the multiplicity itself of the contents (the multiplicity of the Ideas). Here is one of the more important passages in this regard:

> Seeking nothing, possessing nothing, lacking nothing, the One is perfect and, in our metaphor, has overflowed, and its exuberance has produced the new: this product has turned again to its begetter and been filled and has become its contemplator and so Mind.

> That station towards the One (the fact that something exists in presence of the One) establishes Being; that vision directed upon the One establishes the Mind standing towards the One to the end of vision, it is simultaneously Mind and Being; and, attaining resemblance in virtue of this vision, it repeats the act of the One in pouring forth a vast power.[3]

But there is still a further point to be clarified. The birth of the second hypostasis is the *birth of multiplicity* or, if you wish, of the One-Many, not only, as we have previously hinted, in the sense that the Mind (Nous) is Intelligence and Intelligible, but also in the sense that the Cognizable is a multiplicity, although indeed unified (it is, as we will see, an Intelligible cosmos, a world of Ideas). It may be possible to explain the genesis of this multiplicity through the inadequacy or incapacity of the second hypostasis to accept the One in its infinitude. Actually, some texts in a first reading seem to require such an interpretation:

> Good is the source from which the objects of contemplation come to be seen in the Mind, Mind has produced them by its vision of the Good. In the very law, never, looking to That, could it fail of Intellectual Act; never, on the other hand, could its objects be in the Good otherwise it (the Mind would not produce them itself. *Thence it must draw its power to bring forth, to teem with offspring of itself; but the Good bestows what itself does not*

> *possess. From the Unity came multiplicity to Mind it could not sustain the power poured upon it and therefore broke it up;* it turned that one power into variety so as to carry it piecemeal. [4]

But in reality the position of Plotinus is more complex and the same passage previously quoted, if read with attention reveals it. *The Mind (Nous), in fact, does not know the One, but knows itself filled and fecundated by the One.* The multiplicity is born *only within the second hypostasis in the sense that the Mind (Nous) does not see the One as multiple, but sees itself as multiplied.* Here is a most interesting passage:

> The best way of putting the question is to ask whether, when Mind looked towards The Good, it had Intellection of that unity as a multiplicity and, itself a unity, applied its Act by breaking into parts what it was too feeble to know as a whole.

> At first it was not Mind looking upon the Good; it was a looking void of Intellection. We must think of it not as looking but as living; dependent upon That, it kept itself turned Thither; all the tendance taking place There and upon That must be a movement teeming with life and must so fill the looking Mind there is no longer bare Act, there is a filling to saturation. Forthwith it becomes all things, knows that fact in virtue of its self-knowing and at once becomes Mind filled so as to hold within itself that object of its vision, seeing all by the light from the Giver and bearing that light with it. [5]

2. The Mind (*Nous*) as Being, Thought, and Life

The One is "the power of all things"; the Mind (Nous) is, in turn, "all things." [6] What does this mean?

First, the Plotinian Mind, as we have previously pointed out, is an inseparable union of Being and Knowledge, the Object of Knowledge and Mind (Nous). The Mind (Nous) for Plotinus is like the pure Being of Plato, that being which fully is and is not in any way affected by not-being and at the same time it is like the Self-Knowing Knower of which Aristotle speaks. [7]

As we have had occasion many times to point out, Aristotle, in carrying on the Platonic "second voyage," had conceived Mind as immaterial and had also said that it was the *primary ousia,* the supreme being, the pure form; but at the same time he had in a certain sense impoverished its content while he thought he had enriched it by assigning as object of its cognitive activity only itself (itself as known) and reserving to human intelligence the prerogative of being the "*place of forms,*" which are immanent in the sensible (the human Mind is the "place of the forms," insofar as it can receive all of them, "drawing them" from the sensibles). But Plotinus denies that the forms can be immanent in the Aristotelian manner, claiming for them a transcendent nature, and in the wake of the Middle Platonists, the Neo-Pythagoreans, and especially Philo of Alexandria he made Mind the place of the Platonic world of the Ideas. Mind

(Nous) is thus, for Plotinus, the dwelling-place of all beings (Ideas), without exception:

> When we affirm *the reality of the Real Beings and their individual identity of being and declare that these Real Beings exist in the Intellectual Realm, we do not mean merely that they remain unchangeably self-identical by their very essence as contrasted with the fluidity and instability of the sense realm*; the sense realm itself may contain the enduring. No; we mean rather that *these principles possess, as by their own virtue, the consummate fullness of being.* The Being described as the primally existent cannot be a shadow cast by Being, but must possess Being entire; and Being is entire when it holds the form and idea of intellection and of life. *In a Being, then, the existence, the intellection, the life are present as an aggregate. When a thing is a Being, it is also an Mind when it is a Mind it is a Being; intellection and Being are co-existents.*[8]

This identification of Being and Thought involves a radicalization of the tenet previously maintained by Philo, by the Middle Platonists, and the Neo-Pythagoreans according to which the *Ideas are the thoughts of God*. In fact in the Plotinian context the Ideas come to be understood *not only as the content of Thought, but they are themselves the thought* in the sense that each and every Idea is *not only is in the Mind (Nous), but is itself Mind (Nous) in a precise way.* Here is a very interesting passage:

> If, then, the Intellection is an act upon the inner content (of the Mind that content is the Form, and the Form is the Idea.
>
> What, then, is that content?
>
> A Mind and an Intellective Being, *no Idea is distinguishable from the Mind each actually being that Mind. The Mind entire is the total of the Ideas*, and each of them Ideas is the (entire) Mind in a special form. Thus, a science entire is the total of the relevant considerations each of which, again is a member of the entire science, a member not distinct in space yet having its individual efficacy in a total.
>
> This Mind therefore, is a unity while by that possession of itself it is, tranquilly, the eternal abundance.
>
> If the Mind were envisaged as preceding Being, it would at once become a principle whose expression, its intellectual Act, achieves and engenders the Beings: but, since we are compelled to think of existence as preceding that which knows it, we can but think that the very act, the intellection, is inherent to the Beings, as fire stands equipped from the beginning with fire-act; in this conception, the Beings contain the Mind as one and the same with themselves, as their own activity. But Being is itself an activity: *there is one activity, then, in both or, rather, both are one thing.*
>
> Being, therefore, and Mind are one Nature: the Beings, and the Act of that which is, and Mind thus constituted, all are one: and the resultant Intellections are the Ideas of Being and its shape and its act.
>
> It is our separating habit that sets the one order before the other: for there is a separating intellect, of another order than the true, distinct from the

Intellect, inseparable and unseparating, which is Being and the universe of things.[9]

Naturally the Mind (Nous) is also Life, it is "the perfect Living Being," "the Living Being which is purely such." It is "infinite Life."[10]

Plotinus took care[11] to emphasize that life is not necessarily linked to physical dimensions and that in us there is also a life distinct from that of a physical organism. The life of the second hypostasis is a life in the sphere of the immaterial; it is a spiritual life, outside of temporality. Moreover, Aristotle had previously characterized his immobile Movent as the highest form of life that is possible, which is the life of thought and intelligence, located exactly in the sphere of the eternal.[12]

3. The Mind (*Nous*) as the "intelligible cosmos"

In the new context of the hypostatic doctrine of Mind (Nous), the Platonic *hyperouranos* becomes the "intelligible cosmos" (νοητὸς κόσμος). The expression was coined by Philo of Alexandria who, as we have seen, had accomplished the most significant re-interpretation of the doctrine of the Ideas prior to Plotinus. In addition to this expression our philosopher drew again from Philo a series of starting-points which he develops in an original way and on the bases of his totally new conception of Mind (Nous) as a structural unity of Being and Knowledge, proceeds beyond Philo to the most daring reform of the theory of Ideas proposed by ancient thought.

Here in summary form are the essential traits of the Plotinian reform of the theory of Ideas:

(1) The chief change, previously noted, consists in a transformation of the Idea from mere *intelligible* to *intelligence*, or better, into something which is *at the same time Intelligible and intelligence in one "thinking substance"* (νοερὰ οὐσία), *in which knower and known are identical.* The ideas become "powers" or "intelligent powers" (νοεραὶ δυνάμεις), and hence alive, that is, "Minds" or "Spirits."[13] In sum, just as Ideas are *the multiplicity of the Intelligible Beings* in which Being is determined within the interior of Being itself, so they are *by that fact a multiplicity of Minds* in which Mind (Nous) is determined within itself.

(2) Closely connected to this notion is a further change of the conception of the *relationship existing between the Ideas*, between each Idea and the totality of the Ideas, and vice versa. Plato, as we have seen, had maintained the existence of a skein of relations (both positive and negative) among the various Ideas, but Plotinus goes beyond Plato in saying that *each Idea is in a certain sense all the other Ideas.* In fact, because the Mind (Nous) is a grasp not of one thing but of all things and is identified with them, it is necessary that all of its "parts" also grasp or have a knowledge of all things, because otherwise, if any part were to remain outside (have knowledge of only some things), since each and all parts are Mind (Nous), the absurdity would follow that part of Mind

(Nous) would be outside of Mind (Nous). In this sense, Plotinus says that Mind (Nous) is *One-Many*, and a *Many-One*, a *unified multiplicity* and a *multiplied unity*.

This characteristic of the Ideas, which sound paradoxical in this way, in reality is plausibly explained by keeping in mind the two essential traits of Mind (Nous) in general (of which Minds are particular moments), namely, (*a*) *immateriality* or *incorporeality* and (*b*) *infinitude* (in the sense of the inexhaustability of its power).

(*a*) Thus, insofar as they are incorporeals, Being and Mind (Nous) cannot be understood *as many*, as if they were *divided* into various Ideas like physically separated parts. Such parts are multiplied inasmuch as they occupy different places and their differences can be traced to their physical attributes. The many Ideas which constitute Being and Mind (Nous), instead, are such by way of their *Intelligible otherness* (which Plato had previously discussed in the *Sophist*):

> We are agreed that diversity within the Authentic *depends not upon spatial separation* but sheerly upon differentiation; all Being, despite this plurality, is a unity still; "Being neighbors Being"; "all holds together"; and thus the Mind (which is Being and the Beings) remains an integral, multiple by differentiation, not by spatial distinction.[14]

This "differentiation," or "otherness" (ἑτερότης), in sum, in the measure in which it is not the otherness of physical and corporeal parts but is a *purely spiritual differentiation*, enters into being (it is the otherness of Being and not in Being); but Being is a unity in such a way that in this sense the Ideas are a unified multiplicity and a multiplied unity, as we said above. Here is a very suggestive point:

> But would not this indicate that the Authentic is diverse, multiple?

> That diversity is simple still; that multiple is one; for it is a Mind which is to say a unity in variety: all Being is one; the differing being is still included in Being; the differentiation is within Being, obviously not within non-being. Being is bound up with the unity which is never apart from it; wheresoever Being appears, there appears its unity; and the unity of being is self-standing, for presence in the sensible does not abrogate independence.[15]

(*b*) The same conclusions are obtained by considering the paradoxes of the One-Many and of the All-in-All according to the parameters of the infinite. If Mind (Nous) is infinite (and it is infinite insofar as it is fecundated by the infinite power of the One, although simply refracted in the way seen above), it possesses each individual, and, vice versa, in each individual there must be all the other individuals, otherwise, in the individual Being (Mind) would be diminished and impoverished and *hence not infinite*. Here are two texts which illustrate these concepts:

The Intellectual Beings, thus, are multiple and one; *in virtue of their infinite nature their unity is a multiplicity,* many in one and one over many, *a unit-plurality.* They act as entire upon entire; even upon the partial thing they act as entire; but there is the difference that at first the partial accepts *this working only partially though the entire enters later.* [16]

The one principle reaches to the individual but none the less contains all souls and all intelligences; this, because it is at once a unity and an infinity; it holds all its content as one yet with each item distinct, though not to the point of separation. Except by thus holding all its content as one—life entire, soul entire, all intelligence—it could not be infinite; *since the individualities are not fenced off from each other, it remains still one thing.* [17]

(3) The attribute of the eternality of Mind (Nous) (and hence of the Ideas) came to assume a new meaning and rather than being understood simply as *immobile present, as static atemporality,* it was conceived dynamically in connection with perfection, and with infinitude, *i.e., with the inexhaustability of its power,* and hence in connection with the notion of "all in all." In the Mind (Nous) (which Plotinus called God) the "was" and the "will be" are in the "is" *insofar as each thing which looks to the Mind (Nous) must be always entirely contained actually in the Mind (Nous).* In sum, the future is in the "is" of the present (as is the past) *because all is in all,* because Nous (Mind) is all things, in need of nothing and is inexhaustible (infinite power):

No: all turns on the necessary completeness of Act; we cannot think anything belonging to God to be other than a whole and all and therefore in anything of God's that all must be contained; *God therefore must take in the future, present beforehand. Certainly there is no later in the divine; what is There as present is future for elsewhere. If then the future is present,* it must be present as having been fore-conceived for later coming to be; at that divine stage therefore it lacks nothing and therefore can never lack; all existed, eternally and in such a way that at the later stage any particular thing may be said to exist for this or that purpose; the All, in its extension and so to speak unfolding, is able to present succession, but while it is bound up together, it is a single total fact: in other words, it contains its cause (as well as everything else) within itself. [18]

(4) Plato, as you will remember, had introduced the Ideas as the "true causes," as the "reason" and the "why" of sensible things, but he had a great deal of difficulty explaining in what sense they are the cause of things. Plotinus discusses this issue, with new results. In sensible things the *what* (i.e., the being of things) and the *why* (i.e., the reason of the being of things) generally do not coincide; the *why* is always further, compared to the factual being of things. Vice versa, in the world of Mind (Nous) the *what* and the *why* coincide. And this is true not only for the Mind (Nous) in its wholeness, but also for each of the beings which are in Him, that is, for each Idea. In every Idea, thus as in the Mind (Nous), the "what" is coincident with the "why," since the Mind (Nous) is "the all in all" (the Mind (Nous) is each single being contained in it). [19] In

sum: the Ideas (as Mind [Nous] in general) do not *have* but *are* the cause of their being, and therefore *on this ground are the cause of all the rest.*

(5) In the measure in which the Mind (Nous) includes in itself all things, there are *Ideas of all things*, and not only of the species, but likewise of all the possible differences in which the species can appear. There is not, hence, a single Idea of man, but as many Ideas of man as *there are different appearances of men, as many as there are "individual differences."* The same is likewise true for animals and for all other things.

Plotinus is forced by his purely negative conception of matter (which is non-being) to this position which differs from Plato's conclusion. In fact, this conception prevented him from attributing to matter any capacity of "individuating" the species and to determine the different individual appearances in which the species are manifest in multiple individuals (as, for example, the man with an aquiline nose, snub-nose, etc.). For Plotinus, only ugliness and privations (as for example, to be crippled, cross-eyed, and the various disabilities are derived) and everything that can be considered an inadequacy in the empirical realization of the Idea are derived from matter.

Some scholars have concluded, consequently, that Plotinus admitted the existence of Ideas of *all individual things*, namely, the Ideas of each individual. But this is not really correct, or, at least, it is very misleading, since Plotinus *lacked a exact concept of the individual as an unrepeatable singularity.* In fact, on the one hand, for Plotinus, the world has a cyclical history in which the various cosmic periods occur during each of which the same things return again in such a way that the same model is repeated many times; therefore that very particular type of man or animal which, for example, in a given cycle is produced only once with these very particular differences, in each case is repeated more times in the succession of the cycles. On the other hand, with respect to the individual man the issue is made even more complex by reason of the Plotinian doctrine of metempsychosis. In fact, in the context of this doctrine the soul of Socrates *is not always Socrates* because it is reborn in other times and circumstances; in this sense, there cannot be an Idea of Socrates. Here is the most explicit text on this point:

> We have to examine the question whether there exists an ideal archetype of individuals, in other words whether I and every other human being go back to the Intellectual, every (living) thing having origin and principle There.
>
> If Socrates, Socrates' soul, is eternal, then the Authentic Socrates—to adopt the term—must be There; that is to say, the individual soul has an existence in the Supreme as well as in this world. If there is no such permanent endurance—and what was Socrates may with change of time become another soul and be Pythagoras or someone else—then the individual Socrates has not that existence in the Divine.[20]

(6) Plato, in his esoteric doctrine [the unwritten doctrines], posited ideal Numbers as principles from which the Ideas themselves are derived, and

posited as principles of the same ideal Numbers the One and the Dyad. The same doctrine, was previously revived by the Neo-Pythagoreans; we find it again also in Plotinus, in part deepened and clarified, even if not given a place of eminence. The ideal Numbers (which are quite distinct from mathematical numbers, from numbers which arise in the mind of a calculating subject, i.e., one who counts) derive from the One itself. The Dyad (in the Plotinian sense) arises from the One itself, as many Neo-Pythagoreans have also maintained. The Dyad is, of itself, unlimited and receives a limit from the One itself. The ideal Numbers arise from this delimitation of the Dyad by the One:

> Number is not primal: obviously before even duality, there must stand the unity.
>
> The Dyad is a secondary; deriving from unity, it finds in unity the determinant needed by its native indetermination: once there is any determination, there is Number, in the sense, of course, of the real (the archetypal) Number. And the soul is such a number. For the Primals are not masses or magnitudes; all of that gross order is later, real only to the sense-thought; even in seed the effective reality is not the moist substance but the unseen— that is to say—Number (as the determinant of individual being) and the Mind (of the product to be).
>
> Thus by what we call the Number and the Dyad of that higher realm, we mean Reason Mind and the Mind but while the Dyad is undetermined— representing, as it were, the underlie (or Matter) of the Intellectual World— the number which rises from the Dyad and the One is always a Form-Idea: thus the Mind is, so to speak, shaped by the Ideas rising within it ... [21]

These ideal Numbers are further characterized by Plotinus as *the power which divides Being and produces the multiplicity of Being, the rule according to which the multiplicity of beings is born from being,* and in this sense, as the *foundation and root of beings*:

> The truth is that it existed within the Authentic Being but not as applying to it, for Being was still unparted; the potentiality of Number existed and so produced the division within Being, put in travail with multiplicity; Number must be either the substance of Being or its Activity; the Life-Form as such and the Mind must be Number. [22]
>
> Next we come to Being, fully realized, and this is the seat of Number; by Number Being brings forth the Beings; its movement is planned to Number; it establishes the numbers of its offspring before bringing them to be, in the same way as it establishes its own unity by linking pure Being to the First: the numbers do not link the lower to the First; it suffices that Being is so linked; for Being, in taking form as Number, binds its members to itself. [23]

(7) Everything which has been stated above (and especially the principle according to which Mind (Nous) or Being is One and Many, many Ideas, together harmoniously, unity in variety, simplicity in difference, all in all) explains the reason why Plotinus denominates Mind (Nous) with a Philonian expression as the "intelligible cosmos" (νοητὸς κόσμος), a world of order and

of spiritual harmony, hence a world of *beauty*.[24] In fact, for Plotinus, beauty in general is identical with form: a thing is beautiful insofar as it possesses a form. The Mind (Nous), which is the world of the Forms and of the Ideas, that is to say, the system completely ordered of the Forms in their totality (a totality in which each single Form is all the others and in which all are unified, although being diverse), is the supreme Beauty.[25]

4. The categories of the Intelligible world

We said above that the distinction made between the corporeal world and the incorporeal world is one of the cornerstones of the Plotinian system. In fact, Plotinus, forcing to extreme consequences the conclusions which arise from such distinctions, affirms that *the Aristotelian system of the categories is not valid for the incorporeal*, and establishes, consequently, completely different categorical systems for the two spheres of reality.

Since the One is absolutely simple, any categorical system would not be applicable to Him. The One is a trans-categorical Mind The categories of the incorporeal are applicable to the other two hypostases and especially to Mind (Nous).

These categories, taken by Plotinus from the *Sophist* of Plato, with the appropriate reforms which are derived from the base of his new metaphysics, are: (*a*) *being* or *ousia*, (*b*) *stability* or *stasis*, (*c*) *movement*, (*d*) *identity*, and (*e*) *diversity*.

Everything in the world of Mind (Nous) is *ousia*. In addition, the cognitive acts of Mind (Nous) imply *movement* (obviously it is a spiritual, not a physical, movement). But the cognitive acts of Mind (Nous) likewise imply *stability* and *stasis*, owing to their contents. Nous (Mind), in addition, is *identical* with itself and of itself, thus there is in it a *distinction* between knower and known.

These categorical distinctions in the world of Mind (Nous) were obviously conceived in the dynamic of the One-Many and of the All-in-All, as Plotinus expressly noted.[26]

The doctrine of the categories, although diffusely treated, does not play a primary role in the Plotinian system. But keep in mind that to have expressly established that there are diverse spheres of being which postulate categorical systems formally distinct constitutes a substantial achievement in the history of metaphysics.

III. The Third Hypostasis: the Soul

1. The procession of the Soul from the Mind (Nous) and the two-fold relation which occurs between Soul and Mind (Nous)

The Mind (Nous), as we have seen, is an *infinite inexhaustible power*, and precisely because it is such it "overflows," as it were, and generates another reality, hierarchically inferior, which is the Soul. How does the "procession" of the Soul from the Mind (Nous) occur?

Plotinus began again with the same models which he used *in order to explain the procession of the Mind (Nous) from the One*. He distinguishes, in fact (analogously to what we have seen apropos of the One), (*a*) an activity *of* the Mind, meaning an activity which the Mind (Nous) addresses to itself and (*b*) an activity *from* the Mind, meaning an activity which comes from the Mind (Nous) and exists outside of Him. The second activity derives from the first and is, in fact, a consequence of the first, insofar as it is precisely in function of its return to itself that the Mind (Nous) produces something which is other than itself. Here is one of the most significant texts in this regard:

> In the Mind the Being is an Act and in the absence of any other object it must be self-directed; by this self-intellection it holds its Act within itself and upon itself; all that can emanate from it is produced by this self-centering and self-intention; first self-gathered, it then gives itself or gives something in its likeness; fire must first be self-centered and be fire, true to fire's natural Act; then it may reproduce itself elsewhere. [1]

Here is a no less important text:

> Soul too is a part of a part, though in the sense of being an Act (actuality) derived from it. When the Act of Mind is directed upon itself, the result is the manifold (particular) minds; when it looks outwards, Soul is produced. [2]

All this, however, is still not sufficient. The result of the activity which proceeds from the Mind (Nous) is certainly not *immediately* the Soul. *It is necessary*, as we have already seen in regard to Mind in relation to the One, *that even the product of the activity which proceeds from Mind returns to look at and contemplate Mind (Nous) itself*: the Soul, in fact, as produced by the activity of the Mind, in relation to the Mind (Nous) towards that which it is turned in contemplation, is as "matter" with respect to form or, as Plotinus also says, as the "indeterminate" with respect to formal determination. Here are some texts which are helpful in this regard:

> Soul, for all the worth we have shown to belong to it, is yet a secondary, an image of the Mind reason uttered is an image of the reason stored within the Soul, and in the same way Soul is an utterance of the Mind it is even the total of its activity, the entire stream of life sent forth by that Mind to the production of further being; it is the forthgoing heat of a fire which has also

heat essentially inherent. But within the Supreme we must see energy not as an overflow but in the double aspect of integral inherence with the establishment of a new being. Sprung, in other words, from the Mind soul is intellective, but with an intellection operating by the method of reasonings: for its perfecting it must look to that Divine Mind, which may be thought of as a father watching over the development of his child born imperfect in comparison with himself.

Thus its substantial existence comes from the Mind and the Reason within it becomes Act in virtue of its contemplation of that prior; for its thought and act are its own intimate possession when it looks to the Supreme Intelligence; those only are Soul-acts which are of this intellective nature and are determined by its own character; all that is noble is foreign (traceable to Matter) and is accidental to the Soul in the course of its peculiar task.

In two ways, then, the Mind enhances the divine quality of the Soul, as father and as immanent presence; nothing separates them but the fact that they are not one and the same, that there is succession, that over against a recipient there stands the Ideal-Form received; but this recipient, Matter to the Supreme Mind, is also noble as being at once informed by divine Mind and uncompounded.³

We have the example of the Soul itself in its relation to the Mind and to the Divine Reason, taking shape by these and led so to a nobler principle of form.⁴

...the Soul, for example, being an utterance and act of the Intellectual is Mind as that is an utterance of the One. But in Soul the Utterance is obscure, for Soul is an image and must look to its own original: that Mind on it must the contrary, looks to the First without mediation—thus becoming what it is—and has that vision not as from a distance but as the immediate next with nothing intervening close to the One as Soul to it.⁵

But there is more. By turning around to Mind (Nous) and contemplating it, Soul, precisely "through the Mind" itself, "sees the Good," the One, and becomes "full of goodness" and enters "into possession of the Good itself."⁶ In the ultimate analysis, it is precisely in this union with the One through Mind (Nous) that the supreme foundation of the reality of the Soul consists. Plotinus writes:

But since the beauty and light in all come from That which is before all, it is Thence that Mind took the brilliance of the Intellectual Energy which flashed its nature into being; Thence Soul took power towards life, in virtue of that fuller life streaming into it.⁷

This linking up of Soul to the One, as we will see, constitutes one of the hinges of the entire Plotinian system, that is to say, the foundation, in addition to its creative activity, of the possibility of the "return to the One."

2. The essential characteristic and the fundamental role of the Soul in the Plotinian system

But what is the specific characteristic of the Soul and its reason for being and how is it differentiated from the Mind (Nous), of which nevertheless it is the "image" and "simulacrum"?

The essential characteristic of Mind (Nous) consists in knowing (and it is for this reason—let us remember—that Plotinus choose the term Mind (Noûs), which means Mind and Thought), whence its duality (given that thought is always thought about Being) and also its multiplicity (given that Being is a multiplicity of Ideas). Duality and multiplicity, for the reasons seen, coincide with unity (the Mind [Nous] is essentially One-many). The One, says Plotinus, if He wishes to know must become Mind (Nous),[8] given that the One as such—for the reasons explained above—cannot know. But the soul also does know at least in the measure in which it looks to and contemplates the principle which has generated it, that is to say, the Mind (Nous); but its essence consists not in knowing (because, likewise, it would not be distinguished from the Mind [Nous]) *but in producing and in the giving of life to all the other things which are (i.e., all sensible things), in ordering them, and in governing them.* Here is an unusually explicit text:

> No doubt the task of the Soul, in its more emphatically reasoning phase, is intellection: but it must have another as well, or *it would be undistinguishable from the Mind To its quality of being intellective it adds the quality by which it attains its particular manner of being:* it ceases to be an Mind and has thenceforth its own task, as everything must that exists in the Intellectual Realm.
>
> It looks towards its higher and has *intellection, towards itself and orders, administers, governs* its lower.
>
> The total of things could not have remained stationary in the Intellectual Cosmos, once there was the possibility of continuous variety, of beings inferior but as necessarily existent as their superiors.[9]

Now consider that Soul's "looking to" the things which come after it, this "ordering," "ruling," and "commanding" is identical with its producing, generating, and vivifying of these very things. The Soul, as we have previously pointed out, is the first born productive cause, the creative and vivifying principle of all things.[10] Here are some of the numerous affirmations of Plotinus in this regard:

> Soul, then, in the same way, is intent upon a task of its own; in everything it does it counts as an independent source of motion ...[11]
>
> Let every Soul recall, then, at the outset the truth that Soul is the author of all living things, that it has breathed the life into them all, whatever is nourished by earth and sea, all the creatures of the air, the divine stars in the sky; it is the maker of the sun; itself formed and ordered this vast heaven and conducts all that rhythmic motion: and it is a principle distinct from all

these to which it gives law and movement and life, and it must of necessity
be more honorable than they, for they gather or dissolve as Soul brings them
life or abandons them, but Soul, since it never can abandon itself, is of
eternal being.[12]

The Soul is consequently not only a principle of movement, but it itself is
movement:

> This second outflow is an image or representation of the Divine Mind as the
> Divine Mind represented its own prior, The One.
>
> This active power sprung from essence (from the Mind [Nous] considered
> as Being) is Soul.
>
> Soul arises out of the motionless Mind (Nous)—which itself sprang from its
> own motionless prior—*but the Soul's operation is not similarly motionless;
> its image is generated from its movement.* It takes fullness by looking to its
> source; but it generates its image by adopting another, a downward, move-
> ment.
>
> This image of Soul is Sense and Nature, the vegetal principle.[13]

In conclusion, we may say that as the One had to become Mind in order
to know, *in the same way He had to become Soul in order to generate all the
things of the visible world.* Soul constitutes the extreme moment of the process
of expansion of the infinite power of the One, the cosmogonic hypostasis
which is identical with the moment when, as last self-gifting, the incorporeal
generates the corporeal, revealing himself in the sensible dimension.

It must not be overlooked that the hypostases following the One *are*, on
the one hand, *the One Himself*, as long as He is the source and power of all
and, on the other hand, *they are not the One*, but are differentiations of the
power of the One in which the rising new does not destroy the old, but flows
from the very persisting of the old:

> All in that region [of the Mind (Nous) and of the Soul] is *the One and not
> the One*-nothing else because deriving thence, *yet not that because the One
> in giving it forth is not merged into it.*
>
> There exists, thus, a life, as it were, of huge extension, a total in which each
> several part differs from its next, all making a self-continuous whole under
> a law of discrimination by which the various forms of things arise with no
> effacement of any prior in its secondary.[14]

3. The Soul and its intermediate position

From what has been said above, the significance of the "intermediate
position" which Plotinus assigns to the Soul is clear. She is "the final goddess,"[15] the ultimate intelligible reality, and consequently she is the reality
which borders on the sensible and she is, in fact, the cause itself which produces
the sensible:

> The Kind, then, with which we are dealing is twofold, the Intellectual against
> the sensible: better for the Soul to dwell in the Intellectual but, given its

proper nature, it is under compulsion to participate in the sense-realm also. There is no grievance in its not being, through and through, the highest; *it holds mid-rank among the authentic existences, being of divine station but at the lowest extreme of the Intellectual and skirting the sense-known nature; thus, while it communicates to this realm something of its own store, it absorbs in turn whenever—....*[16]

The Soul is, so to speak, "two-faced," [17] [a Janus] aimed in one direction as well as in another.

This does not mean that the nature of the Soul is in some way a mixture of the incorporeal and corporeal. Plotinus, in fact, makes every effort to reject any conception which in any way places the nature of the Soul on par with the nature of the corporeal. Not only, in fact, does he reject the extreme conception of the Stoa, but the Pythagorean conception of the Soul as a harmony as well and even the Aristotelian conception of the Soul as an *entelechy*. He maintains the purely immaterial Spiritual and eidetic character and therefore, the *transcendent* being of the Soul. The Soul has an intermediate position and hence has "two faces" because in generating the corporeal, although it continues to be and to perdure as an incorporeal reality and hence continues to enjoy all the prerogatives of the incorporeal, *"it happens" to have relations with the corporeal that it produced and consequently "it happens" to have some characteristics of the corporeal, but not in precisely the way in which these characteristics inhere in the corporeal itself.*

Let us explain this rather important point from another perspective. The Soul, by producing the sensible and entering into relations with the sensible (we will see in what way this is to be understood), even if it is not originally and primarily divisible, "it becomes divided into bodies." When bodies are divided, it *happens* that the Soul which is in them is also divided, not in the manner in which bodies are divided, but by remaining "in its entirety in each of the parts." [18] The division of the Soul, in sum, does not mean its breaking up into separate parts as occurs in bodies, but its being in its wholeness in all the parts of the divided bodies, since the Soul does not have magnitude. Therefore, divisibility remains a characteristic specific to bodies, while the Soul has *the capacity to enter totally into all its parts.* Plotinus writes:

> To have penetrated this idea is to know the greatness of the Soul and its power, the divinity and wonder of its being, as a nature transcending the sphere of Things.

> Itself devoid of mass, it is present to all mass: it exists here and yet is there, and this not in distinct phases but with unsundered identify: thus it is "parted and not parted," or better, it has never known partition, never become a parted thing, but remains a self-gathered integral, and is "parted among bodies" merely in the sense that bodies, in virtue of their own sundered existence, cannot receive it unless in some partitive mode; the partition, in other words, is an occurrence in body, not in Soul. [19]

In this sense, the Soul can be said to be *divisible and indivisible, a One-and-a-many*, insofar as it is the Mind which produces, rules, and governs the sensible world: with its multiple unity and divisibility it lavishes life on all things, with its indivisible unity it reunites and governs them. The Soul is wholly and everywhere identical. The Soul is thus, One-and-many, a unity-and-plurality; while the First Mind is exclusively One, the Mind (Nous) is One-many, and bodies are exclusively many.

4. The multiplicity of the Soul

The question of the unity and multiplicity proper to the Soul that we have been discussing actually is even more complicated if we begin from another viewpoint. Plotinus, in fact, speaks of the multiplicity of the Soul not only, so to speak in the horizontal sense, but likewise in a vertical sense, meaning *in a hierarchical sense*. Our philosopher admits in short a true and proper hierarchical gradation within the sphere of the *psyché*. The characteristic of One-many which we have seen to be proper to Mind (Nous) differs, therefore, also in this sense from the characteristics of One-and-many proper to the Soul. In the Mind (Nous), every Idea is wholly Nous (and vice versa), because if it were not so Nous (Mind) would be diminished and impoverished in each Idea. Therefore, *in the sphere of Being and Nous (Mind) there is no hierarchy, while in the sphere of the Soul a hierarchical multiplicity is also present.*

Scholars are hardly in agreement in specifying this hierarchy of Souls, given the extreme flexibility and variety of the Plotinian expressions in this regard. Nevertheless, despite this polyvalence of the expressions used in the *Enneads* about the Soul, which borders many times on pure equivocity, it still seems that by the hierarchy of Souls, or better, in the sphere of Soul, Plotinus is referring to the following. (*a*) First there is the *supreme Soul, universal Soul*, Soul in its entirety and purity: this Soul is considered as a pure hypostasis of the intelligible world, in close union with the Mind (Nous) from which it proceeds outside of its relations with the sensible world. (*b*) There is then the *Soul of the totality*, which is the Soul of the world and the sensible universe which places, rules, and governs the universe itself. The Soul of the universe comes thus to have a precise relationship with the corporeal, but does not "descend" into the corporeal; it puts on the corporeal while remaining above it, says Plotinus, or better, it has a body which *is attached to it by being illuminated by it* while it remains up above without being in any way affected by body. (*c*) There are, finally, particular Souls which do not create but animate and govern individual bodies, that is, the Souls of the stars and Souls of human beings and of particular living things which (especially those of humans and terrestrial beings) "descend" into bodies and hence they have closer relations with bodies than even the Soul of the universe. All the other Souls are derived from the first Soul, both those of the universe and of the individual Souls. The latter are hence of the same nature as the former and are differentiated, as we said, *through greater or lesser proximity to bodies or,* to speak in terms which we will fully explain, *through greater or lesser levels of contemplation* (the attachment to the body and the descent into the body on the part of the Soul becomes greater insofar as the contemplation of the Mind (Nous) grows weaker). Here is a particularly significant text which summarizes it all:

> Thus the gist of the matter is established: one Soul the source of all; the many founded in that one, on the analogy of the Mind those many are at once divided and undivided; that Soul which abides in the Supreme is the one expression or Logos of the Mind and from it spring other Mind partial but immaterial, exactly as in the differentiation of the Supreme.

> But how comes it that while the All-Soul has produced a cosmos, the Soul of the particular has not, though it is of the one ideal Kind and contains, it too, all things in itself?

> We have indicated that a thing may enter and dwell at the same time in various places; this ought to be explained, and the inquiry would show how an identity resident simultaneously here and there may, in its separate appearances, act or react—or both—after distinct modes; but the matter deserves to be examined in a special discussion.

> To return, then: how and why has the All-Soul produced a Cosmos, while the particular Souls simply administer some one part of it?

> In the first place, we are not surprised when men of identical knowledge differ greatly in effective power.

> But the reason, we will be asked.

> The answer might be that there is a similar difference of degree among Souls, *the one never having fallen away from the All-Soul, but dwelling within it and assuming body therein, while the others received their allotted spheres when the body was already in existence,* when their sister Soul was already in rule and, as it were, had already prepared habitations for them. Again, the reason may be that the *One (the creative All-Soul) looks towards the universal Mind (the exemplar of all that can be) while the others are more occupied with the Intellectual within themselves, that which is already of the sphere of their part*; perhaps, too, these also could have created, but that they were anticipated by that originator—the work accomplished before them—an impediment inevitable whichsoever of the Souls were first to operate.

> But it is safer to account for the creative act *by nearer connection with the over-world; the souls whose tendency is exercised within the Supreme have the greater power; immune in that pure seat they create securely*; for the greater power takes the least hurt from the material within which it operates; and *the power of these souls derives from their remaining enduringly attached to the over-world*: it creates, therefore, self-gathered and the created things gather round it; the other Souls, on the contrary, *themselves go forth*; that can mean only that they have deserted towards the abyss; a main phase in them is drawn downward and pulls them with it in the desire towards the lower.[20]

It is hardly necessary to note that the multiplicity of Souls is not contrasted entirely with their unity and vice versa when considered in this hierarchical sense. Not only is the Soul One and many, but it is indivisible and divisible not only in the sense that it is present in various bodies and in various parts of them insofar as it can be "wholly everywhere," but also in the sense that *the many "particular Souls"* (both that of the universe and those of individual beings) *are present in the unique All-Soul in act, distinct without being separate.*

Here is a more explicit text:

> Now as in Soul unity does not debar variety, so with Being and the Beings; in that order multiplicity does not conflict with unity. Multiplicity. This is not due to the need of flooding the universe with life; nor is the extension of the corporeal the cause of the multiplicity of Souls; before body existed, Soul was one and many; the many Souls fore-existed in the All not potentially but each effectively; that one collective Soul is no bar to the variety; the variety does not abrogate the unity; the Souls are apart without partition, present each to all as never having been set in opposition; they are no more hedged off by boundaries than are the multiple items of knowledge in one mind; the one Soul so exists as to include all Souls; the nature of such a principle must be utterly free of boundary.[21]

5. Soul, *Physis*, and *Logos*

We must turn again later to some particular problems concerning the Soul of the universe and particular Souls, for the treatment of cosmological and anthropological problems. But in order to conclude the discussion on the Soul in general considered as a hypostasis, two concepts require clarification: that of *physis* and that of *logos*, which Plotinus relates, in a very original way, to the concept of *psyché*.[22]

We have seen that the activity of the Soul turns, so to speak, in two different directions: on the one hand it tends to contemplation of Mind (Nous), and on the other it looks to producing something other than itself and to creating the sensible world. We have seen, in addition, that of the three Souls that which properly produces the sensible world is the Soul of the universe, since the supreme Soul (or All-Soul, which is the Soul which contains all the other Souls) remains perennially in the intelligible world along with Mind (Nous), while the particular Souls find the bodies already made by the Soul of the universe and are limited to animating and ruling these bodies. Hence that two-fold activity about which we spoke is a special characteristic of the Soul of the universe. Consequently, the inferior part, the "border" or "extreme edge" of this Soul, to use the images of Plotinus, *the aspect by which this Soul produces the physical world, constitutes physis (nature).* "Nature" for Plotinus represents, therefore, the extreme edge of the world of the incorporeal and that part of the intelligible which is reflected in matter, and hence represents the extreme limit in which true beings terminate. Here is the most important passage in this respect:

But what is the difference between the Wisdom thus conducting the universe and the principle known as Nature?

This Wisdom is a first (within All-Soul) while Nature is a last: for Nature is an image of that Wisdom, and, as last in the Soul, possesses only the last reflection of the Mind we may imagine a thick waxen seal, in which the imprint has penetrated to the very uttermost film so as to show on both sides, sharp cut on the upper surface, faint on the under. Nature, thus, does not know, it merely produces: what it holds it passes, automatically, to its next; and this transmission to the corporeal and material constitutes its making power: it acts as a thing warmed communicating to what lies in next contact to it the principle of which it is the vehicle so as to make that also warm in some less degree....

Thus the Mind possesses: the Soul of the All eternally receives from it; this is the Soul's life; its consciousness is its intellection of what is thus eternally present to it; *what proceeds from it into Matter and is manifested there is Nature, with which—or even a little before it—the series of real being comes to an end, for all in this order are the ultimates of the intellectual order and the beginnings of the imitative.*

There is also the decided difference that Nature operates towards Matter, and receives from it: Soul, near to Nature but superior, operates towards Matter but without receiving in turn; and there is the still higher phase (the purely Intellectual) with no action whatever upon body or Matter. [23]

Evidently, "nature" conceived in this way is not a mere irrational productive activity, but on the contrary, it is a productive activity accompanied by reason and in fact deriving from reason. Previously, Aristotle had indicated through the notions of *form, eidos* and *logos* one of the meanings of *physis*; Plotinus carries this conception to extreme consequences: *physis is eidos* and *logos, i.e.,* "rational form," in fact it is *logos or rational form [the eidetic form] which produces other logoi, that is, other rational forms*; instead, the *eidos* [form or shape] which is included in matter is now devitalized and hence no longer capable of producing another. *Nature, in sum, is a logos which supplies rational forms to sensible matter*:

Nature is a Mind [logos or rational form] producing a second Mind its offspring, which, in turn, while itself, still, remaining intact, communicates something to the underlie, Matter.

The Mind [form or shape presiding over visible Shape] is the very ultimate in its order, a dead thing unable to produce further: that which produces in the created realm is the living Mind [logos = rational form] brother, no doubt, to that which gives mere shape, but having life-giving power. [24]

In this context it is easy to understand how Plotinus comes to attribute to *physis* itself its "contemplation." First, that *physis* derived from contemplation (of the Soul) we knew previously. *Physis* is *contemplation in itself* in the measure in which it is a living rational form, and in fact *precisely insofar as it is contemplating it is creating, in the measure in which it is a vision of forms, it is productive of forms in matter*. Also nature, as all intelligible realities, *produces by contemplating*. Here is the passage in which Plotinus, maintaining and widening the concepts presented above, caps the vision of *physis* more boldly than all of previous Greek thought:

...what we know as Nature is Soul, offspring of a yet earlier Soul of a more powerful life; that it possesses, therefore, in its repose, a vision within itself; that it has not tendency upward nor even downward but is at peace, steadfast, in its own Being; that, in this immutability accompanied by what may be called Self-Consciousness, it possesses—within the measure of its possibility—a knowledge of the realm of subsequent things perceived in virtue of that understanding and consciousness; and, achieving thus a resplendent and delicious spectacle, has no further aim.[25]

IV. The Procession of the Sensible from the Intelligible, the Meaning and the Value of the Physical Cosmos

1. The problem of the deduction of the physical world

The series of hypostases of the incorporeal and intelligible world has ended with the Soul. The corporeal, the sensible world, the physical world unfold after and below the Soul.

How and why does the physical universe exist? Why does reality not terminate in the world of the incorporeal? Why does a further world also exist? What is the destiny of the sensible? What are its formal characteristics? What is its meaning and its power?

These are the basic questions of any metaphysics; but they acquire a wholly unique importance in the context of Plotinian speculation because of the deductive character of his procedure from higher to lower. After all, it is helpful to see that these questions are closely associated with the general problem, about which we spoke at the beginning: *why did the One not remain One and why are the many also derived from the One?*

These questions virtually constitute the formulation of the most delicate and, in a certain sense, the most dramatic aspect of that general problem: how and why from the *incorporeal One* is there, in addition to the *incorporeal multiple, likewise the corporeal multiple?*

The replies which Plotinus gives to these questions are without doubt among the most productive of difficulties which can be read in the *Enneads*, but are, at the same time, *among the most interesting which have been given to us in the history of Western philosophy,* and for this reason we must try to clarify them insofar as we are able.

Let us begin from an examination of the specific trait which distinguishes the incorporeal from the corporeal world, from *sensible matter.*

2. The procession of the matter of the sensible world and its characteristics

We have now said that the characteristic element of the corporeal world is *sensible* matter; but attention is to be focused on the adjective and not on the substantive. In fact, as we well know, "matter" exists also in the incorporeal world, but it is a purely *intelligible* matter. We have seen, indeed, that the activity or power which derives from the One is not directly the second hypostasis, the Mind (Nous), but rather something, so to speak, indeterminate and unformed (an indeterminate and unformed thought) which is determined and becomes a noetic cosmos, or world of forms, by looking to the One Himself and being fecundated by Him; the power which derives from the One is hence like an indefinite matter which is determined only by turning to the One. We have also seen something analogous in relation to Soul.¹ The result of the activities of Mind (Nous) is not directly Soul; in order to be Soul she must turn toward Mind (Nous), in comparison with which she is like matter with respect to form, the indeterminate in relation to the determinate.

But intelligible matter has the characteristics proper to the intelligible itself, simplicity, immutability, and eternality, while *that of the sensible reveals opposite characteristics.*

Why does this happen? A preliminary response is given by Plotinus using the notions of "exemplar" and "image" (model and copy).

The characteristics of each type of matter are to be *indefinite, indeterminate,* and *unlimited.*

Sensible matter is an *image of the intelligible one*, and insofar as it is an image or copy its distance from the being of the original grows and it is therefore more indeterminate and hence consigned to the negative and to evil:

> The Matter even of the Intellectual Realm is the Indefinite (the undelimited); it must be a thing generated by the undefined nature, the illimitable nature, of the Eternal Being, The One—an illimitableness, however, not possessing native existence There (not inherent) but engendered by The One.
> But how can Matter be common to both spheres, be here and be There?
> *Because even Indefiniteness has two phases.*
> But what difference can there be between phase and phase of Indefiniteness?
> The difference of archetype and image.
> So that Matter here (as only an image of Indefiniteness) would be less indefinite?
> On the contrary, more indefinite as an Image-thing remote from true being. Indefiniteness is the greater in the less ordered object; the less deep in good, the deeper in evil. The Indeterminate in the Intellectual Realm, where there is truer being, might almost be called merely an Image of Indefiniteness: in this lower Sphere where there is less Being, where there is a refusal of the Authentic, and an adoption of the Image-Kind, Indefiniteness is more authentically indefinite.²

But this is not yet sufficient to explain the radical metaphysical difference between intelligible matter (model) and sensible matter (image and simulacrum of it). Since in the intelligible world, each hypostasis is also a copy or simulacrum of the preceding one, nevertheless it maintains the same nature as the preceding one, insofar as it derives from it. Also, matter derives from a cause preceding it, and hence from the intelligible, thus *it is not something which is eternally opposed to the intelligible* (as in Plato). The solution to our problem, then, moves us to look into the *"way"* in which the hypostasis derives from the preceding hypostasis and into *"why"* it is not more successful in constituting a further hypostasis: only then will the reasons, as with the origin of sensible matter, be comprehended, why its being is dispersed in coming to be. First, that matter is also deduced by Plotinus from prior causes is clear from more than one text. Here, for example, is an explicit one. After having said that each reality (each hypostasis) brings in itself the impulse to always create something right up to the limits of possibility, and that each thing participates in the Good in the measure in which it is capable, Plotinus writes:

> If, therefore, Matter has always existed, *that existence is enough to ensure its participation in the being which, according to each receptivity, communicates the supreme Good universally: if, on the contrary, Matter has come into being as a necessary sequence of the causes preceding it,* that origin would similarly prevent it standing apart from the scheme as though it were out of reach of the principle to whose grace it owes its existence.[3]

Sensible matter derives from its cause as ultimate possibility, as the extreme stage of that process in which the impulse to create and the power of producing *are weakened* to the point of complete exhaustion. Sensible matter becomes thus the total emptying and hence the *extreme privation of the power of the One and therefore of the One itself, or, in other words, the privation of the Good* (which identical with the One). *In this sense, it becomes evil* (note that evil is understood not as a negative force opposed to a positive one, *but as the absence and privation of the positive!*). And here is how Plotinus accomplishes the deduction of matter by using these concepts:

> There is another consideration establishing the necessary existence of Evil. Given that The Good is not the only existent thing, it is inevitable that, by the outgoing from it or, if the phrase be preferred, the continuous down-going or away-going from it, there should be produced a Last, *something after which nothing more can be produced*: this will be Evil.
> As necessarily as there is Something after the First, *so necessarily there is a Last: this Last is Matter*, the thing which has no residue of good in it: here is the necessity of Evil.[4]

It is easy to understand, therefore, how Plotinus was able to define sensible matter as *non-being*; this expression does not at all mean nothing, the non-existent, but rather, as he expressly notes, it means "the other (= the different) than being]."[5] In fact, given that intelligible matter is being (ὄν) sensible matter to be distinguished from intelligible matter must necessarily be *different* (ἕτερον) from being (it must not be that being which is characteristic of intelligible matter):

> But the matter [= intelligible matter] There is something real (ὄν), for that which is before it is beyond being (ἐπκενα ὄντος). Here, however, that which is before matter is real, and so matter itself is not real (οὐ ὄν); it is something other (ἕτερον ὄν), over and above the excellence of real being.[6]

Matter, in sum, does not belong to the spheres of Being, of Mind (Nous), of Soul, and in general of the intelligible. For this reason Plotinus must turn chiefly to images in order to characterize it, as for example in the following passage, which is among the most significant ones:

Matter is not Soul; it is not Intellect, it is not Life, is no Mind, it is no limit or bound, for it is mere indetermination; it is not a power, for what does it produce?

It lives on the farther side of all these categories and so has no title to the name of Being. It will be more plausibly called a non-being, and this not in the sense that movement and station are Not-Being (i.e., as merely different from Being) but in the sense of veritable Not-Being, so that it is no more than the image and phantasm of Mass, a bare aspiration towards substantial existence; it is stationary but not in the sense of having position, it is in itself invisible, eluding all effort to observe it, present where no one can look, unseen for all our gazing, ceaselessly presenting contraries in the things based upon it, it is large and small, more and less, deficient and excessive; a phantasm unabiding and yet unable to withdraw—not even strong enough to withdraw, *so utterly has it failed to accept strength from the Intellectual Mind so absolute its lack of all Being.*

Its every utterance, therefore, is a lie; it pretends to be great and it is little, to be more and it is less; *and the Being with which it masks itself is no Being but a passing trick making trickery of all that seems to be present in it, phantasms within a phantasm; it is like a mirror showing things as in itself when they are really elsewhere,* filled in appearance but actually empty, containing nothing, pretending everything. Into it and out of it move mimicries of the Authentic Being images playing upon an image devoid of Form, visible against it by its very formlessness; they seem to modify it but in reality effect nothing, for they are ghostly and feeble, have no thrust and meet none in Matter either; they pass through it leaving no cleavage, as through water; or they might be compared to shapes projected so as to make some appearance upon what we can know only as the Void.[7]

Plotinus tries to determine the reason for this absence of any metaphysical heft proper to matter. It is produced by the Soul, not by the supreme Soul, which is entirely fixed in contemplation, but at the extreme edge of the Soul of the universe, in which contemplation has grown weak, in the measure at least in which Soul turns more to itself than to Mind (Nous). Here are two more significant passages:

The particular Soul is illuminated by moving towards the Soul above it; for on that path it meets Authentic Being.

Movement towards the lower is towards non-Being: and this is the step it takes when it is set on self; *for by willing towards itself it produces its lower, an image of itself—a non-Being—and so is wandering, as it were, into the void, stripping itself of its own determined form.*

And this image, this undetermined thing, is blank darkness, for it is utterly without reason, untouched by the Mind far removed from Authentic Being. As long as it remains at the mid-stage it is in its own peculiar region; but when, by a sort of inferior orientation, it looks downward, it shapes that lower-image and flings itself joyfully thither.[8]

The true doctrine may be stated as follows.

In the absence of body, Soul could not have gone forth, since there is no other place to which its nature would allow it to descend. Since go forth it must, it will generate a place for itself; at once body, also, exists.

While the Soul (as an eternal, a Divine Being) is at rest—in rest firmly based on Repose, the Absolute—yet, as we may put it, that huge illumination of the Supreme pouring outwards comes at last to the extreme borne of its light and dwindles to darkness [this is matter]; this darkness now lying there beneath, the Soul sees and by seeing brings to shape [that is, as we will see, transformed it into a body endowed with form in a physical cosmos]; for in the law of things this ultimate depth, neighboring with Soul, may not go void of whatsoever degree of that Mind it can absorb, the dimmed reason of reality at its faintest.[9]

Finally, Plotinus tries to further clarify the reason for the different nature of matter with respect to the realities which preceded it with his typical concept of contemplation.

The superior Soul contemplates, and from this contemplation arises the creative power of the cosmic Soul.

Consequently, this creative power in reality is only *a weakened form of contemplation*: a contemplation which is the same as that of the higher Soul, but gradually dissipating in intensity, such that, "in that dissipation it goes almost to evanescence."[10]

And thus matter, produced by this activity which is a relaxed contemplation, no longer has the power to turn toward the One who generated it and to contemplate in its turn, so that it is up to the Soul itself to support it, so to say, and hence to order it, inform it, keep it in some way hanging on to being. And thus the sensible cosmos arises as we will see in further detail.

3. The forms and rational design of the world, their origin, and their relations with matter

The sensible world is constituted in its totality as well as in its parts, of matter and form. But, while differing from intelligible matter which is a power or potency perennially trying to gain its form and which perpetually and factually possesses it and is acted on by it, sensible matter *is not a positive capacity to receive form, but only the inert possibility of reflecting it, without being basically truly in-formed and vivified by it*. In sum, sensible matter is incapable of constituting a true unity with form.[11]

For this reason one cannot say that the form truly enters into matter, but only enters "in a deceptive way," superficially and almost as an appearance like an object which is reflected in a mirror:

But, at least, in a true entry [the forms into matter]?

No: how could there be a true entry into that which, by being falsity, is banned from ever touching truth?

> Is this then a pseudo-entry into a pseudo-entity something merely brought near, *as faces enter the mirror, there to remain just as long as the people look into it*?

> Yes: if we eliminated the Authentic Existents from this Sphere, nothing of all now seen in sense would appear one moment longer.

> Here the mirror itself is seen, for it is itself an Ideal-Form of a kind (has some degree of Real Being); but bare Matter, which is no Idea, is not a visible thing; if it were, it would have been visible in its own character before anything else appeared upon it. The condition of Matter may be illustrated by that of air penetrated by light and remaining, even so, unseen because it is invisible whatever happens.[12]

What we have said up to now permits us to understand thoroughly the twofold activity with which the Soul creates the physical world.

(*a*) At first it posits the matter, which is like the extreme edge of a circle of light which at that point becomes obscured, (*b*) next it gives form to this matter, almost piercing the darkness and illuminating it.

Naturally, the two operations are not chronologically distinct, but only logically so.[13] The first action of the Soul derives from the extreme weakening of "contemplation," the second from the ultimate recovery, so to speak, of contemplation.

We have thereby indicated the origin of the form which reverberates in the sensible world: it is what of Mind (Nous) passes through the highest contemplating Soul to the creating Soul.

In other words: the Ideas which constitute, as we know, Being and Mind (Nous) are contemplated and thought by the Soul as Forms and then descend into the physical world as rational determinations, as *logoi* or the rational design of the world, as Plotinus says with the terminology taken from the Stoa, but which he transforms in its conceptual content in a Platonic sense. Here is an important text:

> These considerations oblige us to state the Logos (the Mind of the Universe) once again, and more clearly, and to justify its nature.

> This Mind then—let us dare the definition in the hope of conveying the truth—this Logos is not the Mind unmingled, not the Absolute Divine Mind; nor does it descend from the pure Soul alone; it is a dependent of that Soul while, in a sense, it is a radiation from both those divine Hypostases: the Mind and the Soul—the Soul as conditioned by the Mind this Logos which is a Life holding restfully a certain measure of Reason.[14]

And here is a second text no less explicit. After having underlined that all things are composed of matter and form which is sovereign over it, Plotinus asks "whence this forming Idea comes" and replies:

> ...you will ask whether in the Soul we recognize a simple or whether this also has constituents, something representing Matter and something else

representing Form, namely, the Mind within it, this corresponding both to the shape on the statue and to the artist giving the shape.

Applying the same method to the total of things, here too we discover the Mind and this we set down as veritably the maker and creator of the All. The underlie has adopted, we see, certain shapes by which it becomes fire, water, air, earth; *and these shapes have been imposed upon it by something else. This other is* Soul which, hovering over the Four (the elements), imparts the pattern of the Cosmos, the Ideas for which it has itself received from the Mind as the Soul or mind of the craftsman draws upon his craft for the plan of his work.

The Mind is in one phase the Form of the Soul, its shape; in another phase it is the giver of the shape—the sculptor, possessing inherently what is given—imparting to Soul nearly the authentic reality while what body receives is but image and imitation.[15]

The conclusion which Plotinus arrives at can be understood in this sense: in the sensible universe not only does form have clear domination but, as far as it is able, the cosmos is reduced almost entirely to form:

From the beginning to end all is gripped by the Forms of the Intellectual Realm: Matter itself is held by the Forms of the elements and to these Forms are added other Forms and others again, so that it is hard to work down to crude Matter beneath all that sheathing of Form. Indeed since Matter itself is, in its degree, a Form—the lowest—all this universe is Form and there is nothing that is not Ideal Form as the archetype was.[16]

4.   The origin of temporality

The passage from the intelligible world to the sensible world involves the passage from being to becoming, from eternity to temporality. How does temporality come into being?

Plotinus has also tried to give us an explicit answer to this question. Temporality results from the work of the Soul conjointly with the production of the universe. Temporality is identical with the same activity with which the Soul creates the physical world, *with that activity which produces something which is other than Mind (Nous) and Being, which are instead in the sphere of the eternal.*

Eternity, for Plotinus, is life without change, a life which is totally, entirely, and simultaneously present. The life of Mind (Nous) is life eternal precisely because it is the presence of the totality of Being, which is always, all in all.

The Soul then, through a sort of "recklessness" and a "desire to belong to itself"[17] or, to use another image of Plotinus, "through a desire to transfer into something different the vision of the above,"[18] is not satisfied in seeing the whole simultaneously. So it departs from unity, advances and spreads, so to speak, *in a prolongation and in a series of acts which succeed one another,* and it creates a sensible world which is made on the model of the intelligible, but which inevitably *turns and posits in temporal succession what of the above which was wholly possessed in a united and simultaneously way.* In this way, the Soul makes itself temporal and hence its product as well. The world is structurally in time, in the same way as it is *in* Soul and *through* Soul.

When it is said that the typical characteristic of the Soul for Plotinus is *life*, it is understood as *life in the realm of temporality different than the life of Mind (Nous) which is in the province of the eternal.* And life as temporal is life which flows in successive moments or, if you prefer, which by creating flows or by flowing creates the successive moments and which hence *is always turning to some further moments and is always charged with past moments.* With these remarkable additions, Plotinus restates the Platonic definition of time as an image of eternity:

> Would it, then, be sound to define Time as *the Life of the Soul in movement as it passes from one stage of act or experience to another?*

> Yes; for Eternity, as we have said, is Life in repose, unchanging and identical, always endlessly complete; and there is to be an image of Eternity—Time— such an image as this lower All presents of the Higher Sphere. Therefore over against that higher Life there must be another life, known by the same name as the more veritable Life of the Soul; over against that Movement of the Intellectual Soul there must be the movement of some partial phase; over against that Identity, Unchangeableness and Stability there must be that which is not constant in the one hold but puts forth multitudinous acts; over against that Oneness without extent or interval there must be an image of oneness, a unity of link and succession; over against the immediately Infinite and All-comprehending, that which tends, yes, to *infinity* but by tending to a *perpetual* futurity; over against the Whole in concentration, there must be that which is to be a whole by stages never final. The lesser must always be working towards the increase of its Being; this will be its imitation of what is *immediately complete, self-realized, endless without stage*: only thus can its Being reproduce that of the Higher.[19]

Three corollaries are worth noting about this conception of becoming.

First, becoming loses all characteristics of drama and tragedy insofar as to be born and to die is nothing other than the mobile play of the Soul which reflects its forms as in a mirror: of a play in which all is preserved, nothing perishes, because Plotinus says "nothing can be eliminated from being."[20]

Second, the universe itself, including its parts, will not perish, just as it was not born in a given moment from nothing. The genesis of the world is eternal, or better, it is from eternity (*ab eterno*) in the sense that *ab eterno* the Soul is temporalized, wishing *ab eterno* to make what it has contemplated in Mind (Nous) live in something other than it, according to the "necessary" law of the procession.[21]

Third, because it is the Soul which generates and rules the world and all its parts, and because the Soul is, through its essence, life, *all is alive,* even what does not have the appearance of it, even the earth and all the elements: in sum, "there is nothing which is not alive."[22]

5.   The origin of the corporeal and of spatiality and their nature

As time depends on the activity of Soul, so corporeality (and consequently spatiality) depends on form, on the activity of form on matter.

Matter, in fact, conceived in the way which is seen above, is neither mass nor extension and hence it is not corporeality. The body in general comes to be from the union of form and matter and is the result of *quality united to matter*. In particular, Plotinus says specifically that "corporeality" as such is form, is *logos*, is productive *seminal reason* which generates the concrete body in union with matter. This is a very interesting doctrine because it represents the extreme attempt to attribute to the *logos* and to the form some positive determination. Previously, the Stoics defined the body as qualified matter (matter plus quality), but they understood the quality as immanent to the matter, that is, in a materialistic sense, while Plotinus transposed the doctrine onto a spiritual plane in which matter is a reflection of the form.[23] The body is hence, in the ultimate analysis, a creation of form.[24]

6.   The positive character of the corporeal world

This conception of the origin and structure of the physical world could give rise, to two opposed evaluations of it.

In the measure in which it is concerned with a world which in some way has to be made with matter, which is a *privation of the Good*, or evil, it could be concluded that the world is *evil*.

Instead, in the measure in which the aspect of matter is emphasized as the shadow of the form and the derivation of the world in general by the Soul, and hence by Mind (Nous) and in the ultimate analysis by the One itself, it must be concluded that the world is *good*.

This latter position is the conclusion which, although not free from difficulties, Plotinus drew from his principles and defended strenuously against the opposed Gnostic tenets.[25]

First, the ancient Platonic intuition according to which it is not the Soul which is in the world, but the world in the Soul is carried by Plotinus to extreme limits: the Soul not only produces the cosmos, but embraces it, binds it up, and clasps it to itself:

> Imagine that a stately and varied mansion had been built; it has never been abandoned by its architect, who, yet, is not tied down to it; he has judged it worthy in all its length and breadth of all the care that can serve to its Being as far as it can share in Being or to its beauty, but a care without burden to its director, who never descends, but presides over it from above: this gives the degree in which the Cosmos is ensouled, not by a Soul belonging to it, but by one present to it; it is mastered, not master; not possessor, but

possessed. The Soul bears it up, and it lies within, no fragment of it unsharing.

The Cosmos is like a net which takes all its life, as far as ever it stretches, from being wet in the water; it is at the mercy of the sea which spreads out, taking the net with it just so far as it will go, for no mesh of it can strain beyond its set place: the Soul is of so far-reaching a nature—a thing unbounded—as to embrace the entire body of the All in the one extension; so far as the universe extends, there Soul is; and if the universe had no existence, extension would be no concern of the Soul; it is eternally what it is. The universe spreads as broad as the presence of Soul; the limit of its expansion is the point at which, in its downward egression from the Supreme, it still has Soul to bind it in one: it is a shadow as broad as the Mind proceeding from Soul; and that Mind is of scope to generate a cosmic bulk as vast as lay in the purposes of the Idea (the Divine forming power) which it conveys.[26]

It is clear, taken in this context, that the Stoic doctrines of the *universal sympathy* and of *providence* take on a new spiritual significance, with unexpected consequences.

As a result, for example, the doctrine of the Demiurge and the many questions raised by the Platonists in this respect change their meaning. The Demiurge, in a certain sense, is the Soul, because this latter is the true productive cause of the world: but the Soul produces *not only insofar as it is life and generator of life (which is its special characteristic), but insofar as it possesses in itself the forms which derive from the Ideas of Mind (Nous)*. In this sense the Demiurge is also Mind.[27] In its final form, then, it enters into the issue of the One itself if it is true that the physical cosmos must be born so that all the power of the One may be realized. But more generally, as we will see, the concept of "creative contemplation" had to transform completely the problematic of the Demiurge.[28]

The anti-Gnostic polemic only reinforced the conviction of Plotinus about the positive nature of the physical cosmos. For our philosopher anyone who judges the world *as born evil* commits a basic error of judgment, the result of an optical illusion: the world is not to be seen and not to be judged as a *model*, that is, as Mind (Nous), but as *a copy which imitates the model*. If it is judged as a copy, as an image, then it is necessary to conclude that *it is the most beautiful image of the original*.[29] Moreover, Plotinus even says that the sensible world "exists for Him and looks above."[30]

In fact, he affirms not only that the world looks to God, but that *in a certain sense the world itself is in God*, since the world is in the Soul, the Soul is *in Mind (Nous)*, Mind is in the One, and the One is not in something else but encloses everything entirely within itself.[31]

The dematerialization of the cosmos is really pushed by Plotinus to the point of being an acosmism: matter is reduced to the activity of the diminished

Soul, the body to form, the world to the mobile play of forms which move as reflections in a mirror, and finally the form is linked to Mind (Nous) and Mind to the One.[32]

V. The Origin, Nature, and Destiny of Man

1. Man prior to his descent into the corporeal world

Man is not produced at the same time as the corporeal world, but he pre-ëxists it, although in another condition, in the state of being a pure Soul.

First, Plotinus says with all requisite clarity that before our birth "we were above," in the world of Being and Mind (Nous), we were "other men," in fact "we were Gods," participants in the spiritual life of all, without the separations and the wounds which belong to terrestrial life. Here are the exact words of our philosopher:

> But we ourselves, what are We?
>
> Are we that higher or the participant newcomer, the thing of beginnings in time?
>
> Before we had our becoming Here we existed There, men other than now, some of us gods (ἄνθρωποι ἄλλοι ὄντες καὶ τινες καὶ θεοί): we were pure Souls, Intelligence inbound with the entire of reality, members of the Intellectual, not fenced off, not cut away, integral to that All. Even now, it is true, we are not put apart; but upon that *primal Man* there has intruded another, a man seeking to come into being and finding us there, for we were not outside of the universe. This other has wound himself about us, foisting himself upon the Man that each of us was at first. Then it was as if one voice sounded, one word was uttered, and from every side an ear attended and received what was present and active upon it: now we have lost that first simplicity; we are become the *dual* thing, sometimes indeed no more than later foisting, with the primal nature dormant and in a sense no longer present. [1]

In fact Plotinus states clearly that our Souls were *in the beginning associated with the universal Soul* (evidently in that condition of unity-distinction which we know is peculiar to the world of the intelligible) in governing the world as kings along with the supreme Ruler:

> So it is with the individual Souls; the appetite for the divine Mind urges them to return to their source, but they have, too, a power apt to administration in this lower sphere; they may be compared to the light attached upwards to the sun, but not grudging its bounty to what lies beneath it. *In the Intellectual, then, they remain with the All-Soul, and are immune from care and trouble; in the heavenly sphere, inseparable from the All-Soul, and are immune from care and trouble; in the heavenly sphere, inseparable from the All-Soul, they are administrators with it, just as kings, associated with the supreme ruler and governing with him, do not descend from their kingly stations*: the Souls indeed are thus far in the one place. [2]

It is hardly necessary to emphasize that in this phase the Soul knows intuitively and simultaneously the totality of the things which are in the Mind (Nous) and through the Mind (Nous), the Good itself. In this context, in the unity with Mind (Nous) and with the Good, it also has a self-awareness. [3] But why do the Souls of human beings descend into bodies?

This is an ancient problem which troubled Plato and to which he was unable to give a simple answer. He vacillated between two opposed tenets: one involving an *metaphysical necessity*, the other a *"fault."* [4] Plotinus takes up these opposed views and tries to reconcile them on the basis of the advantages given to him by his metaphysics.

Let us see how he tried to reconcile them and in addition let us attempt to establish if and up to what point he succeeded in his attempt.

2. The descent into bodies

First it is very important to keep in mind that the principal reason for the descent of individual Souls into particular bodies is sought chiefly in the same law which regulates the "procession" of all things from the One. According to this law hence the All-Soul, must articulate all its possibilities and hence must produce the universe in general not only through the Soul of the cosmos but likewise through individual Souls, all the individual living things. Among those there are human beings: and all of this happens, indeed it must happen, so that the infinite power of the One can achieve its total unfolding and so that the perfection of the whole can be guaranteed, as we have seen. In short, as the All-Soul cannot remain as pure thought, because it would not be distinct from Mind (Nous), so individual Souls cannot remain as individual Minds, but in order to distinguish themselves from pure Mind (Nous) must take on their special functions, which are ordering, ruling, and governing sensible things. [5] Consequently, it is obvious that in this way the "descent" of the Soul into bodies is not voluntary, since it does not depend on a choice nor on deliberation of the Soul itself and hence cannot constitute a "fault." In fact, Plotinus even admits that if the Soul succeeds in fleeing rapidly from the body not only is it not damaged from having taken on a body, but it is enriched, because it has contributed, to the actualization of the potentialities of the universe as well as having suffered the experience of evil (in its contact with the corporeal). This makes it acquire more clearly an awareness of the good and permits all its virtues to unfold. [6] Nevertheless, precisely while he says this Plotinus likewise affirms the doctrine that for the Soul it is "better" to live near Mind (Nous) and that its descent, although necessary, is nevertheless a "worsening" and hence an evil and a fault (a kind of "audacity," or "hubris").

Shall we return thus to the uncertainty of Plato?

Plotinus tries to solve the problem by distinguishing two different kinds of fault belonging to the Soul.

(a) The first type of fault, in general, involves *the "descent" but insofar as it is unavoidable, it is involuntary. The punishment which accompanies this involun-*

tary fault is the painful experience of the descent into the body. The "desire of being within one's competence" or the "centering within one's self," of which Plotinus speaks is identical with this involuntary fault involving the necessary descent. Souls in this "descent" come to dwell in individual or particular bodies. [7] The second kind of fault is connected instead *to the Soul which has already taken up a body and manifests itself in its excessive concern for the body with all the consequences therefrom, viz., being distant from its origin in order to put itself at the service of exterior things and hence to forget itself.* [8] It is not, therefore, the first kind of fault, but the second which is the great evil for the Soul. It is evil which makes it forget itself, its origins, and hence God (and makes it worthy of particular punishments). Here is a very clear passage:

> What can it be that has brought the Souls to forget the father, God, and though members of the Divine and entirely of that world, to ignore at once themselves and It?

> The evil that has overtaken them *has its source in self-will, in the entry into the sphere of process, and in the primal differentiation with the desire for self-ownership.* They conceived a pleasure in this freedom and *largely indulged their own motion; thus they were hurried down the wrong path, and in the end, drifting further and further, they came to lose even the thought of their origin in the Divine.* A child wrenched young from home and brought up during many years at a distance will fail in knowledge of its father and of itself: *the Souls, in the same way, no longer discern either the divinity or their own nature; ignorances of their rank bring self-depreciation; they misplace their respect, honoring everything more than themselves;* all their awe and admiration is for the alien, and, clinging to this, they have broken apart, as far as a Soul may, and they make light of what they have deserted; *their regard for the mundane and their disregard of themselves bring about their utter ignoring of the Divine.* [9]

We will see further on what are the ethical and eschatological consequences of these Plotinian affirmations. First it is necessary to examine in general what is the situation of the Soul which takes a body and what are the relations between individual Souls and individual bodies.

3. Man and the relations between Soul and body

We have so far spoken about human beings, taking for granted the equality of human beings and Soul, as indeed Plotinus does in the texts we have read. This equality was established for the first time as we know, by Socrates, [10] it was metaphysically developed by Plato, [11] and Plotinus took it to its limits. Nothing prohibits, says our philosopher, what is called "ego," or man, from being identified with the composite of body and Soul, but it is always true that a "true human being" is the Soul alone, indeed, "the separated Soul" and, as we will see, also "separable" on earth. [12]

Actually, in many more places in the *Enneads* it is stated that there are *three men* present in us, not simply an interior man and an empirical man. This view, which at first might cause surprise, becomes much less jarring, not only if understood within the parameters of Plotinus's metaphysics, but likewise if located within the Middle Platonic tradition from which the Neo-Stoic Marcus Aurelius had taken his threefold distinction within man, of *Nous, psyché*, and *body.* It is essentially this tripartition from which Plotinus begins the transformation in terms of his metaphysics and giving man, so to speak, an unusual metaphysical status, thanks to his theory of procession. Here is a paradigmatic text:

> If material things [scil., the Ideas of material things, as there are also the Ideas of elements water, fire, etc.] existed There, the Soul would perceive them; Man in the Intellectual, Man as Intellectual Soul, would be aware of the terrestrial. This is how the secondary Man, copy of Man in the Intellectual, contains the Mind in copy; and Man in the Mind contained the Man that existed before any man. The diviner shines out upon the *secondary* and the secondary upon the *tertiary*: and even the latest possesses all—not in the sense of identifying itself with them all but as standing in under-parallel to them. Some of us act by this lowest; in another rank there is a double activity, a trace of the next higher being included; in yet another there is a blending of the third (i.e. highest) grade with the others: each is that Man by which he acts while each too contains all the grades, though in some sense not so. On the separation of the third life and the third Man from the body, then if the second also departs—of course not losing hold on the Above— the two, as we are told, will occupy the same place.[13]

The tripartition (on which we insist because it is absolutely fundamental for understanding the ethics, ascetics, and the mysticism of our philosopher) is proposed again in terms of "Soul," in the sense that the "three men" can be considered as three Souls, or better, "three powers" of the Soul, since the "first man" is simply the Soul considered in its contact with the Mind (Nous) (a contact which is never lost), the "second man" is the Soul or discursive thought which is halfway between the intelligible and sensible, and the "third man" is the Soul which vivifies the terrestrial body:

> And as to our own Soul we are to hold that it stands, in part, always in the presence of the Divine Beings, while in part it is concerned with the things of this sphere and in part occupies a middle ground. It is one nature in graded powers; and sometimes the Soul in its entirety is borne along by the loftiest in itself and in the Authentic Existent; sometimes the less noble part is dragged down and drags the mid-Soul with it, though the law is that the Soul may never succumb entire.

> The Soul's disaster falls upon it when it ceases to dwell in the perfect Beauty—the appropriate dwelling-place of that Soul which is no part and of which we too are no part—thence to pour forth into the frame of the All

whatsoever the All can hold of good and beauty. There that Soul rests, free from all solicitude, not ruling by plan or policy, not redressing, but establishing order by the marvelous efficacy of its contemplation of the things above it.

For the measure of its absorption in that vision is the measure of its grace and power, and what it draws from this contemplation it communicates to the lower sphere, illuminated and illuminating always. [14]

In another text, Plotinus continues to examine the notion that our "ego" is our Soul, as well as the intermediate man (discursive thought) capable of tending toward the better (Nous [Mind]) as well as the worse (the sensible, the third man):

Again; we perceive by means of the perceptive faculty and are not, ourselves, the percipients: may we then say the same of the understanding (the principle of reasoning and discursive thought)?

No: our reasoning is our own; we ourselves think the thoughts that occupy the understanding—for this is actually the We—but the operation of the Mind enters from above us as that of the sensitive faculty from below; the We is the Soul at its highest, the mid-point; between two powers, between the sensitive principle, inferior to us, and the Mind superior. We think of the perceptive act as integral to ourselves because our sense-perception is uninterrupted; we hesitate as to the Mind both because we are not always occupied with it and because it exists apart, not a principle inclining to us but one to which we incline when we choose to look upwards.

The sensitive principle is our scout; the Mind our King. [15]

It is clear, therefore, that for Plotinus man is comprehensible only in the dynamic of these three aspects. It remains true for him that man is a Soul which uses a body. Nevertheless, on the one hand, the body is simply "a fallen Soul" in the sense seen, and the Soul as reason governing the body is superior to the body not only when it is in the body, but it also firmly maintains a link to the Absolute, a connection which is never diminished:

And—if it is desirable to venture the more definite statement of a personal conviction clashing with the general view—*even our human Soul has not sunk entire; something of it is continuously in the Intellectual Realm* ... [16]

We decide our destiny according to whether we allow the sensible part to predominate or we transcend the sensible clinging closely to the superior part.

But before taking this up we ought to clarify further the activities of the individual Soul, both in its relations with the body and taken in itself.

4. The activities and functions of the Soul

The elementary activities of the vegetative and sentient life are dependent on the All-Soul. We have seen, in fact, that the creation of the world is produced by this Soul, while the task of vivifying and ruling individual bodies is the concern of individual Souls.

Consequently, all activities which seem to belong to bodies in general are in reality characteristic of the Soul which produces them. Thus all the activities which would seem to belong to particular bodies are, in reality, under the direct rule of the Soul which governs them or even are activities characteristic and peculiar to this Soul itself. And note that at all levels the Soul is conceived as *impassible* and as *capable only of acting*, because the incorporeal cannot be affected in any way by the corporeal.

How, then, is sensation to be explained? Does it suppose, perhaps, not only an action on the part of bodies on bodies, but likewise an action of bodies on Soul, or, at least a mutual interaction between Soul and body, and hence a *being acted upon* of the Soul? The reply of Plotinus is quite ingenious. He distinguishes, fundamentally, two aspects of sensation: "exterior" sensation, which is simply the affection and the impression which bodies produce on bodies (and which is explained in terms of the general rule of *sympatheia* which mutually joins all the things of the universe), and sense perception, which is, on the other hand, an act of Soul, an act of knowledge of the Soul which effectively grasps corporeal impressions and affections.

Hence, on the one hand, when *we sense, our body receives an affection* through another body; on the other hand, when we sense *our Soul enters into action*, not only in the sense that *"it does not avoid"* [17] *the corporeal affection*, but even in the sense that it "judges" these affections. [18] In fact, for Plotinus, in the sensory impression which is produced in our body the Soul sees (although on the most weakened and feeble level) *the mark of the intelligible forms. Hence, the sensation itself is, for the Soul, a form of contemplation of the intelligible in the sensible.* Here is a quite important text in this regard:

> The faculty of perception in the Soul cannot act by the immediate grasping of sensible objects, but only by the discerning of impressions printed upon the Animate by sensation: these impressions are already Cognizables, while the outer sensation is a mere phantom of the other (of that in the Soul) [19] which is nearer to Being as being an impassive reading of Ideal-Forms.

Nevertheless, this is only a corollary which arises from the Plotinian conception of the physical world according to which bodies are produced from the *logoi*, that is, from the rational powers of the Soul of the universe (which are a reflection of the Ideas) and in the ultimate analysis are reduced to them, so that sensations are, in a certain sense, simply "obscure thoughts," while thoughts of the pure intelligibles are "clear sensations." [20]

In fact, for our philosopher sensation is possible inasmuch as the lower *Soul which feels is connected to the higher Soul which perceives pure intelligibles* (the Platonic *anamnesis* or reminiscence, for Plotinus, is *an original intuitive vision* or *a possession of the pure intelligible*. The sensing of the lower Soul accepts the sensible forms by illuminating them with a light which proceeds from it and *which comes precisely from that original full grasp which the higher Soul has of the pure forms*. The passage which follows expresses in a complete way this complex conception, which deepens and carries to extreme consequences the original Platonic doctrine:

> The Soul is in its essential nature the Mind of all things; it is ultimate among Intellectual Beings and the ultimate Mind of the Beings of the Intellectual Realm, and it is the primal Mind of the entire realm of sense.
>
> *Thus it has dealings with both orders*—benefited and quickened by the one, but by the other beguiled, falling before resemblances, and so led downward as under a spell. *Poised midway, it is aware of both spheres.*
>
> Of the Intellectual it is said to have intuition by memory upon approach, for it knows them by a certain natural identity with them; its knowledge is not attained by besetting them, so to speak, but by in a definite degree possessing them; they are its natural vision; they are itself in a more radiant mode, and it rises from its duller pitch so that greater brilliance in a sort of awakening, a progress from its latency to its Act.
>
> *To the sense-order it stands in a similar nearness and to such things it gives a radiance out of its own store and, as it were, elaborates them to visibility: the power is always ripe and so to say, in travail towards them, so that, whenever it puts out its strength in the direction of what has once been present in it, it sees that object as present still; and the more intent its effort the more durable is the presence.* [21]

Analogously, Plotinus also attributes to the Soul the capacities of *imagination* and *memory*. The body of itself is not capable of memory, nor is the body considered in its union with the Soul, but only the Soul alone; the body, on the contrary, is a hindrance and obstacle to remembering and hence rather a cause of forgetting:

> Memory, in point of fact, is impeded by the body: even as things are, addition often brings forgetfulness; with thinning and clearing away, memory will often revive. The Soul is a stability; the shifting and fleeting thing which body is can be a cause only of its forgetting, not of its remembering—Lethe stream may be understood in this sense—and memory is a fact of the Soul. [22]

This is obvious, Plotinus says, especially in the case of memory and recollection of scientific doctrines in which the body clearly has no role.

In spite of this, memory and recollection have a formal relation with temporality, with the coming *before* and *after*, and the Soul, in the measure in which it has relations with the corporeal also has relations with the temporal. Instead, all that which remains in the identity and the equality of eternity has no memory, but participates in the *simultaneous presence of the totality of things*. God and Mind (Nous) do not have memory therefore, but the Soul possesses such an activity insofar as it has business with the temporal.

Recollection (*anamnesis*) is formally different from memory, about which we have previously spoken: it consists in a permanent preserving in the Soul of what is co-natural to the Soul itself insofar as it derives it from its original and formal contact with the supernal realities. Our higher Soul, in fact, is eternally bound to Mind (Nous). [23]

Consequently, in the hereafter the Soul tends to lose the memories linked to the body and to the temporal, while in the here and now the recollection of supernal things can never be entirely obscure. [24]

The highest cognitive activity of the Soul consists, hence, in the thought which grasps the Ideas and Mind (Nous). Beyond this the Soul also possesses the meta-rational power of accepting the One itself and "uniting itself" with Him. But we will speak of this later.

Also the feelings, the passions, the volitions, and everything linked to them are interpreted by Plotinus as sensations, perceptions, and memory, in sum as *activities of the Soul*. In fact, for our philosopher it is the body, viz., the animal part, which suffers, while the Soul is, properly speaking, immune to feelings and *it acts on the body being aware of* the passions of the body and consequently being concerned with them. An Italian scholar summarizes this point of Plotinian doctrine well: " ...we can say that what suffers is the living composite of body and Soul, but it suffers in the body and never in the Soul, both that the suffering may ascend from the impressions suffered by the body up to the Soul (being found there in the form of a vision and judgment) and that from the opinion of the Soul it must descend toward the body. If the Soul is in a certain way struck by passion, it is because it is interested itself in the body, destined as it is to govern it by being impassible itself. The Soul perceives the passion but the body seems to be the indispensable condition, because passion itself can become true. If we refer the passion to the Soul, we can only do it through a certain analogy, extending to an unextended and incorruptible substance, which is of itself number and reason, what can only be said of the body." [25]

5. Man and his liberty

The highest activity of the Soul is liberty. Actually, Plotinus essentially repeats the traditional Platonic doctrines and, as all his pagan predecessors, he does not entirely succeed in freeing himself from the burden of Socratic intellectualism. Nevertheless, it seems to us that he made substantial progress based on his new conception of the Absolute.

We have, in fact, seen that the One, the unconditioned, is necessarily free (liberty), a volition and cause of itself. The One wishes itself (and hence posits itself) because it is Good, and that Good (positive absolute) is self-willing and self-positing. Therefore, in the Absolute, *(absolute) liberty is identical with the volition of the (absolute) Good, or in willing to be like the (absolute) Good.*

If this is so, the liberty of man and of the Soul also will be sought in the same direction, and those affirmations of an intellectualistic flavor are to be read in this perspective.

Therefore, Mind (Nous) itself is *free* only thanks to the Good, as is shown in this exemplary text:

> In principle, act and essence must be free. No doubt Mind itself is to be referred to a yet higher; but this higher is not extern to it; Mind is *within the Good*; possessing its own good in virtue of that indwelling, *much more will it possess freedom and self-disposal which are sought only for the sake of the good. Acting towards the good, it must all the more possess self-disposal,* for by that Act it is directed towards the Mind from which it proceeds, and this its act is self-centered and must entail its very greatest good. [26]

So, as the liberty of the Mind (Nous) consists in following the trail of the Good, thus analogously liberty of the Soul consists in its turn in the placing of the proper operating force on the trail of the Mind (Nous) and acting consequently according to those ways which carry it to union with the Mind (Nous) and through the Mind (Nous) to the One and the Good itself.

Liberty, consequently, for Plotinus, cannot consist in practical activity, in exterior acts, but in the highest virtue, contemplation, and within limits, in ecstasy.

Liberty and sovereign will, hence, for Plotinus consists in the immaterial (τὸ αὔλον). [27]

But while the One is liberty which is self-posited as absolute Good, Nous (Mind) is free in the sense that its act coincides with willing the Good, insofar as it is indissolubly tied to the Good; the Soul, finally, is free in the measure in which through the Mind (Nous) itself it tends to Good. Here is a text which clearly illustrates this last point:

> Soul becomes free when it moves without hindrance, through Mind towards The Good; what it does in that spirit is its free act; Mind is free in its own right. That principle of Good is the sole object of desire and the source of self-disposal to the rest when it fully attains, to Mind by connate possession. [28]

The liberty of man therefore is always and only the liberty of soul which wills and tries to reach the Good. [29]

6. The eschatological destiny of the soul and the supreme goal of man

But what does it mean for our soul to will and to reach the Good? And by willing and searching for the Good, when and how does the soul reach it?

In response to these questions, Plotinus in part takes up and in part goes beyond the traditional conceptions of the Greeks.

Therefore, note that Plotinus, both when he goes back to the traditional Orphic, Pythagorean, and Platonic conceptions as well as when he proposes viewpoints which are more peculiar to him and taken from the Alexandrine ambience and especially from Philo, [30] generally puts the accent on the separation from the corporeal and the material as the outstanding goal to be achieved (moreover, as we have seen, liberty for him is dependent on the immaterial).

This being his most deeply held conviction (which is inserted in the general system and in particular in the conception of matter as the privation of the good), it is evident that Plotinus must firmly reject the Christian doctrine of *the resurrection of the body*, which he considers as an expression of a form of materialism. Here is a text not well known, but very important in this respect:

> Thus far we have been meeting those who, on the evidence of thrust and resistance, identify body with real being and find assurance of truth in the phantasms that reach us through the senses, those, in a word, who, like dreamers, take for actualities the figments of their sleeping vision. The sphere of sense, the Soul in its slumber; for all of the Soul that is in body is asleep and the *true getting-up is not bodily but from the body: in any movement that takes the body with it there is no more than a passage from sleep to sleep, from bed to bed; the veritable waking or rising is from corporeal things; for these, belonging to the Kind directly opposed to Soul*, present to it what is directly opposed to its essential existence: their origin, their flux, and their perishing are the warning of their exclusion from the Kind whose Being is Authentic. [31]

There remains hence nothing for Plotinus but the alternative of metempsychosis, which he maintained and upheld, basing it upon Plato and therefore, falling back into all the difficulties this belief entails. [32]

But the belief that the Souls of men can be reincarnated in the bodies of animals or even in plants (based on the type of life led in the preceding existence) is explained better in the context of Plotinian metaphysics than in the context of the Platonic metaphysics, since the soul itself creates, vivifies, and governs all the physical world and is *the principle of every form of life*. [33]

In any case, Plotinus states more often than Plato, that the ultimate destiny of Souls which have lived better lives is to be re-united to God:

> Souls, body-bound, are apt to body-punishment; clean souls no longer drawing to themselves at any point any vestige of body are, by their very being, outside the bodily sphere; body-free, containing nothing of body—there where Being is, and Being, and the Divine within the Divinity, among Those, within That, such a soul must be.
>
> If you still ask Where, you must ask where those Beings are—and in your seeking, seek otherwise than with the sight, and not as one seeking for body. [34]

But the novelty of Plotinus with respect to the classical Greek tradition is in having pointed out *the possibility of realizing the separation from the sensible and from the corporeal and of realizing fully the union with the One already in this life by means of the mystical-ecstatic union with the Absolute.*

This doctrine in some way agreed with those doctrines of Greek ethics which, in part, Socrates and Aristotle had given value to and which especially the philosophers of the Hellenistic Age had brought into the foreground, that is, *that happiness (which is the achievement of the ultimate end of man) must be possible already in this life.* [35] But in the same instance in which the doctrine of Plotinus agreed with them, it overturned them: man also can attain his highest *telos in this life* by separating himself completely, by means of Mind (Nous), from all that is material and in this way entering into intimate union (although only occasionally and for a brief period) with the transcendent Absolute (as Philo had previously maintained, although on other bases). And further, Plotinus notes that it is possible, inasmuch as there is a component of a wholly diverse nature from the physical in man. Being happy among torments in the "bull of Phalaris" is also possible, because it is possible even among physical torments to unite with the incorporeal soul to the incorporeal Divine, but, it is possible only on this condition:

> The characteristic activities are not hindered by outer events but merely adapt themselves, remaining always fine, and perhaps all the finer for dealing with the actual. In the activities of the mind particular applications may find him in difficulties: he may not be able to put his vision into act without searching and thinking, but the one "greatest principle of knowledge" (the Good) is ever present to him, like a part of his being—most of all present, should he be even a victim in the much-talked-of Bull of Phalaris. No doubt, despite all that has been said, it is idle to pretend that this is an agreeable lodging; but what cries in the Bull is the thing that feels torture; in the Proficient there is something else as well, something which associates with that other, but which, so long as the association is not of its own choice, can never be robbed of the vision of the All-Good. [36]

What the highest ideal of the preceding age had been remains thus shattered and its illusory nature is laid bare. *What the Hellenistic Age had vainly searched for in the immanent dimension is only possible through a firm connection to the transcendent.*

7. The reform of the list of values

The classic list of values which was clearly treated by Plato in the *Laws*, [37] put the Gods in the first place, the Soul in second, the body, in third, the body, and exterior goods in general in fourth. The Peripatetics also referred to this list. And Plotinus himself had referred to the same list, but in order to reform it considerably. Both Plato and Aristotle had proclaimed and cultivated the values of the soul without denying the lower values, but subordinating them to those of the soul. But Plato himself, even in his mystical dimension, had hardly given a privileged place to values concerning the Gods, the religious values as such. On the contrary, these very values move in Plotinus into a position of prominence. The values of soul are subordinated to them, while the values of the body and exterior values lose all relevance. In brief: the preceding Greek spirit and tradition had attributed a meaning to the physical values in the measure in which, in some way, they could be joined to the values of the soul, which were the values par excellence. Plotinus did not attribute any more significance to physical values ("he was ashamed to be in a body," says Porphyry, and he refused the remedies which the doctors prescribed when he was sick). [38] He attributed an instrumental significance to the values of the Soul, he cultivated them in the measure in which it became possible through them to achieve religious values, the assimilation to the Divine in the new meaning about which we will speak. [39] Plotinus, in sum, judged that true wisdom was not simply to live the life of an *upright man,* but the life of the Gods. He explicitly writes:

> ...but our concern is not merely to be "sinless," but to be God. [40]

8. The ways of returning to the Absolute

It is clear that in this new context the ways that lead to the achievement of the highest values and the Absolute had to be proposed again.

First of all, the doctrine of the virtues is restricted by Plotinus. The "civic virtues," those which are the basis of classical ethics and on which Plato himself had based his *Republic,* are for Plotinus simply a point of departure and not of arrival. Justice, wisdom, fortitude and temperance understood in the "political" sense, *i.e.,* in a "civic" sense, they are capacities only of assigning limits and measure to the desires and of eliminating false opinions, hence are only *an indication of the highest Good.* They are a *condition* for becoming like the Gods, but assimilation to God is something higher than them. [41]

Higher than "civic virtues" are the virtues understood as "purifications." In fact, while civic virtues are limited to moderating the passions, the virtues in sense of purifications *liberate us from them* and, consequently, permit the soul to unite itself to what it is akin to, *i.e.,* to the Mind (Nous), since such a union can be achieved only by separating oneself from the sensible, [42] and even from the soul itself (from its lower parts). Plotinus, in fact, writes:

> Virtue, in the same way, is a thing of the Soul; it does not belong to the Mind or to the Transcendence. [43]

When the soul has achieved the Mind (Nous) and contemplated it, then the virtues in this contemplation and imitation of the Mind (Nous), so to speak, are transformed. In Mind (Nous) "virtues" are like *the models of which those of the soul are images and copies.* In fact, on this higher level, *wisdom* becomes contact of the soul with Mind (Nous), *justice* is the willing of the act of soul to Mind (Nous), *temperance* the intimate adherence of soul to Mind (Nous), and *fortitude* the impassible perseverance of the soul in the impassible Mind (Nous) without being subject to any passion of the body. In sum: at this level the paradigm virtues are precisely the way for the soul to live, which separates it from sensible things and enters it again wholly into itself, living in absolute purity, the very life of the Gods, assimilating itself to Mind (Nous), living the very life of the Mind (Nous). [44]

But the virtues are not the only way to reach unity with the Divine. In fact, going back to Plato, Plotinus gives value also to the erotic and dialectic which are, although purely for a different reason and in a different measure, diverse ways with which the soul separates, liberates itself from the corporeal, and approaches the Absolute.

The Plotinian erotic is, as the Platonic, closely connected to beauty. [45] Now we know already that beauty is fundamentally form at all levels. Even sensible beauty is form: it is the translucence of the intelligible form in the sensible. In the measure in which the beautiful is form, it is connatural to the soul, and it is hence a capacity to make the soul re-enter into itself and of bringing it back to the recollection of its divine origins. And the "rapture" that the lover shows in seeing the beautiful is simply that metaphysical recollection of its own spiritual origins. [46]

Also for Plotinus, as well as for Plato, there is a "ladder of beauty" which needs to be mounted in order to achieve the Absolute. From sensible beauty it is necessary to ascend to beautiful customs, to works of virtue, and to beauty of the purified soul. In fact the purified soul becomes Idea and hence beauty itself by realizing that identification with what is the source of all beauty. Through this way, in sum, the soul moves from beauty, and by transcending the sensible beautiful things by means of those energies which the beautiful itself awakened in it, the soul progresses through the various grades of incorporeal beauty up to becoming wholly beautiful itself and to being identified with absolute Beauty (the Mind [Nous]) and with the principle itself of Beauty (the Good or the One). Here is a very explicit passage in this regard:

> The Soul thus cleansed is all Idea and Reason, wholly free of body, intellective, entirely of that divine order from which the wellspring of Beauty rises and all the race of Beauty.

> Hence the Soul heightened to the Mind *is beautiful to all its power.* For Intellection and all that proceeds from Intellection are the Soul's beauty, a graciousness native to it and not foreign, *for only with these is it truly Soul.* And it is just to say that in the Soul's becoming *a good and beautiful thing is its becoming like to God,* for from the Divine comes all the Beauty and all the Good in beings.

> We may even say that *Beauty is the Authentic-Existents* and Ugliness is the Mind contrary to Being and the Ugly is also the primal evil; therefore its

contrary is at once good and beautiful, or is Good and Beauty: and hence the one method will discover to us the Beauty-Good and the Ugliness-Evil.

And Beauty, this Beauty which is also The Good, must be posed as The First: directly deriving from this First is the Mind which is pre-eminently the manifestation of Beauty; through the Mind Soul is beautiful. The beauty in things of a lower order—actions and pursuits for instance—comes by operation of the shaping Soul which is also the author of the beauty found in the world of sense. For the Soul, a divine thing, a fragment as it were of the Primary Beauty, makes beautiful to the fullness of their capacity all things whatsoever that it grasps and molds. [47]

We have spoken fully, in the preceding section, about dialectic as the path to the Absolute showing that it is distinguished into three stages: the first consists in the journey from the corporeal to the incorporeal, the second consists in moving gradually within the sphere of the incorporeal, and the third, which is the terminus of the process, is the total and complete achievement of the ultimate goal, the ecstatic union of the Soul with the Absolute. We must now go into some detail about the final stage. [48]

9. The reunification with the One

The way of returning (*reditus*) to the One described above is essentially going back on the same path the reverse of the metaphysical "procession" (*exitus*) from the One. And because the successive hypostases are derived from the One through a kind of "differentiation" and *metaphysical alteriety* to which is add-ed the moral differentiations in man, it is evident that the return to the One will consist *in the destruction of every differentiation and otherness, i.e., in a kind of "simplification."* [49]

Now, note, this is possible because "otherness" (= differentiation and alteriety) is not in the hypostasis of the One, but rather in what follows on the One, especially in us. Thus, immune as it is from any otherness, *the One is present always to us, but we are present to Him only when we eliminate otherness.* Plotinus expressly writes:

> Thus the Supreme [the One] as containing no otherness is ever present with us; we with it when we put otherness away. [50]

To cut away every alteriety necessarily means for human beings to reenter into themselves, into their souls. It means, hence, to separate from the corporeal and from the body and from everything which is connected to it. It means, in addition, to separate oneself from the affective parts of the soul and whatever is connected to it. It means, in sum, to purify the soul of all that which is extraneous to it:

> But why have we to call in Philosophy to make the Soul immune if it is thus (like the Melodic Mind of our illustration) immune from the beginning?

Because representations attack it at what we call the affective phase and cause a resulting experience, a disturbance, to which disturbance is joined the image of threatened evil: this amounts to an affection and Reason seeks to extinguish it, to ban it as destructive to the well-being of the Soul which by the mere absence of such a condition is immune, the one possible cause of affection—the representation of the Soul—not being present.

Take it that some such affections have engendered appearances presented before the Soul or Mind from without but taken (for practical purposes) to be actual experiences within it—then Philosophy's task is like that of a man who wishes to throw off the shapes presented in dreams, and to this end recalls to waking condition the mind that is breeding them.

But what can be meant by the purification of the Soul that has never been stained and by the separation of the Soul from the body to which it is essentially a stranger?

The purification of the Soul is simply to allow it to be alone; it is pure when it keeps no company; when it looks to nothing without itself; when it entertains no alien thoughts—be the mode or origin of such notions or affections what they may, a subject on which we have already touched—when it no longer sees in the world of image, much less elaborates images into veritable affections. Is it not a true purification to turn away towards the exact contrary of earthly things?

Separation, in the same way, is the condition of a soul no longer entering into the body to lie at its mercy; it is to stand as a light, set in the midst of trouble but unperturbed through all.

In the particular case of the affective phase of the Soul, purification is its awakening from the baseless visions which beset it, the refusal to see them; its separation consists in limiting its descent towards the lower and accepting no picture thence, and of course in the banning of all that it ignores when the pneuma (finer-body or spirit) on which it is poised is not turbid from gluttony and surfeit of impure flesh, but is a vehicle so slender that the Soul may ride upon it in tranquility. [51]

The soul besides must cut away words, discourse and discursive reason, every obstacle or what in any way separates it from the One, even the conscious reflection of its own being:

If the mind reels before something thus alien to all we know, we must take our stand on the things of this realm and strive thence to see. But in the looking beware of throwing outward; this Mind does not lie away somewhere leaving the rest void; to those of power to reach, it is present; to the inapt, absent. In our daily affairs *we cannot hold an object to mind if we have given ourselves elsewhere, occupied upon some other matter*; that very thing, and nothing else, must be before us to be truly the object of observation. *So here also; preoccupied by the impress of something else, we are withheld under that pressure from becoming aware of The Unity*; a mind gripped and fastened by some definite thing cannot take the print of the very contrary. As Matter, it is agreed, must be void of quality in order to accept the types of the universe, so and *much more must the soul be kept formless if there is to be no inherent impediment to prevent it being brimmed and lit by the Primal Mind.*

In sum, we must withdraw from everything external, pointed wholly inward; no leaning to the outer; the total of things ignored, first in their relation to us and later in the very idea, [and precisely, at first, only towards our deepest attitudes, then, towards our interior mind-set]; *the self put out of mind in the contemplation of the Supreme; all the commerce so closely There that, if report were possible, one might become to others reporter of that communion.* [52]

The phrase which summarizes, in a very realistic way, the process of total purification of the soul that wishes to unite itself to the One is, thus:

Cut away everything (ἄφελε πάντα). [53]

This is, undoubtedly, the most radical conception that one meets in the history of ancient thought.

Actually, the philosophers of the Hellenistic Age had already preached the necessity of cutting away all exterior things, and Pyrrho had even tried to "cut away from man," i.e., to liberate him from all which was not essential to him. But none of these philosophers came so far. In fact, as we have seen, in the attempt to save the individual as the true absolute they each fell into individualism. Plotinus wishes man to also cut away what the Hellenistic philosophers still wanted to preserve, insofar as they considered it essential to man as such. Only in this way is it possible for him to achieve the supreme goal of happiness.

It will be objected that in this way Plotinus arrives at nullifying not only the external world, but likewise the "ego," and hence he nullifies man himself and that consequently his happiness ends by being equivalent to the happiness of being lost in nothingness. [54]

But actually, exactly the opposite is true for Plotinus.

To cut away everything does not mean entirely to impoverish or even to nullify oneself, but it means, on the contrary, to increase oneself by being refilled by God, hence by the All, by the infinite. Here is a fine text:

It is not by some admixture of non-being that one becomes entire, but by putting non-being away. By the lessening of the alien in you, you increase.

Cast it aside and there is the All within you; engaged in the alien, you will not find the All. Not that it has to come and so be present to you; it is you that have turned from it. And turn though you may, you have not severed yourself; it is there; you are not in some far region: still there before it, you have faced to its contrary. [55]

"To cut away everything," means to return the soul to itself, the finding of that metaphysical connection which unites it not only to Being and to Mind (Nous) (the second hypostasis), but to the One itself (to the first hypostasis).

The soul would go toward non-being precisely by *not cutting away things*, but by attaching itself to them, since things are made of matter, hence of non-being. (But it is clear that the soul, however it proceeds through this descent, cannot arrive at absolute non-being, for the metaphysical reasons that we know.) Instead, by cutting away all things, it achieves itself, it reaches Being (second hypostasis), and then it transcends Being itself up to achieving non-being in the meaning of what is beyond Being, *i.e.*, to the One:

> It is not in the soul's nature to touch utter nothingness; the lowest descent is into evil and, so far, into non-being; but utter nothing, never. When the soul begins again to mount, it comes not to something alien but to its very self; thus detached, it is in nothing but itself; self-gathered it is no longer in the order of being; it is in the Supreme.
>
> There is thus a converse in virtue of which the essential man outgrows Being, becomes identical with the Transcendent Being. [56]

Far, then, from being brought to the point of being lost in nothingness, the cutting away of all things from the soul brings it not only to the fullness of being, but to the One which is beyond Being, to contact with the Absolute. This last passage that we shall quote shows this is in a very clear way:

> No longer can we wonder that the principle evoking such longing should be utterly free from form, even Intellectual form. The soul itself, once it has conceived the yearning love towards this, lays aside all the form it has taken, even to the Intellectual form that has informed it. There is no vision, no union, for those handling or acting by any thing other; the soul must see before it neither evil or good nor anything else, that alone it may receive the Alone.
>
> Suppose the soul to have attained: the highest has come to her, or rather has revealed its presence; she has turned away from all about her and made herself apt, beautiful to the utmost, brought into likeness with the divine— by those preparings and adornings which come unbidden the divine—by those preparing and adornings which come unbidden to those growing ready for the vision—she has seen that presence suddenly manifesting within her, for there is nothing between: here is no longer a duality but a two in one; for, so long as the presence holds, all distinction fades: it is a lover and beloved here, in a copy of that union, long to blend; the soul has now no further awareness of being in body and will give herself no foreign name, not man, not living being, not being, not all; any observation of such things falls away; the soul has neither time nor taste for them; This she sought and This she has found and on This she looks and not upon herself; and who she is that looks she has not leisure to know. Once There she will barter for This nothing the universe holds; not though one would make over

the heavens entire to her; than This there is nothing higher, nothing more good; above This there is no passing; all the rest however lofty lies on the downgoing path: she is of perfect judgment and knows that This was her quest, that nothing higher is. Here can be no deceit; where could she come upon truer than the truth? and the truth she affirms, that she is herself; but all the affirmation is later and is silent. In this happiness she knows beyond delusion that she is happy; for this is no affirmation of an excited body but of a soul become again what she was in the time of her early joy. All that she had welcomed of old—office, power, wealth, beauty, knowledge—of all she tells her scorn as she never could had she not found their better; linked to This she can fear no disaster, nor even once she has had the vision; let all about her fall to pieces, so she would have it that she may be wholly with This, so huge the happiness she has won to.[57]

10. Ecstasy

This contact with the One is called, at least in one text (which we will read below), "ecstasy."

So on the basis of what we said it is evident that ecstasy cannot be a form of science nor of rational or intellectual knowledge. It is, on the contrary, a contemplation which implies close contact (without reflecting the subject-object distinction) with the contemplated, a co-presence, a union, a total unification with it.

Also in this regard, not a few interpreters have fallen into error and have confused this ecstasy with a state of *unconsciousness*, or something irrational or hypo-rational.[58]

In reality, Plotinian ecstasy is not a state of unconsciousness but a state of *hyper*-awareness; not something irrational or hypo-rational but *hyper*-rational. In ecstasy *the soul sees itself filled, so to speak, sees itself filled up with the One*, and in the measure possible fully assimilated to Him. Therefore, its ecstatic contemplation is a participation in the subsistence of the One with all the characteristics that are peculiar to Him, as we have seen above, *what is beyond Being, and hence is likewise beyond Thought, Reason, and Awareness*. Here is the text which summarizes very well the Plotinian thought about ecstasy:

> This is the purport of that rule of our Mysteries: "Nothing Divulged to the Uninitiate": the Supreme is not to be made a common story, the holy things may not be uncovered to the stranger, to any that has not himself attained to see. *There were not two; beholder was one with beheld*; it was not a vision compassed but a unity apprehended. *The man formed by this mingling with the Supreme* must—if he only remember—carry its image impressed upon him: he is become the Unity, nothing within him or without inducing any diversity; no movement now, no passion, no outlooking desire, once this ascent is achieved; *reasoning is in abeyance and all Intellection and even, to dare the word, the very self: caught away, filled with God, he has in perfect*

stillness attained isolation; all the being calmed, he turns neither to this side nor to that, not even inward to himself; utterly resting he has become very rest. He belongs no longer to the order of the beautiful [which belongs to the second hypostasis]; *he has risen beyond beauty; he has surpassed even the choir of the virtues* [which belongs to the third hypostasis]; he is like one who, having penetrated the inner sanctuary, leaves the temple images behind him—though these become once more first objects of regard when he leaves the holies; for There his converse was not with image, not with trace, *but with the very Truth* in the view of which all the rest is but of secondary concern.

There, indeed, it was scarcely vision, unless of a mode unknown; *it was a going forth from the self, a simplifying, a renunciation, a reach towards contact and at the same time a repose, a meditation towards adjustment.* This is the only seeing of what lies within the holies: to look otherwise is to fail.

Things here are signs; they show therefore to the wiser teachers how the supreme God is known; the instructed priest reading the sign may enter the holy place and make real the vision of the inaccessible.

Even those that have never found entry must admit the existence of that invisible; *they will know their source and Mind since by principle they see principle and are linked with it, by like they have contact with like and so they grasp all of the divine that lies within the scope of mind.* Until the seeing comes they are still craving something, that which only the vision can give; this Term, attained only by those that have surpassed all, is the All-Transcending. [59]

That the doctrine of ecstasy was spread in Alexandria by Philo is indubitable (but it is likewise certain that Plotinus many times had direct personal experience of it). Nevertheless, while Philo in a Biblical spirit intends ecstasy to be understood as grace, that is, as a "gratuitous gift" from God in harmony with the Biblical concept of God who makes gifts of himself and of things created by Him to man, [60] Plotinus places it within a vision which maintains connections to the categories of Greek thought: God does not make a gift of Himself to men and men can rise to Him and unite themselves to Him *through their natural powers.* This point has been noticed by a French scholar better than anyone else, in a passage worth reading in full: " ...the difference between the *Enneads* and the *Commentary on the Holy Laws* [of Philo] is great. The radical impotency of man to raise himself by his efforts to God, the benevolence and the initiative of God who guides man and is his collaborator, are concepts unknown to Plotinus; also, when he speaks of an influence illuminating and fortifying the soul from the One which it contemplates, it is an influence which is naturally and necessarily exercised, so that he can promise to anyone who is prepared, that God will inevitably show himself. In effect, here, God does not truly give, since He does not give Himself; Plotinus thinks that this would signify an extrinsic activity, a tendency incompatible with his notion of the simplicity and transcendent unity of the One. The success of the initiative is wholly in the hands of man, who, with his powers, is the artificer of his own salvation and perfection: nothing is more opposed to the thought of Plotinus than the notion of grace." [61]

VI. Nature and Originality of Plotinian Metaphysics

1. Plotinian metaphysics is not a form of emanationism of an Eastern
    type, or a form of pantheism, or a form of creationism

The term with which Plotinian metaphysics is most frequently identified
is "emanationism"; but, it is merely mentioned for the most part without any
adequate analyses and hence it leads to a series of equivocations.

Every form of emanationism seems to be characterized by three essential
characteristics:

(*a*) First, emanationism implies that all things (or some) *flow from the
substance* of the first Mind and that such a flow is, in some way, a flow of the
substance itself of the Mind (*b*) In this flowing *from the substance* of the Mind
there takes place *a gradual and successive weakening of the substance itself* in
the sense that the Mind insofar as it is such, is inexhaustible, while the flow is
progressively weakened as it gets further from the Mind (*c*) This flowing from
the Mind is a process which is not reducible to an act of the will, nor to an
activity of reason, but rather has the character of a *physical necessity.*

So Plotinus speaks of "emanation" only in his images, while his doctrine
is the negation of it.[1] Thus what follows should be carefully kept in mind.

(*a*) The hypostases subsequent to the One are not, in fact, an *outflow of
the substance of the One.*

(*b*) Consequently, they are not the *diminished substance* of the One.

(*c*) Finally, they are not derived from the One *by a merely physical necessity.*

Zeller[2] has clearly seen the indefensibility of interpreting Plotinus's
philosophy in an emanationistic manner and has proposed instead the notion
of "dynamic pantheism."

What does Zeller mean by this phrase?

(*a*) That from the One flows not His substance, but His "power," His
dynamis (the One is the power of all things).

(*b*) In this outflow, consequently, there takes place a gradual weakening
not of the substance, but of the *power* of the One.

(*c*) This process is not a free act or a logical necessity, but an action which
arises *of necessity* from the nature of the One (and in this way emanationism
and pantheism are identical).

(*d*) In relation to the Absolute, the phenomenal world does not have any
autonomy, but is a simple manifestation of the Divine.

The definition of Zeller did not meet with success.[3] Actually, the concept
of "dynamic pantheism" is quite ambiguous. What does it mean exactly? It
means not only that *everything is God*, but that everything is *a power* (a *dynamis*)
of God. So there is a great difference between saying that *everything is God* and
everything is the power of God, since the former statement implies the identity

of the substance of God and the world, while the latter implies that the world is an *effect* and God is the *cause*. The former is a pantheistic affirmation, but not the latter, precisely because the latter maintains the distinction between the *substance* and the *power* of God by identifying all things not with the former but precisely with the latter. Consequently, the phrase *dynamic pantheism* ends by being a real contradiction in terms. [4] In every instance, the affirmations of Plotinus are une-quivocal.

The One is transcendent at two levels: (*a*) it is transcendent (as is the whole incorporeal world) with respect to the corporeal world and (*b*) it is transcendent in the confines of the realm of the incorporeal with respect to Soul and Mind (Nous) themselves.

In addition, when Plotinus affirms that all things are in God he means to say, as we have previously noted, not that they are identical with the substance of God but that they derive and depend wholly on his power.

Finally, that the flowing out of the power of the One is a sort of "natural action" is not true, but, as we have seen and will state below in our conclusions, the "procession" implies such a complexity of elements that it cannot be in any way spoken of as a mere "natural action." [5] Evidently, the Plotinian metaphysics is also clearly different from a creationistic metaphysics for the following reasons:

(*a*) Plotinus does not admit in any instance that the procession of all things from the One can be the *result of a free choice and decision*. Posit the One, the other things follow "of necessity" (we have seen and we will say immediately that it is a question of a quite unusual "necessity").

(*b*) Consequently, the aspect of the structural *contingency* of things which derives from God is wholly unknown to Plotinus. Instead, it is fundamental in creationistic metaphysics (in the context of the metaphysics of our philosopher, to speak of production *ex nihilo sui et subjecti* [*out of nothing*] does not make sense).

(*c*) Finally, God is Good, but He is not the Love that gives gratuitously, through "grace."

Nevertheless, it would be a mistake to maintain that creationism (which he knew from Mosaic philosophy and from Ammonius himself) did not have some influence on Plotinian metaphysics. Actually, the Plotinian metaphysics is not reduced to any of the three positions examined above, *yet it contains some elements of each of them*, put together in a very original way in a complex synthesis which is a real *unicum* [singularity] in the history of philosophy. [6] Let us recapitulate the essential elements of this Plotinian singular event (*unicum*).

2. The liberty of the One, the "procession," and the "return"

The metaphysical question par excellence for the Greeks was a single one: "How do the many exist?" that is, "How is a multiplicity derived from the One?"

With Plotinus, the basic metaphysical question becomes two questions:

(1) Why does the One exist?

(2) Why and how are the many derived from the One?

(1) The first of these questions is quite novel, given that in the context of classical theory of being it was completely inconceivable. If the One is the principle, to ask why there is the One means to ask why there is a principle, that is, the Mind of the principle: a question which Aristotle rejected as absurd. In fact (in the context of his *ousiology* [inquiry into *ousia* or entity]) the reply to this question would end in a process to infinity (the "why" of the Mind would imply a further question *on the "why" of the "why" of the principle*, and so on to infinity).

Plotinus proposes the question under the influence of a certain problematic aroused by the Christians and in particular arising from the "rash arguments" of the Gnostics. And his unforeseeable reply is numbered, as we have previously said, among the high points of Western metaphysics. The cause or reason of the One is *liberty*. The One exists because it is a *free, self-producing activity*, a free *causa sui* [self-caused being], a self-creating liberty. The One is liberty in the sense that He is what He wishes to be, or in other words, He wishes to be what He is. And what He wishes to be *is the highest there can be, the Absolute Positive, the Absolute Good.* The whole eighth treatise of the sixth *Ennead* develops, in a most clear and profound manner, these new concepts.

The "why" of the One is therefore Liberty. [7] Now it is evident that this answer to the first question must also radically alter the answer to the second by permitting a series of new understandings.

(2) Why, therefore, are the many derived from the One?

Plotinus distinguishes in the One (and then also in the successive hypostases) *two forms* of activity: (*a*) the proper activity *of* the One and (*b*) the activity which arises *from* the One. (*a*) The first is and remains *in* the One, (*b*) the other proceeds *from* the One. It is evident that the two activities are structurally linked in such a way that by positing the first (the activity *of*) as a consequence, the second (the activity *from*) will arise from it.

Consequently, (*a*) the activity *of* the One cannot be identified with *liberty*, for the reasons examined above. Instead, (*b*) the activity which proceeds *from* the One follows of *necessity*. But it is certainly not a "physical," or "natural," necessity which is *blind*. In every instance it is not a necessity which can be interpreted in terms of the traditional categories of the Greeks. In fact, it is a necessity in a certain way *willed*, and *freely willed*, or better, *a necessity consequent on an act of liberty*. The One *posits itself freely*, and by positing itself it *necessarily* produces the other things which could not be derived by Him who is freely self-posited as infinite power.

It is clear, as a result, that the activity *from* the One differs from the creative activity of the Biblical divinity who *"wills" the things* and thus produces them (from nothing) as a gratuitous "gift." But it is likewise clear that things are derived *from* the One, *because the One has freely willed to be what He is.* And if the conclusion, reached by some scholars that the creation of things on the part of the One is no less free than the One itself, can appear exaggerated (or at the least paradoxical), it is true, nevertheless, that the source of the procession *from* the One is the liberty itself *of* the One (the activity *of* the One).[8] But this is not all.

The origin of the many from the One is not even explained with the activity *from* the One alone, in a linear fashion, quasi-mechanically. The activity which derives *from* the One (and from the other hypostases) is able to produce *Nous* (or the next hypostasis and physical reality itself) only if it turns around to *contemplate.* The *theoria*, the "creative contemplation" to which scholars have only recently called attention,[9] *becomes one of the axes around which Plotinian metaphysics revolves,* if not the very key to this metaphysics. In fact, in one of his most mature writings, Plotinus posits a precise equivalence between "contemplation" (θεωρία) and "creation" (ποίησις). *To create is to contemplate or, if you prefer, it is an effect of contemplation.* Creative contemplation is the characteristic which is common to all the hypostases, the key which unlocks the secret of the "procession" *from* the One and the "return" to that One "contemplation."

In the light of this concept (which, as is well known, is no longer Greek and not yet Christian) the traditional confines into which the Plotinian system has often been imprisoned are shown to be truly inadequate.

3. Creative contemplation

An Italian scholar has written that "Plotinus takes *contemplation* out of the shadow and hypostatizes it: θεωρία is the unique, the creative Hypostasis: the mythic Demiurge is submerged in contemplation."[10]

This statement which is often asked to bear too large a burden in explanations, nevertheless does bear a basic truth too often neglected by scholars.

Moreover, Plotinus himself beginning the eighth treatise of the third *Ennead* in which he explains the concept of *theoria*, which overturns all the traditional schemas, uses a tone of humor in order to soften the impact of the new doctrine on the reader, which could only succeed in provoking a violent reaction:

> Supposing we played a little before entering upon our serious concern and maintained that all things are striving after Contemplation, looking to Vision as their one end—and this, not merely beings endowed with reason but even unreasoning animals, the Mind that rules in growing things, and the Earth that produces these—*and that all achieve their purpose in the measure possible to their kind, each attaining Vision and possessing itself of the End in its own way and degree, some things in entire reality, others in mimicry and in image*—we would scarcely find anyone to endure so strange

a thesis. But in a discussion entirely among ourselves there is no risk in a light handling of our own ideas. [11]

But the playful tone is quickly put aside, and Plotinus concentrates on showing the two final points of the doctrine respectively concerning nature and practical activity. In fact, that the Mind (Nous) contemplates the One and the Soul, the Mind (Nous) (and, through the Mind [Nous], the One itself) seems paradoxical, being in fact quite clear considered in itself, given the structure of these hypostases. Instead, (*a*) *nature*, and (*b*) *praxis*, or *action* should seem on the whole or in part extraneous to "contemplation." On the contrary, for our philosopher, *nature, action, praxis, are contemplation and the results of contemplation.* Here are the conclusions of Plotinus on the first point:

> Nature does not lack; it creates because it possesses. Its creative act is simply its possession of its own characteristic Being; now its Being, since it is a Mind is to be at once an act of contemplation and an object of contemplation. In other words, the Mind produces by virtue of being an act of contemplation, an object of contemplation, and a Mind on this triple character depends its creative efficacy.
>
> *Thus the act of production is seen to be in Nature an act of contemplation, for creation is the outcome of a contemplation which never becomes anything else, which never does anything else, but creates by simply being a contemplation.* [12]

Plotinus further clarifies his conception by imaging an interrogation of nature and putting in her mouth the replies which represent the synthesis of his thought in this regard:

> And Nature, asked why it brings forth its works, might answer if it cared to listen and to speak:
>
> "It would have been more becoming to put no question but to learn in silence just as I myself am silent and make no habit of talking. And what is your lesson? This; that whatsoever comes into being is my vision, seen in my silence, the vision that belongs to my character who, sprung from vision, am vision-loving and create vision by the vision-seeing faculty within me. The mathematicians from their vision draw their figures: but I draw nothing: I gaze and the figures of the material world would take being as if they fell from my contemplation. As with my mother (the All-Soul) and the Beings that begot me so it is with me: they are born of a Contemplation and my birth is from them, not by their Act but by their Being; they are the loftier Mind they contemplate themselves and I am born." [13]

It is clear (and with this we take up the second point) that Nature contemplates and creates insofar as it is Soul. It is the same also in individual souls, contemplation and action are structurally connected together. Not only does action depend on contemplation and is much richer insofar as the contemplation is richer (an obvious tenet in the context of the Plotinian system), but it tends likewise to return to contemplation. Praxis, even in its lowest grade, without even being aware of it tends to contemplation:

> Action, thus, *is set towards contemplation and an object of contemplation*, so that even those whose life is in doing have seeing as their object; what they have not been able to achieve by the direct path they hope to come at by the circuit.

> Further: suppose they succeed; they desired a certain thing to come about, not in order to be unaware of it but know it, to see it present before the mind: their success is the laying up of a vision. [14]

The true creative force therefore is not *praxis*, but is *theoria*, "contemplation." As Souls in the Platonic *Phaedrus* have an interior richness proportioned to the "vision" of what they have contemplated in the "plain of truth"[15] so in a way without a greater comparison this Platonic intuition, carried to the extreme, becomes in Plotinus a general metaphysical concept. *The spiritual activity of "seeing" is transformed into an act of creating.*

The One is a kind of self-contemplator; Mind (Nous) is contemplation of the One and of itself filled up with the One; the Soul is contemplation of the Mind (Nous) and of itself filled up with Mind (Nous); Nature, the extreme edge of Soul, is contemplation; action is nothing but a more diminished form of contemplation. [16]

Contemplation is silence.

All reality is hence "contemplation" and "silence." [17]

In this context, the "return" to the One by means of ecstasy becomes simply the return by means of contemplation to the One. Let us remember that "ecstasy" is a term used only one time in the *Enneads*, and that the more appropriate term would be "simplification," which as we have seen, is the elimination of otherness, separation from all that which is terrestrial and multiple, a contemplation precisely in which the contemplating subject and the contemplated object are melted into one: it is the famous "passing of solitary to Solitary":

> This is the life of gods and of the godlike and blessed among men, liberation from the alien that besets us here, a life taking no pleasure in the things of this earth, the passing of solitary to solitary. [18]

On the one hand, therefore, the concept of *liberty* as "the why of the One" throws new light on the *necessity* of the procession and, on the other hand, the concept of "contemplation" as a cosmogonic concept, in fact, ontogonic, *viz.*, the concept of creative contemplation, helps us to recover the true character of the metaphysics of Plotinus (one of the most complex and noble creations of the human mind), whose richness certainly has not yet been wholly plumbed, since to use an image dear to Plotinus himself,[19] it is like a jewel interiorly shimmering with innumerable facets. And the succeeding history of philosophy has concentrated, at least up until now, only on some of them. [20]

Third Section

THE DEVELOPMENTS OF NEOPLATONISM
AND THE END OF ANCIENT GREEK-PAGAN PHILOSOPHY

«πάντα πλήρη θεοῦ.»

"Everything is full of Gods."
Thales, Test. 22 [*D-K* I.79.27]

«μεστὰ δὲ πάντα θεῶν.»

"Everything is overflowing with Gods."
Proclus, *Elements of Theology* 145

I. A Comprehensive Overview of the Schools, the Exponents, and the Tendencies of Neoplatonism

1.   Some methodological remarks concerning the reconstruction of the history of Neoplatonism

The history of Neoplatonism after Plotinus is particularly difficult to write for many reasons.

First, the contributions of individual thinkers tend to become, on the speculative level, always more analytic and tend frequently to complicate the Plotinian system, especially through the multiplication of hypostases reaching to almost imaginable extremes.

Secondly, it tends more and more to spread the literary genera of the commentary in which the above noted analytical character is taken to the extreme limits.

Thirdly, beginning chiefly with Iamblichus, the Neoplatonists espouse the cause of polytheism and hence adopt a series of reasons belonging to pagan religion with the further complication that arises from the fact that this or that God or this or that Goddess is claimed to correspond to various hypostases and, in general, the world of the hypostases tends to become, beside including the totality of metaphysical realities, an actual Olympus, a *pantheon*.

Fourthly, while on the one hand pagan philosophers made of Neoplatonism the theoretical foundation of polytheism, the Christian philosophers used the same Neoplatonic principles in order to rethink the new religion on a theoretical level with quite original results. There also exists, hence, a Christian Neoplatonism: that of Origen, of Ammonian derivation, that of Victorinus, of Porphyrian derivation, that of Saint Augustine, of Plotinian and Porphyrian derivation, and that of Pseudo-Dionysius, of Proclean derivation.

Consequently, in a synthesis like this volume those peculiarities which we have noted in the first three points could only be adequately considered in specialized and full monographs. In addition, in a history of ancient philosophy as we have understood it (in accord, moreover, with the majority of scholars), that is, as a history of Greek-Roman philosophical thought which was unacquainted or has not accepted the Christian message, a place cannot be found for the exposition of the philosophical elaborations of Christianity made on the bases of Neoplatonic categories. In fact this elaboration, as we have previously said, constitutes the necessary premise of the history of medieval philosophy, not the crown of classical and Hellenistic thought.

By reserving for another time a return in another work to discuss the two-fold way of pagan and Christian Neoplatonism, we mean to restrict ourselves here to tracing a general framework which permits us to embrace without distortion the various schools, the exponents, and the tendencies of pagan Neoplatonism. Also, the citations of texts of the authors in this section are necessarily restricted, since the most beautiful aspect of these philosophers (if one excludes the *Elements of Theology* by Proclus) is found chiefly in the analytical nature of their writings; but we will not now proceed into the depths of these analyses, for the reasons explained.

2. The schools and the exponents of Neoplatonism

A quite fortunate interpretive schema of the history of Neoplatonism (accepted for a long time and not yet wholly absent from the writers of textbooks, however now largely superseded by specialized studies) is that proposed by Zeller.[1]

The Neoplatonic schools, according to the German scholar, were three in number, and to them would correspond likewise three different tendencies: the first was that of Plotinus, characterized by a prevalently philosophical interest; the second is that of Iamblichus (Syriac school), characterized by a prevalently religious interest; the third was that of the school of Athens, characterized by a combination of these two interests. But Praechter, in one of his works which dates from 1910 and then also in other works,[2] showed the inadequacy of this schema and that it gave rise to many difficulties; in fact, it is evident that Zeller has made use of the Hegelian schema of thesis-antithesis-synthesis: Plotinus corresponds in a certain sense to the thesis, Iamblichus and his school to the antithesis, Proclus and the school of Athens to the synthesis. Praechter showed that the reality is much more complex. He distinguishes *six schools and three tendencies*. In his schema he does not include the schools and the tendencies of Christian Neoplatonism, and this is correct for the reasons explained above; but he did not even include the school of Ammonius Saccas, an omission open to strong objections and, in fact, in our judgment, not justifiable, since as we have seen, the gestation of Neoplatonism occurred in the circle of Ammonius. By updating, therefore, the conclusions of Praechter (which in their substance successive studies have in various ways reconfirmed), we can trace the following outline of the Neoplatonic schools.

(1) First school of Alexandria, founded by Ammonius Saccas probably around 200 CE, flourished in the course of the first half of the third century CE (circa 200-250 CE). The most famous members of this school, as we already know, were Erennius, the pagan Origen, in addition to the well-known erudite, Longinus (probably also the Christian Origen was a hearer of Ammonius).

(2) A school founded by Plotinus at Rome in 244 CE which flourished in the course of the second half of the third century CE. The most important members of this school were Amelius and Porphyry (the latter also spent some time in Sicily).

(3) A school in Syria, founded by Iamblichus a little after 300 CE, which flourished in the course of the first decades of the fourth century. Exponents of this school were Theodorus of Asine, Sopater of Apamea, and Dexippus.

(4) A school at Pergamum, founded by Aedesius, follower of Iamblichus, a little after his death. Exponents of this school were Maximus, Chrysanthius, Priscus, Eusebius of Mindus, Eunapius, the Emperor Julian called the Apostate, and his collaborator, Sallustius. The dissolution of the school can be made to coincide with the death of Julian (363 CE).

(5) The school of Athens, founded by Plutarch of Athens between the end of the fourth century and the beginning of the fifth century and consolidated by Syrianus. Proclus was the most important figure. Other representatives were Domninus, Isidore, Damascius, Simplicius, and Priscianus. The school was closed following the Edict of Justinian in 529 CE.

(6) A second school of Alexandria; among its exponents are Hypatia, Synesius of Cyrene, Hierocles of Alexandria, Hermias, Ammonius son of Hermias, John Philoponus, Asclepius, Olympiodorus, Elias, David and Stephen of Alexandria. This school arose or better was revived, contemporaneously with the school of Athens and survived up to the beginning of the seventh century CE.

(7) A circle apart, if not a real school, is constituted by the so-called Neoplatonists of the Latin West of the fourth and fifth centuries CE among whom are numbered in erudite supremacy Chalcidius, Marius Victorinus, Marcrobius, Martianus Capella, and Boethius. Almost all of these thinkers were, or became, Christians: nevertheless, they were not successful (if Victorinus and Boethius are excluded) in their attempts at a synthesis between Platonism and Christianity and they were important (sometimes very much so) especially as intermediaries between the philosophical thought of antiquity and the Middle Ages.

3. The various tendencies of the Neoplatonic schools

The tendencies of the Neoplatonic schools, according to Praechter, are *reducible to three*: (1) a speculative tendency, (2) a theurgic tendency, (3) a chiefly erudite tendency. The speculative tendency would be represented by the school of Plotinus, by the school of Syria, and that of Athens; the theurgic tendency is found especially in the school at Pergamum; the erudite tendency is found instead in the school of Alexandria and in the Neoplatonists of the Latin West. The principal merit of Praechter, in this regard, consists in a particular way in having completely re-evaluated the role of Iamblichus and having shown that precisely with this philosophy the essential turning-point occurs in the history of second Neoplatonism. These characteristics that Zeller maintained were typical of Iamblichus and of the Syrian school, that is, the reduction of the speculative and philosophical interests to the mystical-theurgic interest are instead, according to Praechter typical of the school of Pergamum. In effect, the extant documents show that Zeller is mistaken and Praechter is largely correct, as the most recent research has again more clearly demonstrated.[3]

The schema of the tendencies, nevertheless, in our judgment needs a further correction. In fact, there exists a rather clear difference between the school of Plotinus and that of Iamblichus and of Proclus insofar as *only in the former* does pure speculation prevail while in the other two the speculative interest is linked to the religious-theurgic interest, as we will see. It will therefore be appropriate to distinguish not three, but *four tendencies*:

(1) Plotinus with his school (as perhaps also Ammonius with his circle)[4] represents the *speculative-metaphysical tendency*. He, in fact, maintained his philosophy as quite detached both from "positive" religion as well as from theurgic practice and his religious nature itself was of a uniquely speculative character. His reply to Amelius's invitation to a religious ceremony is well known: "It is up to the Gods to come to me; not for me to go to them."[5] Also, the immediate followers of Plotinus, although showing some accommodation, did not succeed in ameliorating except in a partial way the position of the master, as we will see.

(2) The school of Iamblichus and that of Athens represented, instead, *a combination between the speculative tendency and that mystico-religious theurgic*: Neoplatonism, besides philosophical speculation, becomes foundation and apologetic defense of polytheistic religion and even assumes theurgy as complement, if not even as crown, of philosophy.

(3) *The school of Pergamum represents a moment of accentuated religious-theurgic turning inward* and of a clear decline of the speculative-philosophical component.

(4) In the Alexandrine Neoplatonists and in those of the Latin west, finally, the *erudite component* prevails and the metaphysical system is notably simplified and sometimes reduced in a Middle Platonic sense. Let us now examine, in a more specific way, each of these schools and their related tendencies.

II. The Immediate Followers of Plotinus

1. Amelius

We have spoken amply in the preceding section of the school of Ammonius (first Neoplatonic school of Alexandria) just as we did of the school and the system of Plotinus. However we still need to speak about the immediate followers of Plotinus, Amelius and Porphyry, whom we have mentioned many times above but only in passing. Amelius,[1] who was deeply intimate with the thought of Numenius before becoming a very faithful follower of Plotinus, remained poised between two masters. Notwithstanding the facts he began to develop some points of the philosophy of Plotinus, anticipating, in his own way, a tendency which was then largely followed by successive Neoplatonists. He maintained that it was necessary to proceed to a tripartition of the second hypostasis, the *Nous*. Proclus says:

> Amelius posits a threefold Demiurge, three Nous and three Kings: that which exists, that which contains, and that which contemplates [τὸ ὄντα = the existent; τὸ ἔχοντα = the container or possessor; τὸν ὁρῶντα = the contemplator]. They differ insofar as the first *Nous* is being in the fullest sense, the second is the Intelligible in itself, possesses that which is prior to Him and entirely participates in that and for such a reason indeed is second. The third is simply Intelligible in itself, because every Intelligence is identical to the Intelligible to which it is strictly conjoined.[2]

Amelius called this triad with names of the Gods: *Phanes, Ouranos*, and *Kronos*.[3] That the complex second Plotinian hypostasis could give rise to such distinctions is undeniable; but it is likewise undeniable that Plotinus insisted on its unity, while beginning precisely from Amelius the Neoplatonists would insist more and more on the distinctions and, as we will see, introduced distinction after distinction and multiplied the hypostases and the stages of the various hypostases in a mode and measure which, far from enriching, ended in disintegrating Neoplatonic metaphysics.

Amelius (at least to judge from the few extant fragments) apparently did not introduce the tripartition of *Nous*, since he did not reinterpret the three Plotinian hypostases in a unified way but rather remained under in the influence of Middle Platonism and of Numenius who, as we have seen, distinguished a gradation of minds.[4] This would seem to be confirmed again by the fact that Amelius had an attitude toward the Soul opposite to that taken in relation to *Nous*, insisting on the unity of the Soul contrary to Plotinus. In fact, while Plotinus spoke of the unity of the Soul with respect to genus and species, Amelius spoke of the unity of the Soul with respect to number as well, and held that the differentiations of the Soul would depend only on the different relations into which the Soul can enter.[5]

The general schema of the hypostases of the Amelian system seem thus to be the following:

The One

$$\text{Mind or Nous} \begin{cases} \text{First } Mind & = \text{Being } (= \text{Phanes}) \\ \text{Second } Mind & = \text{Having } (= \text{Ouranos}) \\ \text{Third } Mind & = \text{Contemplating } (= \text{Kronos}) \end{cases}$$

Soul

Amelius had a strong attachment to philosophy as well as to positive religion and to the practices of pagan worship. Porphyry says:

> Amelius was scrupulous in observing the day of the New-Moon and other holy-days.[6]

Evidently, at least on the existential level, philosophy was not sufficient for him to achieve the ultimate goal. Nevertheless, he did not defend (or did not know how to defend) on the speculative level the positions which were implicit in this practical attitude, and therefore, as we have previously said, he did not change the general direction that Plotinus had impressed on the school.

2. Porphyry

Porphyry for a long time was scarcely taken seriously as a thinker, instead, he was valued as a learned man and as a communicator of the thought of Plotinus.[7] The judgment of Bidez is typical and is accepted by many scholars: "If we want to characterize Porphyry" writes the French scholar with expressions which we would use for a writer of our time, "we would say of him that he possessed the lively and flashy attitude of an excellent publicist, a lively pen, sharp scissors and he placed these instruments each in turn at the service of the credulity and superstition of eastern cults, of the 'scientific' and literary criticism of Longinus, finally at the service of the religiousness of Plotinus. In all that remains of his writings there is not a thought or an image which one can say with certainty belongs to him. Not only does he contradict himself as he gets old and discovers new thinkers and new ambiences, but also, in the most beautiful and fecund period of his life, after having undergone the influence of Plotinus, he did not succeed in establishing communications rapid and complete enough to suppress the discords and to make of the whole a perfect harmony between the two different compartments of his intelligence."[8]

For some time, nevertheless, scholars have noted a repair of the break and they have made a remarkable effort, in part crowned by success, at re-evaluating Porphyry from an essentially philosophical viewpoint.[9]

The most conspicuous originality emerges in the sphere of his metaphysics. In the last century, some scholars had noted that Being, Life and

Mind, which in Plotinus are traits essentially characterizing Mind (Nous), in Porphyry tend to become true and proper hypostases.[10] But recently, Pierre Hadot has shown that actually Porphyry had forged further ahead than others.[11] As is drawn from some testimonies, compelled by the doctrine of the *Chaldean Oracles*, along with that derived from Plotinian metaphysics, our philosopher placed at the apex of his theology *nine hypostases*, i.e., three hypostases characterized each by a triad, by three distinct moments. By using all the extant testimonies in this regard, Hadot succeeded in establishing that "all three triads were probably described in the same terms and Porphyry did not distinguish among them except for the predominance of one term over the others,"[12] according to the following schema:

Father or Sustainer [= One]
$\begin{cases} \text{Subsistence} \\ \text{Life (=power)} \\ \text{Mind} \end{cases}$

Life [= Power]
$\begin{cases} \text{Subsistence} \\ \textbf{Life} \\ \text{Mind} \end{cases}$

Mind
$\begin{cases} \text{Subsistence} \\ \text{Life} \\ \textbf{Mind} \end{cases}$

Hadot has also explained the meaning of this schema as follows: "At the level of Father, Mind is reduced to a state of pure subsistence [ὕπαρξις]; life and Mind are mixed up with the first term. Rising from subsistence, Mind becomes life, and this is the second triad; it is, then, in a state of alteriety and infinitude. Mind is truly itself only in the third triad, when it predominates over life and subsistence. In this ennead, the Father or subsistence is therefore the first moment of the self-generation of Mind."[13]

The One, according to Porphyry, does not stand above the triad (or of the ennead) but is identical with its first term, as is expressly stated. The One, for our philosopher, would be pure being (absolute power) from which Mind is derived and developed.[14]

Porphyry, in sum, seems not to be wholly stripped of the Middle Platonic mentality,[15] linking the One to Mind in a way which, as we will see, the succeeding Neoplatonic pagan thinkers could not accept (while, for a different reason, the Porphyrian position lends itself to be used fruitfully by Christian thinkers for the elaboration of trinitarian doctrine).

In addition, it has been noted that Porphyry, with regard to the question of the origin of the world in a certain way is close to the conception of creation from nothing, expressly rejecting the necessity of matter for the generation of the world and maintaining the temporal origin of the world.[16] Nevertheless, on the basis of the extant evidence,[17] it is not possible to evaluate the occurrence and nature of these tenets in the general plan of the metaphysics of Porphyry.

Our philosopher has a particular sensitivity for the moral problematic. It seems, in fact, that he valued the ethical component greatly, conceiving philosophy as "a salvation of the soul," as a way of becoming pure and a means of rising to God.[18] "Salvation" consists in being liberated from the burden of the body, hence of being freed from the passions of the soul and finally in rising to God through the soul itself. This is possible according to Porphyry since "what is saved" as well as "what saves" simultaneously exists within us. And what saves is "a true teacher"[19] present in our soul, God and His Law, or if you prefer, the Mind which recognizes in itself the imprint of God and of His Law. Here are two significant texts:

> The intellect is master, savior, nourisher, guardian and guide: it aims at truth in silence and discovering the divine law through the contemplation of itself it recognizes in its interior depths the law impressed, known from all eternity.[20]

> God is chiefly reflected in pure minds, but he cannot be seen by the body or by an evil soul covered in vice. The beauty of God is unblemished, his light is a life effulgent with truth; vice is falsity because of ignorance and is deformation because of an ugly way of life. Therefore you should desire and ask of God what he himself wishes and *is*, because you are well acquainted with the fact that the more man loves the body and bodily things so much the more will he cover over the vision of him, even if you are honored by all men as a God. The wise man is known to a few, or even, if you wish, is unknown to the many, but he is known to God. The intellect follows, therefore, God and contemplates his image in itself; the soul follows the intellect; the soul preserves, insofar as it is possible, the body, made pure by its purity: likewise, the body becomes impure through the passions of the soul, and it will revert in its turn to its own filth.[21]

The Porphyrian distinctions of the virtues are present which also indicates an undoubted clarity and a certain deepening of the corresponding Plotinian doctrine.

The virtues are divided into four grades.

(*a*) The lowest grade is the "political virtues," which consist "in moderating the passions" (or, as Porphyry likewise says, in "following the guidance of reason in the duties and actions of life"). These are: *wisdom* understood as moderation of the irrational part, *fortitude* as moderation of the irascible part, temperance as moderation of the concupiscible part, and *justice* as that which "sees to it that all the individual virtues perform their proper function both in commanding and in obeying."

(*b*) The political or civic virtues are only a stage preparatory to the further virtues, the "cathartics," which consist in the separation from the body and the actions of bodies. In this sphere, *wisdom* consists in working without following the body, *temperance* consists in not being disturbed by the qualitative changes in the body, *fortitude* in not being fearful of the separation from the body (as though this were to mean to dissipate into nothingness), *justice* in undisputed power of reason. These virtues are not only *virtues which purify the soul*, but are the *virtues of the purified soul* and their goal is "to make us like God."

(*c*) The third kind of virtue is that of "intellectual operating soul," or, we can say, the kind of *virtue of the spiritualized soul*. At this level, *wisdom* is contemplation of what the Mind possesses, *justice* is to act according to the Mind, *temperance* is the internal conversion of the Mind, *fortitude* its impassiveness.

(*d*) The fourth level is the "paradigmatic" or "exemplary virtues" which are proper to the Mind (Nous) and are the exemplars, of the virtues which are in the soul. Here are the conclusions which Porphyry draws in this regard:

> There are, therefore, four kinds of virtue. One belongs to the mind, that is, to the exemplars, which participate in the intelligible substances themselves; another belongs to the soul which turns to the mind and from this is filled; the third type belongs to the soul of the man occupied in purifying himself or already purified from the body and its base passions; the fourth, finally, adorn man insofar as he places restraints on the irrational and tries to moderate the passions. The one which has the greater virtue as well as the lesser does not act principally according to the lesser but only according to the various circumstances. The aims, then, as was said, differ according to their type. The aim of the civic virtues is to be able to moderate the emotions in the tasks which belong to them naturally; characterized by erasing of all the memories of the emotions; of the others then to act in conformity with the intellect, having abandoned the emotions. The aims of the others are analogous to what was said. Therefore, he who acts according to practical virtue is an conscientious man; one who acts according to a divine character and a good daimon; one who acts solely according to the intellect is a God; and one who acts as the exemplars is father of the Gods. Because it is appropriate that we first of all be concerned with character, trying to possess it in this life, and through these gradually we will come to the highest.[22]

Porphyry was also known as a commentator of Plato as well as of Aristotle. He was convinced, as previously Ammonius Saccas, of the possibility of reconciling the two philosophers: A work of his, unfortunately lost, says so with its significant title: *On the Unity of the Sects of Plato and Aristotle.*

Within the sphere of this activity, the commentary to the works of Aristotle is of signal importance; it will become an obligatory point of reference for all succeeding Neoplatonists.[23] Of particular importance is the attitude taken by Porphyry in relation to the Aristotelian categories. These, in fact, were subjected to a cutting criticism on the part of Plotinus, who considered them from a metaphysical perspective; our philosopher, instead, proposes and discusses them anew on the logical level, and in this sphere he considers them of great usefulness. Porphyry, in this way, re-introduces the logic of Aristotle within the sphere of Neoplatonic speculation. The *Isagoge*, which is a short but succinct introduction to the problematic of the categories, is explicit on this point through the study of the five "predicaments":

> To understand Aristotle's categories, Chrysaorius, one must know the nature of *genus, difference, species, property,* and *accident. This knowledge is also useful for giving definitions and generally for division and demonstration.* I shall make for you a concise review of this traditional teaching as befits an introduction and try to recount what our predecessors said. I shall avoid the deeper issues and in a few words try to explain the simpler notions. For example, I shall put aside the investigation of certain profound questions concerning genera and species, since such an undertaking requires more detailed examination: *(1) whether genera or species exist in themselves or reside in mere concepts alone; (2) whether, if they exists, they are corporeal or incorporeal; and (3) whether they exist apart or in sense objects and in dependence on them. Instead, I shall try to make clear to you how in logic the ancients, and especially the Peripatetics, dealt with genus, difference, and the rest.*[24]

This is the celebrated passage which will give rise in the medieval period to the well-known dispute about universals.

Porphyry was, in addition, the first to comment on the *Chaldean Oracles* using Neoplatonic categories.[25] With this commentary he put in place the foundation for the birth of that tendency which will become dominant immediately after him, especially in the works of Iamblichus. The *Chaldean Oracles*, together with the Orphic *Songs* (and the great poets of the past such as Homer[26] and Hesiod), became a kind of pagan *"Bible."* These texts are considered expressions of a divine revelation which philosophy had to welcome as points of departure for its own reflection.

Porphyry conducted a sharp polemic against the Christian religion in a vast work of fifteen books entitled *Against the Christians.* (The work is not extant, but, to judge from fragments and testimonies, it was not a counter-positing of the ancient vision of the world to the new, but it was engaged in a clever criticism of the texts of the *Bible.*)[27] He therefore did not embrace the cause of paganism in an indiscriminate manner and, at least after meeting Plotinus, he criticized, in the *Letter to Anebo,* that theurgy and those superstitions in which he believed in his youth and which he had extolled in his *Philosophy of the Oracles.*[28] A speculative spirit prevailed in Porphyry which is particularly Plotinian even if, after the death of Plotinus, he turned to making concessions to theurgy in his work *On the Return of the Soul:*[29] the theurgic practices would act only on an inferior part of the soul, on the pneumatic soul, meaning the heavenly "vehicle" (ὄχημα) in which each soul is clothed. Taking everything into account it would seem that Porphyry, although recognizing in theurgy a certain efficacy, did not judge it in favorable light.[30]

III. Iamblichus and the Syriac School

1. Iamblichus and the new course of Neoplatonic Philosophy

A great turning-point in the history of Neoplatonism took place with Iamblichus and his school. A turning point which permits Hellenic philosophy to survive for two more centuries, by exploiting all the residual energies of the Greek spirit which were by then flagging.

Iamblichus was born in Chalcis, in Coele Syria, toward the end of the first half of the third century CE.[1] Before coming in contact with Neoplatonic philosophy, he knew and admired Neo-Pythagorean as well as Aristotelian philosophy. He probably became acquainted with Neo-Pythagorean philosophy, of which he was a fervent admirer,[2] at Alexandria, and Aristotelian philosophy at the school of the Peripatetic Anatolius, who later became Bishop of Laodicea.[3] Only at a second stage did Iamblichus make contact with Porphyry (perhaps introduced by Anatolius himself).[4] The meeting with Porphyry must have been decisive, since it meant his first contact with Neoplatonic thought. The relationship between the two thinkers, which at first were good, must have deteriorated before Porphyry died. The crux was the interpretation and proper evaluation of the relationship between philosophy and positive religion, and in particular between rational thought and theurgy. The rupture became irreparable and Iamblichus adopted an attitude not only critical, but positively hostile to Porphyry.[5] Those aspects and practices of pagan religion that Porphyry had criticized and in great part rejected, for Iamblichus instead must have been an essential stage or even the crowning moment of philosophy. It was precisely this conception which inspired the school (founded in Syria at the beginning of the fourth century)[6] and the most important works of our philosopher.[7]

The different direction that Iamblichus had impressed on Neoplatonism was correctly understood by the ancients. Olympiodorus, for example, expressly opposed the position of Plotinus and Porphyry to that of Iamblichus, Syrianus, and Proclus, as follows:

> Some rank *philosophy* first, like Porphyry, Plotinus and many other philosophers; others, instead, rank the *priestly arts* (ἱερατική) first, like Iamblichus, Syrianus and Proclus...

The importance of the thought of Iamblichus was noted even more by the ancients. Frequently enough, in fact, the later Neoplatonists called Iamblichus "divine," praising him and extolling him without reserve.

The modern reader who encounters as much of this thinker as came down to us would undoubtedly be surprised by these exalted eulogistic terms and remain disappointed or even irritated, as for example happened to Zeller and to those scholars who followed him. But apart from the fact (although in itself important enough) that the extant works of Iamblichus are (if we exclude *De mysteriis*) the less important ones, it needs to be emphasized that the thought of our philosopher cannot be understood according to the abstract canons of Hegelian dialectic, *but only by bearing in mind the concrete historical situation in which he moves*.

Consequently, considered from this perspective Iamblichus is actually an important thinker, because he knew how to interpret the problems of the learned pagan of his time and he was able to adopt solutions which were considered to be quite effective.

The originality of our philosopher is particularly important in at least three different directions.

(1) Plotinus criticized in particular the doctrinally unorthodox Christian sect known as the Gnostics. Porphyry, in his massive work *Against the Christians*, was limited to a kind of historico-erudite criticism. So then it was not sufficient to criticize the Christians, it was also necessary to present paganism again positively in that Greco-eastern syncretistic understanding which he had accepted and to further the cause by providing it with a theoretical foundation. The polytheism of the last Greeks had to be established again on a conceptual level.

Consequently, in the Neoplatonic metaphysics appropriately reinterpreted in function of the stimuli of the *Chaldean Oracles*, our philosopher found the theoretical foundation of polytheism. Note that in this reform Iamblichus succeeded easily, since the multiplication of the metaphysical hypostases and the multiplication of the Gods have the same source, arising, in the ultimate analysis, from the same intellectual attitude, as has been correctly acknowledged for a long time.

On the other hand, as we have seen previously, the school of Plotinus, although timidly had opened a way to Iamblichus: Amelius had distinguished three hypostases in Mind [Nous] giving it the names of Gods and Porphyry had introduced his metaphysical innovations inspired by the *Chaldean Oracles*.[9]

(2) But final paganism could not be content with this ontological refoundation of polytheism, pervaded as it was by soteriological anxieties and by a thirst for the rites, magic, and theurgic practices which would be capable of placating and propitiating the Gods.

As we have previously said, while Plotinus does not mention theurgy, Porphyry, after having practiced it in his youth, criticized it in his *Letter to Anebo* (Egyptian priest). The fulcrum of the Porphyrian criticism consisted in the denunciation of the fallaciousness of the pretenses of theurgy on the basis of the principle that the Gods are "impassible." Evidently, if the Gods are impassible, it is inconceivable that theurgists can act on them with practices of the kind as those which are performed in theurgy. (The admission of a certain efficacy of theurgy that Porphyry made in the *De regressu animae* was of a very limited character, as we have said above.)[10]

It was hence necessary to defend theurgy from these criticisms and to also provide it with a theoretical aspect, inspired by the desire to find an adequate place in the life of the spirit for it.

This task was taken up by Iamblichus in the work previously cited many times *On the Mysteries of Egypt*, which received the subtitle "The Reply of Abammon to Porphyry's *Letter to Anebo* and a Solution of the Difficulties which are Found Therein." (Abammon is the name of a priest which Iamblichus used as a pseudonym, practically indicating his function as interpreter of the Gods.)

The particular attachment to theurgy which is encountered not only in later Hellenic popular paganism, but likewise in late Hellenic philosophy is particularly suggestive. The pure *logos* as such was judged insufficient to guarantee the achievement of the ultimate goal without the use of meta-rational powers. And the way in which Iamblichus made interpretations based on this attitude, as we will see, is truly exemplary.

(3) In the final phase of Greek philosophy, as we know, the literary form of the commentary especially to Aristotle and Plato had a very wide diffusion. Plotinus is an exception. But Porphyry had returned to the literary form of the commentary with which he re-read Homer, the *Chaldean Oracles*, the *Dialogues* of Plato, and the works of Aristotle. But Porphyry adopted a criterion of commenting freely and often arbitrarily, as can be clearly seen in his interpretation of the Homeric *The Cave of the Nymphs*. So in this area Iamblichus also was an important innovator. He introduced some exact exegetical canons which were quite effective.

Let us see in a more specific way how our philosopher achieved these reforms.

2. The metaphysics and theology of Iamblichus

The speculative foundation of polytheism, as we have pointed out above, is substantially connected with the complex activity of the multiplication of the hypostases.[11]

The first novelty in this regard consists in having reversed the course followed by Porphyry in the reinterpretation of the Neoplatonic metaphysics. We have seen, in fact, that Porphyry (at least toward the end of his life) tended to relate the One to the intelligible triad and to conceive the former as the first member of the latter (this then being determined according to the enneadic rhythm). Iamblichus, on the contrary, not only re-affirmed the transcendence of the One with respect to the Intelligible, as Plotinus had done, but affirmed the necessity of introducing between the One and the intelligible cosmos a second One. Damascius says:

> After this let us go to the inquiry concerning this other point: are the first principles prior to the first intelligible triad, two, that is to say, what is absolutely ineffable [= the first One] and what is not coordinate to the triad [= the second One], as the great Iamblichus states in the twenty-eighth book of his most perfect *Chaldean Theology*? Or as most of the philosophers preceding him maintained does the ineffable cause [= the One] comes immediately after the first intelligible triad? Or let us not forget this hypothesis and do we say with Porphyry, that the father of the intelligible triad is the single principle of all things?[12]

The position of Iamblichus, taking into account this passage, seems to have been judged as too radical by most of the later Neoplatonists (most preferred to uphold the unique One of Plotinus; Damascius, as we will see, instead, followed our philosopher). Evidently Iamblichus felt the need to distinguish the two characteristic aspects of the Plotinian One (namely, that by which He is said to be absolutely transcendent, wholly ineffable, and unsayable and that through which he is proclaimed the power that produces all things) by making two different hypostases.[13]

What was in Plotinus the second hypostasis, the Mind (*Nous*), is transformed into a complex of hypostases and moments. It is not possible to be describe this complex except in a general way because of the present state of research. First, Iamblichus held that it was necessary to distinguish the sphere of the "intelligible"(νοητόν) from the sphere of the "intellective," or better, the "intellectual"(νοερόν), separating in this way the two essential traits of the Plotinian *Mind* and *Intelligible*. But there is more. The sphere of the intelligible is divided into three triads and he later also divided the intellective sphere.[14]

It seems possible, in addition (at least based on a text of Proclus although somewhat conjectural), that Iamblichus had previously introduced, anticipating in some way a doctrine which will become technical with the philosophers of the school of Athens, an intermediate sphere between that of the intelligible and that of the intellective, that is, the sphere of the *intelligible-and-intellective* (νοητόν-καὶ νοερόν), and distinguished this also into triads.[15]

The sphere of the Soul, according to the general triadic schema, was also distinguished into three orders.[16]

All the hypostases were presented within the ontological-metaphysical perspective and likewise under a religious perspective and were considered Gods. And in this way polytheism came to be rationally justified by Iamblichus

Here is a synoptic listing which can aid the easy comprehension of the system of the hypostases of Iamblichus:[17]

Supreme, absolutely ineffable Principle (first One)
Second principle (second One)

Mind
(Nous)
{
Sphere of the intelligible, distinguished into three triads
(Sphere of the intelligible-and-intellective distinguished into three triads)
Sphere of the intellective, distinguished into one triad (if the correction of the testimony of Proclus referred to in note 15 is accepted), or in three triads, or one hebdomad if we follow the traditional reading

Soul
{
Hypercosmic Soul
Soul of the Whole
Individual Souls

Naturally, the number of these hypostases was able to be increased without limits by multiplying *ad libitum* [freely] the number of souls which are in the world. And thus, besides the Gods of the *other-world*, Iamblichus also introduces a great number of Gods of the *intra-world* and then still more Angels, Daimons, and Heroes. The intramundane Gods were then divided into complex orders and categories and were multiplied and systematized in such a way to make room for the entire *pantheon* of late-pagan belief.[18]

In the light of what we said, the statement is clear that the conception of the multiplicity of hypostases and the conception of the multiplicity of the Gods depend on the same mental attitude. In fact, as the pagan Gods are nothing but the personified and individualized forces and aspects of nature and man, so the new hypostases, endlessly multiplied, are fundamentally nothing but the reification and substantialization (precisely the hypostatization) of what in Plotinus were simply conceptual determinations. It seems to us that on this point Zeller hits the mark (nevertheless, on the whole, as we previously said, he judged our philosopher incorrectly): "The better way for holding on to the divine seems to him [scil., Iamblichus] that of multiplying it as much as is possible and placing the concepts which determine its essence and its relations with the finite, as autonomous forms, one by the other and one above the other. *But such is the distinctive character of religion and particularly of polytheistic religion: what for philosophical thought is simply a conceptual element is for the religious sensibility a concrete form*; what has the form of universality there has the sensible form of individuality here; and while the monotheistic religions preserve the unity of the divine being and posit the numerous forms of religious intuition only in the history of its revelation, the natural polytheistic religion instead has the characteristic tendency to cut up the divine being into a plurality of particular Gods."[19]

3. Iamblichus and theurgy

In the justification of polytheism, Iamblichus could exploit many of the results which had come down to him from preceding Middle and Neoplatonic, as well as Neo-Pythagorean, thought. But how was it possible to justify that theurgy which in certain respects seems to be the antithesis of philosophy and whose pretensions Porphyry had thus lucidly contested?

Let us see in the first place what is the exact conception that Iamblichus had of theurgy.[20] In the *De mysteriis* it is presented as a practice and an art with which, by means of appropriate acts, symbols, and formulas not understood by human reason but understood by the Gods, man can join himself to the Gods themselves and benefit from their influence and power. The theurgic union with divinity and the related practices necessary for the realization of it were thus conceived as something that was decisively meta-rational. Our philosopher writes:

> Is it not reason (ἔννοια) which unites the theurgist to the Gods; since, in that case, what would impede theoretical philosophers from achieving theurgic union with the Gods? But this is not the truth. The theurgic union is produced by the completion of ineffable actions which they perform beyond any possibility of understanding by the intelligence and by the power of unutterable symbols understandable only by the Gods. Therefore it is not by reason that we grasp these things; in fact, in that case, if we did they would be effects of our intelligence and would depend on us; but both options are untrue. In fact, without our exercising our reason the signs themselves act by their own power, accomplishing their own work, and the ineffable power of the Gods, about which these things are concerned, recognizes by itself their own images without the signs being hidden from the activity of our reason...[21]

Moreover, this passage is an indication of something further; besides forming a complete definition of theurgy, it likewise contains the foundation on which the reply to the objections of Porphyry is based and reveals the remarkable distance that separates the position of Iamblichus (and late Neoplatonism which will follow Iamblichus) from that of Plotinus and his school.

The objections of Porphyry fail, according to Iamblichus, if it is held firmly that *theurgy is an activity beyond intellect and reason of human beings and hence beyond rational powers*. In theurgy, there is no activity of man which rises to the Gods and reaches them, since in such a case it would compromise the impassibility of the Gods themselves, as Porphyry precisely said; it is a question, instead, of the same divine power which descends to men, or better, which frees men from this world and carries them again to the Gods; *it is, in sum, an initiative of the Gods more than one of men.*

Hadot clarifies these concepts very well: "If we could achieve the perfect union with the Gods by means of contemplation, then it would be by means of our powers that we would reach the divine. The Gods would be then moved by lower beings. On the contrary, if they themselves choose the practice, incomprehensible to men, by means of which it can be hoped to be united to them, they remain immobile in themselves and maintain their initiative."[22]

Whoever has followed us up to this point should easily be able to understand that the cost of this operation attempted by Iamblichus was very great. It meant *the explicit admission of the incapacity of philosophy, classically understood, to lead men to the achievement of their supreme goal.* Still Plotinus, as we have noted above, held the wholly Greek conviction that it is possible for man to realize the "union" (ἕνωσις) with the divine by means of his own powers, while Iamblichus consistently denies this possibility.

It is evident that in theurgy and in the "acts and unspeakable symbols" of theurgy, which rational man cannot grasp but which the Gods can comprehend, the pagan searched for what reason *alone* clearly could not give and that the Christians achieved through grace and through the sacraments, but on a very different foundation and with very different guarantees.[23]

4. The canons for the interpretation of classical texts

Praechter[24] has noted that it was a great merit of Iamblichus to introduce some canons and rules for the interpretation of classical texts and in particular for the Platonic dialogues, and the most recent studies have confirmed the soundness of this thesis.

First, according to Iamblichus, a Platonic dialogue must be interpreted *in view of its goals or its unitary aim.* And accordingly not only the whole of the dialogue but likewise the prologue and the individual parts must be interpreted in terms of this goal.

Secondly, according to Iamblichus, it is possible to read a dialogue of Plato's on various levels. He conceived metaphysics, mathematics, physics, and ethics as closely united according to the relation of "model," of "image," or of "copy." More precisely: metaphysics was the model, mathematics the image; in its turn, mathematics was the model in relation to physics and physics was the image of mathematics; ethics was closely connected to mathematics. On the basis of this schema, it was possible to interpret the dialogues *at a different level, without breaking the rule of the principal aim, by passing from image to model,* that is, from a presentation of physics to its mathematical model and from this to the later metaphysical model (or also by passing from parts to the whole).[25]

For all these contributions the final pagan philosophers acclaimed our philosopher by using the epithet "divine." He breathed some life into expiring Hellenic thought. All the other Neo-platonic schools, as we will see, depend on Iamblichus in various ways.

5. Theodorus of Asinus and other followers of Iamblichus

After the death of Iamblichus his school dissolved. Sopater of Apamea, whom Eunapius considered the outstanding thinker among the followers of Iamblichus, remains for us little more than a name, since there are no remaining testimonies that permit us to reconstruct his thought. He went to Constantinople, where he was at first very influential at the imperial court, but then he was executed, being accused of magic.[26]

There is, however, a not very important commentary to the *Categories*, which is extant.[27]

Instead, a certain number of testimonies (only recently collected and systematically arranged) were handed down to us about Theodorus of Asinus.[28] He had some contacts with Amelius and, perhaps through Amelius, also with the thought of Numenius. He was at first a follower of Porphyry and then a follower of the school of Iamblichus, towards whose doctrine he kept a critical attitude. In particular, he did not seem to be interested in the practice of theurgy. But his metaphysics undoubtedly depends on the reform of Iamblichus.

He posited a First, inexpressible and unutterable, as "source of all things and cause of happiness." From the First he deduced a triad which exhausts the "sphere of the intelligible," and he called it the One. It is a *triadic One*, so to speak, a unitary triad. The members of this triad were named by exploiting the symbolism of the three sounds of ἕν = hen, that is, of the One (which are the breath spirit corresponding to the "h" aspirate, the epsilon, and the "nu"), according to the Neo-Pythagorean fashion. Theodorus followed this triad with that which exhausts the "intellectual sphere," characterized by being, by thinking, and by living. Further, he deduced a triad of Demiurges characterized respectively by entity, by thought, and by life (note that in order to characterize this triad Theodorus used the substantives corresponding to the verbal forms (participles) with which he indicated the members of the preceding triad, evidently wanting to signify that these were products of their activity), and he also divided each member of this triad into other triads. Finally, he also distinguished three hypostases in the sphere of the soul.[29] Here is a schema which clarifies this intricate construct:

The First

	Sphere of the Intelligible	= One, divided into three triads, deduced from the three sounds of ἕν (*hen* = One)
World of Mind	Sphere of the Intellective	Being (= being prior to entity) Thinking (= thinking prior to thought) Living (= living prior to life)
	Sphere of the Demiurge	Entity or substantial thought Thought or intellective substance Life or source of life
Sphere of Soul		Soul in itself Universal Soul Soul of the Whole

Theodorus used complex distinctions in relation to Soul considered in itself and in its relations with the corporeal by introducing, once again, Pythagoreanizing considerations taken from the letters of the word *psyché* and from the corresponding number.[30]

The thought of Theodorus has a limited importance and is historically interesting chiefly in the measure in which, in consolidating the system of the triadic dialectic, he ultimately prepared the way for the definitive systematization of Proclus.

IV. The School of Pergamum

1.   Characteristics and exponents of the school of Pergamum

At the death of Iamblichus, Aedesius, one of his more esteemed followers, took up residence at Pergamum in Mysia and there he founded a school. At first, following an oracle that he had received in sleep, he fled into the solitude of a rustic life in Cappadocia. But the information leaked out and many joined him, desirous of hearing his teaching, and he was forced to return to a social form of living. He chose Pergamum as the seat of his school, which very quickly flourished and redounded to the fame of Aedesius.[1]

Among the followers of Aedesius was Maximus, Chrysanthius of Sardis, Priscianus and Eusebius of Mindus.[2] Julian, the future Emperor, also came to Pergamum, attracted by the fame of Aedesius. Among the followers of Aedesius, Julian chose as his teachers: Maximus, who became his teacher in Ephesus, and Chrysanthius.[3] Eunapius (follower of Chrysanthius), who has left a work on the lives of these philosophers, was also connected to this school.[4]

Libanius, the famous rhetorician whose philosophical interests were minimal, was linked to Julian[5] and to Sallustius, who actively collaborated with the Emperor for the restoration of pagan polytheism.[6]

The special characteristics of this school are: (1) the strong reduction of the metaphysical-theoretical dimension; (2) likewise, a strongly accented religious-mystical theurgic component, carried to extremes by some exponents, chiefly by Maximus;[7] (3) the almost total disinterest in the works of Plato and Aristotle, or at least for systematically reading them by means of commentaries.

Eusebius of Mindus, with his dialectical ability and with his strong reservations about the theurgic art, considered it an mindless abuse of certain powers that derive from matter and by his defense of the capacity for reasoning is the exception which proves the rule.[8]

We are hardly in a position to speak about any of the specific doctrines of many of the exponents of this school. Eunapius is limited to narrating the facts about the lives of these philosophers and makes only somewhat elusive hints couched in general terms about their thought. We have, on the contrary, extant works of Julian and Sallustius, but they give us only a partial glimpse of the conceptions of this school.

But let us briefly see the intellectual direction of these two figures.

2.   Julian (the Apostate)

The person and the work of Flavius Claudius Julianus,[9] known to history as Julian the Apostate, belong more to the history of politics and religion than to the history of philosophy. His fame is connected chiefly to the desperate attempt with which he, in his political activity (first in the position of governor of Gaul and then as Emperor), tried to revive the spirit and the religion of Hellenism. It was an attempt which lasted as long as a shooting star.[10]

In whatever way this attempt is judged (on which we will not elaborate), it remains evident that Julian, for a series of reasons in part deriving from circumstances of which he was the victim, did not basically understand Christianity and hence the reasons why history would grant Christianity an enduring posterity. His enterprise was a headlong flight into the past. Even if it is true, as some think, that he did not want to reject Christianity as such, but was intent rather on opposing the attitude of exclusivism of the new religion toward all other religions and he really desired to inaugurate a universal religion which would embrace everyone, what we have said above is still quite sound.

Here are some of his affirmations which are particularly revealing:

> It is opportune, it seems to me, to show here all the reasons by which I have become convinced that the sectarian doctrine of the Galileans is an invention produced by human maliciousness. Nothing of it is from the divine and is the result of the irrational part of our soul which tends toward the fabulous and the puerile, it succeeds in making the truth a construction of monstrous fictions.[11]

Paradoxically, the very one who accused Christianity of rampant irrationality and of being a constructed from a monstrous falsehood was himself overcome by a fanatic attachment of the most irrational kind to the currents of late Greek thought and showed an almost morbid fascination with theurgic practices. Eunapius relates a very significant fact. Eusebius of Mindus, when Julian was at Pergamum, continued to insist on the superiority of the rational method in philosophy in comparison with theurgic practices, so much so that Julian importuned him until he revealed the reasons for his insistence. Eusebius then presented him his own reasons. He tried to warn Julian about the magical arts of Maximus, who rejected rational demonstrations in order to practice theurgy and magic, and he related some exceptional magical works of Maximus, for example, making the statue of the Goddess Hecate laugh and the torch which she held between her hands catch fire. Eusebius thus concludes:

> But you must not marvel at this, as I do not marvel at it, and consider instead the purification which is achieved by means of reason a great thing.[12]

Julian, without hesitation, replied:

> I salute you, you are attached to your books: I have had revealed that which I sought.[13]

Julian did not pursue the *logos*, but rather the murky theurgic arts, in which Maximus was clearly an expert. In a letter to Priscianus, in addition, he himself writes:

> Look for all the books of Iamblichus about my namesake [Julian the Theurgist]. Only you can do that....I have a foolish passion for Iamblichus

in philosophy and for my namesake in theosophy, and I judge the others as nothing...in comparison with them.[14]

Notice that the actual Neoplatonic doctrine is only a general framework in which both allegorizing and theurgy are found together. The two most famous discourses of Julian, *To the Sun King* and *To the Great Mother of the Gods*, are an excellent illustration of the speculative results of the thought of the Emperor.[15]

3. Sallustius

The treatise of Sallustius[16] *On the Gods and the World* quite probably enters into the framework of the politics of the restoration of pagan polytheism started by Julian and is a kind of manifesto of polytheistic faith or a catechism of its essential articles, as has been acknowledged for a long time.

The writing is truly exceptional in its clarity and lucidity and is a rather conspicuous effort to purify pagan beliefs in order to make them competitive with the Christian religion.

Most of the ideas expressed in the brief treatise are not original. In some points, however, the author, trying hard to compete with Christian conceptions, upholds some unusual positions. Thus, for example, he affirms that Providence exists for the people, for the city, "as well as for each individual man."[17]

The interpretation of the origin of evil is very fine. In the world, says Sallustius, *nothing is evil by its nature*, but *it only becomes evil through the actions of men*, in fact, of some men. In addition, evil is not committed by men *for itself*, but because it is falsely presented under the appearance of a good. Evils arise and only because of a false evaluation of a good and the soul can be a victim of this false evaluation "because it is not a primary reality"; we would say *because of its finitude.*[18]

The knowledge of the existence of the Gods for Sallustius, as for all Neoplatonists, is *natural*. Atheism is explainable, then, only as a kind of "punishment." It can be conceived that those who have known but despised the Gods in a succeeding reincarnation are punished with the privation of the knowledge of the Gods, banished, as it were, from them. The Demons, writes Sallustius, are not the only ones to punish souls, but it is also the soul itself which "gives itself its proper punishment."[19]

These are the limited areas of interest in which the Neoplatonists of the school of Pergamum move. At a far higher level the message of Iamblichus, as we will now see, is heard in the school at Athens.

V. Proclus and the School at Athens

1. The origin of the school at Athens

We have examined above what happened at the closing of the Academy during the conquest of Athens by Sulla (86 BCE) and at the dissipation of the inheritance of the School at the time of Antiochus of Ascalon.[1] At the end of the pagan era and at the beginning of the Christian era the center from which the most significant philosophical ideas emanated, as we know, was Alexandria, where Neo-Pythagoreanism, Middle Platonism, the Mosaic philosophy of Philo, and Neoplatonism took shape.

Certainly at Athens, even after the end of the glorious institution founded by Plato himself, although in a somewhat non-continuous way, there were revivals of Platonism owing to the works of some of the masters who gathered around themselves a certain number of students. Let us recall Ammonius of Chaeronea, the Egyptian teacher of Plutarch, and Calvenus Taurus, teacher of Aulus Gellius, who must have imparted their teaching in a private fashion and not under the aegis of an institution.[2] In the third century CE, we have news of two Platonist "diadochai," Theodotus and Eubulus.[3] But they probably had no more than a publicly financed "chair" in Platonic philosophy.

Probably only toward the end of the fourth and the beginning of the fifth century CE was a Platonic school revived and systematically organized in Athens, with its own resources and funds and with a regular succession of scholarchs[4] which continued for another century up to 529 CE, the year in which the Emperor Justinian prohibited public teaching to the pagans.

With this new school pagan Neoplatonism produced its final fruit, and then remained definitively overcome by Christian thought, which in the meantime was established and was consolidated and diffused in the East and West. In the city in which it reached its greatest splendor, ancient philosophy hence returned in order to live its final significant state and to pass from the stage of history.

The reasons for this return to Athens of the final pagan philosophy has long ago been well stated.[5] In Constantinople Christianity's domination by then was uncontested. In Alexandria the "catechetical school" had furnished a speculative base to the Christian message and was a consistent pole of attraction. In the Latin world, then, Greek philosophy did not have any possibility of being proposed and put on its feet again. Instead, as Vacherot noted, "in Greece and especially at Athens, although the new religion penetrated into souls, it had not turned the men away from the worship of antiquity: Christians and pagans untied in a common admiration of the art and science of Greece."[6] Political events connected with the pagan reaction promoted by the Emperor Julian and the succeeding Christian retaliation after the death of Julian would produce moderate effects in Athens. In sum, Greece (and especially Athens) "while becoming Christian still remained the sanctuary of the Muses; the love of antiquity then brought men closer.... The new religion, absolute sovereign in the East, was contented for the moment to have destroyed the schools of philosophy and polytheism at the center of the empire and allowed the school of Athens in its isolation and impotency to temporarily continue in existence."[7]

The philosophers of the school of Athens are therefore authentic "survivors." A date is particularly significant in this regard. In 430 CE, Saint Augustine died. Precisely around this time Proclus, the man who was destined to give greater consistency to the school, arrived in Athens, where he met the founders: Plutarch, son of Nestorius, now old, and his disciple and friend Syrianus and with them he joined in a last desperate attempt to revive a world which had already sunk into the mists of the past.

2.   The predecessors of Proclus: Plutarch of Athens, Syrianus, and Domninus

The initiator of the Neoplatonic school at Athens was Plutarch, son of Nestorius, as we have already pointed out.[8] We do not know who his teachers were, nor do we know with precision his doctrines. From extant testimonies, nevertheless, it is possible to recover what were the general directions of his intellectual interests and his problematic, which was essentially identical with the parameters within which the whole school moved.

In his lectures, the texts which constituted the landmarks were those of Aristotle and Plato. He dedicated specific commentaries to some of these texts. The philosophy of Aristotle was interpreted by Plutarch as a propaedeutic to that of Plato, as a kind of "initiation preparatory to the little mysteries," as a condition for being initiated into the higher mysteries of Plato.[9]

The problematic which Plutarch seems to have probed with great success was that of psychology.[10] He also cultivated with jealous attachment the theurgic art which he probably considered the crown of philosophy.[11]

We are also poorly informed about Syrianus, who succeeded Plutarch. There is a commentary to some books of the *Metaphysics* of Aristotle by him and some testimonies which permit us to construct a very approximate idea of his thought.[12]

In his commentary to the *Metaphysics*, he consolidated that interpretation probably arising with Plutarch which saw in the philosophy of the Stagirite a conception of reality which was located on a different plane from that of the Platonic. The reconciliation of these two philosophers could not be resolved in an eclectic accommodation of their thought, but through the distinction and the specification of the diverse planes on which they think. Thus, according to Syrianus, the criticisms Aristotle leveled at Plato do not reach their target, since they do not rise to the level on which Plato's thought lives. The distinction of these levels also explains why the Stagirite can be the first stepping stone to further Platonic levels (which, for our philosopher, is identical with Pythagoreanism).

At the higher level, according to Syrianus, the poems of Homer (understood, naturally, in an allegorical sense) are to be placed as well as the songs of Orpheus and the *Oracles*, which are the real "sacred texts" of the final pagan period. The project cherished by Syrianus of writing a commentary on the songs of Orpheus or to the *Oracles* (or to both) was not realized.[13]

Proclus says to cling in all things to the master; this fact would lead us to believe that Syrianus had anticipated many of the ideas which are found in his disciples. But it is not possible to give anything but a much wider meaning to this statement since, as we know, the Neoplatonists believed that all their doctrines are to be found in Plato. In any case, Syrianus has probably specified, at least partly, the law of procession (to which Proclus, as we will see, gave maximum prominence) consisting in the triadic relation of permanence-procession-return. There is evidence, in fact, that Syrianus applied it to the development of the soul.[14]

It is not quite clear whether Domninus succeeded Syrianus for some time before Proclus. Domninus was a cultivated man and a scientist more than a metaphysician, as is shown by his two extant works.[15]

3. Proclus and his philosophical, theological, and religious synthesis

Proclus is the best of the post-Plotinian Neoplatonists,[16] and some of his works (especially the synthesis in the *Elements of Theology*) reveal the presence of a speculative genius of the first order. But with respect to Proclus, it can truly be said that, like the owl of Minerva, genius arrived when it was already evening and night was falling.

The Proclean synthesis, in fact, aimed at embracing in a systematic way the whole spiritual life of the Greeks, at taking on all aspects of it, and at furnishing it with a specific justification: from philosophy, to poetry, to popular religion, to the mysteries, to myths, and in general to all the beliefs which are embraced within the faith of the Hellenes as it had been shaped in the Imperial Age. He found a solid revelation of the truth in all these components.

Actually, our thinker is convinced that man is brought to the Truth and to God not only by (*a*) philosophy by means of reason (understood in the widest sense), but also (*b*) by myth through fantasy and (*c*) by faith through an immediate and transcendent union with the Absolute.

(*a*) The way that philosophical reason carries us to the Absolute is the key notion throughout the whole of his philosophy, as we will show in detail below.

(*b*) Through myth Proclus remarks that the soul, in addition to reason, is endowed with imagination. Consequently, myth, which involves fantastic conceptions, can present the truth to the soul in this way. In fact, nature itself represents the supersensible model in images or sensible copies, true eternity in the passing of time, the One in multiplicity. And thus myth also points to the supersensible with sensible representations, and through its apparent contradictions it drives men to what transcends reason and provokes a movement which, for one who understands it, achieves the truth.[17]

(c) With respect to faith, then, Proclus expressly points out that it is established as the arcane, transcendent, ineffable union with the Absolute: a union which not only binds man to the Absolute, but everything together to the Gods and to the Absolute:

> What therefore is it which unites us to the Good? What is it which causes in us a cessation of action and motion? What is it that establishes all divine natures in the primary and ineffable unity of the Good? And how does it happen that every thing being in that which is each prior to itself, according to the Good which is in itself, again establishes things posterior to itself according to cause. It is, in short, the faith of the Gods which unites, in an ineffable way, all the genera of the Gods, of daimons, and of souls which are happy to the Good. For it is necessary to seek the Good, not by way of knowledge, not by an incomplete way, but with the help of the divine light, after having contemplated themselves and having closed the eyes of the soul in such a manner to become established in the unknown and arcane unity of beings. For such a type of faith as this is more ancient than the gnostic energy not in us only, but with the Gods themselves, according to this all the Gods are united, and around a single center uniformly collect the whole of their powers and progressions. And if it is necessary to give a particular definition of this faith, let no one suppose that it is such a kind of faith as that which is conversant with the wandering about sensible things. For this falls short of science and so much more of the truth of beings. But the faith of the Gods transcends every form of knowledge, and according to the highest union conjoins secondary with first natures. Nor again, let him conceive a faith of a similar kind with the famous belief in common notions; for we believe in common notions prior to all reasoning. But, the knowledge of these is divisible and is by no means equivalent to divine union; and the science of these is not only posterior to faith, but also to intellectual simplicity. The mind is established beyond all science, both the first science and that which is posterior to it. Neither, therefore, must we say that the activity according to mind is similar to such a faith as this. For intellectual activity is multiform, and is separated from the objects of intellectual through difference; and in short, it is intellectual motion about the intelligible. But it is necessary that divine faith should be uniform and quiet, being perfectly established in the port of Goodness.[18]

Faith is identified for Proclus therefore, with *theurgic power*, which is *a wisdom higher than human wisdom*, a kind of *meta-rational union with the Divine*, as we know.

It is understandable, on the basis of these premises, why the activity of our philosopher develops in this threefold direction: (*a*) reading and commenting on philosophers, especially on Plato; (b) commenting on the poets (from Hesiod to Homer to Orpheus) and in general of Greek and non-Greek theology; (c) the practice of theurgy.

It is, as can be clearly seen, the same program inaugurated by Iamblichus which Proclus had completely achieved.

4. The structure of the incorporeal, or the Proclean system of the hypostases

Before touching on the most original points of the Proclean system, we will make a quick survey together with what, according to our philosopher, is the structure of the incorporeal.

We have seen that the triadic division tended to distinguish and to multiply the Plotinian hypostases, but was then consolidated from Amelius to Porphyry to Iamblichus to Theordorus of Asinus. Proclus brings this tendency to its extreme consequences almost to the point of paradox.

First, he was convinced, as was Iamblichus, that between the highest Principle and the hypostases of the intelligible world there are intermediaries. For Iamblichus it was a second One, and for Proclus it became a series of henads, which are identical with the highest Gods. Here is a revealing text in which Proclus summarizes his conception of the One and, in part, of the henads:

> Again, therefore, the arcane doctrine concerning the One must be resumed by us, so that by proceeding from the first principle we may celebrate the second and the third principles of the whole of things. Of all beings, therefore, and of the Gods that produce beings, one exempt and imparticipable cause pre-exists,an ineffable cause indeed by all language, unknown by all knowledge and incomprehensible, unfolding all things into light from itself, subsisting ineffably prior to and converting all things to itself, but existing as best end of all things. This cause Socrates in the *Republic* calls the Good; and it is a cause which truly transcends, separated from all the other causes; a cause which gives unity to all the divine monads, to all the genera of beings and their processions, and through its analogy with the sun, reveals its admirable and unknown transcendence in relation to every knowable thing. But again, in the *Parmenides* he calls it the One. And showed the transcendent and ineffable subsistence of this One which is the cause of the whole of things through the use of negative characteristics. But the argument in the *Letter to Dionysius* couched in hidden and enigmatic statements speaks about it as the cause of all that which exists and of all beautiful things. Socrates, then, in the *Philebus*, refers to it as the foundation of the whole of things, because it is the cause of all deity. For all the Gods, by means of this primary God, have their existence. So is it called the source of all divinity, or the king of beings, or the henad of all henads, or the goodness generative of truth, or the transcendent subsistence of all things, and beyond all paternal or generative causes; let us venerate it in silence and prior to silence by union, and of the mystic goal may it impart by illumination a portion adapted to our souls.[19]

It is easy to see that the Henads existing between the One and the first stage of the intelligible (which is Being), as has been noted, could be drawn doctrinally from Plotinus himself and in particular from his doctrine of numbers, which we examined above. Actually, for Plotinus number was "pre-existent to beings" and "it was not beings." Plotinus said likewise that "Being is a number contracted in a unity," while beings are "developed numbers.'[20]

It is understandable, then, on the basis of these preceding considerations and the further reflections of Iamblichus, applying the hypostatic dialectic, how Proclus did not have very far to go in order to arrive at his "Henads," which are not the primary entities but are above being and have characteristics very similar to the One. In contrast, it is the One, they are "unity" while the One is Good, they are "Goodness." Like the One, Proclean Henads are beyond the intelligible and hence are not only, as we have previously said, beyond Being, but likewise beyond Life and Thought. These Henad-Gods are therefore super-essence, super-vital, and super-intellectual.[21] Polytheism prior to Proclus never elevated the qualities of the Gods (or some of the properties of the Gods) to this level.

The hypostases of the sphere of the Nous followed on the Henads, which Proclus distinguished in the following way:

He distinguished three great spheres of the spiritual world: (1) that of the *intelligible*; (2) that of the *intelligible-intellective*; (3) that of the *intellective*. These correspond basically to the three characteristics with which Plotinus had tried to define *Nous*, meaning *Being, Life, and Thought*. But while in Plotinus they were conceptual and definitional distinctions with respect to the hypostases themselves, in Proclus they are also hypostases. Perhaps, however, Iamblichus previously made additions to this tripartition, as we have seen. It is nevertheless certain that only with Proclus did it reach its full development. Let us read a very clear text in this regard:

> All things which participate intelligence are preceded by the unparticipated Intelligence, those which participate life by Life, and those which participate being by Being; and of these three unparticipated principles *Being is prior to Life and Life to Intelligence*. For in the first place, because in each order of existence unparticipated terms precede the participated, there must be Intelligence prior to things intelligent, Life prior to living things, and *Being prior to things which are*. And secondly, since the cause of more numerous effects precedes the cause of fewer among these principles, Being will stand foremost; for it is present to all things which have life and intelligence (since whatever lives and shares intellection necessarily exists), but the converse is not true (since not all that exists lives and exercises intelligence). *Life has the second place*; for whatever shares in intelligence shares in life, but not conversely, since many things are alive but remain devoid of knowledge. *The third principle then is Intelligence*; for whatever is in any measure capable of knowledge both lives and exists. If, then, Being gives rise to a greater number

of effects, Life to fewer, and Intelligence to yet fewer, Being stands foremost, next to it Life, and then Intelligence.[23]

But, again, the first two hypostases in the sphere of Nous are distinguished by Proclus into further triads, and then again into other triads. In the third hypostasis, instead, a subdivision into hebdomads emerges.[24]

It is impossible, in this setting, to follow our philosopher in the meandering deduction of all these triads and hebdomads, as he redesignates the complex branches of the relationships that link them, showing, according the Neoplatonic axiom of all in all, the multiple play of the reciprocal reflections of the various hypostases and their moments. On the other hand, note that his interest does not lay so much in the results as in the dialectical ability with which Proclus achieved them. But in order to adequately illustrate this ability, it would require a full-blown monograph and its concomitant analysis.

Naturally, these hypostases are Gods, as were the Henads; in fact, Proclus does not hesitate to specify some of them with the traditional Greek names of divinity.[25]

The sphere of the soul was also conceived as a plurality of hypostases and is distinguished into: divine souls, daimonic souls, "partial" souls. Proclus made still further distinctions within the totality of these distinctions, especially within the sphere of the divine Souls, he distinguished triads of Psychic Gods with different functions, and specified and individualized in some of them the Gods of Olympus. Our philosopher distinguishes the Daimons, then, into three classes: Angels, Daimons in the senses specified, and Heroes. The "partial" souls are those that "admit changing from intelligence to senselessness"; to this group belong human souls.[26]

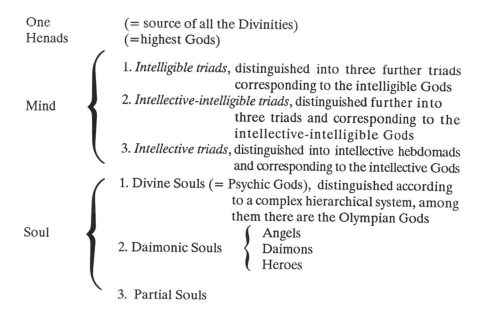

One   (= source of all the Divinities)

Henads   (=highest Gods)

Mind

   1. *Intelligible triads*, distinguished into three further triads corresponding to the intelligible Gods

   2. *Intellective-intelligible triads*, distinguished further into three triads and corresponding to the intellective-intelligible Gods

   3. *Intellective triads*, distinguished into intellective hebdomads and corresponding to the intellective Gods

Soul

   1. Divine Souls (= Psychic Gods), distinguished according to a complex hierarchical system, among them there are the Olympian Gods

   2. Daimonic Souls   Angels / Daimons / Heroes

   3. Partial Souls

5. The laws which govern the procession of reality from the One according to Proclus

The greatness of Proclus is not only due to the perfection of this plan, in part previously traced out by his predecessors, but in the deepening of the laws which govern the procession of the real, specifically in the deepening of that point which, as we have seen, indicated the essential results of Neoplatonism.

First is the perfect specification achieved by Proclus of the general law which governs the generation of all things, understood as a cyclical process made up of three stages: (1) the "maintenance" (μονή) i.e., the remaining or perduring in itself of the principle; (2) the "procession" (πρόοδος) or the exiting from the principle; (3) the "return" or the "turning around" (ἐπιστροφή), i.e., the rejoining of itself to the principle. We have seen that Plotinus had previously specified these three stages and that they play a function in his system which is much more complex than is commonly believed to be the case. Nevertheless, Proclus goes beyond Plotinus, bringing this triadic law to an unusual level of speculative refinement. The law is valuable not only in general, but also in particular: it expresses the *very rhythm of reality both in its totality and in all its individual stages.*

The One, as every other reality which produces something else, also produces by reason "of its perfection and superabundance of power." Consequently, every productive entity (1) *remains what it is* (precisely in virtue of its perfections) and, owing to this immobile and inexhaustible permanence, it produces. (2) The "procession" is not a *transition*, as if the product was derived as *a part separated from the producer*. Procession is to be conceived, instead, as a *multiplication of itself on the part of the producer in virtue of its power*. Besides, what proceeds is similar to that from which it proceeds and the likeness is prior to the unlikeness: the unlikeness consists only in the producer being the *better*, or *more powerful* than the product. In other words, the producer has the same nature as the product, but not *in the same way*. (3) Consequently, the things derived have a structural affinity with their causes; in addition, they aspire to stay in contact with them and hence to "return" to them. The hypostases, therefore, arise through a likeness and not through unlikeness.

The triadic process is conceived like a circle; not, however, in the sense of a succession of moments, as if between *permanence, procession, and return* there were a distinction of a *first* and of a *next* but in the sense of the co-existence of the moments, that is, in the sense that each process is *perennially permanent, perennially proceeding, perennially returning*. In addition, since according to *the principle of likeness* not only does the *permanent* cause as cause, but *also the product, in a certain sense*, remains *in the cause in the same moment in which it leaves it*, because the process is not a "separation," i.e., a becoming totally other; the *permanent* is substantially *the likening of the product to the producer,* and this likeness is the reason why the product aspires to "return" to the cause. Let us read the five theorems [which are italicized] and their proofs from the *Elements of Theology* which fully illustrate these concepts:

30. *All that is immediately produced by any principle both remains in the producing cause and proceeds from it.* For in every procession the first terms remain steadfast, and if the procession is accomplished by means of likeness, like terms coming to existence before unlike, then the product in some sense remains in the producer. For a term which proceeded completely would not have identity with that which remained: such a term is wholly distinct from the prior. If it is to be united by any common link with its cause, it must remain in the latter as we saw that the latter remained in itself. If, on the other hand, it should remain only, without procession, it will be indistinguishable from its cause, and will not be a new thing which has arisen while the cause remains. For if it is a new thing, it is distinct and separate; and if it is separate and the cause remains steadfast, to render this possible it must have preceded from the cause. Insofar, then, as it has an element of identity with the producer, the product remains in it; insofar as it differs, it proceeds from it. But being like it, it is at once identical with it in some respect and different from it: accordingly it both remains and proceeds, and the two relations are inseparable.

31. *All that proceeds from any principle reverts in respect of its being upon that from which it proceeds.* For if it should proceed yet not revert upon the cause of this procession, it must be without appetition of that cause, since all that has appetition is turned towards the object of its appetite. But all things desire the Good, and each attains it through the mediation of its own proximate cause: therefore each has appetition of its own cause also. Through that which gives being it attains its well-being; the source of its well-being is the primary object of its appetite; and the primary object of its appetite is that upon which it reverts.

32. *All the reversion is accomplished through a likeness of the reverting terms to the goal of reversion.* For that which reverts endeavors to be conjoined in every part with every part of its cause, and desires to have communion in it and be bound to it. But all things are bound together by likeness, as by unlikeness they are distinguished and severed. If, then, reversion is a communion and conjunction, and all communion and conjunction is through likeness, it follows that all reversion must be accomplished through likeness.

33. *All that proceeds from any principle and reverts upon it has a cyclic activity.* For if it reverts upon that principle whence it proceeds, it links its end to its beginning, and the movement is one and continuous, originating from

the unmoved again returning. Thus all things proceed in a circuit, from their causes to their causes again. There are greater circuits and lesser, in that some revert upon their immediate priors, others upon the superior causes, even to the beginning of all things. For out of the beginning all things are, and towards it all revert.

35. *Every effect remains in its cause, proceeds from it, and reverts upon it.* For if it should remain without procession or reversion, it will be without distinction from, and therefore identical with, its cause, since distinction implies procession. And if it should proceed without reversion or immanence, it will be without conjunction or sympathy with its cause, since it will have no communication with it. And if it should revert without immanence or procession, how can that which has not its being from higher revert existentially upon a principle thus alien? And if it should proceed and revert, but not remain, how comes it about that being parted from its cause it endeavors to be conjoined with it, although before the severance there was no conjunction (since if it was conjoined with the cause it certainly remained in it)? Finally, if it should remain and revert, but not proceed, how can there be reversion without distinction (since all reversion seems to be the resolution of a principle into something from which its being divides it)?

But the effect must remain simply, or revert simply, or proceed simply, or combine the extreme terms, or combine the mean term with one of the other two; or else combine all three. By exclusion, then, every effect remains in its cause, proceeds from it, and reverts upon it.[27]

A second law, closely connected to this one just illustrated, is that of the so-called "tertiary." By the time such a law was uncovered by specialized studies as the "key to the philosophy of Proclus," it still was not accepted by *communis opinion* [commonly-held opinion]; but now in some more recent studies it is simply stated and then used as a hermeneutic principle.[28]

Proclus maintained that every reality, at every level from incorporeal to corporeal, is made up of two essential components: (1) the "limit" (πέρας) and (2) the "unlimited" (ἀπεῖρον), or infinite (which is like form and matter); (3) every entity, consequently, is like the "mixture", or the synthesis, of them (this is a position which is evidently derived from the Platonic *Philebus*. Let us read the *Elements of Theology*:

> 159. *Every order of gods is derived from the two initial principles, limit and infinity; but some manifest predominantly the causality of limit, others that of infinity.* For every order must proceed from both, because the communications of the primal causes extend through all derivative ranks. But at some points *Limit* is dominant in the *mixture*, at others *Infinity*; accordingly there results one group of a determinative character, that in which the influence of Limit prevails; and another characterized by infinitude, in which the element of Infinity preponderates.[29]

The third law consists in each entity being constituted by *limit* and the *unlimited* and by different mixtures of these elements. The law, note, cannot only be applied to every true *entity* and in general to the higher hypostases, but also to the soul, to mathematical entities, to everything, in sum without exception.[30] Proclus, note again, conceived the "mixture" of finite and infinite both as an effect as well as a cause. In fact, except for the One, everything is a synthesis of two principles; so after the One, every cause is a mixture, and then it is correct to say that "the mixture is a result of the activity of the One, who unites infinite and finite; but insofar as it manifests the One, it is a principle both in relation to the finite and to the infinite."[31]

It is fairly obvious that the *infinite*, or the *unlimited*, corresponds to the *processive moment*, while the *finite*, or *limited*, corresponds to the *turning around*, or to *the moment of returning*.[32]

In this context, (sensible) matter comes to be the *ultimate infinitude* (or unlimitedness), and hence "in a certain sense is good"[33] (contrary to what Plotinus thought), insofar as it is the ultimate effusion of the One according to the unitary law of reality.

A final remark involves the radical exploitation of the principle of "all in all according to an appropriate manner," which is encountered in the dialectic of Proclus. "All is in all," according to our philosopher, refers to the high as well as the low. This may be of some help in understanding this statement.

The lower is *causally* present in the higher hypostases, insofar as the one is a cause of the other. On the other hand, the lower is present by means of *participation* in the higher, that is, insofar as the lower, although being the effect of the higher, remains in the cause by means of the aforesaid relationship (namely, it does not leave the cause, but rather stays in it and keeps a likeness with it). In particular, if we consider the "all in all" from the high to low (according to the way of participation), the One is in the various hypostases of the world of *Nous*, i.e., in the hypostases of Being, Life, and Intelligence, and these are in the hypostases of the Soul, which recapitulate in themselves the universe of the incorporeal and then make it manifest as an appearance by sharing it with the corporeal.[34]

The Elements of Theology, dedicated to the illustration of these principles and to the general laws of the system, remains the most lively work by Proclus, insofar as the philosopher, by eliminating most of the dominant concerns in the *Platonic Theology* of defending to the bitter end pagan religion as well as transferring his preoccupation with constructing the metaphysical Olympus, the metaphysical *pantheon* capable of accepting all the Gods, then concentrates on the essential and presents us with a metaphysical treatise of the first rank. It is precisely this fact which guarantees this work a great future in the Middle Ages as well.[35]

6. Theurgic virtue

Marinus, in writing of the *Life of Proclus*, ends with examples of the "theurgic powers" (which are conceived as hierarchically superior to all the other powers), virtues which Proclus possessed in conspicuous measure.[36] These powers, as we know, are identical with the capacity to be reunited with the Divine. Proclus even placed this power above every human wisdom and made it identical with that "faith" which is involved in all the powers.

From what we have seen above, we ought not be surprised by the fact that Proclus, in order to achieve this union with God, thought that theurgic practices were in order and was thoroughly convinced that they were efficacious.

From the son of Plutarch he had learned the rites and secret formulas of the theurgic art and made frequent use of them. By practicing the Chaldaic lustrations [purificatory rites], he was assured that he had seen apparitions of the Gods in luminous forms and in general of having seem apparitions of Gods and Daimons. Marinus even says that Proclus had absolutely incredible powers, like being able to provoke rain, to foresee earthquakes, and other things of that kind. Finally, let us remember that Proclus was convinced that he belonged to the *catena Hermetica* (i.e., to chain of life among which are numbered those who live the philosophic life), and after a vision he had in sleep, "he was persuaded that he had the soul of the Pythagorean Nicomachus."[37]

All the components of the final stage of Neoplatonism can easily be seen in Proclus in their extreme form almost to the point of breaking out beyond it.

What further can be said after him by the school of Athens?

7. Man and his re-union with the absolute.

Proclus systematically takes up again the typical conceptions of his school about man, who is identified essentially with his soul.

In particular, our philosopher develops the idea of the ὄχημα, i.e., of the "vehicle," or heavenly body, with which every human soul is furnished as incorruptible and eternal as the soul itself, indivisible and impassible, and of which the soul can never be stripped.[38] Proclus maintained, in addition (but this idea is also ancient and was encountered, for example, in Numenius), that before entering into a material corruptible body on this earth the soul puts on like successive layers "more material cloaks."[39] After death it is stripped of these, but not of the ethereal "vehicle" which, as we said, is eternal.

It is noteworthy that Proclus emphasized the presence of the Divine in the soul, which is not identical with the life of the soul, nor with its thought, but is like *a presence or a participation in the One*, which makes the mystical union with the One possible. The mystical intuition of the One, in fact, is possible, just as the various forms of knowledge are, by means of the union of like with like. In the context of the Proclean system this idea, which is very ancient, is influenced by new relationships since for our philosopher the soul recapitulates and contains in itself, according to the law of "all in all," all the preceding hypostases and hence in some way must even contain the One. In effect it constitutes the extreme unfoldedness of the power of the One and in the sensible world it develops, analogously, that function which the One has in the incorporeal: the soul is the immanent link among beings while the One is the transcendent link. Here is a most important page illustrating the chief theme:

> Hence if it be admitted that the divine nature can be known in some way, then it must be known by the substance of the soul, and only by that means is it known insofar as it is possible. For we say that like is always known by like, and evidently, the sensible by sense, the opinable with opinion, the discursive with discursive thought, the intelligible by the mind. So that also by the One, what is in the highest grade One, and the ineffable by that which is ineffable. That is why Socrates rightly observes in the *Alcibiades*, that the soul entering into itself will behold not only all other things but the Gods as well. For inclining towards its own unity and towards the center of all life, and laying aside all plurality and all the variety of the all multiform powers it contains, the soul ascends to the highest watch-tower of beings. And as in the most sacred of the mysteries, it is said that the initiates at first meet with some infinitely varied in species and forms, which are hurled before the Gods but on entering the interior of the sanctuary, unmoved and protected by the sacred rites, they genuinely receive in their depths divine illumination: and like a soldier bereft of his armor (as they would say) participate of a divine nature: -in the same way I believe, also in the contemplation of the whole universe of things. For the soul, when looking at things posterior to herself, beholds only the shadows and images of beings, but when she enters into herself, she unfolds then her own being and her reason. And at first, she only as it were beholds herself; but when she penetrates more deeply into the knowledge of herself, she finds in herself both mind and the order of beings. But when she proceeds into the interior recesses, and into the inaccessible holy place of the soul, she can contemplate, with eyes closed, the general of the Gods, and the unities of beings. *In fact, all things are also in us psychically: and for this reason our nature can know all things; by awakening the powers and the images of wholes which we contain. And this is the best employment of our energy, to be extended to a divine nature itself, having our powers at rest, to revolve harmoniously round it, to excite all the multitude of our soul to this union*, and laying aside all such things as are posterior to *the One*, to become seated and conjoined with that which is ineffable, and beyond all things.[40]

8. The successors of Proclus: Marinus, Isidore, Damascius, and Simplicius

In 485 CE, Marinus of Neapolis (the ancient Sichem), a Jew who lapsed into paganism became the successor to Proclus.[41] He acquired this position because of his great capacity to work and for his perseverance.[42] From what

Damascius says it can easily be understood how much the thought of Marinus lacked profundity.[43] We know that this philosopher did not follow Proclus in the interpretation of the *Parmenides*, but instead understood it as a work wholly concerned with the Ideas and not about hypostases.[44]

Nor was Isidore of greater importance; he held the position only for a brief period and seems to have interests which were more mystical and theosophical than philosophical.[45]

On the contrary, Damascius, who first studied at Alexandria and then directed the school of Athens, was of an entirely different stature.[46] Damascius had talents like Proclus. Nevertheless, although he possessed considerable dialectical talent, he could not proceed beyond Proclus. Actually, with Proclus, Neoplatonism became an *hortus conclusus* [closed garden], lacking any outlet. And under such conditions the attempt to reinterpret a system which had reached the limits of its possibilities would open up the possibility of weakening it rather than strengthening it. This is precisely what happened with Damascius.

First, however, the very title of his major work is significant: *Questions and Solutions concerning the First Principles*. It concerned the issue of doubts and aporias which gathered about the principles of the system and which had to be resolved. Understandably, a positive solution prevailed in Damascius. Like or not, aporias leave their traces, fracturing the certainty which in his predecessors had remained unshaken. Here and there Damascius let slip expressions of doubt about he possibility of man achieving the true Absolute, which is an inheritance of the Gods.

In addition, in order to maintain the Proclean schema Damascius attempted to add other hypostases. At the bottom he adds the "*material Gods*, who elaborate matter as such."[47]

But his most important contributions are concerned with the realities which are at the apex of the system. While Proclus speaks of the One and the Henads, Damascius tends to place the Absolute, in a certain sense, above the One itself, followed by a One-Whole (ἕν-πάντα) and then by an All-One (πάντα-ἕν), which are evidently hypostases introduced with the illusory hope of better explaining the deduction of multiplicity. In this multiplying of hypostases in order to "mediate" the Absolute and what is made to follow upon it, Damascius actually ends up even further away from it, almost placing it, in a certain sense, outside the realm of reality. Our philosopher, consequently, writes of the Absolute:

> It is not necessary to call it Principle, or cause, or first, or prior to all, or beyond everything, much less must we call it the All. In conclusion: it is not necessary to give it any names: for it is not possible to conceive it or think it.[48]

Of this ineffable Absolute which is still beyond the One, nothing can be said; but it cannot even properly be qualified as ineffable or unknowable. With these terms and with others, in fact, we simply verify *the state of our thought in its relationships, not its nature.* Our ignorance in this regard is total. He is "that which is not absolutely by any part," in the sense that he is absolutely transcendent: it is nothingness which is beyond being, but not evidently the nothingness which is the negation of being. It is obvious that the procession could only be ineffable from this ineffable Absolute (in the sense specified).[49]

Damascius, on the one hand, truly empties almost all the support for they system, and on the other hand he risks obscuring the system itself under the accumulation of multiple hypostases, which after wrecking the first Principle as we have seen, ends with the loss of any meaning and just becomes a pile of ruins.

Simplicius called himself a follower of the school of Athens but yet concentrated his efforts on the commentary, especially on commentaries to the works of Aristotle, following for the most part the footsteps of the Alexandrines (at Alexandria, he had heard Ammonius). Among the extant commentaries, that on the *Physics* of Aristotle remains even today an indispensable landmark (given that he followed objective canons of interpretation) and a source of information of the first order.[50]

VI. The Second Neoplatonic School of Alexandria

1.   Characteristics of the final phase of Alexandrine Neoplatonism

We have noted above the necessity to distinguish two Neoplatonic schools of Alexandria or, to a somewhat lesser degree, two distinct phases of Neoplatonism in this city. In fact, after the death of Ammonius (toward the middle of the third century CE) his circle dispersed: Plotinus founded his own school at Rome; the pagan Origen and Heremius, as it seems, did not provide any particular reason for staying together.

The conditions did not exist at Alexandria which would encourage further speculative developments of Neoplatonism in the directions towards which we have seen the other Neoplatonic schools moving. In this city Christian thought had rapidly taken deep roots and, as we have previously recorded, the "catechetical school" with Clement and the Christian Origen had begun to elaborate a powerful philosophical-theological system of Christian provenance, destined to constitute the victorious alternative.

In addition, it should be mentioned that the spirit of the particular sciences and empirical-scholarly research had been forming and consolidating at Alexandria for a long time. Hence, all those who were thirsty for knowledge could move in this direction, in a moment in which the ancient vision of the world was dissolving and a new one was arising, although it was not easy in the general disorientation of the times to work out another choice.

These historical conditions explain the peculiar characteristics which Neoplatonism took on in the fifth and sixth centuries CE.

(*a*) On the one hand we find some thinkers who pursue Christian ideas and who are even converted to Christianity.

(*b*) On the other hand, we have a group of thinkers and students who seem to have a taste for learning more than for speculation; they dedicate themselves to commentaries in which exegesis prevails over the elaboration of philosophical doctrines.

(*c*) In both of these groups we encounter a kind of "simplification" of Neoplatonism. The first reinterpret Neoplatonic thought in order to make it agree with the Christian message, or in order to make it capable of explaining Christian teachings. In fact, some of them even tend *to return Platonism to Middle Platonic positions, or in some way to simplify it is much as possible.*[1] It is true, moreover, that from two representatives of this current come the only testimonies that we possess concerning the teachings of Ammonius Saccas. The positions of Ammonius Saccas note are the simplest form of Neoplatonism, although influenced by Christian creationism.[2] On their side, the commentators are oriented toward understanding the texts in a fundamentally historical and philosophical sense or, in a more objective sense, rejecting, as we have noted above, many of the accretions which are encountered in the school of Iamblichus and in that of Athens.

(*d*) We also encounter a preference for the works of Aristotle in the commentators. This implies a choice, in a certain sense, a "neutrality" on the programmatic level. We see, in fact that from its very origin the school of Athens understood Aristotle as a path leading to Plato and hence in a way which was somewhat "instrumental," or, propaedeutic-instrumental. Therefore, the reading or commenting on Aristotle could be tolerated or even utilized by Christians. It is easy to comprehend, therefore, how the school of Alexandria was able to survive even the closing of the school of Athens.

(*e*) The Alexandrine Neoplatonists had contacts with the school of Athens from the very beginning. Hierocles was a disciple of Plutarch of Athens, Hermias listened to Syrianus, and Ammonius spent time studying with Proclus. Later members of the school of Athens heard exponents of the school of Alexandria, so Damascius and Simplicius listened to Ammonius. But despite such contacts the differences are rather clear, and there was, as a matter of fact a certain antipathy between the two schools.

2. The Neoplatonic Alexandrine thinkers and the interaction between Platonism and Christianity

The Alexandrine school was revived toward the end of the fourth and the beginning of the fifth century CE,[3] chiefly through the drive of an exceptional woman, the famous Hypatia. Daughter of a scientist, Hypatia first learned and mastered the mathematical and astronomical sciences. She then devoted herself to philosophy and in her teaching she chiefly followed Plato and Aristotle. Her vast knowledge and her remarkable influence provoked the negative concern of Christians, to which she fell victim in 415 CE.[4]

Among her numerous followers there was one of particular importance Synesius of Cyrene, who then converted to Christianity and became a Bishop. Synesius greatly admired Hypatia, he was thoroughly convinced beyond his relationship to her as a follower that a union of philosophy with Christian faith was possible. His Neoplatonism was rather elementary. Some influences of the *Chaldean Oracles* are visible and the only new aspect he presents in regard to the Neoplatonic tradition is the insertion, quite fragmentary, of Christian ideas.[5]

Hierocles of Alexandria, who was a younger contemporary of Synesius, at first spent time studying with Plutarch at Athens.[6] In his lectures, which he held with great success at Alexandria, as well as in his writings, he concentrated his attention chiefly on moral problems. His *Commentary on the Golden Verses of Pythagoras*[7] is an excellent testament of his ideas and of his refined style of exposition and writing. Also in Hierocles those characteristics which we have indicated above as peculiar to the second Alexandrine school are clearly recognizable, as the most recent research has more and more confirmed.[8] Our philosopher tends, in fact, on the one hand, to a simplification of

Neoplatonism and on the other, to accept some Christian ideas, as for example creation and the role of the liberty of God in creation itself. The conviction of Hierocles that God helps men in the way of salvation and that human liberty is a divine gift also denoted evident Christian influences.[9]

An analogous interest in ethical problems is encountered in Theosebius, a follower of Hierocles. That fact alone explains why he focused on the philosophy of Epictetus.[10]

Enea of Gaza was linked to this ambiance. A Platonic Christian, he lived between the fifth and sixth century CE and was the author of a still extant dialogue by the title of *Theophrastus*.[11]

Nemesius, Bishop of Emesa, is also to be remembered in this context. His work *On the Nature of Man*, composed probably at the beginning of the fifth century CE, utilized Neoplatonic concepts (simplified in the Alexandrine manner) and ideas of Greek science in order to show the reasonableness and credibility of the Christian religion.[12]

3. The Alexandrine Neoplatonic Commentators

The enriching group of commentators who gave life to the final stage of Alexandrine culture has a founder in Hermeas (a contemporary of Proclus, a follower, together with him, of Syrianus), of whom there is extant a commentary to the *Phaedrus*.[13]

But the true head of the school was the son of Hermeas, Ammonius, who was a follower of Proclus after the premature death of his father. (Ammonius, besides being a commentator on Plato and on Aristotle, is also remembered for his knowledge of mathematics and astronomy.) Asclepius and Olympiodorus were followers of Ammonius, while Elias and David were disciples Olympiodorus.[14] A certain number of commentaries of these authors are extant. The above-mentioned judgment about these philosophers is clearly drawn from them.[15]

Note that in addition to "neutralizing" the commentated philosophical texts in the sense explained, some of these authors converted to Christianity. John Philoponus, in particular, not only was converted, but also wrote works in defense of some essential concepts of the *Bible*, e.g., the creation of the world. Plato was considered by Philoponus to be close to Christianity and this closeness is explained with the conviction, rather wide-spread in the Alexandrine ambiance, that the Athenian philosopher had derived many concepts from the *Bible*. The treatise of Philoponus *On the Eternity of the Cosmos* [*de Aeternitate Mundi*], which is extant, was composed about 529 CE and was chiefly aimed at Proclus.[16]

Perhaps Olympiodorus was also converted to Christianity, while the names of Elias and David attest as such to the Judaic-Christian origins of these men.

With Stephen of Alexandria, the series of commentators of this school ends. After 610 CE having taught at Alexandria, Stephen went on to Byzantium.[17]

VII. The Neoplatonists of the Latin West in Outline

In order to complete the outline, we take a very brief look at the so-called Neoplatonists of the Latin West.

They do not constitute an identifiable school; nevertheless, certain traits that they have in common permit considering them in a unitary enough manner.

In almost all of them learning prevails over speculation. In fact they are in general authors of translations of Platonic and Aristotelian works and commentaries.

In addition, almost all were Christians from the beginning of their activity or were soon converted to the new religion. In these authors, just as with some exponents of the school of Alexandria, there can be found a remarkable speculative contraction of Neoplatonism and even the return, in some respects, to Middle Platonic positions.

Among them, Chalcidius is especially to be remembered as the author of a translation and commentary to the Platonic *Timaeus* (first half of the fourth century), which was of very influential in the Middle Ages.

In the same century lived Marius Victorinus, converted to Christianity in the last years of his life (about 357 CE). He translated into Latin some logical treatises of Aristotle, the *Isagoge* of Porphyry and some Neoplatonic writings. He also composed logical, grammatical, and rhetorical treatises as well as commentaries to Cicero and to Aristotle. The theological writings composed after his conversion contain an attempt at an original synthesis, which makes him worthy of a place in the history of the Fathers of the Church.

Macrobius lived between the fourth and fifth centuries. He was famous chiefly because of his *Commentary to the Dream of Scipio [Commentarii in Somnium Scipionis]* of Cicero, in which a form of simplified Neoplatonism typically predominates. He cited Plato very frequently as well as Plotinus. Macrobius does not cite (and this is very indicative) names of Neoplatonists later than Porphyry. From the *Commentary* Macrobius appears to be a pagan, nevertheless, some scholars think that he was converted at the end of his life.

Martianus Capella lived in the first half of the fifth century, he was the author of a work of encyclopedic character by the title of *The Marriage of Mercury with Philology* [*De Nuptiis Mercurii et Philologiae*], in which is contained a treatment, in a compendium, of the seven liberal arts: grammar, dialectic, geometry, arithmetic, astronomy, and music, i.e., what will then become known as the arts of the "trivium" and of the "quadrivium." This work was also of great influence in the Middle Ages.

Some historians have put back in this list also the name of Boethius, who lived between the fifth and sixth century CE, considering him chiefly in his activity as translator and interpreter of the logical works of Aristotle, and the best mediator between antiquity and the Middle Ages. But Boethius, considered as a whole (see in particular his theological *opuscula*, is rightly to be seen as concerned with other spheres of interest.

The treatment of these authors, does not belong so much in the concluding chapter of a history of ancient philosophy, as in a chapter on the sources of Medieval thought and culture, where they will be appreciated and where they will be seen in their proper perspective. Their function and their historical importance is in fact almost on the whole, in having been an intermediary and channel between two civilizations and two cultures.[1]

VIII. The End of Ancient-Pagan Philosophy

1. The Edict of Justinian and the prohibition of the public teaching of Pagans

The end of ancient-pagan philosophy has an official date, that is, 529 CE, the year in which Justinian prohibited to pagans any public office and hence of having Schools and teaching. Here are two significant extracts of the Codex Justinianus:

> In what regards all the other heresies (and we call heresies those sects which think and practice a worship in contrast with the catholic and apostolic church and orthodox faith), we wish that there be strongly entered a law promulgated by us and by our divine father, in which are established adequate dispositions not only with regard to the said heresies, but also with regard to the Samaritans and the Pagans. No one who has been contaminated by such heresies can occupy ranks in power or can exercise public office, nor in quality of teaching can he fill any discipline, can he influence the souls of persons more simple in their error and can he render them more weak in true and pure faith of the orthodox. We only permit the teaching and the receiving of public support to those who are of the orthodox faith.[1]

> We prohibit that anyone learn any of the doctrines aside from those who are affected with the madness of the impious pagans. Therefore no pagan pretend to instruct those who by chance frequent them, while in reality he does nothing other than to corrupt the souls of the disciples. In addition, he does not receive any public subsistence, since he does not have any right derived from divine scripture or from the statutes in order to pretend to have a license for things of this kind. If anyone, here [scil., at Constantinople] or in the provinces, has fallen in this way and he should not be afraid to return into the bosom of our holy church, together with his family, that is, together with his wife and children, he will fall under the sanctions, and his property confiscated and he will be sent into exile.[2]

This Edict of Justinian is undoubtedly quite important, as likewise is the date on which it was promulgated, for the destiny of Greek-Pagan philosophy. Nevertheless, it is to be noted that 529 CE, like all the dates which close and open epochs, do nothing other than confirm with a outstanding event that which by now was a reality produced wholly by a series of preceding events. As we have seen, in fact, at Alexandria as well as in the Latin West, not only was there a process of simplification of the Neoplatonic system so that the friction with the Christians was less and less sharp, but many thinkers ended by accepting the Christian message and being converted to it. The School of Athens endured, it is true; but, by now it was only an isolated stronghold, undermined in every respect, and perhaps left to itself it was close to collapse:

certain doubts aroused by Damascius and the position of Simplicius himself are very symptomatic of this malaise, as we have noted previously above.

The Edict of 529 CE in reality only accelerated and sanctioned, directly, that end to which, as a matter of fact, ancient-pagan philosophy was, already left to itself, inexorably destined. But we still need to make some clarifications about the nature and the effects of the Edict.

2. The destiny of the Neoplatonists of the School of Athens after the Edict of Justinian

As has been noted by recent scholarship, the passages of the Edict read above establish a general prohibition, and do not name any school in particular.[3] Actually, this only lends credence to some testimonies, of clearly hostile stamp, of the ancient historians and chroniclers, and thus it could be argued that the School at Athens was closed and its members dispersed that same year.[4] Also the information reaching us about the confiscation of the property of the school (which was rather conspicuous) should not be immediately and necessarily referred to the year 529 CE. On the other hand, we know that the famous members of the School of Athens did not leave the city immediately, but only in 531/532 CE. In fact, in 531 King Chosroës ascended the Persian throne, an admirer of Greek culture, who had placed many hopes in the soul of the Athenian Neoplatonists and the dream of founding in Persia political conditions similar to those longed for in the Platonic *Republic*. And precisely to the court of Chosroës, Damascius, Simplicius, and five other Neoplatonists moved: Priscianus Lidus, the Phoenician Hermias, and Diogenes, the Phrygian Eulamius, and Isidore of Gaza, as the historian Aegatia tells us.[5]

But what had attracted these men to Persia turned out to be pure illusion. Chosroës had a moral stature very different from the tyrants Dionysius I and Dionysius II of whom Plato was the repeated victim in Sicily. He was in fact truly a lover of Greek wisdom; but, as to capacity and talent he was far from the ideal of the philosopher-king, and the conditions of his court and of his reign were very far from the ideal of the Platonic *Republic*.

The sojourn in Persia of the Neoplatonists of the school of Athens was hence brief. In 533 CE Persia made a peace treaty with the Roman emperor, in which there was guaranteed among other things the possibility for these philosophers, besides returning to their homeland, of living according to their customs and "not to be forced to change their ancestral faith."[6] The desire of Chosroës to keep philosophers at his court came to nothing. The delusion, the discomfort, and perhaps nostalgia for their homeland forced them to return to Greece.

The activity of the seven philosophers during the Persian sojourn was limited to a translation of Platonic and Aristotelian works,[7] to the compilation of some manuals, and to the composition of works useful to beginners. The

Solutiones eorum de quibus dubitavit Chosroës Persarum rex [The Solutions of the Doubts of Chosroës King of Persia] by Priscianus Lidus, which has come down to us in a Latin translation,[8] is an important enough verification of what we said.

It would seem that after the return to Athens Simplicius continued his writing activity, composing his commentaries, but privately and probably without having any following. Moreover, as has been noted for a long time, it cannot be said that Simplicius "produced anything more than consciously elaborating a previously existing doctrine, and essentially he arrived at its already definitive conclusions."[9]

Some scholars think that the activity of some Neoplatonists in Athens may even have continued up to the invasion of the Slavs, i.e. up to 580 CE.[10] But, if this were so, things did to change substantially, since it would be closer to a state of survival like death throes.

Philosophical thought had by now undergone a most radical μετάνοια, a most radical spiritual revolution. The "second voyage" had ended a long time before and what we can call the "third voyage" had already begun and was far along.

Plato, in a passage of the *Phaedo* which we chose as the epigraph of this work, had written:

> For he must do one of two things; either he must learn or discover the truth about these matters [scil., those which touch on the supreme destiny of man], or if that is impossible, he must take whatever human doctrine is best and hardest to disprove and, *embarking upon it as upon a raft, sail upon it through life in the midst of dangers...*[11]

And to this he added:

> ...unless he can sail upon some stronger vessel, some divine revelation, and make his voyage more safely and securely.[12]

But neither Plato, nor any Greek, could possibly have imagined what the "solid ship" and what "the secure voyage through the sea of life" was to be. The Christian message, appeared in this regard, as a great deal more disconcerting, more radical, and ultimate: but precisely as such, it had conquered. Saint Augustine says, with evident reference to the Platonic passage read above:

> No one...can traverse the sea of this century, except he is carried by the cross of Christ.[13]

Thus the "third voyage" is to be completed on the wood of the cross.

ABBREVIATIONS

Ammonios: F. Heinemann, "Ammonios Sakkas und der Ursprung des Neuplatonismus" in *Hermes* 61 (1926) 1-27.

Ariston: F. Wehrli, *Die Schule des Aristoteles. Heft VI: Lykon und Ariston von Keos* (Basel, 1952, 1969 ²).

Aristotle: I. Düring, *Aristotle in the Ancient Biographical Tradition* (Göteborg, 1957).

Aristotle's School: I. P. Lynch, *Aristotle's School, A Study of Greek Educational Institution* (Berkeley-Los Angeles: University of California Press, 1972).

Atomos Idea: V. E. Alfieri, *Atomos Idea, l'origine del concetto dell'atomo nel pensiero greco* (Florence: F. Monnier, 1953; rev. ed. Galatino: Congedo Editore, 1979).

Corpus Hermeticum: Walter Scott, ed. *Hermetica* (Boston: Shambhala, 1985). 2 volumes.

Der Aristotelismus: P. Moraux, *Der Aristotelismus bei den Griechen von Andronikos bis Alexander von Aphrodisias. Erster Band: Die Renaissance des Aristotelismus im I.Jh.V.Chr.* (Berlin, 1973).

DL: Diogenes Laertius, *The Lives of Eminent Philosophers* ed. R. D. Hicks 2 vols. "The Loeb Classical Library," (Harvard University Press, Cambridge, Mass.: W. Heinemann, London 1959).

DK: H. Diels-W. Kranz, *Die Fragmente der Vorsokratiker Griechisch und Deutsch*, 3 vols. (Berlin: Weidemann, 1951-1952⁶.

DPG: E. Zeller, *Die Philosophie der Griechen in ihrer geschichtlichen Entwicklung* 3 vols. (1844-52); ed. W. Nestle (Leipzig, 1920⁶, Hildesheim: G. Olms, 1963).

Due precursori: G. Martano, *Due precursori del neoplatonismo* (Naples, 1979).

EPG: J. Burnet, *Early Greek Philosophy* (London, 1892).

Empirikerschule: K. Deichgrüber, *Die griechische Empirikerschule, Sammlung der Fragmente und Darstellung der Lehre* (Berlin, 1930).

Epicurea: H. Usener, *Epicurea* (Leipzig: Teubner, 1887; republished Rome 1963 and Stüttgart, 1966).

Epitteto: G. Reale, "La filosofia di Epitteto come messaggio de liberazioni," in the volume: *Epitteto. Diatribe, Manuale, Frammenti* (Milan: Rusconi, 1982) 5-50.

GT: Th. Gomperz, *Greek Thinkers. A History of Ancient Philosophy*. Trans. L. Magnus and G. G. Berry, 4 vols. (London: J. Murray, 1906-1).

Hermétisme: A. J. Festugière, *Hermétisme et mystique païenne* (Paris: Auber-Montaigne, 1967).

Hieronymos: F. Wehrli, *Die Schule des Aristoteles Heft X: Hieronymos von Rhodos Kritolaos und seine Schüler* (Basel, 1959, 1969^2).

Histoire critique: E. Vacherot, *Histoire critique de l'école d'Alexandrie*, 3 vols. (Paris, 1846-1851; republished Amsterdam, 1965).

Iamblichi Chalcidensis: J. M. Dillon, *Iamblichi Chalcidensis In Platonis dialogos commentariorum fragmenta* ("Philosophia antiqua" 23) [Leiden: J. Brill 1973).

Il Didaskalikos: G. Invernizzi, *Il Didaskalikos, di Albano e il medioplatonismus. Saggio di interpretazione e commento del Didaskalikos*, 2 vols. (Rome: Edizione Abete, 1976).

Jamblique: Dalsgaard Larsen, *Jamblique de Chalcis exégète et philosophe, Appendice: Testimonia et fragmenta exegetica* (Universitets forlaget i Aarhus, 1972).

Kritolaos: F. Wehrli, *Die Schule des Aristoteles Heft X: Hieronymos von Rhodos, Kritolaos und siene Schüler* (Basel 1959, 1969^2).

La Révélation: A. J. Festugière, *La Révèlation d'Hermès Trismégistus* 4 vols. (Paris: Gabalda, 1944-1954).

LCL: "The Loeb Classical Library," Harvard University Press, Cambridge, Mass.: W. Heinemann, London.

Le désir: R. Arnou, *Le désir Dieu dans la philosophie de Plotin* (Paris, 1921; Rome, 1967^2).

Le scuole: P. L. Donini, *Le scuole, l'anima, l'impero: la filosofia antica da Antioco a Plotino* (Turin: Rosenberg and Sellier Editori, 1982).

LFG: E. Zeller-R. Mondolfo, *La filosofia dei Greci nel suo sviluppo storico*, Parte Prima, vol. III, ed. Giovanni Reale (Florence: La Nuova Editrice, 1967)

Melisso: G. Reale, *Melisso, Testimonianze e frammenti* (Florence: La Nuova Italia, 1970) [Biblioteca di Studi Superiori, 50].

Monopsychism: Ph. Merlan, *Monopsychism, Mysticism, Metaconsciousness. Problems of the Soul in the Neo-Aristotelian and Neoplatonic Tradition* (The Hague, 1963).

Oracles: É. des Places, *Oracles Chaldaïques, avec un choix de commentaires ancien* (Paris: Les Belles Lettres, 1977).

Paideia: W. Jaeger, *Paideia: the Ideals of Greek Culture*, trans. Gilbert Highet (Oxford: Basil Blackwell, 1954).

Plotinus: J. Rist, *Plotinus, the Road to Reality* (Cambridge, 1967).

Posidonius: L. Edelstein-I. G. Kidd, *Posidonius, I, The Fragments* (Cambridge: Cambridge University Press, 1972).

Pyrrhon: L. Robin, *Pyrrhon et le scepticisme grec* (Paris, 1944).

Reale: G. Reale, *A History of Ancient Philosophy* 5 vols. (Albany: State University of New York Press, 1980-) [translation of *Storia della Filosofia Antica* (Milan: Vita e Pensiero, 1975-9), volumes 1 through 5, only volumes 3 and 1 have been translated and the present volume 4, volumes 2 and 5 will published in the near future Ed.]

RE: *Realencyclopëdie der classichen Altertumswissenschaft*, ed. Pauly-Wissowa-Kroll-Mittelhaus-Zeigler (Stüttgart, 1984 and following years).

Richtungen: Praechter "Richtung und Schulen im Neuplatonismus" in *Genethliakon Carl Robert* (Berlin, 1910) 103-156.

Saggi: V. Cilento, *Saggi su Plotino* (Milan, 1973).

Le scepticisme: J. P. Dumont, *Le scepticisme et le phénomène* (Paris 1972).

Studien: Theo Kobusch, *Studien zur Philosophie des Hierokles von Alexandrien* (Munich, 1976).

Theodorus: W. Deuse, *Theodorus von Asine, Sammlung der Testimonien und Kommantar* (Weisbaden, 1973).

Theology: W. Jaeger, *The Theology of Early Greek Philosophers* (Oxford: Clarendon Press, 1947) trans. R. Robinson.

Thesleff: H. Thesleff, *The Pythagorean Texts of the Hellenistic Period* (Abo, 1965).

Tre studi: P. L. Donini, *Tre studi sull'aristotelismo nel II secolo d.c.* (Turin, 1974).

Zeller-Martano: see above, *DPG* (Florence: La Nuova Italia, 1961).

NOTES

*See the fifth volume, *Lexicon, Indices, and Bibliography*, forthcoming.

(pp. 7-9) (1-21)

1. Lycon was born in the Troads at the beginning of the third century BCE. He was designated by Strato himself as his successor and he directed the Peripatos from about 270/268 to 226/224 BCE (cf. *Diogenes Laertius* 5.68). He was an able and refined man of the world. The Peripatos, during the headship of Lycon, rested more on the personal qualities of the director than on his philosophical thought, which must have been very thin. The fragments of Lycon have been collected and commented on by F. Wehrli, *Die Schule des Aristoteles* Heft 6: *Lykon und Ariston von Keos* (Basel 1952, 1959^2).

2. Cicero, *De finibus* 5.5.13; Wehrli, *Lykon* frag. 17.

3. Cf. Clem. Alex., *Strom.* 2.21.129.9; Wehrli, *Lykon* frag.20.

4. Cicero, *Tusc. disp.* 3.32.78; Wehrli, *Lykon* frag. 19.

5. Cf. *Diogenes Laertius* 5.65; Wehrli, *Lykon* frag. 22; cf. also *Diogenes Laertius* 5.66; Wehrli, *Lykon* frag. 23.

6. Hieronymus is said by many sources to be a native of Rhodes. His *acmé* was placed about the middle of the third century BCE. He was a contemporary of both Timon and Lycon. His fragments are collected with commentary by F. Wehrli, *Die Schule des Aristoteles* Heft X: *Hieronymos von Rhodos, Kritolaos und seine Schüler.*

7. Cicero, *De finibus* 2.3.8; Wehrli, *Hieronymos,* frag. 8a.

8. Cicero, *De finibus* 2.13.41; Wehrli, *Hieronymos,* frag. 8b.

9. Cicero, *De finibus* 5.5.14; Wehrli, *Hieronymos,* frag. 8c.

10. Ariston was born on the island of Ceos. His *acmé* fell probably toward the end of the second half of the third century BCE. His fragments with commentary are collected by F. Wehrli, *Die Schule des Aristoteles* Heft 6: *Lykon und Ariston von Keos*(Basel, 1952, 1969^2).

11. Cicero, *De finibus* 5.5.13; Wehrli, *Ariston*, frag. 10.

12. Cf. Wehrli, *Ariston*, frags. 14-16.

13. Critolaus (Kritolaos) was born at Phaselis in Lycia, probably around two hundred BCE. We know with certainty that in 156/155 BCE he was at Rome, together with Carneades scholarch of the Academy and Diogenes scholarch of the Stoa (cf. *Reale* 3.443 n. 3). Lucian (*De longaevis* 20.223) tells us that he died at eighty-two years of age. The fragments with commentary are collected by F. Wehrli, *Die Schule des Aristoteles* Heft X: *Hieronymos von Rhodos, Kritolaos und siene Schüler* (Basel 1959, 1969^2). For the embassy at Rome cf. ibidem, frags. 5-10.

14. Cf. Wehrli, *Kritolaos,* frags. 12, 13, and 15.

15. Cf. Wehrli, *Kritolaos,* frags. 16 and 17.
16. Aulus Gellius, *Noctes atticae,* 9.5.6; Wehrli, *Kritolaos,* frag. 23.
17. Cicero, *Tusc. disp.* 5.17.51; Wehrli, *Kritolaos,* frag. 21.
18. We only know that Diodorus was born at Tyre, that he was a follower of Critolaus and scholarch of the Peripatos. The few extant testimonies have been collected with commentary by Wehrli, in the volume cited above in note 13.
19. Aetius, *Plac.* 1.7.21; Wehrli, *Diodorus von Tyros,* frag. 2.
20. Cf. Wehrli, *Diodorus von Tyros,* frags. 3a; 4a; 4b.
21. Cf. Posidonius quotes Atheneus 5.211ff.; Edelstein-Kidd, *Posidonius,* frag. 253.221; Theiler, Posidonios, frag. 247, 180.

(pp. 11-19) (1-53)
1. Cf.*Reale* 2.244, n.1 [Italian ed.] *Reale* 3.107ff.
2. *Diogenes Laertius* 5.52f.
3. Cf. *Reale* 3.103ff.
4. See the evidence of Strabo (13.1.54) which we reported above on pp. 13ff.
5. Here is what Plutarch writes *Life of Sulla* 12, "As for Sulla, he at once received deputations and invitations from the other cities, but Athens was compelled by the tyrant Aristion to side with Mithridates. Against this city, therefore, Sulla led up all his forces, and investing the Piraeus, laid siege to it, bringing to bear upon it every sort of siege-engine, and making all sorts of assaults upon it. And yet if he had been patient a little while, he might have captured the upper city without hazard, since it lacked the necessities of life and was already reduced by famine to the last extremity. But since he was eager to get back to Rome, and feared the spirit of revolution there, he ran many risks, fought many battles, and made great outlays that he might hasten on the war, in which, not to speak of his other munitions, the operation of the siege-engines called for ten thousand pairs of mules, which were employed daily for this service. And when timber began to fail, owing to the destruction of many of the works, which broke down of their own weight, and to the burning of those which were continually smitten by the enemy's fire-bolts, *he laid hands upon the sacred groves, and ravaged the Academy, which was the most wooded of the city's suburbs, as well as the Lyceum.* See, in addition, what Plutarch says in chapter 14.
6. Cf. I. P. Lynch, *Aristotle's School, A Study of a Greek Educational Institution.* (Berkeley-Los Angeles-London: University of California Press, 1972), pp. 205f.
7. The succession of the scholarch as we know them is as follows: Aristotle, Theophrastus, Straton, Lycon, Ariston, Critolaus, Diodorus, Erinneus. Now, both Ammonius (*In Arist. De interpret.* 5.28) and Elias (*In Arist. Cat.* 117.22ff.; cf. also 113, 18ff.) say that Andronicus was the eleventh

scholarch (the tenth successor after Aristotle); therefore at least two names between Erinneus and Andronicus are certainly missing.

8. On this Strabo and Plutarch completely agree, as can be seen in the two documents which we reported above (pp. 13-15) and the related notes.

9. Cf.above, pp. 15ff. There is a rather strange sequel to the story in modern times with reference to the meaning of the title *Metaphysics* of which few scholars seem to be aware, cf. J. Owens, *Elementary Christian Metaphysics* (Milwaukee: Bruce Publishing Co., 1963), p. 1, note 1.

10. Strabo 13.1.54.

11. Plutarch, *Life of Sulla*, 26.

12. Cf. Atheneus 5.211d-215b; Edelstein-Kidd, *Posidonius,* frag. 253; Theiler, *Posidonios*, frag. 247, 180.

13. Cf. about this argument, the works of Moraux which we cite below note 16.

14. About Eudemus, cf. *Reale* 3.101ff.

15. Porphyry, *Life of Plotinus,* 24.

16. Cf. P. Moraux, *Les listes anciennes des ouvrages d'Aristote*, (Louvain, 1951), and especially by the same author, *Der Aristotelismus bei den Griechen von Andronikos bis Alexander von Aphrodisias* Erster Band: *Die Renaissance des Aristotelismus im I.jh.v.Chr.*, (Berlin, 1973).

17. Cf. P. Moraux, *Der Aristotelismus,* I.93.

18. Cf. I. Düring, *Aristotle in the Ancient Biographical Tradition* (Göteborg, 1957), p. 423.

19. Cf. Philoponus, *In Arist. Cat.* 5.18-23; Elias, *In Arist. Cat.* 117.22-24.

20. For a probing analysis of these questions cf. Moraux, *Der Aristotelismus,* I.58-94.

21. About Tyrannion, cf. I. Düring, *Aristotle*, pp. 393ff., 412f.

22. The reader will find the state of the problem well presented by Moraux, *Der Aristotelismus,* I.45-58. Moraux, following the German tradition begun by F. Littig, *Andronikos von Rhodos* 3 vols., (München: Erlangen, 1890), defends the later dating. See, on the other side, the arguments of I. Düring, *Aristotle*, pp. 420ff. which Moraux did not succeed in refuting. The fact that Cicero, did not know Andronicus, as we will immediately see, is a determining element in favor of the earlier dating.

23. Cf. Cicero, *De orat.* 1.22.104; *De finibus* 5.3.8; 5.25.75; *Acad. pr.* 2.4.12; *De officiis* 1.1.1; 3.2.5.

24. Cf. Cicero, *Epist.* 12.16 and 14.21; cf. the correct remarks made in this regard by Lynch, *Aristotle's School*, pp. 204ff.

25. Simplicius, *In Arist. Cat.* 159, 31f.

26. Cf. Strabo 17.5.790. This is also admitted, although simply in a hypothetical way, by Moraux, *Der Aristotelismus*, I.182.

27. This is a datum that seems to us to emerge clearly, if the suppositions are left aside, and we base ourselves only on what is expressly attested.

28. The above dating is obtained from some indications which Cicero, (*De orat.* 1.22.106; *De finibus* 5.25.75; furnishes about the contacts which our philosopher had with noted contemporaries (he was a friend of Licinius Crassus and a teacher of Piso).

29. Cf. Cicero, *De finibus* 5.25.75.

30. Cf. *Reale* 3.445-46 n. 1.

31. Cf. Cicero, *Acad. pr.* 2.4.12).

32. Cf. above p. 16, note 25.

33. These observations can be seen in Moraux, *Der Aristotelismus,* I.182ff.

34. On this point of the doctrine of Ariston we found detailed information in a work attributed to Apuleius (cf. *Apulei Opera quae supersunt* vol. 3 *De philosophia libri recensuit P. Thomas* [Lipsiae, 1908], pp. 176-94).

35. See the indications in all the documents used to reconstruct the chronology and the life of Cratippus in Moraux, *Der Aristotelismus,* pp. 223ff.

36. Cf. Cicero, *De officiis* 1.1.1; 3.2.5.

37. Cf. above note 24.

38. Cf. Cicero, *De divinatione* 1.3.5; 1.32.70ff.

39. Cf. above pp. 12ff.

40. Cf. above p. 12, note 7.

41. I. P. Lynch (*Aristotle's School,* pp. 198-207) maintains that the Peripatos, as an institution, must have ceased to exist in 96 BCE. This view is undoubtedly erroneous. It is true that, as we have previously noted many times, in this period, as a consequence of the damages by Sulla to the places in which the school arose and to the hard times inflicted on Athens, the Peripatos almost certainly ceased to function for a certain period of time, but it must have been briefly. But it is also true that the activity of the Peripatetics must return to the places in which the original Peripatos arose, as is shown, among other things, in a passage of Lucian (second century CE). He refers to the acerbic quips of the Cynic philosopher Demonax (of whom we will speak above pp. 229ff.), he writes: "*Seeing Rufinus of Cyprus*—the gimp of the Peripatos—*who spent a lot of time in the ambulatory of the Peripatos*, Demonax said: Pretty cheeky, I'd say—a gimp as a Peripatetic'." Now with the term περίπατος (used twice, in the singular and plural) Lucian undoubtedly indicates the school itself (cf. *Life of Demonax* 54).

42. Cf. Moraux, *Der Aristotelismus,* I.97-113.

43. Cf. Themistius, *In Arist. de an.* 31.1ff.; 32.24ff.; cf. also Galen, *Quod an. mor. temper. sequantur,* 4 (4.782ff. Kühn-44.12ff. Müller).

44. From Strabo (16.2.24.757), we learn that Boethos was among his contemporaries (Strabo was born in 63 BCE and died in 21 CE). Strabo mentions

"that he studies Aristotle together with him," by using the expression συμφιλοσοφεῖν, which can be understood both in the sense of "to study under the guidance of," as well as in the sense of "to study together" (in the sense of being a co-disciple). That Boethos has been a disciple of Andronicus confirmed by Philoponus, (*In Arist. Cat.* 5.18); and that he has also been his successor can be gathered from Ammonius, (*In Arist. anal. pr.* 1.31.12).

45. Cf. Philoponus, *In Arist. Cat.* 5.16ff.; Elias, *In Arist. Cat.* 117.22ff.
46. Cf. Simplicius, *In Arist. Cat.* 78.4ff.; Dexippus, *In Arist. Cat.* 45.12ff.
47. Cf. Alexander of Aphrodisias, *De anim. mantissa* 150.19-153.27. For a discussion and interpretation of all the extant testimonies about Boethos cf. Moraux, *Der Aristotelismus* I.144-79.
48. About Strabo (14.5.4.670) we know that Xenarchus left his native Seleucia quickly, that he taught at Alexandria, at Athens, and at Rome, that he was a friend of Arius Didymus and of the Emperor Augustus and that he died in old age. He, therefore, must be approximately a contemporary of Boethos, with which, among others, he has in common some Stoicizing tendencies.
49. Cf. the reconstruction of the doctrine contained in this writing in Moraux, *Der Aristotelismus* I.198.
50. Julian, *Orat.*5.8 [5].162 c; 2.1.107 Rochefort.
51. Cf. above note 47. About Xenarchus, see Moraux, *Der Aristotelismus* I.197-214.
52. For a reconstruction of the life and works of Nicolaus see Moraux, *Der Aristotelismus* I.445-514 and the work cited in the following note.
53. The fragments of the first five books extant in a Syriac translation have been collected with a translation and commentary in English by H. J. Drossaart Lulofs, *Nicolaus Damascenus on the Philosophy of Aristotle*, (Leiden, 1965, 1969²). In a fine introduction (pp. 1-57) Drossaart Lulofs fully discusses the various problems concerning Nicolaus, his work, his thought, and his influence in the East.

(pp. 21-25) (1-25)
1. The classic interpretation is to be found in Zeller, *Die Philosophie der Griechen* 3.1.805-30. The breakthrough work which has put in doubt that interpretation is rather recent and is by a specialist in the thought of late antiquity Ph. Merlan, *Monopsychism, Mysticism, Metaconsciousness. Problems of the Soul in the Neoaristotelian and Neoplatonic Tradition* (The Hague, 1963). In Italy P. L. Donini proceeded along Ph. Merlan's way in his recent work, *Tre studi sull' aristotelismo nel II secolo d. c.* (Turin, 1974), and recently P. Moraux, *Der Aristotelismus bei den griechen.* Zweiter Band: *Der Aristotelismus im I. und II. Jh. v. Chr.*, Berlin 1984. This work, which is the most important written so far on this subject and a masterpiece in

this field (and in a sense also the first such), should have been concluded and published in the 80s with a third volume about Alexander. Unfortunately Moraux died suddenly in 1985.

2. We will speak above about these Neoplatonic commentaries.

3. Cf. Simplicius, *In Arist. Cat.*10.19ff.; *In Arist. De Caelo* 430.29ff. Cf. Moraux, *Der Aristotelismus* II. 222-25.

4. What remains of this commentary is published by G. Heylbut, *Aspasii in Ethica Nicomachea quae supersunt commentaria,* in the great collection *Commentaria in Aristotelem Graeca* t.19, Pars I (Berlin, 1889). Cf. Moraux, *Der Aristotelismus* II. 226-93.

5. Cf. Zeller, *DPG* 3.1.809ff.

6. Lucian reports that this Peripatetic was a scoundrel: "His reply to Herminus the Aristotelian deserves mention. Aware that, although he was an out-and-out scoundrel and had done a thousand misdeeds, he sang the praises of Aristotle and had his Ten Sentences (the categories) on his tongues' tip, Demonax said: "Herminus, you really need ten sentences [which also means ten accusations] (*Life of Demonax*). Cf. Moraux, *Der Aristotelismus* II. 361-98.

7. On this writing of Aristocles, of which Eusebius, (in his *Praep. evang.*) has preserved fragments see F. Trabucco, "Il problema del *de philosophia* di Aristocle di Messene e la sua dottrina" *Acmé* 11 (1958) 97-150. Cf. Moraux, *Der Aristotelismus* II.83-207.

8. See, above p. 27, note 2.

9. Influenced by the Peripatetic doctrines are two great scientists of this epoch, the astronomer and geographer Claudius Ptolemy and the physician Galen, who, however, did not make significant contributions in the area of philosophical inquiry.

10. Bignone, *L'Aristotele perduto*, 1.35ff.

11. Cf. *Reale* 3.87-108 and above especially pp. 7-20.

12. See above pp. 205-34.

13. Aristocles quoted in Eusebius, *Praep. evang.* 11.3.1.

14. Aristocles quoted in Eusebius, *Praep. evang.* 10.3.6.

15. Aristocles quoted in Eusebius, *Praep. evang.* 15.2.1.

16. A great part of the *Astronomy* of Theon of Smyrna (see more in addition below p. 498, n. 37) according to modern scholars is derived from this commentary of Adrastus.

17. Cf. Simplicius, *In Arist. De caelo* 380.3ff.

18. Cf. Donini, *Tre studi,* pp. 98ff.

19. Aspasius, *In Arist. Eth. Nicom.,* 1.14-20.

20. Aspasius, *In Arist. Eth. Nicom.,* 4.4-10.

21. Aspasius, *In Arist. Eth. Nicom.,* 99.4-5. Here is the basic text: δοκεῖ θεῖόν τι εἶναι ἡ ἀρετὴ καὶ ὁμοίωσίς τις τῷ θεῷ.

22. Cf. Aspasius, *In Arist. Eth. Nicom.*, 157.12ff. Cf. Donini, *Tre studi*, pp. 118ff.
23. Aspasius, *In Arist. Eth. Nicom.*, 33.10ff.; cf. Donini, *Tre studi*, pp. 112ff.
24. Donini, *Tre studi*, p. 124.
25. Many scholars place the work, which came down to us under the name of Aristotle entitled, *Treatise on the Cosmos for Alexander* in this epoch and they give it a certain amount of attention, and consider it, mostly an attempt to eclectically reconcile Peripatetic and Stoic doctrines. Recently instead the influence of Neo-Pythagoreanism and even Middle Platonism has been identified (the treatise was translated by Apuleius into Latin). We have tried in a recent volume (supplying the text also to the reader, as well as a translation and commentary) to show how it is traceable back to the first Peripatos (advancing also the hypothesis, supported by numerous proofs, that it may be actually a work of Aristotle, retouched by Theophrastus); it, in fact, reflects the ideas and the spiritual climate of the works of the early Aristotle in a quite accentuated manner. See G. Reale, *Aristotle Trattato sul cosmo per Alexandro*, passim. Recently, P. Moraux, *Der Aristotelismus*, II.5-82, again upholds the thesis of the inauthenticity of this work. In fact he says he is not convinced by our arguments, even if he recognizes our volume as "indispensable" and seems to be "grateful" (p. 6 note 3) for the information and the material we supply and even refers to and discusses it in a number of cases. Moraux, however, fails to answer the strictly philosophical and metaphysical questions we posed and therefore he does not affect our opinions.

(pp. 27-33) (1-25)

1. We know very little about the life of Alexander. It seems that he held a chair in philosophy in Athens between 198 and 211 CE under Septimus Severus.
2. Numerous commentaries by Alexander are extant, that to the *Prior Analytics* (Book I), to the *Topics*, to the *Meteorologica*, to the *Metaphysics* (according to scholars, only the part concerning Books 1-4 are authentic), and to the small treatise *De Sensu et Sensato*. All these commentaries are published in the great collection *Commentaria in Aristotelem Graeca*: to the *Analytics* by M. Wallies in 1883, to the *Topics* again by M. Wallies in 1891, to the *Meteorologica* by M. Hayduck in 1899, to the *Metaphysics* again by M. Hayduck in 1891 and to the *De sensu et Sensato* by P. Wendland in 1901. Some theoretical works of Alexander are extant (among which *De anima* stands out), published in the above cited series: *Alexandri Aphrodisiensis Praeter commentario scripta minora: De anima liber cum mantissa* edidit I. Bruno, *Supplementum Aristotelicum*, 2, 1, Berolini 1887; *Alexandri Aphrodisiensis Praeter commentaria scripta minora: Quaestiones, De fato, De mixtione*, edidit I. Bruns, *Supplementum Aristotelicum*, 2, 2, Berolini 1892.

3. Simplicius, *In Arist. Cat.* 85.6.
4. Cf. Alexander of Aphrodisias, *De anima* 89.13ff; 108.3.
5. Cf. Alexander of Aphrodisias, *De anima* 12.7; 17.9.
6. Simplicius, *In Arist. Cat.* 82.6.
7. Simplicius, *In Arist. Cat.* 90.31ff.
8. Cf. *Reale* 3.103-5.
9. It is necessary to distinguish the logical sense of the universal (the abstract universal) from the ontological sense (universal = first principle). Cf. for example, Aristotle, *Metaphysics* E 1 end.
10. The first study to throw light on this question was P. Moraux, *Alexandre d'Aphrodise exégète de la noétique d'Aristote* (Liège-Paris, 1942). The theses of this volume ought to have been thoroughly rethought and completed in order to appear in the third volume of the great work *Der Aristotelismus*, but even as they are, they are still very important. Cf. what we said on page 459, note 1 above.
11. Note the use of the term assimilation (scil., to God) which is typically Middle Platonic.
12. Cf. above pp. 32-33.
13. For a brief, but well-documented analysis of the noetic of Alexander see G. Movia, *Alessandro di Afrodisia tra naturalismo e misticismo* (Padua, 1972).
14. Cf. *Reale* 2.338 [Italian edition].
15. Alexander, *De anima* 89.11ff.
16. Alexander, *De anima* 88.24-89.8.
17. Cf. Merlan, *Monopsychism*, pp. 39ff.
18. Alexander, *De anim. mantissa* 107.29ff.
19. Cf. Aristotle, *De generatione animalium* B 3.736b27ff.
20. Alexander, *De anim. mantissa* 111.29ff.
21. Alexander, *De anim. mantissa* 108.19ff.
22. With respect to the doctrine of the "intellect which comes from the outside" Alexander (in *De anim. mantissa* 110.4) says he had "heard it from Aristotle." Now, given the evident absurdity of the text, it was thought to be necessary to emend Aristotle to Aristocles (cf. Zeller *DPG* 3.1.815. note 3, which is followed by many scholars). Moraux at first in the volume *Alexandre d'Aphrodise,* 144ff., argued soundly against the possibility of such an emendation; on a second occasion, in the article "Aristoteles, der Lehrer Alexanders von Aphrodisias," *Archiv für Geschichte der Philosophie* 49 (1967) 169-82, he showed that actually there existed an Aristotle of Mytilene, in the second century CE, who was a Peripatetic and that he studied the *De anima*, the *De caelo*, and the *Metaphysics*. This Aristotle of Mytilene (and not Aristocles) was the true master and precursor of Alexander of Aphrodisias.

23. Alexander, *De anima*, 89.21ff.
24. Alexander, *De anima*, 21.22ff.
25. Alexander, *De anima*, 90.13-23.

(pp. 37-43) (1-26)

1. Cf. *Reale* 3.183-204.
2. Cicero, *Ad fam.*, 13.1.
3. Seneca for example writes: "Itaque tot familiae philosophorum sine successore deficiunt" (*Nat. quaest.* 7.32); ["*Therefore whole families of philosophers are lacking successors.*"] It is true that, immediately after, he refers to the Academics, but it is also true that he does not name exceptions.
4. The testimonies of Numenius and Aristotle of whom we speak, are preserved by Eusebius, *Praep. evang.* 14.5.3; 14.21.
5. Cf. *Inscriptiones Graecae* 2.1097.
6. *Diogenes Laertius* 10.9.
7. Cf. *Inscriptiones Graecae* 22.1099.
8. Cf. Philostratus, *Vit. soph.* 2.2.566 and Lucian, *The Eunuch* 3.
9. Seneca, *Epist.* 79.15ff.; Pliny, *Nat. Hist.* 35.2.4ff.
10. Cf. Lucian, *Alexander*, 25.
11. Cf. Usener, *Epicurea*, p. lxxiv.
12. Cf. above pp. 45-47.
13. Cf. *Reale* 3.183ff.
14. Numenius, *frag.* 24, des Places p. 63.23ff.
15. Cf. *Reale*. 3 passim.
16. Cf. *Diogenes Laertius* 10.18.
17. Pliny, *Nat. Hist.*, 35.2.4.
18. Seneca, *Epist.* 2.8; Usener, *Epicurea*, frag. 211.
19. Lucretius, *De rerum natura*, 5.1ff.; Lucian, *Alexander*, 61.
20. Cf. above pp. 7.
21. Seneca, *Epist.*, 8.8.
22. Seneca, *Epist.*, 12.11. Consult also Seneca, *Epist.*, 14.17; 16.7; 21.9.
23. Seneca, *Epist.*, 79.15ff.
24. Cf. Marcus Aurelius, *Meditations*, 7.64; 9.41.
25. Lucian, *Alexander*, 38.
26. Lucian, *Alexander*, 47.

(pp. 45-47) (1-19)

1. We know Diogenes of Enoanda only by what has been recovered from the inscriptions he ordered cut into the marble of his portico (he was completely unknown before the discovery of the inscriptions). When the portico was made he was already old and had a bad heart (cf. *frags*. 2, col.2 and 66). The second century CE is the epoch in which his life can be placed

most probably, but we are not in possession of the elements which would permit us to proceed to a more precise chronological determination.

2. There were two French scholars (Holleaux and Paris) who in 1884 discovered the first fragments. Between 1885 and 1889 the research was taken up by Diehl and Cousin and in 1895 it was followed up by Heberdey and Kalinka.

3. A first complete edition of the fragments was published by William 1907 (*Diogenis Oenoandensis Fragmenta, ordinavit et explicavit* Johannes William, Leipzig) it has recently been re-edited by C. W. Chilton, *Diogenis Oenoandensis Fragmenta* (Leipzig, 1967). The fragments of Diogenes were translated into English with commentary by C. W. Chilton, *Diogenes of Enoanda, The Fragments. A Translation and Commentary*, London-New York: Oxford University Press, 1971. [This is the translation we used with kind permission of the publisher. Ed.] The numbering of the fragments (and of the columns) is William's (when necessary we will indicate also the lines). We will also give further bibliographical indications in the fifth volume.

4. Diogenes of Enoanda, *frag.* 2.2-6 (C. W. Chilton, trans.).

5. Diogenes of Enoanda, *frag.*, 24.2 (C. W. Chilton, trans.).

6. Cf. Diogenes of Enoanda, *frags.*, 4 and 5.

7. Cf. Bignone, *L'aristotele perduto*, 1.1ff.

8. Cf. *Reale* 3.113ff.

9. Diogenes of Enoanda, *frag.*, 5.3 (C. W. Chilton, trans.).

10. Cf. Diogenes of Enoanda, *frags.*, 3-21.21; cf. also *frags.*, 35-37.

11. Cf. Diogenes of Enoanda, *frag.*, 8; on this problem consult what is said in *Reale* 3.147ff.

12. Cf. Diogenes of Enoanda, *frag.*, 12 passim.

13. Diogenes of Enoanda, *frag.*, 12.1.5-7 (C. W. Chilton, trans.).

14. Diogenes of Enoanda, *frag.*, 25.2.9ff. (C. W. Chilton, trans.).

15. Diogenes of Enoanda, *frag.*, 25.3.

16. Diogenes of Enoanda, *frag.*, 29.1.6ff.

17. Diogenes of Enoanda, *frags.*, 35 and 36.

18. Diogenes of Enoanda, *frag.*, 33.1-3.

19. Diogenes of Enoanda, *frags.*, 67-72.

(p. 49) (1-6)

1. The fragments of Diogenianus are collected and published by A. Gercke in *Jahrbücher für klassische Philologie*, Suppl. 14 (1885) 748ff. Cf. *OCD*[2], *s.v.* (1), p.349a.

2. In order to grasp the very sympathetic attitude of Diogenes Laertius toward Epicurus see especially what he wrote in *Diogenes Laertius* 10.9ff.

3. Cf. Dionysius, Bishop of Alexandria, quoted by Eusebius, *Praep. evang.*, 14.23-27 (Dionysius was Bishop between 249 and 265 CE).

4. Lactantius, *Div. Instit.* 3.17.306.
5. Cf. Lynch, *Aristotle's School*, p. 192.
6. Cf. Julian, *Epist.* 89.301 c-d; 1.1.169.15ff. Bidez.

(pp. 53-55) (1-13)

1. This Hierocles is not to be confused with the Neoplatonic Hiereocles. K. Praechter, *Hierokles der Stoiker* (Leipzig, 1901) demonstrated that the fragments of the *Philosophoumena* recorded by Stobeus should be attributed to Hierocles the Stoic.
2. On the allegorical interpretation of polytheistic mythology consult *Reale* 3.246ff.
3. On Cornutus, Heraclitus, and Chaeremon consult Pohlenz, *La Stoa*, 2.10ff. and note 10.
4. Manilius was author of a poem entitled *Astronomica*, the first book of which is especially of interest (the other four are concerned with astrology). Cf. OCD^2 *s.v.* p. 644 (a).
5. On Cleomedes consult Pohlenz, *La Stoa*, 2.41ff.
6. It is enough to consider, for example, Traseus Petus and Barea Soranus condemned to death in 66 CE by Nero.
7. In this period, the Portico survived at Athens, as is demonstrated by certain epigraphic evidence which has preserved the names of some of the scholarchs (see in this regard Lynch, *Aristotle's School* p. 190) but which did not leave traces in the literary tradition.
8. Consult *Reale* 3.291ff.
9. Consult Pohlenz, *La Stoa*, 2.3ff.
10. Consult Seneca, *De beneficiis*, 4.25.1; 4.26.2.
11. Consult above pp. 71f.
12. Consult above pp. 93ff.
13. Epictetus, *Arrian's Discourses of Epictetus*, 2.14.9-13; consult also 1.12.22.

(pp. 57-68) (1-37)

1. Lucius Annaeus Seneca, was born in southern Spain, at Cordoba [Cordova], between the end of the pagan era and the beginning of the Christian era. At Rome he was initiated into Stoic philosophy by the teachers Attalus and Sotion, who had a great influence on him, and later by Papirius Fabianus. He spent some time in Egypt, for reasons of health, living with a maternal aunt. He returned to Rome and participated actively and successfully in the political life. In 41 CE Seneca, because of the shady maneuvers of Messilina was sent into exile in Corsica. Only in 49 CE could he return to Rome, when after the elimination of Messilina, Agrippina recalled him to supervise the education of her son Nero.

In 54 Nero became Emperor, from then on for many years Seneca, together with Burrus (prefect of the praetorium) had great political influence and responsibility, but without taking on any official public office, simply in their role as counselors to the Emperor. In 62 CE Burrus died, Seneca, retired from public life, being by this time out of favor with Nero, as well as because of the malificent influence of Poppea. This however did not allay the suspicions of Nero, who discovered, in 65 CE, the plot organized against him by Calpurnius Piso. Seneca was accused of secret dealings with Piso and he was condemned to suicide. Seneca took his life with Stoic fortitude and great equanimity of soul. The works of Seneca are very rich, notwithstanding that many works have been lost (of this group some few fragments have been preserved), a remarkable group of philosophical and moral writings are extant, collected under the general title of *Dialogorum libri*. Here are the individual titles of these writings: *De providentia, De constantia sapientis, De ira, Ad Marciam de consolatione, De vita beata, De otio, De tranquillitate animi, De brevitate vitae, Ad Polybium de consolatione Ad Helviam matrem de consolatione*. Besides these there have come down to us: *De clementia, De beneficiis, Naturales quaestiones* (in eight books), and the imposing collection of *Letters to Lucilius* (124 letters divided into 20 books). We also have some tragedies, which more than in the presentations of the letters, present persons who exemplified the ethics of Seneca, (*Hercules furens, Troades, Phoenisse, Medea, Phaedra, Oedipus, Agamemnon, Thyestes, Hercules oetaeus*). Marchesi (*Storia della letteratura latina* 2.227) judges Seneca, "the most modern writer of Latin literature...the only one who still can speak to us as if he were alive in the dead language of Rome." The editions and the translations of the works of Seneca are numerous all over the world. Further bibliographical indications may be found in *Reale* 5 under "Seneca." Cf. *OCD*^{2} *s.v.* pp. 976-77.

2. Seneca, *De vita beata*, 3.2.
3. Seneca, *De otio*, 3.2.
4. Seneca, *De brev. vitae*, 14.2.
5. Seneca, *De vita beata*, 13.4.
6. Seneca, *Epist.* 58.16-22.
7. Seneca, *De beneficiis*, 4.7.1-2.
8. Consult Pohlenz, *La Stoa*, 2.92 and note 60.
9. Seneca, *Epist.* 41.1-5.
10. Seneca, *De providentia*, 1.1.5.
11. Seneca, *Ad Helviam matrem* 11.6-7.
12. Seneca, *Epist.* 65.12.
13. Seneca, *Epist.* 92.30.
14. Seneca, *Epist.* 102.24-29.
15. Seneca, *Epist.* 106.4.
16. Seneca, *Epist.* 54.6.
17. Consult Pohlenz, *La Stoa*, 2.85. On Sextus consult above 383ff.

18. Seneca, *De ira* 3.36.1-4.
19. Seneca, *De vita beata*, 20.4.
20. Seneca, *Epist.* 97.12-16.
21. Pohlenz, *La Stoa*, 2.89ff.; for the last two passages consult Seneca, *Epist.*,71.36; 20.5.
22. Seneca, *De ira*, 2.28.1-3.
23. In *De ira*, 2.10.3. Seneca, says that it is a structural condition of man to be subject to as many ills of the soul as those of the body.
24. Consult Pohlenz, *La Stoa*, 2.70 and the passages indicated, there, at note 25.
25. In Seneca, *Epist.* 31.6 read, for example: "What therefore is good? The knowledge of things (*rerum scientia*). And vice versa what is evil? The ignorance of things (*rerum imperitia*)."
26. Seneca, *Epist.* 44.1-3; *LCL* 1.287.
27. Seneca, *Epist.* 44.5-6.
28. Seneca, *Epist.* 31.11.
29. Seneca, *Epist.* 47.1.
30. Seneca, *Epist.* 47.11.
31. Analogous evangelical maxims will be found also in Musonius Rufus, in Epictetus, and in Marcus Aurelius. Consult above pp. 73ff.; pp. 87ff.; pp. 101ff.
32. Seneca, *Epist.* 95.51-53;
33. In Seneca, *De ira*, 3.43.5; we read: "we are not for nothing object of fears, for nothing objects of danger, we scorn damage, the offenses, the verbal insults, the bites ..."; consult Seneca, *De vita beata*, 20.5; *De benef.* 4.26.1ff.
34. The apocryphal letter is edited by C. W. Barlow, *Epistulae Senecae ad Paulum et Pauli ad Senecam* (Rome, 1938); consult on the question J. N. Sevenster, *Paul and Seneca*, (Leiden, 1961).
35. St. Paul, *First Letter to the Corinthians* 2.4-5.
36. St. Paul, *First Letter to the Corinthians* 3.18.
37. Marchesi, *Storia della letterature latina* 2.254.

(pp. 69-73) (1-15)

1. Musonius was born at Volsinii (Etruria) about 31 CE. He belonged to the class of knights as attested by Tacitus (*Hist.* 3.81). He was often in exile. In 60 CE, he accompanied Rubellius Plautus who was sent into exile by Nero. In 65 CE he was banished to the inhospitable island of Gyaros again by Nero. In 71 CE when Vespasian banished the philosophers, Musonius was spared, but, a little after, he was subjected to the fate of the other philosophers. It seems that he was repatriated by Titus. He died toward the end of the first century CE.

   The lectures of Musonius, the *Diatribes* were collected by his disciple Lucius. Perhaps they were collected also in a book of the *Sayings* of the philosopher by a Pollionus, who is difficult to identify. What remains of the works of our philosopher have been published by O. Hense, *C. Musonii Rufi Reliquiae* (Lipsia, 1905). R. Laurenti has edited an Italian translation with a good introduction: *C. Musonio Rufo, Le Diatribe e i frammenti minori*, (Roma: Signorelli, 1967), also M. P. Charlesworth, *Five Men* (1963), 33ff.

2. Musonius, *Diatribe*, 1; 1.17-2.4 Hense.

3. Epictetus, *Arrian's Discourses of Epictetus*, 1.7.30-33.

4. Musonius, *Diatribe*, 1; 5.11-6.4 Hense.

5. Musonius, Diatribe, 5; 21.17-23.3 Hense.

6. Musonius, *Diatribe*, 2, 4, and 5.

7. Musonius, *Diatribe*, 6; 25.14-26.5 Hense.

8. Musonius, *Diatribe*, 7; passim (and especially 31.9-11 Hense).

9. Musonius, *Diatribe*, 9; 42.1-13 Hense.

10. Musonius, *Diatribe*, 11 passim.

11. Musonius, *Diatribe*, 13 and 14 passim.

12. Musonius, *Diatribe*, 10; 56.6-57.2 Hense.

13. Musonius, *Diatribe*, 17; 90.4-17 Hense.

14. Musonius, *Diatribe*, 16; 86.18-87.18 Hense.

15. Musonius, *Diatribe , frag.* 38;124ff. Hense. Naturally the fact needs to be kept in mind that this fragment is preserved by Stobaeus (2.8.30) who took it from one of *Arrian's Discourses of Epictetus*, (which we no longer possess). The strongly Epictetian tone of the fragment is also explained by this circumstance.

(pp. 75-87) (1-38)

1. Epictetus was born in Hierapolis, in Phrygia, between 50 and 60 CE. A little after 70 CE, when he was still a slave, he began to frequent the lectures of Musonius who revealed to him his calling to be a philosopher. Banished from Rome by Domitian together with other philosophers (in 88/89 or in 92/93 CE) he left Italy and retired to the city of Nicopolis in Epirus, where he found a school (consult Aulus Gellius, *Noctes atticae* 15.11.5) which was a great success and attracted listeners from all over. The strong personality of Epictetus, his natural tendency to teach, the humane character of his teaching, and the importance of his teaching were the causes of the exceptional favor that the school achieved. The date of his death is not known (some place it around 138 CE). Epictetus wrote nothing, wishing to emulate the ideal of Socrates's philosophizing. Fortunately, the historian Flavius Arrianus frequented his lectures, and (perhaps around 120 CE) had the happy thought of putting them in writing. In this way the *Arrian's Discourses of Epictetus*, were produced, in eight books, of which four have survived. Arrian also compiled a *Manual (Encheiridion)* extracted from the *Arrian's Discourses of Epictetus*, using the most important ones. *Arrian's Discourses of Epictetus*, are very faithful reflections of the

thought of Epictetus. Arrian expressly notes: "I have not compiled the lectures of Epictetus as material of such a kind that could be compiled and I have not placed them before the public. I say that I have not even compiled them. But everything that I heard said by him, I wrote down, insofar as possible with the very same words, I have tried to keep for the future a record of his thought and of his outspoken speech." To the eight books of the *Arrian's Discourses of Epictetus*, it seems that there are to be added twelve books of *Homilies*. Consult: G. Reale, "La filosofia di Epitteto come messaggio de liberazioni," in the volume: *Epitteto. Diatribe, Manuale, Frammenti* (Milan: Rusconi, 1982) 5-50. *Arrian's Discourses of Epictetus*, and the fragments are translated in a bilingual edition of the Loeb Classical Library Series by W. A. Oldfather [the translation of the passages which we used is by this author with minor changes]. For further bibliographical indications consult *s.v. Reale.*5.

2. About Musonius, see above, pp. 71-75.

3. Consult J. Souilhé, *Epictète, Entretiens* (Paris, 1948) 1.54; W. A. Oldfather, *Epictetus, The Discourses* (London-New York, 1925) 17, who observes that the word liberty occurs in the text of our philosopher 130 times.

4. Consult A. Bonhöffer, *Epictet und die Stoa* (Stüttgart, 1890) as well as his *Die Ethik des Stoikers Epictet* (Stüttgart, 1894) both reprinted, (Stüttgart-Bad Cannstatt, 1968).

5. On the relationship between Epictetus and Socrates consult F. Schweingruber, "Sokrates und Epiktet" *Hermes* 78 (1943) 52-79. On the relationship between Epictetus and Plato consult A. Jagu, *Epictète et Platon: Essai sur les relations du stoïcisme et du platonisme à propos de la morale des Entretiens* (Paris, 1946). On the relationship between Epictetus and Christianity consult the second volume of A. Bonhöffer which we will cite below at note 22; cf. also G. Reale, *Epitteti*, pp. 5-55.

6. Epictetus, *Manual* 1. The things *which are in our power* are said by Epictetus to be τὰ ἐφ' ἡμῖν, while those *that are not in our power* are said to be τὰ οὐκ ἐφ' ἡμῖν.

7. Epictetus, *Manual* 1.3.

8. Epictetus, *Arrian's Discourses of Epictetus* 3.15.13; [*Manual* 29.7].

9. Epictetus, *Arrian's Discourses of Epictetus* 4.10.25.

10. Epictetus, *Arrian's Discourses of Epictetus* 4.1.144ff.

11. Epictetus, *Arrian's Discourses of Epictetus* 4.1.1ff.

12. Epictetus, *Arrian's Discourses of Epictetus* 4.1.151-58.

13. Epictetus, *Manual* 8. See also the passage quoted below in p. 508, note 3.

14. Epictetus, *Arrian's Discourses of Epictetus* 3.2.1-2.

15. Epictetus, *Arrian's Discourses of Epictetus* 3.2.3.

16. Epictetus, *Arrian's Discourses of Epictetus* 3.2.3.

17. Epictetus, *Arrian's Discourses of Epictetus* 3.2.4.

18. Epictetus, *Manual* 30; *LCL* 2.511.
19. Epictetus, *Arrian's Discourses of Epictetus* 4.5.30; *LCL* 2.343.
20. Epictetus, *Arrian's Discourses of Epictetus* 3.2.5.
21. Consult *Reale.*2, ad loc.
22. Consult A. Bonhöffer, *Epictet und die Stoa*, pp. 118ff., 159ff. as well as his *Epiktet und das neue Testament* (Geissen, 1911; Berlin, 1964[2]), 235.
23. Consult Pohlenz, *La Stoa*, 2.113ff.
24. Epictetus, *Arrian's Discourses of Epictetus* 3.1.40; 1.30.3; [We changed the Italian translation of R. Laurenti which renders [προαίρεσις] as Souihlé, with "moral person," which is a paraphrasis which inadequately expresses both the Greek term as well as the corresponding concept].
25. The ancient Stoa, we recall, spoke instead of a correct interior disposition.
26. Epictetus, *Arrian's Discourses of Epictetus*, 2.23.5-19.
27. Epictetus, *Arrian's Discourses of Epictetus*, 1.17.25.
28. Epictetus, *Arrian's Discourses of Epictetus*, 4.8.3-4.
29. Pohlenz, *La Stoa*, 2.117ff.
30. Epictetus, *Arrian's Discourses of Epictetus*, 1.28.6-8.
31. Here is a very important passage: "The good and the excellent man must, therefore, inquire into all these things [that is, the problem of the existence of God and the relationship between Him and us] before he subordinates his own will to him who administers the universe, precisely as good citizens submit to the law of the state...And he that is being instructed ought to come to his instruction with this aim: "How may I follow the Gods in everything, and how may I be acceptable to the divine administration, and how may I become free?" Since he is free for whom all things happen according to his moral purpose, and whom none can restrain. What then? Is freedom insanity? Far from it; for madness and freedom are not consistent with one another. "But I would have that which seems best to me happen in every case, no matter how it comes to seem so." You are mad; you are besides yourself. Do you know that freedom is a noble and precious thing? But for me to desire at haphazard that those things should happen which have at haphazard seemed best to me, is dangerously near being, not merely not noble, but even in the highest degree shameful. For how do we act in writing? Do I desire to write the name "God" as I choose? No, but I am taught to desire to write it as it ought to be written. What we do in music? The same. And what in general, where there is any art or science? The same; otherwise knowledge of anything would be useless, if it were accommodated to every individual's whim. Is it, then, only in this mater of freedom, the greatest and indeed the highest of all, that I am permitted to desire at haphazard? By no means, but instruction consists precisely in learning to desire each thing exactly as it happens.

And how do they happen? As he that ordains them has ordained" (*Arrian's Discourses of Epictetus*, 1.12.7-16).

32. Epictetus, *Arrian's Discourses of Epictetus*, 1.14.12-17.
33. Epictetus, *Arrian's Discourses of Epictetus*, 3.5.7-10.
34. Epictetus, *Arrian's Discourses of Epictetus*, 2.8.11-14.
35. Epictetus, *Arrian's Discourses of Epictetus*, 1.3.1-8.
36. Epictetus, *Arrian's Discourses of Epictetus*, 1.9.1-7.
37. Epictetus, *Arrian's Discourses of Epictetus*, 1.13.1-5.
38. Epictetus, *Arrian's Discourses of Epictetus*, 1.16.15-21.

(pp. 89-100) (1-55)

1. Marcus Aurelius Antoninus was born 121 CE. While young, he became interested in philosophy and rhetoric, which he then left to give himself over completely to philosophy. He frequented the Roman Stoics as well as the Greek Stoic Apollonius. Marcus Aurelius had a particular affection for Rusticus, who, among other things, made him aware of *Arrian's Discourses of Epictetus*, (in 146) which constituted for him, from that time, a constant point of reference. In 161, at forty, Marcus Aurelius became Emperor. The situation of the empire was particularly delicate, both because of the external pressure of the barbarians as well as internal pressures. Marcus Aurelius held his own with fortitude in the situation, exercising imperial authority with a profound Stoic sense of duty. He never showed levity nor joy nor the satisfaction of holding the highest office in the world at that time; instead, he showed consistently a sense of the tremendous responsibility which he carried, and a Stoic faith from which he derived the energy to keep up with his duties. Marcus Aurelius truly exercised the imperial power as a service for others. He died in 180 CE. His philosophical work is compiled in Greek, the title is τὰ εἰς ἐαυτόν usually translated by the term *Memoirs* or *Meditations*. It is a series of maxims, judgments, and reflections which he composed during difficult military campaigns (and which he did not intend to publish). For further bibliographical information see *Reale* 5, under Marcus Aurelius. Cf. *OCD*[2] s.v. pp. 152-53.

2. That the Heracliteanism of Marcus Aurelius is derived from Aenesidemus is proven especially by the skeptical manner with which the "everything flowing" is precisely developed and its connected corollaries. About Aenesidemus consult above pp. 111-30.

3. Marcus Aurelius, *Meditations*, 2.12.
4. Marcus Aurelius, *Meditations*, 2.17 (G. Long, *MLG*, pp. 500-1).
5. Marcus Aurelius, *Meditations*, 4.35 (G. Long, *MLG*, p. 513).
6. Marcus Aurelius, *Meditations*, 4.43.
7. Marcus Aurelius, *Meditations*, 5.23.
8. Marcus Aurelius, *Meditations*, 6.15.

9. Marcus Aurelius, *Meditations*, 6.36.
10. Marcus Aurelius, *Meditations*, 9.19.
11. Marcus Aurelius, *Meditations*, 9.29.
12. Marcus Aurelius, *Meditations*, 9.33.
13. Marcus Aurelius, *Meditations*, 2.14.
14. Marcus Aurelius, *Meditations*, 6.37.
15. Marcus Aurelius, *Meditations*, 7.1.
16. *Ecclesiastes* 1-2 passim.
17. *Ecclesiastes* 1 passim.
18. Consult note 2 above.
19. Marcus Aurelius, *Meditations*, 4.33.
20. Marcus Aurelius, *Meditations*, 4.48.
21. Marcus Aurelius, *Meditations*, 9.36.
22. Consult further Marcus Aurelius, *Meditations*, 5.10; 8.24.
23. For a profound analysis of these themes consult E. R. Dodds, *Pagan and Christian in an Age of Anxiety* (Cambridge, 1965).
24. Marcus Aurelius, *Meditations*, 4.45.
25. Marcus Aurelius, *Meditations*, 5.8.
26. Marcus Aurelius, *Meditations*, 6.38.
27. Marcus Aurelius, *Meditations*, 7.9.
28. Marcus Aurelius, *Meditations*, 2.2.
29. Marcus Aurelius, *Meditations*, 3.16.
30. Marcus Aurelius, *Meditations*, 12.3.
31. Consult the passages quoted above pp. 93ff. and p. 95.
32. Marcus Aurelius, *Meditations*, 4.4.
33. Marcus Aurelius, *Meditations*, 9.8.
34. Marcus Aurelius, *Meditations*, 12.30.
35. Consult Marcus Aurelius, *Meditations*, 9.9; 12.30.
36. Marcus Aurelius, *Meditations*, 5.27.
37. This is an alternative which also turns up in Seneca.
38. Marcus Aurelius, *Meditations*, 4.21.
39. On the question consult Hoven, *Stoïcisme et Stoïciens face au problème de l'au-delà*, pp. 141-48.
40. Marcus Aurelius, *Meditations*, 6.11.
41. Marcus Aurelius, *Meditations*, 8.48.
42. Marcus Aurelius, *Meditations*, 4.3.
43. Marcus Aurelius, *Meditations*, 5.9.
44. Marcus Aurelius, *Meditations*, 11.1.
45. Marcus Aurelius, *Meditations*, 12.26; also 2.13.
46. Marcus Aurelius, *Meditations*, 5.6.
47. Marcus Aurelius, *Meditations*, 7.22 [consult *Matthew* 5.44; *Luke* 23.44].
48. This is also a common characteristic of other Neo-Stoics as we will see.

49. Marcus Aurelius, *Meditations*, 2.3.
50. Marcus Aurelius, *Meditations*, 6.7.
51. Marcus Aurelius, *Meditations*, 6.2.
52. Marcus Aurelius, *Meditations*, 5.27.
53. Marcus Aurelius, *Meditations*, 9.40.
54. Marcus Aurelius, *Meditations*, 11.3.
55. Marcus Aurelius, *Meditations*, 10.15.

(pp. 101-2) (1-3)
1. Pohlenz, *La Stoa*, 2.191.
2. Porphyry, *Life of Plotinus,* 20, "There have been in our time, Marcellus, many philosophers, especially in the early part of our life; I say this because at the present moment there is an indescribable shortage of philosophy. When I was a boy there were not a few masters of philosophical argument, all of whom I was enabled to see because from childhood I travelled to many places with my parents, and became acquainted in the same way with those who had lived on later in my intercourse with a great number of people and cities. Some of them undertook to set down their doctrines in writing, so as to give posterity the chance of deriving some benefit from them; others thought that all that was required of them was to lead the members of their school to an understanding of what they held. Of the first kind were the Platonists Eucleides and Democritus, and Proclinus, who lived in the Troad, and Plotinus and his Gentilianus Amelius, who are still teaching publicly at Rome, and the Stoics Themistocles and Phoebion and the two who were in their prime a little while ago, Annius and Medius, and the Peripatetic Heliodorus, the Alexandrian. Of the second were the Platonists Ammonius and Origen, with whom I studied regularly for a very long time, men who much surpassed their contemporaries in wisdom, and the Successors at Athens, Theodotus and Eubulus.... Of Stoics in this group there are Herminus and Lysimachus adn the two who lived in town, Athenaeus and Musonius, and among Peripatetics Ammonius and Ptolemaeus, both the greatest scholars of their time, especially Ammonius; there has been no one who has come near him in learning....Of those who wrote, some produced nothing except compilations and transcriptions of what their predecessors had composed, like Eucleides and Democritus and Proclinus; other recalled to mind quite small points of the investigations of the ancients and set to work to compose treatises on the same subjects as they, like Annius and Medius and Phoebion, this last chose to be distinguished for elegance of style rather than coherence of thought. One might class Heliodorus with these, for he too contributed nothing to the ordered exposition of philosophical thought beyond what his elders had said in their lectures. Those who have shown the seriousness with which they took their writing

by the multitude of problems which they treated and have had an original way of thinking are Plotinus and Gentilianus Amelius. Plotinus, it would seem, has expounded the principles of Pythagorean and Platonic philosophy more clearly than anyone before him."

3. Pohlenz, *La Stoa*, 2.263ff.

(pp. 105-23) (1-59)

1. Consult Reale 3.347ff.
2. For a discussion on the documents from which the chronological indications of Aenesidemus are derived see especially Brochard, *Les sceptiques grecs*, pp. 242ff. and Gödeckemeyer, *Geschichte des griechischen Skeptizismus*, pp. 210ff. and especially 211, note 1. That he was a native of Cnossos (in Crete) we know from *Diogenes Laertius* 9.116. That he attempted a systematic overcoming of the eclectic Academy we know from Plotinus, in fact from Aenesidemus himself, whose words Photius faithfully recorded (see the passage of Photius, *Biblioth.*, cod. 212, 169b19ff. which we quote). That he taught at Alexandria we know from Aristocles, quoted by Eusebius, *Praep. evang.* 14, 18, 22.
3. Photius, *Biblioth.* cod. 212 [169b19-170a40].
4. Photius, *Biblioth.* cod. 212 [170a4ff.] (text quoted above).
5. Consult *Reale* 3.314ff.
6. *Diogenes Laertius* 9.78ff; *LCL* 2.491.
7. That not only in *De ebrietate*, in which he quoted eight of the ten tropes, Philo shows traces of the influence of Aenesidemus but also in his other works, as *De Iosepho* 125-44 and *De vita Mosis* 1.31, *Quod deus immutabilis sit* 172-76-in which the Heraclitean component is clearly visible which, as we will see, Aenesidemus fused with skepticism-is a thesis about which many scholars largely agree (the first to have systematically studied the question is H. von Armin, "Quellenstudien zu Philo von Alexandria," *Philologische Unterschungen*, Heft 2, Berlin 1888). For the contrary view see J. P. Dumont, *Le scepticisme et le phénomène*, Paris 1972, 147ff., who prefers to speak of the "Anonymous Philo," without adducing evidence that in our judgment is convincing. For the numbering of the tropes we follow Diogenes Laertius, who seems to be more faithful to Sextus (he seems to have at hand the text of Aenesidemus or anyhow a faithful representation of this text).
8. Philo, *De ebr.*, 171.
9. *Diogenes Laertius* 9.79ff.
10. Sextus Empiricus, *Outlines of Pyrrhonism*, 1.78.
11. Sextus Empiricus, *Outlines of Pyrrhonism*, 1.78-89.
12. *Diogenes Laertius* 9.80ff.
13. Philo, *De ebr.*, 175f.

14. Diogenes Laertius 9.81. Sextus Empiricus (*Outlines of Pyrrhonism*, 1.95ff; makes a very interesting analogy. "he can mention also that the apple possesses a unique quality and is perceived in different ways according to the differences of the senses in which the perception takes place. Instead, the apple may possess more qualities than those which appear to us we infer in this way. Let us imagine a man who possesses from birth the sense of touch, taste, and smell, but can neither see nor hear. This man, then, will believe that there is nothing which is visible or audible, but only those three kinds of qualities which he is capable of grasping. Possibly, then, we also, having only the five senses, perceive only such of the apple's qualities as we are capable of grasping; and possibly it may possess other underlying qualities which affect other senses, although we, not being endowed with those senses, fail to grasp the sensations which come through them."

15. *Diogenes Laertius* 9.82.

16. Philo, *De ebr.*, 193ff.

17. *Diogenes Laertius* 9.84.

18. Philo, *De ebr.*, 189ff.

19. *Diogenes Laertius* 9.85ff.

20. Sextus Empiricus, *Outlines of Pyrrhonism*, 1.129.

21. Philo, *De ebr.*, 186ff.

22. Sextus Empiricus, *Outlines of Pyrrhonism*, 1.141ff.

23. We have systematically avoided stating the conclusion that Sextus Empiricus drew more upon the tropes and thus that we cannot pronounce "on the reality of exterior objects." Such a conclusion supposes the introduction of a dualistic presupposition and the transformation of skeptical phenomenalism into one based on empiricism. Aenesidemus is pays no attention to this issue, as we have seen confirmed many times. It is, instead, interesting what Sextus notes about the possibility of re-grouping the ten tropes under three summarizing titles. These are (*a*) the tropes which depend on the subject, (*b*) those which depend on the object, and (*c*) those that depend on both subject and object. But still more interesting is the remark of Sextus according to which all the tropes are reduced, in the ultimate analysis, "to a relation" (*Outlines of Pyrrhonism*, 1.38 or better to the nature of a relation.

24. Brochard, *Les sceptiques grecs*, p. 126.

25. Sextus Empiricus, *Adv. math.*, 8.40.

26. Consult *Reale* 3.127.

27. Sextus Empiricus, *Adv. math.*, 8.40-48.

28. Consult for example Aristotle, *Metaphysics* A 1-3 passim.

29. Consult *Reale* 3.165ff. and 242ff.

30. Sextus Empiricus, *Adv. math.*, 9.218-27, and *Diogenes Laertius* 9.97.

31. Sextus Empiricus, *Adv. math.*, 9.220.

32. Sextus Empiricus, *Adv. math.*, 9.223.
33. Sextus Empiricus, *Adv. math.*, 9.224.
34. Sextus Empiricus, *Adv. math.*, 9.226.
35. Sextus Empiricus, *Outlines of Pyrrhonism*, 1.180-85.
36. Sextus (and hence Aenesidemus) present eight tropes as "the ways by which the reasoning used to explain the cause is subverted," evidently the reasoning used to explain the cause is reasoning understood to infer the cause, the cause being precisely a meta-phenomena which is reached through an inference.
37. On this expression and its meaning see H. Diller, "ΟΨΙΣ ΑΔΗΛΩΝ ΤΑ ΦΑΙΝΟΜΕΝΑ," *Hermes* 67 (1932) 14-42 (now in *Kleine Schriften zur antiken Literatur* (Munich, 1971) 119-43.
38. Photius, *Biblioth.* cod. 212, 170b12-17.
39. Sextus Empiricus, *Adv. math.*, 8.215.
40. Sextus Empiricus, *Adv. math.*, 8.219.
41. Sextus Empiricus, *Outlines of Pyrrhonism*, 2.97-103; *Adv. math.*, 8.141.
42. Sextus Empiricus, *Outlines of Pyrrhonism*, 1.210.
43. Sextus Empiricus, *Outlines of Pyrrhonism*, 1.210-12.
44. Consult *Reale* 3.187ff. Remember, on this point, in our judgment the contribution of the often previously cited book of Conche, *Pyrrhon ou l'apparence*, is decisive.
45. On the principal positions taken by scholars in relation to the question of the relations between Pyrrhonism and Heracliteanism in Aenesidemus see Dal Pra, *Lo scetticismo greco* 2.392ff. We maintain that only after the recent contribution of Conche, *Pyrrhon ou l'apparence*, cit. is the question is clarified in a plausible way (pp. 123-56).
46. Consult G. Caspone Braga, "L'eraclitismo di Enesidemus," *Rivista di filosofia* 22 (1931) 33-47.
47. Plato, *Theaetetus* 180A-B.
48. Plato, *Theaetetus* 182E-183B.
49. Consult *Reale* 3.314ff. and 317ff.
50. Consult Photius, *Biblioth.* cod. 212 169b29; 170a1ff.
51. Consult Sextus Empiricus, *Adv. math.*, 10.38.
52. Hippolytus, *Philosoph.* 1.23.2; Diels, *DG*, pp. 572.25ff.
53. Conche, *Pyrrhon*, pp. 127ff.
54. Consult Photius, *Biblioth.* cod. 212.170b22ff.
55. Consult Photius, *Biblioth.* cod. 212.170a-b34ff.
56. Consult *Reale* 3.323ff.
57. Consult *Diogenes Laertius* 9.107.
58. Aristocles quoted by Eusebius, *Praep. evang.* 14.19.4.
59. Consult *Reale* 3.324ff.

(pp. 125-28) (1-16)

1. Concerning Sextus Empiricus see above pp. 138-40.
2. Consult *Diogenes Laertius* 9.116.
3. Consult *Diogenes Laertius* 9.106. Apollonidus of Nicea also belonged to the period of Zeuxis and Antiochus, he wrote a *Commentary to the Silli of Timon*, which he dedicated to the Emperor Tiberius. The little that we know about these Skeptics is to be found in Brochard, *Les sceptiques grecs*, pp. 228ff.; Gödeckmeyer, *Geschichte des griechischen Skeptizimus*, pp. 235ff.; Dal Pra, *Lo scetticismo greco*, 2.415-417.
4. Consult Pliny, *Epist*. 4.30; 7.27.
5. Aulus Gellius, *Noctes atticae*, 2.22.20. Concerning Favorinus consult Godeckmeyer, *Geschichte des griechischen Skeptizimus*, pp. 248-57.
6. Consult *Diogenes Laertius* 9.106ff.
7. Consult *Diogenes Laertius* 9.116; "This Antiochus [scil., Antiochus of Laodicea] had as pupils Menodotus of Nicomedia, an empirical physician, and Theiodus of Laodicea; Menodotus was the instructor of Herodotus of Tarsus, son of Arieus. Herodotus taught Sextus Empiricus, who wrote ten books on Skepticism, and other fine works. Sextus taught Saturninus called Cythenas, another empiricist."
8. Consult Brochard, *Les sceptiques grecs*, pp. 231-40.
9. Diogenes Laertius writes (9.88) about Agrippa and expressly attributes to him five "tropes" or modes (which Sextus reports by attributing them generically to the "more recent Skeptics" [more recent with respect to Aenesidemus]). Again Diogenes Laertius, as we have already pointed out informs us that the Skeptic Apellas composed a work entitled *Agrippa* (*Diogenes Laertius* 9.106), which shows the prestige that Agrippa had achieved. He lived, probably, in the second half of the first century CE or between the first and second century CE.
10. Consult *Diogenes Laertius* 9.88ff.; Sextus Empiricus, *Outlines of Pyrrhonism*, 1.164-169.
11. Sextus Empiricus, *Outlines of Pyrrhonism*, 1.166.
12. Sextus Empiricus, *Outlines of Pyrrhonism*, 1.168.
13. *Diogenes Laertius* 9.89.
14. Sextus Empiricus, *Outlines of Pyrrhonism* (1.169 and 1.178) mentions a table consisting of only two tropes or modes, which are nothing more than a maladroit attempt to reduce to two the five modes which are actually irreducible.
15. Sextus Empiricus, *Outlines of Pyrrhonism*, 1.175.
16. Consult Brochard, *Les sceptiques grecs*, p. 306.

(pp. 129-40) (1-39)

1. For a brief but accurate outline of the trends of Greek medicine consult Robin, *Pyrrhon*, pp. 181-96; on the trends of empirical medicine the work

of K. Deichgräber is basic, *Die griechische Empirikerschule, Sammlung der Fragments und Darstellung der Lehre* (Berlin, 1930).

2. Sextus Empiricus, *Outlines of Pyrrhonism*, 1.238.

3. Consult Gödeckmeyer, *Geschichte des griechischen Skeptizimus*, p. 263. In addition K. Deichgräber is basic, *Empirikerschule*, pp. 301ff.

4. The development, which is understood and evaluated in various ways by different interpreters, in our judgment, consists in the transformation of skepticism into a kind of phenomenologic empiricism, as we clarified above on pp. 141ff.

5. The chronology of Menodotus is difficult to reconstruct, lacking any precise indications in the testimonies which have come down to us about him. Perhaps it is not too far from the mark to place him in the first half of the second century CE; consult (Brochard, *Les sceptiques grecs*, p. 311). The most balanced reconstruction of the thought of Menodotus would seem to be that of Gödeckmeyer, *Geschichte des griechischen Skeptizimus*, pp. 247-63.

6. Galen, *De subfig. emp.* 84.1ff. Deichgräber.

7. Consult Sextus Empiricus, *Outlines of Pyrrhonism*, 1.222ff.

8. It is a rather plausible hypothesis maintained by Gödeckmeyer, *Geschichte des griechischen Skeptizimus*, pp. 259ff. and note 5.

9. We have scarcely any chronology and biographical facts for Sextus Empiricus unfortunately. Perhaps he lived in the second half of the second century CE and died at the beginning of the third century CE. Only this chronology accords with what Sextus himself says, namely that at his time the principal adversaries of the Skeptics were the Stoics (Cf. *Outlines of Pyrrhonism*, 1.65 in fact, in the second half of the second century CE, the Stoics were still flourishing while in the next century that were languishing. Diogenes Laertius, who seems to have lived in the first half of the third century CE knows not only about Sextus, but also his follower Saturninus and this fact confirms the chronological hypothesis about which spoke above. Sextus would be therefore, perhaps a little bit younger contemporary, of Galen. The fact that Galen does not cite him (at least in the works which have come down to us) can be explained either with the hypothesis that Sextus was not known in the area of medicine just as in philosophy, or even supposing that he had become the head of the school only after Galen had published his principal writings (consult Brochard, *Les sceptiques grecs*, p. 315). We do not know where Sextus was a teacher, at the period in which he wrote *Outlines of Pyrrhonism*, 3.120 he says, incidentally, that he is teaching in the same place in which his teacher had taught (Herodotus of Tarsus), but he does not name this place. In any case, it would seem by now that it would no longer be Alexandria (cf. *Outlines of Pyrrhonism*, 3.221). Therefore already with the

teacher of Sextus the school was shifted from Alexandria. In addition to the *Outlines of Pyrrhonism*, of Sextus there has come down to us, as we have already noted, two works entitled respectively, *Against the Mathematicians* in six books, and *Against the Dogmatists* in five books, commonly cited under the unified title of *Against the Mathematicians* [*Adversus mathematicos*] (mathematicians are understood, here, as men who profess the arts and sciences) and with the successive numbering of the books from one to eleven. The first two books of the *Against the Dogmatists* (= *Against the Mathematicians* 7 and 8) are also given the title *Against the Logicians*; Books 3 and 4 of *Against the Dogmatists* (= *Against the Mathematicians* 9 and 10) are also given under the title of *Against the Physicists* and the last book of the *Against the Dogmatists* (= *Against the Mathematicians* 11) is also given the title of *Against the Moralists*.

10. See above page 120, note 44 [above, p. 476]
11. Consult *Reale* 3. 317ff., and p. 119 above.
12. Consult Sextus Empiricus, *Outlines of Pyrrhonism*, 1.8.
13. Sextus Empiricus, *Outlines of Pyrrhonism*, 1.9. It is interesting to note how Sextus also interpreted his predecessors in function of this equation and risked misunderstanding them. Consult for example, *Against the Mathematicians* 8.216 where Sextus expressly states: "Aenesidemus here seems (ἔοικε) to call sensible impressions appearances." Which means that Aenesidemus did not make such an identification and that this identification is taken from Sextus as his personal interpretation.
14. Sextus Empiricus, *Outlines of Pyrrhonism*, 1.12.
15. Sextus Empiricus, *Outlines of Pyrrhonism*, 1.13.
16. Sextus Empiricus, *Outlines of Pyrrhonism*, 1.19.
17. Sextus Empiricus, *Outlines of Pyrrhonism*, 1.208.
18. Sextus Empiricus, *Against the Mathematicians*, 8.368.
19. Sextus Empiricus, *Against the Mathematicians*, 8.383.
20. Sextus Empiricus, *Outlines of Pyrrhonism*, 1.208.
21. Sextus Empiricus, *Outlines of Pyrrhonism*, 1.192.
22. Sextus Empiricus, *Outlines of Pyrrhonism*, 1.22ff.
23. Sextus Empiricus, *Outlines of Pyrrhonism*, 2.102.
24. Sextus Empiricus, *Outlines of Pyrrhonism*, 2.246.
25. Sextus Empiricus, *Outlines of Pyrrhonism*, 1.23ff.
26. Sextus Empiricus, *Outlines of Pyrrhonism*, 3.2.
27. For *metropatheia* [= *control of the passions*], consult Sextus Empiricus, *Outlines of Pyrrhonism*, 1.25-30.
28. Sextus Empiricus, *Against the Professors*, 1.50ff.
29. Sextus Empiricus, *Outlines of Pyrrhonism*, 1.28ff.
30. See above page 132, note 9 [above pp. 478-9].

31. Consult A. Russo, in *Sesto Empirico, Contro i logici, Introduzione*, (Bari: Laterza, 1975) p. vii, note 1.

32. Especially Sextus Empiricus, *Against the Professors*, 1, passim which presents this mental attitude in an exemplary way. Consult also *Reale* 3, passim; in addition see also *Reale* 5.2.

33. Consult Sextus Empiricus, *Outlines of Pyrrhonism*, Books 2 and 3, passim and, *Against the Mathematicians*, Books 7 to 11, passim. For the correspondence between the two works consult Robin, *Pyrrhon*, pp. 226-229.

34. Sextus Empiricus, *Outlines of Pyrrhonism*, 3.280ff.

35. Consult, for example, Sextus Empiricus, *Against the Mathematicians*, 7.279, 297ff.; 8.57, 274, 288, 365.

36. Consult Brochard, *Les sceptiques grecs*, 309ff.; and Robin, *Pyrrhon* pp. 181ff.

37. He was not able to construct a new logic of an "inductive" character, that is, the type of logic which will be proper to modern sciences. With good reason A. Russo (*Sesto Empirico, Contro i logici*, pp. xlivff.) speaks of a "logic of negativity." The scholar also states: "Sextus did not give any formulation of that concept of observation παρατήρησις which will be of such importance in modern scientific inquiry" (p. xliv, note 82).

38. Consult Sextus Empiricus, *Outlines of Pyrrhonism*, 2.244ff.

39. Dumont, *Le scepticisme*, p. 235.

(pp. 141-2) (1-5)

1. Consult *Diogenes Laertius* 9.116.

2. Sextus Empiricus, *Outlines of Pyrrhonism*, 1.206.

3. Sextus Empiricus, *Against the Mathematicians*, 8.480.

4. A. Russo in *Sesto Empirico, Introduzione*, pp. xxff.

5. See, for example, how Philo of Alexandria in *De ebrietate* made use of the tropes or modes of Aenesidemus and how Plutarch used the epoch. Concerning this last point consult D. Babut, *Plutarque et le stoïcisme* (Paris, 1969) 279ff.

(p. 145) (1-4)

1. *Reale* 3.21-38.

2. *Reale* 3.35ff.

3. *Reale* 3.36ff.

4. *Reale* 3.35 and 37ff.

(pp. 147-52) (1-25)

1. Demetrius was born probably towards the beginning of the first century CE. He was already known for his espousal of Cynic doctrine and life during the years in which Caligula ruled, to judge from what Seneca, writes in the *De beneficiis*, 7.11; *LCL* 3.483. Perhaps he was forced to leave Rome for the first time after the condemnation of his friend Thrasea Paetus (cf. Tacitus, *Annales* 16.34; *Complete Works of Tacitus*, Modern Library, p.

416) in 67 CE. It is certain that he was expelled from Rome in 71 CE by reason of his opposition to the policies of the Emperor Vespasian. Concerning the final years of his life (probably spent, at least in part, in Greece) we know very little. Our principal source of information is Seneca, who frequented his company devotedly.

2. Seneca, *De beneficiis*, 7.1.3.

3. Seneca, *De beneficiis*, 7.8.2ff.

4. Seneca, *Epist.* 62.3.

5. Seneca, *De beneficiis*, 7.1.7.

6. Seneca, *Epist.* 67.14.

7. Seneca, *De provid.*, 3.3.

8. Seneca, *De provid.*, 5.5ff.

9. Dio was probably born in the last decade of the first half of the first century CE. The nickname Chrysostom, which means "golden mouth,"[in modern terms "golden tongue"] was derived from his ability in speaking and from his persuasive eloquence. He was exiled from 82 CE to the death of Domitian, that is until 96 CE. He was on good terms with Trajan (98-117), to whom he orally presented some of his discourses. Concerning Dio we have the whole of eight orations in which the literary form of the diatribe predominates. The work of H. von Arnim, *Leben und Werke des Dio van Prusa* (Berlin, 1898) is still the fundamental one and he has also edited an excellent critical edition of the works, *Dionis Prusaensis quem vocant Chrysostomum quae existant omnia edidit apparatu critico instruxit H.von Arnim*, 2 vols. Berolini 1893-1896.

10. Consult Dio Chrysostom, *Orat.*, 13, passim. That Diogenes himself had become a philosopher because exiled and deprived of everything was a commonly shared conviction; for example, Musonius Rufus, *Diatribe*, 9.

11. Dio Chrysostom, *Orat.*, 13.11-13.

12. Consult especially *Orat.*, 6, 8, 9, and 10.

13. Dio Chrysostom, *Orat.*, 8.11-16.

14. Dio Chrysostom, *Orat.*, 8.19.

15. Dio Chrysostom, *Orat.*, 8.24.

16. Dio Chrysostom, *Orat.*, 7.81.

17. Dio Chrysostom, *Orat.*, 7.107.

18. Consult the first four *Orations*, passim.

19. Dio Chrysostom, *Orat.*, 4.24.

20. Consult Homer, *Iliad* 1.5.263.

21. Dio Chrysostom, *Orat.*, 1.45.

22. Dio Chrysostom, *Orat.*, 1.37.

23. Consult Dio Chrysostom, *Orat.*, 12.61.

24. See the last passage presented above.

25. Dio Chrysostom, *Orat.*, 4.79.

(pp. 153-58) (1-34)

1. Oenomaus lived in the first half of the first century CE (c. 120 CE). It seems that his *floruit* was placed during the reign of Hadrian (see the documents and the discussion of the issues in Dudley, *A History of Cynicism*, p. 184, note 3.

2. These extracts were preserved by Eusebius, *Praep. evang.* 5.18-36; 6.1-42 (consult P. Vallette, *De Oenomao Cynico*, Paris 1908).

3. Oenomaus, quoted by Eusebius, *Praep. evang.* 6.7.23.

4. Consult Oenomaus, quoted by Eusebius, *Praep. evang.* 6.7.1.

5. Consult *Reale* 3.251.

6. Oenomaus, quoted by Eusebius, *Praep. evang.* 6.7.42.

7. Demonax was born on Cyprus and lived a long time at Athens where he died at almost 100 years of age, allowing himself to starve to death, when he saw that he could no longer be self-sufficient. He had as teachers the Cynics Demetrius and Agathobulus and the Stoic Epictetus (consult Lucian, *Life of Demonax*, 3; *LCL* 1.145). The dates of his birth and death are not known to us. Dudley (*A History of Cynicism*, p. 159, n. 1), on the basis of a few testimonies that are extant, as a conjecture proposes the years 70 to 170 CE (approximately) as the dates which encompass his birth and death. In any case, it seems certain that the activity of Demonax is to be located in the second century CE. Our principal (and almost our only) source of information on this Cynic is the *Life of Demonax*, written by Lucian, or, generally, attributed to him (even if this short work were not by Lucian, its value would not diminish, insofar as the author was very familiar with Demonax [consult note 21, below]).

8. Consult Lucian, *Life of Demonax*, 5.

9. Consult Lucian, *Life of Demonax*, 5 and 62.

10. Consult Lucian, *Life of Demonax*, 4.

11. Consult Lucian, *Life of Demonax*, 3.

12. Consult Lucian, *Life of Demonax*, 19ff.

13. Consult Lucian, *Life of Demonax*, 11.

14. Consult Lucian, *Life of Demonax*, 32.

15. Consult Lucian, *Life of Demonax*, 43.

16. Consult Lucian, *Life of Demonax*, 3.

17. Consult Lucian, *Life of Demonax*, 7.

18. Consult Lucian, *Life of Demonax*, 9f.

19. Consult Lucian, *Life of Demonax*, 63.

20. Peregrinus of Parium in Mysia was probably born at the beginning of the second century CE and died in 165 CE (or in 167 according to the calculations of Nissen in *Rheinisches Museum* 43 (1881) 253ff.).

21. Personally we do not hold that there is sufficient evidence to deny that Lucian, is the author of the *Life of Demonax*, (consult p. 527, note 7 above) and hence we propose to consider it an authentic work of Lucian.
22. Aulus Gellius, *Noctes atticae*, 12.11.1-7.
23. Consult Lucian, The *The Death of Peregrinus*, 11.
24. Consult Lucian, The *The Death of Peregrinus*, 13.
25. Consult Lucian, The *The Death of Peregrinus*, 15.
26. Consult Lucian, The *The Death of Peregrinus*, 16.
27. Consult Lucian, The *The Death of Peregrinus*, 17. (Agathobulus was also a teacher of Demonax [consult *Life of Demonax*, 3 also consult p. 527, note 7 above]).
28. Consult Lucian, The *The Death of Peregrinus*, 18.
29. Consult Lucian, The *The Death of Peregrinus*, 23ff.
30. Consult *Reale* 3.34.
31. Consult Lucian, The *The Death of Peregrinus*, 33.
32. Consult Aulus Gellius, *Noctes atticae* 12.11.
33. Consult Aulus Gellius, *Noctes atticae*, 12.11.1.
34. Consult Aulus Gellius, *Noctes atticae*, 12.11.2.

(pp. 159-63) (1-16)

1. Consult Zeller, *DPG* 3.1.803, note 2.
2. It is difficult to reconstruct the features of the personality of Maximus and the significance of the marriage between Cynicism and Christianity which he produced, since we are informed about him by hostile sources (chiefly by Gregory Nazianzenus, *Orat.*, 23). On Gregory, see Dudley, *History of Cynicism*, pp. 203-06.
3. Consult Damascius, *Vita Isid.* frags. 138-139; 144-154; 159 Zintzen. On Sallustius see Dudley, *History of Cynicism*, p. 207.
4. The expression is that of K. W. Göttling, taken and made famous by Th. Gomperz in his *Greek Thinkers*.
5. Lucian, *The Fugitives*, 12-21.
6. Consult immediately above p. 156 , note 21 [immediately above].
7. Consult Seneca, *Epist.* 51 and *Epist.* 14.14.
8. At the end of *Diatribe*, 16 of Musonius we read: "By doing this [scil., by correctly using reason], you will philosophize yourself, and not indeed by putting on the large cloak, nor by living without a tunic, nor by letting your hair grow long, nor by distancing yourself from the actions of the many: also this suits the philosophers, but to philosophize does not consist in this but in having appropriate thoughts and reasoning about them."
9. Consult Epictetus, *Arrian's Discourses of Epictetus*, 3.22 passim.
10. Consult Epictetus, *Arrian's Discourses of Epictetus*, 3.22.13.
11. Consult Epictetus, *Arrian's Discourses of Epictetus*, 3.22.45-54.
12. Consult Julian, *To the Cynic Heracleios* and *To the Uneducated Cynics*.

13. Consult Julian, *To the Uneducated Cynics* 187 D.
14. Consult Julian, *To the Cynic Heracleios*, 211 Aff.
15. Consult Julian, *To the Uneducated Cynics*, 201 Aff.,
    To the Cynic Heracleios, 226 Cff.
16. The term which Julian used was ἀποτακτικοί, which means that they
    renounced this world; cf. *To the Cynic Heracleios*, 244 B.

(pp. 169-75) (1-29)

1. Philo was born at Alexandria, probably between 15 and 10 BCE. He was
   the son of a rich and influential Jewish family who had settled in
   Alexandria. He was able to receive instruction at the highest possible level
   at that time. He had a complete mastery of Greek culture (and, especially,
   of the intellectual categories of Hellenism), and, at the same time, of the
   cultural and spiritual inheritance of his people, as we will see at some
   length. We know very little about the details of his life. Basically he
   devoted himself to living a kind of life dedicated almost entirely to
   meditation, to study, and to the composition of his books. But this must
   not be understood so as to divorce his life from political burdens which
   he probably accepted as the fulfillment of an obligation he felt toward his
   people. The most well known episode is his voyage to Rome as the head
   of an embassy to protest against the persecutions of the Jews. On his
   return in 41 CE, Philo wrote a full account of his embassy, from which it
   is clear that he was in the prime of his life. Philo wrote numerous works,
   almost all have been preserved. Among them stands out chiefly the
   nineteen allegorical commentaries on *Genesis*. Here are the Latin titles,
   which is the way they are usually cited: 1. *De opifici mundi*; 2. *Legum
   allegoriae*; 3. *De Cherubim*; 4. *De sacrificiis Abelis et Caini*; 5. *Quod deterius
   potiori insidiari soleat*; 6. *De posteritate Caini*; 7. *De gigantibus*; 8. *Quod
   Deus sit immutablilis*; 9. *De agricultura*; 10. *De plantatione*; 11. *De ebrietate*;
   12. *De sobrietate*; 13. *De confusione linguarum*; 14. *De migratione
   Abrahami*; 15. *Quis rerum divinarum heres sit*; 16. *De congressu eruditionis
   gratia*; 17. *De fuga et inventione*; 18. *De mutatione nominum*; 19. *De somniis*.
   Of exceptional interest are also the so-called expository writings about
   the Mosaic Law: *De Abrahamo*; *De Iosepho*; *De Decalogo*; *De specialibus
   legibus*; *De virtutibus*; *De praemiis et poenis*; *De vita Mosis*. A separate
   group which is composed of exegetical and Biblical catechesis writings:
   Quaestiones et solutiones in Genesim; *Quaestiones et solutiones in Exodum*.
   The purely philosophical writings are among the least interesting and
   original: *Quod omnis probus liber sit*; *De providentia*; *De aeternitate mundi*;
   De Alexandro; *Hypothetica*. Linked to his political activities and to the
   Jewish ambiance instead are: *In Flaccum*; *Legatio ad Gaium*; *De vita
   contemplativa*. The most recent critical edition of the Philonian Corpus is
   that edited by L. Cohn and P. Wendland, *Philonis Alexandrini Opera quae*

supersunt, 6 vols., Berlin 1896-1915, completed by an indispensable Index edited by H. Leisegang, in 1926-1930. The following translations are important: in German edited by L. Cohn and I. Heincmann, Breslau, 1909ff. (Berlin 1962-1964[2]), in English edited by F. H. Colson and G. H. Whitaker in the collection "Loeb Classical Library," London-Cambridge 1929-1962. In French, under the editorship of R. Arnaldez, J. Pouillous and C. Mondésert for the "Éditions du Cerf," Paris 1961ff. In Italian there is available: all nineteen allegorical commentaries with the collaboration of C. Kraus Raggiani, C. Mazzarelli, R. Radice, and G. Hense; collected in five volumes, Milan: Rusconi, 1981-1988, with these titles: Vol: I. *La filosofia mosaica* (nn. 1-2) 1987; Vol. II: *Le origini del male* (nn. 3-8), 1984; Vol. III: *La migrazione verso l'eterno* (nn. 9-16), 1988; Vol. IV: *L'erede delle cose divine* (n. 15), 1981; Vol. V: *L'uomo e Dio*, (nn. 16-19), 1986; consult G. Reale and R. Radice, *La genesi e la natura della "filosofia mosaica." Struttura, metodo e fondamenti del pensiero filosifico e teologeo di Filone in Alexandria*, a monograph contained in: *Filone Alexandria filosofia mosaica*, Milan: Rusconi, 1987. In this volume are contained also commentaries to *De opificiis mundi* and *Legum allegoriae*-the last one is the first one written in Italian to date. Consult also *Reale 5* in this series under Philo of Alexandria, bibliography.

2. On this argument, the remarks of E. Vacherot, *Histoire critique de l'école d'Alexandrie*, 3 vols. (Paris, 1846-1851; republished Amsterdam 1965) 1.100-125.

3. Consult above pp. 205-72.

4. Our whole presentation will be a proof of this thesis on which the greater number of interpreters have for some time focused their attention.

5. Consult above pp. 263-272.

6. Consult Clem. Alex., *Stromata* 1.15.72.4; 2.19.100.3.

7. See chiefly Pohlenz, *La Stoa*, 2.193-215.

8. See above pp. 276ff.

9. On the influence of the Aristotelian *exoterica* on Philo see especially: A. J. Festugière, *La révèlation*, 2.520ff.

10. On the position of Philo in comparison to Greek philosophers consult H. A. Wolfson, *Philo, Foundations of Religious Philosophy in Judaism, Christianity, and Islam*, 2 vols., Harvard University Press, Cambridge-Massachusetts 1947 (republished many times) 1.107-115.

11. Consult above p. 171 and note 5 immediately above.

12. The numerous misunderstandings of Philo arise from the fact that many scholars do not pay attention to this element which is fundamental to the correct understanding of our philosopher. By analyzing the writings of Philo with "purely philosophical," that is, purely rationalistic criteria, and pointing out in them only what can appear within the parameters and the dimension of Hellenic thought either prior to or contemporary with Philo,

means to dismember a great mosaic and reduce it solely to its individual tiles, destroying in this way the general design which was realized through these individual tiles.

13. None of the evidence adduced by scholars to the present which attempt to prove that Philo possessed a knowledge of Hebrew yield incontrovertible or decisive results. The variants which are encountered in some citations of the *Bible* made by Philo in reference to the *Septuagint* which we possess today, can be easily explained, as has been long ago remarked, by supposing that these variants were contained in the edition which he used, that is, that the translation of the *Septuagint* which we possess received some slight changes and revisions.

14. Consult Philo of Alexandria, *Moses* 2.12-40; *LCL* 6.457, 459, 461, 463, 465, 467, 469.

15. Philo, sometimes, maintained the dependence of some Greek philosophical theories on Jewish wisdom (consult, for example, *Questions and Answers on Genesis*, 3.5; *On The Special Laws* Book IV, 4.61; he frequently remarks on the correspondence of Greek philosophical ideas with those of the *Bible*, and underlines the priority of the latter. On these questions see Wolfson, *Philo*, 1.138-143.

16. We will also be able to point out a judaizing Platonism or a platonizing Judaism; but this phrase puts to the side the other Greek philosophical components which are surely operative.

17. The core of this *Allegorical Interpretation* is well summarized by Bréhier as follows: "*Genesis* in its totality up to the appearance of Moses represents the transformation of the soul previously morally indifferent, which then abandons itself to a life of evil, and which finally, when the vice is curable, returns in stages to a virtuous life. In this story, every stage is represented by a person. Adam (the indifferent soul) is attracted by sensations (Eve), who is seduced by pleasure (the serpent); consequently, the soul becomes in itself envious (Cain) with all the evil consequences; the good (Abel) is excluded, just as the soul dies to the moral life. But, when the evil is curable, the seeds of goodness which are in it can develop through hope (Enos) and repentance (Enoch) until justice (Noah) is achieved, and then notwithstanding a relapse (the Flood, Sodom), it achieved a secure holiness" (Bréhier, *Les idées philosophiques et religieuses de Philon d'Alexandrie*, Paris 1908 [1950^3] 43).

18. Consult *Reale* 3.246-247.

19. Consult Clem. Alex. *Strom.* 5.8.45; *frag.* 227 O. Kern, *Orphicorum fragmenta*, p. 243.

20. On this parallel between the allegorical method of the *Table of Cebetes* and that of Philo consult Bréhier, *Les idées*, pp. 39ff.; on the Neo-Pythagorean *pseudepigrapha* consult above pp. 263ff. Later he will offer a

particularly important example of an allegorical interpretation of Plutarch's Egyptian mythology, especially in *On Isis and Osiris*.

21. A typical example of the excesses to which this thesis has been forced may be found in the book of E. R. Goodenough, *By Light, Light* (New Haven, 1935).

22. On the thought of Aristobulus and his significance there is quite a bit a disagreement among scholars. Actually, some of them have maintained that the fragments really belong to the Jewish Aristobulus who lived around 100 BCE. Other scholars, instead, think that the fragments attributed to him are not authentic but are forgeries from the post-Philonian period and that furthermore they contain gross misunderstandings of the Philonian thought. The arguments of those who support the non-authenticity of the fragments are not however decisive, as Zeller has already correctly pointed out (*DPG* 3.2.277ff.). In any case, there are two fundamental ideas which this Judaizing "Peripatetic" (thus he is called by the ancient sources) maintained: (1) The anthropomorphism of the *Bible* must be understood in terms of allegory and the expression such as the "hands of God" and similars are to be understood in the sense that they indicate "the divine powers." (2) The Greeks are indebted to Moses for their philosophical wisdom. But the first position is only a very fragmentary anticipation of the results of the Philonian allegorizing and the second position, which is maintained in a rashly stated way, in Philo is instead presented in a very cautious manner. For an analysis of the problem we refer the reader to N. Walter, *Der Thoraausleger Aristobulos. Untersuchungen zu seinem Fragmenten und zu pseudepigraphischen Resten der jüdisch-hellenistischen Literatur* (Berlin, 1964) and C. Kraus Reggiani, *I frammenti di Aristobulo, esegete biblico*, Accademia Nazionale dei Lincei, Boll. da Classici, serie III, fasc. III, 1982 (contains the fragments, translation and commentary).

23. The forger who wrote this letter and attributed it to Aristea, seems actually to have lived around 100 BCE. The point of contact which the document presents with Philo is very tenuous and rather marginal. See the important volume: C. Kraus Reggiani, *La lettera di Aristea a Filocrate*, Università di Roma, Istituto di filologia classica, (Università di Roma, 1979).

24. Also the *Wisdom of Solomon* seems to be composed after 100 BCE, probably by an Alexandrian Jew. But the contact between this text and Philo is not terribly important.

25. Consult Philo of Alexandria, *The Special Laws*, 3.178 and 1.8.

26. Consult Philo of Alexandria, *Every Good Man is Free*, 75ff.

27. Consult Philo of Alexandria, *On the Contemplative Life*, passim.

28. On the texts and problems concerning the Philonian allegorical interpretation consult H. A. Wolfson, *Philo*, 1.115-132 and the fine article of J. Pepin, "Remarques sur la théorie de l'exégèse allégorique chez Philon," in *Philon d'Alexandrie. Colloques nationaux du Centre National de la Recherche Scientifique, Lyon 11-15 Septembre 1966* (Paris: Éditions du Centre National de la Recherche Scientifique, 1967) 131-67.

29. On his own "divine inspiration" in the explanation of the allegorical meaning Philo speaks with pronounced clarity, for example, in *On the Cherubim*, 27.

(pp. 177-80) (1-17)

1. Consult *Reale* 1.13ff.

2. Consult *Reale* 2, ad loc.

3. In particular, it is necessary to point out that Philo carried the Platonic vocabulary into a context which presupposed a Creating and Revealing God who is concerned with individuals, even wicked ones, and hence it involves a kind of relationship between God and man which for Plato was literally inconceivable.

4. Consult *Reale* 2.95ff. [Italian edition].

5. Plato, *Phaedo* 85C-D.

6. H. A. Wolfson, *Philo*, 1.143-163.

7. Philo of Alexandria, *On Mating with the Preliminary Studies*, 79.

8. Philo of Alexandria, *Allegorical Interpretation* 3.228.

9. Philo of Alexandria, *On Abraham* 268.

10. Keep in mind, in order to estimate the nature of this originality that Plato (*Reale* 2. ad loc.) considered *pistis* (= faith, belief) only as an aspect of *doxa*, for Plato, even when it was not in error, could never be true knowledge.

11. Consult above pp. 128 and 141ff.

12. Philo of Alexandria, *On Husbandry*, 14ff.

13. Philo of Alexandria, *On the Change of Names*, 76.

14. Philo of Alexandria, *On Rewards and Punishments*, 81

15. Philo of Alexandria, *On the Unchangeableness of God*, 140-145.

16. Philo of Alexandria, *On the Posterity and Exile of Cain*, 102.

17. H. A. Wolfson *Philo*, 1.147ff., and 183ff.

(pp. 181-196) (1-67)

1. It would be well to consider, at this point, the positions of the Hellenistic schools with respect to this question, in order to understand the novel character of Philo's notion; consult *Reale* 3.135ff., 151ff., 358ff.

2. Consult the indices of Leisegang *s.v.* ἀσώματος.

3. Philo of Alexandria, *Allegorical Interpretation*, 2.1-3.

4. Philo of Alexandria, *Allegorical Interpretation*, 1.44.

5. Consult, for example, Philo of Alexandria, *On the Creation*, 25; *Questions and Answers on Exodus*, 2.52; *Moses*, 2.74.

6. Consult Philo of Alexandria, *The Special Laws*, 1.327-329.

7. Consult above pp. 197ff.

8. Consult Philo of Alexandria, *The Special Laws*, 1.32.

9. Consult Philo of Alexandria, *The Special Laws*, 1.331ff., consult also *The Decalogue*, 52ff.

10. Consult Philo of Alexandria, *The Special Laws*, 1.330.

11. Consult Philo of Alexandria, *The Special Laws*, 1.332, consult also the passages cited above in note 9.

12. Consult for Socrates *Reale* 1.340-46; with respect to Plato see *The Laws* 10, passim; and concerning Aristotle see chiefly *De Philosophia* and *Treatise on the Cosmos* 6 passim (our edition pp. 168-85).

13. Consult Philo of Alexandria, *The Special Laws*, 1.32-35.

14. Philo of Alexandria, *On Abraham*, 75-76.

15. Philo of Alexandria, *On Rewards and Punishments*, 43.

16. Philo of Alexandria, *On Rewards and Punishments*, 43.

17. Philo of Alexandria, *Allegorical Interpretation*, 3.100.

18. Philo of Alexandria, *On Rewards and Punishments*, 45.

19. Consult Philo of Alexandria, *The Special Laws*, 1.43ff.

20. Consult, for example, Philo of Alexandria, *On Dreams*, 1.73, *Allegorical Interpretation*, 2.1.

21. Consult Philo of Alexandria, *On the Creation*, 8; *On Rewards and Punishments*, 40; *On Flight and Finding*,198; *On the Contemplative Life*, 2.

22. For the discussion of some texts in which this attribute is affirmed and for their interpretation consult H. A. Wolfson *Philo* 2.101-10.

23. Consult, for example, Philo of Alexandria, *Allegorical Interpretation*, 1.44, 3.4, 3.51; *On the Confusion of Tongues*, 136ff.; *On Dreams*, 1.61ff.

24. Consult Philo of Alexandria, *On the Change of Names*, 9-28.

25. Consult H. A. Wolfson, *Philo*, 2.110-26 and 158ff.

26. Consult Philo of Alexandria, *The Special Laws*, 1.36-40. See, in addition, *On the Creation*, 8; *On the Change of Names*, 7-15; *On Rewards and Punishments*, 36-46; *On Abraham*, 75-79.

27. It would betray the Philonian conception of God to give to these attributes and to others which could also be listed an excessive importance, the nature of God is beyond all these attributes.

28. Consult Philo of Alexandria, *Moses*, 1.75.

29. Philo of Alexandria, *On Dreams*, 1.230ff.

30. Philo of Alexandria, *The Worse attacks the Better*, 160.

31. Philo of Alexandria, *On the Cherubim*, 77.

32. Philo of Alexandria, *Allegorical Interpretation*, 1.5.

33. Philo of Alexandria, *On the Creation*, 7-9.

34. Philo of Alexandria, *On the Creation*, 21ff.
35. Philo of Alexandria, *Who is the Heir*, 156-60.
36. Philo of Alexandria, *On Providence*, 1.625-26 and 2.48-50.
37. Consult H. A. Wolfson, *Philo*, 1.295-324 and G. Reale, "Filone di Alessandria e la prima elaborazione della dottrina della creazione," in *Paradoxos Politeia* (Milan: Vita e Pensiero, 1979) and G. Reale-R. Radice, op. cit. pp. 247-97.
38. Consult Philo of Alexandria, *Moses*, 2.267.
39. Philo of Alexandria, *Allegorical Interpretation*, 3.10.
40. Philo of Alexandria, *On Dreams*, 1.76.
41. Philo of Alexandria, *Allegorical Interpretation*, 3.78.
42. Cf. Philo of Alexandria, *On the Unchangeableness of God*, 107.
43. Philo of Alexandria, *On the Creation*, 19.
44. Philo of Alexandria, *On the Creation*, 24.
45. This has already been pointed out by M. Heinze, *Die Lehre vom Logos in der griechischen Philosophie* (Aldenburg, 1872 and Aalen 1961^2) 218ff. H. A. Wolfson (*Philo*, 1.226-40) maintains that it is the first and highest meaning of *Logos*.
46. For an adequate comprehension of the various aspects of *Logos* consult these three classical works: M. Heinze, *Die Lehre vom Logos*, 204-97; E. Bréhier, *Les idées*, 83-111; H. A. Wolfson, *Philo*, 1.226-82.
47. In this immanent meaning of the Philonian *Logos* is taken up some of the meanings of the Stoic notion of *Logos*, which, therefore, in the new general context changes its original connotations.
48. Consult above pp. 341-50.
49. Let us keep in mind that Bréhier has correctly underscored that "to study the theory of *Logos* means to study the whole of Philonism according to a certain point of view" (*Les idées*, p. 83). Moreover, it is perhaps the Philonian theme which has been given the most attention.
50. Also for an analysis of the thematic of the Powers consult, H. A. Wolfson, *Philo*, 1.217-26 and 2.138-49.
51. Consult Philo of Alexandria, *Questions and Answers on Exodus*, 2.68.
52. Philo of Alexander *On Abraham*, 119-23. Here the "second voyage" has a meaning which is wholly unusual.
53. Philo of Alexandria, *Questions and Answers on Exodus*, 2.68.
54. Philo of Alexandria, *On the Cherubim*, 27.
55. We will find the expression in Plotinus; consult above pp. 345-50.
56. Concerning the problem consult R. M. Jones "The Ideas as the Thoughts of God" *Classical Philology* 21 (1926) 317-26 and A. N. M. Rich, "The Platonic Ideas as the Thoughts of God" *Mnemosyne* Ser. 4, 7 (1954) 123-33.
57. Consult above pp. 187ff.

58. Consult especially Philo of Alexandria, *Allegorical Interpretation*, 3.96; *On the Creation*, 19; *Who is the Heir*, 231.
59. Concerning atemporal creation consult Philo of Alexandria, *On the Creation*, 13ff.; on creation in time on the part of God consult, for example, *On the Unchangeableness of God*, 30ff.
60. Consult, for example, Philo of Alexandria, *The Special Laws*, 1.327, 329 (see the passage mentioned above on pp. 182ff.).
61. The most satisfactory treatment of the problem of the Ideas in Philo is that of H. A. Wolfson *Philo*, 1.200-394.
62. Consult above pp. 201ff.
63. Philo thus gives reasons for the Platonic Ideas (transcendent), the Aristotelian forms (immanent) and the intermediate position.
64. Consult Philo of Alexandria, *On Dreams*, 1.141.
65. Consult Philo of Alexandria, *On Dreams*, 1.143.
66. Philo of Alexandria, *Allegorical Interpretation*, 3.177.
67. Philo of Alexandria, *Allegorical Interpretation*, 3.177.

(pp. 197-204) (1-26)
1. Philo of Alexandria, *On the Creation*, 69ff.
2. Philo of Alexandria, *On the Creation*, 134ff.
3. It seems to us that the best of all those who have refocused attention on the meaning of Spirit is A. Maddalena, *Filone Alessandrino* (Milan, 1970) 21-43.
4. Philo of Alexandria, *Allegorical Interpretation*, 1.31ff.
5. Philo of Alexandria, *Allegorical Interpretation*, 1.36-38.
6. Concerning this paragraph and the succeeding ones consult G. Reale, "L'itinerario a Dio in Filone di Alessandria," Introduction to *L'erede delle cose divine* (cited on page 485, note 1 above).
7. Philo of Alexandria, *On the Sacrifices of Abel and Cain*, 2.
8. Consult Philo of Alexandria, *On the Posterity and Exile of Cain*, 35-38; *On the Confusion of Tongues*, 122-27 (consult *Allegorical Interpretation*, 1.49).
9. Philo of Alexandria, *On Drunkenness*, 2
10. Philo of Alexandria, *On the Unchangeableness of God*, 47.
11. Consult especially *On Abraham*, 262-76.
12. For the theme of the "assimilation to God" consult Philo of Alexandria *The Special Laws*, 4.188; *On Flight and Finding*, 63; *On the Virtues*, 168; *On the Creation*, 144.
13. On faith, hope, and love in Philo consult Maddalena, *Filone*, pp. 381-95.
14. Philo of Alexandria, *On Flight and Finding*, 58.
15. Consult *On the Migration of Abraham*, passim; *Who is the Heir*, passim.
16. Aristotle, *Nicomachean Ethics* Z 7.1141a34-b2.
17. Philo of Alexandria, *On the Migration of Abraham*, 185.
18. Philo of Alexandria, *On the Migration of Abraham*, 2-12.

19. Philo of Alexandria, *Who is the Heir*, 73.
20. Philo of Alexandria, *Who is the Heir*, 84.
21. Philo of Alexandria, *Who is the Heir*, 75.
22. Philo of Alexandria, *Who is the Heir*, 69-70 and 263-65.
23. Philo of Alexandria, *On Dreams*, 1.60.
24. Philo of Alexandria, *Who is the Heir*, 30.
25. Philo of Alexandria, *On the Preliminary Studies*, 134.
26. Philo of Alexandria, *Who is the Heir*, 111.

(pp. 207-14) (1-54)

1. Consult *Reale* 3.347ff.
2. Consult Sextus Empiricus, *Outline of Pyrrhonism*, 1.220.
3. Consult *Reale* 3.59-83; 329-65.
4. Cicero, *Acad.* passim.
5. Consult, for example, R. E. Witt, *Albinus and the History of Middle Platonism* (London: Cambridge University Press, 1937; republished at Amsterdam in 1971). For a contrary view consult G. Invernizzi, *II Didaskalikos di Albino e il medioplatonismo. Saggio di interpretazione storico-filosofico con traduzione e commento del Didaskalikos*, 2 vols. (Rome: Edizione Abete, 1976) passim; H. Dörrie, *Platonica minora* (Münich, 1976).
6. Consult *Reale* 3.445-46, note 1.
7. Plutarch, *Life of Sulla*, 12.
8. Plutarch, again in the *Life of Sulla*, 14 writes: "At any rate, the city was taken at this point, as the oldest Athenians used to testify. And Sulla himself, after he had thrown down and levelled with the ground the wall between the Piraic and the Sacred Gate, led his army into the city at midnight. The sight of him was made terrible by blasts of many trumpets and bugles, and by the cries and yells of *the soldiery now let loose by him for plunder and slaughter, and rushing through the narrow streets with drawn swords*. There was therefore no counting of the slain, but their numbers are to this day determined only by the space that was covered with blood. For without mention of those who were killed in the rest of the city, the blood that was shed in the market-place covered all the Cerameicus inside the Dipylon gate; nay, many say that it flowed through the gate and deluged the suburb. But although those who were thus slain were so many, there were yet more who slew themselves, out of yearning pity for their native city, which they thought was going to be destroyed. For this conviction made the best of them give up in despair and fear to survive, since they expected no humanity or moderation from Sulla)."
9. The Peripatos was subjected also to an analogous fate, for the same reasons, as we have mentioned above (consult page 12, note 5 [above p. 455]).

10. Cicero, *De finibus* 5.1.1-2.

11. Consult *Index Academicorum*, col. xxv, p. 110 Mekler; Cicero, *Brutus*, 97, 332; *Acad. post.*, 1.3.12; *De finibus* 5.3.8; *Tusc. disp.* 5.8.21.

12. Seneca, *Naturales quaestiones*, 7.32.2: "Academici et veteres et minores nullum antistitem reliquerunt." ["Academics both old and minor no masters leave."]

13. Consult above pages 212ff.

14. The great merit of having contributed to the acceptance of the term "Middle Platonism" belongs to K. Praechter, who analyzed this current of thought in a series of philosophical works and articles as well as the problems related to it. He has especially furnished us with a panoramic view of "Middle Platonism in his *Die Philosophie des Altertums* (volume 1 of the famous *Grundiss der Geschichte der Philosophie* of F. Ueberweg) 524-56. Praechter had also projected a systematically arranged collection of the fragments which unfortunately he did not accomplish. The shortcoming of the works of Praechter is their use of chiefly philological criteria which did not always permit the comprehension of the philosophical meaning of the problems (we will give a list of these works in the bibliography in the final volume of the series). Zeller, on this point, offered a somewhat disordered and pedestrian treatment (consult *DPG* 3.831-45; 3.2.175-254); he lacked, in fact, the concept of "Middle Platonism" which alone would have allowed him to see synthetically and unitarily those thinkers whom he presented in such a disconnected sequence. He spoke of "Platonic commentators" and of "Pythagoreanizing Platonists" of whom he treated in separate volumes. Then, next to these volumes, he presented the Platonizing aspects and themes of the Stoics of the Imperial Age (consult *DPG* 3.2.706-91) of whom, analogously, he had already treated basically in the preceding volume (*DPG* 3.1.254-61).

15. Consult above pages 181ff.

16. Consult above pages 219ff. and 221ff.

17. Consult above pages 16ff. and 21ff.

18. Consult Invernizzi, *Il Didaskalikos*, passim.

19. Consult above pages 219-21.

20. Consult above pages 226ff.

21. Consult above pages 229ff.

22. Consult *Reale* 3.353-56.

23. Dercyllides, as Simplicius informs us (*In Arist. Phys.*, 246.31ff.), wrote a work on Platonic philosophy divided into many books (at least eleven it would seem). We know very little about his thought.

24. It is from Strabo's testimony (who was born in 63 BCE and died about 21 CE) that we locate Eudorus in the second half of the first century BCE, since he presents him as his contemporary (17.1.5.790). Some scholars

conjecture that Eudorus heard Antiochus of Ascalon when he taught at Alexandria. His relations with Ariston are instead more certain (on which see above pages 8ff.) this latter was linked for a certain time to Antiochus and then he moved on to Aristotelianism (consult Strabo in the same place). From the few fragments that are extant, however, the distance which separated Eudorus from the Stoicizing Antiochus is evident. Eudorus was concerned with Pythagoreans, the Platonic *Timaeus* and the Aristotelian *Metaphysics*. Some scholars maintain that he tended to read Plato (according to a tradition which goes back to the "unwritten dialogues" and to the earliest Academy) in a Pythagoreanizing manner, in particular by trying to deduce entities from the supreme One. But the extant testimonies are very uncertain and do not permit us to draw any conclusions except those which are chiefly conjectural. On the thought of this philosopher consult H. Dörrie, "Der Platoniker Eudoros von Alexandreia," *Hermes* 79 (1944) 25-39, now in *Platonica minora*, pp. 297ff. The fragments of Eudorus are collected by C. Mazzarelli, "Raccolta i interpretazione delle testimonianze e dei frammenti del medioplatonica Eudoro di Alessandria," *Rivista di Filosofia neo-scolastica* 22 (1985) 197-209; 535-55. Cf. Moraux, *Der Aristotelismus*, 2.509-827 (a good analysis).

25. Consult above, pp. 169ff.
26. Thrasyllus (perhaps a native of Rhodes) was an astrologer at the court of Tiberius (consult, for example, Tacitus, *Annales* 6.20; *MLCE*, p. 206). He died in 36 CE (consult Dio Cassius 58.27). On the division of the Platonic dialogues into tetralogies attributed to him consult *Diogenes Laertius* 3.56; Albinus, *Prologue*, 4. Porphyry (*Life of Plotinus*, 20) puts him (together with Numenius, Cronius, and Moderatus) among the philosophers who profess "Platonic and Pythagorean principles."
27. Suidas (*s.v.*) records Thrasyllus as the author of a commentary on the *Republic* of Plato which has been lost.
28. Plutarch is one of the most important Middle Platonists. Born in Chaeroneia towards the middle of the first century CE, he died probably in the third decade of the second century CE (consult the documents and the related discussion in K. Ziegler, "Plutarchos von Chaironeia" in *Pauly-Wissowa-Kroll* 21, 1 [1951] coll. 636-962. The quite well-to-do circumstances of his family permitted him to come to Athens to complete his studies, where his meeting with the Platonists Ammonius was decisive in his formation. Under this teacher he began his mathematical and philosophical studies, as well as Egyptian religion (Ammonius is presented as an interlocutor in *De E apud Delphi* and in *De defectu oraculorum*; consult also *Quaestiones convivialium*, 8.3.720C). Plutarch also visited Alexandria (consult *Quaestiones convivalium*, 5.5.1.678C) and came, especially in order to fulfill political duties placed on him by his

native city, more than once to Rome. His teaching activity was done chiefly at Chaeroneia, in the confines of a restricted circle: "Correctly it is spoken of," writes Ziegler, *Plutarchos*, p. 38, "as a simple private and intimate academy which Plutarch had not so much created on purpose, as much as it had spontaneously formed itself around his personality." Plutarch wrote a fair number of works. An ancient catalogue of them (the catalogue purportedly made up by his son Lamprias) lists 227 works (of which 83 have come down to us) but it is incomplete since there are 18 other works extant which are not mentioned in that catalogue, in addition we also know of 15 more works which are not mentioned in that catalogue (consult F. C. Babbit, *Plutarch's Moralia*; LCL 1.xviii-xix. The topics of these writings range from philosophy in the wide sense, to religion, science, politics, rhetoric, literary exegesis, and biography. The extant works are divided into two large divisions: the famous *Parallel Lives*, and *Moralia*. The title *Moralia* is sufficiently justified, since the ancients preferred it and hence the work came down to us, in addition to the *Lives*, as writings of a popular but philosophical character concerned chiefly with moral issues. It is to be noted that the more technical philosophical writings have been almost completely lost and hence it is unjust to characterize Plutarch, as some have done, as being superficial, since indeed the writings on the basis of which we judge him are not those in which he goes to the bottom of the problems treated, because of the limitations of the nature of a popular work. The citations from his works are made on the basis of the edition of Xilander (Venice 1560) repeated in the margins of successive editions (consult the bibliographical information in *Reale* 5). There are translations in English of the *Moralia* in the Loeb Classical Library in 15 volumes which we have consulted in our translation

29. From the testimonies of Plutarch it is clear that Ammonius was one of the Athenian civil authorities [*strategos* in that period], (consult *Quaestiones conviviaiium* 8.3.720Cff. and 9.1.736D).

30. Calvenus Taurus was some years younger than Plutarch and seems to have been a follower of his (consult Aulus Gellius, *Noctes atticae*, 1.26.4). He engaged in polemics against the Epicureans and the Stoics and probably also against those who attempted to produce a mediation between Plato and Aristotle since he wrote a work on the differences existing between their doctrines (consult Aulus Gellius, *Noctes atticae*, 9.5.8; 12.5.5; Suidas *s.v.* Taurus). It would seem he had written among others a commentary on the *Gorgias* and a treatise (of which the title alone is quite important) *On the Corporeal and Incorporeal Realities*.

31. Consult Aulus Gellius, *Noctes atticae*, 1.2 passim, 9.2 passim, 18.10.1.

32. The connection of Aulus Gellius with Calvenus Taurus is evident when we read, for example, Aulus Gellius, *Noctes atticae*, 1.9.8; 10.19; 17.20.4-5.

33. Gaius according to the testimony of Proclus (*In Plat. Remp.* 2.96.11ff. Kroll) was one of the most well-known Platonists [consult R. T. Wallis, *Neo-Platonism*, (London: G. Duckworth, 1972), pp. 30ff.]. This is confirmed by the fact that Plotinus lectured on his commentaries (consult Porphyry, *Life of Plotinus,* 14). We know very little about him. His commentaries on the Platonic doctrine were published by Albinus (consult the following note), as can be seen from the Index of the codex *Parisinus Gr. 1962.* All the testimonies on Gaius have been carefully studied by Praechter, "Zum Platoniker Gaios" in *Hermes* 51 (1916) 510-29. To attempt to reconstruct the doctrines of Gaius on the basis of the agreements existing between Albinus and Apuleius, according to some, by supposing that Gaius is the common source (consult T. Sinko, *De Apulei et Albini doctrinae Platonicae adumbratione* (Cracoviae, 1905), is undoubtedly a risky business. However, we would be committing the opposite excess, if we were to deny, on the one hand, the connections existing between Gaius and Albinus, to which our sources attest in varying degrees, and on the other, the comparable doctrinal affinities between Albinus and Apuleius, and the *Anonymous Commentary on the Theaetetus*. It does not seem, therefore, out of place to speak of the "school of Gaius," or of the "circle of Gaius," or of the "associates of Gaius" giving to these phrases the widest meaning.

34. A certain point for the reconstruction of the chronology and biography of Albinus is offered by the famous Galen who is said to come from Smyrna to hear the lectures of the "Platonic" Albinus in 151/152 CE (Galen, *De libr. Prop.* 2.16 Kühn; = 97.66ff. Müller). At this period, hence, Albinus was a teacher eminent enough to appeal to Galen. Therefore he must have been born toward the end of the first century CE or toward the beginning of the second century CE. We know, in addition, (consult the preceding note) that he published the lectures of Gaius from which we may correctly assume that he was probably his student. Of his writings only two are extant: the *Prologue* and the *Didaskalikos*, which is a synthesis of the doctrines of Plato. Actually, this latter work has come down to us under the name of Alcinous, but J. Freudenthal (*Der Platoniker Albinus und der falsche Alkinoos Hellenistische Studien II*, Berlin, 1879) has shown that Alcinous is simply an orthographical corruption of Albinus. (Recently M. Giusta has again taken up this issue as subject to dispute, which had up to now been the universally accepted opinion of scholars, in his work "Albínou Epitomé o Alkinóou Didaskalikós?" in *Atti dell'Accademia delle Scienze di Torino, Classe di Scienze morali, storiche e filologiche* 95 [1960-1961] 167-94, but with unconvincing arguments [consult C. Mazzarelli, *Rivista di Filosofia neo-scolastica* [1980] 606-19; he pointed out

that the only Alcinous of this period whose memory has survived is an obscure Stoic to whom in any case the doctrines of the *Didaskalikos* cannot be attributed). Recently E. Orth has also attempted to attribute to Albinus the anti-Stoic work entitled *De qualitatibus incorporeis*, which has come down to us among the works of Galen, but judged for a long time to be inauthentic; consult E. Orth, "Les oeuvres d'Albinos le Platonicien," *L'Antiquité Classique* 16 (1947) 113-14. The *Prologue* and *Didaskalikos* have been published by C. Hermann in 1853 in an appendix to the *Opera* of Plato in the Teubner edition volume 6, 147-89; the *Didaskalikos* has been re-issued, with introduction and French translation with notes by P. Louis, *Albinos Epitomé* (1945). A good critical edition of the work *De qualitatibus incorporeis* with Italian translation and notes has been edited recently by M. Giusta, *L'opusculo pseudogalenico* ὅτι αἱ ποιότητες ἀσώματοι (Torino: Accademia delle Scienze, 1976). Concerning Albinus in relation to Aristotle, consult Moraux, *Der Aristotelismus*, 2.441-80.

35. Apuleius was born at Madaurus in the first half of the second century CE. Scholars give 125 CE as a possible date, on the basis of the fact that around 158 he was involved in a trial (he was charged with being a magician) and that at the time he was a little more than thirty years old. But this is conjecture. The well-off character of his family allowed him to go to Carthage for his studies and to embark on numerous travels. He came to stay at Athens, where he became familiar with Platonism. He was also concerned with Aristotle and the Peripatetics (consult his *Apology* 36) and he studied the special sciences with great relish. He prized, however, the mentality and taste for literature, although he boasted of being accomplished in all the arts (consult Apuleius, *Florida* 4.20.5). He naturally came to spend time at Rome where he succeeded in making himself appreciated, without staying there for a long period of time. During a voyage to Alexandria, he became sick and had to disembark at Oea (Tripoli), where he was married rather fortuitously to a rich widow named Pudentilla, who was rather older than he, the mother of Sicinius Pontianus, his companion in studies at Athens. Because of obscure and complex occurrences following his marriage he was accused of magic (according to his accusers, he had seduced Pudentilla with his magical arts and with a love potion). The accusation was not grounded but it did seem plausible due to the fact that Apuleius had been initiated into a number of Eastern and Greek mystery religions (consult *Apology* 55) and was well-known for his knowledge of the occult sciences (consult *Apology* 51). He settled down at Carthage for the rest of his life. Of his philosophical works which are extant: *De Platone et Eius Dogmate* (which treats of metaphysics and ethics), *De Deo Socratis* (which is concerned with

daimonology), *De Mundo* (which is a translation/paraphrase of the *Treatise on the Cosmos for Alexander* attributed to Aristotle. Apuleius expressly refers to Aristotle and Theophrastus). A recent good critical edition, with French translation and accompanying Latin text and commentary of these works has been edited by J. Beaujeu, *Apulée Opuscules philosophiques et fragments* (Paris, 1973).

36. Consult *Anonymer Kommentar zu Platons Theaetet (Papyrus 9782) nebst drie Bruchstücken philosophischen Inhalts (pap. N. 8; pap. 9766-9769)* unter Mitwirkung von J. L. Heiberg, bearb. v. H. Diels und W. Schubart, Berliner Klassidertexte, Heft II, Berlin 1905. This commentary has been analyzed by K. Praechter in a famous edition published in *Göttingische Gelehrte Anzeigen* 171 (1909) 530-47, now in *Kleine Schriften* (New York: Hildesheim, 1973) 264ff.

37. Theon of Smyrna (lived at the time of Emperor Hadrian) developed chiefly the mathematical aspects of Platonism, in the work *Expositio rerum mathematicarum ad legendum Platonem utilium*, placing in relief the purificatory aspects, moral and religious of mathematics. In Theon hence the influences of Pythagoreanism are particularly apparent. The *Expositio rerum mathematicarum ad legendum Platonem utilium* was published by E. Hiller, Leipzig 1878 and in a French translation by J. Dupuis, Paris 1892.

38. On Nigrinus we are only given information by Lucian who dedicated to him a work which carries his name. Nigrinus stayed at Rome, living a very temperate life and teaching philosophy. Lucian presents him as a very severe critic of the customs of Rome about which: "For my part," said he, "when I first came back from Greece, on getting into the neighborhood of Rome I stopped and asked myself why I had come here, repeating the well-known words of Homer [*Odyssey* 11.93ff.] Why left you, luckless man, the light of day'-Greece to wit, and all that happiness and freedom and came to see' the hurly-burly here-informers, haughty greetings, dinners, flatterers, murders, legacy-hunting, feigned friendships? And what in the world do you intend to do, since you can neither go away nor do as the Romans do?" After communing with myself in this vein and pulling myself out of bowshot of Zeus did Hector in Homer, "From out of the slaughter, blood, and battle-din" [*Iliad* 11.163]. I decided to be a stay-at-home in the future. Choosing thereby a sort of life which seems to most people womanish and spiritless, I converse with Plato, Philosophy, and Truth and seating myself, as it were, high up in a theater full of untold thousands, I look down on what takes place, which is of a quality sometimes to afford much amusement and laughter, sometimes to prove a man's true steadfastness (*The Wisdom of Nigrinus* 17ff. That Nigrinus, as some have thought, was a person invented by the imagination of Lucian has very little

plausibility. It is certain, instead, that little can be recovered about the philosophical thought of Nigrinus from Lucian and that the positions in part Stoic and in part Cynic of the reflections put in the mouth of this "Platonic philosopher" (*The Wisdom of Nigrinus* 2) are due to the particular angle from which Lucian viewed the philosophical problematic.

39. Nicostratus flourished in the second half of the second century CE. On this Middle Platonist the article of K. Praechter "Nikostratos der Platonike," *Hermes* 57 (1922) 481-517 is basic. It is a study and commentary on what is extant of his works. Nicostratus merits a special place in the history of Middle Platonism because of his acerbic criticism of the doctrine of the *Categories* of Aristotle. He pointed out that the Aristotelian system of the Simplicius *In arist. Cat.* 1.9ff; 73.15ff; 76.14ff.), anticipating, in this way, the position which on this question Plotinus would carry to extreme consequences.

40. Atticus lived in the second half of the second century CE. Sincello (*Chronographia* 666.11ff. Dindorf) informs us that our philosopher was famous in the 239 Olympiad, that is, in 176-80 CE. Atticus was one of the most esteemed interpreters of Plato. His literary productions must have been extensive. The most well-known work entitled (*Against Those Who Try to Interpret Plato by means of Aristotle*) ample fragments of which are preserved by Eusebius. He was a relentless defender of the teachings of Plato and was a fierce adversary of Aristotle (not that his thought is "orthodox" Platonism even though the criticism of those who judge him to be a closet-Stoic is not correct (consult the anonymous commentary to the *Nicomachean Ethics* of Aristotle published under the editorship of G. Heylbut in volume 20 of the *Commentaria in Aristotelem Graeca* 248.25). Plotinus read his writings in his own lectures (consult Porphyry, *Life of Plotinus,* 14). Eusebius of Caesarea thought well of him and used him often, presenting many fragments from his works. Proclus also cited our philosopher frequently in his commentary on the *Timaeus*. A good critical edition of the fragments of Atticus, with French translation and notes has been recently published by É. des Places, *Atticus, Fragments* Paris 1977. Consult also R. T. Wallis, *Neo-Platonism* (London: G. Duckworth, 1972) 31-32. An important analysis of the thought of Atticus is found in Moraux, *Der Aristotelismus*, 2.564-82.

41. Harpocration was born at Argos and was the pupil of Atticus (consult Proclus, *In Plat. Tim.* 1.305.6ff. Diehl). According to the information given us in Suidas (*s.v.*) he wrote a *Commentary on Plato* in 24 books, as well as a Platonic *Lexicon* in two books. He was strongly influenced in addition to Atticus, by Numenius, especially in his doctrine of the Hypostases (consult Proclus, *In Plat. Tim.* 1.304.22ff. Diehl) and in his ethics (consult Stobaeus *Anth.* 1.375.14ff.; 380.14ff. Wachsmuth).

42. Celsus became famous chiefly by the fact that he wrote a book directed against the Christians entitled *True Account* ' Ἀληθὴς λόγος which intended to refute the new vision of the world which they defended and to reaffirm the correctness of the vision of the world of antiquity, especially that of Platonism. As is known, Origen refuted, in the work *Contra Celsum*, the theses maintained by the *True Account* in a detailed analytical mode so much so that it is possible to reconstruct from Origen the essential positions of the work of Celsus which has been lost. Scholars, on the basis of Origen's *Contra Celsus*, 8.68ff., conjecture that Celsus had written his work in the last years of the rule of Marcus Aurelius, that is, around 178-80 CE. The philosophical categories which Celsus used are not only generically Platonic but specifically Middle Platonic. A reconstruction of the *True Account* in a critical edition is edited by O. Glöckner, *Celsus, Alethes logos* (Bonn, 1924).

43. Maximus of Tyre was active in the second half of the second century CE (our sources place the beginning of his activity around 155 CE; consult the evidence in Zeller, *DPG* 3.2.219, note 1). Maximus was chiefly a rhetorician and his Platonism is of a popular character. We possess 41 of his *Discourses* or *Orations* edited many times in the modern period. The most accurate edition is that of H. Hobein, *Maximi Tyrii Philosophumena* (Leipzig, 1910).

44. The placement of Severus in the second half of the second century CE is a conjecture, but not wholly arbitrary. In fact, from Porphyry (*Life of Plotinus*, 14) we know that the commentaries of Severus were read (together with those of Cronius, Numenius, Gaius, Atticus, Aspasius, Alexander of Aphrodisias, and Adrastus) by Plotinus in his lectures. In addition to Proclus, Severus is cited by Iamblichus, while Eusebius also quotes a fragment of his. These texts are found gathered together by G. Martano in an Appendix to the small monograph previously cited *Due precursori del neoplatonismo*, pp. 63-68, and are translated in the notes of the first of these two works which are put together under the title *Severo, filosofo platonico del II sec. d.c.* pp. 9-21.

45. Praechter in an article "Hierax der Platoniker," *Hermes* 41 (1906) 593-618 has analyzed the fragments reported by Stobaeus from a work *On Justice* of a Platonists by the name of Hierax, who shows some contacts with Albinus, and who, therefore, probably belonged to this period. To the group of Middle Platonists must also belong Iuncos, author of a dialogue *On Old Age*, of which Stobaeus reports some fragments. Finally let us record the exposition of Plato by Diogenes Laertius in book three (67-80) redolent with Middle Platonic influences. Also the pseudo-Plutarchian treatise *De fato* is a document typical of Middle Platonic thought. A good edition of this work, with full introduction, Italian translation and notes

has been edited by E. Valgiglio, *Ps.-Plutarco, De fato* (Rome: Signorelli, 1964).

46. A work systematically collecting all the testimonies and fragments of the Middle Platonists would fill one of the most serious lacuna remaining in the sphere of the study of ancient thought, which in addition prejudices the comprehension of two centuries of the history of Western thought.

47. Consult above notes 28, 34, 35, 37, 43.

48. For the demonstration of this assertion check Invernizzi, *Il Didaskalikos*, passim.

49. The distinction between an "orthodox" and a "syncretistic" current was made by Praechter (consult *Die Philosophie des Altertums*, 524ff.). Among those who have most effectively contributed to the demise of this thesis, which had become canonic, we cite C. Moreschini "La posizione di Apuleio e della scuola di Gaio nell'ambito del medioplatonismo," *Annali della Scuola Normale Superiore di Pisa* 33 (1964) 15-56.

50. Consult especially Plutarch, *On Isis and Osiris*, passim.

51. The first method ends in reducing the exposition to a catalogue, as occurs in the very valuable exposition of Praechter (*Die Philosophie des Altertums*, pp. 524-56). The second method would be of value only if we possessed a greater number of the works of the various Middle Platonists; Albinus, for example, who, to judge from what remains, would be sensitive to the purely philosophical positions, could appear in a totally different light, if we possessed his work in which, as Tertullian writes (*De anima 28.1*), "the ancient discourse" on metempsychosis was considered of divine origin.

52. Consult the passage of Porphyry cited many times from the *Life of Plotinus*, 14 in which the names of Severus, Gaius, and Atticus are mentioned.

53. Consult the preceding note. The names of the Peripatetics mentioned are: Aspasius, Alexander, and Adrastus. The sense in which Middle Platonism has exercised its influence on them has been discussed above on pages 23-25.

54. It should be noted that scholars of early Christian thought realized the importance of Middle Platonism and they illuminated its historical significance better than the scholars of ancient-pagan thought.

(pp. 215-27) (1-63)

1. Consult *Reale* 3.238ff.
2. Plutarch, *De E apud Delphi*, 393E.
3. Plutarch, *Ad princ. iner.* 781F.
4. Plutarch, *On Isis and Osiris* 382F. On the relationship between Plutarch and Stoicism a solid contribution has been made by D. Babut, *Plutarque*

et le stoïcisme (Paris, 1969) concerning the specific issues that we are considering consult pages 453ff.

5. Plutarch, *De E apud Delphi*, 392A-93B.

6. Albinus, *Didaskalikos*, 11.2 Louis.

7. Albinus, *Didaskalikos*, 10.7-8 Louis.

8. Apuleius, *De Platone*, 1.193. Let us briefly note that Apuleius a little before (190) defines God as "incorporeal, one" and "ἀπερίμετρος," that is, infinite, using an obsolete Greek term which has a parallel (although not identical), for example, in Philo of Alexandria (consult, for example, *Sacrif.* 59 where the term ἀπερίγραφος is used).

9. Consult above pages 183-88.

10. Albinus, *Didaskalikos*, 10.4 Louis.

11. See above pages 221ff.

12. Consult *Reale* 2.250ff. [Italian edition].

13. Let us note that some of the Middle Platonists called metaphysics, with a name taken from the Elusian mysteries, *"epoptica"* which has many meanings (consult Plutarch, *On Isis and Osiris*, 382C; *LCL* 5.181 and note e; Theon of Smyrna, *Expositio* 14 Hiller).

14. Consult especially H. J. Krämer, *Der Ursprung der Geistmetaphysik* (Amsterdam, 1967²) 21-45 which is chiefly based on fragments 15 and 16 of the collection of Heinze.

15. In Stoicism the antecedent doctrine is the "seminal reasons" *(logoi spermatikoi)* which are included in the *Logos*; consult *Reale* 3.255.

16. Consult especially W. Theiler, *Die Vorbereitung des Neuplatonismus* (Berlin-Zurich, 1964²) 16ff.

17. Consult Varro, quoted in Augustine, *De civit. Dei* 7.28; Seneca, *Epist.* 65.7.

18. Consult *Reale* 2 passim.

19. Albinus, *Didaskalikos*, 10.3.

20. Albinus, *Didaskalikos*, 9.3.

21. Albinus, *Didaskalikos*, 4.7.

22. The position of Atticus, who revives and accepts this interpretation of the Ideas, is interesting. He argues, as he typically does, against Aristotle giving to the argument a nuanced account in which the achievements of the Stagirite do not seem to play any role. Here is fragment nine: "The central doctrine of Platonic philosophy, that is, the theory of the Intelligibles, has been argued against, trampled on, and enmeshed within the possibilities of Aristotle's philosophy. In fact he did not understand that great, divine, and excellent realities in order to be known require some power similar in nature. He relied instead upon the rather small and narrow capacity for quibbling-which, even if it could investigate physical realities and grasp their truth, was not accustomed to grasp the most pure

light of that which is really the truth-and, by using himself as the criterion and judge of things which stay above himself, rejected the reality of those ideal natures which Plato had recognized, and dared to define that most high reality as unimportant matters, monotonous songs or childish tales: whereas the summit, the supreme among Platonic truths consists in that which concerns this intelligible and eternal essence of the Ideas, which by extreme and toilsome work becomes present to the soul. In fact, those who have aspired to it and have achieved it will be wholly happy, while those who have not succeeded in achieving this contemplation are wholly deprived of happiness. Therefore Plato endeavored to demonstrate everything about the power of these ideal natures. He affirmed that the causes of things can not be attained, except by recourse to the theory of "participation" of these realities, neither can there be had according to him a knowledge of truth except in relation to them; nor again can there by any participation in this reasoning, unless the realities of the Ideas is accepted. Those who have maintained the necessity of upholding the Platonic doctrine must see in this argument the greatest cohesive force for their discussions. In fact, nothing further remains of the Platonic, if the reality is not conceded to these primary and sovereign natures, in defense of Plato. These then are the doctrines in which he chiefly surpassed all others. By conceiving a father god, demiurge, father and guardian of all things, and by grasping by analogy with his activities that the primary constructor has in mind all that which he is going to construct, so that the vision which he has in his mind can likewise be transformed into things; in the same way Plato conceived the thoughts of god, most ancient of things, as exemplary cause of the realities which are generated, incorporeal and intelligible, realities in themselves and always permanently in the same condition-in the first place, primarily, equal to themselves-and the cause of other things because they are of such a nature, which they manifest simply through the likenesses of things with their principles; and he saw, in addition, that those entities are not easily visible, and they are in no way clear neither through the way of reasoning, what can be said and thought about them, in order to prepare the way to those who were going to follow him, and being prepared and conformed to that objective all the principles of his philosophy maintain that in them are found both intelligence, and wisdom and science, through which the human goal and happy life is achieved."

23. Consult above pp. 345f.
24. Consult Aristotle, *De anima*, passim; *Reale* 2.324-39 [Italian edition].
25. Consult pages 198f. above for what has been stated here.

26. It is appropriate to read in its entirety fragment 7 of Atticus which is quite interesting (des Places, *Atticus*, pp. 61ff.).
27. Consult the passages reported above pp. 215f.
28. Apuleius, *De Plat.* 1.193: "Et primae quidem substantiae vel essentiae (1) primum deum esse (2) et mentem formasque rerum (3) et animam." ["*And first are certain substances or essences (1) first God's being (2) and mind the form of things (3) and soul.*"]
29. Consult Albinus, *Didaskalikos*, 10.2 (consult the passage which is quoted in the text above).
30. Consult Albinus, *Didaskalikos*, 10.2-3; consult the passage which is quoted in the text above p. 225).
31. Consult Invernizzi, *Il Didaskalikos*, 1.62ff. and related note.
32. Consult, for example, Plutarch, *De def. orac.* 425F-26A; *LCL* 5.435: "...one only God, who in absolute priority governs, [consult above, note 46] who is ruler of the whole universe, endowed with mind and reason [ἔχοντα καὶ νοῦν καὶ λόγον], such as to be called among men Lord and father of all things"; consult Maximus of Tyre, *Orat.* 8.10; 17.8, etc. Also Atticus, *frag.* 9 (quoted in note 22 above).
33. Consult Origen, *Contra Celsum*, 7.45: "That which the sun is in the sphere of sensible realities...God is in the sphere of the intelligible realities, he is neither intellect, nor intellection, nor science, but the cause for the intellect of his thinking....and for the substance itself is the cause of being; being above everything, he is conceivable by a kind of unutterable power."
34. Consult Plato, *Republic* 509B.
35. Here is the passage of Simplicius, *In Arist. Phys.* 181.7ff. which presents the fragments of Eudorus in which he seems much more to explain and interpret the Pythagoreans than to present his own doctrine: "The Pythagoreans, not only of physical things, but also of all things in an absolute sense, after the One, which they say is the principle of all, have placed the contraries as secondary and elementary principles, and to them, which however are not principles in the primary sense, they subordinate the two series. Thus Eudorus writes about these things: In a first and higher sense (κατὰ τὸν ἀνωτάτω λόγον) it is enough to say that the Pythagoreans say that the One is principle (ἀρχήν) of all things, while in a second sense (κατὰ δὲ τὸν δεύτερον λόγον) they say that there two principles of existing things, the One and the nature contrary to it. Concerning all things thought as opposed they say to that what is good is subordinated to the One, which that which is evil is subordinated to the nature which is opposed to the One. Therefore, according to them, these are not the common principle (τὸ σύνολον ... ἀρχάς). If in fact one is the principle of somethings, the other is of the others, they are not universal (κοιναί) principles of all realities, as instead the One is." And again:

'So—he says—from another point of view (κατ' ἄλλον τρόπον) they affirm that the One is the principle of all things because both the matter and all the beings are derived from him. And this they say is also the supernal God (τὸν ὑπεράνω θεόν).' Hence, speaking precisely, Eudorus says that they posit the One as principle and that from the One they derive the elements (στοιχεῖα), which they call by many names. In fact he says: 'I say therefore that Pythagoreans maintain that the One is the principle of all things, but from another point of view they introduce two principles, the highest elements. And they call these two elements with many names: the first of them they call in fact "ordered," "defined," "knowable," "masculine," "odd," "right," "light," the other contrary to this, "disordered," "undefined," "unknowable," "feminine," "even," "left," "dark," so that the principle is the One, the elements are the One and the indefinite Dyad, both the Ones again in their turn being principles. It is clear that the One which is the principle is different than the One which is opposed to the Dyad and which they call the Monad.' "

36. Consult Plutarch, *De def. orac.* 428Fff.; Plutarch, *On Isis and Osiris*, 354Fff.

37. A "monistic" schema, but it seems to be of different origin than that of Severus. Proclus (*In Plat. Tim.* 1.227.15ff. Diehl) writes that Severus maintained that "...something (τὸ τί 3,18) is the genus of being and becoming and that by it is meant the whole (τὸ πᾶν); just as it would be both that which becomes, and that which is always..." This doctrine of "something" as the supreme genera derives undoubtedly from the Stoa (consult *Reale* 3:243ff.), but goes further than the Stoa. In fact, the "something" of Severus, far from being that indeterminate and indeterminable *quid [what]* of the Stoa, is the Whole τὸ πᾶν including being (= eternal being, and, hence the intelligibles) and becoming (= sensible beings). Perhaps (but this is purely a conjecture) Severus deduced from the Whole eternal (intelligible) being and becoming (sensible) being, in a hypostatic-hierarchical manner. Again from Proclus (*In Plat. Tim.* 1.255.3ff. Diehl) we know that Severus understood *noesis* as the organ of the *Logos* or Thought, and that to it he subordinated (and hence probably, from it he deduced it). Also the position of our philosopher on the origin of the cosmos is special (consult what we state above pp. 350ff. and note 49).What we can say about the doctrine of the soul of Severus is that he is influenced by the Pythagoreans (consult the testimonies 6ff. in Martano, *Due precursori*, pp. 64ff.; also 16ff. for the exegesis of the testimonies). Unfortunately all these testimonies are too thin and too problematical to permit us to establish whether the "monism" of Severus represents an advance or a retreat, compared to the other Middle Platonists of the second century CE, with respect to Neoplatonism. The fact that Plotinus would read it in his lectures is, in any case, very significant.

38. On the "doctrine of the three principles" and on its relevance within the sphere of Middle Platonism, consult Invernizzi, *Il Didaskalikos*, 1.31-42 and the related notes on pp. 171-78 where the documents and bibliography will be found.
39. Consult Albinus, *Didaskalikos*, 8.2-3.
40. Consult Apuleius, *De Plat.* 2.191ff.
41. Plutarch, *On Isis and Osiris*, 372Fff.
42. Consult *Reale* 2.8ff. [Italian edition] and *Reale* 3.76 and 80-81.
43. Consult Plutarch, *De anim. procreat.* 1013A-B. The passage of Plutarch has now been re-interpreted by H. Cherniss in a different way (*Plutarch's Moralia* in Seventeen Volumes 13.1.999C-1032F with an English translation by H. Cherniss [Cambridge, Mass.-London, 1976] 169ff. so that the revival of this interpretation on the part of Eudorus can no longer be maintained as certain, as was believed in the past.
44. Consult Albinus, *Didaskalikos*, 14.3.
45. Consult Apuleius, *De Platone* 1.198; Calvenus Taurus, quoted by John Philoponus, *De aeternitate mundi* 145.13ff. Rabe (for further particulars see Moreschini, *La posizione di Apuleio* 32-39).
46. Consult Plutarch, *Plat. quaest.* 4.1002Eff.; *De anim. procreat.* 13.1.1014Bff. The opinion of Plutarch about the plurality of worlds (which he maintained as Platonic) is worth noting: "...it is more consistent with reason that the world should not be the only-begotten of God and quite alone. For he, being consummately good, is lacking none of the virtues, and least of all in those which concern justice and friendliness (φιλία); for these are the fairest and are fitting for gods.

   Nor is it in the nature of God to possess anything to no purpose or for no use. Therefore there exist other gods and other worlds outside, in relation with which He exercises the social virtues..." (*De def. orac.* 423D). The worlds are five in number. The five elements would correspond, according to Plutarch, to the five categories of the *Sophist* (being, identity, alteriety, movement, and rest), which would in their turn correspond to the five primordial geometrical solids (428Cff.) and the worlds would be indeed "as many as there were primordial existing bodies" (430E). All the worlds are produced and governed by the unique Reason-God (consult above note 32).
47. Read in this regard the fourth fragment (des Places, *Atticus*, pp. 50-54).
48. Consult Plato, *Statesman* 269Aff.
49. Consult Proclus, *In Plat. Tim.* 1.289.7 and 2.95.29 Diehl (testimonies 3 and 4, in Martano, *Due precursori*, pp. 63ff.
50. Consult Stobaeus, *Anth.* 4.1108.7ff.
51. Consult Plutarch, *Plat. quaest.* 4.1003A.
52. Consult Plato, *Laws* 10.896Dff.

53. Consult in particular Plutarch, *On Isis and Osiris*, 370F.
54. Proclus, *In Plat. Tim.* 1.391.6ff. Diehl) writes that Atticus and his followers "posit many principles which bound among them the Demiurge and the Ideas, and they say that matter also, moved by an ungenerated irrational, evil soul, without order of rule is agitated, and they place according to time, matter before the sensible, irrationality before the rational disorder prior to order." (frag. 26 des Places, *Atticus*, p. 76).
55. Consult Origen, *Contra Celsum* 4.65.
56. See also what is written about Harpocration in Stobaeus, *Anth.* 1. 375.14ff.; 380.14ff. Wachsmuth; consult also Maximus of Tyre, *Orat.* 41.4.
57. Plutarch, *On Isis and Osiris*, 360D-E. Consult Apuleius, *De deo Socratis* 147ff.
58. Consult Apuleius, *De deo Socratis* 150ff.; Plutarch, *De def. orac.* 415B-C.
59. Plutarch, *De def. orac.* 415C-D and 419Aff.
60. Consult Apuleius, *De deo Socratis* 153ff.; Plutarch, *On Isis and Osiris*, 361E.
61. Consult Plutarch, *On Isis and Osiris,* 360E and 361A-B.
62. Consult Plutarch, *On Isis and Osiris*, passim.
63. Consult Plutarch, *De def. orac.* passim.

(pp. 229-34) (1-32)

1. This is the point in our judgment which has scarcely been mentioned by scholars. On the Platonic antecedents consult, *Theaetetus* 176A; *Phaedrus* 253A-B; *Republic* 10.613A; *Timaeus* 90A; *Laws* 4.716C.
2. Consult Stobaeus, *Anth.* 2.48,8ff. Wachsmuth, on which see H. Dörrie, "Der Platoniker Eudoros von Alexandreia" *Hermes* 79 (1944) 28ff.
3. Consult Plutarch, *De superst.* 169E; *De ser. num. vind.* 550D.
4. This is possible to infer, as a conjecture, from the fact that the thesis in question is maintained by all the thinkers who seem to have been connected to him.
5. See the passage which is above on pp. 229.
6. Consult Apuleius, *De Platone*, 2.25ff.
7. Theon of Smyrna, in his *Expositio*, maintained that in order to achieve the imitation of God, man must traverse a pathway involving five levels, which moves from the purification through the mathematical sciences, to the grasping of philosophical doctrines (logic, politics, and physics), to the knowledge of the intelligibles, to the acquisition of the capacity to be initiated also into the other highest knowledges, to the fifth and last level, which is "the most perfect," and which consists, in fact, in the "imitation of God in the measure it is possible" (14.18ff. Hiller) according to the expression used by Plato himself (*Theaetetus* 176A).
8. Consult Maximus of Tyre, *Orat.*, 26.9; 13.1 Hobein.
9. Consult Stobaeus, *Anth.*, 4.1064.4 Wachsmuth.

10. Consult note 13 below.
11. Consult *Diogenes Laertius* 3.78; Hippolytus, *Philosoph.* 1.19.17 (Diels, *DG*, 569.14ff.).
12. Albinus, *Didaskalikos*, 28.1-4.
13. *Anonymer Kommentar* col. 7.14.
14. Albinus, *Didaskalikos*, 13.1.
15. Consult, for example, Apuleius, *De deo Socratis*, 168.
16. See, for example, the passage of Albinus cited above on pp. 229ff.
17. Consult Atticus, *frag.* 7.13 (des Places, p. 64).
18. Plutarch, *De genio Socratis*, 391E; consult also *De facie*, 943A.
19. Albinus, *Didaskalikos*, 27.3.
20. Albinus, *Didaskalikos*, 26.2; 31.1; Apuleius, *De Platone*, 2.236.
21. Albinus, *Didaskalikos*, 26.1-2. Concerning these themes see also Ps.-Plutarch, *De fato*, 5.
22. Consult *Reale* 2. 141-43 [Italian edition].
23. Consult Apuleius, *De Platone*, 2.219ff.
24. Albinus, *Didaskalikos*, 27.2; consult also the remainder of the chapter.
25. Plutarch, *Quaest. plat.*, 1009A-B; consult Albinus, *Didaskalikos*, 30.
26. Albinus, *Didaskalikos*, 27.3.
27. Consult Albinus, *Didaskalikos*, 27, passim.
28. Consult Albinus, *Didaskalikos*, 27.5.
29. Plutarch, *Vita Agesil.*, 36.2.
30. Consult Albinus, *Didaskalikos*, 30, passim.
31. Consult Albinus, *Didaskalikos*, 31.1.
32. For a detailed presentation of the various exponents of Middle Platonism, consult J. Dillon, *The Middle Platonists, 80 B.C. to A.D. 200* (Ithaca: Cornell University Press, 1977). See also in addition Donini, *Le scuole*, cited above, pages 100-159 and the further information which we provide in *Reale* 5.433 [Italian edition].

(pp. 237-48) (1-59)
1. Consult *Reale* 1.57-73.
2. Consult *Diogenes Laertius* 8.84; *D-K* 44A1; *Diogenes Laertius* 3.9; Eusebius, *Adv. Hierocl.* 64.380.8 Kayser; Iamblichus, *Life of Pythagoras* 199; *D-K* 44A1.
3. Consult *Reale* 2 ad loc. and note 1 [Italian edition].
4. Consult *Reale* ad loc. [Italian edition], where we show that the Pythagorean concept of "measure" is transformed on the basis of the new metaphysics.
5. Consult *Reale* 3.67ff.
6. Consult Aristotle, *Metaphysics* A 6.987b10ff.
7. Consult Aristotle, *Metaphysics* A 9, and books M and N, passim.

8. Let us remember the treatises *On the Pythagoreans*, and *On the Philosophy of Archytas* which arc unfortunately lost.

9. This is the thesis which is canonical, chiefly for Zeller, *DPG* 3.2.92ff.

10. Consult Aristoxenus, quoted by Iamblichus, The *Life of Pythagoras* 248ff.; (frags. 18 and 19, *Aristoxenus*, Wehrli; frag. 34 *Dikaiarkos*, Wehrli). Already some authors of the Imperial Age spoke not only of "*ancient* Pythagoreans" and of "*recent* Pythagoreans" (Plutarch, *Quaest. conviv.* 8.8.1 [728D]) but even of the "*ancient* Pythagoreans" and "*new*," that is, Pythagoreans (consult Syrianus, *In. Arist. Metaph.* 151.17ff.).

11. We will give a longer and complete list of these names in *Reale* 5 s.v. Middle Platonists. The whole of the extant pseudepigrapha, fragments and testimonies relative to them have been collected by H. Thesleff, *The Phythagorean Texts of the Hellenistic Period*, (Abo, 1965). A few years prior, Thesleff also published an introductory work, *An Introduction to the Pythagorean Writings of the Hellenistic Period*, (Abo, 1961) which contains the state of the question, catalogue of names, description of the various writings and fragments, and a new interpretation of the development and chronology of the pseudepigrapha, which is somewhat controversial but interesting. See also: W. Burkert, "Hellenistische Pseudopythagorica," *Philologus* 105 (1961) 16-42, 226-46; also articles in *Pseudepigrapha I, vol. 18, "Entretiens sur l'Antiquité Classique" (Vandoeuvres-Genève)* 21-102, which contains further contributions by Burkert and Thesleff. See also: Moraux, *Der Aristotelismus* 2.605-83, which shows the connections between the pseudepigrapha and the Aristotelianism.

12. See this treatise in *Thesleff*, pp. 21-32. A second treatise on the categories is attributed to Archytas: *On the Ten Universal Concepts* in (*Thesleff*, pp. 3-8); but this work is considered a forgery of the humanistic age (consult Th. A. Szlezák, *Pseudo-Archytas über die Kategorien*, Berlin 1972, pp. 19ff.), hence it is completely outside of the historical period with which we are concerned.

13. Consult *Thesleff*, p. 19ff. Here is, for example, the most important passage. After having stated that matter is not simply of itself united to the form, or vice versa, and that hence a third cause is necessary, who is God, the author writes: "So there are three principles: God, material substance, and the form. God is the maker and principal mover, the material substance is the matter and that which is moved, and the form is art and that in function of which the material substance is moved by the principal mover" (*Thesleff*, 19.25ff.).

14. *Thesleff*, pp. 20.11ff.: "The principles will necessarily be three: the material substance of things, the form and that which is moved of itself and that which is first through its power. And this principle must be not only Mind, but something superior to Intellect: that which we call God, evidently is

superior to Intellect." Consult Aristotle, *On Prayer*, frag. 1 Ross (p. 58): "That Aristotle has the notion of something further reason and being is shown by his saying clearly, at the end of his book On Prayer, that God is either reason or something even beyond reason" (Simplicius, *In de caelo* 485.19-22).

15. Consult *Thesleff*, pp. 36ff.
16. Consult *Thesleff*, pp. 125-38ff. Concerning this text, there is also an excellent edition with commentary and full introduction edited by R. Harder, *Ocellus Lucanus. Text und Kommentar* (Berlin, 1926).
17. *Thesleff*, pp. 203-5. Also in this document, the author, after having begun with the assertion that "there are two causes of the totality of things," that is, the matter and the paradigm-Idea, and after having added, as third, the composite of the two, that is, the sensible concrete thing, he restates the doctrine of the three principles, stating that before the birth of heaven "there was the Idea, matter, and the demiurgic God" (pp. 206.11ff.). An accurate critical edition with a full introduction and German translation has recently been edited by W. Marg, *Timaeus Locri, De natura mundi et animae* (Leiden, 1972).
18. Pseudo-Archytas seems to refer to the Aristotelian ethics in the treatise, *On the Good and Virtuous Man, Thesleff*, pp. 8ff.); *metropatheia* is maintained in the treatise, *On Moral Education*, again attributed to Archytas (*Thesleff*, pp. 40ff.). See then, the *Treatise on Virtue* attributed to Metopus (*Thesleff*, pp. 116ff.) which is particularly important. Political conceptions of a Platonic lineage are found in Zaleucus (*Thesleff*, pp. 225ff.), in the treatise *On the Art of Ruling* attributed to Diotegenes, Ecphantus and Stenides (*Thesleff*, pp. 71ff., 79ff., 187ff.).
19. Consult the Pseudo-Callicratidas, in *Thesleff*, pp. 103.11ff.
20. Consult the Pseudo-Brontinus, in *Thesleff*, 56.1-10, and the text in note 14. Consult on the Monad in general Pseudo-Buterus, in *Thesleff*, p. 59; the text cited in the preceding note; Pseudo-Opsimus, in *Thesleff*, p. 141 the texts attributed to Pythagoras, in *Thesleff*, pp. 164ff., 173.11, 186.
21. It is clear that the practice of writing books and attributing them to ancient Pythagoreans, once begun and consolidated, can continue indefinitely, even when some Pythagoreans came on the scene with their name and doctrine, and hence in the Christian era, as we have already noted further.
22. Consult above pages 259-61.
23. Consult Olympiodorus, *In Arist. Categ.* 13.13ff. King Juba II lived in the second century CE.
24. We propose to understand the term in both the temporal sense and also in its philosophical sense; consult above pp. 246ff.

25. Thesleff is guilty of the opposite excess, collecting all the pseudepigrapha between the fourth and second centuries BCE, but has the merit of having re-opened fruitfully the terms of the complex question. It is certain, in any case, that the general tendency is to pre-date these writings; consult the positions of various scholars after Zeller in *Thesleff, Introduction*, pp. 30ff.

26. On the origin of these writings in southern Italy, consult *Thesleff, Introduction*, pp. 46ff.

27. Reported by *Diogenes Laertius* 8.24-33.

28. Photius, *Biblioth.* cod. 249.438b-41b (quoted also in *Thesleff*, pp. 237-42).

29. Sextus Empiricus, *Adv. math.* 10.249-84, consult also *Outlines of Pyrrhonism*, 3.152-57.

30. Ovid,*Metamorph.* 15.1-478; Diodorus 10.3-11 (quoted also in *Thesleff*, pp. 229-37.

31. For the sake of completeness, we must also mention Eudorus (consult above pages 222-3, n. 35 [above p. 504-5] Alexandria (consult above pages 169-204) whose sources are unknown to us, but are securely circumscribed within the Alexandrian ambiance. The treatise *On Numbers* of Philo has been reconstructed by K. Staehle, *Die Zahlenmystik bei Philon von Alexandreia* (Leipzig and Berlin, 1931).

32. *Diogenes Laertius* 8.25.

33. *Diogenes Laertius* 8.27.

34. Photius, *Biblioth.*, cod. 249.438b33-93a8.

35. Photius, *Biblioth.*, cod. 249.439a19-24.

36. Consult Photius, *Biblioth.*, cod. 249.440a30-33.

37. Consult Photius, *Biblioth.*, cod. 249.438b8ff.

38. Consult Photius, *Biblioth.*, cod. 249.440a33ff.; 440b29ff.

39. Consult Photius, *Biblioth.*, cod. 249.440b20-27.

40. Sextus Empiricus, *Outlines of Pyrrhonism*, 3.152-57. Remember that *Adv. math.* (10.249-84 is considered by everyone (beginning from P. Wilpert, *Zwei platonische Frühschriften über die Ideenlehre*, Regensburg 1949) as a testimony referring to the unwritten doctrine of Plato. Sextus spoke of Pythagoreans, because evidently the source with which he is in contact (directly or indirectly) is a Pythagorean who has taken over Academic material, according to the practice with which we are familiar. On the other hand, keep in mind that, in general, the Neo-Pythagoreans do not refer to the original Pythagoreans, but to those of the Academy, as, moreover, modern scholars are today in agreement. Also the reduction of all things to the three highest categories, that is, to *the things which are of themselves*, to *the opposites* and to the *relatives* in order to reduce them to the Monad and the Dyad, which we read in Sextus, has a parallel although rather a rough one, in the Pseudo-Callicratides (in *Thesleff*, pp. 103.12ff.), and hence is not a problem.

41. Sextus Empiricus, Outlines of Pyrrhonism 3.152-55.
42. Nigidius Figulus was between the end of the second and the beginning of the first century BCE and died in 45 BCE. Cicero says of him directly in *Tim.* 1.1: "Denique sic iudico, post illos nobiles Pythagoreos, *quorum disciplina extincta est quodammodo*, cum aliquot saeculo in Italia Siciliaque viquisset, hunc extitisse, qui illam revocaret." ["Therefore as I judge, after the noble Pythagoras, *of whose discipline is somewhat extinct*, that some time in Italy and Sicily flourished, then ceased, which is called to mind"]. The fragments of Nigidius Figulus have been collected by A. Swoboda, *Publii Nigidi Figuli operum reliquiae* (Prague, 1889) and A. della Casa, *Nigidio Figulo* (1963).
43. On the tradition of Roman Pythagoreanism see L. Ferrero, *Storia del pitagorismo nel mondo romano (dalle origini alla fine della Repubblica)* [Turin, 1955]. On the legend of Numa and on the pseudo-Numa consult Ferrero, pages 142ff. The forgery of books attributed to Numa arose around 181 BCE.
44. Publius Vatinius and Appius Claudius belonged to the group. Concerning the former, Cicero delivers a decidedly negative judgment, consult *In Vat.* 6.14.
45. Quintus Sextius was a (a little older) contemporary of Augustus, as we can gather from Seneca, *Epistle* 98.13. He was born of a noble and well-off family, retired from active political life and dedicated himself entirely to philosophy (Plutarch, *De profect. in vi.* 77E. Sotion was one of the teachers who stimulated the enthusiasm of the young Seneca (consult *Epist.* 108.17). Crassicus, before he went over to the school of Sextius, was a grammarian (consult Seutonius, *De gramm.* 18). Seneca also heard Fabianus Papirius (consult *De brev. vitae* 10.1, *Epist.* 11.4.)
46. Here are some statements of Seneca, *Epist.* (64.1-3: "We then had read to us a book by Quintus Sextius the Elder. He is a great man, if you have confidence in my opinion, and a real Stoic, though he himself denies it. God, what strength and spirit one finds in him! This is not the case with all philosophers; there are some men of illustrious name whose writings are sapless. They lay down rules, they argue, and they quibble; they do not infuse spirit simply because they have no spirit. But when you come to read Sextius, you will say: 'He is alive; he is strong; he is free; he is more than a man; he fills me with a mighty confidence before I close his book.' "
47. Consult Claudianus Marmertius, *De statu animae* 2.8; for the doctrine of Sotion consult Seneca, *Epist.* 108.17ff. For the *incorporeality* of the soul, in addition to which *inlocalitas [not-being-in-place]* is also attributed consult F. Bömer, *Der lateinische Neuplatonismus und Neupythagoreismus und Claudianus Mamertus in Sprache und Philosophie* (Leipzig, 1936) 110ff.

48. Consult Seneca, *De ira* 3.36.1; *Versei aurei* 40ff. (consult Porphyry, *Life of Pythagoras* 40).

49. It is reckoned that Moderatus lived at the time of Nero or Flavius based on the fact that Plutarch, in the *Quaest. conviv.* 8.7.1 [720A], introduces a pupil of Moderatus. His work in eleven books on the teachings of the Pythagoreans was enjoyed by Porphyry, who, as we will see, used them on some essential points in his *Life of Pythagoras*.

50. Nicomachus was of Arabian origin (Gerasa, modern *Jerash* in Jordan). He could not have lived very much after the first half of the second century CE since Apuleius translated two of his works. Of his works extant, there are: *Introduction to Arithmetic* (ἀριθμητικὴ εἰσαγωγή) published by R. Hoche (Leipzig 1866) and *Manual of Harmony* ('Εγχειρίδιον ἁρμονικῆς) published by C. Jan, *Musici scriptores Graeci* (Leipzig, 1895) in addition, there are extracts of the *Theological Arithmetic* in Photius (*Biblioth.*, cod. 187), and in Iamblichus (V. de Falco 1922).

51. On Numenius, consult above p. 263, note 1 and [below p. 516].

52. Cronius was a contemporary and friend of Numenius (consult Porphyry, *The Cave of the Nymphs* 21). He is frequently cited together with Numenius. We know very little about him. He was one of the authors read by Plotinus in his lectures (Porphyry, *Life of Plotinus*, 14).

53. Apollonius was born at the beginning of the first century CE at Tyana, in Cappadocia and took up his studies at Tarsus, "according to our only full account, Philostratus" Τὰ ἐς τὸν Τυανέα 'Απολλώνιον (time of Septimus Severus, see Rose, *Handb. of Gk. Lit.* 403, W. Nestle, *Griechsiche Religiosität* (1930-3), iii.123ff.). Although Philostratus is highly untrustworthy (*PW* xx. 139ff., F. Solmsen), and references elsewhere are scanty, Apollonius's existence and Pythagoreanism need not be doubted. An anti-Christian writer, Hierocles of Nicomedia, paralleled Apollonius with Christ, which provoked a reply (extant) from Eusebius. According to our source, he made many voyages to the East and to the West preaching the Pythagorean doctrine and doing extraordinary things, living, that is, the same kind of life that is attributed to Pythagoras. Of his writings (see *Suda, s.v.* 623 Berhardy) we have only a fragment of his work *On Sacrifices* [Τελεταὶ ἢ περὶ θυσιῶν]," (*OCD*[2] p. 86) while the extant *Letters* attributed to him are doubtfully authentic. He seems to have died during the reign of Emperor Nerva.

54. Julia Domna died in 217 CE, consult *OCD*[2] *s.v.* p. 567. Among the editions of the *Life of Apollonius*: F. C. Conybeare, *Philostratus. The Life of Apollonius of Tyana, the Epistles of Apollonius and the Treatise of Eusebius with an English translation*, 2 vols. London-Cambridge, Mass. 1912 [Loeb Classical Library]. Βίοι σοφιστῶν, W. C. Wright (Loeb, 1922); Εἰκόνες, A. Fairbanks (Loeb, 1931); *Letters*, A. R. Benner and F. H. Fobes (Loeb,

1949); Translation, *Life of Apollonius*, J. S. Phillimore, 1912. There is a
new edition in Italian by D. Del Corno, *Filostrato, Vita di Apollonio di
Tiana* (Milan: Edizioni Adelphi, 1978).

55. Consult Zeller, *DPG* 3.2, esp. pp. 129-51.
56. Consult Zeller, *DPG* 3.2, esp. pp. 113ff.
57. Photius, *Biblioth.*, col. 249, 438b17-19.
58. Porphyry, *Life of Pythagoras* 53.
59. Consult above pp. 263ff.

(pp. 251-62)   (1-47)

1. Consult *Thesleff* 186.5-20; consult also Sextus Empiricus, *Adv. math.*
   9.127.
2. See the passages already cited above p. 222-3, note 35 [above p. 504-5].
3. Photius, *Biblioth.*, cod. 249.438b34.
4. Sextus Empiricus, *Adv. math.*, 10.249-58.
5. Consult above the passage quoted on page 257.
6. Nicomachus, *Intro. arith.* 1.1.1-2.
7. Consult the passage quoted on page 264.
8. Consult the passage quoted on page 245, note 47 [above p. 512].
9. Sextus Empiricus, *Adv. math.*, 10.258.
10. Consult *Reale* 1.61-65.
11. Moderatus, quoted by Porphyry, *Life of Pythagoras*, 48ff.
12. Moderatus, quoted by Porphyry, *Life of Pythagoras*, 48.
13. Moderatus, quoted by Porphyry, *Life of Pythagoras*, 49.
14. Moderatus, quoted by Porphyry, *Life of Pythagoras*, 51ff.
15. Moderatus, quoted by Porphyry, *Life of Pythagoras*, 52.
16. Consult Nicomachus, *Intro. arith.*, passim.
17. Photius, *Biblioth.*, cod. 187.142b40ff.
18. Photius, *Biblioth.*, cod. 187.143a22-28.
19. Consult below note 7, pages 539-40.
20. Consult Iamblichus, *Theol. arith.*, 3.21ff. De Falco.
21. The error of many scholars is that they maintain that the lexical contacts
    also imply the necessity of conceptual contacts. Here in the Neo-
    Pythagoreans, just as in the authors of Middle Platonism, with the identity
    of some terms taken from the vocabulary of the Stoa there is present a
    novelty of philosophical content, which is just as distinct from Stoicism as
    the metaphysics of the incorporeal is distinct from a materialistic ontol-
    ogy.
22. Aetius, *Plac.*, 1.3.8 (Diels, *DG* 281b5ff.).
23. Pseudo-Galen, *Hist. philos.*, 35 (Diels, *DG* 618.12ff.).
24. Sextus Empiricus, *Adv. math.*, 10.277.
25. *Diogenes Laertius* 8.25.
26. Consult above page 222-3, note 35 [p. 505-5].

27. Sextus Empiricus, *Adv. math.*, 10.261.
28. Syrianus, *In Arist. metaph.*, 151.17ff.
29. Syrianus, *In Arist. Phys.*, 230.34ff.
30. The entire passage can be read in Simplicius, *In Arist. Phys.*, 230.34-31.27 Diels. On the interpretation of this passage consult E. R. Dodds, "The *Parmenides* of Plato and the Origin of the Neoplatonic One," *Classical Quarterly* 22 (1928) 129-42; A. J. Festugière, *La Révèlation d'Hermès Trismégiste*, vol. 4 (Paris, 1954) 22ff. and 38ff.
31. Cf. above page 239, note 14 [above p. 509-10].
32. Cf. above page 240, note 20 [above 510].
33. Cf. Nicomachus quoted by Iamblichus, *Theol. arith.*, 57.21ff. De Falco, where the One is described as "first-begotten" which proceeds through imitation of the supremely Beautiful (that is, of the One which is above everything).
34. Cf. Nicomachus, *Introd. arith.*, 1.4.1-2 Hoche; Iamblichus, *In Nicom. arith. intro.*, 10 Pistelli; *Thesleff*, 165.1-5.
35. Cf. above page 256; also Photius, *Biblioth.*, cod. 187.143a32ff.
36. Cf. above pages 226-7.
37. Cf. above page 240, note 18 [above p. 510].
38. The *Table of Cebes*, for example, is Stoicized in the way it distinguishes *goods, evils*, and *indifferents*, but it places the doctrine in a mystical milieu, presenting it as an explanation of an allegorical picture, in order to conclude, in the end, with the re-affirmation of the Socratic principle that only wisdom is good and ignorance is evil. For the *Table of Cebes*, Italian reader has at his disposal the best translation with Greek text on facing pages, with notes in addition to a fine introduction and an index terms edited by D. Pesce (*La tavola di Cebete. Testo, traduzione, introduzione commento* [Brescia: Paideia Editrice, 1982]), the Greek text used is the Praechter's edition.
39. Cf. Zeller, *DPG*, 3.2.153 and note 5.
40. Thesleff assigns them to the fourth century BCE, Nauck, who produced an exemplary edition, assigns them to the fourth century CE.
41. The translation is based on the Italian taking into account the Greek text.
42. Cf. Photius, *Biblioth.*, cod. 249.439a8-19.
43. Cf. Apollonius quoted by Eusebius, *Praep. evang.*, 4.13.
44. Philostratus, *Life of Apollonius*, 1.2.
45. Philostratus, *Life of Apollonius*, 1.1.
46. Cf. Porphyry, *Life of Pythagoras* 2. Porphyry speaks of getting information from Apollonius.
47. Cf. Iamblichus, *Life of Pythagoras* 90ff.

(pp. 263-72) (1-30)

1. We know very little about the life of Numenius. He was born at Apamea (or the second century CE), in Syria which is the same city that gave birth to Posidonius. The single chronological reference that we possess and which serves as a time before which is the mention that is made by Clement of Alexandria. Probably Numenius lived in the second half of the second century CE. His knowledge of Philo and of Egyptian wisdom postulate a long stay at Alexandria, where presumably he studied, or, even taught (but this is a conjecture drawn from the fact that the school of Ammonius, of which we speak in the next section, has doctrinal connections to Numenius). Some say that Numenius must have spent some time at Athens, since he exhibits very solid knowledge of the history of the Academy, to which he dedicated work entitled *On the Infidelity of the Academy to Plato* of which there a extant many fragments. Important fragments of another work of his have been preserved, which must have been his masterpiece the treatise *On the Good*. testimonies and the fragments have been collected by F. Thedinga (*De Nume philosopho Platonico* [Bonn, 1875]) and by E. A. Leemans (*Studie over den Wijsger Numenius van Apamea met Uitgave der Fragmenten* [Brussels, 1937]), and recently by É. des Places, with a French translation and notes (*Numénius Fragments* [Paris: Société d'Éditions "Les Belles Lettres," 1973]). The first work of Thedinga has been already surpassed by the excellent edition of Leemans and des Places. Since all modern scholars cite Numenius on the basis of the edition of Leemans, so will we, for the convenience of the reader we will cite as well the edition of des Places which in the future will become the most important edition especially for his commentary and indices of Greek terms which is lacking in Leeman's edition. The Leeman's edition because of its different structure, which in some cases is very easy to use, is not completely substitutable for the des Places edition. In the edition of des Places, fine bibliographical information is given for the interpretation of the subject matter of each fragment.

2. Cf. testimonies 4 and 5 Leemans (which are presented by des Places).

3. Cf. frags. 1-8 Leemans; frags. 24-28 des Places. See in particular the first of these fragments.

4. On this problem see especially, H. C. Puech, "Numénius d'Apamée et les théologies orientales au second siècle," *Mélanges Bidez*, Brussels 2 (1934).

5. Leemans, *test.* 17, 36, 43; *frags.* 9a, 9b, 17, 18, 19, 22, 36, 39; des Places, *frags.* 1c, 44, 31, 1a, 1b, 8, 9, 13, 1c, 55, 60.

6. Consult *frags.* 11-16 Leemans; *frags.* 2-7 des Places.

7. Consult *frag.* 14 Leemans; *frag.* 5 des Places.

8. Consult *frag.* 15 Leemans; *frag.* 7 des Places.

9. Consult *frag.* 16 Leemans; *frag.* 7 des Places.

10. Consult *frag.* 16 Leemans; *frag.* 7 des Places.
11. Consult *test.* 17 Leemans; *frag.* 1c des Places.
12. Consult *frag.* 17 Leemans; *frags.* 8 (p. 51.9-13) des Places.
13. Proclus, *In Plat. Tim.*, 1.303.27ff. Diehl (= test. 24 Leemans; frags. 21 des Places.
14. Consult *frag.* 25 Leemans; *frag.* 16 des Places.
15. Consult *frag.* 24 Leemans; *frag.* 15 des Places.
16. Consult *frag.* 22 Leemans; *frag.* 13 des Places.
17. Consult *frag.* 27 Leemans; *frag.* 18 des Places.
18. It should be noted, in addition that this position of Numenius according to which the Demiurge, which is "good," is such by imitating the Good, that is, the first God, and he derives his capacity to judge by contemplation again the first God, that is, the eternal Ideas which are produced by him requircs, as our ancient sources point out, that not only sensible things but even the intelligible things (the second God and the contents of his thought) "participate" in the highest Ideas, and that, hence also, among intelligible things there are besides models, even images of them, that is *eternal images* of eternal models (Cf. Syrianus, *In Arist. Metaph.* 109.12-14 Proclus, *In Plat. Tim.* 3.33, 33-34.3 Diehl; *test.* 27 Leemans; *frags.* 46b, 46c des Places). This is explained quite well by having recourse to the position of Philo of Alexandria (to whom Numenius owed a great deal, as we know) who was the first to introduce this hierarchical notion of the intelligible, in which what comes after God is *an image of Him*, and in it turn, is a *model for succeeding realities*, as we have seen above (pp. 495 498).
19. Chalcidius, *In Plat. Tim.* capp. 295ff. page 297.7ff. Waszink.; *test.* 30 Leemans; *frag.* 52 des Places.
20. Consult *frag.* 20 Leemans; *frag.* 11 des Places.
21. Iamblichus quoted by Stobaeus, *Anthol.* 1.49.32 (365.6-21 Wachsmuth); *test.* 33 Leemans; *frag.* 41 des Places. Remarkable, but much discussed, the testimony of Proclus, *In Plat. Tim.* 3.103.28-33 Diehl; *test.* 25 Leeman *frag.* 22 des Places in which he says that the first God is *the Living in Himself*, which thinks using the assistance of the second God, who is Nous exercises in its turn the demiurgic activity using the help of the third which is discursive thought. Now discursive thought (*dianoia*) is indeed precisely a characteristic peculiar to the soul.
22. The first God is said to be the One = the Good in the 28th fragment of Leemans; (*fragment* 19 des Places), the second God is said to imitate the first God in the 25th fragment of Leemans and the 16th fragment of des Places and *only* the second God is said to enter into contact with the Dyad (become thus himself two-folded; in the 20th *fragment* of Leemans and the 11th of des Places) so that the Monad which orders the Dyad, of which the 30th *testimony* of Leemans speaks (and *fragment* 52 of des Places)

cannot in any way be the first God. Therefore, the hypothesis which we propose is the more logical one.

23. Chalcidius, *In Plato. Tim.* capp. 297, page 299.14ff. Waszink; *test.* 30 Leemans; *frag.* 52 des Places.

24. Consult *test.* 33 Leemans; *frag.* 41 des Places.

25. Proclus, *In Plat. Tim.* 2.153.17ff. Diehl; *test.* 31 Leemans; *frag.* 39 des Places.

26. On the conception of the soul, consult all the testimonies which Leemans collected under numbers 31-51.

27. Consult the passages which we present above on page 272.

28. Consult *frag.* 23 Leemans; *frag.* 14 des Places.

29. Iamblichus quoted by Stobaeus, *Anthol.* 1.49.32 (pp. 365.5-21ff.) Wachsmuth *test.* 33 Leemans; *frag.* 41 des Places.

30. Consult *frag.* 11 Leemans; *frag.* 2 des Places.

(pp. 275-83) (1-31)

1. Consult Plato, *Phaedrus* 274Cff., a passage quoted in *Reale* 2.9ff. (Theuth is a variant of Thoth).

2. In this respect, the representation of Hermes with the inscription *Hermes Mercurius Trismegistus Contemporaneus Moysi* in which he is represented in the act of giving to an Easterner, a book with the inscription *Suscipe...litteras et leges Aegyptii [Take...the books and laws of the Egyptians]* which is found on the pavement of the cathedral of Siena (end of the fifteenth century) is very interesting. Consult A. J. Festugière, *Herméticisme et mystique païenne* (Paris: Auber-Montaigne, 1967) 28.

3. All the problems relative to the Hermetic writings in all their implications and influence have been studied by A. J. Festugière in the monumental work, *La révèlation d'Hermès Trismégiste*, 4 vols. (Paris: Gabalda, 1944-54). By the same author see also the volume cited in the preceding note (where, on pages 28-87, the results of the studies of the author can be found briefly and effectively summarized) and those which are also cited in note 5 below. In the volumes of Festugière information can be found on the preceding literature.

4. For everything which concerns these writings (which are of interest only marginally for the history of philosophy) consult the work of Festugière, *La révèlation.* The first volume has the subtitle *L'astrologie et les sciences occultes* and is entirely devoted to this subject.

5. These writings have been published with English translation and commentary by W. Scott and A. D. Ferguson (Oxford, 1924-36). Even better is the successive edition, under the editorship of A. D. Nock with respect to the critical text and the translation, as well as the individual introductions to each treatise and the notes of the commentary by A. J. Festugière mentioned in the previous note. An excellent instrument is the recent

Index du Corpus Hermeticum edited by L. Delatte, S. Govaerts, J. Denooz (Rome: Edizioni dell'Ateneo e Bizzarri, 1977). Concerning the *Corpus Hermeticum*, there is a recent Italian edition by B. M. Tordini Portogalli, *Discorsi di Ermete Trismegisto* (Turin: Boringhieri, 1965). Keep in mind that the writings of the *Corpus Hermeticum* which we have said are seventeen, are numbered in an odd way as if there were eighteen of them. This must be due to the fact that in the *editio princeps* of Turnèbe of the sixteenth century, as treatise fifteen, a work had been inserted containing extracts taken from Stobaeus which are absent from the manuscript tradition. The modern editions have rightly eliminated this irrelevant insertion of Turnèbe, but in order to maintain the numbering of the *editio princeps*, which has become canonical, they have left the treatise number fifteen without content, and so our numbering is from one to fourteen and then from sixteen to eighteen, with a blank fifteen.

6. Festugière, *Hermétisme*, pp. 39ff.
7. Festugière, *Hermétisme*, p. 42.
8. Festugière, *Hermétisme*, p. 41.
9. Xenophon, *Memorabilia* 1.1.9; *LCL* 7, consult the passage which we quoted in *Reale* 1.103.
10. Festugière, *Hermétisme*, p. 44.
11. *Corpus Hermeticum*, 10.4-6 (Scott-Ferguson trans.).
12. *Corpus Hermeticum*, 4.10ff.
13. *Corpus Hermeticum*, 2.5; 4.9.
14. *Corpus Hermeticum*, 5 passim.
15. *Corpus Hermeticum*, 2.14 (Scott-Ferguson trans.).
16. *Corpus Hermeticum*, 1.7-8.
17. *Corpus Hermeticum*, 1.18.
18. *Corpus Hermeticum*, 1.18 (Scott-Ferguson trans.).
19. On this point, consult the remarks of Festugière, *Hermétisme*, pp. 72ff.
20. It is a question of a kind of fall through the sin of "narcissism" (*Anthropos*, who is in love with his own image reflected in nature), as has been correctly remarked.
21. *Corpus Hermeticum*, 6.4.
22. *Corpus Hermeticum*, 7 passim.
23. *Corpus Hermeticum*, 1.21 (Scott-Ferguson trans.).
24. *Corpus Hermeticum*, 10.13 (Scott-Ferguson trans.).
25. *Corpus Hermeticum*, 12.2 (Scott-Ferguson trans.).
26. Consult, for example, *Corpus Hermeticum*, 1.21; 10.21-24.
27. Consult Festugière, *Hermétisme*, pp. 58-61.
28. *Corpus Hermeticum*, 10.24 (Scott-Ferguson trans.).
29. *Corpus Hermeticum*, 4.3 (Scott-Ferguson trans.).
30. *Corpus Hermeticum*, 13.3 (Scott-Ferguson trans.).

31. *Corpus Hermeticum*, 1.26.

(pp. 285-91) (1-27)

1. The *Chaldean Oracles* have been edited by W. Kroll, *De Oraculis Chaldaicis* (Breslau, 1894) and photostatically reproduced in Hildesheim, 1962. A new critical edition with French translation and commentary has been completed recently by É. des Places, *Oracles Chaldaïques, avec un choix de commentaires anciens,* "Les Belles Lettres" (Paris, 1977). An excellent interpretation of the doctrine of the *Oracles* is to be found in H. Lewy, *Chaldean Oracles and Theurgy* (Paris, 1978³). On the theurgy of the *Oracles* and its development, the article of E. R. Dodds, "Theurgy and its Relationship to Neoplatonism," *Journal of Roman Studies* 37 (1947) 55ff., published also in the appendix to *The Greeks and the Irrational* (Berkeley and Los Angeles, 1951; republished in Boston: Beacon Hill Press, 1957 this is the edition to which we will refer for convenience). The translation of the fragments in the Italian edition is that of des Places (some are to be found already translated into Italian in the recent volume of this author entitled, *Platonismo e tradizione cristiana*, ed. P. A. Carozzi (Milan: Celuc Libri, 1976); others we have translated by referring to the French version of des Places, which is to be found in the critical edition cited above [for the English translation we have consulted various sources including the French and Italian translations of the *Oracles*, Ed.].

2. Consult the references in Lewy, *Chaldean Oracles*, pp. 3ff. In his critical edition des Places prefers to suspend judgment: "All things considered, it does not seem to be too far afield to admit that the collection came down from Julian the Theurgist, a contemporary of Marcus Aurelius; but it is still more certain to maintain that the *Oracles* are from an anonymous author or authors (p. 7).

3. Consult E. R. Dodds, *The Greeks and the Irrational*, pp. 284ff. Appendix II.

4. Consult des Places, *Oracles*, p. 11.

5. Consult des Places, *Oracles, frag.* 37, p. 75ff.

6. Consult des Places, *Oracles, frag.* 39, p. 77ff.

7. Consult des Places, *Oracles, frag.* 5, p. 67.

8. Consult des Places, *Oracles, frag.* 7, p. 68.

9. Consult des Places, *Oracles, frag.* 8, p. 68; for the parallels with Numenius, consult above, pp. 283-92.

10. Consult des Places, *Oracles, frag.* 53, p. 80. For the problem of the identification of Hecate with the Anima hypostasis and the role of Hecate, consult des Places, *Oracles*, pp. 13 and the related notes; also page 133.

11. For the documentation, consult des Places, *Oracles*, p. 14ff.

12. Consult des Places, *Oracles, frag.* 21, p. 71.

13. Consult above, pp. 271-2.

14. Consult des Places, *Oracles,frag.* 26, page 72.
15. Consult des Places, *Oracles,frag.* 31, page 73.
16. Consult des Places, *Oracles,frag.* 7, page 68.
17. Consult des Places, *Oracles,frag.* 22, page 71.
18. Consult des Places, *Oracles,frag.* 23, page 72.
19. Consult des Places, *Oracles,frag.* 27, page 73.
20. P. Hadot,*Porphyre et Victorinus*, 2 vols. (Paris, 1968); the passage reported here is from volume 1.261 (consult the documentation in the notes also).
21. Consult des Places, *Oracles,frag.* 1, p. 66.
22. Consult des Places, *Oracles,frag.* 2, pp. 66ff.
23. Consult E. R. Dodds, *The Greeks and the Irrational*, p. 291. Appendix.
24. Consult E. R. Dodds, *The Greeks and the Irrational*, p. 291. Appendix.
25. Consult E. R. Dodds, *The Greeks and the Irrational*, p. 295-96. Appendix II, see also references given there.
26. Consult des Places, *Oracles,frag.* 110, page 94.
27. M. Psello, "Commentario degli Oracli Caldaici," *Patrologia Graeca* 122, col. 1132a found in des Places, *Oracles*, p. 169.

(pp. 285-91) (1-26)
1. Theodoret (*Gr. affect. cur.* 6.96) states that Ammonius's *floruit* was during the rule of Commodus (180-92 CE).
2. Consult Theodoret, in the place cited in the previous note, and Ammianus Marcellinus 22.528.
3. Consult, for example, E. Seeberg, "Ammonius Sakkas," *Zeitschrift für Kirchengeschichte* 61 (1941) 136-70.
4. Consult Porphyry quoted by Eusebius, *Hist. eccles.* 6.19.7.
5. Consult Eusebius, *Hist. eccles.* 6.19.7ff.
6. Consult H. Langerbeck, "The Philosophy of Ammonius Saccas and the Connection of Aristotelian and Christian Elements therein," *Journal of Hellenic Studies* 77 (1957) 67-74. The hypothesis that Ammonius may be the author of the writings attributed to Pseudo-Dionysius was made by E. Elorduy, "Es Ammonio Sakkas el Seudo-Areopagita," *Estudios Eclesisticos* 18 (1944) 501-7, and in many other articles and works.
7. Porphyry, *Life of Plotinus*, 3.
8. Porphyry, *Life of Plotinus*, 3.
9. Porphyry, *Life of Plotinus*, 14.
10. Porphyry, *Life of Plotinus*, 3.
11. Consult above, pp. 302ff.
12. Consult the erudite W. Theiler, "Ammonios der Lehrer des Origenes," in the collection of essays by the same author entitled, *Forschungen zum Neuplatonismus* (Berlin, 1966) 1-45, where, however, the demonstration of the thesis is not sufficiently clear.

13. See also the interesting article of H. Dörrie, "Ammonios, der Lehrer Plotins," *Hermes* 83 (1955) 439-78 which, on the contrary, interprets Ammonius in a Pythagoreanizing way.

14. Consult Hierocles quoted by Photius, *Biblioth.*, cod. 214 and 251; Nemesius, *De nat. hom.* cc. 2 and 3. Priscianus Lydus speaks of our Ammonius in his *Solut. ad Chosroen* which can be found in the "Supplementum Aristotelicum" to the *Commentarium in Aristotelem Graeca* 1.2.42.15ff.

15. Concerning these sources see: H. von Arnim, "Quelle der Überlieferung über Ammonius Sakkas," *Archiv für Geschichte der Philosophie* 7 (1894) 295-312. An excellent reconstruction of the thought of Ammonius on the basis of these sources has been completed by F. Heinemann, "Ammonios Sakkas und der Ursprung des Neuplatonismus," *Hermes* 61 (1926) 1-27, although the author sins through excess and ends with drawing much that is not stated as such.

16. Consult Hierocles quoted by Photius, *Biblioth.*, cod. 251.461a24ff.; and cod. 214.172a9ff.

17. Consult Photius, *Biblioth.*, cod. 251.461b6ff.

18. Consult Photius, *Biblioth.*, cod. 251.461b17ff.

19. Nemesius, *De nat. hom.* 3.129ff. Matthaei.

20. Nemesius, *De nat. hom.* 3.133ff. Matthaei.

21. F. Heinemann, *Ammonios*, pp. 21ff.

22. Consult Porphyry, *Life of Plotinus,* 3; F. Heinemann, *Ammonios*, p. 19.

23. Consult Porphyry, *Life of Plotinus*, 14; 20.

24. Consult Porphyry, *Life of Plotinus*, 18; and Proclus, *In Plat. Tim.* 1.322.24 Diehl. This is a confirmation again of what we stated above, that is, that Ammonius did not profess the doctrine of the second hypostasis as Nous, understood as the unity of the essence (Idea) and thought, which we will find in Plotinus.

25. See the edition of D. A. Russell, *Longinus, On the Sublime* (Oxford, 1964) with introduction and commentary.

26. Consult the work of W. Theiler cited above p. 521, note 12.

(pp. 303-6) (1-15)

1. We know about the life of Plotinus almost exclusively from what has been written by Porphyry in the famous *Life of Plotinus*. In fact, not only does Plotinus never speak about himself in his works, but he did not wish to speak even with his intimate friends. Porphyry writes *Life of Plotinus*, 1. "Plotinus, the philosopher of our time, seemed ashamed of being in the body. As a result of this state of mind he could never bear to talk about his race or his parents or his native country. And he objected so strongly to sitting to a painter or sculptor that he said to Amelius, who was urging him to allow a portrait of himself to be made, 'Why really, is it not enough

to have to carry the image in which nature has encased us, without your requesting me to agree to leave behind me a longer-lasting image of the image, as if it was something genuinely worth looking at?' " Of the particular events in the life of Plotinus referred to by Porphyry, we will speak in the text. Here we limit ourselves to tracing the chronology and to complete what we do not mention in the text. Plotinus was born at Lycopolis (modern Asyut) in Upper Egypt, according to Suidas (*s.v.*). The date is given by Porphyry as 205 CE. In 232 CE, he began to dedicate himself entirely to philosophy at Alexandria. In 243, he left Alexandria to follow the Emperor Gordian in his Eastern expedition against the Persians. In 244, he came to Rome, where he established a school. He wrote his works between 253 and 269 CE. He died in 270 at the age of sixty-six as a result of an illness (not well identified) which gave him sores in his hands and feet and a hoarse voice. In his final years, because of his illness, he abandoned his school and his friends and retired to the estate of an old friend in Campania where he died alone. The Plotinian *Enneads*, (we will discuss in the text their origin and arrangement) have recently been edited in an excellent critical edition by P. Henry and H. R. Schwyzer, *Plotini Opera*, 3 vols. Paris-Brussels, 1951-1973) and Oxford 1964-1982 (editio minor). The only complete English translation until recently was that S. MacKenna-B. S. Page published by the Medici Society 1917-1930; published in a new revised edition 1956 by Faber and Faber, London (4th revised, 1964). Beginning in 1966 and ending in 1989 A. H. Armstrong has presented a new and excellent translation in the Loeb Classical Library Series, which we have consulted throughout of our translation which was made from the Italian. Very important also is the *Lexicon Plotinianum*, ed. J. H. Sleeman and G. Pollet (Leiden-Louvain, 1908).

2. Consult Porphyry, *Life of Plotinus*, 3.
3. Consult Porphyry, *Life of Plotinus*, 3.
4. Consult Porphyry, *Life of Plotinus*, 3. Cf. OCD^2, *s.v.*, Philippus (1), Julius Verus, p. 816 (b).
5. Consult Porphyry, *Life of Plotinus*, 4-6.
6. Consult Porphyry, *Life of Plotinus*, 8.
7. Consult Porphyry, *Life of Plotinus*, 7.
8. Consult Porphyry, *Life of Plotinus*, 24-26.
9. Consult Porphyry, *Life of Plotinus*, 9.
10. Consult Porphyry, *Life of Plotinus*, 12.
11. Consult Porphyry, *Life of Plotinus*, 1.
12. Consult Porphyry, *Life of Plotinus*, 9.
13. Porphyry writes that the books written by Plotinus "few people people had received copies of them. The issuing of copies was still a difficult and

anxious business, not at all simple and easy; those who received them were most carefully scrutinised."

14. Consult Porphyry, *Life of Plotinus*, 23.
15. Consult Porphyry, *Life of Plotinus*, 2.

(pp. 307-17) (1-24)

1. Consult Porphyry, *Life of Plotinus*, 14.
2. E. R. Dodds, *The Ancient Concept of Progress and other Essays on Greek Literature and Belief* (Oxford, 1973) 129.
3. See above, pp. 169-291.
4. Consult Porphyry, *Life of Plotinus*, 14.
5. Here is what Porphyry has written about this point: "Some of the Greeks began to accuse Plotinus of appropriating the ideas of Numenius. Amelius, being informed of this charge by the Stoic and Platonist Tryphy, challenged it in a treatise which he entitled *The Differences between the Doctrines of Plotinus and Numenius*." (*Life of Plotinus*, 17). Note that Amelius is well acquainted with the thought of Numenius, as Porphyry himself writes: "Amelius...surpassed all his contemporaries in industriousness of which he gave proof, he presented almost all the doctrines of Numenius in writing, summarized them, and he almost learned by heart the greater part of them" (*Life of Plotinus*, 3).
6. No philosopher later than Epicurus is cited.
7. Consult Plotinus, *Enneads*, 5.1.8.
8. That Plotinus never mentions Ammonius, who was no less to him than what Socrates must have been to Plato, is amazing. However, Heinemann (*Ammonios*, p. 2) correctly remarks that even if Plato had been at the school of Ammonius, he would have behaved differently than he behaved with Socrates. In the third century CE and in the philosophical milieu of the circle of Ammonius, a hymn to the Teacher, meaning to the *man* himself and to others (and in a special way a man inspired as Ammonius was) almost alone as the expression of the supersensible Divine. Hence, it was necessary to exalt the Divine and not any one who is simply a vehicle for the Divine. Moreover, Plotinus almost never wished to mention himself or his own life (consult above page 303, note 1 [above p. 522]).
9. Consult Porphyry, *Life of Plotinus*, 3.
10. Consult Zeller, *DPG*, 3.2 (pp. 468-500).
11. See above pages 169-204.
12. V. Cilento, *Plotino, Paideia Antignostica. Ricostruzione d'un unico scritto Enneadi*, 3.8, 5.8, 5.5, 2.9 (Florence, 1971) 23ff.
13. Consult above pp. 332ff.
14. Consult Porphyry, *Life of Plotinus*, 16 .
15. Consult Plotinus, *Enneads*, 3.6.6.
16. In order to analyze the very complex question of the historical sources and the development and theoretical foundation for Plotinian thought, see, in

addition to the cited works: *Les sources de Plotin* (which contains contributions by E. R. Dodds, W. Theiler, P. Hadot, H. C. Puech, H. Dörrie, V. Cilento, R. Harder, H. R. Schwyzer, A. H. Armstrong, P. Henry), the following contributions which are in many respects stimulating: W. Theiler, *Die Vorbereitung des Neuplatonismus* (Berlin, 1930; Berlin-Zürich, 1964²); Ph. Merlan, *From Platonism to Neoplatonism* (The Hague, 1953; 1960²); H. J. Krämer, *Der Ursprung der Geistmetaphysik. Untersuchungen zur Geschichte des Platonismus zwischen Platon und Plotin* (Amsterdam, 1964; 1967²).

17. Consult Plotinus, *Enneads*, 5.1.8 and Numenius, *frag.* 2 des Places; *frag.* 1 Leemans.
18. Consult *Reale* 2 ad loc.
19. Consult Plotinus, *Enneads*, 1.3.1.
20. Consult Plotinus, *Enneads*, 1.3.1-3.
21. Consult Plotinus, *Enneads*, 1.3.4.
22. Consult Plato, *Phaedo* 99E-100D.
23. Consult Plotinus, *Enneads*, 1.3.5.
24. Consult above pp. 390ff.

(pp. 319-22) (1-9)
1. They make the first component the most important one, for example, M. Wundt (see below note 4) and R. Arnou, *Le désir de Dieu dans la philosophie de Plotin* (Paris, 1921; Rome, 1967²); instead the second component is given importance by Zeller, *DPG*, 3.2 (pp. 500-687).
2. Bréhier, *La philosophie de Plotin* (Paris, 1968⁴).
3. Bréhier, *La philosophie de Plotin*, p. 44.
4. See, for example, M. Wundt, *Plotin. Studien zur Geschichte des Neuplatonismus* 1 (Leipzig, 1919); F. Heinemann, *Plotin. Forschungen über die plotinische Frage, Plotins Entwicklung und sein System* (Leipzig, 1921).
5. Consult, for example, Bréhier, *La philosophie de Plotin*; C. Carbonara, *La filosofia di Plotino* (Rome 1938-1939); Naples, 1964³).
6. Consult, for example, Zeller cited above in note 1; A. H. Armstrong, *The Architecture of the Intelligible Universe in the Philosophy of Plotinus* (Cambridge, 1940; republished Amsterdam, 1967).
7. H. R. Schwyzer, in his otherwise very accurate article, "Plotinus" in *Pauly-Wissowa-Kroll*, 21.533ff. begins from the middle hypostasis.
8. Consult Plotinus, *Enneads*, 1.3.6.
9. Heinemann, *Ammonios*, p. 27. Heinemann refers all this again to Ammonius. Perhaps, in this respect, he is excessive; it is certain, in any case, that this is the true "movement" of Plotinian thought.

(pp. 325-39) (1-43)

1. On this argument see C. J. De Vogel "On the Neoplatonic Character of Platonism and the Platonic Character of Neoplatonism" in the volume of essays entitled *Philosophia* (Assen: Van Gorcum, 1970) 355-77.
2. Consult above pp. 207-350.
3. Plotinus, *Enneads*, 6.9.1.
4. Plotinus, *Enneads*, 6.9.1.
5. Plotinus, *Enneads*, 6.9.2.
6. Plotinus, *Enneads*, 5.3.16; also 3.8.10.
7. Consult Anaximander, Anaximenes, Melissus and Anaxagoras.
8. Consult *Reale* 2 ad loc.
9. Consult *Reale* 2 ad loc.
10. We need not be deceived by the fact that Philo does not use the term ἄπειρον in referring to God, since he reserves this term for matter. But from everything he says about God this characteristic emerges all the same.
11. Plotinus, *Enneads*, 5.5.10 and f.
12. Plotinus, *Enneads*, 6.9.6.
13. Plotinus, *Enneads*, 6.5.12.
14. Plotinus, *Enneads*, 5.5.6.
15. Consult above pp. 183ff. The position is also in Albinus, but somewhat modified, see above pp. 218ff.
16. Plotinus, *Enneads*, 5.3.13.
17. Plotinus, *Enneads*, 5.4.1.
18. Plotinus, *Enneads*, 5.3.15.
19. Plotinus, *Enneads*, 2.9.1, "We have seen elsewhere that the Good, the Principle, is simplex, and, correspondingly, primal-for the secondary can never be simplex: that it contains nothing: that it is an integral Unity. Now the same nature belongs to the Principle we know as The One. Just as the goodness of The Good is essential and not the outgrowth of some prior substance so the Unity of The One is its essential. Therefore: When we speak of The One and when we speak of The Good we must recognize an identical nature; we must affirm that they are the same-not, it is true, as venturing any prediction with regard to that (unknowable) Hypostasis but simply as indicating it to ourselves in the best terms we find."
20. Plotinus, *Enneads*, 5.5.13.
21. Plotinus, *Enneads*, 6.9.6.
22. Plotinus, *Enneads*, 6.8.16.
23. Plotinus, *Enneads*, 6.8.14.
24. Plotinus, *Enneads*, 6.8.16.
25. Plotinus, *Enneads*, 5.4.2.
26. Plotinus, *Enneads*, 6.7.38.

27. Plotinus, *Enneads*, 6.8.7.
28. Plotinus, *Enneads*, 6.8.13.
29. Plotinus, *Enneads*, 6.8.10.
30. Plotinus, *Enneads*, 6.8.15.
31. Plotinus, *Enneads*, 6.8.16.
32. Plotinus, *Enneads*, 6.8.14.
33. Plotinus, *Enneads*, 6.1.6.
34. Plotinus, *Enneads*, 4.3.17.
35. Plotinus, *Enneads*, 5.1.6.
36. Plotinus, *Enneads*, 3.8.10.
37. Plotinus, *Enneads*, 4.4.16.
38. Plotinus, *Enneads*, 6.8.18.
39. Consult for example, *Enneads*, 5.3.12 passim. This is one of the cardinal points of Plotinian ontology.
40. The first studies which focused attention on this point in an adequate way seems to be that of A. Covotti, *Da Aristotele ai Bizantini* (Naples, 1935) 134-41. Very clear also is J. M. Rist, *Plotinus, The Road to Reality* (Cambridge, 1967) 70ff. who, however, seems to ignore Covotti.
41. Plotinus, *Enneads*, 5.4.2.
42. Rist, *Plotinus*, p. 83.
43. For further analyses of the Plotinian conception of the One consult Arnou, *Le désir* passim; Armstrong, *The Architecture*, pp. 1-47; Rist, *Plotinus*, pp. 21-83.

(pp. 341-50) (1-26)

1. Plotinus, *Enneads*, 2.4.5.
2. Plotinus, *Enneads*, 5.3.7.
3. Plotinus, *Enneads*, 5.2.1.
4. Plotinus, *Enneads*, 6.7.15.
5. Plotinus, *Enneads*, 6.7.16.
6. Plotinus, *Enneads*, 5.4.2.
7. The reasons are therefore evident why it is not enough to translate the term Nous (Νοῦς) simply by the term Intellect or Intelligence, precisely because the Plotinian Nous is a polyvalent term, insofar as it includes, in addition to the conceptual connotations of Thought, likewise those of Being and Life. It would seem, therefore, that Spirit is the least inadequate translation, precisely because, in this way, it would suggest this two-fold connotation. The Plotinian Nous is frequently rendered in French by the term Esprit, in English by the term Spirit, in German by Geist, terms which exactly correspond to Spirito in Italian. (It was the complexity of the connotations of the term Spirit which induced the later Neoplatonists to break it down into further hypostases). Consult in addition what we will say about *Enneads*, 5.3.5. [In the American edition, we have decided to

use Mind instead of Intellect or Spirit in order to avoid ambiguities, and *Nous* is put in parentheses following Mind for the sake of clarity Ed.]

8. Plotinus, *Enneads*, 5.6.6.
9. Plotinus, *Enneads*, 5.9.8; consult also 6.6.6.
10. Plotinus, *Enneads*, 5.9.9; 6.4.14 ; 6.6.7; 6.6.15; 6.7.8; 6.7.12.
11. Plotinus, *Enneads*, 6.6.8.
12. Aristotle, *Metaphysics* Λ 7 and 9.
13. Plotinus, *Enneads*, 4.8.3; 5.9.8; 6.2.20 ; 6.7.17; 6.8.3.
14. Plotinus, *Enneads*, 6.4.4.
15. Plotinus, *Enneads*, 6.4.11.
16. Plotinus, *Enneads*, 6.5.6.
17. Plotinus, *Enneads*, 6.4.14.
18. Plotinus, *Enneads*, 6.7.1; consult also 5.1.4.
19. Plotinus, *Enneads*, 6.7.2.
20. Plotinus, *Enneads*, 5.7.1, also consult 5.9.12
21. Plotinus, *Enneads*, 5.1.5.
22. Plotinus, *Enneads*, 6.6.9.
23. Plotinus, *Enneads*, 6.6.15.
24. Plotinus, *Enneads*, 1.6 passim; 5.8 passim.
25. Note in this respect that the One, that is, the first hypostasis, is not properly speaking Beauty because it is not a form, but is above the form insofar as it is the principle of Form and hence it is "Beauty which transcends all Beauty," insofar as it is "the potency of all beautiful things" (*Enneads*, 6.7.22).
26. Consult the first three treatises of the *Sixth Ennead*.

(pp. 351-60) (1-25)

1. Plotinus, *Enneads*, 5.3.7, consult also 5.1.7.
2. Plotinus, *Enneads*, 6.2.22, consult also 5.2.1.
3. Plotinus, *Enneads*, 5.1.3.
4. Plotinus, *Enneads*, 2.4.3.
5. Plotinus, *Enneads*, 5.1.6.
6. Plotinus, *Enneads*, 1.7.2 and 4.4.4.
7. Plotinus, *Enneads*, 6.7.31.
8. Plotinus, *Enneads*, 5.6.2.
9. Plotinus, *Enneads*, 4.8.3.
10. Plotinus, *Enneads*, 3.1.8; 4.3.10; 4.7.9.
11. Plotinus, *Enneads*, 2.3.8.
12. Plotinus, *Enneads*, 5.1.2.
13. Plotinus, *Enneads*, 5.2.1. It is hardly necessary to point out that the creation of the soul does not happen by an act of the procession, in the sense seen above. Here is a text which is very clear: "The soul does not create by means of a faculty drawn from the outside nor attending to

counsel or to deliberation; because this would mean to create not according to nature but according to an art acquired from the outside. Art, to speak truthfully, is posterior to the creating Soul and only imitates it by producing pallid and feeble images, playthings, perhaps, without great value and adopting many expediences in order to produce these vain phantasms" (*Enneads*, 4.3.10; consult also 3.2.1).

14. Plotinus, *Enneads*, 5.2.2; consult also 3.2.2.
15. Plotinus, *Enneads*, 4.8.5.
16. Plotinus, *Enneads*, 4.8.7.
17. Plotinus, *Enneads*, 4.6.3.
18. Plotinus, *Enneads*, 4.1.1-2.
19. Plotinus, *Enneads*, 4.2.1; consult also 4.9.4.
20. Plotinus, *Enneads*, 4.3.4-6; consult also 2.3.9; 2.3.18; 3.4.4.
21. Plotinus, *Enneads*, 6.4.4.
22. The interpretation of the two concepts of *logos* and *physis*, in Plotinus, made by Rist, *Plotinus*, pp. 84-102 is especially clear.
23. Plotinus, *Enneads*, 4.4.13.
24. Plotinus, *Enneads*, 3.8.2.
25. Plotinus, *Enneads*, 3.8.4.

(pp. 361-71) (1-32)
1. Consult above pp. 341ff; and pp. 351ff.
2. Plotinus, *Enneads*, 2.4.15; consult also 2.4.4.
3. Plotinus, *Enneads*, 4.8.6.
4. Plotinus, *Enneads*, 1.8.7.
5. Plotinus, *Enneads*, 1.8.3.
6. Plotinus, *Enneads*, 2.4.16.
7. Plotinus, *Enneads*, 3.6.7.
8. Plotinus, *Enneads*, 3.9.2.
9. Plotinus, *Enneads*, 4.3.9.
10. Read the whole of Plotinus, *Enneads*, 3.8.5.
11. Plotinus, *Enneads*, 1.8.14.
12. Plotinus, *Enneads*, 3.6.13.
13. Plotinus, *Enneads*, 4.3.9; 5.8.7.
14. Plotinus, *Enneads*, 3.2.16.
15. Plotinus, *Enneads*, 5.9.3.
16. Plotinus, *Enneads*, 5.8.7.
17. Plotinus, *Enneads*, 5.1.1.
18. Plotinus, *Enneads*, 3.7.11.
19. Plotinus, *Enneads*, 3.7.11.
20. Plotinus, *Enneads*, 4.7.15.
21. Plotinus, *Enneads*, 2.9.8; 2.9.12.
22. Plotinus, *Enneads*, 4.4.36; consult also 6.7.11.
23. Plotinus, *Enneads*, 2.7.3.

24. On the concept of sensible object in Plotinus, consult Rist, *Plotinus*, pp. 103-111.
25. Plotinus, *Enneads*, 2.9 passim.
26. Plotinus, *Enneads*, 4.3.9.
27. Consult the correct observations of Covotti, *Da Aristotele ai Bizantini*, pp. 153ff.
28. Plotinus, *Enneads*, 3.8.
29. Plotinus, *Enneads*, 2.9.4.
30. Plotinus, *Enneads*, 2.9.9.
31. Plotinus, *Enneads*, 5.5.9.
32. The conceptions of Plotinus, about the structure of the world are less interesting. Here we limit ourselves to pointing some relations between cosmogony and daimonology. The heavens, which are the better part of the visible cosmos, "restricts" with the ultimate degrees of the world of the Spirit, and it is made of light (different than terrestrial fire). And the heavens are the first region in which souls penetrate (*Enneads*, 4.3.17). Stars and celestial bodies are animated and are second or visible Gods, which are like images or copies of the spiritual and intelligible Gods. In addition to the conception of the visible Gods, Plotinus, likewise presents Daimons, understood as the agents between the Gods and human beings. The Daimons do not belong to the world of the Spirit (to this belongs only their eternal and spiritual model, which, as such, is a God), they have an intelligible matter, which can permit them to take on airy and fiery bodies (*Enneads*, 3.5.6). The Daimons have affections and can make sounds in the air (*Enneads*, 4.3.18). The Daimons are generated by the Soul of the universe according to the various needs of the universe. In fact "...they alone give him fullness and support, in common with all things, to each individual thing; since it is necessary that the Soul of the universe take care of the world, indeed by the production of daimonic forces which would for a time be useful for its own totality" (*Enneads*, 3.5.6). A particular species of Daimons is constituted from "Loves," from Erotes, which are produced by Soul in its aspiring to the beautiful, while the other Daimons are generated from other powers of the Soul, not from its power of love.

(pp. 373-91) (1-61)

1. Plotinus, *Enneads*, 6.4.14.
2. Plotinus, *Enneads*, 4.8.4; consult also 4.8.2.
3. Plotinus, *Enneads*, 4.4.2.
4. Consult *Reale* 2 ad loc.
5. Plotinus, *Enneads*, 4.8.3.
6. Plotinus, *Enneads*, 4.8.5ff.
7. Plotinus, *Enneads*, 5.1.1.

8. Plotinus, *Enneads*, 4.8.4ff.
9. Plotinus, *Enneads*, 5.1.1.
10. Consult *Reale* 1.201ff.
11. Plato, *Alcibiades* I and *Phaedo* passim.
12. Plotinus, *Enneads*, 1.1.10.
13. Plotinus, *Enneads*, 6.7.6.
14. Plotinus, *Enneads*, 2.9.2.
15. Plotinus, *Enneads*, 5.3.3.
16. Plotinus, *Enneads*, 4.8.8.
17. Plotinus, *Enneads*, 3.4.2.
18. Plotinus, *Enneads*, 3.6.1; 4.3.11.
19. Plotinus, *Enneads*, 1.1.7; consult also 3.8.7.
20. Plotinus, *Enneads*, 6.7.7.
21. Plotinus, *Enneads*, 4.6.3.
22. Plotinus, *Enneads*, 4.3.26.
23. Plotinus, *Enneads*, 4.3.25.
24. Plotinus, *Enneads*, 4.3.27.
25. Carbonara, *La filosofia di Plotino*, pp. 267ff.
26. Plotinus, *Enneads*, 6.8.4.
27. Plotinus, *Enneads*, 6.8.6.
28. Plotinus, *Enneads*, 6.8.7.
29. For an analysis of the problem of liberty in Plotinus, see P. Henry, "La liberté chez Plotin," *Revue Néoscolastique de Philosophie* 8 (1931) 50-79; 180-215; 318-39.
30. Consult above pp. 202-4.
31. Plotinus, *Enneads*, 3.6.6.
32. Plotinus, *Enneads*, 3.2.16.
33. Plotinus, *Enneads*, 4.3.10; 4.7.6.
34. Plotinus, *Enneads*, 4.3.24.
35. Consult *Reale* 3 passim.
36. Plotinus, *Enneads*, 1.4.13.
37. Consult *Reale* ad loc.
38. Consult Porphyry, *Life of Plotinus*, 1-2.
39. Consult above pp. 386-91.
40. Plotinus, *Enneads*, 1.2.6.
41. Plotinus, *Enneads*, 1.2.1.
42. Plotinus, *Enneads*, 1.2.2ff.
43. Plotinus, *Enneads*, 1.2.3.
44. Plotinus, *Enneads*, 1.2.7.
45. Consult *Reale* 2 ad loc.
46. Plotinus, *Enneads*, 1.6.4; 3.5 passim.
47. Plotinus, *Enneads*, 1.1.6. Plotinus in the context of these arguments, does not hesitate to call the Absolute itself the Supreme and Primordial

Beautiful (*Enneads* 1.6.7); but immediately afterwards (*Enneads*, 1.6.9) he says that the Beautiful is Spirit and that the One or the Good, which is above Spirit, "*radiating Beauty before it.* So that, treating the Intellectual-Cosmos as one, *the first is the Beautiful*: if we make distinction there, the Realm of Ideas constitutes the *Beauty of the Intellectual Sphere; and The Good, which lies beyond, is the Fountain at once and Principle of Beauty...*"

48. Let us remember that dialectic and the erotic are in Plotinus strictly fused no less than in Plato. But in Plotinus both dialectic (as we have seen) and the erotic are amplified in the context of the hypostatic doctrine. Note in fact that Eros insofar as it is a power which arises from the tension of the soul towards the beautiful, *is not only hypostatized in Plotinus in a way which is more complete than in Plato, but it is multiplied.* In fact, to the First Soul (the universal Soul), which loves the Spirit, is made to correspond the *Love-God* (the highest love which lives in the sphere of the Spirit), to the Soul of the universe is made to correspond "in company with this second Soul, also a second Eros," endowed through aspiration of this to the beautiful, which is a *Daimon included in the world* and assisting everywhere the soul of the world (*Enneads*, 3.5.1-3). And *to human souls, finally, Plotinus makes correspond "Aphrodites" "Love-Daimons,"* endowed by aspiration to the beautiful of each of them, and companions to individual soul: "Does each individual Soul, then, contain within itself such a Love in essence and substantial reality? Since not only the pure All-Soul but also that of the Universe contains such a Love, it would be difficult to explain why our personal Soul should not. It must be so, even, with all that has life. This indwelling love is no other than the Spirit which, as we are told, walks with every being, the affection dominant in each several nature. It implants the characteristic desire; the particular Soul, strained towards its own natural objects, brings forth its own Eros, the guiding spirit realizing its worth and the quality of its Being" (Plotinus, *Enneads*, 3.5.4).

49. Plotinus, *Enneads*, 6.9.11 (ἅπλωσις).

50. Plotinus, *Enneads*, 6.9.8.

51. Plotinus, *Enneads*, 3.6.5.

52. Plotinus, *Enneads*, 6.9.7.

53. Plotinus, *Enneads*, 5.3.17 (consult also 4.3.32).

54. This basically is the thesis of A. Drews, *Plotin und der Untergang der antiken Weltanschauung* (Jena, 1907; republished Aalen, 1964) , pp. 271-90.

55. Plotinus, *Enneads*, 6.5.12.

56. Plotinus, *Enneads*, 6.9.11.

57. Plotinus, *Enneads*, 6.7.34.

58. Add to these conclusions those which they who read Plotinus in an Eastern perspective reach.

59. Plotinus, *Enneads*, 6.9.11.
60. Consult above, pp. 202-04.
61. Arnou, *Le désir*, pp. 228ff.

(pp. 393-8) (1-20)

1. The best arguments against the emanationistic interpretation were made by H. F. Müller, "Platonische Studien I. Ist die Metaphysik des Plotinos ein Emanationssystem?" *Hermes* 48 (1913) 408-25.
2. Zeller, *DPG* 3.2.560-65.
3. Consult, for example, the sharp criticism made by Covotti, *Da Aristotele ai Bizantini*, pp. 125-70.
4. Zeller has referred this formula for the first time to the theology of the *Treatise on the Cosmos* attributed to Aristotle (to which we have many times alluded), which he maintained was a work of a Stoicizing Peripatetic, where he says that the substance or *essence* of God is transcendent, while its *power* is immanent to the world. Now, such a position is the exact negation of pantheism (see the whole of chapter six of this small work with our comments, already cited many times).
5. What is very clear especially in the light of the conception of the "creative contemplation" about which we have spoken above, pp. 396-8.
6. Already Covotti pointed out that the conjunction of the various elements which come into play in the Plotinian procession "form a whole *sui generis*, which can hardly be reduced to a unique general category. This whole is not pantheism, nor is it even emanationism, but it is Plotinianism" (*Da Aristotele ai Bizantini*, pp. 170).
7. The best reflections on the concept of the liberty of the One are found in Cilento, *Saggi*, pp. 97-122.
8. Moreover Plotinus in *Enneads*, 6.8.6 expressly writes as follows: "herein lies our will which remains free and self-disposing in spite of any orders which it may necessarily utter to meet the external."
9. Consult Arnou, *Praxis et theoria* (Paris, 1921); Cilento, *Saggi*, pp. 5-27; P. Prini, *Plotino e la genesi dell'umanesimo interiore* (Rome, 1968).
10. Cilento, *Saggi*, p. 9.
11. Plotinus, *Enneads*, 3.8.1.
12. Plotinus, *Enneads*, 3.8.3.
13. Plotinus, *Enneads*, 3.8.4.
14. Plotinus, *Enneads*, 3.8.6.
15. Plato, *Phaedrus* 246A-249D.
16. All these statements have been documented above.
17. Whence the fruitfulness also on the ethico-practical level of silence itself. Prini writes, "Plotinus has based his doctrine of wisdom above intuition of the immense 'practical' value of silence, of concentration, of interior wealth" (*Plotino*, p. 139).

18. Plotinus, *Enneads*, 6.9.11.
19. The image is referred by Plotinus to Mind (*Nous*) in the *Enneads*, 6.7.15.
20. For an analysis of the documentation of the interpretations which we have presented consult M. L. Gatti, *Plotino e la metafisica della contemplazione* (Milan: CUSL, 1982).

(pp. 401-4) (1-5)

1. Zeller, *DPG* 3.2.735-931. This part of the work of Zeller has also been translated into Italian by E. Pocar with rather limited additions and edited by G. Martano (Florence: La Nuova Italia, 1961). In particular, Martano does not seem to be aware of the revolutionary character of the studies of Praechter, about which we will immediately speak, and hence does not bring into the light the second line according to which the Zellerian schema was subsequently restructured. All the up-to-date studies have in fact followed the lines laid down by Praechter.

2. K. Praechter, "Richtungen und Schulen im Neuplatonismus," *Genethliakon Carl Robert* (Berlin, 1910) 103-56; *DPG* 590-655.

3. See chiefly the following basic contributions of B. Dalsgaard Larsen, *Jamblique de Chalcis exégète et philosophe*, 2 vols. (Aarhus, 1972); the second volume of this work (*Appendice: testimonia et fragmenta exegetica*) contains the first collection of the testimonies and the fragments extant relative to the commentaries of Iamblichus on Aristotle's and Plato's works. In the next year a second collection of the fragments of Iamblichus was published relative to the dialogues of Plato with an English translation, introduction and a fruitful commentary by J. M. Dillon, *Iamblichi Chalcidensis in Platonis dialogos commentariorum fragmenta* (Leiden, 1973) (it was part of the collection "Philosophia antiqua" directed by W. J. Verdenius and J. H. Waszink published by the house of E. J. Brill [Dillon is preparing the collection of the fragments of the other works of Iamblichus]). Again by B. Dalsgaard Larsen is the work entitled, "La place de, Jamblique dans la philosophie antique tardive" in the volume of essays *De Jamblique á Proclus*, which is the twenty-first volume in the series "Entretiens sur l'Antiquité Classique," (Vandoeuvres-Genéve 1975) 1-34. This work and the introduction of Dillon shows well enough the path that has been followed in the interpretation of Iamblichus after Zeller, and in the direction pointed out by Praechter. As an example of this approach see what A. C. Lloyd writes in *The Cambridge History of Later Greek and Early Medieval Philosophy* edited by A. H. Armstrong (Cambridge, 1970) making direct reference to Praechter, he speaks of Iamblichus as the second founder of Neoplatonism and as "the Chrysippus of the School" (p. 273).

4. Given the scarcity of the documents, it is difficult to speculate about the tendency proper to the School of Ammonius. However, from the tes-

timonies which we discussed above (consult pp. 299ff.) the positions of the School of Ammonius would seem to be analogous to that of Plotinus.

5. Porphyry, *Life of Plotinus*, 10.

(pp. 405-10) (1-30)

1. Amelius or Amerius Gentilianus and came from Etruria (consult Porphyry, *Life of Plotinus*, 7). He stayed at the school of Plotinus for twenty-four years, from 246 to 269 CE. Then he went on to Apamea in Syria. We possess only a few extant testimonies of him.

2. Proclus, *In Plat. Tim.* 1.306.1 Diehl. Probably the logical reasoning which supports this distinction is as follows: in order *to think* it is necessary *to be able* and in order to be able it is necessary *to be* [to possess reason] (consult Vacherot, *Histoire* 2.8). To each of these functions there must therefore be a corresponding hypostasis.

3. Consult Proclus, *In Plat. Tim.* 1.306.10ff. Diehl.

4. Also in the ancient sources we find the name of Amelius expressly associated with that of Numenius; consult for example, Proclus, *In Plat. Tim.* 3.33.33ff. Diehl; Syrianus, *In Arist. Metaph.* 109.12ff.

5. Consult Stobaeus, *Anthol.* 1.372.25ff. and 376.2ff. Wachsmuth.

6. Porphyry, *Life of Plotinus*, 10.

7. Porphyry was born at Tyre in 233/234 CE, as can be determined from the information which he himself furnishes us in his, *Life of Plotinus*, 4. He was, first of all, a student of Loginus at Athens. From 263 to 268 CE he was at the school of Plotinus, where his philosophical thought came to maturation. Stricken by a serious crisis of an emotional nature (a deep depression) he wanted to end his life, taking the advice of Plotinus he left Rome and went to Sicily, at Lilibeus, where he recovered his spiritual equilibrium. Then he came back to Rome. Only in the last years of his life (perhaps after 298 CE) was he ready to publish the edition of the Plotinian, *Enneads*, which as we know, he edited under the will of his teacher. He died around 305 CE. Porphyry wrote a great deal. J. Bidez in his work (which to this point is basic) *Vie de Porphyre le philosophe néo-platonicien* (Ghent, 1913; Hildesheim, 1964) 65-73 has reconstructed a catalogue of seventy-seven titles. R. Beutler has recently given us a new one of sixty-eight titles, completing it in the light of more recent research, in his article "Porphyrios" (1953) in *Realenzyclopädie der classischen Altertumswissenschaft Pauly-Wissowa-Kroll*, 22.1.278-301 (each title of the Beutler catalogue is described in detail). Of this remarkable oeuvre relatively little has come down to us: eleven complete works and fragments of various lengths of about thirty others. The eleven extant works are: *The Cave of the Nymphs, Isagoge, Commentary to the Categories of Aristotle* (a commentary on the *Categories* in the form of question and answer), the famous *Life of Plotinus, Sentences Leading to the Intelligible World, The Life of Pythagoras*, treatises *On the Animation of the Embryo* and *On the*

Abstinence from Eating Animals, Letter to Marcella, Commentary to the Harmonics of Ptolemy, Isagoge to the Apotelsmatico of Ptolemy. Further information can be taken from the catalogue of Beutler. We reserve the bibliography to its proper place [in the fifth volume] where we will give a list of all that has been published up to the present. We mention finally that P. Hadot has traced back to Porphyry an anonymous commentary on the Parmenides of which Kroll has published a large fragment (W. Kroll, "Ein neuplatonischer Parmenideskommentar in einem Turiner Palimpsest," *Rheinisches Museum* 57 [1892] 599-627); Hadot has also published an article entitled "Fragments d'un commentaire de Porphyre sur le *Parménide*," *Revue des études grecques* 74 (1961) 410-38 and a new edition, with French translation and commentary, in *Porphyre et Victorinus* 2.60-113. Consult for further information volume *Reale* 5 *s.v.*

8. Bidez, *Vie de Porphyre*, 132ff.

9. We here indicate the principal works that have contributed to the radical renovation of studies and research on Porphyry: W. Theiler, *Porphyrios und Augustin* (Halle, 1933) [Schriften der Königsburger Gelehrten Gesellschaft, Geisteswissenschaftliche Klasse. 10.1]; the previously cited article of Beutler in *Pauly-Wissowa* (consult note 7 above); H. Dörrie, *Porphyrios' Symmikta Zetemata* (München, 1959) [Zetemata 20]; the twelfth volume of the "Entretiens sur l'Antiquité Classique," which is entirely devoted to our philosopher: *Porphyre huit exposés suivis de discussions par H. Dörrie, J. H. Waszinck, W. Theiler, P. Hadot, A. R. Sodano, J. Pépin, R. Walzer* (Vandoeuvre-Genève, 1966); P. Hadot, *Porphyre et Victorinus* already cited in note 7 above (this last volume presents the most original perspectives of the author).

10. Consult Vacherot, *Histoire critique*, 2.39ff. and Zeller, *DPG* 3.2.705 and note 1.

11. See the volume *Porphyre et Victorinus* already cited and especially the article "La métaphysique de Porphyre" in the volume of essay entitled *Porphyre* in the collection "Entretiens sur l'Antiquité Classique" (cited above in note 9) 127-63.

12. Hadot, *La métaphysique de Porphyre*, p. 138 (in the schema which we used on page 435 above, the terms in bold indicate the term that predominates in each of the triads).

13. Hadot, *La métaphysique de Porphyre*, p. 141.

14. For an analysis of this point as well as the complex documentation see Hadot, *La métaphysique de Porphyre*, pp. 148-57.

15. A. C. Lloyd, *Cambridge History of Later Greek Philosophy and Early Medieval Philosophy*, pp. 287ff. speaks of a "monistic tendency" of Porphyry. In our judgment, the thesis is arguable and the account is better understood with reference to the doctrine of the Intelligence of Middle

Platonism and even the fact that the Chaldean Oracles on which Porphyry commented and by which he was inspired resonate quite loudly with the Middle Platonic metaphysics (consult above pp. 285).

16. Consult Beutler, *Porphyrios* coll. 303ff.

17. See what Beutler, *Porphyrios* says in coll. 303ff.

18. Consult Eusebius, *Praep. evang.*, 4.7.1; 4.8.1.

19. Porphyry, *Letter to Marcella* 9.

20. Porphyry, *Letter to Marcella* 26.

21. Porphyry, *Letter to Marcella* 13.

22. Porphyry, *Sentences* 32.6-7 (17ff. Mommert). According to Beutler Porphyry had given the will a central role, to which he coupled the notion of sin. The German scholar even goes on to assert that not Augustine (as is believed by many) but in fact Porphyry, in the ambit of Western thinkers, has given the will a specific place. If this were so, the importance of Porphyry in the history of ethics would be considerable. But the evidence that Beutler adduces (*Porphyrios* coll. 306ff.) does not support this thesis.

23. Let us remember that Plotinus had an ambiguous attitude with respect to Aristotle, although he was not a little in his debt. It was Porphyry who was the first to point out that in the *Enneads*, there were present Peripatetic doctrines and "there were compressed questions of Aristotelian metaphysics," (*Life of Plotinus*, 14). It was then the great merit of Porphyry to banish all ambiguities and to have definitively recovered Aristotle for Neoplatonism.

24. Porphyry, *Isagoge* 1.

25. The writing in which Porphyry commented on the *Chaldean Oracles* is not to be confused with *The Philosophy of the Oracles* which we mentioned below and which was a youthful work written in any case in a pre-Plotinian period.

26. An important work of allegorical interpretation of Homer done by Porphyry is contained in the extant *The Cave of the Nymphs*.

27. The fragments and the testimonies of this work are collected by A. von Harnack (Berlin, 1916).

28. Consult G. Wolff, *Porphyrii de philosophia ex oraculis haurienda librorum reliquiae* (Berlin, 1856; republished Hildesheim, 1962).

29. See the fragments of this work which are collected by Bidez, *Vie de Porphyre*, pp. 25-44 and the fine interpretation given by Bidez on pp. 88-97.

30. On theurgy see what we said above pp. 289-91 and at pp. 416-7.

(pp. 411-9) (1-30)

1. While in the previous century the date of birth of Iamblichus was placed for the most part around 280 CE, scholars tend today to favor an earlier date. Even Bidez proposed to put Iamblichus's date of birth around 250 CE (consult "Le philosophe, *Jamblique* et son école" *Revue des études*

grecques 32 [1919] 32; A. Cameron proposes 245-50 CE ("The Date of Iamblichus' Birth" *Hermes* 96 [1968] 374-76; J. M. Dillon proposes 242 CE (*Iamblichi Chalcidensis* 7 [previously cited above p.534 note 3]; B. Dalsgaard Larsen thinks it may be 240 CE (*La place de Jamblique*, p. 27 [previously cited above p. 264, note 3]). The arguments in favor of this later dating is taken from the information extant about the marriage of a daughter of our philosopher.

2. Iamblichus was acquainted with Neo-Pythagorean philosophy (he was influenced chiefly by Nicomachus of Gerasa) probably at Alexandria, as Dalsgaard Larsen notes. Actually, if Iamblichus was born somewhere around 240 CE (or a little after), then it could no longer be said that Porphyry was his first teacher. "It is to Alexandria-notes the Danish scholar-that his teachers need to be sought. Nothing would be more natural for a Hellenized Syrian intellectual" (*La place de Jamblique*, p. 3). Dillon also speaks of a "Pythagorean-Hermetic" period in the development of the thought of our philosopher (*Iamblichi Chalcidensis*, p. 18).

3. We know from Eunapius (*Vitae Sophistarum* 5.1.2) that Iamblichus had as teachers Anatolius and then Porphyry. That this Anatolius was the Peripatetic, and not as Zeller claims, an anonymous follower of Porphyry (consult *Zeller-Martano*, p. 2) is the thesis at this time accepted by more scholars. Not only the shifting of the date of his birth (consult note 1 above) makes the thesis probable, but also the massive presence of the Aristotelian component in our philosopher (from the *Protrepticus* to the *De anima* commentaries to the works of the Stagirite) decisively settles the matter in favor of it (consult Dalsgaard Larsen, *Jamblique*, pp. 37ff.; also *La place de Jamblique*, p. 4).

4. Consult J. M. Dillon, *Iamblichi Chalcidensis*, p. 9 who formulates the hypothesis that Porphyry was known to Anatolius at Athens in the 50s, and that this is the Anatolius to whom Porphyry dedicated his *Homeric Questions* (a work that arose indeed in the period in which Porphyry was a follower of Longinus at Athens).

5. That the relations between the two philosophers were primarily good can be easily seen based on the fact that Porphyry dedicated to Iamblichus the work entitled *On Self-Knowledge* (consult Stobaeus, *Anthol.* 3 [579.21 Hense]). The seriousness of the succeeding rupture is proven, limiting ourselves to the most evident documents, by the *De mysteriis* (which is a refutation of the Porphyrian *Letter to Anebo*) and from extant fragments of the *Commentary to the Timaeus*. Dillon remarks that of the thirty-two fragments extant of this work in twenty-five of them Iamblichus dissents from Porphyry's views by name. Iamblichus goes to the point of accusing Porphyry of "crude boasting" (consult Proclus, *In Plat. Tim.* 1 [152.12ff. and especially 153.10 Diehl]).

6. From Malala (*Chronographia* 12 [312.11-12 Dindorf]) there is evidence that Iamblichus did his teaching at Daphne (near Antioch) in the period of the Emperors Maximianus and Galerius (305-12). If this is so, our philosopher would have opened his school in Syria only in his advanced old age. The date would coincide with that of the death of Porphyry. However some think that Iamblichus left the company of Porphyry very quickly, and that he settled himself at Alexandria and stayed there for a long period of time, before returning to Syria (consult Dalsgaard Larsen, *Jamblique* 40-42; also *La place de Jamblique*, pp. 4ff.). The date of death of our philosopher is conjecturally placed in the third decade of the fourth century (around 325 CE).

7. A detailed catalogue of the works of Iamblichus has been done and can be found in Dalsgaard Larsen, *Jamblique* 42-65, and in Dillon, *Iamblichi Chalcidensis* 18-25. Let us record the most important titles. First, the imposing *A Collection of Pythagorean Doctrines*, in ten volumes, which is like a wide-ranging introduction to philosophy (to Pythagorean philosophy which he considered as paradigmatic). *On the Egyptian Mysteries* [*De Mysteriis*] is attributed at present by most scholars to our philosopher (Zeller still attributed it to a follower of the Syriac school; but after attentive research was conducted by K. Rasche, *De Jamblicho libri qui inscribitur de mysteriis auctore* (Münster, 1911) and the solid proof brought forward by him, the most competent scholars have pronounced in favor of its authenticity), and, as we will see, it constitutes a work of a very important programmatic character. *The Chaldean Theology, The Platonic Theology* and *Treatise on the Gods* must probably be considered the *summa* of our philosopher (the first must be of a remarkable proportions, since as a result of a passage of Damascius [see note 12 below], it was made up of at least twenty-eight books). His commentaries on Plato and Aristotle were of great importance for reasons that we will give above. Iamblichus commented on the Platonic *First Alcibiades, Phaedo,* perhaps *Cratylus, Sophist, Phaedrus, Philebus, Timaeus,* and *Parmenides.* Iamblichus also commented on the Aristotelian *Categories,* and *Prior Analytics* and probably also other works. Of Aristotelian content is also the *Treatise on the Soul,* of which there extant fragments. Finally his *Letters* must be mentioned addressed for the most part to his followers, and of which Stobaeus has preserved important fragments (see the list compiled by Dalsgaard Larsen, *Jamblique* 50ff.). Of the rich production little has come down to us. Of the ten volumes, we possess some volumes (a fourth or perhaps a fifth) of *A Collection of Pythagorean Doctrines,* and *De vita pythagorica* (ed. Teubner, Leipzig, 1937) reproduced with improvements by M. von Albrecht with German translation, (Zürich-Stüttgart, 1963), *Protrepticus* or *Adhortatio ad Philosophium* ed. H. Pistelli, (Leipzig, 1888), *De communi mathematica scientia* ed. N. Festa (Leipzig, 1891), *In Nichomachi Arithmeticam Introduc-*

tionem ed. H. Pistelli (Leipzig, 1894). Probably Iamblichus is the author of at least a part of the content of the work entitled *Theologumena Arithmeticae anonymous* (ed. De Falco, Leipzig 1922); in fact Iamblichus himself (*In Nicom.* [125.15ff. Pistelli] says that a work of this title must constitute the seventh volume of *A Collection of Pythagorean Doctrines* and in the extant anonymous work with this title at least a part reveals linguistic similarities with the writings of our philosopher which we know with certitude are authentic. *De mysteriis* which has been edited and translated many times has come down to us complete (consult M. Sicherl, *Die Handschriften, Ausgaben und Uebersetzungen von Jamblichos de mysteriis* [Berlin 1957]; the most recent edition is that edited by É. des Places, with French translation, introduction and notes [Paris, 1966]. Of the editions of the fragments of the commentaries we already mentioned them above p. 534, note 3. The fragments of the *De anima* are found in a French translation, with commentary, in A. J. Festugière, *La Révèlation d'Hermès Trismégiste* [Paris, 1953] 3.177-248. For further information consult *Reale 5 s.v.*

8. Olympiodorus, *In Plat. Phaed.* 123.4ff Norvin.
9. Consult above 406-7ff.
10. Consult above 410ff.
11. Dalsgaard Larsen has remarked in this respect that it is necessary to explain the historical process through which this "multiplication" was accomplished: Iamblichus did not start from Plotinus but from Middle Platonism, from Neo-Pythagoreanism, from the revelations of the *Chaldaic Oracles*, from the Hermetic treatises, from the Gnosis (*La place de Jamblique*, p. 14). But this is true only in part, since without the mediation of the Plotinian categories, the system of Iamblichus would be inconceivable.
12. Damascius, *De principiis* 43.1.86.3-10 Ruelle.
13. Consult the remarks of Dillon, *Iamblichi Chalcidensis*, pp. 30-33.
14. Consult Proclus, *In Plat. Tim.* 1. 308.17ff.; Dalsgaard Larsen, *Jamblique*, *frag.* 230. Owing to the traditional text, the division of the levels of the intelligible would be in three triads and one hebdomad; but correcting the text as Festugière has proposed, results in a totally different systematization (consult the following note).
15. A. J. Festugière (*Proclus, Commentaire sur le Timée traduction et notes*, 5 vols. [Paris, 1966-1968] 2.164, note 3) emends the text of Proclus (*Proclus In Plat. Tim.* 1 [308.20ff Diehl]) "it is necessary to read...μετὰ τὰς νοητὰς <τρεῖς?> τριάδας καὶ τὰς τῶν <νοητῶν καὶ> νοερῶν θεῶν τρεῖς τριάδας ἐν τῇ νοερᾷ ἑβδομ<ῃ τρι>άδι (ἑβδόμαδι codd. correxi) τὴν τρίτην ἐν τοῖς πατράσιν ἀπονέμει...τάξιν." "Iamblichus attributed to the Demiurge, after the three triads of the Intelligible Gods and the three triads of the Intelligible and Intellectual Gods, the third rank among the

Fathers in the seventh triad, the Intellectual." Hence there would exist three intelligible triads, three intelligible-intellectual triads, and one intellectual (a seventh counting the others).

16. Consult Dillon, *Iamblichi Chalcidensis*, frags. 50 and 54; Dalsgaard Larsen, *Jamblique frags.* 248 and 253. Iamblichus insisted on the structural difference between the soul and the other hypostases (consult Stobaeus, *Anthol.* 1.362.24-85.10 Wachsmuth).

17. For completion sake let us remember that according to Dillon in Iamblichus there would already be present the doctrine of the Enneads which would have been developed by Proclus, as we will see (consult "Iamblichus and the Origin of the Doctrine of the Henads," *Phronesis* 17 [1972] 102-6, reproduced also in *Iamblichi Chalcidensis*, Appendix B 412-16). But the role of these Henads in Iamblichus is not yet sufficiently clear.

18. Consult *De mysteriis* and Dillon, *Iamblichi Chalcidensis*, frags 75-79 (with the related commentary). To Iamblichus probably can be attributed the inspiration for Sallustius, *De Diis* and Julian in his famous *Or.* (consult also above pp. 421-3).

19. *Zeller-Martano*, pp. 44ff.

20. On this theme see also what we stated above pp. 289-91 and the work of Dodds cited above p. 520, note 1.

21. Iamblichus, *De mysteriis*, 2.11.95ff.

22. Hadot, *Porphyre et Victorinus*, 1.94.

23. Iamblichus, of course, must have joined to the theurgy his ethics, at least in part. In fact, we know that to the classes of the virtues distinguished by Porphyry he added also the *hieratic virtue* or *priestly virtue*, realized in the mystical union with the Absolute and the theurgic virtue which similarly coincided with these (consult Olympiodorus, *In Plat. Phaed.* [114.22ff. Norvin; Marinus, *Life of Proclus* 28). Perhaps also the emphasis on the structural differences existing between the soul and the higher hypostases (consult note 16) at least in what concerns the soul of man, must place in prominence the necessity of recourse to the aid of theurgy. (Let us remember that Iamblichus also conceived the souls clothe in the ὄχημα, *ethereal body* destined to remain also after death, except in these souls which knew how to achieve the maximum purification, which becomes angels. In addition, for our philosopher, reincarnation can happen only in a human body.

24. Praechter, *Richtungen*, pp. 128ff.

25. On Iamblichus the exegete see the volume of Dalsgaard Larsen, *Jamblique*, passim, which contains, at the moment, the last word on the matter.

26. Eunapius, *Vitae Sophistarum*, 5.1.5; 6.2.7; 6.2.10ff.

27. It has been published in the great collection *Commentaria in Aristotelem Graeca* 4.2 edited by A. Busse in 1888.
28. See W. Deuse, *Theodoros von Asine, Sammlung der Testimonien und Kommentar* (Weisbaden 1973). Theodorus born in the last thirty years of the third century and died "a little after 360 CE," says Deuse (p. 1). In his younger years, he could have listened to Porphyry and then, perhaps only for a short time, Iamblichus (Theodorus of whom Eunapius speaks *Vitae Sophistarum* 5.1 [Deuse, *Theodorus*, test. 3] is probably our philosopher).
29. Deuse, *Theodoros*, test. 6 and 12 and the related commentary.
30. Deuse, *Theodoros*, pp. 3-11.

(pp. 421-4) (1-19)

1. Consult Eunapius, *Vitae Sophistarum*, 6.4.1ff.
2. We are informed about them chiefly by Eunapius (consult note 4 below).
3. Consult Eunapius, *Vitae Sophistarum*, 7.1.5ff.
4. Concerning the life of Eunapius there is a recent edition edited G. Giangrande, *Eunapii Vitae sophistarum* (Rome, 1956) which substitutes for the old edition of Boissonade. There is a very old Italian translation in the fourth volume of the *Storici minori volgarizzati ed illustrati* (Milan, 1831) edited by S. Blandi.
5. Libanius was born around 314 CE and died in 393 CE. His extant works are edited by R. Förster (Leipzig, 1903-1922) in eleven volumes.
6. See below note 16.
7. Consult Eunapius, *Vitae Sophistarum* 7 passim. Maximus was condemned to death by Christians in 372 CE.
8. Consult Eunapius, *Vitae Sophistarum* 7.2.2-13.
9. Julian was born in 332 CE. He was made Caesar in 355 CE (at only twenty-four years of age), and received the supreme rank of Emperor in 361. He died in battle in 363. His meeting with Maximus must have occurred around 351. We have listed the editions of his works in *Reale* 5, *s. v.*
10. The image is from G. Negri, *L'imperatore Giuliano l'Apostata* (Milan, 1902[2]) 485ff., 517ff.
11. Julian, *Against the Christians, frag.* 1.
12. Consult Eunapius, *Vitae Sophistarum* 7.2.11.
13. Consult Eunapius, *Vitae Sophistarum* 7.2.12.
14. Julian, *Epist.* 12 (1.2.19.2-4 Bidez).
15. For further analyses see R. E. Witt, "Iamblichus as a Forerunner of Julian," in the already cited volume of essays (p. 534, note 3) *De Jamblique á Proclus*, pp. 35-67.
16. On the basis of the most recent studies it would seem that this Sallustius is to be identified with Saturninus Sallustius Secundus, elevated by Julian in 361 CE to the position of prefect of the East (and to whom he dedicated

the work entitled *Ad Helios Re*). See the excellent introduction of G. Rochefort, *Des Dieux et du monde* (Paris, 1960) ix-xxi. On the basis of a series of plausible elements this scholar has fixed the date of the composition of the treatise between March and June of 362 CE (pp. xxi-xxv).

17. Sallustius, *Concerning the Gods and the World* [*De Dis et Mundo*], 9.7.
18. Sallustius, *Concerning the Gods and the World*, 12.5.
19. Sallustius, *Concerning the Gods and the World*, 19.1.

(pp. 425-40) (1-50)

1. Consult above, pp. 207ff.
2. Consult above, pp. 212ff. and the related notes.
3. Consult Porphyry, *Life of Plotinus*, 20.
4. Consult Lynch, *Aristotle's School*, pp. 184ff.
5. Consult Vacherot, *Histoire critique*, 2.192ff.
6. Consult Vacherot, *Histoire critique*, 2.193ff.
7. Consult Vacherot, *Histoire critique*, 2.194ff.
8. Concerning what Marinus says in the, *Life of Proclus* 12 we can say that Plutarch died in 431/432 CE, when Proclus was twenty-two years old. On the beginnings of the School of Athens consult É. Évrard, "Le maître de Plutarque d'Athènes et les origines du néoplatonisme athénien," *L'Antiquité Classique* 29 (1960) 108-33; 391-406.
9. Consult Marinus, *Life of Proclus*, 13.
10. On the theme consult H. J. Blumenthal, "Plutarch's Exposition of the *De anima* and the Psychology of Proclus," in the previously cited volume of essays (consult above p. 601, note 3) *Jamblique á Proclus*, pp. 123-47.
11. He received from his father Nestorius the secrets of these arts and he gave them to his daughter, who then revealed them to Proclus (Marinus, *Life of Proclus*, 28).
12. Syrianus lived between the fourth and firth centuries CE. He came from Alexandria. His commentaries to some of the books of the *Metaphysics* of Aristotle are edited in the collection *Commentaria in Aristotelem Graeca* 6.1 by W. Kroll published in 1902.
13. Consult Marinus, *Life of Proclus*, 26.
14. Consult Proclus, *In Plat. Tim.* 2.218.20ff. Diehl.
15. One of the writings has the title *Manual of the Arithmetic Introduction* and has been published by J. F. Boissonade, *Anecdota Graeca* 4.413-29 (Paris, 1832; republished Hildesheim 1962). The other title, *How Discourse can be Deduced from Discourse* has been published by C. E. Ruelle in *Revue de Philologie* 7 (1883) 82-94 with French translation.
16. Proclus was born at Constantinople of parents who were Lycian from the city of Xanthus. For the information which Marinus furnishes and from the horoscope of our philosopher that Marinus himself had preserved (consult, *Life of Proclus*, 35ff.) it can be determined that Proclus was born

on the eighth of February of 412 and died the seventeenth of April of 485 CE. Except that Marinus (*Life of Proclus*, 3, 26) says also that Proclus died at seventy-five years of age, so that the account does not turn out exactly. É. Évrard, who has recently re-examined the problem ("La date de la naissance de Proclus le néoplatonicien," *L'Antiquité Classique*) 29 [1960] 137-41), comes to the conclusion that the date of the death is certain, but the date of the birth can be calculated to be either 409/410 or 411/412 CE (In favor of 410 as a date of birth are scholars such as Zeller, Freudenthal, Praechter). After a period of studies spent in Alexandria, Proclus, not yet twenty, went to Athens, where he remained all his life (except for a period of about a year in which he must have left the city, probably for political reasons). He wrote numerous works (R. Beutler has reconstructed a detailed descriptive catalogue of fifty titles: see the name "Proklos" in the *Realenzyclopädie der classischen Altertumswissenschaft* (Pauly-Wissowa-Kroll, 23.190-208) many of which (about twenty some odd) are extant. We will give extensive bibliographical information in *Reale 5 s.v.*, for now we will only be concerned with those of philosophical interest. The two most important theoretical works are: *The Elements of Theology*, ed. E. R. Dodds (Oxford, 1933, 1963^2) and *In Platonis theologiam*, ed. Portus (Hamburg, 1618; new edition begun by H. D. Saffrey and L. G. Westerink [Paris 1969ff.]). Of minor importance is instead the *Elementatio physica*, ed. H. Boese (Berlin, 1958). The commentaries to the Platonic dialogues preserved are as follows: *In Alcibiadem*, ed. L. G. Westerink (Amsterdam, 1954), *In Cratylum* ed. G. Pasquali (Leipzig, 1908), *In Parmenidem*, ed. V. Cousin (Paris, 1864; reproduced Hildesheim, 1961), *In Rem Publicam*, ed. W. Kroll (Leipzig, 1899-1901), *In Timaeum*, ed. E. Diehl (Leipzig 1903-1906). Among the commentaries let us record also *In primum Euclidis elementarum librum commentarii*, ed. G. Friedlein (Leipzig, 1873). In Latin translation there are extant the following small works: *De decem dubitationibus circa providentiam, De providentia et fato, De malorum subsistentia*, ed. H. Boese (Berlin, 1960). Let us remember finally the *Eclogae de philosophia Chaldaïca*, ed. A. Jahn (Halle, 1891) and the *Hymni*, ed. E. Vogt (Weisbaden, 1957). Consult G. *Reale*, "L'estremo messaggio spirituale del mondo antico nel pensiero metafisico e teurgia di Proclo," in *Proclo, I Manuali* (Milan: Rusconi, 1985) pp. v-ccxxiii. For further information consult *s.v.* Proclus in *Reale 5*.

17. Consult Proclus, *In Plat. Rempub.*, 2.107.14ff. Kroll.
18. Proclus, *Platonic Theology*, 1.26 (based on T. Taylor trans., *Proclus: The Platonic Theology*, pp. 79-80).
19. Proclus, *Platonic Theology*, 3.47 (based on T. Taylor trans., *Proclus: The Platonic Theology*, pp. 165-66).
20. Proclus, *Enneads*, 6.6.9. Consult above note 17.

21. Consult Proclus, *Elements of Theology*, 115.
22. Consult Proclus, *Elements of Theology*, 101.
23. Consult Proclus, *Elements of Theology*, 113 (E. R. Dodds, *Proclus: The Elements of Theology*, p. 93).
24. Consult Proclus, *Platonic Theology* 5.2.
25. Consult Proclus, *Platonic Theology* 5.3ff.
26. Consult Proclus, *Platonic Theology* 6 passim; *Elements of Theology* 184.
27. Consult Proclus, *Elements of Theology* 30-33; and 35 (E. R. Dodds, *Proclus: The Elements of Theology*, p. 35, 37, 39).
28. The law has been specified by Vacherot quite well in his *Histoire critique* 2.282ff. but Zeller maintains the contrary: "It must not therefore be inferred that Proclus considered the limited and the unlimited, rather than as substances in the proper sense, only as a universal principle of all being" (*Zeller-Martano*, p. 151). But the text damages Zeller's position. Limit, Unlimited, and the Mixture are both a triad (the first intelligible triad) and also a general law of reality, as new studies have fully confirmed. Consult J. Trouillard, *L'Un et l'âme selon Proclos* (Paris, 1972) 71-89 and passim.
29. Consult Proclus, *Elements of Theology* 159 (E. R. Dodds, *Proclus: The Elements of Theology*, p. 139, 141).
30. Consult respectively Proclus, *Elements of Theology* 89 and ff.; *In Plat. Parm,* 4.937a39ff. Cousin; *In Euclid* 6.7-19 Friedlein; *In Plat. Tim.* 2.196.30ff. Diehl.
31. Consult Vacherot, *Histoire critique*, 2.287.
32. Consult Trouillard, *L'Un et l'âme*, pp. 78ff.
33. Consult Proclus, *In Plat. Tim.* 1.384.27-85.17 Diehl.
34. Consult Proclus, *Elements of Theology* 103. On the interpretation of the soul in this sense consult Trouillard, *L'Un et l'âme*, passim.
35. Consult on the theme E. R. Dodds, *Proclus, The Elements of Theology*, pp. xxviff.
36. Consult Marinus, *Life of Proclus*, 28.
37. Consult Marinus, *Life of Proclus*, 28.
38. Consult Proclus, *Elements of Theology* 196.
39. Consult Proclus, *Elements of Theology* 209.
40. Consult Proclus, *Platonic Theology* 1.3 (based on T. Taylor trans., *Proclus: The Platonic Theology*, pp. 8-10).
41. Consult Damascius, *Life of Isidorus* 42e, 141 (66.8 and 196.1 Zintzen).
42. Consult Damascius, *Life of Isidorus* 142 (196.8-10 Zintzen).
43. The work of Marinus devoted to the *Life of Proclus* is the most eloquent proof of the speculative thinness of this author. This work has been edited by Boissonade at Leipzig in 1914 and republished at Amsterdam in 1966. Consult also R. T. Wallis, *Neoplatonism* (London: Duckworth, 1972) 138

who writes "Proclus's successor and biographer Marinus was by contrast a man of little philosophical talent (consult Damascius, *Life of Isidorus* 144.).''

44. Consult Damascius, *Life of Isidorus* 275 (304.12-15 Zintzen).

45. From the same *Life of Isidorus* written by Damascius, his follower, which was to be a panegyric, we indeed can draw forth this impression.

46. Damascius was born at Damascus (*Life of Isidorus* 200 [274.4-9 Zintzen]). We do not know the dates of his birth and death. On the basis of conjecture it is thought that 470 CE is the year of his birth and 544 the year of his death. Besides Marinus, he had Ammonius as a teacher, son of Hermias (of whom we will speak in the next chapter) who brought him to study the works of Plato. There is extant a monumental work of his entitled *Problems and Solutions concerning the First Principles* (the edition commonly used is that of C. A. Ruelle [Paris, 1889; reproduced Amsterdam 1966; furthermore, we have the commentary *On Plato's Parmenides*, edited also by Ruelle, Paris 1883. [Consult also the French translation of A. E. Chaignet, *Damascius le Diadoque. Problèmes et solutions touchant les premiers principes*, 3 vols. [Paris, 1898]; which according to some is a continuation of the first work. Of the *Life of Isidorus* there is a new edition of C. Zintzen (Hildesheim, 1967). To Damascius now are attributed the *Commentary on the Philebus* and the *Phaedo* once attributed to Olympiodorus (consult Damascius, *Lectures on the Philebus wrongly attributed to Olympiodorus, Text, Translation, Notes and Indices*, L. G. Westerink (Amsterdam, 1959). See the further information in *Reale* 5, sub voce.

47. Damascius, *De principiis*, 134 (2.13.26 Ruelle).

48. Damascius, *De principiis*, 2 (1.4.7ff. Ruelle).

49. Damascius, *De principiis*, 3-8 (1.5ff. Ruelle).

50. The extant commentaries are published in the collection *Commentaria Aristotelem Graeca*, we will give detailed information about them in *Reale* 5.

(pp. 441-3) (1-17)

1. This thesis was maintained for the first time by Praechter, *Die Philosophie des Altertums*, pp. 635-47, and has been subsequently been confirmed. Consult note 8 below.

2. Consult above, pp. 297-301.

3. Hence at the same time as the beginnings of the School of Athens.

4. Consult under the name Hypatia in *Suidas*.

5. He seems to have been elected Bishop around 410 CE. We give a list of his extant works in *Reale* 5, sub voce.

6. The activity of Hierocles is to be placed chronologically towards the middle of the fifth century CE (consult Damascius, *Life of Isidorus* 54 [80.1ff. Zintzen]).

7. Consult the recent edition edited by F. W. Köhler (Stüttgart, 1974).

8. Consult Theo Kobusch, *Studien zur Philosophie des Hierokles von Alexandrien* (Münich, 1976). Kobusch gives eminence expressly to the "pre-Neoplatonics" treatises of our philosopher. Hadot moves in another direction instead in his, *Le problème du néoplatonisme alexandrin Hiéroclès et Simplicius* (Paris, 1978).

9. Consult Kobusch, *Studien*, pp. 193-96.

10. Consult *Suidas* under the name Epictetus.

11. See also the edition with Italian translation of M. E. Colonna, *Enea di Gaza, Teofrasto* (Naples, 1958).

12. The edition of *De natura hominis* has been edited by C. F. Matthaei (Magdeburgicae: Halae, 1802; republished Hildesheim, 1967). For a recent analysis of the doctrines contained in the treatise see the recent work of A. Siclari, *L'antropologia di Nemesius di Emesa* (Padua, 1974).

13. The commentary is published by P. Couvreur, *Hermiae Alexandrini in Platonis Phaedrum Scholia* (Paris, 1901).

14. We will give information on the extant commentaries of these authors and of their related editions in *Reale 5*, sub voce.

15. The commentaries of these authors are generally utilized as instruments for the interpretation of Aristotle and are not studied for themselves. Only recently is there beginning to be some steps in this direction. We cite, for example, the contribution of K. Kremer, *Der Metaphysikbegriff in den Aristoteles-Kommentaren der Ammonius-Schule* (Münster-Westfalen, 1960).

16. *De opificio mundi* has been edited by G. Reichardt (Leipzig, 1897) and *De aeternitate mundi contra Proclum* by G. Rabe (Leipzig, 1899).

17. John Lydus (sixth century CE), who was in attendance at the Byzantine court is to be found within the Alexandrian ambiance. There are two works preserved *De mensibus* (an extract in form) and *De ostentis*, in which the author refers to Platonic and Neoplatonic texts. *De mensibus* is edited by R. Wünsch (Leipzig, 1898) and *De ostentis* by C. Wachsmuth (Leipzig, 1863).

(p. 446) (1)

1. For lack of space, we will give a list of the works of these authors, who are significant to the goals of this work, in *Reale 5*, sub voce.

(pp. 447-49) (1-13)

1. *Justianian Code* 1.5.18.4ff. (57 Krueger).

2. *Justinian Code* 1.11.10.2ff. (64 Krueger).

3. Consult Lynch, *Aristotle's School*, pp. 165ff. and the bibliographical information which he gives to notes 2-5.

4. Consult Procopius, *Anecdota* 26.74b.1ff. (143.3ff. Dindorf) and Malala, *Chronographia* 18.187 (451.16ff. Dindorf).

5. Agathias, *Historiae* 2.30 (80.5ff. Keydell).
6. Agathias, *Historiae* 2.31 (81.15-19 Keydell).
7. Consult Agathias, *Historiae* 2.28 (77.9ff. Keydell).
8. Consult above, p. 522, note 14.
9. Zeller-Martano, pp. 225ff.
10. Consult Lynch, *Aristotle's School*, p. 167.
11. Plato, *Phaedo* 85C.
12. Plato, *Phaedo* 85D.
13. Augustine, *Commentary on the Gospel of St. John*, Homily 2.3.